ALSO BY THE EDITORS OF COOK'S ILLUSTRATED
HOME OF AMERICA'S TEST KITCHEN

The America's Test Kitchen Family Cookbook
The Best of America's Test Kitchen Cookbook 2007

The Best Recipe Series:
The Best 30-Minute Recipe
The Best Light Recipe
The Cook's Illustrated Guide to Grilling and Barbecue
Best American Side Dishes
The New Best Recipe
Cover and Bake
Steaks, Chops, Roasts, and Ribs
Baking Illustrated
Restaurant Favorites at Home
Perfect Vegetables
Italian Classics
The Best American Classics

Cooking at Home with America's Test Kitchen
America's Test Kitchen Live!
Inside America's Test Kitchen
Here in America's Test Kitchen
The America's Test Kitchen Cookbook

834 Kitchen Quick Tips

The Complete Book of Pasta and Noodles
The Cook's Illustrated Complete Book of Poultry

How to Barbecue and Roast on the Grill
How to Cook Chicken Breasts
How to Cook Chinese Favorites
How to Cook Garden Vegetables
How to Cook Shrimp and Other Shellfish
How to Grill
How to Make an American Layer Cake
How to Make Cookie Jar Favorites
How to Make Ice Cream
How to Make Muffins, Biscuits, and Scones
How to Make Pasta Sauces
How to Make Pot Pies and Casseroles
How to Make Salad
How to Make Sauces and Gravies
How to Make Simple Fruit Desserts
How to Make Soup
How to Make Stew
How to Sauté

To order any of our books, visit us at
http://www.cooksillustrated.com
http://www.americastestkitchen.com
or call 800-611-0759

THE BEST SOUPS & STEWS

A BEST RECIPE CLASSIC

THE
BEST
SOUPS
& STEWS

A BEST RECIPE CLASSIC

BY THE EDITORS OF

COOK'S ILLUSTRATED

ILLUSTRATIONS
JOHN BURGOYNE

PHOTOGRAPHY
CARL TREMBLAY

AMERICA'S TEST KITCHEN

BROOKLINE, MASSACHUSETTS

Paperback edition copyright © 2006 by The Editors of Cook's Illustrated

All rights reserved. No part of this book may be reproduced or transmitted in any manner whatsoever without written permission from the publisher, except in the case of brief quotations embodied in critical articles or reviews.

America's Test Kitchen
17 Station Street
Brookline, Massachusetts 02445

Library of Congress Cataloging-in-Publication Data
The Editors of Cook's Illustrated

The Best Soups & Stews
Would you make 30 versions of French onion soup to find the one with the richest broth and the deepest onion flavor? We did. Here are more than 200 foolproof recipes for the best soups and stews plus no-nonsense kitchen tests and equipment ratings.
1st Paperback Edition

ISBN-13: 978-1-933615-02-8
ISBN-10: 1-933615-02-8 (paperback): $19.95 US/$24.95 CAN
I. Cooking. I. Title
2006

Manufactured in the United States of America

10 9 8 7 6 5 4 3 2 1

Distributed by America's Test Kitchen, 17 Station Street, Brookline, MA 02445

Designed by Amy Klee
Edited by Jack Bishop

Pictured on front cover: French Onion Soup (page 147)
Pictured on back cover: Corn Chowder (page 128), Hearty Beef Stew (page 201), French Onion Soup (page 147),
Chicken Cacciatore with Portobellos and Sage (page 234)

Contents

WELCOME TO AMERICA'S TEST KITCHEN viii

PREFACE BY CHRISTOPHER KIMBALL ix

ACKNOWLEDGMENTS xi

HOW TO USE THIS BOOK xiii

PART 1: THE BASICS

CHAPTER 1   Buying Guide to Equipment 3

CHAPTER 2   Stocks 15

PART 2: SOUPS

CHAPTER 3   Chicken Soups 41

CHAPTER 4   Meat Soups 71

CHAPTER 5   Seafood Soups 87

CHAPTER 6   Vegetable Soups 105

CHAPTER 7   Pasta and Bean Soups 151

CHAPTER 8   Chilled Soups 177

PART 3: STEWS

CHAPTER 9   Meat Stews 197

CHAPTER 10   Chicken Stews 229

CHAPTER 11   Seafood Stews 249

CHAPTER 12   Vegetable Stews 263

CHAPTER 13   Chilis, Gumbos, and Curries 275

PART 4: ACCOMPANIMENTS

CHAPTER 14   Rice, Potatoes, Polenta, Breads, and Biscuits 307

INDEX 335

A NOTE ON CONVERSIONS 351

WELCOME TO AMERICA'S TEST KITCHEN

THIS BOOK HAS BEEN TESTED, WRITTEN, AND edited by the folks at America's Test Kitchen, a very real 2,500-square-foot kitchen located just outside of Boston. It is the home of *Cook's Illustrated* magazine and *Cook's Country* magazine and is the Monday through Friday destination for more than two dozen test cooks, editors, food scientists, tasters, and cookware specialists. Our mission is to test recipes over and over again until we understand how and why they work and until we arrive at the "best" version.

We start the process of testing a recipe with a complete lack of conviction, which means that we accept no claim, no theory, no technique, and no recipe at face value. We simply assemble as many variations as possible, test a half dozen of the most promising, and taste the results blind. We then construct our own hybrid recipe and continue to test it, varying ingredients, techniques, and cooking times until we reach a consensus. The result, we hope, is the best version of a particular recipe, but we realize that only you can be the final judge of our success (or failure). As we like to say in the test kitchen, "We make the mistakes, so you don't have to."

All of this would not be possible without a belief that good cooking, much like good music, is indeed based on a foundation of objective technique. Some people like spicy foods and others don't, but there is a right way to sauté, there is a best way to cook a pot roast, and there are measurable scientific principles involved in producing perfectly beaten, stable egg whites. This is our ultimate goal: to investigate the fundamental principles of cooking so that you become a better cook. It is as simple as that.

You can watch us work (in our actual test kitchen) by tuning in to *America's Test Kitchen* (www.americastestkitchen.com) on public television or by subscribing to *Cook's Illustrated* magazine (www.cooksillustrated.com) or *Cook's Country* magazine (www.cookscountry.com), which are each published every other month. We welcome you into our kitchen, where you can stand by our side as we test our way to the "best" recipes in America.

PREFACE

THE ARGUMENT OVER WHETHER COOKING is subjective or objective, a matter of individual taste or scientific principle, comes to a head in the preparation of soups and stews. Few cooks would claim independence from the laws of chemistry when baking a cake, but when putting together a pot of soup on a gray November day, one is tempted to throw caution to the wind and simmer up whatever is in the vegetable bin that afternoon.

This reminds me of a gentleman in our town in Vermont who was known for his lack of attention to natural laws. On one occasion, while he was riding a tractor out of gear down a steep driveway, the hay wagon he was pulling ended up in twisted pieces across the road, but the tractor remained upright, the driver no worse for the ride and as unconcerned as ever about his brush with disaster.

I often feel like that headstrong neighbor of mine when concocting a batch of soup or stew. After all, what is there to know about such simple preparations? Well, having spent several years developing the recipes in this book, the staff at *Cook's Illustrated* can honestly say that there is a great deal to know if you want to turn out a great bowl of soup or stew.

Did you know that the best chicken stock is made by first sautéing chicken parts and that it's possible to prepare rich-tasting chicken stock in just one hour? Many sources swear that bones are the key to beef stock. In fact, we found that meat makes the difference between decent beef stock and rich, flavorful, beefy beef stock. Most cooks let stews simmer on the stovetop, but we determined that oven heat is gentler and more consistent, guaranteeing that stews simmer at an even rate.

When developing recipes for this book, we often tested conventional wisdom—the kinds of declarations you find in many classic cookbooks—as well as old wives' tales and other tips your grandmother might have known. For instance, we found that spent Parmesan rinds are just the thing to enhance a minestrone made without stock. We also learned that frozen peas can make a delicious pea soup and that flambéing the shells is the secret to great shrimp bisque.

As is our custom, we tested dozens of pieces of equipment to find those tools that work and those that don't. Did you know that the blender, not the food processor, is the best tool for pureeing vegetable soups? Or that a fine-mesh strainer, such as a chinois, will yield the silkiest lobster bisque imaginable?

These prescriptions may seem simple—as indeed most of the techniques in this book are—but they can dramatically enhance flavor, which is the key to memorable soups and stews. Although soups and stews may not be as formulaic as bread or pie dough recipes, they require the use of quality ingredients and sound technique. Use this book, and we will show you how to make the best recipes for chicken noodle soup, clam chowder, and French onion soup as well as bouillabaisse, chicken gumbo, and chili.

Christopher Kimball
Founder and Editor
Cook's Illustrated and *Cook's Country*
Host, *America's Test Kitchen*

ACKNOWLEDGMENTS

ALL OF THE PROJECTS UNDERTAKEN AT AMERICA'S Test Kitchen are collective efforts, the combined experience and work of editors, test cooks, and writers, joined in the search for the best cooking methods. This book is no exception.

Executive Editor Jack Bishop spearheaded this project. Food editor Kay Rentschler supervised the recipe development process. Elizabeth Germain was the main test cook and researcher for the book. Shannon Blaisdell, Matthew Card, Julia Collin Davison, Rebecca Hays, Bridget Lancaster, Raquel Pelzel, Kay Rentschler, Adam Ried, Shona Simkin, and Dawn Yanagihara also developed recipes and wrote portions of the text.

Art director Amy Klee and graphic designer Nina Madjid transformed computer files and digital scans into a book. Keller + Keller took the front cover photo and Carl Tremblay captured the black-and-white images that appear at the beginning of each chapter. Daniel van Ackere took step photographs and John Burgoyne turned these pictures into illustrations.

The following individuals on the editorial, production, circulation, customer service, and office staffs also worked on the book: Ron Bilodeau, Barbara Bourassa, Jana Branch, Rich Cassidy, Sharon Chabot, Mary Connelly, Cathy Dorsey, Daniel Frey, Larisa Greiner, India Koopman, Jim McCormack, Jennifer McCreary, Nicole Morris, Henrietta Murray, Juliet Nusbaum, Jessica Quirk, and Mandy Shito. And without help from members of the marketing staff, readers might never find our books. Steven Browall, Adam Dardeck, Connie Forbes, Jason Geller, Robert Lee, David Mack, and Jacqui Valerio all contributed to marketing and distribution efforts.

Several of the recipes and techniques in this book are based on work that has appeared in *Cook's Illustrated* magazine. Thanks to Pam Anderson and Stephanie Lyness for those contributions.

HOW TO USE THIS BOOK

THIS BOOK IS DIVIDED INTO FOUR SECTIONS. The first part covers the basic equipment and ingredients (in this case, homemade stocks) you will need to make the recipes in this book. We suggest that you read through these chapters before making any recipes in the other sections.

The second part of the book covers the wide range of soups popular in this country. For the most part, we have organized soup recipes by the main ingredient—chicken, meat, seafood, vegetables, or pasta and beans. We have collected the recipes for soups that are served chilled in a separate chapter.

The third part of the book covers stews. Again, we have organized most chapters by the main ingredient—meat, chicken, seafood, or vegetables. A final stew chapter looks at chilis, gumbos, and curries—three types of stew made with a variety of ingredients and their own unique techniques. Lamb curry and shrimp curry are closely related, so it made sense to put these recipes in the same chapter rather than assign them separately to the meat stew and seafood stew chapters.

The fourth and final part of the book covers the accompaniments usually served with soups and stews—such as rustic country bread, baguettes, mashed potatoes, rice, and cornbread.

So what exactly is a stew, and how does it differ from a soup? There is some disagreement in the food world, but for our purposes a stew starts with small chunks of meat, chicken, seafood, and/or vegetables that are cooked in liquid. That liquid is usually thickened and served as a sauce. A stew is a one-dish meal that can be eaten with a fork and usually without a knife.

Soup can start with the same ingredients as a stew, but the liquid is often not thickened. Even in cases where the liquid is thickened, it is not reduced to a sauce. The liquid component in a soup retains equal footing with the solid ingredients. Soup is eaten with a spoon and can be served either as a main course, first course, or lunch entrée. We have divided soup from stew recipes according to these criteria.

PART I

THE BASICS

1

BUYING GUIDE TO EQUIPMENT

SOUPS AND STEWS CAN BE PREPARED IN even the most primitive kitchen. Other than a pot, a spoon for stirring, and a ladle for serving, most of the other equipment recommended here is either optional or recipe-specific. That said, good strainers, knives, and cheese graters will make the preparation of soups and stews (as well as other foods) easier and more enjoyable. Likewise, you may not need a blender to make chicken noodle soup, but it is essential when preparing pureed squash soup. What follows are notes from the *Cook's Illustrated* test kitchen on various pieces of equipment used to prepare the recipes in this book.

BAKING SHEETS

BAKING SHEETS, ALSO KNOWN AS COOKIE sheets, are occasionally used to toast ingredients or prepare croutons for soups and stews. Most baking sheets have the same basic design. They are made from metal and are usually slightly longer than they are wide. (A standard size is 16 inches long and 14 inches across.) Some are dark, some are light. Some have rims on all four sides. Others have rims on only one or two sides and otherwise have flat edges. We tested 11 sheets in a variety of materials and came to some surprising conclusions.

First of all, shiny light-colored sheets do a better job of evenly browning the bottoms of bread slices (as well as cookies) than dark sheets. Most of the dark sheets are nonstick, and we found that these pans tend to overbrown foods. Shiny, silvery sheets distribute heat much more evenly, and if sticking is a concern we simply use parchment paper.

In our tests, we also came to prefer sheets with at least one rimless edge. This way we could slide toasted croutons or other ingredients onto a cooling rack without actually touching the hot food. Our favorite cookie sheet is made by Kaiser out of tinned steel. At just $7, it was also the cheapest sheet we tested.

BLENDERS

THE TEXTURE OF A PUREED SOUP SHOULD be as smooth and creamy as possible. With this in mind, we tried pureeing several soups with a food mill, a food processor, a hand-held immersion blender, and a regular countertop blender.

Forget using the food mill for this purpose. We tried all three strainer plates (coarse, medium, and fine), and the liquid ran right through each plate as we churned and churned only to produce baby food of varying textures. The liquid and pureed solids were separated and could not be combined with a whisk.

The food processor does a decent job of pureeing, but some small bits of vegetables can get trapped under the blade and remain unchopped. Even more troubling is the tendency of a food processor to leak hot liquid. Fill the workbowl more than halfway and you are likely to see liquid running down the side of the food processor base. Even small quantities of

BUYING A BLENDER

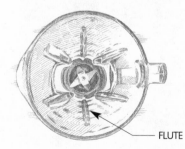

In our testing, we preferred blender jars with flutes on the sides. This design produces smoother soups.

WIDE-MOUTH

Many new blenders have a wide-mouth jar with straight sides.

CLASSIC

On a classic blender, the jar tapers at the bottom. In our tests, this design promoted a smoother consistency in pureed soups.

soup must be pureed in batches, and that's a hassle.

The immersion blender has more appeal because it can be brought directly to the pot, eliminating the need to ladle hot ingredients from one vessel to another. However, we found that this kind of blender also leaves unblended bits of food behind. If you don't mind a few lumps, use an immersion blender.

For perfectly smooth pureed soups, we rely on a standard blender. The blade does an excellent job with soups because it pulls ingredients down from the top of the container. No stray bits go untouched by the blade. And as long as plenty of headroom is left at the top of the blender, there is no leakage.

When choosing a blender, you have several options. Modern blenders have electronic touch-pad controls, a wide range of speeds, and new jar designs. We wondered how these newfangled options compared with the features on a basic blender, the kind your mother might have owned. We put nine blenders through a series of tests to find out.

We found that blender jars with flutes (vertical protrusions on the inside of the container) were especially efficient at pureeing soups. These flutes (see illustration on page 4) cause the vortex created by the spinning blade to collapse, thus redirecting food matter being thrown against the jar walls back down onto the blade.

A modification to the standard angled shape of the classic blender jar was not received as positively in the test kitchen. Some companies now make a wide-mouth blender with straight sides (see illustration on page 4). Because these jars are wider at the base, there's more room between the blade and the walls of the jar. Extra space gives bits of food a place to hide, and the texture of soups can suffer. In contrast, the tapered bottom on the classic blender jar is quite narrow and thus promotes more contact between food and blade (see illustration on page 4). This results in pureed soups with a finer, smoother consistency.

An apparent wide range of speeds (as indicated by countless buttons) did not necessarily track with the actual range of speeds observed by our test cooks. Some blenders with just two speeds (high and low) actually had more (and less) power than blenders with 15 speeds.

Our test cooks also remained unimpressed by electronic touch-pad controls. The flat touch pad is easier to clean than a control panel with raised buttons (around which it is difficult to maneuver a sponge or cloth), but it is not easier to operate. On several models, we found it necessary to press down on the electronic touch pad quite forcefully. Traditional buttons are easier to engage.

So when shopping for a blender, focus on the design of the jar (a jar that tapers at the base and has flutes on the inside is preferred), steer clear of electronic touch-pad controls, and don't be swayed by a seeming multitude of speeds.

CHEESE GRATERS

A DUSTING OF PARMESAN CHEESE CAN BE the crowning glory on a bowl of great minestrone or pasta and bean soup. As any cook knows, cheese can be grated quickly or slowly, with minimal or maximum effort.

In the old days, you grated cheese on the fine teeth of a box grater. Now cheese graters come in several distinct designs. Unfortunately, many of them don't work all that well. With some designs you need Herculean strength to move the cheese over the teeth with sufficient pressure for grating; with others you eventually discover that a large portion of the grated cheese has remained jammed in the grater instead of sitting where it belongs, on your food. Whether you are dusting a bowl of soup or grating a full cup of cheese to use in a recipe, a good grater should be easy to use and efficient.

We rounded up 15 models and set about determining which was the best grater. We found five basic configurations (see illustrations on page 6). Four-sided box graters have different size holes on each side to allow for both fine grating and coarse shredding. Flat graters consist of a flat sheet of metal that is punched through with fine teeth and attached to some type of handle. Grater designs based on the rasp, a small, maneuverable wood-working tool, are similar to flat graters but are generally much thinner and longer. With rotary graters, you put a small chunk of cheese in a hopper and use a handle to press it down against a crank-operated grating wheel. Porcelain dish graters have raised teeth in the center and a well around the outside edge to collect the grated cheese.

After grating more than 10 pounds of Parmesan, we came to some conclusions. Success, we learned, was due to a combination of sharp grating teeth, a comfortable handle or grip, and good leverage for pressing the cheese onto the grater. Our favorite model was a flat, rasplike grater. Shaped like a ruler but with lots of tiny, sharp raised teeth, The Cheese Grater (as it is called) can grate large quantities of cheese smoothly and almost effortlessly. The black plastic handle, which we found more comfortable than any of the others, also earned high praise. Standard flat graters also scored well.

What about traditional box graters? Box graters can deliver good results, and they can do more than grate hard cheese. However, if grating hard cheese is the task at hand, a box grater is not our first choice. These graters are too large and bulky to use at the table, and they can't be used to shower cheese directly over a bowl of soup.

We also had good results with rotary graters made from metal but did not like flimsy versions made from plastic. A metal arm is rigid enough to do some of the work of pushing the cheese down onto the grating drum. The arms on the plastic models we tested flexed too much against the cheese, thus requiring extra pressure to force the cheese down. Hand strain set in quickly. A rotary grater can also chop nuts finely and grate chocolate.

The two porcelain dish graters we tested were duds. The teeth were quite ineffective, and the design made it almost impossible to avoid scraping your knuckles.

DUTCH OVENS/LIDDED CASSEROLES

WE FIND THAT A DUTCH OVEN (ALSO CALLED a lidded casserole) is almost essential to making stew and works beautifully when browning chicken or beef to make stock. You can try to use a large pasta pot or stockpot for these jobs, but they are most often too narrow and tall. Many are also quite light, thin, and cheap—designed to heat up water quickly, not to brown meat. Since most stew recipes begin with browning to develop flavor, it's imperative to use a pot with a heavy bottom.

A Dutch oven (see illustration below) is nothing more than a wide, deep pot with a cover. It was originally manufactured with "ears" on the side (small,

FIVE TYPES OF CHEESE GRATER

RASP

FLAT

A rasplike grater has very sharp teeth and a long, solid handle. It is our favorite tool for grating Parmesan and other hard cheeses.

A typical flat grater does a decent job grating small amounts of Parmesan and other hard cheeses.

BOX

ROTARY

PORCELAIN

A rectangular box grater can grate hard cheeses (albeit a bit slowly) and shred soft cheeses, such as mozzarella.

A rotary grater can work well. We had better luck with metal than with plastic models.

A porcelain grater with tiny raised teeth is ineffective and is a hazard to your knuckles.

round tabs used to pick up the pot) and a top that had a lip around the edge. The latter design element was important because a Dutch oven was heated through coals placed both underneath and on top of the pot. The lip kept the coals on the lid from falling off. One could bake biscuits, cobblers, beans, and stews in this pot. It was, in the full sense of the word, an oven. And this "oven" was a key feature of chuck wagons and an essential in many Colonial American households, where all cooking occurred in the fireplace. This useful pot supposedly came to be called "Dutch" because at some point the best cast iron came from Holland.

Now that everyone in America has an oven, the Dutch oven is no longer used to bake biscuits or cobblers. However, it is essential for dishes that start on top of the stove and finish in the oven, like many stews. To make some recommendations about buying a modern Dutch oven, we tested 12 models from leading makers of cookware.

We found that a Dutch oven should have a capacity of at least six quarts to be useful. Eight quarts is even better. As we cooked in the pots, we came to prefer wider, shallower Dutch ovens because it's easier to see and reach inside them, and they offer more bottom surface area to accommodate larger batches of meat for browning. This reduces the number of batches required to brown a given quantity of meat, and, with it, the chances of burning the flavorful pan drippings. Ideally, a Dutch oven should have

CHOOSING A DUTCH OVEN

The ideal Dutch oven is twice as wide as it is high. It also should have handles on both sides (which make it easy to lift the pot in and out of the oven) as well as a lid with a handle. Because this pot often goes into the oven, make sure the handles are ovenproof.

a diameter twice as wide as its height.

We also preferred pots with a light-colored interior finish, such as stainless steel or enameled cast iron. It is easier to judge the caramelization of the drippings at a glance in these pots. Dark finishes can mask the color of the drippings, which may burn before you realize it. Our favorite pot is the 8-quart All-Clad Stainless Stockpot (despite the name, this pot is a Dutch oven). The 7-quart Le Creuset Round French Oven, which is made of enameled cast iron, also tested well. These pots are quite expensive, costing at least $150, even when on sale. A less expensive alternative is the 7-quart Lodge Dutch Oven, which is made from cast iron. This pot is extremely heavy (making it a bit hard to maneuver), it must be seasoned (wiped with oil) regularly, and the dark interior finish is not ideal, but it does brown food quite well and costs just $45.

FOOD PROCESSORS

YOU CAN CERTAINLY MAKE THE VAST MAJORITY of soup and stew recipes in this book without a food processor. In fact, a blender is a better option for pureeing soups. However, a food processor can come in handy when trying to slice, grind, or chop ingredients. A food processor is also our preferred tool for kneading bread dough, and what goes better with soup than a hunk of good bread?

So how do you go about buying a food processor that can blend pesto for minestrone, grate beets for borscht, grind shells for lobster bisque, and knead dough to make bread? We evaluated seven food processors based on their performance in five general categories: chopping and grinding, slicing, grating, pureeing, and kneading.

We found that most food processors chop, grind, slice, grate, and puree at least minimally well. Of course, there are differences in models, but they were not as dramatic as the results of our bread-kneading tests. A food processor won't knead bread dough fully, but it can bring together the dry and wet ingredients beautifully to form the dough. If a recipe calls for a smooth, satiny ball of dough, you will have to knead the dough by hand on the counter after processing, but this should take only a few minutes.

We found that successful kneading in a food processor was linked directly to large bowl size and the weight of the base. The 11-cup machines were best because they provided ample space in which the ball of dough could move around. A heavy base provided stability, and the nods went to KitchenAid and Cuisinart, with their substantial, 10-pound-plus bases. These machines also turned in the best performances in the other basic food processor tests.

If you are in the market for a food processor, we recommend that you look beyond the obvious tasks of slicing and chopping. Focus on the machines' capacity for kneading, the test that separates adequate food processors from truly great ones.

KNIVES

A LARGE CHEF'S KNIFE AND A SMALL PARING knife are essential tools for most cooking jobs, the preparation of soups and stews included.

A good chef's knife is probably the most useful tool any cook owns. It can be used not only to chop vegetables but also for such jobs as cutting up poultry, mincing herbs, and slicing fruit. What separates a good knife from an inferior one? To understand the answer to this question, it helps to know something about how knives are constructed.

The first pieces of cutlery were made about 4,000 years ago, when it was discovered that iron ore could be melted and shaped into tools. The creation of steel, which is 80 percent iron and 20 percent other elements, led to the development of carbon steel knives—the standard for 3,000 years. While this kind of steel takes and holds an edge easily, it also stains and rusts. Something as simple as cutting an acidic tomato or exposure to the salt air of the seacoast can corrode carbon steel.

In this century, new alloys have given cooks better options. Stainless steel, made with at least 4 percent chromium and/or nickel, never rusts. Still used for many cheap knives, stainless steel is also very difficult to sharpen. The compromise between durable but dull stainless steel and sharp but corrosive carbon steel is something called high-carbon stainless steel. This blend, which is now used by most knife manufacturers, offers both durability and a sharp edge.

Until recently, all knives were "hot drop forged"—that is, the steel was heated to 2,000 degrees, dropped into a mold, given four or five shots with a hammer, and then tempered (cooled and heated several times to build strength). This process is labor-intensive (many steps must be done by hand), which explains why many chef's knives cost almost $100.

A second manufacturing process feeds long sheets of steel through a press that punches out knife after knife, much like a cookie cutter slicing through dough. These blades are referred to as stamped. They require some hand finishing but are much cheaper to produce since a machine does most of the work.

While experts have long argued that forged knives are better than stamped ones, our tests did not fully support this position. We liked some forged knives but not others. Similarly, we liked some stamped knives but not others. The weight and shape of the handle (it must be comfortable to hold and substantial but not too heavy), the ability of the blade to take an edge, and the shape of the blade (we like a slightly curved blade, which compared with a straight blade is better suited to the rocking motion often used to mince herbs or garlic) are all key factors in choosing a knife.

When shopping, pick up the knife and see how it feels in your hand. Is it easy to grip? Does the weight seem properly distributed between the handle and blade? In our testing, we liked knives made by Henckels and Wüsthof. Inexpensive knives by Forschner and Friedr. Dick, which have stamped blades, also scored well.

In general, our test cooks prefer chef's knives with molded plastic handles (grease and dirt tend to collect in the rivets on wooden handles). As for length, an 8-inch blade is the most useful size. If your hands are particularly small or large, you may want to consider a 6-inch or 10-inch blade.

Paring knives are easier to buy, especially because they are so much less expensive than chef's knives; the stakes are not quite so high. That said, there are still plenty of choices. Blades and handles come in different sizes and shapes and are made from different materials. Some are marketed for specific tasks, such as trimming, fluting, or mincing, but most are designed to be "all-purpose." Prices range from a modest $5 plus change to a grand $50, which invites the obvious question for a home cook: Is the most expensive knife really 10 times better than the cheapest model? To find, out we put seven all-purpose paring knives through a series of kitchen tests, including peeling and slicing shallots, peeling and slicing turnips, coring tomatoes, peeling and mincing fresh ginger, and slicing lemons and limes.

The way the knives were made (by forging or stamping) wasn't much of a factor in our ratings of paring knives. By definition, a paring knife is used for light tasks in which weight and balance are not terribly important (it doesn't take huge effort to peel an apple). The way the handle felt in testers' hands was much more important. Most testers preferred medium-sized, ergonomically designed plastic handles. Slim wooden handles were harder to grasp. Testers also preferred paring knives with flexible blades, which make it easier to work in tight spots. Peeling turnips or sectioning oranges is much easier done with a flexible than a stiff blade. Stiffer blades are slightly better at mincing and slicing, but these are secondary tasks for paring knives. Among the knives tested, expensive forged knives from Wüsthof and Henckels performed well, as did an inexpensive stamped knife made by Forschner.

Of course, buying good knives is only half the challenge. You must keep their edges sharp. To that end, we recommend buying an electric knife sharpener. Steels are best for modest corrections. All knives require more substantial sharpening at least several times a year—if not more often, if you cook a lot. Stones are effective but can be difficult to use; to sharpen a knife properly with a stone, you must maintain a perfect 20-degree angle between blade and stone. An electric knife sharpener (we like models made by Chef's Choice) takes the guesswork out of sharpening and allows you to keep those edges sharp and effective.

LADLES

ONCE YOUR POT OF SOUP OR STEW IS DONE, a good ladle is essential for dividing portions among individual bowls. After spending so much effort to make soup or stew, you certainly don't want any precious liquid dripping onto the stove.

Ladles can be made from stainless steel, plastic, or, occasionally, wood. Wood may look great, but it is impractical because it absorbs flavors and odors. We don't like plastic, either. Ladles made from this material can stain and will melt if placed too close to a lit burner. Metal is the way to go. It's lightweight, nonporous, and durable.

There are two other major considerations when choosing a ladle: the size of the bowl and the length of the handle. We find that an 8-ounce bowl allows us to fill an individual serving bowl in just one attempt. Smaller ladles require several dips to fill each bowl, increasing the likelihood of spills or drips. As for the handle, it should be long enough to stand up inside even the deepest stockpot. We recommend a handle that measures a minimum of 12 inches. Finally, make sure the handle is bent at the end so that the ladle can hook onto the side of a pot or hang from a pot rack.

DRIP-FREE LADLING

Here's an easy way to keep drips and spills to a minimum when ladling soups or stews. Before lifting the filled ladle up and out of the pot, dip the bottom back into the pot, so the liquid comes about halfway up the ladle. The tension on the surface of the soup grabs any drips and pulls them back into the pot.

POULTRY SHEARS

ALTHOUGH YOU CAN USE A HEAVY CHEF'S knife to cut up a whole chicken into parts, a pair of poultry shears makes the task much easier. While a chef's knife will slip and slide on the skin and often get stuck in bone, poultry shears cut with precision. They also are much safer to use. And if you want to cut up chicken backs for stock, poultry shears are a must.

Poultry shears should feel comfortable in your hand and work efficiently and quickly. Even cooks with small hands should be able to squeeze the blades together. Good shears will cut through bone the first time, without tearing skin or meat. We tested four brands of poultry shears, cutting up several chickens with each pair, to see if we could discern important differences.

Because your hands become greasy and slippery when cutting up a chicken, it is imperative that poultry shears have good handles. Some models have textured stainless steel handles (made from the same material as the blades), while others have plastic handles. We found that stainless steel handles, even textured ones, were slippery and hard to grip. Plastic handles were not always better, although we found one model with a bulbous and soft plastic grip that was especially comfortable and secure. Testers with medium-to-large hands found this model to be the best. However, testers with small hands had a hard time squeezing the extralarge handles.

Most poultry shears have regular scissor blades, although we found a few with serrated blades. The blades are attached by a spring that adds to their power. We preferred straight-edged blades to serrated blades. The latter tend to tear poultry skin. In addition to sharpness, we found that some blades were so tightly coiled that it was nearly impossible for some cooks to close them. If you have small hands, make sure that the spring isn't too tightly coiled and that you can close the blades without too much exertion.

Because of the spring that connects the blades, poultry shears have a mechanism for locking the blades shut when they are not in use. Some shears have a latch at the end of the handles. Others have a push-button closure or a lever that can be engaged to close the blades.

Unfortunately, some of these mechanisms cause other problems. The latch at the bottom of the handles on one model kept closing as we cut up chickens. Several times we had to stop cutting and unlatch the handles. We had the opposite problem with another pair of shears with a latch closure. The closing mechanism was so ineffective that the shears kept springing open during storage. Push-button and lever-style closures weren't much easier to operate.

Our advice is to pay attention when storing shears and not rely solely on the closing mechanism. If possible, keep shears in a plastic sleeve, not loose in a drawer.

ROASTING PANS

THOUGH MOST COOKS HAUL OUT THEIR roasting pan infrequently, when you do need this large pan, nothing else will do. A roasting pan is a must for a turkey or prime rib. It's also sometimes essential when browning meat or vegetables for use in soups or stews.

A roasting pan should promote deep, even browning of food. It should be easy to maneuver in and out of the oven. And it should be able to travel from oven to stovetop, so that you can deglaze the pan and loosen drippings.

Roasting pans can be made from stainless steel, stainless steel with an aluminum core, enameled steel, nonstick-coated aluminum, or anodized aluminum, all of which we tested. We decided not to test pans lined with copper, which are prohibitively expensive; cast-iron pans, which when loaded with food are too heavy to lift; and pans made from Pyrex, ceramic, or stoneware, all of which seem better suited to lasagne and casseroles because they can't be used on top of the stove.

We tested eight roasting pans and preferred the materials we like in other cookware—stainless steel with an aluminum core (for better heat conduction) and anodized aluminum. These materials are heavy and produce excellent browning. Although nonstick coatings made cleanup easier, roasting racks slid around in these pans. For instance, when one test cook tilted a nonstick pan ever so slightly to remove it from the oven, a turkey and rack slid sharply to one side, which threw off her balance and nearly landed the hot turkey at her feet.

Roasting pans generally come in two different styles—upright handles and side handles (see illustrations below). Upright handles tend to be square in shape, while side handles are generally oval loops. We found upright handles to be easier to grip. The problem with side handles is that their position, coupled with the large size of the pan, can cause you to bring your forearms perilously close to the hot oven walls. We tested one pan without handles, which was by far the most difficult to take out of the oven.

We tested pans ranging in length from 16 to 20 inches and in width from 11 to 14 inches. We preferred pans that measured about 16 inches long and 12 to 14 inches across. Larger pans made for an awkward fit in the oven, and, because of their large surface area, tended to burn pan drippings more easily.

In terms of weight, heavier pans performed better in all tests, especially on top of the stove. Lightweight pans buckled, and the meat browned quite spottily.

To summarize, heavy-duty pans made from stainless steel with an aluminum core or anodized aluminum work best to brown foods, especially if the pan is to be used on top of the stove as well as in the oven. Expect to spend $150 for a top-flight pan.

TWO KINDS OF HANDLES FOR ROASTING PANS

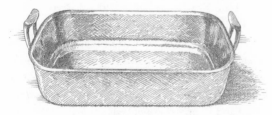

The handles on this roasting pan are upright and easy to grasp.

Side handles, like those on this roasting pan, are more difficult to grasp than upright handles and seem more likely to cause burns.

SCALES

EVERY SERIOUS COOK NEEDS AN ACCURATE scale for weighing fruits, vegetables, and meats. For example, four potatoes can weigh 1 pound or 3 pounds, depending on their size. The former will make a thin soup, the latter a thick soup, so many recipe writers specify quantities in weight.

Two types of kitchen scales are worth considering. Mechanical scales operate on a spring and lever system. When an item is placed on the scale, internal springs are compressed. The springs are attached to levers, which move a needle on the scale's display (a ruler with lines and numbers printed on a piece of paper and glued to the scale). The more the springs are compressed, the farther the needle moves along the ruler.

Electronic, or digital, scales have two plates that are calibrated to a fixed distance. The bottom plate is stationary, the top plate is not. When food is placed on the platform attached to the top plate, the distance between the plates changes slightly. The movement of the top plate (no more than one thousandth of an inch) causes a change in flow of the electricity in the scale's circuitry. This change is translated into a weight and expressed in numbers displayed on the face of the scale.

We tested 10 electronic scales and nine mechanical scales. As a group, our test kitchen staff vastly preferred the electronic scales. Their digital displays are much easier to read than the measures on most mechanical scales, where the lines on the ruler are so closely spaced it's impossible to nail down the precise weight within half an ounce. Also, many mechanical scales could only weigh items within a limited range—usually between 1 ounce and 5 pounds. What's the point of owning a scale that can't weigh a large chicken or roast? Most electronic scales can handle items that weigh as much as 10 pounds and as little as ¼ ounce. Among the electronic scales we tested, we found that several features make the difference between a good electronic scale and a great one.

Readability is a must. The displayed numbers should be large. They should also be steeply angled and as far from the weighing platform as possible. If the display is too close to the platform, the numbers can hide beneath the rim of a dinner plate or cake pan.

An automatic shut-off feature will save battery life, but this feature can be annoying, especially if the shut-off cycle kicks in at under two minutes. A scale that shuts off automatically after five minutes or more is easier to use.

A large weighing platform (that detaches for easy cleaning) is another plus. Last, we preferred electronic scales that display weight increments in decimals rather than fractions. The former are more accurate and easier to work with when scaling a recipe up or down.

SKIMMERS

WHEN MEAT, CHICKEN, OR FISH IS SIMMERED to make stock, foam is released by the bones and will rise to the surface, along with other impurities. To improve the appearance and flavor of the finished stock, we sometimes found it necessary to skim off this foam as the stock simmered. A mesh skimmer is the best tool for the job, removing only the impurities and leaving all the liquid behind. (A large spoon can be used, but invariably this tool removes some precious stock along with the foam.)

We like a long-handled metal skimmer that ends in a flat, mesh-covered spoon. Choose a spoon covered with a fine-mesh screen; it will trap more impurities than more loosely woven mesh.

STOCKPOTS

IF YOU WANT TO MAKE CHICKEN STOCK OR enough soup to feed a crowd, you will need a large pot, usually called a stockpot. A stockpot is tall and narrow to minimize the amount of evaporation that occurs across the small surface area of the liquid. This pot is also great for cooking pasta.

Stockpots can be made from numerous materials, including stainless steel (often with an aluminum layer sandwiched inside to promote heat conduction), aluminum, anodized aluminum, copper, and enameled steel. Some stockpots are coated with a nonstick finish. Stockpots can range in size from 5½ quarts to 20 quarts or more. Stockpots can weigh as little as 2 pounds or as much as 10 pounds.

A good stockpot will do more than just boil water. The bottom should be heavy enough to permit even browning without scorching, especially since many soup recipes begin by sautéing aromatic vegetables and many stock recipes begin by browning meat.

We rounded up six stockpots in a variety of materials. (We decided not to test copper, since a stockpot made from this material often costs $500.) We chose 12-quart pots—a size that we find convenient for most uses. (Only cooks who make extralarge batches of soup will want something bigger.) We boiled pasta in each pot, noting the time it took for 6 quarts of water to come to a boil and prepared vegetable stock in each pot, starting with a slow sauté of onions, carrots, celery, and garlic.

The pasta test proved inconclusive. Water came to a boil in all six pots in about the same amount of time. This result makes sense since the water—not just the pot material—is responsible for conducting heat. In a related test, we brought water to a boil, reduced the heat to low, and checked to make sure each pot could maintain a gentle simmer. All the pots performed well. Since water is water, the type of material hardly matters when boiling or simmering in a stockpot.

The vegetable stock test, in particular the sautéing step, was much more informative. When making vegetable stock, we find it best to sauté the vegetables slowly to soften their texture and extract as much flavor as possible. However, you don't want the vegetables to brown too much or the stock will taste scorched. We sweated the vegetables in a covered pot for half an hour over low heat, hoping that the vegetables would emerge tender and lightly caramelized.

Even with the heat set to low, the vegetables burned in the inexpensive aluminum, stainless steel, and enameled steel pots. The lightest pots (those weighing just under 2 pounds) turned in the worst performance on this test, burning the onions in just 15 minutes. Even in a slightly heavier pot (about 3 pounds), the onions were burned by the 23-minute mark.

The heavier (and more expensive) pots in our testing did not overheat and allowed us to sweat the vegetables for a full 30 minutes and achieve proper caramelization. We particularly liked the anodized aluminum pot (it weighed more than 6 pounds) as well as the stainless steel pot with an internal layer of aluminum to promote even heat conduction (this pot weighed just under 6 pounds).

In the end, testers preferred to sweat vegetables in the shiny stainless pot because it was easier to see what was happening to the vegetables. Sautéing on the anodized aluminum finish takes an act of faith, as it's very hard to discern the color of the vegetables against the dark cooking surface. We had the same problem when sautéing on the nonstick surface.

As for cleanup, the nonstick pot was the easiest to wash, although the heavy pots weren't bad. Forget about the light pots—the vegetables burned so badly that they all required a lot of soaking and elbow grease to clean.

The bottom line is that you get what you pay for. We loved all the pots we tested with prices above $150. A $20 pot is fine for cooking pasta and simmering stock, but forget about sautéing or browning in it—the bottom is so thin that everything burns. You could buy a cheap stockpot and then start soup and stock recipes that call for sautéing in a heavy-duty sauté pan, but this compromise is cumbersome.

STRAINERS

STRAINERS ARE USED IN A VARIETY OF SOUP and stew recipes. In some cases, you need only separate solid ingredients from liquids (pasta and water, meat and stock). In this case, a common bowl-shaped colander (with small perforations in the metal) or a standard strainer covered with coarse mesh will do just fine.

In some instances clarity is important, and you will want to use a strainer covered with fine mesh to separate the solids completely from the liquid. For instance, clarity is one measure of a good vegetable stock. When it comes time to remove the flavor-exhausted vegetables from the savory liquid, your choice of strainer is an important consideration. By passing the stock through a colander or a regular strainer, you may create a mess as the liquid sloshes out the sides, and you will probably find that some small pieces of vegetable will find their way into the

strained stock. The best tool to use for this purpose is a conical strainer with a functional funnel shape that draws liquid through its pointed base.

There are two types of conical strainers—a chinois and a china cap (see illustrations below). A chinois is covered with several layers of fine mesh (finer than the screens on your windows). No solids can pass through the mesh. A chinois is often used to produce perfectly smooth sauces and custards.

A china cap has a perforated metal body, a long handle for easy gripping, and a hook for resting on the rims of pots or bowls to facilitate use. The perforations come in two sizes, coarse and fine. We found that fine perforations work best for straining stocks—they are small enough to allow the liquid to pass through relatively particle-free, leaving the mass of spent vegetables behind.

Between a chinois and a china cap, we prefer a china cap for straining stock. It is more affordable and just as effective as a fine-mesh chinois for this

A CHINOIS VERSUS A CHINA CAP

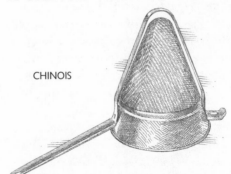

CHINOIS

A chinois is covered with fine woven mesh and will trap all solids, even small bits. It's ideal for producing a perfectly smooth pureed soup or bisque.

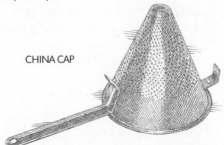

CHINA CAP

A china cap has the same conical shape as a chinois but consists of metal perforations rather than mesh screen. It's best for straining hot, thin liquids through bones and vegetables; it will allow tiny solids to pass through. We use it to strain solids from stock.

task. However, a chinois is a must for flawless pureed soups. The cook who makes soups often should own both.

VEGETABLE PEELERS

YOU MIGHT IMAGINE THAT ALL VEGETABLE peelers are pretty much the same. Not so. In our research, we turned up 25 peelers, many with quite novel features. The major differences were the fixture of the blade, either stationary or swiveling; the material of the blade, carbon stainless steel, stainless steel, or ceramic; and the orientation of the blade to the handle, either straight in line with the body or perpendicular to it. The last arrangement, with the blade perpendicular to the handle, is called a harp, or Y, peeler because the frame looks like the body of a harp or the letter Y. This type of peeler, which is popular in Europe, works with a pulling motion rather than the shucking motion of most American peelers. (See illustrations at right.)

To test the peelers, we recruited several cooks and asked them to peel carrots, potatoes, lemons, butternut squash, and celery root. In most cases, testers preferred the Oxo Good Grips peeler with a sharp stainless steel blade that swivels. Peelers with stationary blades are fine for peeling carrots, but they have trouble hugging the curves on potatoes.

The Y-shaped peelers tested well, although they removed more flesh along with the skin on potatoes, lemons, and carrots and therefore did not rate as well as the Oxo Good Grips. The one case where this liability turned into an asset was with butternut squash. The Y-shaped peelers took off the skin as well as the greenish-tinged flesh right below the skin in one pass. With the Oxo Good Grips, it was necessary to go over the peeled flesh once the skin had been removed.

ZESTERS

CITRUS ZEST—THE COLORED PEEL FROM oranges, lemons, and the like—is often added to soups and stews. The zest can take many forms. Some recipes use narrow strips; others call for minced or grated zest.

There are a variety of tools designed to remove citrus zest. The conventional zester has a flat blade that is curved at the end. On this curved section there are small holes (usually five, but sometimes more). You pull the zester over the fruit so that the holes remove long, thin strands of zest. The long strips can be used as is or minced.

Among the zesters we tested, we liked ones with short handles (about 3 inches long). We felt that these models gave us better control. Zesters with long handles (some have handles that measure 6 inches) are harder to control.

Many recipes call for grated zest. We find that flat, very fine graters work better than flat, coarse cheese graters or four-sided box graters. The design for flat, very fine graters was inspired by a rasp, a woodworking tool. These graters are shaped like a ruler (long and narrow) and covered with hundreds of tiny holes. (The same tool can be used to grate hard cheese. See the illustration on page 6.) Run a lemon across these sharp blades and within seconds you have a dry mound of grated zest that can be added directly to many recipes.

TWO STYLES OF VEGETABLE PEELER

CLASSIC

The classic vegetable peeler has a blade that is straight in line with the handle. We found that this model, with its bulbous handle, is particularly easy to grip.

HARP

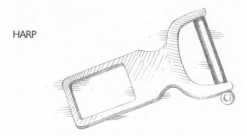

On some vegetable peelers, the blade is perpendicular to the handle. Because of this alignment, it is called a harp, or Y, peeler.

2

STOCKS

AS THE FRENCH MASTER CHEF ESCOFFIER proclaimed, "Stock is everything . . . without it nothing can be done." In professional kitchens, stocks are the basis of almost every savory dish and sauce. Many restaurants make duck, veal, and goose stocks along with basics like chicken and fish stocks.

When making soups and stews at home, stocks are just as important. However, the home cook is more likely to focus on four classic stocks—chicken, beef, vegetable, and fish. Homemade stocks are essential in brothy soups. Homemade stocks have richness, body, and flavor that canned versions will never possess. For instance, wonton soup or beef noodle soup made with commercial broth is vastly inferior to versions made with good homemade stock. If we don't have homemade stock on hand, we would rather not make these soups than eat pale imitations.

Canned broths do have their place in the home kitchen. They can be used in stews or soups that contain plenty of vegetables, pasta, grains, or beans. However, when you need real homemade stock, there is no other option. Preparing your own stock is one of the best culinary investments you can make.

There are plenty of myths and lore surrounding the making of good stocks. In French kitchens, many chefs would rather go out of business than reveal their secret formulas. After making hundreds (if not thousands) of batches of stock, we have some thoughts on some of the most popular notions about stock making.

Good stock starts with good ingredients. Although this sounds obvious, many sources suggest saving up scraps of meat and bits of leftover vegetables until you have enough to make stock. Tired vegetables and less-than-fresh meat will make a poor stock. In our tests, we found that you can taste the difference between stocks made from a mass-market chicken and a premium brand. Soft carrots, wilted cabbage, and moldy onions cannot be magically transformed into delicious stock. Use common sense, and don't put anything in the stockpot that you would not otherwise cook and eat.

When bones (whether from meat, chicken, or fish) simmer in water, they release tiny impurities—bits of meat and protein. The impurities become trapped in foam, which rises to the surface of the liquid as the stock cooks. (See page 17 for scientific information on what causes the formation of foams.) Some sources say that skimming this foam is mandatory, while others say not to bother. Classic sources not only suggest skimming the foam as the stock cooks but also recommend straining finished stocks through cheesecloth for absolute clarity.

We wondered if it's truly necessary to skim this grayish foam. We put this cookbook commandment to the test with two pots of beef stock and two pots of chicken stock, skimming just one pot of each as they cooked. After cooking, we strained and skimmed away the surface fat of all four pots. When it came to taste, we found that skimming the foam during cooking made no difference in the beef or chicken stock. As for appearance, the unskimmed chicken stock was more cloudy than the skimmed chicken stock, while there was no discernible difference in the two beef stocks.

Our conclusion? When making a hearty,

INGREDIENTS: Stock versus Broth

The terms stock and broth have become synonymous in recent years. At least technically, though, there are differences between them.

According to classic culinary reference books, broth is something that can be served on its own. Broth is made with meat (sometimes supplemented with bones) or a whole chicken and simmered until the meat or chicken is done. The meat or chicken is pulled from the pot and is used in the soup or reserved for sandwiches or salads.

In contrast, stock is always destined to be a component in another dish, such as a soup, sauce, gravy, or risotto. Stock is made from meaty bones, usually from the leg if making beef stock or from the back, neck, and wings if making chicken stock. The bones are simmered until they are completely spent, having given every ounce of their flavor to the liquid. The bones (and any meat attached to them) are discarded once the stock is strained.

Still, these are technical distinctions. Home cooks are more likely to categorize soup liquid as either a stock or a broth depending on whether it is homemade or commercial. In this book, we have followed this popular convention, using the term stock when referring to the homemade liquid base for soup. We use the term broth when referring to commercial products.

ingredient-rich soup, you can skip skimming. Small chunks of vegetable and meat will hide any imperfections in the unskimmed stock. However, in a brothy soup based on chicken stock, such as matzo ball or wonton soup, the difference between the unskimmed and skimmed stocks will be quite noticeable. The unskimmed will contain bits of sediment that settle at the bottom of each bowl. Because you may not always know how you will eventually use stock, we recommend skimming the foam as the stock simmers. That said, it's fine if a few impurities get left behind. We find that straining most stocks through cheesecloth to remove every last solid speck is too much of a bother. Many home cooks don't have cheesecloth, and for those who do the straining process can be tedious and messy.

Most experts agree that the rate at which a stock cooks is key, but not all sources suggest the same cooking temperature. Common wisdom says that stocks should simmer slowly. In our tests, we found that rapid simmering or boiling causes fat droplets released by meat or chicken to become more finely dispersed and thus more difficult to remove. Our tasters found that chicken stock made by rapidly boiling the liquid was greasy and unpalatable.

So what, exactly, is a gentle or slow simmer? When liquid is gently simmering, you see a few small bubbles breaking the surface every few seconds. As the heat rises, the bubbles become larger and break the surface more rapidly. At this point, the liquid is simmering briskly.

Finally, we noted that most sources advise against salting stock as it cooks. For chefs, this caveat makes sense, as stock is often greatly reduced and concentrated for use in sauces. For the home cook, who is

likely to make stock strictly for soups and stews, this logic doesn't quite hold up. In our tests, we found that stocks taste better when salt is added during the cooking process. Adding salt later (when using the stock to make soup) isn't quite as effective, tending to produce a one-dimensional (and salty-tasting) soup. When added during the stock-making process, salt brings out more flavors in the stock and blends more easily with other ingredients.

Once your stock is done, it must be strained to remove solids and cooled quickly. Stock left at room temperature for long periods of time is a perfect growth medium for bacteria. We generally portion out strained stock into several small containers so that it cools rapidly. We then refrigerate the stock as soon as possible. Once chilled, it's easy to defat stock. Simply use a spoon to skim off the congealed fat on the surface.

Stock freezes beautifully, and the efficient cook will always have some on hand. Try freezing stock in very small airtight containers, or try one of the freezing stock in portions tips on page 20. We find portions of one cup or so allow for the most flexibility in later use.

STRAINING STOCK

Once the solids have given up their flavor, they must be strained from the liquid. Because the solids can cause lots of splashing during straining, it's easy to lose some precious stock in the process. We thus recommend using a large pot with a pasta insert when making stock. When the solids are ready to be strained, simply lift the insert and its cargo out of the pot easily and neatly. For clarity, the remaining liquid should be strained, but this job becomes much simpler when there aren't any large solids in the pot. Note that this tip works best with stocks that don't involve sautéing, such as the Traditional Chicken Stock on page 23.

SCIENCE: What Causes Foam?

What is that gray foam that forms on the surface of some liquids, especially stocks, as they cook? All foams consist of tiny pockets of air surrounded by a thin layer of water. In the case of stock, protein molecules leach into the water as the meat and bones are heated. When bubbles are formed by heat agitation, the proteins unwind and embed themselves in the thin layer of water that surrounds each air bubble. This network of unfolded proteins acts to stabilize the foam.

CHICKEN STOCK

CHICKEN STOCK IS THE BASIS FOR COUNTLESS soups. It is the most important stock in any cook's repertoire. Most standard chicken stocks are not flavorful enough for a robust chicken soup. They are fine if ladled into risotto or stew but not strong enough for a broth-based chicken soup such as wonton soup or matzo ball soup. Our goal was simple: create a chicken stock with as much unadulterated chicken flavor as possible. We also wanted to streamline and speed up the process as much as we could.

We started with the most common technique for making stock—the simmering method. We placed all the ingredients (chicken, vegetables, aromatics, and water) in a pot, simmered everything for hours, then strained and defatted the stock. We tested a tremendous number of ingredients—everything from thyme and parsley to carrots and parsnips—and found that we preferred stock with fewer ingredients. Onions, salt, and bay leaves complemented the flavor of the chicken; everything else was a distraction. The exceptions were ginger and scallions, which we like to use in place of the onion and bay leaves when making stock for an Asian soup. (For more details, see page 24.)

We tried making stock with a whole cut-up chicken, with whole legs, as well as with the more traditional necks and backs using the simmering method. While the necks and backs yielded a rich stock, tasters preferred stocks made with a cut-up chicken or whole legs, which had more flavor and

CHILLING STOCK QUICKLY

Here's a quick way to cool down stock quickly so it can be refrigerated. Fill a large, clean plastic beverage bottle almost to the top with water, seal it, and freeze it. Use the frozen bottle to stir the stock in the pot. The ice inside the bottle will cool the stock rapidly without diluting it.

body. Because whole legs are much less expensive, they are our first choice when using the traditional simmering method.

Some other findings emerged during our testing of traditional stock making:

1. Skim any impurities that rise to the surface as the water comes to a boil. Continue to skim any foam, once every hour or so, as the stock simmers. We found that removing the foam gave our stock a clearer appearance.

2. Reduce the heat once the stock comes to a boil. Boiling breaks the fat into tiny droplets that a gravy skimmer will not be able to trap. The result is greasy stock. While refrigerating the stock will allow the fat to congeal, at which point it can be removed, you may not always have time for this step. For the best results, gently simmer the stock—small bubbles will slowly and gently break through the surface.

3. Let the stock simmer as long as possible, up to five hours. We tried simmering stocks from one to six hours. When we tasted the various stocks, it was clear that more time yields a better stock. In fact, our favorite stock simmered for five hours. (After that we could not taste any improvement; evidently the bones were spent, having given up all their flavor to the stock.) Our long-cooked Traditional Chicken Stock has a rich, intense chicken flavor, just what you want when making a simple chicken soup with a few dumplings or matzo balls. Although you may be tempted to short-cut this process, don't. While stocks simmered for at least 2½ hours were fine (stocks simmered for less time were insipid), they lacked the intensity and flavor of longer-cooked stocks. Time, and a lot of it, is needed to extract the full flavor from the chicken.

Our testing had produced a great stock and we had reached some interesting conclusions about traditional stock making, but we wondered if there was a quicker route to good stock. While throwing everything into the pot and letting it simmer for hours is easy (the hands-on work is no more than 10 minutes), you do need to be around the house. There are times when you need stock in a hurry or don't want to hang around the house for five hours. We were willing to try almost anything.

We tried blanching a whole chicken based on the theory that blanching keeps the chicken from releasing foam during cooking. The blanched chicken was then partially covered with water and placed in a heatproof bowl over a pan of simmering water. Cooked this way, the chicken never simmered, and the resulting stock was remarkably clear, refined, and full-flavored. The only problem: It took four hours to develop sufficient flavor. We also noted that our 4-pound chicken was good for nothing but the compost heap after being cooked so long.

A number of recipes promote roasting chicken bones or parts and then using them to make stock. The theory, at least, is that roasted parts will flavor stock in minutes, not hours. We tried this several times, roasting chicken backs, necks, and bones—

TWO WAYS TO DEFAT STOCK

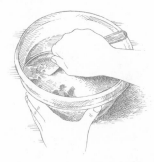

Stock should be defatted before being used. The easiest way to do this is to refrigerate it until the fat rises to the surface and congeals. Use a spoon to scrape the fat off the surface of the stock. When skimming chicken stock, you may want to save this fat, which makes a flavorful replacement for oil or butter when cooking. Chicken fat can be kept refrigerated in an airtight container for several days.

If you don't have time to refrigerate the stock and allow the fat to congeal, use a gravy skimmer. Pour the stock into the gravy skimmer, then pour it out through the spout attached to the bottom of the skimmer. The fat floating on top of the liquid will remain behind.

with and without vegetables. We preferred the roasted stock with vegetables. The resulting stock was dark in color and had a nice caramelized onion flavor, but it still wasn't the full-flavored stock we were looking for. While the roasted flavor was quite strong, the actual chicken flavor was too tame.

At last, we tried sautéing a chicken, hacked into small pieces, with an onion until the chicken was slightly browned. The pot was then covered and the chicken and onion cooked over low heat until they released their rich, flavorful juices, which took about 20 minutes. Only at this point did we add water, and the stock was simmered for just 20 minutes more. We knew we were onto something when we smelled the chicken and onions sautéing, and the finished stock confirmed what our noses had detected. It tasted pleasantly sautéed, not boiled. We had some refining to do. For once, we had too much flavor.

We substituted chicken backs and wing tips for the whole chicken and used more water. This stock was less intense, but just the right strength to serve as a base for some of the best chicken soup we've ever tasted. We made the stock twice more—once without the onion and once with onion, celery, and carrot. The onion added a flavor dimension we liked; the extra vegetables neither added nor detracted from the final soup, so we left them out.

After much trial and error, we had a master recipe that delivered liquid gold in just 60 minutes. While this recipe requires more hands-on work (hacking up parts, browning an onion, then chicken parts), it is ready in a fraction of the time required to make a traditional, long-cooking stock.

The question before us now: How do you come up with these chicken parts for stock? The Buffalo chicken wing fad has made wings more expensive than legs and thighs. For those who can buy chicken backs, this is clearly an inexpensive way to make stock. Our local grocery stores usually sell them for almost nothing, but in many locations they may be difficult to get. Luckily, we found that relatively inexpensive whole legs make incredibly full-flavored stocks. In a side-by-side comparison of stocks, one made from backs and one from whole legs, we found the whole leg stock to be more full-flavored. Just don't try to salvage the meat once the stock is finished. After 5 minutes of sautéing, 20 minutes of sweating, and another 20 minutes of simmering, the meat is void of flavor.

If you are making a soup that needs chicken meat, use a whole chicken as directed in Quick Chicken Stock with Sautéed Breast Meat (page 23). The breast is sautéed separately and then set aside while the rest of the bird—legs, back, wings, and giblets—is sautéed and sweated. The breasts are added back to the pot along with the water, and the result is perfectly cooked breast meat, ready to be skinned and shredded when cool. The remaining chicken pieces are discarded. We like the tidiness of this method; one chicken yields one pot of soup.

One note about our recipe for quick stock: We found it necessary to cut the chicken into pieces small enough to release their flavorful juices in a short period of time (see "Hacking Up a Chicken for Stock" on page 22). A cleaver or poultry shears speeds up this process. Don't try to cut through chicken bones with a chef's knife. The blade isn't strong enough to cut through bone, and you may hurt yourself as the knife slips and slides. Even if you do manage to cut through the bone, your knife may become nicked in the process.

BUYING CHICKEN

GREAT CHICKEN STOCK STARTS WITH A GREAT chicken. Most markets offer consumers several choices, which can be divided into two broad categories: mass-market and premium.

Mass-market producers, such as Tyson and Perdue, aim to offer a good chicken at a low cost.

TWO WAYS TO FREEZE STOCK IN CONVENIENT PORTIONS

Here are two easy ways to freeze defatted stock in small portions without relying on plastic containers, which always seem to be in short supply.

1. Ladle the stock into an oversized nonstick muffin tin (each hole holds just about one cup) and freeze.

2. When the stock is frozen, release it by twisting the muffin tin in the same manner you twist an ice cube tray, using a knife to loosen each block, if necessary. Place the blocks of frozen stock in a plastic bag, seal tightly, and use as needed.

1. Line a coffee mug with a quart-sized zipper-lock plastic bag. (This keeps the bag open so both hands will be free for pouring.)

2. Fill the bag almost to the top with room-temperature stock, and seal it. Repeat until all the stock has been placed in bags.

3. Stack the bags flat in a large, shallow roasting pan and freeze. Once the stock is solidly frozen, the bags can be removed from the pan and stored in the freezer. When frozen this way, stock takes up very little room.

These birds are the most widely available, especially if you want to buy parts such as backs and wings.

The premium category includes kosher chickens, which have always been popular in urban areas with Jewish populations and have become increasingly available owing to concerns about cleanliness in chicken processing. In accordance with religious law, kosher chickens are bathed in saltwater to remove blood. This process also seasons the meat slightly and is thought to improve flavor. All kosher chickens must be grown and processed according to a standardized protocol and are clearly labeled.

The remaining premium chickens are harder to categorize. Many small chicken farms have returned to the animal-raising practices of the past and are now producing "free-range" chickens. Although there is no clear definition of this term, most operations that allow their birds access to the outdoors use it. Many free-range chickens are also labeled "organic" or "natural." Again, definitions can be hazy, but most farmers that rely on organic feed and reject the use of antibiotics to treat disease in their flocks are using one or both of these terms.

To make some sense of the vast array of choices, we pitted four of the leading supermarket chickens (all mass-market brands) against five premium chickens. This last group included kosher, free-range, and organic chickens, all of which have one thing in common—they cost more than mass-market brands.

We purchased one bird from each company and then roasted it plain, without seasonings, until the internal temperature was 160 degrees. Half of each bird was carved, and the rest was left on the carcass so panelists could judge the bird's overall appearance. The results of this tasting were quite clear. The mass-market brands received uniformly negative marks. Several panelists said they would rather swear off chicken than eat these tasteless, mushy birds. In comparison, most of the premium chickens were thoroughly enjoyed. The flavor of these birds was stronger and sometimes even a bit gamey. The texture was also firmer but not tough.

So a premium chicken tastes better than a mass-market bird. That's not really a shocking revelation. Although the difference was clear on a roasted chicken, could we tell the difference when making stock? We chose the top-rated bird (Bell & Evans, a popular East Coast brand) and the lowest-rated bird (Perdue) and made stock from each.

Right from the start, we noticed significant differences in the two stocks. When we unwrapped the chickens, we noticed that the Perdue bird was yellow and released a lot of pink watery liquid. In contrast, the Bell & Evans chicken appeared plumper, the skin was whitish, and there was no liquid released. We hacked up both chickens and started to sauté each for our Quick Chicken Stock recipe. It was clear that more fat was being released from the Perdue chicken. We continued with the recipe, adding the water, simmering, and then straining out the solids. The stock made with the Perdue chicken was lighter in color.

We cooled each stock. A thick layer of yellow fat formed on top of the Perdue stock. It was solid and easy to remove. The Bell & Evans stock had a much thinner layer of yellow-tan fat on top, which had not fully solidified. We spooned it off with no problem. Removing the fat revealed a huge difference in the texture of the two stocks. The Perdue stock was thin and pure liquid. The Bell & Evans stock had gelatinized and was thick, almost like Jell-O.

A taste test confirmed that the Bell & Evans stock was far superior. It was rich in flavor and had a great mouthfeel. It tasted very chickeny, like a stock that was well made and had been cooking for hours on the stovetop. The Perdue stock had little substance and had a thin feeling in the mouth. It was very weak in flavor, almost like a stock that hadn't finished cooking. Although each stock was prepared with 2 teaspoons of salt, tasters wanted to add salt to the Perdue stock in an attempt to improve its flavor.

Our conclusion was simple: Whether you are roasting a chicken or using it to make stock, buy a premium bird. When we talked to industry experts, they offered several explanations as to why premium chickens taste so much better.

First, many small companies have invested heavily in livestock gene pool development. Some specialty companies are using French birds; others use old-fashioned American varieties known for their superior flavor. (Larger companies may be more concerned with the size of the breast or other breeding characteristics that involve keeping costs down or appealing to perceived consumer interests, such as skin color.)

Second, some of the premium chickens have access to the outdoors or at least have the freedom to wander in a fairly large indoor area. Exercise is directly linked to flavor development and any hint of gaminess. The more a bird exercises, the leaner and more flavorful (and darker) the muscles—especially in the legs—become.

Third, many small outfits take extra steps in processing (another reason for their higher cost). Bell & Evans ships chickens loose on ice so that they can weep fluids and blood as they make their way from processing plant to supermarket. The net weight of each bird is reduced, so the company actually earns less for every chicken. In contrast, mass-market brands are usually shrink-wrapped at the plant and then frozen to keep moisture from accumulating in the packages. But many experts believe that a chicken must lose these fluids to develop a stronger, meatier flavor.

Fourth, many smaller companies "grow out" their birds for eight or nine weeks instead of slaughtering them at six or seven weeks, as the industry giants do. The older the bird, the more flavorful its muscles are likely to have become.

In sum, we think it's worth spending a little extra money to get a chicken that tastes great. In addition to Bell & Evans chickens, our panel gave high ratings to kosher chickens from Empire (which are sold nationwide), free-range, natural chickens from D'Artagnan (available in some markets, mostly in the East, as well as by mail), and free-range chickens from La Belle Rouge (raised without growth stimulants or antibiotics and available in select locations around the country). These premium chickens range in price from $1.59 to $3 a pound, but we have found that you get what you pay for when it comes to chicken.

Whether buying a premium or mass-market brand, make sure the chicken you buy is fresh. If you detect off odors—strong enough to permeate plastic wrap—or see excess liquid in the package, walk away. Since poultry is shrink-wrapped, you must rely mostly on "sell-by" dates rather than your senses. Many supermarkets label birds with a sell-by date that is a week or more away from the day they arrive in the store. You don't want to buy a bird that has been sitting in the supermarket for a week. Always check the sell-by date and try to get a chicken that still has plenty of shelf life left.

HACKING UP A CHICKEN FOR STOCK

You can hack up a chicken with a cleaver (see pages 24 and 25) or use poultry shears (see page 10). If using a whole chicken, start by removing the whole legs and wings from the body; set them aside. Separate the back from the breast, then split the breast and set the halves aside. Hack or cut the back crosswise into three or four pieces, then halve each of these pieces. Cut the wing at each joint to yield three pieces. Leave the wing tip whole, then halve each of the remaining joints. Because of their large bones, the legs and thighs are the most difficult to cut. Start by splitting the leg and thigh at the joint, then hack or cut each to yield three or four pieces. If using just backs and wing tips, or whole legs, follow the directions above for those parts.

Quick Chicken Stock
MAKES ABOUT 2 QUARTS

Chicken pieces are sautéed and then sweated before being cooked in water for a rich but very quick stock. This is our favorite all-purpose stock. It takes about an hour to prepare.

- 1   tablespoon vegetable oil
- 1   medium onion, chopped medium
- 4   pounds whole chicken legs or backs and wing tips, cut into 2-inch pieces (see "Hacking Up a Chicken for Stock," left)
- 2   quarts boiling water
- 2   teaspoons salt
- 2   bay leaves

1. Heat the oil in a large stockpot or Dutch oven over medium-high heat. Add the onion; sauté until colored and softened slightly, 2 to 3 minutes. Transfer the onion to a large bowl.

2. Add half of the chicken pieces to the pot; sauté both sides until lightly browned, 4 to 5 minutes. Transfer the cooked chicken to the bowl with the onions. Sauté the remaining chicken pieces. Return the onions and chicken pieces to the pot. Reduce the heat to low, cover, and cook until the chicken releases its juices, about 20 minutes.

3. Increase the heat to high; add the boiling water, salt, and bay leaves. Return to a simmer, then cover and barely simmer until the stock is rich and flavorful, about 20 minutes.

4. Strain the stock; discard the solids. Before using, defat the stock (see page 19). The stock can be refrigerated in an airtight container for up to 2 days or frozen for several months.

Quick Chicken Stock with Sautéed Breast Meat

MAKES ABOUT 2 QUARTS

Choose this stock when you want to have some breast meat in your soup.

I	tablespoon vegetable oil
I	whole chicken (about 4 pounds), breast meat removed on the bone, split, and reserved; remaining chicken cut into 2-inch pieces (see "Hacking Up a Chicken for Stock" on page 22)
I	medium onion, chopped medium
2	quarts boiling water
2	teaspoons salt
2	bay leaves

1. Heat the oil in a large stockpot or Dutch oven over medium-high heat. When the oil shimmers and starts to smoke, add the chicken breast halves; sauté both sides until lightly browned, about 5 minutes. Remove the chicken breast pieces and set aside. Add the onion to the pot; sauté until colored and softened slightly, 2 to 3 minutes. Transfer the onion to a large bowl.

2. Add half of the chicken pieces to the pot; sauté both sides until lightly browned, 4 to 5 minutes. Transfer the cooked chicken to the bowl with the onions. Sauté the remaining chicken pieces. Return the onions and chicken pieces (excluding the breasts) to the pot. Reduce the heat to low, cover, and cook until the chicken releases its juices, about 20 minutes.

3. Increase the heat to high; add the boiling water, the chicken breasts, salt, and bay leaves. Return to a simmer, then cover and barely simmer until the chicken breasts are cooked through and the stock is rich and flavorful, about 20 minutes.

4. Remove the chicken breasts from the pot. When cool enough to handle, remove the skin from the breasts, then remove the meat from the bones and shred into bite-sized pieces; discard the skin and bones. Strain the stock; discard the solids. Before using, defat the stock (see page 19). The shredded chicken and stock can be refrigerated separately in airtight containers for up to 2 days.

Traditional Chicken Stock

MAKES ABOUT 2 QUARTS

Long-cooked traditional stock is easy to prepare (you can do it in just a couple of steps) but requires five hours of cooking

---

SCIENCE: Chicken Safety

Given the prevalence of bacteria in the poultry supply in this country, it's probably best to assume that the bird you buy is contaminated. That means you need to follow some simple rules to minimize any potential danger.

Keep poultry refrigerated until just before cooking. Bacteria thrive at temperatures between 40 and 140 degrees. This also means leftovers should be promptly refrigerated. When handling poultry, make sure to wash hands, knives, cutting boards, and counters (and anything else that has come into contact with the raw bird, its juices, or your hands) with hot, soapy water. Be especially careful not to let the chicken, its juices, or your hands touch foods that will be eaten raw (like salad ingredients). Finally, cook poultry to an internal temperature of 160 degrees or higher to ensure that bacteria have been killed. (When making stocks, soups, and stews, this will not be a problem.)

time. If you would rather not stand over the stove and brown parts, this method is ideal. The stock tastes more like boiled chicken than the quick stock, which has the flavor of sautéed chicken. Most of our tasters preferred the quick stock ever so slightly. If you have a large pot (at least 12 quarts), you can double this recipe.

4	pounds whole chicken legs or backs and wing tips
3½	quarts water
1	medium onion, chopped medium
2	teaspoons salt
2	bay leaves

1. Place the chicken and water in a large stockpot (with an insert, if you have one; see "Straining Stock" on page 17) over medium-high heat, using a mesh skimmer to remove any foam that rises to the surface. Once the stock reaches a boil, reduce the heat, and simmer gently for 3 hours. Continue to skim foam occasionally.

2. Add the onion, salt, and bay leaves and simmer for another 2 hours.

3. Strain the stock; discard the solids. Before using, defat the stock (see page 19). The stock can be refrigerated in an airtight container for up to 2 days or frozen for several months.

ASIAN CHICKEN STOCK

WHEN WE DEVELOPED OUR BASIC RECIPES for stock, we found onion and bay leaves to be essential supporting flavor elements. When we began testing Chinese soups, however, tasters thought this stock tasted too "European." Consequently, we set out to test ways to infuse the stock with Asian flavors that would support but not overwhelm the flavor of the chicken. We identified a number of basic ingredients that could replace the onion and bay leaves, including garlic, ginger, scallions, rice wine, dry sherry, soy sauce, star anise, and Sichuan peppercorns.

We found that garlic—even just a single clove—was overpowering. Garlic not only reduced the chicken flavor but also made it impossible to taste any other flavors. We decided to omit garlic. Ginger was another story. It added a subtle perfume to the stock and was well liked by tasters. Many sources suggest smashing thin slices of ginger to release their flavor. We tested this tip and found it worked well. We also found scallions to be a welcome addition, serving as a more traditional Asian source of the sweet allium flavor supplied by onions.

While some tasters liked spices (such as star anise and Sichuan peppercorns), everyone in the test kitchen agreed that their flavors were too distinctive for a basic stock. The same was true of liquids such as rice wine, sherry, and soy sauce. The latter presented the additional problem of muddying the color of the stock.

EQUIPMENT: Cleavers

When making our Quick Chicken Stock or the variation with breast meat, you need to cut the chicken into small pieces that will release their flavor as quickly as possible. (In our traditional stock recipe the chicken simmers for such a long time that there is no need to cut up the parts.) We prefer to use a meat cleaver to hack the chicken into 2-inch pieces (see illustration on page 25).

The cleaver on the left is designed for chopping vegetables. It tapers gently to a slender cutting edge, while the meat cleaver on the right is more like a wedge, tapering within the last 2 centimeters. The hole at the top corner of the meat cleaver is for hanging the cleaver on a hook.

With ginger and scallions added to our homemade stock, we turned our attention to canned broth. (For information on buying canned chicken broth, see page 27.) We wondered if the same ingredients could be simmered in canned broth to improve its flavor. The answer was yes. Tasters found that decent canned broth was actually pretty good after being simmered for 15 minutes with ginger and scallions.

Asian Chicken Stock

MAKES ABOUT 2 QUARTS

The addition of ginger and scallions creates a traditional-tasting Chinese soup base.

1	tablespoon vegetable oil
4	pounds whole chicken legs or backs and wing tips, cut into 2-inch pieces (see Hacking Up a Chicken for Stock on page 22)
1	chunk (about 1 inch) unpeeled fresh ginger, sliced thin and lightly smashed (see illustration on page 26)
2	medium scallions, halved lengthwise and lightly smashed
2	quarts boiling water
2	teaspoons salt

1. Heat the oil in a large stockpot or Dutch oven over medium-high heat. Add half of the chicken pieces to the pot; sauté until both sides are lightly browned, 4 to 5 minutes. Transfer the cooked chicken to a bowl. Sauté the remaining chicken pieces. Return the first batch of chicken pieces to the pot. Reduce the heat to low, cover, and cook until the chicken releases its juices, about 20 minutes.

2. Stir in the ginger and scallions and cook for 1 minute. Increase the heat to high and add the boiling water and salt. Return to a simmer, then cover and barely simmer until the stock is rich and flavorful, about 20 minutes.

3. Strain the stock; discard the solids. Before using, defat the stock (see page 19). The stock can be refrigerated in an airtight container for up to 2 days or frozen for several months.

Asian Chicken Stock with Sautéed Breast Meat

MAKES ABOUT 2 QUARTS

Choose this stock when you want to have some breast meat in your soup.

1	tablespoon vegetable oil
1	whole chicken (about 4 pounds), breast meat removed on the bone, split, and reserved; remaining chicken cut into 2-inch pieces (see Hacking Up a Chicken for Stock on page 22)
1	chunk (about 1 inch) unpeeled fresh ginger, sliced thin and lightly smashed (see illustration on page 26)

USING A CLEAVER

1. To hack through bone, place your hand near the far end of the meat cleaver's handle, curling your fingers securely around it in a fist. Handle the meat cleaver the way you would a hammer, with the motion in the arm rather than the wrist and the weight of the blade's front tip leading the force of the chop.

2. If you cannot chop the bone in one strike, place the cleaver in the groove of the first chop, then strike the blade's blunt edge with a heavy mallet.

2   medium scallions, halved lengthwise and lightly
    smashed
2   quarts boiling water
2   teaspoons salt

1. Heat the oil in a large stockpot or Dutch oven over medium-high heat. When the oil shimmers and starts to smoke, add the chicken breast halves; sauté both sides until lightly browned, about 5 minutes. Remove the chicken breast pieces and set aside.

2. Add half of the chicken pieces to the pot; sauté both sides until lightly browned, 4 to 5 minutes. Transfer the cooked chicken to an empty bowl. Sauté the remaining chicken pieces. Return the chicken pieces (excluding the breasts) to the pot. Reduce the heat to low, cover, and cook until the chicken releases its juices, about 20 minutes.

3. Stir in the ginger and scallions and cook for 1 minute. Increase the heat to high; add the boiling water, the chicken breasts, and salt. Return to a simmer, then cover and barely simmer until the chicken breasts are cooked through and the stock is rich and flavorful, about 20 minutes.

4. Remove the chicken breasts from the pot.

SMASHING GINGER

To release flavorful oils from fresh ginger, thinly slice an unpeeled knob and then use the end of a chef's knife to smash each piece. Use the same technique to release flavorful oils from scallions that have been halved lengthwise. This technique works best when you want to infuse the flavor of ginger (or scallion) into a liquid, especially stock.

When cool enough to handle, remove the skin from the breasts, then remove the meat from the bones and shred into bite-sized pieces; discard the skin and bones. Strain the stock; discard the solids. Before using, defat the stock (see page 19). The shredded chicken and stock can be refrigerated separately in airtight containers for up to 2 days.

Improved Canned Chicken Broth

MAKES ABOUT 2 QUARTS

This broth is fine in soups with plenty of other flavorful ingredients. The shortcomings of canned broth are quite noticeable in a soup that puts broth center stage. We do not recommend canned broths, even when doctored up, in wonton soup, for instance. It is fine in most bean and vegetable soups. Unlike homemade stock, this broth is best used right away, since the added flavors start to fade quickly.

2   quarts low-sodium canned chicken broth,
    defatted (see illustrations on page 28)
1   carrot, peeled and sliced thin
1   medium onion, chopped medium
1   stalk celery, cut into chunks
1   bay leaf
    Several sprigs fresh parsley

1. Place all ingredients in a medium saucepan. Bring to a simmer. Simmer gently for 15 minutes.

2. Strain the broth; discard the solids. Use the stock as soon as possible; the improvement offered by the vegetables is temporary.

➤ VARIATION

Improved Canned Chicken Broth with Asian Flavors

Replace the carrot, onion, celery, bay leaf, and parsley with a 1-inch chunk of unpeeled fresh ginger, sliced thin and lightly smashed (see illustration, left), and 2 medium scallions, halved lengthwise and lightly smashed.

INGREDIENTS : Canned Chicken Broth

Like homemade stocks, commercial broths are made from the meat and bones of chickens, only chicken of a kind that's different from what we are accustomed to cooking at home. We mainly cook with meat birds, meaty breeds of chickens raised for about eight weeks and subsequently sold as roasters and broilers in the butcher section of the supermarket. The chickens used in commercial broths are hens, or egg layers. Hens are effectively productive for only one to two years. After that they are not suited to be sold as meat because they are typically skinny birds, having spent all their energy producing eggs. But because they are older and have been more active than young meat birds, they can be more flavorful, and, most important, they contain a higher density of the connective tissue known as collagen. When heated with moisture, collagen converts to gelatin and provides broth with body. So, basically, the food industry makes use of retired hens to flavor their broths—much like our grandmothers did.

But they sure must not be using the same ratio of bird to water as our grandmothers used. Few of the commercial broths in a tasting conducted in our test kitchen came close to the full-bodied consistency of a successful homemade stock. Many lacked even a hint of chicken flavor. Interestingly, the top four broths are all products of the Campbell Soup Company, of which Swanson is a subsidiary. In order, they were Swanson Chicken Broth, Campbell's Chicken Broth, Swanson Natural Goodness Chicken Broth (with 33 percent less sodium than regular Swanson chicken broth), and Campbell's Healthy Request Chicken Broth (with 30 percent less sodium than regular Campbell's chicken broth).

We tried to find out more about why Campbell's broths are superior to so many others, but the giant soup company declined to respond to questions, explaining that its recipes and cooking techniques are considered proprietary information. Many of the answers, however, could be found on the products' ingredient labels. As it turned out, the top two broths happened to contain the highest levels of sodium. Salt has been used for years in the food industry to make foods with less than optimum flavor tastier. The top two products also contained the controversial monosodium glutamate (MSG), a very effective flavor enhancer. (For more information about MSG, see page 32.)

Sadly, most of the products that had lower levels of salt and did not have the benefit of other food industry flavor enhancers simply tasted like dishwater. Their labels did indicate that their ingredients included "chicken broth" or "chicken stock" or sometimes both. But calls to both the U.S. Food and Drug Administration and the U.S. Department of Agriculture revealed that there are no standards of definition for chicken broth or stock, so that an ingredient label indicating that the contents include chicken broth or chicken stock could mean anything as long as some chicken is used.

Ingredients aside, we found one more important explanation for why most commercial broths simply cannot replicate the full flavor and body of a homemade stock. Most broths are sold canned, which entails an extended heating process carried out to ensure a sterilized product. The immediate disadvantage of this processing is that heat breaks down naturally present flavor enhancers found in chicken protein. And prolonged heating, which is necessary for canning, destroys other volatile flavors at the same time that it concentrates flavor components that are not volatile, such as salt.

A few national brands of chicken broth have begun to offer the option of aseptic packaging. Compared with traditional canning, the process of aseptic packaging entails a flash heating and cooling process that is said to help products better retain both their nutritional value and their flavor.

We decided to hold another tasting to see if we could detect more flavor in the products sold in aseptic packaging as compared to traditional cans. We tasted Swanson's traditional and Natural Goodness chicken broths sold in cans and in aseptic packages. The results fell clearly in favor of the aseptically packaged broths; both tasted cleaner and more chickeny than their canned counterparts. So if you are truly seeking the best of the best in commercial broths, choose one of the two Swanson broths sold in aseptic packaging. An opened aseptic package is said to keep in the refrigerator for up to two weeks (broth from a can is said to keep refrigerated for only a few days).

Until there are some unforeseen new advances in food science, we recommend either making your own chicken stock or sticking with one of the Campbell's products, preferably in an aseptic package. We did wonder, though, if there was some way to improve the flavor of commercial broth. The answer is yes. We found that simmering some aromatic vegetables in the broth removed some of the harshness typical of even the best commercial broths. If you have stray chicken parts around, such as clipped wing tips or a single back, add them as well. For more details, see the recipe on page 26.

DEFATTING CANNED BROTH

1. Most canned chicken broth contains a blob of fat that should be removed. While you can try to skim the fat off with a small spoon, the spoon can sometimes break the fat into smaller pieces. We find the following method is foolproof: Using a manual can opener, punch a small hole in the top of the can without turning. Rotate the can 180 degrees and make a second opening about ½ to 1 inch long.

2. Pour the stock through the larger opening. The liquid will pass through, but the more viscous fat will remain trapped in the can.

BEEF STOCK

BEEF STOCK SHOULD TASTE LIKE BEEF— almost as intense as pot roast jus—and be flavorful enough to need only a few vegetables and a handful of noodles or barley to make a good soup. We wanted a stock that could be made from the usual store of meat in the supermarket, and we didn't want to spend all day making it.

These goals notwithstanding, we thought it would be wise to start with a traditional stock to establish a baseline for testing. So we began with a traditional recipe calling for 4 pounds of beef bones fortified with a generous 2 pounds of beef as well as celery, carrot, onion, tomato, and fresh thyme, all covered with 4 quarts of water. Our plan was to taste the stock after 4, 6, 8, 12, and 16 hours of simmering.

At hours 4, 6, and even 8, our stock was weak and tasted mostly of vegetables. And while the 12- and 16-hour stocks were richly gelatinous, the flavors of vegetables and bones (not beef) predominated. Not willing to give up on this method quite yet, we found a recipe that instructed us to roast and then simmer beef bones, onions, and tomatoes—no celery or carrots—for 12 hours. During the last 3 hours of cooking, 3 pounds of beef was added to the pot. This, we thought, might be our ideal—one with great body from the bones, minimal vegetable flavor, and generous hunks of beef to further enhance the flavor of the rich, reduced stock. Once again, however, the stock was beautifully textured but had very little flavor; the vegetal taste was gone, but there was no real, deep beef flavor in its place. Time to move on.

Knowing now that it was going to take more meat than bones to get great flavor, we started our next set of tests by making stocks with different cuts of meat, including chuck, shank, round, arm blade, oxtail, and short ribs. We browned 2 pounds of meat with 1 pound of small marrowbones and then 3 pounds of bone-in cuts like shank, short ribs, and oxtails, also adding an onion to each pot. We covered the browned ingredients and let them "sweat" for 20 minutes. We added only a quart of water to each pot and simmered them until the meat was done.

With so little added water, these stocks were more braiselike than stocklike. But because more traditional methods yielded bland stocks, we decided to start with the flavor we were looking for and add water from there.

After a simmer of 1½ hours, our stocks were done, most tasting unmistakably beefy. Upon a blind tasting of each, we all agreed that the shank stock was our favorite, followed by the marrowbone-enhanced brisket and chuck. Not only was the stock rich, beefy, and full of body, the shank meat was soft and gelatinous, perfect for shredding and adding to a pot of soup. Because it appeared that our stock was going to require a generous amount of meat, the brisket's price ($3.99 per pound compared with $1.99 for both the shanks and the chuck) knocked it out of the running.

Though not yet perfect, this stock was on its way to fulfilling our requirements. It could be made from common supermarket cuts—shank or a combination of chuck and marrowbones. And it didn't take all day. This stock was done in about 2½ hours and was full-flavored as soon as the meat was tender. Unlike traditional stocks, which require a roasting pan, stockpot, oven, and burner, this was a one-pot, stovetop-only affair. Finally, this stock didn't require a cornucopia of vegetables to make it taste good. To us, the more vegetables, the weaker the beef flavor. At this point, our recipe called for one lone onion.

What we sacrificed in vegetables, however, we were apparently going to have to compensate for in meat. Our 3 pounds of meat was yielding only 1 quart of stock. But now that we had a flavor we liked, we decided to see if we could achieve an equally beefy stock with less meat.

To stretch the meat a bit further, we increased the amount by 50 percent and doubled the amount of water. Unfortunately, the extra water diluted the meat flavor, and though this stock was better than many we had tried earlier, we missed the strong beef flavor of our original formula. To intensify flavor, we tried adding a pound of ground beef to the 3 pounds of meat and bones, thinking we would throw away the spent meat during straining. But ground beef only fattened up the stock, and its distinctive hamburger flavor muddied the waters. Also, fried ground beef does not brown well, and this burger-enhanced stock confirmed that browning had not only deepened the color but beefed up the flavor as well.

We went back to our original proportions, doubling the meat and bones along with the water. Not surprisingly, the stock was deeply colored, richly flavored, and full-bodied. We were finally convinced that a good beef stock requires a generous portion of meat. Though our stock required more meat than was necessary for the soup, the leftover beef was delicious, good for sandwiches and cold salads.

At this point our richly flavored stock needed enlivening. Some stock recipes accomplished this with a splash of vinegar, others with tomato. Although we liked tomatoes in many of the soups we developed for this book, they didn't do much for our stock. And although vinegar was an improvement, red wine made the stock even better. We ultimately fortified our stock with a modest half cup of red wine, adding it to the pot after browning the meat.

Salt was the next issue to consider. We tested various amounts, ranging from none to 1 tablespoon. Stock made with too little salt was flat tasting, and the meat (which would eventually go into the soup) was underseasoned. We found that 2 teaspoons of salt enhances the flavor of the stock and the meat, without making either too salty.

We had followed our method for making chicken stock without giving it much thought—browning then sweating a generous portion of meat and bones, adding water just to cover, and simmering for a relatively short time. We knew the ratio of meat to water was right, but we questioned whether sweating the meat for 20 minutes before adding the water was necessary. Side-by-side tests proved that sweating the meat did result in a more richly flavored stock. Moreover, the sweated meat and bones did not release foamy scum, thus eliminating the need to skim.

After much testing, we came to this inescapable conclusion: If you want to make beef stock right, you just can't skimp on the meat.

INGREDIENTS: The Right Beef

We found that you can make beef stock from shank bones (which have plenty of meat attached) or from a combination of boneless chuck and marrowbones. Although a few tasters preferred the taste and texture of the chuck meat to the shank, the differences were slight. Boston-area supermarkets are more likely to have marrowbones than shank. Let availability influence your decision about which cuts to use here.

In addition to cuts, we wondered if the grade or type of meat would matter. In previous tests, we had found that premium chickens make better stock than mass-market birds. Would premium beef outperform regular beef?

We prepared two pots of stock, one with Coleman beef (a well-regarded national brand of natural beef), the other with regular (nonbranded) Grade A supermarket beef. We used shanks in both cases. The Coleman stock was extremely gelled and very thick, with a luscious full body. The Grade A stock was somewhat gelled and thick, with good body. In terms of flavor, tasters gave the nod to the Coleman stock. It was meatier and more complex. The Grade A stock tasted good but not quite as rich. Although the differences were not nearly as dramatic as with chicken, we found that spending a little extra money for premium beef certainly isn't frivolous.

Rich Beef Stock

MAKES SCANT 2 QUARTS

Both meat and bones contribute flavor to the final product. You can buy shank (sometimes labeled beef shin) and cut the meat away from the bones before adding both to the pot or use bone-less chuck (cut into cubes) and small marrowbones. Because meat makes such an important contribution to the flavor of this stock, a generous amount is required no matter the cut used. You need only half of the meat for use in any of the soup recipes elsewhere in the book. Use the remaining meat in sandwiches or cold salads.

2	tablespoons vegetable oil
6	pounds beef shank, meat cut from bone in large chunks (see illustration below), or 4 pounds chuck, cut into 3-inch chunks, and 2 pounds small marrowbones
1	large onion, halved
1/2	cup dry red wine
2	quarts boiling water
2	teaspoons salt

1. Heat 1 tablespoon oil in a large stockpot or Dutch oven over medium-high heat. Brown the meat, bones, and onion halves on all sides in three or four batches, making sure not to overcrowd the pan, and adding the remaining oil to the pan as necessary. (It will take 15 to 20 minutes to brown all the meat.) Set the browned meat, bones, and onion aside on a platter.

2. Add the red wine to the empty pot. Cook, using a wooden spoon to scrape up the browned bits, until wine reduces to a syrup, 1 to 2 minutes. Return the browned bones, meat, and onion to the pot. Reduce the heat to low, cover, and sweat the bones, meat, and onion until the meat has released its dark juices, about 20 minutes. Increase the heat to medium-high and add the boiling water and salt. Bring to a simmer, reduce the heat to low, partially cover, and simmer gently until meat is tender, about 2 hours.

3. Strain the stock, discard the bones and onion, and set the meat aside, reserving half for use in sandwiches or salads. Cool the remaining meat to be used in the soup, then shred into bite-sized pieces. Before using, defat the stock (see page 19). The stock and meat to be used in the soup can be refrigerated separately in air-tight containers for up to 3 days.

SCIENCE: So Much Beef, So Little Stock

Before we actually began testing, we would not have believed how much meat was required to make a rich, beefy flavored stock. Why, we questioned, did a good beef soup require 6 pounds of beef and bones when a mere 3-pound chicken could beautifully flavor the same size pot of soup?

Though we had always thought of beef as having a heartier flavor, we began to understand chicken's strength while making stocks for both. In one of our time-saving beef stock experiments, we used the 4 pounds of meat called for in the recipe but substituted 2 pounds of quicker cooking hacked-up chicken bones for the beef bones. The result was surprising. Even with twice as much meaty beef as chicken bones, the chicken flavor predominated.

Appearances aside, the flavor compounds in chicken are very strong, possibly stronger than those in beef. It's the browning, or searing, that contributes much of the robust beefy flavor to a good steak or stew. (Think how bland boiled beef tastes.) Skin and bones may be another reason why less chicken is required to flavor a stock. Chicken skin, predominantly fat, tastes like the animal. Beef fat, on the other hand, tastes "rich" but not beefy, as evidenced by french fries cooked in beef tallow. In addition, chicken bones, which are filled with rich, dark marrow, contribute flavor. Beef bones, on the other hand, lend incredible body to a stock but their flavor is predominantly and unmistakably that of bone, not of beef.

Finally, according to the U.S. Department of Agriculture, chicken contains more water than beef does—77 percent in drumsticks and 73 percent to 74 percent for wings and backs compared with 61 percent in chuck. This means that when simmered, chicken is releasing 12 percent to 16 percent more liquid—and flavor—into the pot.

HANDLING SHANK BONES

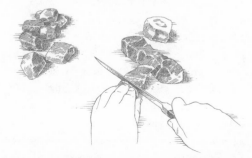

Cut the meat away from the shank bones in the largest possible pieces.

VEGETABLE STOCK

VEGETABLE STOCKS HAVE ALWAYS SEEMED to be a high-maintenance proposition, involving lots of work and little return. Trips to ethnic markets, miles of scrapes and peels, and what do you get? Hot vegetable bath water or hot sweet vegetable tea.

Nonetheless, we sensed there might be promise here, that a careful selection of ingredients and just the right technique could create a stock both nicely balanced and robust, with pleasing color and clarity—something, in short, worth making, even for people who aren't vegetarians. We felt certain, moreover, that a superior vegetable stock could not rise up from the remains in the vegetable drawer, be tossed into a pot with some water and a couple of bay leaves, then subjected to death by boiling. We knew that it might be a time-consuming process and that we might end up with a long and complex ingredient list, but we believed we could come up with a truly good stock.

To kick off, we made five stocks, using different techniques and vegetable combinations for each. In

---

INGREDIENTS: Canned Beef Broth

Beef broth is a traditional European and American staple, a key ingredient in many classic sauces as well as the basis for popular beef soups. Over past years, however, sales of beef broth have lagged. Recent statistics for annual sales show that more than four times as many cans of chicken broth are sold than cans of beef broth.

When we tasted commercial beef broths, it became obvious why this situation has developed: Most beef broths simply do not deliver full-bodied, beefy flavor. There might be subtle beef suggestions, but after tasting nearly all of the selected broths—bouillon-based, canned, gourmet, and organic—there remained one nagging question: "Where's the beef?"

As things stand, U.S. regulations for beef broth do not require much beef. A commercial beef broth need contain only 1 part protein to 135 parts moisture, according to the U.S. Department of Agriculture's standards. That translates to less than about an ounce of meat (or about one-quarter of a hamburger) to 1 gallon of water. Most commercial products are very close to that limit, strictly because of economics. Generally, manufactured beef broth derives its flavor from bare beef bones and a boost of various additives. A glance at the label on the side of any canned broth or boxed bouillon cubes will confirm this.

We wanted to talk to the manufacturers of beef broths to verify our impressions of the way they make their products, but calls to broth giants Hormel Foods and Campbell Soup Company were dead ends. Both declined to answer questions as to how their commercial beef broths are made. But beef bones plus additives would certainly explain why of the 12 commercial broths we tasted, none came even close to the full-bodied, beefy flavor of our homemade stock recipe—made with 6 pounds of meat. Nearly all of the commercial broths were thin and flavorless, with the exception of "off" or artificial flavors.

What seems to distinguish most supermarket broths from homemade, gourmet, or natural foods store broths is a riddling of flavor additives. Monosodium glutamate (MSG) can be found in nearly all supermarket beef broths (see "The Benefits of MSG" on page 32). Disodium guanylate and disodium isonate, both yeast-based, hydrolyzed soy protein, are also typically added to commercial broths. Yeast extracts also find their way into most of these broths. Approved by the U.S. Food and Drug Administration (FDA), additives are intended to "enhance" flavor. As one FDA spokesperson explained, "You've got something that's kind of 'blah,' so to give it a little more taste they add these things."

Salt—and lots of it—also adds to the flavor of these broths. Most beef broth products contain about 35 percent of the daily allowance for sodium per serving. Salt is also added to help extract the needed protein from the bones.

The preferred product in our commercial broth tasting was a jarred beef base, Superior Touch Better Than Bouillon, but even this "winner" had an unflattering score of 4.6 on a scale of 0 to 10. Herb Ox Beef Bouillon Cubes lagged not too far behind. Forget about the more expensive gourmet and organic commercial broths, which not only failed to deliver beef flavor but also proved to be among the least palatable of the pack. Even if you get your hands on one of the "top finishers," we do not recommend that you use it in a recipe where the flavor of beef broth predominates, as in beef soup. However, it would be forgivable used as background in a sauce or gravy, if necessary.

Depending on the recipe, a good alternative might be canned chicken broth, which on the whole tastes better than commercial beef broth (see page 27 for brand recommendations). But if you truly seek beef flavor, bypass the broth aisle in your supermarket and head straight to the meat department for ingredients to make a stock at home.

quick-simmered stocks, on the stove for less than an hour, most of the flavor was left locked in the vegetables. Vegetables simmered in water only—using no dry heat or reduction method—produced a spiritless stock. Roasting vegetables in the oven first did deepen the stock's color and flavor, but deglazing the roasting pan and transferring the vegetables to a pot was a nuisance. We left this method behind. Sweating the aromatic vegetables in a small amount of water before adding the other vegetables and the water produced a stock of perfect clarity and increased flavor. But the best option was sautéing lightly oiled aromatics in the stockpot before adding water. This stock had rich flavor, only slightly compromised clarity, and very little oily residue.

Our review of ingredient choices yielded fewer definitive results. We discovered, to no surprise, that the onion family brought depth and complexity to bear on flavor, that wine tasted out of place, and that salt was essential to palatability. Otherwise, we gleaned no substantive ideas as to which vegetables were expendable, which essential, and which would

play together nicely in a group. Our travails were about to become, in fact, a lengthy treatise on what not to add.

Though we hoped to end up with a grocery list short enough to fit on a piece of scrap paper, lengthy testing lay in our path. Consequently, it seemed prudent to organize potential ingredients into broad categories, starting from the bottom, and to layer flavors one by one. Within the foundation group, for instance (those vegetables that enjoy a slow sauté and lengthy simmer to bring forth their aromatic qualities), we would test members of the onion cartel along with carrots, parsnips, celery, and celery root. Pungent or cruciferous vegetables—cabbage, cauliflower, turnips, peppers, and fennel, to name a few—would come next. Mushrooms and tomatoes had to be tested at some point, as did potential thickening agents such as potatoes, lentils, and rice. Herbs would need to be tested and, at the end, anything from the condiment world we might have to resort to if the vegetables alone proved inadequate.

We began by testing different mixes of yellow and red onions, shallots, garlic, and leeks to see which

---

SCIENCE: The Benefits of MSG

Because so many commercial broths use monosodium glutamate (MSG) as a flavor enhancer, we decided to find out just how this product affects flavor. To provide the most dramatic illustration, we cooked up a batch of the most tasteless liquid in our tasting—a classic French beef stock made with bones and no meat. We then tasted it plain and with ½ teaspoon of MSG per quart.

The difference was more distinct than we had expected. The plain stock was characterized by excessive vegetable and sweet flavors, while beef flavors were indiscernible. By contrast, the stock with MSG had, as one taster described, "higher flavor notes" that included beefy and more savory flavors and a subdued sweetness. What's more, it tasted nothing like the lowest-rated commercial broths.

Just how that half-teaspoon of MSG can make such a difference is something scientists cannot fully explain, says food science professor F. Jack Francis of the University of Massachusetts at Amherst. MSG, like many other flavor enhancers, does not actually change the flavor of the substance to which it is added. Instead, it is believed to enhance the response of a person's taste buds, especially to meats and proteins, says Francis. Exactly how

this happens scientists have yet to learn. Some describe it not only as a taste enhancer but as a stimulator of a fifth taste perception in addition to sweet, sour, salty, and bitter.

While MSG might be popular with many commercial broth makers, it has not been popular with the American public. In the 1980s, people began to associate it with "Chinese restaurant syndrome," which has been reported to include symptoms such as headache, digestive upset, and chest pain. Even though numerous studies have failed to turn up an association between such symptoms and MSG, the reputation has stuck. It has been speculated that a type of bacteria quick to grow on cooked rice left at room temperature and able to cause food poisoning is the real source of trouble for those diners with "Chinese restaurant syndrome."

Nowadays most Chinese restaurants tout "No MSG" on their menus. Yet many people do not realize that it's still lurking in their hot-and-sour soup as well as many other non-Chinese dishes. That's because MSG is the salt form of glutamate, a naturally occurring substance found in such foods as peanut butter, rice, flour, and mushrooms.

combinations would be synergistic. (We were sautéing the onions first and simmering a catholic selection of vegetables in water to finish.) As it happened, these alliums—except the red onion, which brought a dull bruised purple to the group—were most persuasive in concert. Yellow onions offered strong, pure onion presence, shallots were delicate and fragrant, garlic sultry and complex, leeks soft and bright. Sacrifice one, and the efficacy of the whole was diminished. We also learned that unpeeled onions are bitter and that leeks prefer to arrive late and stew a bit; and that their green, horsy tail ends taste horsy. Engaging the stock in a brisk, businesslike simmer to get the job done proved a poor idea—the final product tasted boiled and frayed. We went with the old barbecue adage: low and slow.

We also found that while alliums are critical to flavor complexity, their high sugar content in combination with sustained simmering can result in something far too sweet. In fact, developing flavor while avoiding sweetness became the much sought-after (and nearly unattainable) goal of our testing.

Carrot and celery, both of which are likely to dominate canned or packaged vegetable broths, made enough of an impact with tiny contributions, and we selected them over their respective rivals, parsnip and celery root.

As we advanced to the next round—with the onion family, celery, and carrot on board for the duration—several vegetables dropped out of the running, one by one. Each addition, intended to improve the fragile foundation flavors, instead maligned them. White mushrooms, for instance, were a dastardly bunch, taking up space in the pot but contributing nothing in the way of flavor. Red peppers and tomatoes, tested separately, were dismissed together. Both were differently, inscrutably, and distinctly unpleasant. Fennel bulb contributed what was perhaps the most unequivocally awful flavor to emerge from this mix. We were astounded by the fact that so many singularly tasty vegetables could fare so poorly in a group and that so many of the biggest flavor candidates had failed. "What does this need?" we would wail at tastings. "Some chicken," was the usual answer.

Out of this second tier of vegetables, only two had a strong and positive influence on those already in the pot: green cabbage and cauliflower. Minimal amounts contributed to the flavor-layering effect we were going for—the cabbage fragrant and nutty, the cauliflower earthy and nutty. Hoping they might prove interchangeable, we left each in place and moved on.

Next we approached the starchy candidates, thinking their flavor and body might reward the stock. Nothing could have been further from the truth. We made the basic recipe time and again, adding one by one bits of white rice, potatoes, potato skins, lentils, yellow split peas, and chickpeas, straining them out with the other vegetables at the end. Rather than adding any real body to the stock—which remained stubbornly thin—these ingredients merely turned it murky. Those that added flavor—dry lentils, split peas, and chickpeas—swathed the fresh vegetable flavor in a muddy taste of legumes. A half-hearted gesture toward the East obliged us to throw in some kombu (Japanese dried seaweed), which has gelatinous properties; a nod to the 1970s, some nutritional yeast (thought to improve mouthfeel). Both were ghastly.

In addition to its other flavor problems, the stock was still damnably, persistently sweet. So we tested fresh ginger and lemon juice for their astringent properties. The ginger gave the stock too much of an ethnic flavor, and the lemon juice made it taste like it was going bad.

At this point, we felt as if we had crawled every inch of the produce section on our bellies. One colleague then suggested that we might prevail upon leafy greens for flavor brightness. Why not? Another run to the market and we were back with collards, chard, and kale. Knowing they did not benefit from lengthy cooking, we added about a half pound of each to three separate stocks. Score! Here at last was a breakthrough. The greens brought both depth and brightness to the stock and helped correct the sweetness. Everyone liked the collards best; they were fresh and biting without being bitter.

We now began experimenting with finishing flavors. Fresh thyme and parsley went into the pot with the other greens to simmer briefly; bay leaf earlier, with the water. These simple ingredients alone made a substantial contribution to flavor. We did not care for miso (fermented soybean paste, used in Japanese cooking), as its particulate matter settled to the bottom and kicked up like a dust storm when stirred. But by now people were entering the test kitchen and asking what smelled so good. Sometimes it was our vegetable stock.

Buoyed by these advances, we chopped on. Though lemon juice had been a failure, a bruised piece of lemon grass was a decisive success, adding bright new dimensions to the flavors. The finished stock had a golden, chickeny glow.

Reasonably confident, we put our new recipe to the test by making risotto and an Indian lentil dish. The stock tasted great in risotto but too sweet with the lentils.

Now we became ruthless, stripping the onion family of half its baggage and including only one small carrot. We added some chopped scallions to the stock along with the greens—a compensatory gesture to the onion family. They were piquant and crisp. A splash of rice vinegar and some peppercorns ended our efforts.

Vegetable Stock

MAKES ABOUT 1 QUART

It is important to use a heavy-bottomed Dutch oven or stockpot so that the vegetables caramelize properly without burning. Don't try to double this recipe; there will be too many vegetables in the pot and they won't caramelize fully, resulting in a weak stock. A stalk of lemon grass, available in some grocery stores and most Asian markets, adds a clean, refreshing flavor to the stock. If you cannot find lemon grass, however, the flavor will still be very good. If possible, strain this stock through a china cap (see page 13) to prevent solids from ending up in the liquid.

2	medium onions, peeled and chopped coarse
10 to 12	medium cloves garlic from 1 head, each clove peeled and smashed
8	large shallots (about 8 ounces), sliced thin
1	stalk celery, chopped coarse
1	small carrot, peeled and chopped coarse
	Vegetable cooking spray (see page 131)
4	large leeks, white and light green parts only, chopped coarse (about 5½ cups; see illustrations on page 124 to clean)

8½	cups boiling water
	Stems from 1 bunch fresh parsley
2	small bay leaves
1½	teaspoons salt
1	teaspoon black peppercorns, coarsely cracked
1	pound collard greens, washed, dried, and sliced crosswise into 2-inch strips (about 10 cups packed)
1	small head cauliflower, chopped fine (about 4 cups)
8 to 10	sprigs fresh thyme
1	stalk lemon grass, trimmed to bottom 6 inches and bruised with back of chef's knife (see illustration on page 175)
4	medium scallions, white and light green parts, cut into 2-inch lengths
2	teaspoons rice vinegar

1. Combine the onions, garlic, shallots, celery, and carrot in a large, heavy-bottomed stockpot or Dutch oven. Spray the vegetables lightly with vegetable cooking spray and toss to coat. Cover and cook over low heat, stirring frequently, until the pan bottom shows a light brown glaze, 20 to 30 minutes. Add the leeks and increase the heat to medium; cook, covered, until leeks soften, about 10 minutes. Add 1½ cups boiling water and cook, partially covered, until water has evaporated to a glaze and vegetables are very soft, 25 to 35 minutes.

2. Add the parsley stems, bay leaves, salt, peppercorns, and remaining 7 cups boiling water. Increase the heat to medium-high and bring to a simmer. Reduce the heat to medium-low and simmer gently, covered, to blend flavors, about 15 minutes.

3. Add the collard greens, cauliflower, thyme, lemon grass, and scallions. Increase the heat to medium-high and bring to a simmer. Reduce the heat to low and simmer gently, covered, to blend flavors, about 15 minutes longer.

4. Strain the stock, allowing the liquid to drip through to drain thoroughly (do not press on solids). Discard the solids. Stir in the vinegar. The stock can be refrigerated in an airtight container for up to 4 days or frozen up to 2 months.

FISH STOCK

FISH STOCK, ALSO CALLED FISH FUMET, IS the basis for many fish soups and stews. Since most fish and seafood cooks in a matter of minutes, it can't really flavor the rest of the soup or stew. Therefore, the fish stock (which is the major liquid component in such recipes) must be rich and flavorful. Good fish stock also gives a soup or stew some viscosity, which comes from the gelatin released by the fish bones.

Most recipes for fish stock follow the traditional method for making chicken stock. Fish frames (what's left over once the fillets have been removed—that is, the head, bones, and tail) are simmered in water along with some aromatic vegetables. Most recipes warn that excessive simmering can leech out bitter elements in the fish bones. Therefore, simmering time is usually short—no more than 30 minutes in most recipes.

We tried several classic fish stocks and were unimpressed. They were clear and thin and not nearly flavorful enough. We increased the simmering time to an hour and had better results. We did not encounter any of the bitterness that so many sources warned about. As long as the fish frames are cleaned (to remove the gills) and washed (to remove blood and organs), bitterness isn't a problem.

Even though long-simmered stocks tasted better than short-simmered stocks, the flavor was still lacking and the liquid not as viscous as we wanted. We started to increase the amount of fish frames in the pot. With each increase, the flavor improved. However, fish frames are hard to come by, and developing a recipe that called for 8 or 10 pounds of frames to produce several quarts of stock seemed absurd.

One test cook recalled a technique she had used in restaurants—simmer a modest amount of fish frames and vegetables in stock, strain out the solids, then reduce the stock to improve its flavor and consistency. We tried this method and had good

---

INGREDIENTS: Canned Vegetable Broth

Commercial vegetable broth has become almost as common as chicken and beef broth. There is an array of products in supermarkets and natural foods stores. We wondered if these products were any good. Can they be used in place of homemade stock in a soup or stew? To find out, we lined up 12 samples of readily available vegetable broths for a blind tasting; three in aseptic boxes, three in cans, two in liquid concentrate form, and four in bouillon cubes.

Ten members of the editorial staff sat down to sample these broths. By the grimaces on their faces, you'd think tasters were sampling dishwater. Not one of the samples was well liked. The bouillon cube broths were generally tolerated. While not impressing anyone with their flavor, they were the most palatable of the lot. The only nonbouillon broth that tasters deemed acceptable was Imagine Natural Vegetable Broth, which comes in an aseptic box and looks and tastes more like vegetable soup than broth. Although the taste was inoffensive, several tasters feared that the broth's opaque orange color (owing to a high concentration of carrots) would transfer to whatever dish they were making, be it a creamed soup or risotto. Other aseptic broths did not fare so well, with tasters commenting on their "stale water" and "bland" flavors.

Faring the worst were the canned broths and concentrated liquids. With comments ranging from "tinny and hollow" and "herbal and unpleasant" to "smells like rotten onions," canned broths had no fans. Concentrated forms of broth were deemed "rancid and medicinal."

Why were broths made with bouillon cubes more palatable than the rest of the field? The ingredient labels tell the story. With the other products, water and vegetables top the list. Bouillon cubes don't contain water, and vegetables appear far down on the ingredient list. What seems to make the bouillon cubes more palatable is a combination of higher salt content and a similarity in taste to chicken or beef broth. With salt as the first ingredient—and in one case MSG following close behind—the sodium seemed to cover up the unpleasant dehydrated vegetable taste. All of the bouillon cubes also contained oil, which gave them a richer mouthfeel. Additionally, three of the four bouillon cubes did not contain tomato products, which clouded the appearance and taste of many canned and boxed broths.

Unfortunately, we cannot recommend any of these commercial broths without reservation. Yes, the bouillon cubes were less offensive than others. However, all of our tasters agreed that if cooking for a vegetarian, they would rather start with a base of caramelized vegetables and water than any of these commercial versions. In a pinch, we would use a vegetarian bouillon cube, but begrudgingly.

results. However, the process was tedious and messy, and we wondered if there was an easier way to make good stock.

Most classic fish stock recipes yield a clear finished product. That's because restaurants want maximum flexibility. They may want to use fish stock in consommé or sauce, in which case clarity is important. For our purposes in this book, however, fish stock is used to make things like fish chowder and bouillabaisse. In these cases, clarity doesn't matter, since solid ingredients such as tomatoes and garlic are blended with the stock to create the soup base. Therefore, flavor trumps clarity when making fish stock at home.

At this point, we decided to change course. We wondered what effect sweating the fish frames and vegetables would have on the stock. Since this method worked so well for chicken and beef stock, we had high hopes.

We followed a classic French recipe and sweated chopped aromatic vegetables along with fish frames in melted butter. The principle at work here is that fat will bring out the flavor of the vegetables and frames. Once the vegetables and fish frames have been sweated, wine is added, followed by water.

As this stock cooked, we noticed several differences. First, it smelled more rich and more complex than the simmered versions. We strained and cooled the sweated stock so the fat would have time to solidify. We then skimmed away the fat and tasted the stock. The flavors of the fish and vegetables were much deeper than in any simmered fish stock we had tasted. Just as important, our sweated stock had an excellent mouthfeel. Clearly, this cooking process had unlocked the gelatin in those fish bones. The opaque, almost whitish color was another indication of the stock's body and richness.

We tinkered with the proportions and ran a few more tests. Olive oil did an admirable job in place of the butter and is the best choice if the stock is destined for an olive-oil based soup or stew, such as bouillabaisse. White wine gave the stock a pleasing acidic edge. We ended up using a whole bottle for

---

INGREDIENTS: Fish for Stock

We tested more than a dozen fish when developing our stock recipe and found that bones from mild, white fish generally make the best stock. Within this group, we found a few that make especially gelatinous stock. Other white fish were perfectly acceptable and made good stock, although it was a tad thinner. As expected, our tasters did not like stock made with oily fish, such as salmon or bluefish. The flavors of those fish were much too strong.

Consequently, we have divided fish into three categories—highly recommended, recommended, and not recommend. Feel free to mix and match, using several kinds of fish in the same pot of stock.

There was a time when fishmongers would gladly give away bones, heads, and tails. But no longer, unless perhaps you're an especially good customer. And don't expect the fishmonger to have bones on hand whenever you show up at the market. It's advisable to call one day ahead and reserve what you need.

If freezer space permits, you can pack away fish bones each time you buy seafood. (If the fishmonger fillets some red snapper for you, ask for the bones.) But don't freeze fish frames for more than three or four months; after that amount of time, it is best to go ahead and make the stock, even if you subsequently freeze it.

HIGHLY RECOMMENDED	RECOMMENDED	NOT RECOMMENDED
Blackfish	Cod	Bluefish
Monkfish (especially the heads)	Flatfish (such as sole or flounder)	Mackerel
Red Snapper	Haddock	Pompano
Sea Bass	Pacific Pollack	Salmon
	Rockfish	Smelt
	Skate	

maximum flavor. On the other hand, lemon was too puckery, even in small amounts.

As for the vegetables and herbs, we liked most of the usual suspects—onion, celery, garlic, parsley, thyme, bay leaf, and peppercorns. We found that carrots were too sweet and best left out. We had one surprise addition to the stock—mushrooms. Button mushrooms (as well as a few dried shiitake mushrooms) gave the stock a meaty flavor.

If you can get fish frames (see page 36 for information about choosing the right fish for stock), homemade fish stock is easy to prepare. It takes about an hour of your time and makes a tremendous difference in many seafood soups and stews.

Fish Stock

MAKES ABOUT 3 1/2 QUARTS

Either butter or olive oil can be used to sweat the vegetables and fish frames. Choose one or the other based on how you plan to use the stock. If you are making a soup or stew that calls for butter and/or cream, make stock with butter. If making a soup or stew that calls for olive oil, make stock with olive oil. However, since the fat is skimmed from the stock once it cools, don't fret too much about this fine distinction. A stock made with butter will be fine in bouillabaisse.

4	tablespoons unsalted butter or olive oil
2	large stalks celery, chopped coarse (about 1 1/2 cups)
3	medium onions, chopped coarse (about 3 cups)
7	ounces button mushrooms, quartered (about 3 cups)
5	dried shiitake mushrooms, rinsed (optional)
5	large cloves garlic, crushed
5	pounds fish frames, cleaned (see illustrations below)
1	bottle dry white wine
2	quarts water
1	bunch parsley stems
6	sprigs fresh thyme
10	whole black peppercorns
1	bay leaf
2	teaspoons sea salt

1. Heat the butter or oil in a 12-quart stockpot over medium-low heat until butter foams or oil shimmers. Add the celery, onions, mushrooms, garlic, and fish frames. Increase the heat to high, cover, and sweat ingredients, stirring once or twice, until bubbly, about 10 minutes. Lower the heat to medium and continue to sweat, stirring frequently and pressing on the fish frames with a wooden spoon to break them down, until the vegetables and bones are soft and aromatic, about 10 minutes longer.

2. Add the wine and bring to a simmer. Reduce the heat to low and simmer, covered, for about 10 minutes, skimming foam from the surface as necessary. Add 2 quarts water, parsley stems, thyme, peppercorns, bay leaf, and salt. Increase the heat to high to bring to a simmer. Reduce the heat to low and simmer, uncovered, skimming foam as necessary, until stock is rich and flavorful, about 30 minutes.

3. Strain the stock through a chinois or a china cap lined with damp cheesecloth; discard the solids.

CLEANING FISH FRAMES FOR STOCK

1. Lift the gill cover and detach the gills with shears.

2. Remove and discard the gills. Rinse the fish frame under cool, running water to flush out any blood.

3. Cut the fish frame into small pieces that will fit easily into a stockpot.

Before using, defat the stock (see page 19). The stock can be refrigerated in an airtight container for up to 2 days or frozen for several months.

CHEATER'S FISH STOCK

THERE WILL BE OCCASIONS WHEN YOU need fish stock but have neither the time nor the fish to make it. Using plain water isn't an option. You need a stock with some character. Clam juice is the most common choice.

We wondered if bottled clam juice could be improved, much like canned chicken broth. The answer is yes. Simmering the juice with aromatic vegetables and herbs enhances the salty, briny flavor of bottled clam juice. The result is an acceptable stock. It can't compare with the real thing, but it will do in a pinch.

In our testing, we found that a half cup of white wine rounds out the flavors and gives the impression of depth. Unlike real fish stock, cheater's stock is thin because it contains no dissolved gelatin from any bones. It's best used immediately.

Cheater's Fish Stock

MAKES ABOUT 4 CUPS

We found that doctored clam juice can be used if homemade fish stock isn't at hand. Clam juice is very salty, so don't add any salt to your soup or stew until you have tasted it. We tested several brands of bottled clam juice and found Doxsee to have the cleanest, truest flavor.

1	small onion, chopped coarse
1	medium carrot, chopped coarse
1	stalk celery, chopped coarse
8	sprigs fresh parsley
1/2	cup dry white wine
6	(8-ounce) bottles clam juice
2	bay leaves
8	whole black peppercorns
1/2	teaspoon dried thyme

Bring all ingredients to a boil in a medium saucepan. Simmer to blend the flavors (no skimming is necessary), about 20 minutes. Strain, pressing on the solids with the back of a spoon to extract as much liquid as possible. Use immediately.

PART 2

SOUPS

3

CHICKEN SOUPS

GOOD CHICKEN SOUP STARTS WITH ROBUST stock that tastes like chicken. After much trial and error we developed several techniques for making chicken stocks (see chapter 2). These stocks are so rich and flavorful, you may long for the chance to nurse a cold or flu. The secret to intense chicken stock is extralong simmering (with ingredients thrown into the pot and cooked over low heat for five hours) or a shortcut method that calls for browning and sweating an onion and hacked-up chicken parts to release their flavor and then adding water and cooking for 20 minutes.

If the soup you're making does not contain any chicken meat, start with backs and wing tips or whole legs and use either stock-making method. Egg drop, matzo ball, and wonton soup all fall into this category. Without any chicken meat, these soups are generally served as first courses or for lunch.

If the soup does contain chicken meat, we think tender breast meat is the best choice. Dark meat can be tough and gristly, and the extra fat can make the soup greasy. (Fat from dark meat isn't an issue when making stock because the stock is defatted before being used.) We like to start with a whole chicken and use our quick stock recipe. The breast is simmered just long enough to cook the meat without becoming dry, while the remaining parts are hacked up and cooked long enough to release all their flavor. This stock is ideal for soups like chicken noodle. Soups with chicken meat are sturdier and more filling, and most make a fine main course.

Whether the soup contains chicken meat or not, most chicken soups should be served as soon as they are ready. Chicken soups with eggs, pasta, or rice certainly cannot hold. Soups with just chicken and vegetables can be refrigerated for a day or two and then reheated, but we find that flavors are freshest when the soup is just made. We do suggest that you make the stock at least a day in advance. That way the stock can chill in the refrigerator, making the fat easy to remove.

CHICKEN NOODLE SOUP

WITH HOMEMADE CHICKEN STOCK ON HAND, making chicken noodle soup is a relatively easy proposition. Add some vegetables, herbs, and noodles and you've got a great bowl of soup. We did have several questions, though. Which vegetables are best added to this soup? Should the vegetables be sautéed first, or can diced vegetables simply be simmered in chicken stock? As for the pasta, which kind of noodles work best, and should they be cooked in the soup or in a separate pot of boiling water? We wanted to answer all these questions, develop a basic master recipe, then create some more unusual variations.

We tackled the vegetable issue first. We tested a wide range of vegetables, including onions, carrots, celery, leeks, potatoes, zucchini, tomatoes, and mushrooms. We concluded that the classic mirepoix ingredients (onions, carrots, and celery) should be part of a basic chicken noodle soup. Other vegetables are fine choices, but we concluded that they are more appropriate for variations. For instance, tomatoes and zucchini give chicken noodle soup an Italian character, and spring vegetables are a natural choice with rice.

To settle the issue of how to cook the vegetables, we prepared two batches of soup. For the first batch, we sautéed the onions, carrots, and celery in a little vegetable oil until softened and then added the chicken stock. For the second batch, we simply simmered the sliced vegetables in stock. As might be expected, we found that sautéing brought out flavors in the vegetables and made a big difference in the finished soup.

We saw a few recipes that suggested saving chicken fat skimmed from homemade stock and using this fat as a cooking medium for the vegetables. We tested this and found that chicken fat does in fact add another level of chicken flavor to the soup. Although not essential, it makes sense to use chicken fat if you have planned ahead and saved what you skimmed from the surface of your stock.

In addition to the vegetables, we found that thyme and parsley brightened flavors. We added dried thyme along with the stock to give it time to soften and permeate the stock. To preserve its freshness, the parsley was best added just before serving.

The noodles were the last (and the most important) element that we needed to investigate. Although dried egg noodles are the most common choice, we ran across several recipes that suggested fresh or dried pasta. Before testing various noodles, we decided to clarify the issue of how to cook them. We simmered egg noodles in the soup as well as in a separate pot of salted water. The noodles cooked in the soup pot shed some starch that somewhat clouded the soup. In contrast, noodles cooked in a separate pot and added to the stock left the finished soup completely clear.

The effect on the soup, however, paled in comparison to the effect on the noodles. Noodles cooked separately tasted bland and did not meld with the soup. The noodles cooked in the soup absorbed some of the chicken stock, giving them a rich, well-rounded flavor. We concluded that you must cook the noodles in the soup.

We identified seven possible noodle choices: dried egg noodles (fine, home-style, and extra-broad), dried linguine, dried spaghetti, fresh fettuccine, and fresh linguine. We cooked 2 ounces of each in a pot of chicken soup. Tasters preferred the three egg noodles to both the fresh and dried pastas. The noodles cooked up very soft and yielding. They were tender to the bite and nearly melted in the mouth. In addition to preferring their texture, tasters liked the ridged edges on the noodles, which provide nooks and crannies that can trap pieces of vegetable.

The dried spaghetti and linguine were deemed chewy and the least favorite choice. The fresh fettuccine did have some fans, although the fresh linguine was thought to be too narrow. Fresh fettuccine cooked up fairly soft (but not as soft as the egg noodles), and their width worked better with the vegetables. To make them manageable on a spoon, we recommend cutting them in half and then in half again. Pieces that are 2 to 3 inches long will just fit on a large spoon. (Note that fresh pasta will cook more quickly than dried egg noodles, reducing the simmering time in step 2 of the master recipe to about three minutes.)

Although fresh fettuccine can be used, we think

dried egg noodles are the better choice. In addition to their superior texture when cooked, they are more widely available (every supermarket carries them) and less expensive. Tasters liked all three dried egg noodles tested. The fine noodles cooked up no more than $\frac{1}{16}$ inch wide and gave the soup a delicate character. The extra-broad and home-style noodles cooked up considerably wider and gave the soup a heartier feeling. Although home-style and extra-broad noodles look pretty much the same in the package, the home-style noodles measure about 1½ inches across when cooked, while the extra-broad noodles measure only an inch across when cooked. In addition, the home-style noodles cooked up a bit flatter, while the extra-broad noodles remained twisted. Each noodle had its partisans in the test kitchen. Choose any one of the three based on your preference.

While the recipes that follow are adaptable, we have carefully timed the addition of vegetables, noodles, grains, and other ingredients to make sure that each item is perfectly cooked—not overcooked. You can make adjustments if you keep in mind general cooking times for additional ingredients or substitutions.

THREE KINDS OF DRIED EGG NOODLES

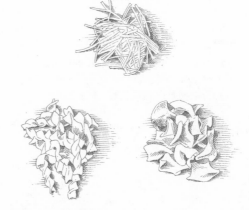

Fine noodles (top) cook up about $\frac{1}{16}$ inch wide and give chicken noodle soup a delicate character. Home-style noodles (right) cook up bigger and flatter than the extra-broad noodles (left), which keep their twisted shape when cooked. Any of these noodles will work well in chicken noodle soup.

Chicken Noodle Soup

SERVES 6 TO 8

Once we figured out how to make good chicken stock, making chicken noodle soup was incredibly easy. The noodles do not hold very well, and this soup is best served as soon as the noodles are tender. If you plan on having leftovers, prepare the recipe through step 1, reserve the portion you want to save for another day, then cook a portion of the noodles in the remaining soup.

2	tablespoons chicken fat (reserved from making stock) or vegetable oil
1	medium onion, chopped medium
1	large carrot, peeled and sliced ¼ inch thick
1	stalk celery, sliced ¼ inch thick
½	teaspoon dried thyme leaves
2	quarts Chicken Stock with Sautéed Breast Meat (page 23), stock and meat separated
2	cups (3 ounces) egg noodles (fine, extra-broad, or home-style; see illustrations on page 43)
¼	cup minced fresh parsley leaves
	Salt and ground black pepper

1. Heat the chicken fat in a large stockpot or Dutch oven over medium-high heat. Add the onion, carrot, and celery and sauté until softened, about 5 minutes. Add the thyme, stock, and shredded chicken meat. Bring the soup to a boil, reduce the heat, and simmer until the vegetables are tender and the flavors meld, 10 to 15 minutes.

2. Stir in the noodles and cook until just tender, about 8 minutes. Stir in the parsley and salt and pepper to taste. Serve immediately.

➤ VARIATIONS

Chicken and Rice Soup with Spring Vegetables

As with noodles, we found that rice tastes best when cooked in the soup rather than a separate pot. Since rice takes more time to soften than do egg noodles, it should be added once the aromatic vegetables have been sautéed.

Follow recipe for Chicken Noodle Soup, replacing the onion with 1 medium leek, rinsed thoroughly, quartered lengthwise, then sliced thin crosswise (see illustrations on page 124 to clean).

Add ½ cup long-grain rice (omit egg noodles) along with the thyme, stock, and chicken meat in step 1 and cook for 10 minutes. Add ¼ pound trimmed asparagus, cut into 1-inch lengths, and simmer until the asparagus and rice are tender, about 8 minutes. Substitute ¼ cup thawed frozen peas and 2 tablespoons minced fresh tarragon leaves for the parsley. Heat through for 1 minute and serve.

Chicken Soup with Shells, Tomatoes, and Zucchini

Zucchini, tomatoes, and pasta shells give chicken soup an Italian flavor. Pass grated cheese at the table, if desired.

Follow recipe for Chicken Noodle Soup, adding 1 medium zucchini, chopped medium, along with the onion, carrot, and celery, and increasing the sautéing time to 7 minutes. Add ½ cup diced canned tomatoes along with the stock. Substitute 1 cup small pasta shells or macaroni for the egg noodles and simmer until they are cooked, about 10 minutes. Substitute ¼ cup chopped fresh basil for the parsley.

Chicken Soup with Wild Rice, Leeks, and Mushrooms

Wild rice and wild mushrooms lend a woodsy flavor to this luxurious take on basic chicken noodle soup. Wild rice takes much longer to cook than regular rice, so it is cooked before being added to the soup.

2	quarts Chicken Stock with Sautéed Breast Meat (page 23), stock and meat separated
½	ounce dried wild mushrooms, such as porcini or shiitake
½	cup wild rice
3	tablespoons chicken fat (reserved from making stock) or vegetable oil
1	medium leek, rinsed thoroughly, quartered lengthwise, then sliced thin crosswise (see illustrations on page 124 to clean)
1	large carrot, peeled and sliced ¼ inch thick
⅓	pound sliced fresh button or wild mushrooms
½	teaspoon dried thyme
¼	cup minced fresh parsley leaves
	Salt and ground black pepper

1. Heat 1 cup of the chicken stock in a small saucepan until almost simmering. Remove the pan from the heat, stir in the dried mushrooms, and let stand until the mushrooms have softened, about 20 minutes. Lift the mushrooms from the liquid, rinse if they feel gritty, and chop. Strain the soaking liquid through a sieve lined with a paper towel. Reserve the mushrooms and their liquid separately.

2. While the mushrooms are softening, combine the wild rice and 1 cup water in a small saucepan set over medium-high heat. Bring to a boil, cover, turn the heat to low, and cook until tender, 30 to 35 minutes.

3. Heat the chicken fat in a large stockpot or Dutch oven over medium-high heat. Add the leek and carrot and sauté until softened, about 5 minutes. Add the fresh mushrooms and continue to sauté until the mushrooms are softened, about 5 minutes. Add the dried mushrooms and sauté to release their flavors, about 1 minute.

4. Add the strained soaking liquid from the dried mushrooms, the thyme, and the remaining chicken stock to the pot. Simmer until the vegetables are tender and the flavors meld, 10 to 15 minutes.

5. Add the chicken meat and cooked wild rice and cook for 5 minutes. Stir in the parsley and add salt and pepper to taste. Serve immediately.

EGG DROP SOUP

EGG DROP SOUP IS BASICALLY THICKENED chicken stock containing ribbons of coagulated egg. Most recipes have simple embellishments, such as scallions, but the focus is on the stock and the eggs.

Ideally, the egg is lightly set in long ribbons that are fully cooked but still tender. There are two schools of thought as to how to accomplish this. In one, the eggs are poured onto the surface of the simmering stock and allowed to set without stirring. The eggs are then broken up with a fork. The other method calls for whisking the eggs into the stock and then allowing them to set without further stirring.

When we laid the eggs on the surface of the soup and allowed them to set up without stirring, some of the egg remained in large blobs. Once the eggs were set, even vigorous stirring with a fork failed to break them up into small enough pieces. The resulting soup looked less than appealing and was not all that easy to eat. The whisking method caused the eggs to break up into small bits that set up into thinner ribbons. We found it best to add the eggs slowly—the process took almost a minute—and then let them cook for another 30 to 60 seconds, undisturbed, to ensure that they were fully set.

Although some sources suggest that the eggs alone will give egg drop soup its characteristic thick texture, we did not find this to be the case. Most recipes added cornstarch to give the soup some viscosity. The texture is important because the ribbons of egg will fall to the bottom of a bowl of thin, brothy soup. We found that 2 tablespoons of cornstarch (dissolved in 2 tablespoons of water) thickened 2 quarts of stock sufficiently to suspend the ribbons of egg.

INGREDIENTS: Eggs

Eggs are often used to flavor and thicken soups. Depending on the breed of the hen and her size, a chicken egg can weigh as much as 3 ounces or as little as 1 ounce. Size is not necessarily a reflection of quality, nor is the color of the shell. The average weight of one egg for each of the common sizes is as follows: jumbo, 2½ ounces; extra-large, 2¼ ounces; large, 2 ounces; and medium, 1¾ ounces. The recipes in this book call for large eggs. You can use other sizes if you approximate the total weight by relying on the preceding figures. For instance, replace four large eggs (weighing 8 ounces) with three jumbo eggs (7½ ounces) rather than four jumbo eggs (10 ounces).

No matter the size, an egg consists of two parts that function quite differently in recipes. The white, or albumin, consists primarily of water (about 90 percent) and layers of protein. The yolk is where most of the fat and cholesterol in the egg are located. The yolk also contains most of the vitamins and nutrients found in the egg, as well as lecithin, the emulsifier that gives sauces and soups with eggs their smooth texture. For soups in which creaminess is paramount, we use yolks only or whole eggs supplemented with extra yolks.

Eggs should always be refrigerated to prolong their shelf life. Since the door is actually the warmest spot in most refrigerators, keep eggs in their container and store them on one of the shelves. The shelves are likely to be colder, and the box acts as a layer of insulation around the eggs.

Our final testing concerned flavorings. We liked the addition of soy sauce as well as scallions and a little cilantro. Both of the latter add color and brighten the flavor. We found that scallion should not be added as a garnish, as many recipes instruct. When used this way, the scallions tasted raw and too strong. Adding the scallions as well as the cilantro just before the eggs gives them time to soften and mellow and give up more flavor to the soup.

Finally, given the importance of the stock in this recipe, we highly recommend that you start with homemade. If you really must use canned broth, take the extra 15 minutes to make our recipe for Improved Canned Chicken Broth with Asian Flavors on page 26.

Egg Drop Soup

SERVES 6 TO 8

Timing is essential in this recipe. Because the cornstarch will lose its thickening power if simmered too long, the remaining ingredients must be added quickly once the cornstarch goes into the pot. (For more information on the science of starches, see right.) Egg drop soup will not hold and should be served immediately.

2   quarts Asian Chicken Stock (page 25) or Improved Canned Chicken Broth with Asian Flavors (page 26)

1   tablespoon soy sauce
      Salt

2   tablespoons cornstarch

2   medium scallions, chopped fine

2   tablespoons minced fresh cilantro leaves

4   large eggs, beaten

1. Bring the stock to a simmer in a large saucepan over medium-high heat. Add the soy sauce and salt to taste.

2. Combine the cornstarch and 2 tablespoons water in a small bowl and stir until smooth. Whisk the cornstarch mixture into the stock until it thickens slightly, about 1 minute. Stir in the scallions and cilantro.

3. Whisk the stock so that it is moving in a circle. Keep whisking as you pour the eggs into the stock

in a slow, steady stream so that ribbons of coagulated egg form, about 1 minute (see illustration below). Let the eggs stand in the stock without mixing until they are set, less than 1 minute. Once they have set, break up the egg ribbons with a fork. Serve immediately.

SCIENCE: How Starches Work

In its natural state, starch exists in the form of essentially insoluble granules. These granules begin to absorb water only with the introduction of energy in the form of heat. As the water begins to seep into the granules, they swell and begin to bump into one another, so that the mixture thickens. The solution reaches its thickest point just past the gelatinization stage, which occurs between 175 and 205 degrees. At this point, the granules begin to leak the starches amylose and amylopectin into the liquid. These molecules, particularly the long amylose chains, form a web that traps the swollen granules, thickening the liquid even further. At a temperature somewhere near boiling, however, the granules have swollen to their maximum size and burst open. This bursting has two consequences: It allows most of the starch molecules to escape, and it also forces the water that had been absorbed by the granules to escape back into the mixture. As a result, the mixture begins to thin out again.

MAKING EGG DROP SOUP

Whisk the stock so that it is moving in a circle. Keep whisking as you pour the eggs into the stock in a slow, steady stream so that ribbons of coagulated egg form, about 1 minute.

Straciatella

MANY CUISINES HAVE A CHICKEN SOUP WITH feathered bits of eggs. Chinese egg drop is the most famous, but the Italian version is equally simple and delicious. This soup is called *straciatella*, which translates as "little rags," and refers to the shape of the egg pieces. While egg drop soup has long, ribbon-like pieces of egg, straciatella usually features elongated shredded rectangles that look like their namesake. Besides this difference, straciatella relies on typical Italian flavorings. The eggs are beaten with grated Parmesan cheese before being added to the soup. As for greens, minced basil or parsley or even spinach or chard are used, not scallions and cilantro.

We figured that straciatella could be made just like egg drop soup. We heated the chicken stock in a saucepan and then started whisking the liquid and slowly drizzled in the egg-cheese mixture and continued to whisk. The results were disappointing—most of the egg mixture stuck to the wires of the whisk. Why had this technique worked for egg drop soup and not for straciatella? The cheese added to the beaten eggs had to be the culprit.

We consulted a number of Italian sources and saw several possible solutions to this problem. Some cookbooks suggested tempering the egg-cheese mixture with the addition of some cold chicken stock. Others suggested pouring the egg-cheese mixture through the large holes of a colander. Although both methods worked, in the end we found a simpler solution. It was the utensil (the whisk), not our technique (adding eggs gradually to moving stock), that was the problem. By using a fork rather than a whisk, we could use the same drizzling technique for straciatella and egg drop without losing too much egg to the utensil. The fork helped shape the egg mixture into elongated, shredded rectangles. (In contrast, a whisk turns eggs into long ribbons.)

Although we liked the idea of adding spinach or chard to this soup, in the end we preferred something less bulky. Chopped fresh basil or parsley adds a pleasing color and perfumes the stock nicely.

Straciatella

SERVES 6 TO 8

Straciatella is a sort of frittata soup—chicken stock with bits of Parmesan and egg floating in it. (See page 60 for more information about buying Parmesan cheese.) Fresh basil is a nice addition, but parsley works equally well.

2	quarts Quick Chicken Stock (page 22), Traditional Chicken Stock (page 23), or Improved Canned Chicken Broth (page 26)
4	large eggs
1/4	cup freshly grated Parmesan cheese
1/4	cup finely chopped fresh basil or parsley leaves
	Pinch freshly grated nutmeg
	Salt and ground black pepper

1. Bring the stock to a simmer in a large saucepan over medium-high heat. Stir the eggs, cheese, basil, and nutmeg together with fork in a medium bowl.

2. Stir the stock with a fork so it is moving in a circle. Keep stirring as you pour the egg mixture into the stock in a slow, steady stream so that shreds of coagulated egg form, about 1 minute (see illustration below). Let the eggs stand in the stock without mixing until they are set, less than 1 minute. Once they have set, break up the egg pieces with a fork. Season with salt and pepper to taste. Serve immediately.

MAKING STRACIATELLA SOUP

Stir the stock with a fork so that it is moving in a circle. Keep stirring as you pour the egg mixture in a slow, steady stream to form shreds of coagulated egg. Don't use a whisk here; the egg-cheese mixture will cling to the wires.

Egg–Lemon Soup

WHEN MAKING EGG DROP SOUP OR STRACIATELLA, eggs are allowed to coagulate and feather in the chicken stock. *Avgolemono,* or Greek egg-lemon soup, uses eggs to yield a very different result. The eggs act as a thickener to create a suave, creamy consistency. You can taste the eggs in the finished soup, but you can't see them.

With only four simple ingredients (chicken stock, eggs, lemon, and rice), egg-lemon soup would seem a cinch to make. For those who have never encountered it, this soup is the essence of simple home cooking, based on ingredients as common in American pantries as they are in Greek ones. Flavorful chicken stock is simmered with rice, accented with lemon, and then thickened with beaten eggs.

Straightforward though it is, we did find issues to investigate. First, the texture must be rich and soft, not thin or frothy or pasty, all of which it sometimes is. Also, the soup should be free of tough bits of cooked egg, which would mar its luxurious texture. Finally, a full, lemony flavor—more than just acidity—should balance the savory flavor of the stock.

That eggs are responsible for the smooth texture of this soup was one point of accord found in all of the recipes we researched, which originated not only in Greece but also in Middle Eastern and North African countries. There was considerable debate, however, over the number of eggs, whether to use them whole or separated, whether to whip separated whites to a foam, how long to beat the yolks, and whether to beat them by hand or with a blender or food processor.

Initial tests based on 2 quarts of stock and 2 eggs demonstrated that whole eggs produced better body than yolks alone but that the yolks produced a superior flavor. At the same time, we ruled out separating the eggs and whipping the whites as well as using a machine to beat yolks or whole eggs; both led to soups that were unappealingly foamy and aerated, with weak body and a pale color. The 2-egg soup was a little too thin for us, though, so from there we tinkered with different numbers of eggs and extra yolks until we finally settled on 2 whole eggs plus 2 yolks as the foundation of our ideal texture and color.

Next we had to ponder even finer points concerning the eggs. First was their temperature. Some recipes warned that the eggs must be at room temperature if they are to marry successfully with the stock. While we had absolutely no problem thickening the soup with eggs right out of the refrigerator, we did find that eggs that sat at room temperature for 15 to 20 minutes yielded a marginally smoother soup. The upshot? Remove the eggs from the refrigerator ahead of time, but don't give it a second thought if you don't. Likewise, several recipes insisted on beating the eggs for up to five minutes before introducing the stock, but we found this extra effort unwarranted. Not only was it harder to do than beating them lightly and quickly, but it created undesirable foam and faded the color of the soup. Like whipping the eggs in a machine, longer beating added too much air.

In classic French cooking, any agent used to thicken or bind a soup, sauce, or stew is called a liaison. Common liaisons include flour, starch, roux (a cooked butter-flour mixture), cream, beurre manié (a mixture of softened butter and raw flour), and, as in the case of egg-lemon soup, eggs and yolks. The method used to introduce the liaison to the stock was the second point of agreement in the recipes we researched. Known as tempering, this process consists of first beating the eggs lightly and then slowly beating in some of the hot stock. This mixture is then added to the remaining hot stock to finish the soup.

The effect of tempering is to elevate the temperature of the eggs gradually so that they don't seize up and form curds in the soup. The added stock dilutes the eggs, with the extra water molecules in effect separating the protein molecules. The protein molecules then have to move faster to find each other and link up, or coagulate, thus raising the temperature at which coagulation occurs. Just to cover all the bases, we tried skipping the tempering process. Sure enough, we produced chunks of scrambled eggs floating in watery soup. Eggs normally coagulate at roughly 150 degrees, and simmering stock can approach 200 degrees.

One recipe offered a variation on the tempering technique. Rather than adding the stock to the eggs in a thin stream, this recipe called for adding all of the stock to the eggs ½ cup at a time. When we tried this method, the eggs didn't curdle, but the texture of the soup did suffer. The smoothest soups resulted from the tried-and-true method of trickling the stock in gradually.

The rice cooked in the stock also plays a role in the thickening process. Rice leaches some of its starch into the stock as the grains swell and cook. Those loose starch molecules act to slightly increase the coagulation temperature of the eggs by becoming part of the network of denatured proteins that join together to do the work of thickening. The presence of the starch in the protein network provides some buffer against curdling the eggs should the soup overheat during the final cooking process. So, in this sense, the rice helps to stabilize the entire mixture.

With the texture just where we wanted it, we turned our attention to the flavor. In most of the soups we'd made so far, the lemon flavor was fleeting. It came and went on the palate in almost the same instant. We tried various amounts of lemon juice, but adding more than ¼ cup made the soup taste harsh. Extra acidity was not the answer. Though none of the recipes we consulted had mentioned it, we tried adding lemon zest—the yellow outermost part of the peel—to the equation. The addition of zest, simmered in the stock with the rice, was a stunning success, giving the soup a refreshing tang and full lemon resonance. This flavor stayed with us. Adding bay leaves and a trace amount of spice to the stock brought even greater depth of flavor. Cardamom, in particular, added a real finesse.

With so few ingredients, the stock plays the leading role when it comes to the flavor of egg-lemon soup. That's why we were sadly disappointed with soup made from canned low-sodium chicken broth. "Weak and tinny" was the consensus of our tasters. There's no question that the very best egg-lemon soup is made with a robust, homemade stock.

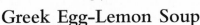

Greek Egg-Lemon Soup
(Avgolemono)
SERVES 6 TO 8

Homemade chicken stock gives this soup the best flavor and body, but in a pinch you can use low-sodium canned broth. The longer the final soup cooks after the eggs have been added, the thicker it becomes. About 5 minutes of heating produces a soft, velvety texture; any longer and the soup begins to turn pasty. Scallions and fresh mint, individually or together, make simple and flavorful garnishes. Serve the soup immediately; it thickens to a gravylike consistency when reheated.

2	quarts chicken stock, preferably homemade
½	cup long-grain white rice
I	bay leaf
4	green cardamom pods, crushed, or 2 whole cloves
	Zest strips from 1½ medium lemons (about twelve ½ inch by 4-inch pieces; see illustration on page 50)
1½	teaspoons salt
2	large eggs, plus 2 yolks, preferably at room temperature
¼	cup juice from zested lemons
I	large scallion, sliced thin, and/or 3 tablespoons chopped fresh mint leaves

1. Bring the stock to a boil in a large saucepan over high heat. Add the rice, bay leaf, cardamom, lemon zest, and salt. Reduce the heat to medium and simmer until the rice is tender and the stock is aromatic from the lemon zest, 16 to 20 minutes. Remove and discard the bay leaf, cardamom, and zest strips. Increase the heat to high and return the stock to a boil, then reduce the heat to low.

2. Whisk the eggs, yolks, and lemon juice lightly in a medium nonreactive bowl until combined. Whisking constantly, slowly ladle about 2 cups hot stock into the egg mixture (see illustration on page 50); whisk until combined. Pour the egg-stock mixture back into saucepan; cook over low heat, stirring constantly, until soup is slightly thickened and wisps

of steam appear, 4 to 5 minutes. Do not simmer or boil. Divide soup among serving bowls, sprinkle with scallion and/or mint; serve immediately.

➤ VARIATIONS

Egg-Lemon Soup with Cinnamon and Cayenne

This variation, the test kitchen favorite, is based on a Tunisian-style egg-lemon soup.

Follow recipe for Greek Egg-Lemon Soup, substituting one 2-inch stick cinnamon and a pinch of cayenne for cardamom.

Egg-Lemon Soup with Saffron

Follow recipe for Greek Egg-Lemon Soup, adding a pinch (about ¼ teaspoon) saffron threads, crushed between fingertips, to stock along with rice, bay leaf, cardamom, zest, and salt.

REMOVING LARGE STRIPS OF LEMON ZEST

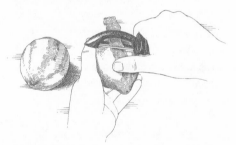

Run a vegetable peeler from pole to pole to remove long, wide strips of zest.

TEMPERING EGGS

Whisking constantly, trickle the hot stock mixture into the beaten eggs with a ladle.

Egg-Lemon Soup with Chicken

Diced breast meat makes this soup especially hearty.

Follow recipe for Greek Egg-Lemon Soup, Egg-Lemon Soup with Cinnamon and Cayenne, or Egg-Lemon Soup with Saffron, adding two boneless, skinless chicken breasts (about 12 ounces total) cut into ½-inch cubes to stock along with rice, seasonings, and zest.

WONTON SOUP

IN MANY RESPECTS, WONTON SOUP IS THE simplest Chinese soup to prepare—that is, if you have dumplings and stock on hand. With our Asian stock recipe developed, our chief concern was the dumplings.

The wrapper is the most important ingredient in the dumplings. We wondered if homemade wrappers (made like pasta, with flour and egg) were better than store-bought. We made our own wrappers and found the process to be unbearably tedious. We also found that store-bought wrappers delivered better results than homemade. Commercial wrappers are moisture-free and much easier to work with than homemade pasta wrappers, which stuck to pots and cooked up gummy in our tests. Buying wrappers allows you to concentrate on making a filling and stock. (For more information on buying wonton wrappers, see page 51.)

The traditional wonton shape is a triangle with two opposing corners brought together. Some sources suggest using the traditional shape, while others state that the filling is less likely to leak in a tortellini-shaped wonton. In tortellini, the top corner is not bound with the others but folded down. We prepared both shapes and had no trouble with leaking in either case, as long as we were careful to brush the edges of the wrappers with water to create a tight seal. The triangular shape was the unanimous favorite for two reasons: tradition and texture. It met people's visual expectations (the tortellini shape evoked comments about Chinese-Italian food), and, when properly cooked, it allows for a large part of the wrapper to turn silky smooth, just as great noodles do in stock. In comparison, the tortellini shape was too chewy and condensed.

The next question was the filling. We tested seven different dumpling fillings, including those made with shrimp, vegetables, meat, chicken, and pork. All were delicious, but the rich pork filling was deemed the most authentic. For a lighter soup, we suggest using chicken or shrimp in place of pork.

Although we tried a variety of seasonings in the filling, tasters preferred classic choices—ginger, garlic, rice wine or dry sherry, soy sauce, sesame oil, sugar, salt, and scallions. The issue of how to bind all the filling ingredients proved to be more complex.

Ground meats and seasonings become a bit watery when cooked inside a wonton wrapper. Some recipes call for some cornstarch to absorb excess water. Other recipes rely on an egg to perform the same function. In our testing, we found that cornstarch did the best job of absorbing excess moisture exuded by the filling as it cooked. This prevents the wrappers from becoming mushy and possibly tearing open.

We found an egg to be less effective at controlling moisture. The flavor of the egg yolk can also be a bit overpowering. That said, we found that an egg white helps the filling to set up into a firm, creamy mass. Although the egg white doesn't absorb moisture, it improves the consistency of the filling and gives it a smoother mouthfeel.

With shape and filling decided, our next concern was cooking the wontons. Boiling the wontons directly in the soup turned them mushy and slimy and clouded the stock. Of the other two options, boiling or steaming them separately, boiling produced the best results. The wrappers retained some body yet remained tender and supple in the mouth. The steamed wontons were chewy by comparison.

Should you want to hold the filled dumplings before cooking them, we found that they can sit refrigerated on a baking sheet for several hours. Line the baking sheet with parchment or wax paper, but don't flour the sheet—flour just made the dumplings gummy when cooked. And don't cover the baking sheet. When we covered it with plastic wrap, the wrappers got moist on the bottom and stuck to the tray. Although the uncovered dumplings dried out a bit, overall the results were better. If you want to hold the dumplings for longer than a few hours, they must be frozen. Freeze the dumplings on a baking sheet lined with parchment or wax paper, and then transfer them to an airtight container to prevent freezer burn. We found it best to cook frozen dumplings straight from the freezer. Add two to three minutes to the cooking time.

The final issue to be tested was what ingredients (if any) to add to the stock and dumplings. This area

INGREDIENTS: Wonton Wrappers

Wonton wrappers (also called wonton skins) are delicate and paper-thin. Several choices are available, especially if you shop in an Asian market. We purchased four different styles of wrappers and proceeded to test them in our wonton soup recipe. We bought both round and square wrappers of varying sizes and thicknesses. Their ingredient lists also differed.

The square wrappers were easier to shape into wontons than round wrappers. If you must buy round wrappers, trim them to make squares and fill them more sparingly, if necessary.

Thickness turned out to be more complicated. Thick wrappers are to be avoided (the wontons will be too doughy), but ultrasheer wrappers can be problematic, too. We tried one brand of Japanese wrapper (called shao mai), which were considerably thinner than the rest (about 85 wrappers in a 12-ounce package). We ripped many of these thin wrappers in the folding and

shaping process. Still more wrappers opened up as they cooked. Stick with wrappers that are about $1/32$ inch thick. A 12-ounce package of $3\frac{1}{4}$-inch square wrappers should contain 50 to 60 wrappers.

Finally, we think it's important to read the ingredient label. Our testers preferred wrappers made with eggs. Wrappers with just flour and salt were white in the package and became translucent when cooked. Traditional Chinese wrappers will be pale yellow in the package and remain opaque when cooked.

Wonton wrappers are sold fresh in the refrigerator case and can be frozen for several months if not used in a week or so. If you decide to freeze them, do so in small batches, since they cannot be separated from each other until completely thawed and, once thawed, do not take well to refreezing. We found that wrappers thaw to room temperature in an hour or so.

is fairly subjective, and we decided to stay close to tradition. Greens and scallions were deemed a must. (Napa cabbage, iceberg lettuce, and spinach are all good choices for the greens.) Carrots, while not absolutely necessary, are a common ingredient and add color to the soup. Testers liked snow peas as well, although this ingredient is optional.

Wonton Soup

SERVES 6 TO 8

Wonton filling is traditionally made with ground pork. For something lighter, try ground chicken, preferably ground at home in a food processor from boneless, skinless thighs. In either case, the wontons are cooked separately in boiling water and then added to the stock. Time it so that the stock is already simmering when you cook the wontons.

WONTONS

4	ounces ground pork
4	peeled water chestnuts (fresh or canned), minced
1	teaspoon minced fresh ginger
1	small clove garlic, minced
1	teaspoon dry sherry or rice wine
1½	teaspoons soy sauce
½	teaspoon Asian sesame oil
¼	teaspoon sugar
⅛	teaspoon salt, plus more for cooking water
1	tablespoon minced greens from 1 medium scallion

½	large egg white, lightly beaten
1	teaspoon cornstarch
32	wonton wrappers

SOUP BASE

2	quarts Asian Chicken Stock (page 25) or Improved Canned Chicken Broth with Asian Flavors (page 26)
1½	teaspoons salt, plus more to taste
½	cup shredded greens (Napa cabbage, spinach, or iceberg lettuce)
2	tablespoons grated carrot (from half a small carrot)
3	medium scallions, chopped fine
4	snow peas cut into ½-inch dice (optional)
	Freshly ground black pepper

1. Mix together all the wonton ingredients, except wrappers, in a medium bowl. (The filling can be covered and refrigerated for 1 day.)

2. Fill and shape the wontons as directed in the illustrations below. Place the filled wontons on a large baking sheet covered with parchment or wax paper and refrigerate, uncovered, for at least 20 minutes or up to a few hours.

3. Bring 4 quarts of water to a boil in a large pot. Add salt to taste and the wontons. Cook until the wontons are tender, 3 to 4 minutes. Lift the wontons from the water with a slotted spoon and set them aside in a single layer on a large plate.

SHAPING WONTONS

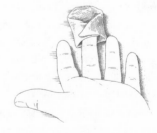

1. Place a wonton skin on a flat, dry work surface with a corner pointing toward you. Place 1 teaspoon of filling in the center of the wrapper. Lightly brush the two edges farthest from you with water.

2. Fold the wonton in half, away from you, making a triangle. Press edges firmly to seal.

3. Lightly brush the two corners nearest you with water, fold them over your finger, and press together to seal.

4. Meanwhile, bring the stock to a simmer in a large stockpot or Dutch oven. Add the salt, greens, carrots, and scallions and cook to blend flavors, 3 to 4 minutes. Add the cooked wontons and snow peas (if using) and simmer until the wontons are heated through, 1 to 2 minutes. Season with salt and pepper to taste and serve immediately.

➤ VARIATION

Shrimp Wonton Soup

Follow the recipe for Wonton Soup, replacing ground pork with 4 ounces shelled raw shrimp, coarsely chopped.

TORTELLINI SOUP

SCHOLARS DEBATE ENDLESSLY WHETHER pasta originated in China or Italy. For cooks, the important issue is that both cuisines make wide use of pasta, even in soups.

The Italian equivalent to wonton soup is *tortellini in brodo,* which translates as "tortellini in broth." Like wonton soup, the recipe is fairly straightforward. Filled pastas are floated in a clear stock, usually flavored with some greens. Although some recipes call for meat stock, we decided to use chicken stock since more cooks are likely to have this ingredient on hand. Since the stock portion of the recipe is so straightforward, we decided to focus on the tortellini first.

Some recipes call for cooking the tortellini right in the stock, although many suggest cooking the pasta in salted water and then adding them to the stock. We tested both methods and preferred cooking the tortellini right in the stock. The pasta picked up more flavor this way, and tortellini don't seem to cloud the stock the way floury wonton wrappers can.

Most commercially made tortellini are tough and doughy, not supple and tender, like homemade versions. We don't think "fresh" tortellini sold in supermarket refrigerator cases are worth buying. These pastas are often quite old (many brands have sell-by dates that are weeks if not months away), and they

don't have any of the delicacy we expect from fresh pasta. High-quality tortellini from a gourmet shop or pasta shop that makes fresh pasta every day is another matter. If you can find this product, by all means use it.

Since not everyone has access to handmade tortellini, we decided to figure out how to make tortellini at home. After testing dozens of recipes, we can honestly say that filled pastas are not difficult to prepare. There is no question, however, that they are time-consuming.

Because most filled pastas have doubled edges where the pasta has been folded over the filling and sealed, it is essential that pasta sheets are rolled as thin as possible. Otherwise, the edges may remain too chewy when the rest of the pasta shape is already cooked through. Use the last setting on a manual pasta machine for the best results.

The biggest problem most home cooks encounter when making filled pastas is that the shapes open up when boiled. There's nothing worse than seeing all the filling floating around the pot, so it's imperative to properly seal the edges on each piece of filled pasta. We tried brushing the edges of the dough with water and with lightly beaten egg. We found that both made the dough sticky and harder to handle, especially the egg.

We had the best results when we used the pasta sheet as quickly as possible, when it was still moist and pliable. Pasta sheets that have been left out to dry (even for just 20 or 30 minutes) will be too brittle to manipulate. If your dough does become dry, brush the edges lightly with water. Be careful to brush lightly or the dough will become very tacky. To guarantee that the pasta does not dry out, we recommend filling and shaping the tortellini as soon as the pasta has been rolled out. This means the filling should be made first, then the pasta.

Take care not to overload the pasta with too much filling, which might cause the pasta shape to burst in the boiling water. As an added precaution, cook the pasta in soup that is at a low boil. Highly agitated stock can rip open delicate shapes.

Tortellini fillings should be kept simple, especially since pasta making requires so much time. Ground meats enriched with cheese, or plain cheese flavored with herbs, are two classic choices. We find it best to add a little egg yolk to help bind filling ingredients.

With the tortellini made and stock on hand, the soup is easy to prepare. Most recipes call for some sort of greens, and we found that any tender leafy greens, including spinach, chard, escarole, and watercress, can be used. Just remove all tough stems and chop the leafy portion into small pieces that will fit on a soup spoon. A shower of grated Parmesan cheese at the table is all that's required to finish this soup.

INGREDIENTS: Homemade Fresh Pasta

Homemade tortellini begins with homemade fresh pasta. (See our recipe on page 56.) Fresh pasta cut into long ribbons, rectangles, or even scraps is a delicious addition to chicken, beef, or vegetable soups.

We wanted to develop a foolproof recipe for basic fresh egg pasta. This meant figuring out the proper ratio of eggs to flour as well as the role of salt and olive oil in the dough. Most recipes start with all-purpose flour, but we figured it was worth testing various kinds of flour. Perhaps most important, we wanted to devise a kneading method that was quick and easy.

Before beginning to develop our pasta dough recipe, we wanted to settle on a basic technique. Pasta dough can be made in one of three ways. Traditionally, the dough is made by hand on a clean counter. The flour is formed into a ring, the eggs are cracked into the center, and the flour is slowly worked into the eggs with a fork. When the eggs are no longer runny, you start kneading by hand. The whole process takes at least 20 minutes and requires a lot of hand strength.

Another option is an electric pasta maker that kneads the dough and cuts it into various shapes. Although these machines have some limited appeal, they are quite expensive. We find that a food processor makes pasta dough much more quickly than the old-fashioned hand method. Since most cooks already own a food processor, we recommend it for making fresh pasta dough.

Most recipes for fresh egg pasta start with three eggs and then add various amounts of flour. A three-egg dough will produce about one pound of fresh pasta, so this seemed like a good place to start our working recipe. We saw recipes that called for as little as $\frac{1}{2}$ cup of flour per egg. Other recipes called for as much as $\frac{3}{4}$ cup of flour per egg. After several tests, we settled on $\frac{2}{3}$ cup of flour per egg, or 2 cups of all-purpose flour for 3 eggs.

In most tests, this ratio produced perfect pasta dough, without adjustments. However, on a few occasions the dough was a bit dry. This seemed to happen on dry days, but it also could be that slight variations in egg size were throwing things off. It was easy enough to add a little water to bring the dough together. The dough was almost never too wet, which was a good thing. It's much harder to add flour to a sticky dough than it is to add a little water to a dry, crumbly dough.

Once the dough comes together, we found it beneficial to knead the dough by hand for a minute or two. The motor on our food processor started to labor before the dough was smooth enough. Taking the dough out as soon as it came together prevented our food processor from overheating.

At this point, we had a recipe and method for making pasta dough that we liked a lot. It seemed time to start testing additional flavorings. We found no benefit from adding salt to the dough. If the pasta is cooked in salted water or stock, it will taste well seasoned. Adding olive oil makes fresh pasta a bit slick, and the olive oil flavor seems out of place in many recipes.

We had been using unbleached all-purpose flour in our tests. We then tested several brands of bleached all-purpose flour and found only minimal differences in the way each flour absorbed the egg. We could not detect any significant differences in flavor. On the other hand, high-protein bread flour and low-protein cake flour had disastrous effects. Bread flour produced a very tough dough that was hard to handle. Pasta dough should be supple and elastic, not stiff and difficult to stretch. At the opposite end of the spectrum, pasta made with cake flour was too soft and crumbly; the dough did not have enough structure. Cake flour also has a sour chemical flavor, which is obscured by sugar and butter in cake but comes through loud and clear in pasta.

With our dough made, it was time to test rolling techniques. Many Italian sources tout the superiority of hand-rolled pasta. However, every time we rolled pasta dough with a pin, it was too thick. Although thick fettuccine is not an abomination, pasta for tortellini, with its doubled edges, must be thin. Perhaps after years of practice we could roll pasta thin enough, but for now we prefer a hand-cranked manual pasta machine.

Tortellini Soup

SERVES 6 TO 8

If you can find high-quality fresh tortellini at a local market, omit steps 1 and 2 and use about 50 small or medium tortellini in step 3.

MEAT AND RICOTTA TORTELLINI

1	teaspoon extra-virgin olive oil
1	small clove garlic, minced
2	ounces ground beef, veal, or pork
1/3	cup ricotta cheese
1	tablespoon freshly grated Parmesan cheese
1	tablespoon minced fresh basil or parsley leaves
	Salt and ground black pepper
1/2	large egg yolk
1/2	pound Fresh Egg Pasta (page 56)

SOUP BASE

2	quarts Quick Chicken Stock (page 22) or Traditional Chicken Stock (page 23)
4	cups stemmed and chopped spinach, chard, watercress, or escarole
	Salt and ground black pepper
	Freshly grated Parmesan cheese

1. Heat the oil and garlic in a small skillet over medium heat. Cook until the garlic is golden, about 2 minutes. Add the meat and raise the heat to medium-high. Cook, using a wooden spoon to break up the larger pieces of meat, until the liquid evaporates and the meat browns, about 3 minutes. Spoon off the fat and transfer the meat mixture to a small bowl. Cool slightly. Stir in the cheeses, basil, and salt and pepper to taste. Stir in the egg yolk. (The filling can be covered and refrigerated for 1 day.)

2. Fill and shape the tortellini as directed in the illustrations below. Place the filled tortellini on a large baking sheet lined with parchment or wax paper. (The tortellini can be refrigerated, uncovered, for up to 2 hours.)

3. Bring the stock to a boil in a large stockpot or Dutch oven. Drop the tortellini and greens into the pot. Simmer until the tortellini are al dente, about 4 minutes. Season the soup with salt and pepper to taste. Serve immediately, passing the Parmesan at the table.

➤ VARIATION

Parsley-Cheese Tortellini in Chicken Stock

This filling requires no cooking and is quite simple to prepare.

Combine 1/3 cup ricotta cheese, 3 tablespoons freshly grated Parmesan cheese, 2 tablespoons minced fresh parsley leaves, 1/2 large egg yolk, and salt and pepper to taste in a small bowl. Follow recipe for Tortellini Soup, omitting step 1. Use ricotta mixture to fill pasta in step 2. Proceed as directed.

SHAPING TORTELLINI

1. Use a pizza wheel or sharp knife to cut sheets of fresh pasta into 2-inch squares. Lift each square and place it on a clean part of the work surface (otherwise squares may stick when stuffed). Place 1/2 teaspoon of filling in the center of each square.

2. Fold each square diagonally in half to make a triangle. Make sure that the top piece of dough covers the filling, but leave a thin border of the bottom exposed. Seal the edges with your fingers.

3. Lift the filled triangle from the counter and wrap the back of the triangle around the top of your index finger. Squeeze the two bottom corners of the triangle together.

4. As you pull back the top peak of the triangle, gently fold over the top ring of pasta so that the stuffing is completely enclosed. Slide the filled pasta off your finger.

Fresh Egg Pasta

MAKES ABOUT 1 POUND

Although the food processor does most of the work, you must finish kneading this dough by hand. Keep pressing and folding the dough until it is extremely smooth. (For more detailed information on making pasta, see page 54.)

2   cups all-purpose flour

3   large eggs, beaten

1. Pulse the flour in the workbowl of a food processor fitted with the metal blade to evenly distribute and aerate. Add the eggs; process until the dough forms a rough ball, about 30 seconds. (If the dough resembles small pebbles, add water, ½ teaspoon at a time; if the dough sticks to the side of the workbowl, add flour, 1 tablespoon at a time, and process until the dough forms a rough ball.)

2. Turn the dough ball and small bits out onto a dry work surface; knead until the dough is smooth, 1 to 2 minutes. Cover with plastic wrap and set aside for at least 15 minutes and up to 2 hours to relax.

3. Cut about ⅙ of the dough from the ball and flatten into a disk; rewrap the remaining dough. Run the dough through the widest setting of a manual pasta machine. Bring the ends of the dough toward the middle and press down to seal. Run the dough, open side first, through the widest setting again. Fold, seal, and roll again. Without folding, run the pasta through the widest setting about two more times, until the dough is smooth. If at any point the dough is sticky, dust lightly with flour. Continue to run the dough through the machine; narrow the setting each time, until you use the last setting on the machine and the outline of your hand is visible through the dough sheet. Lay the sheet of pasta on a clean kitchen towel and cover it with a damp cloth to keep the pasta from drying out. Repeat the process with the remaining pieces of dough.

4. Use pasta immediately to make tortellini. (Extra pasta can be cut into long ribbons or rectangles, frozen on a baking sheet, transferred to a zipper-lock plastic bag, and added directly to simmering soup. Cook several minutes until tender.)

MATZO BALL SOUP

MATZO BALLS ARE JEWISH DUMPLINGS MADE with ground matzo, or matzo meal, and traditionally served during Passover. During the eight days of this Jewish holiday, in commemoration of the exodus of the Jews from Egypt, regular flour and leavening agents are not eaten. Matzo, made with unbleached flour and no yeast, is a substitute for bread and central to the Passover cuisine. Matzo balls, a Passover specialty usually served in chicken stock, are so well liked they are eaten throughout the year.

The most basic matzo ball is prepared with matzo meal, chicken fat or oil, eggs, and water or chicken stock. Yet even with this most traditional recipe, there are many variations in the size and texture of matzo balls. Some people like fluffy, light matzo balls; others prefer something denser and chewier. Flavor variations are also found in most Jewish cookbooks. Matzo balls with bitter herbs, especially parsley, are common, as are matzo balls flavored with ground spices, especially ginger, nutmeg, and cinnamon.

Given the possibilities and strong personal preferences, our goal for this testing was to create a simple, foolproof matzo ball recipe that could be easily varied, both in terms of texture and seasonings.

Our first tests focused on texture, determined first by the ratio of ingredients. We started with 1 cup of matzo meal (a basic measure in most recipes) and tried varying amounts of eggs, fat, and liquid. Testers preferred matzo balls made with 4 eggs for 1 cup of meal. With 5 eggs, the matzo balls were too eggy tasting (you could even see bits of egg white inside the balls). With 3 eggs, the matzo balls were quite heavy and dense. Four eggs produced matzo balls that were noticeably lighter but not overly eggy.

While chicken fat is the traditional choice for matzo balls, many modern cooks are more likely to use vegetable oil. As might be expected, we found that chicken fat does in fact make tastier matzo balls. Solid chicken fat (we suggest skimming fat from cooled homemade stock) also makes a slightly more tender matzo ball. We saw recipes that called for as little as 2 tablespoons and as much as ½ cup of fat for every cup of matzo meal. We found that 4 tablespoons made tasty matzo balls that weren't overly heavy or rich.

Water was the final component to examine. In some respects, this proved the most perplexing element in our testing. Adding too much water makes the matzo meal mixture too soft to shape. However, too little water leaves the texture of the matzo balls dense. To complicate matters, it seems that different matzo meals absorb water at different rates. After running more than a dozen tests, we found it necessary to adjust the amount of water depending on the brand of matzo meal being used and the desired texture. (See page 58 for details on these tests as well as visual clues that you can use to determine when you've added enough water.)

We did find several recipes that replace the water in the batter with chicken stock. We made matzo balls with chicken stock and detected a modest improvement in flavor when tasting the matzo balls on their own. However, once you put these matzo balls in chicken stock, the differences faded. Also, chicken stock seemed to make the texture of the matzo balls more dense and chewy, traits that some tasters liked and others didn't. Our recommendation is to stick with water unless you want an especially chewy matzo ball.

All the recipes we consulted suggested chilling the batter to make it easier to handle and shape. Recommended times in the refrigerator ranged from 15 minutes to 24 hours. We found that chilling the batter for at least one hour makes it easier to handle. The batter becomes firmer and, as long as your hands are moistened with water, shaping the mixture into 1-inch balls should be easy. For especially easy handling, leave the batter in the refrigerator for four hours. Refrigeration longer than four hours did not change the consistency of the batter and yielded overly dense matzo balls.

We next moved on to cooking the matzo balls. Although they tasted marginally better when cooked in stock, we found that matzo balls are best cooked in water. They make chicken stock very cloudy, something all of our tasters disliked. By definition, matzo ball soup should be clear and golden. You could cook the matzo balls in a separate pot of stock and then transfer the cooked matzo balls to the soup. However, matzo balls absorb a surprisingly large amount of liquid. Given the relative scarcity of homemade stock in most kitchens, it seems silly to use stock when the benefit is so modest. We recommend simmering matzo balls in water and then transferring them to the soup just before serving.

As for cooking the matzo balls, don't let the water boil too vigorously. A modest simmer is best. Use a wide pot and distribute the matzo balls evenly across the bottom of the pan. This ensures even cooking. Don't let matzo balls pile up on top of each other. We found that covering the pot (and thus trapping steam) creates a lighter, airier texture. If you like dense matzo balls, leave the cover off.

Once the matzo balls are cooked through (cut one in half to make sure the center is not dark or raw looking), they can be transferred directly to the soup pot with a slotted spoon. Another option is to place the cooked matzo balls in a single layer in a large container and then cover them with room temperature or cold chicken stock. The matzo balls will stay moist in the refrigerator for a day or so. To reheat, add them to the boiling stock along with the carrots. By the time the carrots are done, the matzo balls will be heated through.

Carrots and dill are traditional additions to the stock. We found that the carrots are best sliced into thin rounds that can be easily eaten with a spoon. Dill adds a characteristic flavor, but parsley can pinch-hit if necessary.

SHAPING MATZO BALLS

Lightly moisten your hands. Take 1 level tablespoon of the matzo mixture and use your palms to quickly and gently shape the mixture into a 1-inch ball.

Chicken Soup with Matzo Balls

SERVES 6 TO 8

Matzo balls made with chicken fat are more flavorful than those made with vegetable oil, but either can be used. All matzo meals are not created equal (see below). Flavor, texture, and ability to absorb liquid vary from brand to brand. If using Streit's, reduce the water to 6 tablespoons. This recipe creates light and fluffy matzo balls that are about 1½ inches in diameter when cooked. To create chewier and denser balls, reduce the water by 1 tablespoon. (An easy way to measure 7 tablespoons of water is to start with ½ cup and then remove 1 tablespoon—8 tablespoons equals ½ cup.) To create large matzo balls (2½ inches in diameter when cooked), use 2 tablespoons of raw mixture and increase the cooking time to 35 to 40 minutes.

4	large eggs
¼	cup vegetable oil or chicken fat
7	tablespoons water
I	cup matzo meal
I½	teaspoons salt
¼	teaspoon freshly ground black pepper
2	quarts Quick Chicken Stock (page 22) or Traditional Chicken Stock (page 23)
3	small carrots, peeled and cut into rounds ⅛ inch thick
2	tablespoons finely chopped fresh dill or parsley

1. Lightly beat the eggs with a whisk in a medium bowl. Whisk in the fat, then the water. In a separate bowl, mix together the matzo meal, salt, and pepper. Stir the matzo mixture into the liquids. The consistency will initially be like pancake batter, but it will immediately begin to thicken. After 2 to 3 minutes the batter will be like soft mashed potatoes or soft polenta. Cover and refrigerate for at least 1 hour or up to 4 hours.

2. Bring 4 quarts of water to a boil in a large stockpot or Dutch oven over medium-high heat. With moistened hands, form 1 level tablespoon of matzo mixture into balls about 1-inch diameter (see the illustration on page 57). Drop the balls into the boiling water so that each falls into the pot in a different place. When all of the balls are added, reduce to a simmer over medium-low heat and cook,

---

INGREDIENTS: Matzo Meal

There are three major national brands of matzo meal: Goodman's, Manischewitz, and Streit's. We wondered if all brands are created alike. We made three batches of matzo balls to find out.

Straight from the box, we noticed some differences in the three products. Goodman's and Manischewitz appeared to be more finely ground that Streit's. Goodman's is also a bit darker and more toasted than the other two brands.

Once we added the other ingredients, we noticed that Streit's absorbed the liquid more slowly than the finer meals. We proceeded with our recipe, allowing the batter to firm up in the refrigerator. With 7 tablespoons of liquid in the batter, the Streit's batter was still too loose and thus very difficult to shape. Clearly, this meal would require less liquid.

We then cooked all three kinds of matzo balls. Tasters preferred the matzo balls made with Goodman's, which tasted more toasted and complex than matzo balls made with the other brands. The biggest differences were in texture, though. Matzo balls made with Goodman's and Manischewitz held together nicely. They were fluffy but not soft. In contrast, the loose Streit's batter made ragged-looking matzo balls that were nearly falling apart.

Given that many cooks will use whatever matzo meal they have on hand, we needed to devise some independent method for gauging the consistency of an ideal batter. When the dry ingredients are first mixed into the wet ingredients, the texture resembles pancake batter. Run a wooden spoon through the middle of the batter to divide it in half. When the batter is first mixed together, the two sides will run back together. After two to three minutes, perform this test again. The texture of the batter will now be similar to soft mashed potatoes. When separated at the bottom of the bowl, the mixture will very slowly come back together. This is the ideal consistency for fluffy, light matzo balls.

If after two to three minutes the batter is still runny, stir in some matzo meal. If the batter barely moves after being divided with a wooden spoon, the texture of the cooked matzo balls will be dense. It's fine to leave the batter as is. However, if you want lighter matzo balls, stir in another tablespoon or so of liquid so that the divided batter will slowly come back together again.

covered, for 20 minutes. With a slotted spoon, remove one matzo ball, cut in half and check for doneness and seasoning. The matzo ball is done when the inside is not dark or wet. If more seasoning is desired, add 2 teaspoons salt to the water. If necessary, cook 5 to 10 additional minutes, or until the color is uniform throughout and the texture is light and fluffy.

3. While the matzo balls are cooking, bring the stock to a boil in a large saucepan. Add the carrots, reduce the heat to medium-low, and cook until tender, about 6 minutes. Use a slotted spoon to transfer the matzo balls to the soup. Stir in the dill and serve immediately.

➤ VARIATIONS

Chicken Soup with Herbed Matzo Balls
Follow recipe for Chicken Soup with Matzo Balls, adding ¼ cup minced fresh dill or parsley to the liquids, after the eggs are mixed with fat and water, in step 1.

Chicken Soup with Spiced Matzo Balls
Follow recipe for Chicken Soup with Matzo Balls, mixing ½ teaspoon ground nutmeg, ½ teaspoon ground ginger, and ½ teaspoon ground cinnamon with the matzo meal and salt and pepper in step 1.

CHICKEN SOUP WITH PASSATELLI

PASSATELLI ARE ITALIAN DUMPLINGS MADE with cheese and bread crumbs. They are similar to matzo balls, although much less widely known, at least outside of Italy. That's a shame given how simple and delicious these dumplings can be.

The combination of cheesy dumplings and chicken stock is irresistible. Dumplings made with bread crumbs, eggs, and grated cheese are cooked in chicken stock just until tender. The soup is often garnished with parsley and more grated cheese, but vegetables are not commonly used.

We tried a variety of bread crumbs, including commercial crumbs from the supermarket, homemade crumbs from fresh bread, and homemade crumbs from stale bread. The commercial crumbs made bland-tasting, gummy dumplings. Homemade crumbs were better tasting. The stale crumbs absorbed the eggs better and gave the dumplings a pleasing texture. We found that fresh crumbs could be used as long as they were dried out in a warm oven for five minutes. Since most cooks have a few slices of fresh bread on hand, we developed the recipe with this in mind.

With the bread crumb component decided, the other issues were easy to resolve. Good cheese (real Parmigiano-Reggiano) makes a difference in this recipe. Dumplings made with domestic Parmesan were bland in comparison. (See page 60 for more information on Parmesan cheese.) A pinch of grated nutmeg added more flavor and highlighted the buttery, nutty flavor of the cheese.

As with matzo balls, we found it easier to shape cold batter. Just 15 minutes in the refrigerator is sufficient to firm up this batter and make the shaping process much easier. In Italy, many cooks rely on a special tool to form the batter into thick, cylindrical strands. A food mill or ricer is another common option. The batter is pushed through the holes on the coarsest disk, directly into a pot of simmering stock. We found that these authentic dumplings sometimes fall apart in the soup. Shaping the batter into small rounds (the size of grapes) ensures that the dumplings hold their shape. Although not strictly traditional, this modest change makes sense for cooks who have never made this soup before.

Chicken Soup with Passatelli
SERVES 6 TO 8

Make sure to use homemade bread crumbs in this recipe. Commercial crumbs are bland and too fine to make proper dumplings. For the Parmesan, we highly recommend Parmigiano-Reggiano.

2	slices white bread, torn into rough chunks
2	large eggs
I	cup freshly grated Parmesan cheese, plus more for the table
	Pinch freshly grated nutmeg
	Salt and ground black pepper
2	quarts Quick Chicken Stock (page 22) or Traditional Chicken Stock (page 23)
2	tablespoons minced fresh parsley leaves

INGREDIENTS: Parmesan Cheese

When it comes to grated Parmesan cheese, there's a wide range of options—everything from the whitish powder in green jars to imported cheese that costs $14 a pound. You can buy cheese that has been grated, or you can pick out a whole hunk and grate it yourself. We wondered if "authentic" Parmigiano-Reggiano would be that much better when tasted side by side with a domestic Parmesan at half the price.

Parmesan is a grana—a hard, grainy cheese. The grana cheese category is composed mostly of Italian grating cheeses. Parmigiano-Reggiano is the most famous (and expensive) of the granas, and its manufacture dates back 800 years. Parmigiano-Reggiano has become an increasingly regulated product; in 1955 it became what is known as a certified name (not a brand name). Since that time the name has indicated that the cheese was made within a specific region of northern Italy and approved by a certifying consortium.

American cheese makers need not abide by any more stringent regulations than basic U.S. Department of Agriculture standards. There is no lack of pregrated products, but only a handful of domestic Parmesans come in wedges. Other granas considered Parmesan types are Grana Padano (from Italy) and Reggianito (from Argentina).

The samples in a tasting conducted in our test kitchen included five pregrated Parmesan cheeses (domestic and imported), three wedges of domestic Parmesan, a wedge of Grana Padano, one of Reggianito, and two of Parmigiano-Reggiano. To see if differences in store handling could affect the quality of the latter two, one was purchased at a specialty cheese store that cuts from the wheel per order and has controlled humidity; the other was purchased precut and wrapped in plastic at a large supermarket. All of the cheeses were tasted grated, at room temperature.

To get an idea of what the tasters should look for when tasting the different cheeses, we spoke to a number of cheese experts. All recommended that the tasters rate cheeses on the basics: aroma, flavor (particularly depth of flavor and saltiness versus sweetness), and overall texture. The Parmesans should also be left to sit on the tasters' tongues to see if the cheeses melt smoothly into creaminess in the mouth. All of the experts we spoke to expressed confidence that Parmigiano-Reggiano would be the hands-down winner.

This time the experts were correct. Parmigiano-Reggiano had a depth and complexity of flavor and a smooth, melting texture that none of the others could match. Parmigiano-Reggiano owes much of its flavor to the unpasteurized milk used to produce it. It is a "controlled-district" cheese, which means not only that it must be made within the boundaries of this zone but also that the milk used to make it and even the grass, hay, and grain fed to the cows that make the milk must come from the district. Consequently, just like good wine, a lot of character comes from the soil and climate where it was made. In the tasting we found that none of the other cheeses had the sweet, nutty, creamy flavor of Parmigiano-Reggiano.

We found almost all of the cheeses in the tasting—except the Parmigiano-Reggiano—to be extremely salty. In fact, Parmigiano-Reggiano contains about two-thirds less sodium than the other Parmesans. This is because wheels of Parmigiano-Reggiano are so large that they do not become as saturated with salt during the brining process that is one of the final steps in making the cheese. (The average wheel weighs 75 to 90 pounds; domestic Parmesan wheels average 24 pounds.)

The low-salt content of Parmigiano-Reggiano makes it more perishable once cut from the wheel than other cheeses. Once cut, the cheese will also begin to dry out. This was evident in the Parmigiano-Reggiano sample purchased at the grocery store. Tasters rated this a few tenths of a point lower than the sample purchased at the specialty cheese store because of a chalky finish. This drying effect was even more glaring with the chalky pregrated products, which received consistently poor ratings.

Another benefit of the larger wheel is that Parmigiano-Reggiano can age longer. Parmigiano-Reggiano ages for about 24 months, while domestic Parmesan ages for about 10 months. The longer aging allows more complex flavors and aromas to develop.

The aging also makes a difference in texture, creating a distinctive component that tasters described as "crystal crunch." The crunch stems from proteins breaking down into free amino acid crystals during the latter half of the aging process. The crystals are visible, appearing as white dots in the cheese. No other Parmesan had this effect.

Other textural differences are created by the fact that the curds for Parmigiano-Reggiano are cut into fragments the size of wheat grains, much finer than the fragments created in the manufacture of domestic Parmesan. The benefit of smaller curds is that they drain more effectively. Domestic Parmesans have to be mechanically pressed to get rid of excess moisture. The consequence, as our tasting panel discovered with the domestic Parmesans that were not pregrated, is a cheese that is much more dense. Tasters characterized it as "rubbery," "tough," and "squeaky."

The tasting did not rule out all of the other Parmesans as completely unacceptable—just most. One scored well enough to be recommended: Wisconsin-made DiGiorno. So while there is a somewhat more affordable Parmesan option, Parmigiano-Reggiano was in a class of its own. When added to a dish, it acts as more than a seasoning; it can add a complex spectrum of flavors.

1. Preheat the oven to 300 degrees. Grind the bread in a food processor. Measure ½ cup bread crumbs out onto a small baking sheet. Toast until lightly dried, about 5 minutes. Cool completely.

2. Combine the bread crumbs, eggs, cheese, nutmeg, and salt and pepper to taste in a medium bowl. Refrigerate this mixture until it firms up, about 15 minutes.

3. With moistened hands, roll teaspoonfuls of the dumpling mixture into grape-sized balls.

4. Meanwhile, bring the stock to a boil in a large stockpot or Dutch oven over medium heat. Drop the dumplings into the gently simmering stock and cook until they float to the surface and are cooked through (taste one), 3 to 4 minutes. Stir in the parsley and adjust the seasonings with salt and pepper to taste. Ladle the soup and dumplings into bowls. Serve immediately, passing extra cheese at the table.

CREAM OF CHICKEN SOUP

CREAM OF CHICKEN SOUP (KNOWN AS CHICKEN velouté in France and restaurant kitchens grounded in French traditions) should be rich but not heavy. Tiny bits of chicken should be suspended in a creamy white soup base enlivened with sherry and herbs.

This soup begins with a roux—flour cooked in melted butter. The roux is thinned with stock. Sherry and cream (or another dairy component) add flavor to the soup, as do shallots and thyme. Although the soup contains dairy, the roux is responsible for thickening the stock. The dairy contributes flavor but not the velvety consistency that makes this soup so special. Roux can be a tricky business. Many versions of this soup taste floury or become overly thickened or lumpy. We knew that making the roux and then thinning it out with stock were the central challenges when developing this recipe.

Velouté is the name of a sauce as well as a soup, and the sauce is also made with roux that is then thinned out with stock. To make velouté sauce, several tablespoons of roux are thinned out with about two cups of stock. To make velouté soup, the amount of liquid is doubled. Velouté soup is also enriched with dairy (cream, half-and-half, or milk) just before serving.

Velouté sauce and soup are all about texture. They must be silky smooth to succeed. Our first tests concerned the roux. We found that equal parts butter and flour created a roux that was neither too thick nor too thin; 6 tablespoons of flour (and thus 6 tablespoons of butter) were sufficient to thicken 2½ quarts of liquid for the soup. As for the liquid components, tasters settled on a recipe with 2 quarts of stock and 2 cups of dairy.

Before the liquid can be added, the roux must cook long enough to lose its raw floury flavor. Recipes suggest cooking the roux for as little as 1 minute and as many as 10. Although we want a roux to color and brown when making gravy or any brown sauce, velouté must remain white. Therefore, the flour cannot color. We found that cooking the roux for 2 minutes over medium heat got rid of the floury flavor without coloring the mixture. Higher temperatures caused the roux to burn and caused the starch granules to harden and thus lose their ability to absorb liquid. As an added precaution, some sources recommend cooking velouté for a considerable period of time once the liquid has been added. In fact, we found that letting the velouté simmer for 15 minutes ensured that any traces of bitterness from the raw flour were removed.

Our next series of tests revolved around the temperature of the chicken stock when it was added to the roux. Some cookbooks we consulted said that cold stock would prevent lumps from forming. The problem is that cold stock takes forever to thicken properly. At the opposite end of the spectrum, boiling liquid caused the starches in the flour to gelatinize and form lumps. In the end, we found that we could add hot liquid (and thus speed preparation of the soup) as long as we added the liquid gradually. As a further precaution, we found it best to remove the pot with the roux from the heat when adding the first batches of liquid.

Whisking the liquid in gradually (rather than stirring with a wooden spoon, as many sources suggest) also helps prevent the formation of lumps. Unfortunately, a wire whisk can't reach bits of roux stuck around the edges of the pan. Therefore, we scraped the edges of the pan with a wooden spoon several times as we added the liquid.

Once all the liquid has been incorporated, constant stirring is necessary. Without it, the fully swelled starch can settle on the bottom of the pot and burn. For this reason, use a heavy-bottomed stockpot or Dutch oven. Velouté prepared in a thin pot will burn. If you must use a thin pot, reduce the heat.

With the roux thickened, the rest of the soup is easy to prepare. We added thyme and sherry for flavor and a final swirl of dairy (along with the chicken meat) just before serving. Although tasters loved this soup with cream, it was still quite rich and delicious when made with half-and-half or whole milk. If serving very small portions of velouté as a first course, go ahead and use the cream. The soup is incredibly rich and best eaten in small portions. If serving velouté as a main course, use milk or half-and-half.

Cream of Chicken Soup
(Chicken Velouté)

SERVES 6 TO 8

This is the classic French cream of chicken soup flavored with sherry. Since you need stock and shredded chicken meat, we suggest making the stock recipe listed below that yields both. With some sacrifice in flavor, you could use 2 quarts of low-sodium canned broth along with 4 cups of shredded roasted or poached chicken. This soup can be made with milk, half-and-half, or heavy cream, depending on the desired richness. We like the chive garnish, but parsley or tarragon (use just 1 tablespoon of the latter) are fine alternatives.

2	quarts Quick Chicken Stock with Sautéed Breast Meat (page 23), stock and meat separated
6	tablespoons unsalted butter
3	medium shallots, chopped fine
6	tablespoons all-purpose flour
1	cup dry sherry
2	teaspoons fresh thyme leaves or 1 teaspoon dried thyme
2	cups milk, half-and-half, or heavy cream
	Salt and ground black pepper
2	tablespoons finely chopped fresh chives for garnish

1. Heat the stock in a large saucepan over medium heat until hot but not boiling. Keep the stock warm.

2. Meanwhile, melt the butter in a large stockpot or Dutch oven set over medium-low heat. Add the shallots and cook until soft, 6 to 8 minutes. Do not let the shallots brown. Increase the heat to medium, whisk in the flour, and cook, whisking constantly, until the floury smell has dissipated, 2 to 3 minutes. Do not let the flour brown.

3. Remove the pot from the heat and gradually whisk in several tablespoons of the hot stock. Repeat, adding a few more tablespoons of stock. Use a wooden spoon to scrape the flour from the edges of the pan. Return the pan to very low heat and slowly whisk in the remaining stock, stopping once or twice to scrape flour from the edges of the pan. Whisk in the sherry and thyme.

4. Raise the heat to medium, bring the soup to a gentle simmer, and cook, stirring constantly and skimming any foam on the surface, for 15 minutes. Add the milk and the chicken pieces, and bring the soup back to a simmer. Season with salt and pepper to taste, garnish with the chives, and serve immediately.

TORTILLA SOUP

TORTILLA SOUP IS A CLASSIC "MEAL-IN-A-bowl" served in Mexican homes as well as restaurants. Although there are countless variations, the basic outlines of this soup are consistent. A clear chicken stock is flavored with tomatoes, onions, garlic, chiles, and lime juice. Condiments such as tortilla strips, diced avocado, and cheese are either placed in the bowls before the soup is added or sprinkled into the soup at the table. Either way, the effect is the same. The highly seasoned stock softens but does not really cook these final elements. The tortillas can be thin strips of either soft flour tortillas or fried corn tortillas. The tortillas are usually added with the condiments and give the soup heft and texture.

After testing several recipes, we identified three major areas for exploration: the stock, the condiments, and the tortillas. We decided to focus first on the ingredients that must be added to the chicken stock. We would then handle the issue of condiments, including when to add them. Finally, we would tackle the tortilla element.

We started with the simplest stock possible—homemade chicken stock seasoned with salt and pepper. A few sources indicated that this plain stock could be ladled over the condiments and garnished with tortilla strips. This plan sounded appealing (it was certainly easy), but tasters rejected this soup. The base was not authentic tasting. We concluded that the chicken stock must be infused with Mexican flavors.

The possible choices were fairly obvious—onions, garlic, chiles, tomatoes, lime juice, and herbs—but we uncovered several ways to handle each ingredient. Should the tomatoes be fresh or canned? Should the garlic and onions be roasted on a hot griddle and pureed, or could they simply be sautéed with the soup base? Are dried chiles a must, or are fresh chiles more appropriate? We decided to examine each major ingredient, one at a time.

Onions were included in every recipe we reviewed. Some sources added onions with the condiments; other suggested roasting or sautéing onions and incorporating them into the stock. We tested all three options and preferred sautéing them in the soup pot before adding the chicken stock. Raw onions added with the condiments were too harsh. Onions roasted on a griddle until blackened and then pureed with the soup base left unattractive flecks in the soup. Sautéing the onions gave the stock an earthy flavor, and the bits of browned onion looked appealing in the final soup. Since we decided to sauté the onions, it made sense to handle the garlic in the same fashion.

The chiles proved to be the most complex element because most recipes called for both dried and fresh. Many tasters liked the soups made with dried chiles that had been roasted, soaked, and either pureed or diced before being added to the stock. This process was somewhat tedious, though. We wondered if chili powder could be used instead. We found that sprinkling the sautéed onions and garlic with some chili powder gave the soup base a mildly spicy flavor and reddish-orange color that tasters liked.

Tomatoes were another constant in most recipes, as much for their color as their flavor. Some recipes we consulted added sliced tomatoes with the condiments, while others incorporated the tomatoes into the stock. We tested both approaches and concluded that tomatoes belonged in the stock. As with the onions, roasted tomatoes marred the appearance of the soup. We found that canned diced tomatoes could be added with the chicken stock to provide the soup's characteristic tomato flavor and color.

Tasters responded enthusiastically to lime juice both as an addition to the stock and as a garnish served at the table in the form of lime wedges. We decided to reserve fresh chiles as part of the condiments. Adding sliced jalapeños to the finished soup preserves the bright chile flavor. We came to the same conclusion about cilantro. It lost too much character when simmered with the stock and was best added with the condiments. We quickly decided that diced avocado should also be included in the ingredient list.

At the outset, tasters expressed a strong preference for soups with chunks of chicken. Although some Mexican versions omit this ingredient, our kitchen staff felt that this one-dish soup must include meat. We found it easiest to poach a chicken breast in the stock, then remove and cool it on a plate. The chicken could be shredded and added with the other condiments. (While you can use the recipe for Quick Chicken Stock with Sautéed Breast Meat on page 23 and skip this step, poaching the chicken breast as directed allows you to start with canned broth. Since the stock is so highly seasoned in this recipe, we feel that starting with canned broth sacrifices only a little overall flavor.)

We now needed to decide when to add each condiment to the soup—in the kitchen, placing them in the bowls before ladling in the stock, or letting diners serve themselves at the table. We tried adding each of these condiments—the chicken, avocado, jalapeños, and cilantro—to empty bowls and then ladling the hot stock over them as well as letting each person float the condiments in the soup at the table. In the end, we decided to take a compromise approach. The chicken and avocado tasted best when heated through properly. (The heat enhanced the creamy texture of the avocado, and the chicken was rubbery at room temperature.) This meant adding them in the kitchen. We felt that the chiles and cilantro could be added both ways. Ladling hot stock over these elements released their flavors better, but we felt there was some merit in putting chiles on the table so individuals could adjust the heat to their liking. We decided to add the cilantro to the bowls of soup in the kitchen but to pass the chiles at the table.

We had two last condiments to consider—the cheese and the tortillas. The cheese is typically added to soup bowls right after the hot stock so it can melt. We felt that offering more cheese at the table was a good idea. Queso blanco, a mild white cheese, is the typical choice. This cheese can be hard to find in many parts of the United States. We found mild white cheddar or Monterey Jack to be a fine substitute. Don't use mozzarella or feta, two cheeses sometimes listed as substitutes for queso blanco. We found that mozzarella was too stringy in this recipe, and the sharp feta flavor seemed out of place with the other seasonings.

The tortilla component of this soup provoked some heated debate in the test kitchen. One camp argued for the fried corn tortilla strips added to filled bowls of soup. Crunchy at first, the corn tortillas get soggy as the soup is eaten. The oil absorbed by the tortillas as they are fried is released into the soup, making it heavier and richer. The other camp felt that flour tortillas (placed in the bottom of the bowl before adding the hot soup) were more authentic. The strips of soft flour tortillas become noodle-like and are somewhat easier to eat than the fried corn tortillas. Since the flour tortillas don't involve any work other than slicing, we decided to include them in the master recipe. If you have the time to fry corn tortillas, see the variation. Both versions of this soup are delicious.

Tortilla Soup

SERVES 6 TO 8

There are many renditions of this famous Mexican soup in its homeland. One of the more significant variations pertains to the tortillas. Both flour and corn tortillas are used, but the way they are incorporated differs. Our recipe calls for placing thin strips of flour tortillas on the bottom of the bowls before adding the stock. The tortillas soften, and the soup becomes more of a comforting Mexican-style chicken noodle soup. The other option (outlined in the variation) is to garnish each bowl with fried corn tortillas. These give the soup a crunchy component, but they also require an extra cooking step. Since the chicken stock is so highly seasoned in this recipe, we feel that starting with canned broth sacrifices little overall flavor.

I	tablespoon canola or vegetable oil
I	medium onion, chopped medium
I	large clove garlic, minced
2	teaspoons chili powder
2	quarts homemade chicken stock or canned low-sodium chicken broth
2	tablespoons lime juice, plus I lime cut into wedges
I	whole boneless and skinless chicken breast (12 ounces), cut in half
I	(14½-ounce) can diced tomatoes, drained
6	flour tortillas, cut in half and then crosswise into ⅛-inch-wide strips
2	medium ripe avocados, peeled, pitted, and cut into ½-inch dice (see illustrations on page 65)
1½	cups grated mild white cheddar or Monterey Jack cheese
½	cup packed fresh cilantro leaves
2	medium jalapeño chiles, halved lengthwise, seeded, and sliced thin

1. Heat the oil in a large stockpot or Dutch oven over medium heat. Add the onion, reduce the heat to medium-low, and cook until soft and lightly browned, about 5 minutes. Stir in the garlic and chili powder and cook until aromatic, about 15 seconds.

2. Add the chicken stock, raise the heat to high, and bring to a boil. Reduce the heat to low and add 2 tablespoons lime juice and the chicken. Partially

cover and gently simmer until the chicken is no longer pink, about 15 minutes.

3. Use a slotted spoon to remove the chicken from the stock; cool slightly. Add the tomatoes to the stock and cook over medium heat until stock is very hot, about 5 minutes. With your hands, shred the chicken into bite-sized pieces. (The stock and chicken can be refrigerated separately overnight.)

4. To serve, divide the shredded chicken, sliced tortillas, and diced avocado into the bottom of each bowl and ladle the hot stock on top. Top each bowl with 1 to 2 tablespoons of cheese and a generous sprinkling of cilantro leaves. Place the chiles, remaining cheese, and lime wedges on the table for adding to individual bowls as desired.

➤ VARIATION
Tortilla Soup with Fried Corn Tortillas
Cut 6 corn tortillas in half and then crosswise into ⅛-inch-wide strips. Heat 2 cups of canola or

DICING AN AVOCADO

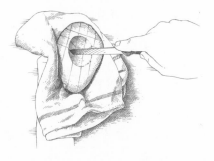

1. Halve and pit the avocado. Hold one half steady in a dish towel. Make ¹/₂-inch crosshatch incisions in the flesh with a dinner knife, cutting down to but not through the skin.

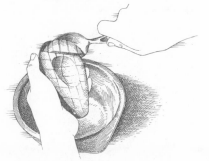

2. Separate the diced flesh from the skin by inserting a soup spoon or rubber spatula between the skin and flesh, gently scooping out the diced avocado.

vegetable oil over medium-high heat in a wide saucepan until the surface is shimmering (the oil should register about 350 degrees on a candy/deep-fry thermometer), about 6 minutes. Add half of the tortilla strips and stir constantly until golden brown and crisp, 1 to 2 minutes. With a slotted spoon, transfer the fried tortillas to a baking sheet lined with paper towels. Fry the remaining tortilla strips. Set the fried tortilla strips aside for up to several hours. Follow the recipe for Tortilla Soup, omitting the flour tortillas. Ladle soup into bowls as directed, sprinkling with cheese, several fried tortillas strips, and cilantro. Place remaining fried tortillas strips on the table along with the chiles, cheese, and limes.

THAI CHICKEN AND COCONUT SOUP

THAI CHICKEN AND COCONUT SOUP IS A velvety soup rich with coconut flavor. Like many Southeast Asian dishes, the soup is aromatic and fresh tasting. A lively contrast of ingredients and flavors is essential. Fragrant lemon grass, pungent fish sauce, fiery chiles, sour citrus juice, peppery ginger, sharp garlic, and aromatic herbs are combined to create a balance of tantalizing flavors. This soup is quite rich and usually eaten in small portions as a first course. The solid ingredients are typically restricted to a few chunks of chicken and several mushrooms floating in the thick stock.

Many traditional versions of this soup rely on ingredients that can be hard to find in American markets: kaffir lime leaves, galangal (a rhizome related to ginger), and lemon grass. Our goal when developing this recipe was to remain as true to the original while recognizing the limitations many American cooks face at their markets. We wanted to figure out which of these ingredients was essential to the stock and which flavors could be approximated with more readily available ingredients.

We also knew that the coconut element would be key: Which kind of coconut product (coconut milk or cream, low-fat or regular) could be used? When should it be added? What is the ideal ratio of chicken stock to coconut product? Finally, we wanted to develop a method for adding chicken chunks that would still allow for the use of canned broth.

We started our testing by focusing on the ingredients necessary to flavor the canned chicken broth. The stock needs a salty boost, which traditionally comes from fish sauce (see page 68 for more information). We found that soy sauce could be used in a pinch, but tasters agreed that the flavor of the fish sauce works better with the other ingredients in this soup. Most supermarkets now carry fish sauce, so make the effort to add this ingredient to your pantry.

We quickly determined that lemon grass is also an essential element in this soup. Its rich but not acidic lemon flavor cannot be left out. Although we found some substitutes for lemon grass (see page 301 for more information), we recommend searching your supermarket, specialty produce store, or local Asian market to find this ingredient.

Galangal has a strong peppery flavor coupled with sour notes. Since this ingredient is available only in Asian markets, we knew that a substitute would be essential. We found that a combination of ginger and lime juice replicated the flavors of galangal nicely.

Kaffir lime leaves have a clean, floral aroma and flavor that's aromatic but not terribly strong. Since these Southeast lime tree leaves are very hard to find, we tried to use lime zest as a substitute. Unfortunately, even a small amount of lime zest (both grated or added in strips that were later removed) proved overpowering. The lemon grass and lime juice would have to supply the citrus flavors in this soup.

The final ingredient we wanted to examine was chiles. Traditionally, this soup is made with tiny Thai chiles that come in a range of colors—green, yellow, orange, and red. These chiles are hot but very flavorful, with strong fruit and floral flavors. Since these chiles can be hard to locate, we set out to find a substitute that would deliver the same combination of heat and rich, aromatic flavor. We tested jalapeño chiles, serrano chiles, dried red chiles, cayenne pepper, chili oil, and Thai curry paste.

The fresh jalapeño and serrano chiles were not spicy enough (even when we left the seeds in the soup) and gave the soup an odd Mexican flavor. Tasters made the same objection about stocks made with dried red chiles. Cayenne pepper was plenty hot, but again the flavor was too Western. The soup

still lacked the floral, fruity chile flavor we desired. Chili oil was better—it provided more heat and did not clash with the other Asian flavors in the soup—but did not blend well with the other ingredients. No one liked the reddish-orange oil slick on the top of each soup bowl. We finally hit upon the right solution when we tried Thai red curry paste (see page 68). When used in sufficient quantities, Thai red curry paste provides plenty of heat as well as those aromatic and fruity chile flavors we wanted.

With the ingredients for our stock in place, we wanted to test methods for infusing their flavors into the liquid. Some recipes suggest smashing large chunks of lemon grass, ginger, and garlic and then simmering them in chicken stock (spiked with fish sauce). Once the bruised aromatics have released their flavors, they are removed from the pot and discarded. The other technique starts by mincing the aromatics and sautéing them in a bit of oil to bring out their flavors. The chicken stock is then added and the minced aromatics remain part of the soup base.

MINCING GINGER

1. Fibrous ginger can be tricky to mince. Start by slicing the peeled knob of ginger into thin rounds, then fan the rounds out and cut them into thin matchstick-like strips.

2. Chop the matchsticks crosswise into a fine mince.

We found that bruising the aromatics did not deliver the knockout flavor we wanted. The coconut is so strong that the flavor of lemon grass, ginger, and garlic was overpowered. We had much better results when we minced these aromatics and sautéed them in oil. Once softened, we added the curry paste and let it cook in the oil to help unlock its flavor.

Our chicken stock was now richly flavored and ready for the coconut element. In Thailand, fresh coconut meat is grated and blended with water to create fresh coconut milk. We wanted to stick with a simpler option, one of the canned coconut products available in most supermarkets. Our choices were unsweetened coconut milk, unsweetened low-fat or light coconut milk, and coconut cream. (See below for descriptions of these products.)

We tested all three and found that unsweetened coconut milk delivers the best combination of strong coconut flavor and velvety texture. Low-fat or light coconut milk is fine if calorie counting is an issue, but it cannot match regular unsweetened coconut milk in terms of flavor or texture. Coconut cream is too thick and rich and did not really offer an extra coconut flavor. Cream of coconut is not appropriate. Its sweet, candy-like flavor does not work in a savory recipe.

After testing various amounts of coconut milk and chicken stock, we settled on a ratio of roughly 4 parts coconut milk to 6 parts chicken stock. The coconut flavor was nicely potent and the texture velvety and smooth. We tried adding the coconut milk with the chicken stock but found that the coconut milk separated and appeared curdled once the soup came back to a simmer. Although whisking alleviated this problem, we found that the coconut taste was more distinct when the coconut milk was added to the stock near the end of the process.

Our last series of tests revolved around the solid ingredients that should be floating in the soup. Typically, this soup is served as a first course (the stock is quite rich) and thus contains just a few chunks of chicken and some mushrooms. It was a fairly straightforward proposition to add the chicken. We tried poaching a whole chicken breast in the stock, removing it, and then shredding the meat. We also tried adding diced and sliced chicken meat at the very end of the process, letting it cook just long enough to lose its pink color.

Poaching a whole chicken breast seemed like more work, and tasters did not like the texture of the shredded meat in the soup. Adding diced or sliced raw breast meat is easier. Of the two, tasters preferred the texture of breast meat cut into strips rather than fine dice.

As for the mushrooms, we tried canned straw mushrooms (fresh straw mushrooms are authentic but very hard to find in the U.S.) and fresh shiitakes. Tasters preferred the soft, silky texture of the canned straw mushrooms. We did find that Asian brands were better than Italian ones, with whole mushrooms that were more uniform in shape and more flavorful. Drain and rinse these canned mushrooms to remove all traces of the packing liquid.

A final garnish of whole cilantro leaves and sliced scallion greens and the soup is ready to be served. Although we prefer to serve this rich soup in small amounts, you can turn it into a meal if you prefer. Simply double the amount of chicken, add some shredded greens (especially bok choy, watercress, or spinach) to the pot with the chicken and mushrooms, and then stir in some cooked rice noodles or jasmine rice just before serving.

INGREDIENTS: Coconut Milk, Coconut Cream, Cream of Coconut

Coconut milk is not the thin liquid found inside the coconut itself—that is called coconut water. Coconut milk is a product made by steeping equal parts shredded coconut meat and either warm water or milk. The meat is pressed or mashed to release as much liquid and flavor as possible, the mixture is strained, and the result is coconut milk. To make light or low-fat coconut milk, slightly more water is used. To make coconut cream, a lot less water or milk is used, usually about 1 part liquid to 4 parts coconut meat. None of these products contains sweeteners or other ingredients.

Cream of coconut—not to be confused with coconut cream—is a sweetened product based on coconut milk that also contains thickeners and emulsifiers. Cream of coconut and coconut cream are not interchangeable since the former is heavily sweetened and the latter is not.

Thai Chicken and Coconut Soup

SERVES 8 AS A FIRST COURSE

This multidimensional soup with tantalizing flavors and aromas is created with a blend of aromatics. Lemon grass imparts a rich, ethereal, lemony essence. If you can't find lemon grass, try 2 pieces of water-packed lemon grass or 1 teaspoon grated lemon zest (see page 301). Fiery Thai chiles typically provide a hot and spicy component, but they are often hard to find, and Mexican hot peppers seem out of place. We found the best substitute to be a Thai red curry paste that includes Thai chiles and other aromatic ingredients favored in this soup. Avoid Indian-style curry pastes that include cumin and other spices. Leftovers can be refrigerated for two days, but the coconut milk will separate. Reheat slowly, not boiling the liquid, to prevent the milk from curdling.

1	tablespoon canola oil
1 to 2	stalks lemon grass, outer sheath removed, bottom 3 inches trimmed and minced (3 tablespoons), see illustrations on page 302
2	tablespoons minced fresh ginger
1	large clove garlic, minced
2 to 3	teaspoons Thai red curry paste
6	cups homemade chicken stock or canned low-sodium chicken broth
3	tablespoons fish sauce or soy sauce
1	tablespoon sugar
2	(14-ounce) cans unsweetened coconut milk
1	whole boneless, skinless chicken breast (about 12 ounces), cut into 1 by ¼-inch strips
1	(15-ounce) can straw mushrooms, drained and rinsed
3	tablespoons lime juice
	Salt
½	cup loosely packed whole fresh cilantro leaves
3	scallions, greens only, sliced thin on an angle (optional)

1. Heat the oil in a large stockpot or Dutch oven over medium heat. Add the lemon grass, ginger, and garlic and cook, stirring constantly, until aromatic, 30 to 60 seconds. Add the curry paste and cook, stirring constantly, for 30 seconds.

2. Add ½ cup chicken stock to the pot and stir to dissolve the curry paste. Add the remaining stock, fish sauce, and sugar and bring to a boil over medium-high heat. Reduce the heat to low, partially cover, and simmer to blend flavors, about 20 minutes.

3. Stir in the coconut milk, chicken, mushrooms, and lime juice. Bring back to a simmer and cook until the stock is hot and the chicken is no longer pink, about 5 minutes. Taste for seasoning and add salt if desired. Serve immediately, garnishing each bowl with cilantro and scallions.

➤ VARIATION

Thai Shrimp and Coconut Soup

Substitute ¾ pound peeled and deveined medium shrimp for the chicken in step 3.

INGREDIENTS: Fish Sauce

Just as Chinese and Japanese cooking rely on soy sauce, Southeast Asian cuisine depends on salty fish sauce. Fish sauce is a clear, brownish liquid that is pressed from salted and fermented fish, usually anchovies. It has a strong fish flavor that can be off-putting straight from the bottle. However, the fish flavor fades when cooked, and this sauce adds unusual (and irreplaceable) depth to countless Thai, Vietnamese, Cambodian, and Malaysian dishes.

If shopping in an Asian food store, look for products labeled *nuoc nam* (Vietnamese) or *nam pla* (Thai). Fish sauce has become a staple in many American supermarkets. It is also sold in natural foods stores.

INGREDIENTS: Thai Red Curry Paste

The average Thai cook may have several commercial and homemade curry pastes on hand. In this country, a thick red curry paste is the most commonly available choice. It is sold in small jars in many markets. Most brands start with red chiles ground to a paste along with lemon grass, ginger, garlic, and onion. Other spices can be added, depending on the brand. The heat level varies from brand to brand, so taste before using.

Don't buy Indian red curry paste. This product usually contains coriander, cumin, turmeric, and tomato puree—ingredients typical in Indian cooking but out of place in a Thai soup.

TURKEY SOUP

THERE IS A PROBLEM WITH TURKEY SOUP.
While chicken soup usually begins with a raw, cut-up chicken carcass, turkey soup tends to start out with only the remnants of a fully roasted bird. Perhaps to compensate for the meager turkey flavor, some cooks load up the stockpot with every vegetable in the crisper drawer, but this only serves to overwhelm any remaining turkey flavor. To boost the turkey flavor, some recipes call for simmering the carcass for up to 20 hours. We wanted to turn a roasted turkey carcass into a soup with big, rich turkey flavor, but we didn't want to spend a whole day making it.

We knew having a great stock was key. We began with the vegetables. After much testing and many rejections, we ended up with the components of a classic stock: carrots, onions, and celery, as well as garlic. But our stock was still a little stodgy. We wondered if adding white wine would brighten it up. We had not seen this in any of the many turkey soup recipes we had consulted, but we knew that it worked nicely in certain classic fish stocks. When we tried it, the improvement was tenfold. The turkey flavor deepened greatly, and the flavor of the vegetables seemed clearer as well.

We then tested the amount of time it would take to extract the maximum flavor from the bones and meat. Were those day-long recipes really necessary? Thankfully, no. After a four-hour simmer, the wine-enriched stock was fully flavored. Anything more made the soup too gelatinous; anything less and the stock was (pardon the expression) too soupy. We found that adding some fresh parsley and thyme halfway through the cooking process infused the stock with plenty of herb flavor.

Once the stock is done, make sure to pick off the bits of meat still clinging to the carcass. They will make a delicious addition to turkey soup.

With turkey stock in hand, making soup is easy. We developed a classic recipe with vegetables and pasta, as well as two soups with bolder, ethnic flavors. So the next time you roast a turkey, don't discard the carcass. Store it in the refrigerator (it will hold for a day or two) and then use it to make stock. Nothing could be more economical or delicious.

Basic Turkey Stock
MAKES 3 QUARTS

Try not to use a barren carcass for the stock. The stock tastes best made with a carcass that has a good amount of meat clinging to it.

- 1 carcass from a 12- to 14-pound turkey, cut into 4 or 5 rough pieces to fit into pot
- 1 large onion, peeled and halved
- 1 large carrot, peeled and chopped coarse
- 1 large stalk celery, chopped coarse
- 3 medium cloves garlic, unpeeled and smashed
- 2 cups dry white wine
- 1 bay leaf
- 4½ quarts water
- 5 sprigs fresh parsley
- 3 sprigs fresh thyme

1. Bring the turkey carcass, onion, carrot, celery, garlic, wine, bay leaf, and water to a boil in a large (at least 12-quart) stockpot over medium-high heat, skimming any fat or foam that rises to the surface. Reduce the heat to low and simmer, uncovered, for 2 hours, continuing to skim the surface as necessary. Add the parsley and thyme; continue to simmer until the stock is rich and flavorful, about 2 hours longer, continuing to skim the surface as necessary.

2. Strain the stock through a large-mesh strainer into a large bowl or container. Remove the meat from the strained solids, shred the meat into bite-sized pieces, and set aside; discard the solids in the strainer. The stock can be refrigerated in an airtight container for up to 2 days or frozen for several months. Before using, defat the stock (see page 19).

Turkey Noodle Soup
SERVES 8 TO 10

This classic soup requires almost no work once the stock has been made. The pasta will break down rather quickly in this recipe and become mushy. Therefore, don't make this soup until you are ready to serve it.

- 1 recipe Basic Turkey Stock and reserved shredded meat

1   medium onion, chopped medium

2   medium carrots, peeled and cut into rounds
      ¼ inch thick

1   large stalk celery, sliced ¼ inch thick

1   tablespoon minced fresh thyme leaves
      Salt and ground black pepper

2 to 3   cups medium pasta shells or other
      medium-sized pasta shape

2   tablespoons minced fresh parsley leaves

1. Bring the turkey stock to a simmer in a large stockpot or Dutch oven over medium-high heat. Add the onion, carrots, celery, thyme, and 1 teaspoon salt. Cover and simmer until the vegetables are just tender, about 10 minutes.

2. Add the pasta and reserved shredded turkey meat from the stock. Simmer until the pasta is al dente, 10 to 12 minutes. Stir in the parsley and adjust the seasonings with salt and pepper to taste. Serve immediately.

➤ VARIATIONS

Turkey Soup with Potatoes, Linguiça, and Kale

Linguiça is a garlicky Portuguese sausage. Chorizo sausage can be used instead.

1   recipe Basic Turkey Stock and reserved
      shredded meat

2   pounds boiling potatoes, scrubbed and cut into
      1-inch pieces

2   teaspoons minced fresh savory or thyme leaves
      Salt and ground black pepper

12   ounces linguiça sausage, cut into rounds
      ¼ inch thick

1   bunch kale (about 12 ounces), washed, stems
      removed, and leaves cut into ¼-inch strips
      (about 9 cups, packed)

1. Bring the turkey stock to a simmer in a large stockpot or Dutch oven over medium-high heat. Add the potatoes, savory, and 1 teaspoon salt. Cover and simmer until the potatoes are tender, about 15 minutes. Off heat, mash the potatoes in the stock with a potato masher until no large chunks remain and the potatoes thicken the soup slightly.

2. Return the soup to medium-high heat and add the sausage and reserved shredded turkey meat from the stock. Bring to a boil, reduce the heat to medium-low, cover, and simmer to blend flavors, about 15 minutes. Add the kale and simmer until tender, about 5 minutes longer. Adjust the seasonings with salt and pepper to taste. Serve immediately.

Spicy Turkey and Jasmine Rice Soup

Jasmine rice is especially fragrant and works well with the Thai seasonings in this recipe. Look for this item in Asian markets as well as many supermarkets. Regular long-grain or medium-grain rice can be used in its place.

1   recipe Basic Turkey Stock and reserved
      shredded meat

1   stalk lemon grass, trimmed to bottom 6 inches
      and bruised with back of chef's knife
      (see illustration on page 175)

1   small piece (about ¾-inch knob)
      fresh ginger, peeled, cut into thirds, and
      bruised with back of chef's knife
      (see illustration on page 26)

2   large cloves garlic, unpeeled and smashed

2   fresh jalapeño or Thai chiles, halved lengthwise
      and seeds removed
      Salt

1   cup jasmine rice

2   tablespoons minced fresh cilantro leaves

3   tablespoons minced fresh basil leaves

5   medium scallions, sliced thin

1. Bring the turkey stock to a simmer in a large stockpot or Dutch oven over medium-high heat. Add the lemon grass, ginger, garlic, chiles, and 1 teaspoon salt. Cover and simmer until the stock is fragrant and flavorful, about 10 minutes. With a slotted spoon, remove and discard the lemon grass, ginger, garlic, and chiles.

2. Add the rice and reserved shredded turkey meat from the stock. Bring to a boil, reduce the heat to medium, and simmer, covered, until the rice is tender, 12 to 15 minutes. Adjust the seasonings with salt and pepper to taste. Ladle soup into individual bowls and sprinkle each with a portion of cilantro, basil, and scallions. Serve immediately.

4

MEAT SOUPS

MOST COOKS ARE LIKELY TO THINK OF MEAT more in terms of stews than soups. And while meat stews are delicious (see chapter 9), there's something to be said for meat soup. In a stew, the meat grabs all the attention. The other ingredients (especially the vegetables) are relegated to supporting roles. As for the liquid, it is almost always thickened and functions somewhat like a sauce. Each person is served a few tablespoons of stew liquid, rarely more. In contrast, meat soups begin with stock—and lots of it. The stock is often gelatinous and heady with the aromas and flavors of meat. The meat itself is usually cut quite small and is often on equal footing with the vegetables. While meat soups can be hearty, they are still soups. You eat them with a spoon, not a fork.

Several of the recipes in this chapter call for homemade beef stock. In these cases, we have found that there's no substitute for the real thing. (For more information about making beef stock, see chapter 2.) Canned beef broth won't work in these soups. If used, the results will surely disappoint.

Since good beef stock relies on meaty cuts rather than bones, making meat soup is actually a neat and tidy process. The meat used to make the stock can be taken off the bone and shredded or cut into bite-sized pieces, then used in the soup. We think the results (as demonstrated in these recipes) are worth the effort.

BEEF NOODLE SOUP

BEEF NOODLE SOUP IS A LOT LIKE CHICKEN noodle soup (see chapter 3). Once you've made homemade stock (and reserved the cooked meat), you've done 90 percent of the work. We assumed the noodle issues here would be similar to those covered in our discussion of chicken noodle soup but wondered if the vegetable choices might be different.

As with chicken noodle soup, sautéed onion, carrots, and celery provided an excellent base for beef noodle soup. The onion adds earthiness, the carrots sweetness, and the celery grassiness. Sautéing the vegetables brought out their flavors and gave the soup more depth.

Thyme and parsley, the duo that worked so successfully in chicken noodle soup, played the same role in this soup. The thyme was added early in the process so its robust flavor could infuse the stock evenly. The parsley was added just before serving to preserve its freshness.

Many beef soups contain some diced canned tomatoes. We found that the tomatoes add complexity and some acidity, which helps balance the richness of the beef stock. While tomatoes can take over in chicken noodle soup, they act as a team player in beef stock when used in moderation.

As expected, we liked dried egg noodles best in this soup. Dried linguine and spaghetti were too chewy, and fresh fettuccine lacked the wavy ridges needed to trap bits of vegetables. While fine, extra-broad, or home-style noodles work well in chicken noodle soup, depending on your inclination, hearty beef soup calls out for extra-broad or home-style noodles (see page 43). The large chunks of meat work better with the wider noodles.

As with chicken noodle soup, we found that the noodles taste best when cooked in the beef soup rather than in a separate pot of salted water. Although you can make the stock for this soup weeks in advance, it's best to assemble beef noodle soup at the last minute. Pasta doesn't hold well and will absorb most of the liquid if you try to hold and then reheat this soup.

Beef Noodle Soup
SERVES 6

Our beef stock is the basis of this quick noodle soup. The soup is best served as soon as the noodles are tender. Don't try to refrigerate leftovers. With time, the noodles absorb more liquid and make the soup more like a stew. If you plan on having leftovers, prepare the recipe through step 1, reserve the portion you want to save for another day, then cook a portion of the noodles in the remaining soup.

1	tablespoon vegetable oil
1	medium onion, chopped medium
2	medium carrots, chopped medium
1	stalk celery, chopped medium
½	teaspoon dried thyme
½	cup drained diced canned tomatoes
2	quarts Rich Beef Stock (page 30), strained and skimmed of fat, plus 2 cups meat shredded into bite-sized pieces

2   cups (3 ounces) extra-broad or home-style
     egg noodles
¼   cup minced fresh parsley leaves
     Salt and ground black pepper

1. Heat the oil in a large stockpot or Dutch oven over medium-high heat. Add the onion, carrots, and celery and sauté until softened, about 5 minutes. Add the thyme, tomatoes, stock, and meat. Bring to a boil, reduce the heat, and simmer until the vegetables are tender and the flavors meld, 10 to 15 minutes.

2. Stir in the noodles and cook until just tender, about 8 minutes. Stir in the parsley and salt and pepper to taste. Serve immediately.

➤ VARIATIONS

Beef Noodle Soup with Spinach and Mushrooms

Cremini mushrooms add more flavor than button mushrooms, but either can be used.

2   tablespoons vegetable oil
1   medium onion, chopped medium
2   medium carrots, chopped medium
12   ounces fresh mushrooms, stems removed, caps
     wiped clean and sliced thin
½   teaspoon dried thyme
½   cup drained diced canned tomatoes
2   quarts Rich Beef Stock (page 30), strained and
     skimmed of fat, plus 2 cups meat shredded into
     bite-sized pieces
2   cups (3 ounces) extra-broad or home-style
     egg noodles
10   ounces fresh spinach, stems removed, leaves
     chopped fine
     Salt and ground black pepper

1. Heat 1 tablespoon oil in a large stockpot or Dutch oven over medium-high heat. Add the onion and carrots and sauté until almost soft, 3 to 4 minutes. Add the remaining tablespoon of oil and the mushrooms and cook until the mushrooms soften and the liquid they throw off evaporates, 4 to 5 minutes. Add the thyme, tomatoes, stock, and meat. Bring to a boil, reduce the heat, and simmer until the vegetables are tender and the flavors meld, 10 to 15 minutes.

2. Stir in the noodles and cook until just tender,

about 8 minutes. Stir in the spinach and cook just until spinach wilts, about 1 minute. Add salt and pepper to taste. Serve immediately.

Beef Noodle Soup with Peas and Parsnips

A little diced parsnip and a handful of frozen peas add some sweetness and color to the soup.

1   tablespoon vegetable oil
1   medium onion, chopped medium
2   medium carrots, chopped medium
1   medium parsnip, chopped medium
½   teaspoon dried thyme
½   cup drained diced canned tomatoes
2   quarts Rich Beef Stock (page 30), strained and
     skimmed of fat, plus 2 cups meat shredded into
     bite-sized pieces
2   cups (3 ounces) extra-broad or home-style
     egg noodles
1   cup frozen peas, thawed
     Salt and ground black pepper

1. Heat the oil in a large stockpot or Dutch oven over medium-high heat. Add the onion, carrots, and parsnip and sauté until softened, about 5 minutes. Add the thyme, tomatoes, stock, and meat. Bring to a boil, reduce the heat, and simmer until the vegetables are tender and the flavors meld, 10 to 15 minutes.

2. Stir in the noodles and cook until almost tender, about 6 minutes. Add the peas and continue cooking until the noodles are just tender and the peas are heated through, about 2 minutes. Add salt and pepper to taste. Serve immediately.

Beef Barley Soup with Mushrooms

We tested cooking barley in a separate pot as well as with the soup. Although the barley does soak up a fair amount of liquid when cooked in the soup, the flavor of the separately cooked barley is quite bland. This thick soup is often seasoned with dill. If you like, replace the parsley with 1 to 2 tablespoons minced fresh dill.

2   tablespoons vegetable oil
1   medium onion, chopped medium
2   medium carrots, chopped medium

12   ounces fresh mushrooms, stems removed, caps wiped clean and sliced thin

½   teaspoon dried thyme

½   cup drained diced canned tomatoes

2   quarts Rich Beef Stock (page 30), strained and skimmed of fat, plus 2 cups meat shredded into bite-sized pieces

½   cup pearl barley (see page 82)

¼   cup minced fresh parsley leaves

Salt and ground black pepper

1. Heat 1 tablespoon oil in a large stockpot or Dutch oven over medium-high heat. Add the onion and carrots and sauté until almost soft, 3 to 4 minutes. Add the remaining tablespoon of oil and the mushrooms and cook until the mushrooms soften and the liquid they throw off evaporates, 4 to 5 minutes.

2. Add the thyme, tomatoes, stock, meat, and barley. Bring to a boil, reduce the heat, and simmer until the barley is just tender, about 45 minutes. Stir in the parsley and salt and pepper to taste. Serve immediately.

OXTAIL SOUP

OXTAIL SOUP IS AN OLD-FASHIONED RECIPE, popular in the nineteenth and early twentieth centuries but now somewhat out of favor. And that's a shame, because this soup is delicious. For many people, oxtail soup conjures up images of medicinal broths used by ancient ancestors to bring forth strength and healing. For others, oxtail soup means fine restaurant dining from an age long gone by. Either way, the qualities that make oxtail soup so appealing are the same.

Oxtail soup is really oxtail stock with a few garnishes added at the last moment. (In fact, we ran across several recipes without any solid ingredients, making them more oxtail consommé than oxtail soup.) As you might then expect, the quality of the stock is paramount when making oxtail soup. The beef flavor must be deep and rich; the body must be thick, almost unctuous; the aroma must be heady, nearly overpowering; and the color must be an intense reddish golden brown. Without question,

the soup must be sparkling clear.

After consulting a dozen or so sources, we soon realized why most cooks (both at home and in restaurants) don't make oxtail soup. Many recipes require 12 hours of simmering. Even though most of this time is unattended, few modern cooks are willing to spend from sunup to sundown in the kitchen. Our goal was clear—figure out how to make great oxtail soup in a reasonable amount of time.

We started our testing by preparing two classic recipes. The first began by roasting oxtails in a 500-degree oven until nicely browned. The oxtails were then placed in a stockpot and covered with water. The roasting pan was deglazed with more water, which was then added to the stockpot. The stock was simmered until the oxtails were tender, about three hours. At this point, the oxtails were fished out of the pot and cooled. The meat was removed, and the picked-over bones were added back to the pot. The stock and bones simmered another eight hours before being strained, cooled, and defatted. This broth was intensely delicious. It jelled to a solid mass in the refrigerator and when heated had a gorgeous deep golden brown color, heady aroma, and rich beef flavor.

Our second classic recipe started by making homemade beef stock—a process that takes about three hours, even if you follow our short-cut method. The oxtails were then browned in a sauté pan, as were carrots and onions. The browned oxtails, browned vegetables, and a bouquet garni (a bunch of herbs tied together for easy retrieval) were placed in a stockpot along with most of the homemade beef stock. (The remaining stock was used to deglaze the sauté pan and then added to the pot.) The stock was simmered for about four hours. This broth was just as rich as the first recipe but with herbal and vegetal flavors in the background. Most tasters liked the onion flavor, while others felt that the carrots made the broth too sweet. No one liked the herbs; they gave the broth a slightly medicinal flavor. Although quicker to make than the first broth, this recipe still required almost eight hours to prepare.

So what had we learned up to this point? First, it takes a long time to extract flavor from oxtail bones. Second, you can shortcut the process slightly by making a double stock—that is, by covering the oxtail bones with beef broth rather than water.

We were now ready to start testing quicker methods. Our first thought was to use our favorite beef stock recipe (see chapter 2) and replace the shanks with oxtail. We made one batch of oxtail stock, using red wine to deglaze the pan after browning the meat (a technique that worked so well when making beef stock). For the other batch, we deglazed the pan with sherry, an ingredient common to many oxtail soup recipes. Both stocks took about three hours to prepare. Unfortunately, they were both thin in flavor and lacking in body. While the stock made with red wine was preferred (the sherry tasted odd when cooked so long), the recipe still had a long way to go.

Taking a clue from the previously tested oxtail stock recipe that used beef stock rather than water, we wondered if we could use oxtail in our beef stock recipe but replace the water with commercial broth. Following our beef stock recipe, we prepared three batches—one with canned beef broth instead of water, one with canned chicken broth instead of water, and a third with an equal blend of canned beef and chicken broths instead of water.

Tasters did not like the "cheater's" recipe made with canned beef broth. The beef flavor was weak, and many tasters detected a tinny taste. The recipe made with canned chicken broth had excellent body, but it lacked the clarity and rich, deep beef flavor that defines good oxtail soup. The third recipe

was the most promising. The color was appealing and the clarity issue faded with the use of less chicken broth. The flavor was decent but needed some help.

We tried three new approaches—replacing some of the oxtail with shank for more beef flavor and body, adding vegetables for more complexity, and simmering tomato paste and/or dried porcini mushrooms with the stock to improve flavors. The shank made the flavor weaker, not stronger; the vegetables detracted from the beef flavor; the tomato paste produced a sour flavor; and the porcini were too strong tasting and easy to identify. We had struck out.

Since no ingredient changes seemed to improve our recipe, we turned to the cooking method. We found that two hours was sufficient time to extract flavor from shank meat when making beef stock. Maybe oxtails needed more time. We increased the simmering time to four hours, and the results were dramatically improved. The beef flavor was incredibly rich, and the body was perfect. One taster commented that his lips "felt sticky" from the high gelatin content.

We tried another batch, increasing the simmering time to six hours. Thankfully, tasters detected no improvement. We had successfully taken a recipe that was thought to require eight to 12 hours of stovetop cooking and reduced that time to just four hours. Not exactly fast food, but most of that cooking time is unattended.

A few minor adjustments completed our work on the stock. Our beef stock recipe calls for salt. With canned broth in the oxtail stock recipe, salt had to be omitted. For maximum clarity, we found it helpful to skim the foam as the oxtails simmered. Oxtails have a lot of fat, and it's best to let the finished broth chill overnight in the refrigerator so that every last bit of fat can be removed.

The heavy lifting was done. Our stock was delicious, and we could focus on the garnishes that would transform it into oxtail soup. From earlier tests, we knew that simpler was better. Duck ravioli, quenelles, and beggars' purses filled with goose confit sound great, but no one is going to make these things at home. Vegetables were the more appealing option, but we knew from our previous testing that we would have to tread lightly. It made no sense to cook too many vegetables in the broth and diminish the oxtail flavor.

BUYING OXTAILS

Depending on which part of the tail they come from, oxtail pieces can vary in diameter from 3/4 inch to 4 inches. (Thicker pieces are cut close to the body; thinner pieces come from the end of the tail.) Try to buy oxtail packages with thicker pieces that will yield some meat for the soup. Thicker pieces also lend more flavor to the broth. It's fine to use a few small pieces—just don't rely on them exclusively.

Carrot, leek, celery, and turnip, all cut into fine dice, are traditional additions to oxtail soup. Tasters found that turnip was too bitter and detracted from the oxtail flavor. Leeks tasted best when sweated in butter, but then the fat clouded the stock, so we chose to omit them. Carrots added some mild sweetness, celery some vegetal flavors and a contrasting color. Tasters liked these vegetables as long as they were diced small enough to become soft (but not mushy) after a few minutes in the pot.

Sherry is a classic addition to many oxtail soup recipes. In fact, sherry even makes it into the recipe name in some of the sources we consulted. Sherried oxtail consommé is a classic, straight from the menu of the Titanic. We found that a medium-dry sherry blended nicely with the stock, adding complexity to

JULIENNING VEGETABLES

1. Long vegetables such as carrots and daikon radish can be cut into long, thin julienne strips that cook quickly. Start by slicing the vegetables on the bias into ovals about ⅛ inch thick.

2. Fan out the pieces and cut them into strips that measure about 2 inches long and ⅛ inch thick.

the final dish. Don't use sweet sherry or harsh cooking sherry, both of which are more jarring than pleasing. (For more details on these tests, see page 77.) A final garnish with parsley and our soup was ready to be served. Because it is elegant and rich, oxtail soup makes a nice first course at a dinner party.

Oxtail Soup
SERVES 6 TO 8

Originally, this soup was prepared with the tail from an ox. Although the name has stuck and the part of the animal used remains the same, it is the tail from a steer raised for meat that is now available. This soup is rich in flavor with a gorgeous golden brown color, full body, and aromatic stock. It is easy to prepare but requires four hours of simmering on the stove. The results are worth the effort. The soup is comforting and warming, and the luscious, tender meat is extremely satisfying. Tradition sometimes calls for placing a large oxtail in the center of each bowl, and, for an informal gathering, some may find it fun to pick away at the meat and gnaw on the bones. We found this approach messy and prefer serving the soup with shredded boneless meat. To easily and properly defat the stock, we suggest making the stock one day (steps 1 through 3) and making the soup the next.

2	tablespoons vegetable oil
6	pounds oxtails (see "Buying Oxtails" on page 75)
1	large onion, halved
½	cup dry red wine
1	quart canned low-sodium beef broth
1	quart canned low-sodium chicken broth
2½	tablespoons medium-dry sherry, amontillado style preferred
1	large carrot, chopped small
1	large stalk celery, chopped small
	Salt and ground black pepper
2	tablespoons minced fresh parsley leaves

1. Heat 1 tablespoon oil in a large stockpot or Dutch oven over medium-high heat. Brown the oxtails and onion halves on all sides in three or four batches, making sure not to overcrowd the pan, and adding the additional oil to the pan when necessary. (It will take 15 to 20 minutes to brown all the oxtails.) Set the browned oxtails and onion aside on a platter.

2. Add the red wine to the empty pot. Cook, using a wooden spoon to scrape up the browned bits, until wine reduces to a syrup, 1 to 2 minutes. Return the browned oxtails and onion to the pot. Reduce the heat to low, cover, and sweat the meat and onion until they have released their juices, about 20 minutes. Increase the heat to medium-high and add the beef and chicken broths. Bring to a simmer, skim the foam, and reduce the heat to low. Partially cover and simmer gently, skimming the foam occasionally, until the meat on the oxtails is tender, about 4 hours.

3. Strain the stock and set the oxtails aside to cool. Pull the meat away from the bones, discarding all fat and gristle as well as the bones. Shred the meat. (You should have about 4 cups.) Refrigerate the stock and meat separately in airtight containers for up to 3 days. When ready to finish the soup, defat the stock (see page 19).

4. Bring the stock to a simmer in a large stockpot or Dutch oven. Add the reserved meat, sherry, carrot, and celery. Simmer until the vegetables are just tender, 8 to 10 minutes. Season with salt and pepper to taste. Ladle the soup into bowls and garnish each bowl with parsley. Serve immediately.

➤ VARIATION
Oxtail Soup with Asian Flavors

Oxtail soup is common in certain regions of China. It's quite easy to give our master recipe an Asian makeover. Aromatics added to the broth and minor changes in the vegetable garnish have a surprisingly profound effect on this soup. Vegetables cut into julienne (thin, long strips) are traditional in this variation. See page 76 for details on preparing the vegetables this way.

Follow the recipe for Oxtail Soup, adding 2 star anise pods, 1 small cinnamon stick, 4 thin slices unpeeled fresh ginger, and 2 peeled garlic cloves to the stockpot in step 2 along with the canned beef and chicken broth. Discard the aromatics when the broth is strained in step 3. In step 4, cut the carrot into thin julienne strips, replace the celery with a 3-inch-long piece of peeled, julienned daikon radish, and replace the parsley with 2 scallions, green parts only, sliced thin on the bias.

INGREDIENTS: Sherry

Sherry is a fortified wine produced in the city of Jerez in southern Spain. There are countless brands and varieties, each with a markedly different color and flavor. Sherry can be syrupy and sweet or dry and nutty. Some varieties are best for cooking, while others are for sipping only.

We found that it is imperative to use the right sherry when making oxtail soup. Dry sherries were too strong, while sweet sherries seemed out of place. A medium-dry sherry is just right—rich but not overpowering, savory but not harsh. There's no need to spend a lot of money here. A $10 sherry is just fine. That said, don't use cooking sherry from the supermarket. It gave our oxtail soup an odd, chemical flavor and ruined the great beef flavor we had worked so hard to create.

How do you know if you are buying the right sherry? Here's a brief primer. Fino and manzanilla sherries are the driest and are usually served chilled as an aperitif. Amontillado is medium-dry and can be used in cooking or served as a cocktail. Cream and oloroso sherries are sweet and best for after-dinner or teatime sipping.

BORSCHT

THE TERM BORSCHT MEANS DIFFERENT things to different people. Soups by this name are made in Russia, the Ukraine, and Poland and can vary significantly. There are two general classes of borscht recipes—hot and cold. The chilled version, which is basically pureed beet soup or cream of beet soup, is served in the summer. It is light and refreshing and is generally eaten as a first course. (For more information on cold borscht, see page 185.) Hot borscht, which is the focus here, can take many forms. At its simplest, borscht can be nothing more than root vegetables (including the obligatory beets) simmered in beef stock. At the opposite end of the spectrum, borscht can contain several kinds of meat (including beef, smoked pork, duck, and even goose), along with almost every root vegetable imaginable and several kinds of cabbage.

After trying several classic recipes, we decided we wanted to pursue a compromise approach. Vegetables simmered in beef stock seemed lacking to our tasters. Hot borscht should be a hearty winter soup that can be served as a meal in a bowl. Everyone agreed that chunks of meat would have to be an element in the final recipe. Beef was the unanimous first choice, although we wanted to consider the possibility of a slightly more complex version with pork. We identified a number of other issues at the outset. How should we make the stock and cook the meat for the soup? What cut of meat is best in this recipe? Is it best to precook the beets or let them simmer in the same pot with the other soup ingredients? How should the beets be cut—grated, diced, or julienned? What other vegetables are essential to this soup and how should they be incorporated? Finally, borscht is characterized by a pronounced but balanced sweet-and-sour flavor. What acid should be used to add the sour notes? Would the addition of sugar be necessary, or would the natural sugars in the beets suffice?

We started our testing with the beef stock and meat. Several traditional sources suggested simmering short ribs or flanken in water to make the stock. The meat was then removed from the bone and used later in the soup. We tried two different variations on this approach and found the stock to be weak in flavor and color. We much preferred our standard recipe for making beef stock, which relies on beef shank. Our recipe starts by browning the meat, a step omitted in the two short rib recipes we had tested.

Although we felt that our beef stock was a good jumping off point, we wondered if there was a shorter (and easier) way to create good borscht. After all, the soup is flavored with so many potent ingredients (beets, cabbage, vinegar, and dill) that it might be possible to start with canned broth. We browned chunks of beef chuck in a little oil, deglazed the pan with red wine, added a little tomato paste for depth and color, and then added canned chicken broth. Unfortunately, borscht made this way lacked flavor. Because the chunks of vegetable float in the liquid base (rather than melding together either naturally or through pureeing), the broth remains an important and separate element in this recipe. We concluded that full-flavored beef stock is essential when making borscht.

SHREDDING CABBAGE

1. It can be hard to figure out how to attack a head of cabbage. We start by placing the heel of the palm on the back of a chef's knife and applying pressure toward the tip of the knife as it goes into the cabbage.

2. Once the blade is completely below the top of the cabbage, move your fingers to the top of the front section of the knife and apply pressure to finish cutting.

3. Cut the cabbage into quarters and remove the tough piece of core attached to each quarter.

4. Separate the cabbage quarters into stacks of leaves that flatten when lightly pressed.

5a. To shred cabbage by hand, cut each stack of leaves diagonally (this creates long pieces) into thin shreds with a chef's knife.

5b. To shred cabbage in a food processor, fit the food processor with the shredding disk. Roll the stacked leaves crosswise and put them into the feed tube.

With our stock and meat elements under control, we decided to focus on the beets. There were several avenues to explore, including baking then dicing or julienning the beets; boiling beets in a separate pot then dicing or julienning and adding both the beets and their cooking liquid to the soup pot; or simply adding raw beets (diced, grated, or julienned) to the soup pot. We tested all three basic approaches and found no advantage to baking or boiling beets before adding them to the soup pot. We concluded that beets are best cooked along with the other ingredients. Raw beets do the best job of flavoring and coloring the stock. In addition, this method is simple and easy.

We peeled the beets and then cut them three ways—dicing, julienning, and grating—and ran three more tests. (Of course, peeling and cutting beets is not an easy proposition. Beets are messy and will turn your hands, cutting board, and counter beet red. See page 80 for tips on minimizing the mess.) Our test kitchen staff felt that beets grated on the large holes of a box grater or with the shredding disk of a food processor blended more easily with the other soup ingredients. Dicing and julienning were both messier, and the larger pieces did not work as well in the soup.

We next explored the addition of other vegetables. Possible choices included cabbage, carrot, and onion (we found all three in most every recipe we consulted), as well as potato, celery, parsnip, celery root, turnip, and leek. We focused on vegetables that were essential—the cabbage, carrot, and onion—and then moved on to other possible players.

Cabbage was well liked by tasters; it added substance and flavor. Shredded cabbage was preferred to chopped, and, surprisingly, tasters liked green cabbage rather than red. The green cabbage turned pink from the beets, but also it offered some subtlety in color. Red cabbage looked so much like the beets it was hard to tell the two apart. It's fine to use red cabbage if you have some on hand, but if shopping specifically for this recipe, buy green cabbage.

Carrots and onion both added a familiar earthy flavor to the soup. Dicing the carrots and onion (rather than grating or slicing them) provided a nice textural contrast with the shredded beets and cabbage. We tried adding raw carrot and onion to the beef stock as well as sautéing these vegetables in butter and then adding the stock. Sautéing these aromatic vegetables extracted more flavor and enriched the stock.

We then tested a long list of other vegetables and found that celery, parsnip, turnip, celery root, and leek did not add much. The soup did not suffer from their inclusion, nor was it much improved. Only potatoes were deemed essential, especially when boiled separately, diced, and mixed into each soup bowl just before serving. When handled this way, the potatoes were creamy and bland and offered a nice textural and flavor contrast with the bright red, sweet-and-sour soup. In contrast, potatoes cooked in the soup pot soaked up the color and flavor of the borscht and became less desirable. Small red-skinned potatoes worked best; they are low in starch and are the best candidates for boiling.

We had one last area to explore: balancing the sweet and sour elements that give borscht its distinctive character. In our research, we uncovered recipes that called for several cups of diced canned tomatoes. Tasters did not like these versions when we prepared them in the test kitchen. The tomatoes seemed out of place. Another possible tack is to add some tomato paste, both for color and acidity. We found that a little tomato paste (added after the carrots and onions have been sautéed) brings another dimension to the soup and starts to build the sour component.

Of course, the defining sour element is vinegar (usually white wine or red wine) or lemon juice. We prepared three more batches of borscht and tested each choice. Lemon juice was too citrusy, while white wine vinegar was harsh and one-dimensional. Red wine vinegar was the hands-down winner. Its sharp but clean taste was perfect in this soup. We found it best to add most of the vinegar early on (so it has time to blend with the other flavors) and then adjust the acidity just before serving by adding a bit more vinegar.

Beets, carrots, and onions provide the bulk of the sweetness in borscht. However, many sources suggest adding sugar as well. After testing borscht with and without sugar, we agree that sugar is a must. Four tablespoons brings out the sweetness in the vegetables and is a necessary counterbalance to the vinegar. Borscht made without sugar tasted bland.

A final flourish of fresh dill and a dollop of sour cream for each bowl completes the picture. Borscht is a symphony of flavors. In the dead of winter, it can seem like a luxury. It puts all the major vegetables available at that time of year into a single bowl. Yet each vegetable remains a distinct element as it floats in a red sea of stock that is meaty, sour, and sweet all at the same time.

Borscht

SERVES 6 TO 8

This hearty, thick, ruby-red soup gets its color from beets. It is known for its characteristic sweet-sour flavor. The sour comes from the addition of vinegar, which also helps to preserve the soup, giving it a long shelf life. It benefits from being made at least a day before eating and will still be excellent five days after it is made. Hold off boiling the potatoes until you are serving the soup. Serve with the traditional accompaniment of sour, dark Russian bread or black bread. Note that the cabbage and beets will rise to the surface of the stock when first added to the pot. As they cook, the vegetables will release their water and sink down.

I	tablespoon unsalted butter
I	medium onion, chopped medium
2	medium carrots, chopped medium
2	medium cloves garlic, minced
2	tablespoons tomato paste
2	quarts Rich Beef Stock (page 30), strained and skimmed of fat, plus 2 cups meat shredded into bite-sized pieces
½	small head green or red cabbage, shredded (about 5 cups; see illustrations on page 78)
1¾	pounds beets, peeled and grated (about 5 cups; see illustrations below)
5 to 6	tablespoons red wine vinegar
4	tablespoons sugar
I	tablespoon salt
I	bay leaf
¾	pound small red potatoes (each I to 1¼ inches in diameter), scrubbed (see illustration on page 81)
	Ground black pepper
½	cup chopped fresh dill
I	cup sour cream

1. Heat the butter in a large stockpot or Dutch oven over medium heat. Add the onion and carrots and cook, stirring occasionally, until softened but not browned, about 5 minutes. Add the garlic and cook until aromatic, about 30 seconds.

2. Add the tomato paste and stir in ½ cup of the stock to dissolve the tomato paste. Add the remaining stock, cabbage, beets, 4 tablespoons vinegar, sugar, 2 teaspoons salt, and the bay leaf. Bring to a boil, lower

HANDLING BEETS

1. Beets can stain counters, cutting boards, and clothes. To minimize the mess, wear tight-fitting surgical gloves and peel the beets over newspaper. Once the beets have been peeled, they can be grated by hand or in a food processor.

2a. To grate beets by hand, use the large holes on a four-sided box grater and set the grater in a large bowl to contain the mess.

2b. To grate beets in a food processor, cut the beets as necessary to fit in the feed tube of a food processor fitted with the shredding disk. If shredding both the cabbage and beets in the food processor, shred the cabbage first, wipe the workbowl clean, and then shred the beets.

the heat, and simmer until the vegetables are soft and tender, 40 to 45 minutes. (The soup can be cooled and refrigerated in an airtight container for up to 5 days.)

3. Meanwhile, place the potatoes in a medium saucepan, cover with cold water, and add the remaining 1 teaspoon salt. Bring to a boil, lower the heat, cover, and simmer, stirring once or twice to ensure even cooking. Cook until a thin-bladed paring knife or metal cake tester inserted into a potato can be removed with no resistance, 10 to 12 minutes. Drain the potatoes, cool slightly, and cut into quarters.

4. Stir the meat into the pot and remove the bay leaf. Taste and adjust the seasonings, adding the remaining 1 to 2 tablespoons of vinegar, pepper to taste, and ¼ cup dill. Place 4 potato quarters in each individual soup bowl and ladle some soup over the potatoes. Top with 2 more pieces of potato, a generous dollop of sour cream, and a generous sprinkling of dill. Serve immediately.

➤ VARIATION

Borscht with Beef and Kielbasa

Many grand borscht recipes contain several kinds of meat. Although duck and goose require too much labor, we found it quite easy to add smoked sausage, such as kielbasa, to our basic recipe. Because this kind of sausage comes precooked, you need only warm it in the soup pot.

SCRUBBING POTATOES

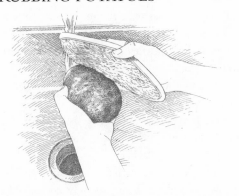

Recipes in which potatoes are not peeled usually instruct the cook to "scrub" the potatoes. We like to use a rough-textured "bathing" or "exfoliating" glove for this task. The glove cleans away dirt but is relatively gentle and won't scrub away the potato skin. We keep a glove in the kitchen especially for cleaning potatoes, turnips, carrots, beets, and other root vegetables.

Follow the recipe for Borscht, adding a ½-pound piece of kielbasa to the pot about 20 minutes before the vegetables are tender. Just before serving, remove the sausage from the pot and cut into slices ¼ inch thick. Arrange the sausage slices in each individual bowl with the potatoes. Garnish with sour cream and dill as directed and serve immediately.

SCOTCH BROTH

THIS HEARTY SOUP, NATIVE TO THE BRITISH Isles, is sometimes called "the porridge of the evening." Contrary to its name, Scotch broth is very thick, more stew-like than brothy. As might be expected, Scotch broth is made not with beef but with lamb, which is very common in Scotland. Barley is added for flavor and heartiness. The soup is generally served as a one-dish meal.

Research revealed various renditions of Scotch broth, with a great variability in the vegetables used and the way they are cooked. Many traditional recipes seem to empty the root vegetable larder into the pot, creating a hodgepodge effect. We identified the following characteristics as central when making Scotch broth: a rich lamb stock, plenty of tender lamb meat, barley that is soft but not mushy to provide substance, and vegetables used sparingly for freshness.

We had a number of initial questions, including which cut of lamb to use, how much barley to add, and which vegetables would be both authentic and complementary. We decided to focus on the stock and meat components first and uncovered three basic approaches.

Some sources suggested using boneless lamb meat—either shoulder meat or leg meat, both of which are often labeled "stew meat" in supermarkets. Typically, the meat is browned, water is added, and the mixture is simmered (skimming for foam) until the meat is tender. The barley and root vegetables are added along the way. This approach does not incorporate the use of a separately prepared stock. We found that Scotch broth prepared this way was lacking in depth and richness.

A second approach is to first make a lamb stock with neck bones, breastbones, and/or leg bones and then prepare the soup according to the method outlined above—meat browned, liquid added, barley and vegetables thrown into the pot—except that in this case the liquid is stock, not water. This method yielded excellent results but was problematic. It's difficult to obtain the bones necessary to make lamb stock, and the process is time-consuming.

A third approach is similar to our preferred method for making beef stock (see chapter 2). A meaty, bone-in cut of lamb is used to make stock. Once the meat is tender, it is removed from the bones and saved for the soup. This method is efficient since the meat and stock are prepared simultaneously—and saves quite a lot of time.

INGREDIENTS: Pearl Barley

Barley has been grown for at least 7,000 years and has a long history in Egypt, Mesopotamia, and China. It was the most important grain in ancient Greece and is referred to countless times in the Bible. Today, barley maintains an important role in many parts of the world, especially Eastern Europe, Russia, Japan, and Korea. In the United States, barley is cultivated mainly for beer production and use in animal feed.

In its most natural form, hulled whole barley contains the bran, germ, and endosperm. Hulled whole barley takes a long time to cook and can be difficult to digest. For this reason, barley is generally polished to remove some of the outer layer of bran. In effect, the grains are rubbed together to remove some bran and thus reduce the amount of time it takes for water to penetrate each grain. Pearl barley is the name given to the polished form of barley. Barley loses some B vitamins and calcium during the polishing process but retains most of its protein content. Pearl barley is sold in coarse, medium, and fine grades, although medium is the most common (and sometimes only) choice in markets.

Pearl barley takes some time to soften (usually about 40 minutes), but it still has plenty of chew, even when cooked for an hour or more. Its ability to hold its shape partly explains the appeal of barley in soups. Unlike rice, it won't fall apart when overcooked. In addition, barley has a pleasant nutty flavor that adds another element to soup recipes. In contrast, rice adds bulk but not much flavor.

For these reasons, barley is ideal in simple soups with strong flavors (such as lamb). Barley adds a distinctive flavor and texture and has no real equal.

When developing our recipe for beef stock, we found that beef shanks were the best cut. It seemed logical to start our tests for lamb stock with lamb shanks—they are meaty, not terribly expensive, and readily available. We followed our recipe for beef stock, replacing the beef shanks with lamb shanks. The resulting stock, made with 6 pounds of lamb shanks, was too rich. Lamb has a much stronger flavor than beef, and it was clear that we could use less lamb to obtain a sufficiently flavorful stock. We found that four lamb shanks (weighing about four pounds total) produced 2 quarts of richly flavored stock.

Four lamb shanks also provided just the right amount of meat for a single batch of Scotch broth. When we removed the meat from the bones and discarded any fat or gristle, we were left with about a pound of tender, flavorful meat—an ideal amount for eight servings of soup. Although we prefer to shred beef for soup, tasters liked the lamb cut into small dice. Meat cut this way made the soup a bit heartier and worked nicely with the barley and vegetables.

With the stock and meat components under control, we turned our attention to the barley and vegetables. As we expected from past tests, barley cooked in the soup pot with the lamb stock was much more flavorful than barley cooked in a separate pot of water. Cooking the barley in the soup pot also created the thick, porridge-like texture characteristic of this dish.

Root vegetables were the most common choices in the Scotch broth recipes we reviewed. Onions, carrots, celery, and turnips add heft and have been grown in the British Isles for centuries. We tested this quartet and found the results satisfactory. Further tests convinced us that leeks were a nice replacement for onions. Although not quite as traditional, their milder flavor was welcome in a soup already packed with other strong flavors.

A few recipes suggested adding cabbage to the pot. We resisted this idea, not only because of cabbage's strong flavor but because our broth was sufficiently thick. Likewise, we felt that parsnips and potatoes would be overkill, adding too much bulk to this already hefty soup. Sautéing the aromatic vegetables (leeks, carrots, and celery) enhanced their flavors. The turnip didn't benefit from a quick sauté and was added along with the lamb stock. Our testers found that a pinch of dried thyme added depth and that a final sprinkle of fresh parsley added color and freshness to the finished dish.

Scotch Broth

SERVES 8

We make our Rich Lamb Stock in the same way we make our Rich Beef Stock (page 30), using lamb shanks instead of beef. For convenience, it's best to make the stock (steps 1 through 3) at least a day in advance so that it can be refrigerated and defatted with ease. With stock on hand, the soup can be prepared in about an hour.

RICH LAMB STOCK

2   tablespoons vegetable oil
4   lamb shanks (about 4 pounds total)
1   large onion, halved
½   cup dry red wine
2   quarts boiling water
2   teaspoons salt

SOUP

1   tablespoon vegetable oil
3   medium leeks, white parts only, rinsed, halved, and sliced thin crosswise (see illustrations on page 124 to clean)
2   medium carrots, chopped medium
1   stalk celery, chopped medium
1   medium turnip, peeled and chopped medium
½   teaspoon dried thyme
2   quarts Rich Lamb Stock (above), strained and skimmed of fat, plus diced shank meat
½   cup pearl barley
½   cup minced fresh parsley leaves
    Salt and ground black pepper

1. FOR THE STOCK: Heat 1 tablespoon oil in a large stockpot or Dutch oven over medium-high heat. Brown the lamb shanks and the onion halves on all sides in two batches, making sure not to overcrowd the pan, and adding the additional oil to the pan when necessary. (It will take 10 to 15 minutes to brown all the meat.) Set the browned lamb shanks and onion aside on a platter.

2. Add the red wine to the empty pot. Cook, using a wooden spoon to scrape up the browned bits, until wine reduces to a syrup, 1 to 2 minutes. Return the browned lamb shanks and onion to the pot. Reduce the heat to low, cover, and sweat the meat and onion until the meat has released its dark juices, about 20 minutes. Increase the heat to medium-high and add the boiling water and salt. Bring to a simmer, reduce the heat to low, partially cover, and simmer gently until lamb shanks are tender, about 2 hours.

3. Strain the stock, discard the onion, and set the lamb shanks aside. Remove the meat from the shank bones, discarding the bones and fat. Cool the meat slightly, and then cut it into ½-inch dice. (The stock and meat can be refrigerated separately in airtight containers for up to 3 days.) Before using, defat the stock (see page 19).

4. FOR THE SOUP: Heat the oil in a large stockpot or Dutch oven over medium-high heat. Add the leeks, carrots, and celery and sauté until softened, about 5 minutes. Add the turnip, thyme, lamb stock, shank meat, and barley. Bring to a boil, reduce the heat, and simmer until the barley is just tender, about 45 minutes. Stir in the parsley and salt and pepper to taste. Serve immediately.

INGREDIENTS: **Lamb Shanks**

Shanks can come from either the front legs (foreshanks) or back legs (hindshanks) of the lamb, and, while usually interchangeable in recipes, hindshank is generally considered more desirable. After talking with about a half dozen butchers, we learned that the hindshank, although smaller (typically, 1 pound per shank instead of 1¼ pounds per foreshank), has more meat on it. The forequarter has a higher proportion of bone. Our test kitchen bought both kinds of lamb shanks and came to the same conclusion—hindshanks are slightly meatier. Unfortunately, this point is often moot when shopping for lamb shanks. Package labels don't differentiate between fore- and hindshanks. In fact, most shanks are likely to come from the forequarters of the animal, because hindshanks are usually sold as part of a leg of lamb. When shopping for lamb shanks, rely on your eyes and buy the meatiest ones you can find.

HOT-AND-SOUR SOUP

HOT-AND-SOUR SOUP MAY NOT STRIKE some people as a meat soup. Many recipes begin with chicken stock (although a few do call for meat stock), and the meat (typically pork) is more an accent than the main focus. However, like the other meat soups in this chapter, hot-and-sour soup is rich and heady. It can be a meal in a bowl. The meat may be used sparingly, but it makes a big impact.

At the outset, we knew we could expect at least three challenges when trying to make hot-and-sour soup in an American kitchen. First, we would need substitutes for a few hard-to-find ingredients. Second, we had to arrive at the correct balance of flavors. Hot-and-sour soup should be complex, with hot, spicy, and sour flavors the most prominent. Third, we had to perfect the texture, which should be silky and thick. We focused first on the hard-to-find ingredients, in particular wood ear fungus (a kind of mushroom) and lily buds (which come from tiger lilies), both of which have a chewy texture and earthy flavor.

We tried fresh button and shiitake mushrooms and were disappointed with the results. Fresh mushrooms did not have the right balance of softness and chewiness. They were either firm (when undercooked) or limp (when fully cooked). Dried mushrooms were a better choice. Dried shiitakes seemed like the best option, not only because of their chewy texture but also because they are available in most supermarkets. Other dried mushrooms, especially oyster mushrooms, can be used, if you prefer.

While dried shiitakes are a good visual replacement for wood ear fungus, the soup looked odd without the thin shredded bits of lily bud. As suggested in some sources, we tested both shredded leeks and bamboo shoots as substitutes. Bamboo shoots seemed more authentic and were easier to prepare.

Almost every recipe we researched included chicken stock flavored with soy sauce, sesame oil, vinegar, and pepper. (The type of vinegar and pepper varied quite a bit, but the soy sauce and sesame oil were constants.) Before exploring these variables, we wanted to test this soup with homemade chicken stock, homemade beef stock, and canned chicken broth. Tasters felt that beef stock was too strong-flavored for this recipe. Although most everyone agreed that the soup made with homemade chicken stock was better, canned chicken broth was thought adequate given the complex flavors added to the liquid base of this soup. Whether making stock or using commercial broth, it's a good idea to add some Asian flavors (ginger and scallions). We decided to stick with our Improved Canned Chicken Broth with Asian Flavors for the rest of the testing.

The next issues to decide were the types of vinegar and pepper. We tested distilled white, rice, white wine, and apple cider vinegars and found that mild rice vinegar provided the necessary sour notes without adding any distracting flavors. Chinese black vinegar (an ingredient available mostly in Asian markets) is also often added for flavor and color. Some sources we consulted suggested using Worcestershire sauce as a substitute, and it worked beautifully, adding the dark color and complex, pungent flavor the soup needed. We tested cayenne, white, and black pepper, alone and in combination. Cayenne was the testers' least favorite. It created a reddish color and an overpoweringly hot flavor. Black and white pepper were equally enjoyed. Since black pepper is a more common item, we chose it for our recipe.

Several recipes we ran across in our research suggested adding the vinegar and pepper to individual bowls. When we tested this tip, we felt that the sour and spicy flavors were not balanced. Adding the vinegar and pepper to the soup during cooking allows the ingredients to blend better with the other flavors.

Thin slices of tofu and pork provide the heft in most hot-and-sour recipes. We tried silken and firm tofu, and testers preferred the chewy texture of firm tofu. As for the pork, most everyone agreed that less is more. Leftover pork loin can be used. However, we wanted to develop a recipe that would begin with a fresh cut of meat. A tenderloin, even a small one weighing just 10 ounces, was too much meat for a single batch of soup. A single pork chop, cut into thin strips, was perfect.

To boost the flavor of the meat, we marinated the strips of pork in a mixture of sherry, soy, and sesame oil. There's no need to brown the meat. We found that it's best to just cook the marinated meat right in the soup. When handled this way, the meat cooks up soft (not crisp), so it blends better with the other ingredients.

The final issue that remained to be tested was thickening the soup. At this point, we knew that a liberal amount of cornstarch would be needed to create a thick liquid base. When we used just two or three tablespoons, the heavy ingredients in the soup (tofu, pork, and vegetables) fell to the bottom of the pot. In the end, we found that ⅓ cup of cornstarch is needed to thicken 8 cups of broth.

The point at which the cornstarch is added is also important. When added after the rice vinegar, an acid, the cornstarch often failed to thicken the soup. Several food scientists we spoke to explained that because acid can prevent starch granules from bonding, it is preferable to add the acid after the

cornstarch has dissolved and its granules have bonded together to form the dense network that thickens the broth. Once the acid is added, the soup must not cook too long, or you again run the risk of causing the soup to thin out.

The other variable affecting the texture of the soup is egg. We found that stirring an egg into the soup made the broth cloudy and unattractive. Stirring also weakened the thickening power of the starch.

Some sources suggested spreading the egg on top of the simmering soup with a spoon. This technique was somewhat challenging and produced large globs of egg. We found the best approach to be drizzling the egg into the pot, stirring gently just once, and then allowing it to cook undisturbed. This technique produced the best results, with small bits of egg floating in the broth. (This method works only with a single egg and thus is not appropriate for egg drop soup.)

REHYDRATING DRIED MUSHROOMS

1. When soaking dried shiitake or porcini mushrooms, most of the sand and dirt will fall to the bottom of the bowl. Use a fork to lift the rehydrated mushrooms from the liquid without stirring up the sand. If the mushrooms still feel gritty, rinse them briefly under cool, running water.

2. The soaking liquid is quite flavorful and should be reserved. To remove the grit, pour the liquid through a small strainer lined with a single sheet of paper towel and placed over a measuring cup.

Hot-and-Sour Soup

SERVES 6 TO 8

If using canned broth, reduce the amount of soy sauce added to the vinegar mixture by 1 tablespoon.

10	dried shiitake mushrooms
1½	cups hot water
1½	teaspoons dry sherry
1	tablespoon Asian sesame oil
3	tablespoons soy sauce
⅓	cup plus 1 teaspoon cornstarch
1	boneless center-cut pork chop (about 4 ounces and ½ inch thick), trimmed of fat
⅓	cup cool water
3	tablespoons rice vinegar
2	tablespoons Worcestershire sauce
1½	teaspoons ground black pepper
6	cups Asian Chicken Stock (page 25) or Improved Canned Chicken Broth with Asian Flavors (page 26)
½	cup bamboo shoots, cut into ⅛-inch strips
½	pound firm tofu, drained and cut into 2 by ¼-inch strips
1	large egg, lightly beaten
2	tablespoons thinly sliced scallions

1. Place the shiitakes in a small bowl, cover with the hot water, and soak until softened, about 20 minutes. Carefully lift the shiitakes from the water, letting any grit stay on the bottom of the bowl (see illustration on page 85). Trim and discard the mushroom stems and slice the caps into ⅛-inch-wide strips. Strain the soaking liquid through a strainer lined with a paper towel and set over a measuring cup (see illustration on page 85). Pour the strained liquid into a large stockpot or Dutch oven. Set aside.

2. Mix the sherry, 2 teaspoons sesame oil, 1 tablespoon soy sauce, and 1 teaspoon cornstarch together in a small bowl. Slice the meat crosswise against the grain into thin strips about 1½ inches long. Toss the pork with the sherry marinade and set aside for at least 10 minutes.

3. Blend the remaining ⅓ cup cornstarch with the cool water in a small bowl. Set aside, leaving a spoon in the bowl. Combine the remaining 2 tablespoons soy sauce with the vinegar, Worcestershire, and pepper in another small bowl and set aside.

4. Add the stock to the pot with the mushroom soaking liquid. Bring to a boil over medium heat. Reduce the heat to a simmer and add the mushrooms and bamboo shoots. Bring back to a simmer and cook for 4 minutes. Gently stir in the tofu and pork, including the marinade. Bring back to a simmer and cook for 2 minutes.

5. Recombine the cornstarch mixture and stir it into the simmering soup until it thickens, about 1 minute. Stir in the vinegar mixture, then turn off heat. Without stirring the soup, slowly drizzle the egg in a circular motion into the pot. Gently stir once so the egg forms into thin ribbons and then cook undisturbed, about 1 minute. Stir in the remaining 1 teaspoon sesame oil. Ladle the soup into individual bowls and garnish with the scallions. Serve immediately.

5

SEAFOOD SOUPS

MANY COOKS ARE NOT QUITE SURE WHAT makes one recipe a seafood soup and another a seafood stew. With meat, chicken, and vegetables, the differences between soups and stews are pretty clear. The broth plays the main role in these soups and the meat, chicken, and vegetables are cut small. The reverse is true in stews; the meat, chicken, and vegetables are cut into large chunks and the amount of liquid is far less. Stew liquid is generally thickened and functions like a sauce.

With seafood soups and stews, these distinctions don't quite hold up. Many seafood stews are quite brothy and not thickened at all. In fact, the liquid in many seafood soups is thicker than the liquid in many seafood stews. (Compare shrimp bisque, which is a soup, with cioppino, which is a stew.) Here's how we like to think of seafood soups and stews.

Seafood soups generally start with a single kind of seafood. The goal is to capture the essence of clams, shrimp, lobster, or oysters in a rich, velvety soup. Often these soups are meant to be served as a first course. They are quite rich, especially soups with cream. Chowders and bisques certainly fall into this category. A chowder is a soup thickened with potatoes and often cream. Bacon plays an important role in almost all chowder recipes. A bisque should be absolutely smooth. It is made rich by the liberal use of cream. Both chowders and bisques are often thickened with flour to give them body. Seafood soups generally don't call for fish stock. In fact, all the recipes in this chapter rely on bottled clam juice (along with wine and tomatoes in several cases) to provide the liquid element. There's so much flavor provided by ingredients such as shrimp shells, cream, lobster carcasses, and bacon that you won't miss the stock.

Seafood stews (see chapter 11) generally start with fish stock and contain several kinds of fish and shellfish. The stock remains a distinct element in these stews, because it is rarely thickened and the ingredients are not pureed. In addition, you would never serve a fish stew, such as bouillabaisse, in small portions. By definition, fish stew is a main course, intended to be a meal in a bowl.

NEW ENGLAND CLAM CHOWDER

WE LOVE HOMEMADE CLAM CHOWDER ALMOST as much as we love good chicken soup. After all, our test kitchen is located just outside of Boston, in the heart of chowder country. But we must confess that many cooks (including some who work in our test kitchen) don't make their own chowder. While they might never buy chicken soup, they seem willing to make this compromise with chowder. We wondered why.

Time certainly isn't the reason. You can actually prepare clam chowder much more quickly than you can a pot of good chicken soup. The real reason why many cooks don't bother making their own clam chowder is the clams. First, clams can be expensive. Second, clams are not terribly forgiving—you must cook them soon after their purchase (chickens can be frozen), and then the soup itself must be quickly consumed (again, chicken soup can be frozen or at least refrigerated for another day). Last, chowders are more fragile (and thus more fickle) than other soups. Unless the chowder is stabilized in some way, it curdles, especially if brought to a boil.

Our goals for this soup, then, were multiple but quite clear. We wanted to develop a delicious, traditional chowder that was economical, would not curdle, and could be prepared quickly. Before testing chowder recipes, we explored our clam options (see page 91 for more information). Chowders are typically made with hard-shell clams, so we purchased (from smallest to largest) cockles, littlenecks, cherrystones, and chowder clams, often called quahogs (pronounced *ko-hogs*).

Although they made delicious chowders, we eliminated littlenecks and cockles, both of which were just too expensive to toss into a chowder pot. Chowders made with the cheapest clams, however, weren't satisfactory, either. The quahogs we purchased for testing were large (4 to 5 inches in diameter), tough, and strong flavored. Their oversized bellies (and the contents therein) gave the chowder an overbearing mineral taste, detracting from its smooth, rich flavor.

Though only a little more expensive than quahogs, cherrystones offered good value and flavor. The chowder made from these slightly smaller clams was distinctly clam-flavored, without an inky aftertaste. Because there are no industry sizing standards for each clam variety, you may find some small quahogs labeled as cherrystones or large cherrystones labeled as quahogs. Regardless of designation, clams much over 4 inches in diameter will deliver a distinctly metallic, inky-flavored chowder.

Some recipes suggest shucking raw clams and then adding the raw clam bellies to the soup pot. Other recipes steam the clams open. We tested both methods and found that steaming clams opened is far easier than shucking them. After seven to nine minutes over simmering water, the clams open as naturally as budding flowers. Ours did not toughen up as long as we pulled them from the pot as soon as they opened and didn't let them cook too long in the finished chowder.

Although many chowder recipes instruct the cook to soak the clams in salt water spiked with cornmeal or baking powder to remove grit, we found the extra step of purging or filtering hard-shell clams to be unnecessary (see page 91 for more details). All of the hard-shells we tested were relatively clean, and what little sediment there was sank to the bottom of the steaming liquid. Getting rid of the grit was as simple as leaving the last few tablespoons of broth in the pan when pouring it from the pot. If you find that your clam broth is gritty, strain it through a coffee filter.

At this point, we turned our attention to texture.

SCRUBBING CLAMS

Many recipes instruct the cook to scrub clams. Don't skip this step; many clams have bits of sand embedded in their shells that can ruin a pot of soup. We like to scrub clams under cold, running water using a soft brush, sometimes sold as a vegetable brush.

We wanted a chowder that was thick but still a soup rather than a stew. Older recipes call for thickening clam chowder with crumbled biscuits; bread crumbs and crackers are modern stand-ins.

Bread crumb–thickened chowders failed to impress. We wanted a smooth, creamy soup base for the potatoes, onions, and clams, but no matter how long the chowder was simmered, bread crumbs or crackers never completely dissolved into the cooking liquid. Heavy cream alone, by contrast, did not give the chowder enough body. We discovered fairly quickly that flour was necessary, not only as a thickener but also as a stabilizer, because unthickened chowders separate and curdle. Of the two flour methods, we opted to thicken at the beginning of cooking rather than at the end. Because our final recipe was finished with cream, we felt the chowder didn't need the extra butter required to add the flour in a paste to the finished soup.

Because most chowders call for potatoes, some recipes suggest that starchy baking potatoes, which tend to break down when boiled, can double as a thickener. In our tests, these potatoes did not break down sufficiently, and instead simply became soft and mushy. We found that waxy red boiling potatoes are best for creamy-style chowders. They have a firm but tender texture, and their red skins look appealing.

We now had two final questions to answer about New England clam chowder. First, should it include salt pork or bacon, and, if the latter, did the bacon need to be blanched? Second, should the chowder be enriched with milk or cream?

Salt pork and bacon both come from the pig's belly. Salt pork is cured in salt, while bacon is smoked, and salt pork is generally fattier than bacon. Salt pork is the more traditional choice in chowder recipes, although bacon has become popular in recent decades, no doubt because of its availability. Jasper White writes in *Fifty Chowders* (Scribners, 2000), his definitive book on the subject, that chowders made years ago with salt pork often had a smoky flavor because they were cooked over an open hearth. For modern cooks, bacon achieves both the pork and smoke flavors.

We made clam chowders with both salt pork and bacon, and tasters liked both versions. Frankly, we ended up using such small amounts of pork in our final recipe that either salt pork or bacon is fine. Bacon is more readily available and, once bought, easier to use up. Blanching the bacon makes it taste more like salt pork, but we rather liked the subtle smokiness of the chowder made with unblanched bacon.

As for the cream versus milk issue, we found that so much milk was required to make the chowder look and taste creamy that it began to lose its clam flavor and became more like mild bisque or the clam equivalent of oyster stew. Making the chowder with clam broth (5 cups of the cooking liquid from the steaming clams), then finishing the soup with a cup of cream, gave us what we were looking for—a rich, creamy chowder that tasted distinctly of clams.

New England Clam Chowder

SERVES 6

If desired, replace the bacon with 4 ounces of finely chopped salt pork. See pages 128 and 129 for information about buying and trimming salt pork.

7	pounds medium-sized hard-shell clams, such as cherrystones, washed and scrubbed clean (see illustration on page 89)
4	slices thick-cut bacon (about 4 ounces), cut into 1/4-inch pieces
1	large Spanish onion, chopped medium
2	tablespoons flour
1 1/2	pounds red potatoes (about 4 medium), scrubbed (see illustration on page 81) and cut into 1/2-inch dice
1	large bay leaf
1	teaspoon fresh thyme leaves or 1/4 teaspoon dried thyme
1	cup heavy cream
2	tablespoons minced fresh parsley leaves Salt and ground black or white pepper

1. Bring 3 cups water to a boil in large stockpot or Dutch oven. Add the clams and cover with a tight-fitting lid. Cook for 5 minutes, uncover, and stir with a wooden spoon. Quickly cover the pot and steam until the clams just open, 2 to 4 minutes (see illustration 1, below). Transfer the clams to a large bowl; cool slightly. Open the clams with a paring knife, holding the clams over a bowl to catch any juices (see illustration 2, below). With the knife, sever the muscle that attaches the clambelly to the shell (see illustration 3, below) and transfer the meat to a cutting board. Discard the shells. Mince the clams; set aside. Pour the clam broth into a 2-quart measuring cup, holding back the last few tablespoons of broth in case of sediment; set the clam broth aside. (You should have about 5 cups. If not, add bottled clam juice or water to make this amount.) Rinse and dry the pots then return it to the burner.

2. Fry the bacon in the empty pot over medium-low heat until the fat renders and the bacon crisps, 5 to 7 minutes. Add the onion and cook, stirring

STEAMING CLAMS FOR CHOWDER

1. Steam clams until they just open, as seen on the left, rather than completely open, as shown on the right.

2. Carefully use a paring knife to open the clams, holding each over a bowl to catch any juices that are released.

3. Once open, discard the top shell and use the knife to sever the muscle that connects the clambelly to the bottom shell.

occasionally, until softened, about 5 minutes. Add the flour and stir until lightly colored, about 1 minute. Gradually whisk in the reserved clam broth. Add the potatoes, bay leaf, and thyme and simmer until potatoes are tender, about 10 to 15 minutes. Add the clams, cream, parsley, and salt (if necessary) and ground pepper to taste; bring to simmer. Remove from the heat, discard the bay leaf, and serve immediately.

➤ VARIATION

Quick Pantry New England Clam Chowder

From late summer through winter, when clams are plentiful, you'll probably want to make fresh clam chowder. But if you're short on time or find clams scarce and expensive, the right canned clams and bottled clam juice deliver a chowder that's at least three notches above canned chowder in quality. We tested seven brands of minced and small whole canned clams and preferred Doxsee Minced Clams teamed with Doxsee brand clam juice as well as Snow's Minced Clams and Snow's clam juice. These clams were neither too tough nor too soft, and they had a decent natural clam flavor.

Follow recipe for New England Clam Chowder, substituting for the fresh clams 4 cans (6½ ounces each) minced clams, juice drained and reserved,

along with 1 cup water and 2 bottles (8 ounces each) clam juice in medium bowl. Reserve clam meat in separate bowl. Omit step 1. Add reserved clam meat and juice at same points in step 2 when fresh clam broth and meat would be added.

MANHATTAN CLAM CHOWDER

NEW ENGLAND CLAM CHOWDER AND MANHATTAN clam chowder both contain clams and potatoes, but the similarities end there. While New England clam chowder is made rich with dairy and bacon, tomatoes and aromatic vegetables complement the clams in the Manhattan version. While New England clam chowder has a smooth consistency (flour and potatoes make it velvety), Manhattan clam chowder is brothy, thickened only by the vegetables themselves.

New England clam chowder is a distinctly American creation, but Manhattan clam chowder has a more tangled pedigree. Although tomatoes appear in a few clam chowder recipes found in New England cookbooks from the mid-1800s, most food historians agree that tomato-based clam chowders

---

INGREDIENTS: Clams

Clams are easy enough to cook. When they open, they are done. However, perfectly cooked clams can be made inedible by lingering sand. Straining the juices through cheesecloth after cooking will remove the grit, but it's a pain. Plus, you lose some of the juices to the cheesecloth. Worse still, careful straining will not remove bits of sand still clinging to the clam meat. Rinsing the cooked clams washes away flavor.

That's why so many clam recipes start by soaking clams in cold salt water for several hours. We tried various soaking regimens, such as soaking in water with flour, soaking in water with baking powder, soaking in water with cornmeal, and scrubbing and rinsing in five changes of water. If the clams were dirty at the outset, none of these techniques really worked. Even after soaking, many clams needed to be rinsed and the cooking liquid strained.

However, during the course of this testing, we noticed that some varieties of clams were extremely clean and free of grit at the outset. A quick scrub of the shell exterior and these clams

were ready for the cooking pot, without any soaking. The cooked clams were free of grit, and the liquid was clean.

Clams can be divided into two categories—hard-shell varieties (such as quahogs, cherrystones, and littlenecks) and soft-shell varieties (such as steamers and razor clams). Hard-shells live along sandy beaches and bays; soft-shells in muddy tidal flats. This modest shift in location makes all the difference in the kitchen.

When harvested, hard-shells remain tightly closed. In our tests, we found the meat inside to be sand-free. The exterior should be scrubbed under cold running water to remove any caked-on mud, but otherwise these clams can be cooked without further worry about gritty broths.

Soft-shell clams gape when they are alive. We found that they almost always contain a lot of sand. While it's worthwhile to soak them in several batches of cold water to remove some of the sand, you can never get rid of it all. In the end, you must strain the cooking liquid. It's a good idea to rinse the cooked clams, too.

were probably inspired by Portuguese and/or Italian immigrants who settled in the Northeast.

Many Manhattan clam chowders are really tomato-vegetable soups with clams added at the last moment. We find these renditions disappointing. Even though Manhattan clam chowder has more ingredients than its northern cousin, we expect the clams to dominate. The briny clam flavor should be the star surrounded by a cast of contrasting and complementary ingredients and flavors.

After making several recipes from classic cookbooks, we knew that clam flavor would be the main focus in other testing. We followed several recipes that turned out to be nothing more than clams swimming in tomato sauce. Our tasters agreed that the broth must taste of the sea, with tomatoes in the background.

It made sense to start our formal testing with the clams. We wondered if the same method for handling clams used in our New England chowder recipe would work here. As expected, steaming the cherrystone clams until they just open, then using their broth and meat to make chowder, worked just fine. In the end, we found it wise to include a few more clams in Manhattan clam chowder to balance the strong flavors of the vegetables and tomatoes. But otherwise, the clams were treated the same way, whether destined for New England or Manhattan chowder.

We tested Manhattan clam chowder with both salt pork and bacon. Tasters preferred the smoky bacon flavor, finding the salt pork too tame. That said, too much bacon will ruin this recipe. Since Manhattan chowder contains so many other flavors, we found that a little bacon went a long way. With just 2 ounces of bacon (rather than the 4 ounces used in our recipe for New England clam chowder), the smoke flavor is subtle, not overwhelming.

We tackled the tomatoes next. Although a few recipes suggested using fresh tomatoes, we quickly dismissed this idea. Manhattan clam chowder is a year-round recipe, more likely to be prepared in winter than during tomato season.

Canned crushed and diced tomatoes were the most common choices in the recipes we reviewed. We made a pot of chowder with each and found that the crushed tomatoes gave the soup more body and a deeper color. Although a few tasters liked these characteristics, most agreed that the crushed tomatoes interfered with the briny flavor of the clams. The soup base was no longer clam broth but, in fact, a thin tomato sauce with clams. The diced tomatoes behaved more like a vegetable, with chunks of tomato floating in the soup rather than a thick, red sea that overwhelmed everything in its path. Diced tomatoes dyed the broth light pink, but their juice did not overwhelm the clam broth; they complemented the clams without hogging the spotlight.

Given the ingredients in crushed and diced tomatoes, these results made sense. Crushed tomatoes contain a lot of tomato puree (it's often the first ingredient listed on labels) as well as fresh tomatoes. Since tomato puree is a cooked tomato product, it has a concentrated, often harsh, flavor. Tomato puree gives crushed tomatoes a consistency and flavor that's not all that different from tomato sauce. In contrast, diced tomatoes are nothing more than fresh tomatoes that have been peeled, chopped, and packed in their own juice. They have a lighter flavor, which is much closer to fresh tomatoes.

Potatoes help to give Manhattan chowder its substance; when used properly, they create body. They also add flavor. We had several questions about the potatoes in this recipe, including what type to use, how to cut the potatoes, and how to cook them. We started by cooking low-starch Red Bliss potatoes, medium-starch Yukon Golds, and high-starch russets in separate pots of chowder. (For more information on types of potatoes and their starch content, see page 125.) The potatoes were diced but not peeled in all three tests.

The red potatoes cooked up quite firm (which tasters liked), but they did not do much for the broth, which remained thin. Russets did a nice job of thickening the soup, but they became mushy. The Yukon Golds were the best choice because they held their shape and also leached some starch into the liquid, providing some thickening power. Even so, tasters would have preferred even more starch to thicken the broth more. We decided to test various ways of preparing and cooking the potatoes to find a method that would accomplish this goal.

We started by peeling the potatoes, then cutting them into fine dice (¼-inch pieces) to provide more surface area which did cause the potatoes to release more starch as they cooked. Although peeled, finely diced potatoes were leaching more starch into the liquid, we still weren't satisfied and wondered if something else was at work in the pot. Could it be the tomatoes?

Acidic ingredients, such as tomatoes, can prevent beans from softening as they cook. We wondered if the same thing was happening here. To find out, we decided to prepare another pot of chowder but hold off adding the tomatoes until the potatoes were fully cooked. As the diced, peeled potatoes became tender, we could see the broth change from clear to dense and milky white. Without tomatoes in the pot, the potatoes were freer to release their starches. We found that smashing some of the tender potatoes against the side of the pot helped thicken the broth even more.

Our recipe was now basically done, with only the vegetables and seasonings remaining on our check-list of items to test. Most Manhattan chowder recipes rely on the classic aromatic vegetables—onions, carrots, and celery. A few add bell peppers, either red or green, to the mix. We tested all five choices and liked everything except the green peppers, which were simply too bitter. Onions and carrots are earthy and add depth to the soup, celery is light and refreshing, and the red pepper is sweet and lively.

We rounded out the seasonings with garlic, dried oregano (added early in the process to bring out its flavor), and fresh parsley (added just before serving to retain its vitality). A little white wine enlivens and brightens all these flavors.

Manhattan Clam Chowder

SERVES 8

Medium-sized hard-shell clams provide the flavor for the broth and the tender clam meat for this hearty soup. This rendition is not like the traditional commercial offerings with a thick broth that resembles tomato sauce. Instead, the broth is briny and clean tasting, flavors from the sea standing out and tomatoes and vegetables offering dimension in flavors and colors. The potatoes provide substance, and cooking them

before adding the tomatoes enables their starch to be released into the broth, lightly thickening it. This soup will hold for two days. Reheat over a low flame, being sure not to boil the chowder, which will toughen the clams.

8	pounds medium-sized hard-shell clams, such as cherrystones, washed and scrubbed clean (see illustration on page 89)
2	slices thick-cut bacon (about 2 ounces), cut into ¼-inch pieces
1	large Spanish onion, chopped small
1	small red bell pepper, stemmed, seeded, and chopped small
1	medium carrot, chopped small
1	stalk celery, chopped small
4	medium cloves garlic, minced
1	teaspoon dried oregano
½	cup dry white wine
1	(8-ounce) bottle clam juice
1¼	pounds Yukon Gold potatoes, peeled and cut into ¼-inch dice
1	large bay leaf
2	(14½-ounce) cans diced tomatoes
	Salt and ground black pepper
2	tablespoons chopped fresh parsley leaves

1. Bring 4 cups of water to a boil in large stock-pot or Dutch oven. Add the clams and cover with a tight-fitting lid. Cook for 5 minutes, uncover, and stir with a wooden spoon. Quickly cover the pot and steam until the clams just open, 2 to 4 minutes (see illustration 1 on page 90). Transfer the clams to a large bowl; cool slightly. Open the clams with a paring knife, holding the clams over a bowl to catch any juices (see illustration 2 on page 90). With the knife, sever the muscle that attaches the clambelly to the shell (see illustration 3 on page 90) and transfer the meat to a cutting board. Discard the shells. Cut the clams into ½-inch dice; set aside. Pour the clam broth into a 2-quart Pyrex measuring cup, holding back the last few tablespoons of broth in case of sediment; set the clam broth aside. (You should have about 5 cups; if not, add water to make this amount.) Rinse and dry the pot, then return it to the burner.

2. Fry the bacon in the empty pot over medium-

low heat until the fat renders and the bacon crisps, 5 to 7 minutes. Add the onion, pepper, carrot, and celery, reduce the heat to low, cover, and cook until softened, about 10 minutes. Add the garlic and oregano and sauté until fragrant, about 1 minute.

3. Add the wine and raise heat to high. Boil the wine until it reduces by half, 2 to 3 minutes. Add the reserved clam broth, clam juice, potatoes, and bay leaf. Bring to a boil, reduce the heat to medium-low, and simmer until the potatoes are almost tender, 8 to 10 minutes. Using a wooden spoon, smash a few potatoes against the side of the pot (see illustration below). Simmer to release the potato starch, about 2 minutes.

4. Add the tomatoes, bring back to a simmer, and cook for 5 minutes. Off heat, stir in the reserved clams and season with salt and pepper to taste; discard the bay leaf. (Chowder can be refrigerated in an airtight container for up to 2 days. Warm over low heat until hot.) Stir in parsley and ladle the chowder into individual bowls. Serve immediately.

➤ VARIATIONS

Manhattan Clam Chowder, Italian Style

Follow recipe for Manhattan Clam Chowder, substituting 2 ounces finely chopped pancetta for the bacon, increasing the garlic to 6 cloves, and adding 1 teaspoon fennel seeds and ½ teaspoon hot red pepper flakes along with the garlic and oregano. Proceed as directed.

Quick Pantry Manhattan Clam Chowder

This variation uses a total of three bottles of clam juice. Two bottles are used to supplement the juice from the canned clams to replace the 5 cups of clam broth in step 1 of the master recipe; the third bottle is used as directed in step 3 of the master recipe.

Follow recipe for Manhattan Clam Chowder, substituting for the fresh clams 5 cans (6½ ounces each) of chopped clams, juice drained and reserved, along with 2 bottles (8 ounces each) clam juice. Add the drained clams and juice at the same points when fresh clam meat and broth would be added.

INGREDIENTS: **Buying Clams by Weight or Number**

Judging by most recipes, there is no consistent, accurate, or easy method to designate the amount of clams needed for a given chowder. Some recipes call for some amount of shucked clams, giving the cook no idea how many whole clams to buy. Other recipes call for "X" number of "hard-shell clams," apparently not taking into account the size differences between a quahog and a littleneck. Likewise, there are no industry sizing standards for each clam variety. Clam size and name vary from source to source, so that one company's cherrystone clam might be another company's quahog.

We wondered if calling for "X" pounds of clams, regardless of size, would yield similar quantities of meat and liquid. Working with 1½-pound quantities, we shucked quahogs, cherrystones, and littlenecks. Although the number of clams per pound varied greatly (two quahogs equaled 1½ pounds, while it took 24 littlenecks to equal the same weight), all three clam sizes consistently yielded a scant ½ cup of clams and ⅔ cup of clam juice.

Even though clams are usually sold by the piece at the fish market, we find it more accurate to buy them by weight rather quantity. Just ask your fish market to weigh the clams as they count them. Regardless of clam size, you'll need about seven to eight pounds to make our clam chowder recipes.

RELEASING STARCH FROM POTATOES

Once the potatoes are tender, use the back of a wooden spoon to press some of the potatoes against the side of the pot. This releases more starch and helps thicken the chowder.

SHRIMP BISQUE

THOUGH A BISQUE BY IMPLICATION IS ANY soup that is rich, velvety, and smooth, by definition it contains shellfish, cream, and the classic French aromatic trio of celery, carrot, and onion known as *mirepoix*. Shrimp bisque, in particular, should be a rich, blushing pastel—delicate in character but deeply intense—with an almost sweet shrimp essence and an elusive interplay of other flavors. Its texture must run unfettered and silky over the tongue. If you are very lucky, there will be tender pieces of poached shrimp and shatteringly crisp, buttery croutons. As is the case with some French food, eating too much may make you feel sick.

We used to believe that a complicated recipe signaled an authentic recipe—a good recipe. Over the years, however, we have realized that while some culinary events require an odyssey of instructions to accompany them, long recipes are often ill-conceived, poorly organized, or simply pompous. That was pretty much our take on the five different modern shrimp bisque recipes the test kitchen put together to begin our work on shrimp bisque. The recipes took hours. They featured a parade of kitchen tools, near-endless numbers of ingredients, and a cacophony of pots and lids. At the end of the day, we had dirtied every pot, spoon, and strainer in the kitchen—and were trying to give away five very average shrimp bisques to our colleagues.

The fundamental challenge in making a shrimp bisque is extracting flavor from the shrimp and shells. The recipes we tested did this in a couple of ways. Some pureed the shrimp meat into the base and left it there, others simmered the shrimp in the base until spent and then strained them out. The bisques made with pureed shrimp were grainy with shrimp curds; the ones in which the shrimp were strained out achieved the velvety texture properly associated with a bisque.

Because the shrimp flavor resides more in the shells than in the meat, a bisque made with shrimp alone is weak and unsatisfying. But trying to deal with shells and meat to the advantage of each tends to induce procedural overkill. The recipes that we tested got carried away by having several pots and pans active at once (here a little pot of simmering aromatics, here fish stock simmering with shells and rice, there a pan to sauté shrimp) rather than proceeding one step at a time in sequence. One recipe, for example, sautéed shell-on shrimp to start and later simmered them in wine, broth, and previously sautéed aromatics. At that point the shrimp were peeled. Because the flavor from the shells had not been sufficiently extracted, a shrimp butter was advised. That involved crushing the shells to a paste, using them to make a butter infusion, and straining them out. The resulting resolidified butter was stirred into the bisque at the end. Though arguably authentic, the technique was absurdly complicated and rendered a finished bisque far too rich for our tastes.

We talked strategy in the test kitchen. The shrimp were key; other ingredients must add background depth and nuance. Fresh shell-on shrimp are virtually unavailable in the United States; those which are not frozen are usually not fresh but simply thawed. Size was not an issue because the shrimp are in effect sacrificed to the bisque. We thought it reasonable to recommend whatever variety of shell-on shrimp could be found in the freezer case or on ice at the seafood counter. (Though differences in shrimp varieties did not prove overwhelming, as it turned out, the nicest bisques were produced with Mexican or Gulf White shrimp. For more on shrimp varieties, see page 97.)

We began by taking 2 pounds of shrimp, shelling 8 ounces worth and putting those aside to use later as a garnish. We then heated a splash of oil in a heavy Dutch oven. Working in two batches, we sautéed the remaining shell-on shrimp until they reached a blistering pink. To wring every drop of flavor from the shells, we then flambéed the shrimp in brandy. Next we took the sautéed shrimp, dumped them into a food processor, and ground them to a pulp. Because we knew the shrimp and the shells were destined to be strained from the bisque, a food processor was the fastest way to cut the shrimp into small pieces and to unlock its flavor potential.

Our next step was to sauté the shrimp pulp with a mirepoix. After five minutes, we stirred in a bit of flour, preferring its convenience to the rice or bread suggested for thickening in some recipes. Next came white wine, diced tomatoes, and some clam juice. After 20 minutes or so we strained the fragrant base through a cheesecloth-lined strainer, pressing to extract every drop. It looked like flowing silk Shantung.

Back on the stove we offered the soup base a bit of cream, a little lemon juice, a sprig of fresh tarragon, cayenne, and then the remaining shrimp, cut into pieces. A brief simmer poached the shrimp garnish and harmonized the flavors. We removed the tarragon sprig and added a splash of sherry. This bisque possessed everything we demanded of it: flavor in spades and a peerless texture and color.

And so it seemed we had a one-pot wonder. But we had to admit, a skillet would beat a Dutch oven at sautéing the shrimp and make the flambéing more manageable. OK. So now it was a two-pot wonder,

TWO WAYS TO FLAMBÉ SHRIMP

To flambé on a gas stove, add the warmed brandy to the pan with the shrimp and shells, tilting the pan toward the flame to ignite it and then shaking the skillet.

To flambé on an electric stove, add the warmed brandy to the pan with the shrimp and shells, waving a lit match over the pan until the brandy ignites and then shaking the skillet.

but a very quick one—and a very good one. No one will ever suspect you used only two pots.

❧
Shrimp Bisque
SERVES 4 TO 6

Shrimp shells contribute a lot of flavor to the bisque, so this recipe calls for shell-on shrimp. A good size to use is large shrimp (about 21 to 25 to a pound; see page 97 for more information on how shrimp are sized). If your food processor is small and your shrimp are extralarge, process them in two batches. For straining the bisque, if you do not own a chinois, use a china cap or large sturdy mesh strainer lined with a double layer of damp cheesecloth. (See page 13 for more information.) Because this recipe contains chunks of shrimp, it cannot be prepared in advance. If you like, you can prepare the soup up to the point that the base is strained and then refrigerate the strained base and the shelled shrimp for several hours. When ready to serve the soup, heat the soup base along with the tarragon, cream, lemon juice, and cayenne, and proceed as directed.

2	pounds large shell-on shrimp, preferably Mexican or Gulf Whites (see page 97)
3	tablespoons olive oil
1/3	cup brandy or cognac, warmed
2	tablespoons unsalted butter
1	small carrot, minced (about 3 tablespoons)
1	small stalk celery, minced (about 3 tablespoons)
1	small onion, minced (about 6 tablespoons)
1	medium clove garlic, minced
1/2	cup all-purpose flour
1 1/2	cups dry white wine
4	(8-ounce) bottles clam juice
1	(14 1/2-ounce) can diced tomatoes, drained
1	small sprig fresh tarragon
1	cup heavy cream
1	tablespoon lemon juice
	Pinch ground cayenne
2	tablespoons dry sherry or Madeira
	Salt and ground black pepper

1. Peel ½ pound shrimp, reserving the shells, and cut each peeled shrimp into thirds. With paper towels, thoroughly pat dry the remaining shrimp and the reserved shells.

2. Heat a 12-inch heavy-bottomed skillet over high heat until very hot, about 3 minutes. Add 1½ tablespoons olive oil and swirl to coat the pan bottom. Add half of the remaining shell-on shrimp and half of reserved shells; sauté until the shrimp are deep pink and the shells are lightly browned, about 2 minutes. Transfer the shrimp and the shells to a medium bowl and repeat with the remaining oil, shell-on shrimp, and shells. Return the first browned batch to the skillet. Pour the warmed brandy over the shrimp and flambé, shaking the pan (see illustrations on page 96). When flames subside, transfer the shrimp and shells to a food processor fitted with a steel blade and process until the mixture resembles fine meal, about 10 seconds.

3. Heat the butter in a Dutch oven or large stockpot over medium heat until foaming. Add the carrot, celery, onion, garlic, and ground shrimp; cover and cook, stirring frequently, until the vegetables are slightly softened and the mixture is fragrant, about 5 minutes. Add the flour and cook, stirring constantly, until combined thoroughly, about 1 minute. Stir in the wine, clam juice, and tomatoes, scraping the pan bottom with a wooden spoon to loosen any browned bits. Cover, increase the heat to medium-high, and bring to a boil; then reduce the heat to low and simmer, stirring frequently, until thickened and flavors meld, about 20 minutes.

INGREDIENTS: Shrimp

It's safe to say that any shrimp you buy have been frozen (and usually thawed by the retailer), but not all shrimp are the same—far from it. The Gulf of Mexico supplies about 200 million pounds of shrimp annually to the rest of the country, but three times that amount is imported, mostly from Asia, Central America and South America.

After several tastings of the commonly available varieties of shrimp, we had little trouble declaring two winners. Mexican Whites *(Panaeus vannamei)*, from the Pacific coast, are usually the best. A close second, and often just as good, are Gulf Whites *(P. setiferus)*. Either of these may be wild or farm-raised. Unfortunately, these are rarely the shrimp you're offered in supermarkets. The shrimp most commonly found in supermarkets is Black Tiger, a farmed shrimp from Asia. Its quality is inconsistent, but it can be quite flavorful and firm. And even if you go into a fishmonger's and ask for white shrimp, you may get farm-raised shrimp from China—a less expensive but decidedly inferior species *(P. chinensis)*. (There are more than 300 species of shrimp in the world and not nearly as many common names.)

All you can do is try to buy the best shrimp available, and buy it right. Beyond choosing the best species you can find, you should also consider some of the following factors. Buy still-frozen shrimp rather than those that have been thawed. Because almost all shrimp are frozen after the catch, and thawed shrimp start losing their flavor in just a couple of days, buying thawed shrimp gives you neither the flavor of fresh nor the flexibility of frozen. We found that shrimp stored in the freezer retain peak quality for several weeks, deteriorating very slowly after that until about the three-month point, when we detected a noticeable deterioration in quality. If you do buy thawed shrimp, they should smell of saltwater and little else, and they should be firm and fully fill their shells.

Avoid buying already peeled and deveined shrimp; cleaning before freezing unquestionably deprives shrimp of some of their flavor and texture; everyone we asked to sample precleaned shrimp found them to be nearly tasteless. In addition, precleaned shrimp may have added tripolyphosphate, a chemical that aids in water retention and can give shrimp an off flavor. When making soups, you will probably want the shells for added flavor.

Shrimp should have no black spotting, known as melanosis, on their shells, which indicates that a breakdown of the meat has begun. Be equally suspicious of shrimp with yellowing shells or those that feel gritty; either of these conditions may indicate the overuse of sodium bisulfite, a bleaching agent sometimes used to retard melanosis.

Despite the popularity of shrimp, there are no strict standards for size. Small, medium, large, extralarge, jumbo, and other size classifications are subjective and relative. Small shrimp of 70 or so to the pound are frequently labeled "medium," as are those twice that size and even larger. It pays, then, to judge shrimp size by the number it takes to make a pound, as retailers do. Shrimp labeled 16/20, for example, require 16 to 20 (usually closer to 20) individual specimens to make a pound. Those labeled U-20 require fewer than 20 to make a pound. Shrimp of 15 or 20 to about 30 per pound usually yield the best combination of flavor, ease of peeling (peeling tiny shrimp is a nuisance), and value (really big shrimp usually cost more than $10 per pound).

4. Strain the bisque through a chinois or fine-mesh strainer into a medium container, pressing on the solids with the back of a ladle to extract all liquid. Wash and dry the now-empty Dutch oven; return the strained bisque to the Dutch oven and stir in the tarragon, cream, lemon juice, and cayenne. Bring to a simmer over medium-high heat; add the reserved peeled and cut shrimp and simmer until the shrimp are firm but tender, about 1½ minutes. Discard the tarragon sprig; stir in the sherry, season to taste with salt and pepper, and serve immediately.

LOBSTER BISQUE

LOBSTER BISQUE IS A CLOSE COUSIN TO shrimp bisque (both contain shellfish, cream, and classic French aromatic vegetables), but this soup is even more luxurious and expensive. And it's a lot more work. While we were able to streamline the process when making shrimp bisque, we knew that such an approach would be much more difficult when dealing with lobsters. Much of the flavor comes from the lobster shells and, let's face it, lobsters are a lot harder to work with than shrimp.

At the outset we rounded up several recipes from classic sources and were underwhelmed by the results. Most of the recipes lacked strong lobster flavor, and they all involved too much work. It was

HARD-SHELL VERSUS SOFT-SHELL LOBSTERS

Hard-shell lobsters are much meatier than soft-shell lobsters, which have recently molted. To determine whether a lobster has a hard or soft shell, squeeze the side of the lobster's body. A soft-shell lobster will yield to pressure, while a hard-shell lobster will feel hard, brittle, and tightly packed.

clear that the fundamental challenge would be extracting the flavor from the lobster shells without backbreaking amounts of work.

We decided to try an adaptation of our shrimp bisque recipe, which started by sautéing raw shell-on shrimp until blistering pink, flambéing them with brandy, then grinding them to a pulp in the food processor. The food processor was the key to unlocking the shrimp's flavor. This pulp gave shrimp bisque great flavor and was easily strained out just before serving. But whereas shrimp are small enough to sauté as is, lobsters are not. We would have to break down the shells before they went into the sauté pan. In addition, we would need to remove the meat from the lobster shells at some point early in the process to prevent it from overcooking.

For our first test, we used two small lobsters (1 pound each, to match the 2 pounds of raw shrimp used in our shrimp bisque recipe). We plunged a knife into the head of each lobster to kill it and separated the tail and claws from the body to remove the meat and reserve it for the finished soup. We then ground the shells in small batches, with the intention of sautéing and flambéing them. Essentially, we intended to reverse the order of sautéing and grinding used in the shrimp bisque recipe.

We had our doubts about this approach. Most cooks, even professionals, don't like killing lobsters with a knife. In addition, removing raw meat from the tail and claws is extremely difficult. We proceeded, removing the meat and then grinding the shells in the food processor. Our heavy-duty food processor started dancing around the counter, and lobster juice and mush oozed and squirted out from the seam where the lid and workbowl meet. This method was not going to work.

We put the shells in a zipper-lock plastic bag and started to smash them with a mallet but were unable to break the shells into really small pieces. Even more troubling, the sharp shells punctured the bag, and lobster juice occasionally shot out all over the place. Although messy, this method eventually broke the lobster shells into pieces that would fit in a pan.

We sautéed and then flambéed the shells, and the results seemed promising. The aroma was certainly strong. We then added the lobster shells to a pot with the sautéed mirepoix (onions, carrots, and celery) and butter and proceeded to make lobster bisque according to our shrimp bisque recipe. Although the finished bisque had a beautiful coral color, the soup was thin and lacking in good lobster flavor. We needed to get more flavor from the shells or perhaps increase the number of lobsters. (We eventually found that three lobsters were the right number to make six servings of bisque.) We also wanted to simplify the process; removing meat from raw lobsters was simply too hard. We would have to cook the lobsters, remove the meat, and then sauté the shells. We saw two ways to cook the lobsters: roasting and steaming.

To roast a lobster, it must first be killed with a knife. We did this, then split the lobsters in half lengthwise, brushed them with olive oil, and placed them on a baking sheet in a 400-degree oven. Tasters found the meat to be too dry and chewy. Worse, the tail and claws did not seem to cook evenly. Dismembering the lobster before roasting, so that each part could be removed when it was done, seemed unnecessarily tedious.

Steaming was much more appealing, both because it was easy and because it would create some lobster broth for use in the soup. (Boiling didn't make much sense because the volume of liquid involved would be too much for use in the bisque.) We steamed the lobsters until partially cooked so that the meat wouldn't become tough. (We wanted to finish cooking the meat in the bisque.) We determined that seven minutes was just enough to time to firm up the meat so it could be removed easily from the shell. The meat was still translucent at this point. We steamed the lobsters in a mixture of wine and bottled clam juice (not water) to pump up the flavor of the broth. With the broth and meat reserved, we ground the cleaned shells and added

REMOVING MEAT FROM STEAMED LOBSTERS

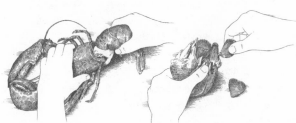   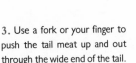

1. Twist the tail to separate it from the body.

2. Twist off the tail flippers.

3. Use a fork or your finger to push the tail meat up and out through the wide end of the tail. Dice the tail meat and reserve.

4. Twist the claw appendages off the body.

5. Twist the claw from the connecting joint.

6. Remove the pincer of the claw. Use a gentle motion; the meat will stay attached to the rest of claw. Otherwise, use a cocktail fork to pick out the meat.

7. Use lobster crackers to break open the claw and, if possible, remove the meat in a single piece. Leave the claw whole or dice as desired.

8. Crack open the connecting joint and remove the meat with a cocktail fork.

them to the pot with the sautéed vegetables.

Although this technique held promise (the lobster was perfectly cooked and the lobster broth was a nice addition to the soup base), it failed to extract enough flavor from the shells. We figured that the lobster shells, like the shrimp shells, would need exposure to dry heat and fat to draw out their full flavor.

We had hoped to avoid using two cooking methods before the shells went into the soup pot, but this course now seemed inevitable. We steamed

some more lobsters, removed the meat, tossed the shells with olive oil, and roasted them until they were incredibly aromatic and brittle. These shells were easily ground up in the food processor, and they gave the bisque a potent lobster flavor. Unfortunately, the flavor of the shells was overpowering the sweet lobster meat. This bisque had a harsh, almost bitter undercurrent.

We decided to try sautéing the steamed empty lobster shells instead of roasting. Although large shell

---

INGREDIENTS: Lobsters

As with most seafood, knowing how to shop for lobster is just as important as knowing how to cook it. Lobsters must be purchased alive. Choose lobsters that are active in the tank; avoid listless specimens that may have been in the tank too long. Maine lobsters, with their large claws, are meatier and sweeter than clawless rock or spiny lobsters, and they are our first and only choice.

When serving whole lobsters, size is really a matter of preference and budget. For soups and stews, we recommend buying small lobsters (about one pound is fine) because they are so reasonably priced. These so-called "chicken lobsters" have plenty of meat for bisques and soups. You might even consider buying "cull" lobsters, which are missing a claw. There will be enough meat in the tail and remaining claw. And remember that the shells are the main source of flavor for the soup base, not the meat.

Another consideration is sex. Many chefs prefer female lobsters because they like to add the roe to soups and other recipes. If you want to add roe to lobster bisque (see variation on page 102), you must buy female lobsters and then get lucky enough to find eggs once you open up the steamed carcasses. (It's more likely than not that at least one of the lobsters will have roe.) To distinguish female from male lobsters at the fish market, look at the fins on the underside of the tail. The first pair (closest to the head) will be soft and feathery on a female, hard and thin on a male. Ask your fishmonger if you are in doubt.

Before working on this topic in the test kitchen, the terms "hard-shell" and "soft-shell" lobster meant nothing to us. Unlike crabs, there's certainly no distinction between the two at the retail level. Of course, we knew from past experience that some lobster claws rip open as easily as an aluminum flip-top can, while others require shop tools to crack. We also noticed the small, limp claw meat of some lobsters and the full, packed meat of others. We attributed these differences to how long the lobsters had been stored in tanks. It seems we were wrong. These

variations are caused by the particular stage of molting a lobster is in at the time it is caught.

As it turns out, most of the lobsters we eat during the summer and fall are in some phase of molting. During the late spring, as waters begin to warm, lobsters start to form new shell tissue underneath their old shells. As early as June off the shores of New Jersey and in July or August in colder Maine and Canadian waters, lobsters shed their hard exterior shell. Because the most difficult task in molting is pulling the claw muscle through the old shell, the lobster dehydrates its claw (hence the smaller claw meat).

Once a lobster molts, it emerges with nothing but a wrinkled, soft covering, much like that on a soft-shell crab. Within 15 minutes, the lobster inflates itself with water, increasing its length by 15 percent and its weight by 50 percent. This extra water expands the wrinkled, soft covering, allowing the lobster room to grow long after the shell starts to harden. The newly molted lobster immediately eats its old shell, digesting the crucial shell-hardening calcium.

Understanding the molt phase clarifies the deficiencies of soft-shell summer lobster. It explains why it is so waterlogged, why its claw meat is so shriveled and scrawny, and why its tail meat is so underdeveloped and chewy. There is also far less meat in a one-pound soft-shell lobster than in a hard-shell lobster that weighs the same.

During the fall, the lobster shell continues to harden, and the meat expands to fill the new shell. By spring, lobsters are at their peak, packed with meat and relatively inexpensive, since it is easier for fishermen to check their traps than it is during the winter. As the tail grows, it becomes firmer and meatier and cooks up tender, not tough. The shells are also more flavorful. For these reasons, give lobsters a squeeze at the market and buy only those with hard shells. As a rule of thumb, hard-shell lobsters are reasonably priced from Mother's Day through the Fourth of July.

pieces were fine on a baking sheet in the oven, we needed to grind the lobster shells before sautéing. We followed the method that had worked so well in shrimp bisque, sautéing and then flambéing the shells. The browned shells were then added to the pot with the other bisque ingredients. Finally, we had achieved a great base for lobster bisque. The flavor of the sweet lobster meat dominated, while the shells added depth and richness. The strong bitter notes that roasting had brought out in the shells were not present in the sautéed shells.

Our recipe was basically done, needing just a few minor revisions. After several more tests, we found that it took 30 minutes of simmering to extract all the flavor from the steamed, ground, and sautéed shells. We wondered if adding the cream in the midst of the simmering time would increase the amount of flavor released by the shells. Since fat extracts flavors from food and cream is loaded with fat, this idea made sense, at least on paper. We made two more batches of bisque, one with cream added at the end, the other with cream added 10 minutes before straining the shells. The latter technique enhanced the lobster flavor, while the former just seemed to dilute it.

The final flavor adjustments that had worked so well in our shrimp bisque—tarragon, lemon juice, sherry, and cayenne—were equally successful in our lobster bisque. Although we were successful in figuring out the best method for extracting maximum flavor from lobster shells, we can't say that our final recipe is all that easy. No single step is difficult, but there are more steps to this recipe than to shrimp bisque. This elegant, luxurious soup takes time to prepare but is nonetheless a splendid choice for a special occasion, especially when served as a first course.

Lobster Bisque

SERVES 6

Chunks of lobster meat are held in a silky smooth, rich flavored cream base. Preparing this soup requires a few steps. First the lobsters are steamed to the point of being slightly undercooked. The meat is removed, the shells ground in a food processor and then sautéed. The shells are flambéed with brandy, a hallmark of this classic recipe, and then added to the steaming liquid, which has been thickened and flavored with browned vegetables. For a classic presentation, float the meat

from one claw in the center of each bowl. To do this, reserve the claws whole and then heat them for 1 minute before adding the diced meat.

1½	cups dry white wine
4	(8-ounce) bottles clam juice
3	lobsters, each about 1 pound
2	tablespoons olive oil
¼	cup brandy or cognac, warmed
6	tablespoons unsalted butter
1	small carrot, chopped fine (about 3 tablespoons)
1	small stalk celery, chopped fine (about 3 tablespoons)
1	small onion, chopped fine (about 6 tablespoons)
1	medium clove garlic, minced
½	cup all-purpose flour
1	(14½-ounce) can diced tomatoes, drained
2	small sprigs fresh tarragon, leaves removed and chopped from 1 sprig
1	cup heavy cream
1	tablespoon lemon juice
	Pinch ground cayenne
1	tablespoon dry sherry
	Salt and ground black pepper

1. Bring the wine and 3 bottles of clam juice to a boil over high heat in a stockpot large enough to hold the lobsters. Rinse the lobsters under cold, running water and put them in the pot. Cover the pot and steam the lobsters for 3 minutes. Shake the pot to redistribute the lobsters and steam for 4 minutes more. Remove the cover, being careful to avoid steam as it escapes. Use large tongs to transfer the lobsters to a large bowl. Strain the liquid through a fine-mesh strainer and set aside.

2. When the lobsters are cool enough to handle, remove meat from the tail and claws and dice (see illustrations on page 99). Place the meat in a bowl, cover with plastic wrap, and refrigerate. Split the lobster body and head in half lengthwise with a heavy knife and remove inedible portions (see illustrations on page 102).

3. Grind the shells in a food processor in 2 or 3 batches. (A small amount of thin pinkish paste will adhere to some of the shells.) Heat a 12-inch heavy-bottomed skillet over high heat until very hot, about

3 minutes. Add 1 tablespoon olive oil and swirl to coat the pan bottom. Add half of lobster shells; sauté until aromatic and lightly browned, about 3 minutes. Transfer the browned shells to a medium bowl and repeat with the remaining oil and shells. Return the first batch of browned shells to skillet. Pour the warmed brandy over the lobster shells and flambé, shaking the pan (see illustrations for on page 96). When the flames subside, turn off the heat and hold the shells in the pan.

4. Meanwhile, heat 2 tablespoons butter in a large Dutch oven over medium heat until foaming. Add the carrot, celery, onion, and garlic and cook, stirring frequently, until the vegetables are slightly softened and lightly browned, 6 to 7 minutes. Add the remaining 4 tablespoons of butter and stir with a wooden spoon until melted. Add the flour and cook, stirring constantly, until combined thoroughly, about 1 minute. Slowly stir in reserved liquid from steaming lobsters, initially adding about ¼ cup at a time. Stir until blended, then continue adding the remaining liquid and scraping the pan bottom with a wooden spoon to loosen browned bits. Add the tomatoes, tarragon sprig, and lobster shells. Pour remaining bottle of clam juice into the skillet once shells have been removed. Turn heat to high and bring liquid to a boil, scraping up browned bits from the pan bottom. Add the clam juice mixture to the pot with the shells. Once the liquid in the Dutch oven comes to a boil, cover the pot, reduce the heat to low, and simmer, stirring frequently, until thickened, about 20 minutes. Stir in the cream and simmer for 10 minutes longer.

5. Strain the bisque through a chinois or a fine-mesh strainer into a medium container, pressing on the solids with the back of a ladle to extract all liquid. Wash and dry the now-empty Dutch oven. Return the strained bisque to the Dutch oven and stir in the lemon juice and cayenne. Bring to a simmer over medium-high heat. When piping hot, add the diced lobster meat (add claws first if serving whole, cook 1 minute, then add remaining meat) and sherry and then season to taste with salt and pepper. Serve immediately, garnishing each bowl with a little chopped tarragon.

➤ VARIATION

Lobster Bisque with Coral

Female lobsters are often loaded with roe—tiny black eggs that turn red when fully cooked. Lobster roe, which is called the coral, can add flavor, texture, and color to this soup.

If you want to add the roe, you must remove it from the steamed lobsters. Look for the roe once the tail has been removed; it should be at the bottom portion of the lobster body. Use a spoon to scrape the purplish-black roe into a small bowl, cover the bowl with plastic, and refrigerate it until needed.

Follow recipe for Lobster Bisque, stirring the reserved roe into the bisque along with the lemon juice and cayenne. Make sure to break apart the roe into individual eggs. By the time the soup comes to a simmer, the roe will turn bright red. Add the lobster meat and proceed as directed.

CLEANING LOBSTER SHELLS

1. Turn the lobster body over and split it in half lengthwise with a heavy knife.

2. Use a spoon to remove and discard the stomach sac.

3. Remove and discard the tomalley (the lobster's green-colored liver).

4. Remove and discard the feathery gills and surrounding cartilage.

Oyster Stew

PEOPLE WHO HAVE NEVER EATEN OYSTER stew often expect that it will be thick and hearty like fish chowder. Nothing could be further from the truth. Oyster stew is thin and elegant, like a Park Avenue matron. Although the name implies thick and hearty, the consistency is really soup-like. Above all, an oyster stew must be well balanced with a delicate interplay of flavors. The recipes we looked at initially, while honoring the thin part of the mandate, ignored the elegant part and skipped the interplay altogether. This was one of the sorriest collections of recipes we had ever tested.

One recipe combined milk, butter, oysters, oyster liquor (the juice exuded by oysters when shucked), and sherry over low heat, then finished with heavy cream and more butter. The resulting soup had a raw, uneven flavor. The oysters cooked so fast that the sherry had no time to cook off. All of the butter floated to the top—another unpleasant touch. A second recipe was made mostly with milk, a touch of cream, and oysters but no wine. Celery seed and paprika gave the soup an awful tinge. Ugh again. A third recipe was better than the others but had too much wine in proportion to the other liquids (water and cream). The addition of parsley, chervil, and chives did make this version look lovely.

At this point, we made some specific conclusions about what we wanted. Oyster stew should be an exercise in minimalism—a knob of sweet butter, sautéed shallots and celery, a splash of white wine or champagne, a moderate amount of dairy, lemon juice, and, finally, a restrained potpourri of the softest possible fresh herbs: parsley, chives, and chervil. That is the course of action we took, using heavy cream for mouthfeel (the milk versions had been watery) and adding a bit of flour for body. A tablespoon of dry sherry gave the stew a soft finish.

Since oysters do not benefit from any sort of lengthy simmering, we chose to finish the base of the soup before adding them. We simply poached the oysters in the hot base and then served the soup immediately. As long as the soup base was simmering when the oysters and their liquor were added to the pot, the oysters were done in about a minute.

Although you can shuck oysters yourself, it's much easier to leave this job to the professionals. When testing this recipe, we found some variation in the shucked oysters available at local fish markets (see below for more details). After buying shucked oysters in several stores, we realized the importance of expressing our needs clearly. Most shucked oysters can be packed to order, so take the opportunity to specify about how many oysters you want and how much liquor you need.

For our recipe, we think that the flavorful oyster liquor, which gives the soup base a rich, briny flavor,

---

INGREDIENTS: Shucked Oysters

Although you can shuck your own oysters (see page 104 for tips on buying an oyster knife), we strongly recommend that you leave this job to your fishmonger. If at all possible, buy freshly shucked oysters at a reputable fish market rather than purchasing oysters packed in a plastic container or in a tin with a plastic lid.

There are advantages to having your oysters shucked to order. First, you'll know that the oysters were just taken out of their shells, which is an indicator of freshness. Second, you'll be able to control the number of oysters per pint. When we purchased already packed pints, we found that the number of oysters per pint ranged from 25 to 50! Finally, when you have oysters shucked to order you'll be able to estimate how much liquor you'll get—a pint container with 25 oysters holds about 1 cup of liquor, and a pint with 50 oysters holds about ½ cup of liquor.

If you can find only packed oysters, make sure that the lid on the container is tightly sealed, and avoid containers that are swelling or blown up—this happens when the oysters are releasing gas and indicates that they are old. Packed oysters should be clearly dated so that you can judge their freshness. Some oysters will be packed with a "pull" date—the date the oysters can no longer be sold. Look for a pull date that is as far in the future as possible.

The oysters themselves should be fairly uniform in size and plump, with a smooth, creamy color. They should also be shiny, but not slimy. Slime indicates that the oysters are way past their prime. The oyster liquor should be clear (it might have a very slight gray tinge), not milky or cloudy. If you can, smell the oysters—superfresh oysters will have a very fresh, salty, ocean smell. Never buy oysters that have a fishy or "low tide" odor.

It's best to use oysters on the same day that you buy them, but, if necessary, oysters can be refrigerated (in a closed container, in their liquor) for up to two days. Store the container in a bowl of ice to keep the oysters well-chilled.

is just as important as the oysters. Avoid oysters that are packed in minimal juices, so your stew won't be shortchanged.

Oyster stew is the perfect way to start a holiday meal. It's rich but still light, special but not difficult to prepare. This stew, which is really soup, certainly deserves wider attention.

Oyster Stew

SERVES 4 TO 6

Be sure to reserve the liquid—or liquor—released when shucking the oysters. Fish stock (page 37) can be substituted if necessary.

3	tablespoons unsalted butter
1	large shallot, minced
1	stalk celery, minced
2	teaspoons all-purpose flour
1/2	cup dry white wine or champagne
2	cups heavy cream, warmed
1	tablespoon dry sherry
1	teaspoon lemon juice
1	teaspoon minced fresh parsley leaves
1	teaspoon minced chives
1	teaspoon minced fresh chervil leaves
	Pinch ground cayenne
	Salt
25	raw oysters, shucked, with 1 cup oyster liquor reserved

1. Heat the butter in a large saucepan over medium-low heat until foaming. Add the shallot and cook, stirring frequently, until fragrant and translucent, about 5 minutes. Add the celery and cook until slightly softened, about 2 minutes. Stir in the flour and cook, stirring constantly, until bubbly, about 20 seconds. Stir in the wine and simmer until thickened and bubbly, about 20 seconds.

2. Stir in the cream and return to a simmer. Simmer to blend the flavors and cook the flour, about 5 minutes. Add the sherry, lemon juice, parsley, chives, chervil, cayenne, salt to taste, oysters, and oyster liquor. Return to a simmer. (The oysters will be cooked at this point. The oyster edges will ruffle and curl up when cooked.) Adjust the seasonings and serve immediately.

EQUIPMENT: Oyster Knives

Shucking oysters is a difficult task best left to the fishmonger. But if you want to serve oysters on the half-shell at home, you must open them yourself. We decided to investigate oyster knives and see if the choice of utensil could make this job any easier.

What should you look for when choosing an oyster knife? First and foremost, an oyster knife must be safe to use. The handle should be easy to grip, even when your hands become slippery or wet. An oyster knife should also be efficient. If it takes five minutes to open every oyster, the knife is nearly useless.

Most knives specifically designed for opening oysters have short handles and short, flat blades that taper to a point. Some models have a round piece of metal that separates the blade from the handle. The guard at the base of the blade is designed to reduce the risk of injury. Many experts claim that an old-fashioned church-key can opener can be used on oysters. These sources suggest using the pointed tip designed for punching holes in cans, not the flat end designed for opening bottles.

We rounded up seven oyster knives, a church-key can opener, and several hundred oysters. We had both experienced shuckers and complete novices open several oysters with each knife. There was unanimous consensus about which knives made this difficult task easier.

Everyone agreed that it's worth spending the money on an oyster knife. Yes, you may eventually open a few oysters with a can opener, but the task will be frustrating and time-consuming. Among oyster knives, testers preferred models with sharp, pointed tips that were angled slightly upward. This design made it surprisingly easy to make that first penetration into the hinge between the top and bottom shells. Testers also preferred plastic handles that were contoured and textured. These handles felt more secure and comfortable than wooden ones. A blade guard between the blade and handle is a useful feature, but not at the expense of blade length. We found that longer blades are better able to detach the oyster meat from the shells.

After opening so many oysters, we have some tips to speed the process along. Hold the oyster cupped-side down in a kitchen towel (to shield your hand) and use the tip of the oyster knife to locate the hinge between the shells. Push between the edges of the shells, wiggling back and forth to pry them apart. Use the oyster knife to detach the meat from the top shell and discard that shell. Slide the blade under the meat to sever the muscle that holds the meat of the oyster to the bottom shell. As you do all this, work over a bowl to catch the precious oyster liquor that is released.

6

VEGETABLE SOUPS

AS THIS CHAPTER DEMONSTRATES, ALMOST any vegetable can be turned into a good soup. The chapter begins with several pureed single-vegetable soups, including pea, asparagus, broccoli, carrot, squash, and tomato. All of these soups are pureed in a blender, and many are strained to create a perfectly smooth texture. (See chapter 1 for information on buying a blender as well as various types of strainers.) Most of these soups are lighter fare, best served as a first course or perhaps at lunch.

The rest of the chapter covers heartier, chunkier soups with multiple vegetables, including potato-leek soup and corn chowder. The chapter ends with some of our favorite ethnic vegetable soups, including minestrone, mulligatawny, and French onion. Note that we've included cheddar cheese soup in this chapter. Although it does contain vegetables, it's not really a vegetable soup. It's here for lack of better placement.

Most of the soups in this chapter call for chicken stock as the liquid base. (In a few recipes, we felt that the chicken flavor overwhelmed the vegetables and opted to use water.) Since many of these soups are pureed, the stock becomes incorporated into the soup and does not remain a distinct element. We found that in these cases either homemade stock or low-sodium commercial broth could be used. (For information on our testing of leading commercial chicken broths, see page 27.) Vegetarians should substitute vegetable stock (see chapter 2) for chicken broth.

Pea Soup

CLASSIC SWEET PEA SOUP WAS ORIGINALLY prepared by briefly stewing fresh blanched peas, leeks, and tendrils of lettuce in butter, moistening them with veal stock, and passing them through a fine-mesh strainer. The soup was then finished with cream and seasoned with fresh chervil.

We wanted to come up with a quick and delicious version of this soup, minus laborious techniques, so we looked at several modern versions. Many introduced new ingredients, largely dismissing veal stock in favor of chicken and adding split peas or sugar snap peas to the mix. Most also moved into the arena of frozen peas. Lacking gelatinous veal stock, these new recipes were obliged to include a bit of thickener in the form of egg yolk, potatoes, or flour. Fresh mint typically replaced chervil. Of the handful of such recipes that we tried, though, most either completely lacked pea flavor or attained this flavor only by sacrificing color or body.

What we were looking for was something different—an easy version of this popular soup that had the same fundamental virtues as the original. Flavor, color, and texture all bear equally on the success or failure of this soup. Our challenge was to cook the peas quickly enough to preserve their vivid color and to achieve a puree of spectacular smoothness without incurring the loss of flavor sometimes associated with sieving away vegetable bits in short-cooked soups.

The obvious starting point was the pea itself. For those of us without gardens, the long-awaited season of fresh peas is often disappointing. Grocery-store pods can conceal tough, starchy pellets worthy of neither the price they command nor the effort they occasion. So when we began this recipe, we headed not down the garden path but up the frozen foods aisle. (For more information on frozen peas, see page 107.)

From the pea, we ventured to aromatics. Because the flavor of the peas is delicate and easily overwhelmed, we wanted to minimize any additions. Experimenting with onions, leeks, and shallots sautéed in butter (unquestionably the most pea-compatible fat in terms of flavor), we found onions too strong but shallots and leeks equally agreeable—delicate and sweet, like the peas themselves.

The means of introducing peas to the soup now became critical. The fun of eating whole peas—breaking through the crisp, springy hull to the sweet pea paste—goes missing in a smooth pea soup, where the listless hulls become an impediment to enjoyment and so must be removed altogether. Simmering peas first to soften their skins, we invariably overcooked them. Additions such as sugar snap peas or snow peas sounded interesting but actually added little flavor.

It occurred to us that if we pureed the peas before putting them into the soup and infused them briefly in the simmering liquid, we might get to the heart of the pea right off. To that end, we chopped partially frozen peas in a food processor and simmered them briefly in the soup base to release their starch and flavor quickly. At this juncture, finding the puree a trifle thin, we doubled back and added two tablespoons of flour to the sautéed aromatics to give the base a little body. A few ounces of Boston lettuce added along with the peas gave the soup a marvelous frothy texture when pureed. (To achieve optimal texture, the soup still needed to be passed through a strainer.) A bit of heavy cream, salt, and pepper were the only finishing touches required.

Creamy Pea Soup

SERVES 4 TO 6

Remove the peas from the freezer just before starting the soup so that when you are ready to process them, as the stock simmers, they will be only partially thawed. To preserve its delicate flavor and color, this soup is best served immediately. A few croutons (see page 108) are the perfect embellishment.

4	tablespoons unsalted butter
8	large shallots, minced (about 1 cup), or 2 medium leeks, white and light green parts chopped fine (about 1⅓ cups; see illustrations on page 124 to clean)
2	tablespoons all-purpose flour
3½	cups homemade chicken stock or canned low-sodium chicken broth
1½	pounds frozen peas (about 4½ cups), partially thawed at room temperature for 10 minutes (see note)
12	small leaves Boston lettuce (about 3 ounces) from 1 small head, leaves washed and dried
½	cup heavy cream
	Salt and ground black pepper

1. Heat the butter in a large saucepan over low heat until foaming. Add the shallots and cook, covered, until softened, 8 to 10 minutes, stirring occasionally. Add the flour and cook, stirring constantly, until thoroughly combined, about 30 seconds. Stirring constantly, gradually add the chicken stock. Increase the heat to high and bring to a boil. Reduce the heat to medium-low and simmer 3 to 5 minutes.

2. Meanwhile, in the workbowl of a food processor fitted with a steel blade, process the partially thawed peas until coarsely chopped, about 20 seconds. Add the peas and lettuce to the simmering broth. Increase the heat to medium-high, cover, and return to a simmer; simmer for 3 minutes. Uncover, reduce the heat to medium-low, and continue to simmer 2 minutes longer.

3. Working in batches, puree the soup in a blender until smooth. Strain the soup through a chinois or fine-mesh strainer into a large bowl; discard the solids. Rinse out and wipe the saucepan clean.

INGREDIENTS: Frozen Peas

Throughout the testing of this soup, we came to depend on frozen peas. Not only are they more convenient than their fresh, in-the-pod comrades, but they also taste better. In test after test, we found frozen peas to be tender and sweet while fresh peas tasted starchy and bland. Trying to understand this curious finding, which flew in the face of common sense, we looked to the frozen food industry for some answers.

Green peas are one of the oldest vegetables known to humankind. Yet despite this long history, they are relatively delicate; fresh peas have little stamina. Green peas lose a substantial portion of their nutrients within 24 hours of being picked. This rapid deterioration is the reason for the starchy, bland flavor of most "fresh" peas found at the grocery store. These not-so-fresh peas might be several days old, depending on where they came from and how long they were kept in the cooler. Frozen peas, on the other hand, are picked, cleaned, sorted, and frozen within several hours of harvest, which helps preserve their delicate sugars and flavors. Fittingly enough, when commercially frozen vegetables first began to appear in the 1920s and 1930s, green peas were among them.

Finding good frozen peas is not hard. After tasting peas from the two major national frozen food purveyors, Birdseye and Green Giant, along with some from a smaller organic company, Cascadian Farm, our panel of tasters found little difference between them. All of the peas were sweet and fresh tasting, with a bright green color. So unless you grow your own or know a reputable local farm stand, your best bet is cruising up the frozen food aisle for a bag of frozen peas.

Return the pureed mixture to the saucepan and stir in the cream. Warm the soup over low heat until hot, about 3 minutes. Season to taste with salt and pepper and serve immediately.

Buttered Croutons

MAKES ABOUT 3 CUPS

The croutons' crisp crunch offers a pleasant contrast with the smooth, velvety texture of a rich pureed soup. Although tasters preferred the flavor of croutons made with butter, olive oil was a close second. If you like, replace the melted butter with an equal amount of extra-virgin olive oil. Be sure to use regular or thick-sliced bread.

6   slices white bread (about 6 ounces), crusts removed and slices cut into ½-inch cubes (about 3 cups)
     Salt and ground black pepper
3   tablespoons unsalted butter, melted

1. Adjust oven rack to the upper-middle position and heat the oven to 400 degrees. Combine bread cubes and salt and pepper to taste in a medium bowl. Drizzle with the butter and toss well with a rubber spatula to combine.

2. Spread the croutons in a single layer on a rimmed baking sheet or in a shallow baking dish. Bake the croutons, turning at the halfway mark, until golden brown and crisp, 8 to 10 minutes. Cool and then store croutons in an airtight container or plastic bag for up to 3 days.

PUREEING SOUP SAFELY

Many vegetable soups are best pureed in a blender to create a smooth texture. Blending hot soup can be dangerous, though. To prevent mishaps, don't fill the blender jar past the halfway point, and hold the lid in place with a folded kitchen towel.

INGREDIENTS: Croutons

A shower of crisp croutons adds flavor, crunch, and, yes, elegance to a humble bowl of pea soup. In fact, most pureed vegetable soups benefit from the addition of a few croutons. We're not talking about the prepackaged croutons sold in the supermarket. Only the real thing will do.

Although croutons are simple fare (cubed bread tossed with fat and toasted in the oven until crisp), we did have some questions. What kind of bread makes the best croutons? Should the crusts be trimmed or left on? Should the bread cubes be coated with butter or oil?

We started with the issue of the bread. We tested several varieties of sliced white bread, Italian bread, and baguette. This test immediately led us to the next variable—the crusts. We quickly determined that croutons are best made with bread cubes that don't have the crusts attached. The crusts are already more crunchy and a deeper brown color than the crumb. Including the crusts results in unevenly cooked croutons, with edges that are darker, drier, and harder. Because Italian bread and baguettes have more crust than sliced white bread, we decided that the latter is the best choice for croutons. Avoid thinly sliced bread, which will make meager croutons. Regular or thick-sliced white bread is the best choice.

We found that half-inch bread cubes create the ideal croutons. Smaller cubes can become too crunchy in the oven and don't absorb soup quite as well. Larger cubes won't fit on a spoon.

We tested both fresh and stale white bread and found that either can be used. Fresh bread is a bit trickier to cut into cubes and takes a bit longer to crisp up in the oven. If you want to use stale bread in the recipe above, simply reduce the baking time by about two minutes. Note that croutons made from stale bread will be a bit more crisp than those made from fresh bread.

Fat adds much of the flavor to croutons. Our tasters preferred butter to the various oils we tested, although extra-virgin olive oil was a close second. An oven temperature of 400 degrees browned the croutons nicely without any scorching. Turning the bread cubes at the halfway mark ensures even cooking, as does arranging the bread cubes in a single layer on the baking sheet.

➤ VARIATION

Garlic Croutons

Finely mince 2 large cloves garlic or press them through a garlic press. Combine with 3 tablespoons extra-virgin olive oil in a small bowl. Let stand 20 minutes, then pour through a fine-mesh strainer; discard garlic. Follow recipe for Buttered Croutons, replacing melted butter with garlic-flavored oil. Proceed as directed.

CREAM OF ASPARAGUS SOUP

CREAM OF ASPARAGUS SOUP IS A CLOSE culinary cousin to creamy pea soup. Both soups should be bright green, bursting with vegetable flavor, and flawlessly smooth. We started with our recipe for pea soup and planned on replacing the peas and lettuce with asparagus. Once we figured out how to handle the asparagus, we were confident that this approach would work.

Unfortunately, the asparagus resisted our early efforts. No matter what we tried, the flavor in soups simmered for fewer than 10 minutes was too mild. Even when we ground the asparagus in the food processor, it took at least 15 minutes to extract sufficient flavor from this vegetable. By that time, the soup was army green. We needed to unlock flavor from the asparagus before it went into the soup pot, without compromising its color too much.

Blanching the asparagus shortened the cooking time in the soup pot but with a huge loss of flavor. Apparently, much of the asparagus flavor went down the drain with the blanching water. We figured that broiling, which concentrates the flavor of many vegetables, including asparagus, might be a better choice. Broiled asparagus remained bright green as long as we didn't let the spears char. Cooked this way, the asparagus quickly contributed its flavor to the soup, but the texture of the soup was a tad stringy. We thought about using fewer asparagus, but we knew that would result in less flavor.

Since the finely chopped raw asparagus had yielded soup with modest flavor but good texture and the broiled asparagus had produced soup with excellent flavor but stringy texture, we wondered if there was some compromise method that would work. What about using half raw asparagus (to promote good texture) and half broiled asparagus (for robust flavor)? Sure enough, by only broiling half the asparagus we eliminated the texture issue. The soup pureed perfectly without a hint of woody texture or strings. Even better, the flavor of this soup was excellent, and the color was brilliant.

The soup seemed a bit thick so we increased the amount of chicken stock slightly from our pea soup recipe. The asparagus called out for some acidity. A tablespoon of lemon juice did the job nicely. With a few minor changes, pea soup had morphed into asparagus soup.

Cream of Asparagus Soup

SERVES 4 TO 6

To preserve its delicate flavor and color, this soup is best served immediately. A few croutons (page 108) are the perfect embellishment.

5	tablespoons unsalted butter
3	pounds asparagus, tough ends snapped off (see illustration on page 110)
8	large shallots, minced (about 1 cup), or 2 medium leeks, white and light green parts, chopped fine (about 1⅓ cups; see illustrations on page 124 to clean)
2	tablespoons all-purpose flour
4	cups homemade chicken stock or canned low-sodium chicken broth
½	cup heavy cream
1	tablespoon lemon juice
	Salt and ground black pepper

1. Adjust the oven rack to the highest position and preheat the broiler. Melt 1 tablespoon butter in a large saucepan and reserve. Place half the asparagus on a rimmed baking sheet, drizzle with the melted butter (do not wash the saucepan), and roll the asparagus back and forth to coat. Broil the asparagus, turning once, until tender and just beginning to color, about 5 minutes. (Do not let the asparagus brown.) Cool and roughly chop the broiled asparagus.

2. Cut the remaining raw asparagus into 1-inch pieces. Pulse the asparagus in the workbowl of a food

processor fitted with a steel blade until finely chopped. (The pieces should be pea-sized.) Reserve with the broiled asparagus.

3. Heat the remaining 4 tablespoons butter in the empty saucepan over low heat until foaming. Add the shallots and cook, covered, until softened, 8 to 10 minutes, stirring occasionally. Add the flour and cook, stirring constantly, until thoroughly combined, about 30 seconds. Stirring constantly, gradually add the chicken stock. Increase the heat to high and bring to a boil. Reduce the heat to medium-low and simmer 3 to 5 minutes.

4. Add the asparagus to the simmering broth. Increase the heat to medium-high and return to a simmer. Reduce the heat to medium-low and simmer, uncovered, until tender, about 5 minutes.

5. Working in batches, puree the soup in a blender until smooth. Strain the soup through a chinois or fine-mesh strainer into a large bowl; discard the solids. Rinse out and wipe the saucepan clean. Return the pureed mixture to the saucepan and stir in the cream. Warm the soup over low heat until hot, about 3 minutes. Add the lemon juice and season to taste with salt and pepper. Serve immediately.

SNAPPING TOUGH ENDS FROM ASPARAGUS

The tough, woody part of the asparagus stem will break off in just the right place if you hold the spear properly. Hold the asparagus about halfway down the stalk; with your other hand, hold the cut end between your thumb and index finger about an inch or so up from the bottom; bend the stalk until it snaps.

CREAM OF BROCCOLI SOUP

ONCE WE HAD FIGURED OUT HOW TO MAKE pea and asparagus soup, we knew that cream of broccoli soup would come together quickly. The issue here is basically the same—how to get full vegetable flavor without any sacrifice in color.

With broccoli, there's an additional worry. When cooked too long, broccoli takes on an unpleasant odor as sulfur compounds in this vegetable react with one another and are released. We knew that quick cooking was key and hoped to achieve it by cutting up the broccoli very fine. Quickly cooked broccoli would not only look better, but it would taste and smell better, too.

For our first test, we replaced the peas in our basic recipe with broccoli that had been chopped very fine in the food processor. We had chopped the florets and peeled stalks separately to account for their different textures. With just a few pulses, the tender florets were cut into pea-sized pieces. The tougher stalks required more pulsing. By separating the florets and stalks, we didn't have to worry about grinding the florets in a puree or leaving large chunks of stalk untouched.

This first test was proceeding nicely. The pureed and strained soup looked fine. However, the flavor was a bit flat. Tasting the strained solids, we realized that they still had some flavor to release even though they were tender. For our next test, we increased the cooking time, but this turned the soup an ugly olive green color. In the end, we decided to leave the pureed broccoli bits in the soup. While pea and asparagus soups should have a silky consistency, tasters did not mind a more rustic broccoli soup with tiny pieces of vegetable in it. (We went back and tested this approach with peas and asparagus and realized that pea skins and woody portions of the asparagus do not puree properly and really must be strained out before serving.)

Like asparagus, broccoli needed a hint of acidity to bring out its flavor. Again, lemon juice fit the bill. With the pureed solids left in, this soup can be quite thick. Once the pureed soup goes back into the pot and the cream has been added, feel free to adjust the consistency as desired. You might want to add as much as a cup of hot tap water to thin the soup.

Cream of Broccoli Soup

SERVES 4 TO 6

To preserve its delicate flavor and color, this soup is best served immediately. A few croutons (page 108) are the perfect embellishment. See illustrations below for tips on preparing the broccoli.

4	tablespoons unsalted butter
8	large shallots, minced (about 1 cup), or 2 medium leeks, white and light green parts, chopped fine (about 1 ⅓ cups; see illustrations on page 124 to clean)
2	tablespoons all-purpose flour
4	cups homemade chicken stock or canned low-sodium chicken broth
1 ½	pounds broccoli
½	cup heavy cream
1 ½	teaspoons lemon juice
	Salt and ground black pepper

PREPARING BROCCOLI

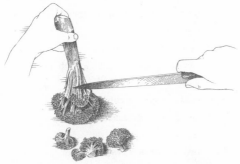

1. Place each piece of broccoli upside down on a cutting board and trim off the florets very close to their heads with a large knife.

2. Trim the tough bottom portion from each stalk and discard. Then stand each stalk up on the cutting board and remove the outer ⅛-inch layer of tough skin from each side with the knife.

1. Heat the butter in a large saucepan over low heat until foaming. Add the shallots and cook, covered, until softened, 8 to 10 minutes, stirring occasionally. Add the flour and cook, stirring constantly, until thoroughly combined, about 30 seconds. Stirring constantly, gradually add the chicken stock. Increase the heat to high and bring to a boil. Reduce the heat to medium-low and simmer 3 to 5 minutes.

2. Meanwhile, separate the broccoli stalks and florets. Trim the tough bottom portion of the stalks and then peel the tough outer skin from the remaining portion. Coarsely chop the stalks and pulse them in a food processor until cut very small but not pureed. (The largest pieces should be pea-sized.) Transfer the stalks to a medium bowl. Coarsely chop the florets and then pulse them in the food processor, in two batches, until cut very small but not pureed. Transfer the florets to the bowl with the stalks.

3. Add the broccoli to the simmering stock. Increase the heat to medium-high, and return to a simmer. Reduce the heat to medium-low and simmer, uncovered, until tender, 7 to 8 minutes.

4. Working in batches, puree the soup in a blender until smooth. Rinse out and wipe the saucepan clean. Return the pureed mixture to the saucepan and stir in the cream. If the soup seems too thick, stir in up to 1 cup hot water. Warm the soup over low heat until hot, about 3 minutes. Add the lemon juice and season to taste with salt and pepper. Serve immediately.

PUREED CARROT SOUP

WE ENJOY THE SMOOTH, SILKY TEXTURE OF creamed carrot soup, but we often find the flavor lacking. The dairy elements (usually lots of butter and cream) mask the taste of the carrots. We wanted a pureed soup with a silky texture that was also redolent of the sweetest carrots.

Most creamy vegetable soups contain flour. While we find flour to be essential when working with more watery green vegetables such as asparagus and broccoli, starchy carrots (as well as winter squash) don't seem to need it. In fact, when flour is added to soups made with dense starchy vegetables, the texture becomes overly thick.

We tested other starches, including cornstarch and potato starch, but found the results to be similar to soups made with flour. The texture was thick and gummy, and the carrots were not the primary flavor. We had seen recipes that used potatoes or rice as thickeners, usually cooked right along with the carrots in the stock. We tried this and found that the potatoes and rice detracted from the carrot flavor and caused the color of the soup to fade.

We decided to switch paths and use a different approach that would eliminate the starch. A classic technique for making cream soups begins by sautéing vegetables, adding some stock and seasonings, and finally adding cream, which is then cooked down to create the proper texture. We found that eliminating the starch improved the texture of the soup, but the dairy component still dominated. We liked the idea of starting with the vegetables, though it seemed that the best idea might be to use a larger quantity of vegetables and puree them for texture.

Most recipes for pureed vegetable soup use equal amounts of vegetables and liquid. We decided to alter this ratio in a big way and cook 4 cups of carrots in 2 cups of stock. We figured we would get more vegetable flavor and could use the vegetables themselves as a thickener.

This effort brought about immediate improvement. By the time the vegetables were cooked, the mixture was thick enough to create a puree with good body. In fact, the pureed carrots and broth were actually a little too thick. Instead of adding cream to the vegetables as they cooked, we now needed to add cream to the blender to thin out the pureed carrots.

We used about one cup of cream to get the right consistency, but this was too much dairy fat for our taste. We tried substituting half-and-half as well as whole and low-fat milk. Half-and-half was good, but a little too rich. Adding skim milk or 2 percent milk was equivalent to adding more stock and was not at all satisfying. Whole milk provided just the right amount of dairy fat to improve the texture, giving the soup a smooth and creamy mouthfeel without overwhelming the carrot flavor.

At this point the soup was bursting with carrot flavor and needed only minor adjustments. We found

that some sautéed onions gave the soup depth and enhanced the flavor of the carrots. A little white wine added some acidity, and white pepper (not black) helped to preserve the pretty color and appearance of the soup.

As for the cooking medium for the carrots, we tested chicken and vegetable stocks, both homemade and canned. Both of the homemade stocks were delicious in this recipe. Chicken stock added more depth, but the vegetable stock was light and pleasant. The canned broths were another matter. The vegetable broth gave the soup a tinny, sweet flavor. The canned chicken broth was mild and unobtrusive. We decided to use chicken stock in our recipe, but you could certainly use homemade vegetable stock (page 34) if you prefer.

Pureed Carrot Soup
SERVES 4 TO 6
If you intend to serve any of this soup cold, use oil; unlike butter, it will not congeal when chilled. If serving the soup hot, use butter for the best flavor.

2	tablespoons unsalted butter or vegetable oil
1	medium onion, chopped medium
1/4	cup dry white wine
1 1/2	pounds (about 8 medium) carrots, peeled, halved lengthwise, and sliced thin (about 4 cups)
2	cups homemade chicken stock or canned low-sodium chicken broth
1	teaspoon salt
1/8	teaspoon ground white pepper
	Pinch freshly grated nutmeg
1 1/4 to 1 1/2 cups whole milk	
2	teaspoons minced fresh parsley, tarragon, or chives

1. Heat the butter in large saucepan over medium heat. Add the onion and sauté until golden, about 5 minutes. Stir in the wine and carrots and cook until the wine evaporates, about 30 seconds.

2. Add the stock, salt, pepper, and nutmeg to the saucepan. Bring to a boil, reduce the heat, cover, and simmer until the carrots are tender, 20 to 25 minutes.

3. Puree the carrot mixture in batches in a

blender, adding 1¼ cups milk; blend until very smooth. Rinse and dry the saucepan. Return the soup to the saucepan and cook over low heat until warmed through. If the soup is too thick, stir in up to ¼ cup more milk to thin it. Adjust the seasonings. (Soup can be refrigerated for up to 3 days. Warm over low heat until hot; do not boil.) Serve immediately, garnishing bowls with the minced herb.

➤ VARIATIONS

Pureed Carrot Soup with Ginger

Follow recipe for Pureed Carrot Soup, adding 1 tablespoon finely minced fresh ginger to the onions after they have sautéed for 4 minutes. Proceed as directed, omitting the nutmeg and garnishing with parsley or chives.

Pureed Curried Carrot Soup

Follow recipe for Pureed Carrot Soup, adding 1½ teaspoons curry powder to the onions after they have sautéed for 4 minutes. Proceed as directed, omitting the nutmeg and garnishing with parsley.

Pureed Carrot Soup with Orange

This variation is particularly good served cold.

Follow recipe for Pureed Carrot Soup, using oil instead of butter and adding 2 teaspoons minced orange zest to the onions after they have sautéed for 4 minutes. Proceed as directed, stirring in 2 tablespoons fresh orange juice when adjusting the seasonings in step 3.

BUTTERNUT SQUASH SOUP

BUTTERNUT SQUASH SOUP IS ESSENTIALLY a simple soup. With squash, a cooking liquid, some aromatic ingredients, and a blender, the soup can be made without much commotion. But many squash soups hardly live up to their potential. Rather than being lustrous, slightly creamy, and intensely "squashy" in flavor, they are vegetal or porridge-like, and sometimes taste more like a squash pie than a squash soup.

Knowing that our basic method would be to cook the squash and then purée it with a liquid, our first test focused on how to cook the squash for the soup. Some recipes suggest boiling the squash in a cooking liquid, others roasting it in the oven, others sautéing it on the stovetop.

We tried boiling the squash, but having to peel the tough skin away before dicing it seemed unnecessarily tedious. We eliminated the sauté technique for the same reason. While the roasting was infinitely more simple than our attempts at boiling or sautéing (all we had to do was slice the squash in half, scoop out the seeds, and roast it on a rimmed baking sheet), it produced a caramel-flavored soup with a gritty texture. Roasting also took at least one hour—too long for what should be a quick, no-nonsense soup.

In an effort to save time without sacrificing the quick preparation we liked from the roasting test, we decided to try steaming the squash. In a large Dutch oven, we sautéed shallots in butter (we tried garlic and onion but found them too overpowering and acrid with the sweet squash), then added water to the sautéed shallots and brought the mix to a simmer. We seeded and quartered the squash and placed it into a collapsible steaming insert, then added the squash and insert to the Dutch oven. We covered the pan and let the squash steam for 30 minutes until it was tender enough to show no resistance to a fork. This method proved to be successful. We liked it because all of the cooking took place in just one pot, and, as a bonus, we ended up with a squash-infused cooking liquid that we could use as base for the soup.

But there was a downside. Essentially, steaming had the opposite effect of roasting: Whereas roasting concentrated the sugars and eliminated the liquid in the squash (which is what made the roasted squash soup gritty), steaming added liquid to the squash and diluted its flavor. As we were preparing squash one morning, it occurred to us that we were throwing away the answer to more squash flavor—the seeds and fibers. Instead of trashing the scooped-out remnants, we added them to the sautéed shallots and butter. In minutes, the room became fragrant with an earthy, sweet squash aroma, and the butter in our Dutch oven turned a brilliant shade of saffron. We added the water to the pan and proceeded with the steaming preparation. After the squash was cooked through, we strained the liquid of seeds, fibers, and spent shallot, then blended the soup.

To intensify the sweetness of the squash (but not make the soup sweet), we added a teaspoon of dark brown sugar just before serving. Not only was this batch of squash soup brighter in flavor, but it was more intense in color as well. We tested using canned chicken broth instead of water as the steaming liquid, but tasters felt that the chicken flavor overwhelmed the squash. To round out the flavor and introduce some richness we added ½ cup of heavy

cream. Now the soup was thick, rich, and suffused with pure squash flavor.

As is true with many creamed soups, texture is almost as important as flavor. We found blending the squash in batches with just enough liquid to make a thick puree worked best—the thicker base provided more friction and made it easier for the blender to smooth out any lumps or remaining squash fibers. Once all the squash was pureed to a silken texture, we added the remaining liquid and cream and briefly pulsed the soup to combine. We heated the soup briefly over a low flame, and stirred in a little freshly grated nutmeg. In under one hour and with only one pot, we made a squash soup that sacrificed no flavor and offered autumn in a bowl.

CUTTING BUTTERNUT SQUASH

With its thick skin and odd shape, butternut squash is notoriously difficult to cut, even with the best chef's knife. We prefer to use a cleaver and mallet.

1. Set the squash on a damp kitchen towel to hold it in place. Position the cleaver on the skin of the squash.

2. Strike the back of the cleaver with a mallet to drive the cleaver deep into the squash. Continue to hit the cleaver with the mallet until the cleaver cuts through the squash and opens it up.

Butternut Squash Soup

SERVES 4 TO 6

If you don't own a collapsible metal steaming basket, the removable insert from a pasta pot works well, too. See page 115 for information on other squash varieties that can be used in this soup. Some nice accompaniments are lightly toasted pumpkin seeds, a drizzle of aged balsamic vinegar, or a sprinkle of paprika.

4	tablespoons unsalted butter
I	large shallot, chopped fine
3	pounds butternut squash (about I large squash), cut in half lengthwise (see illustrations, left), and each half cut in half widthwise; seeds and strings scraped out and reserved (about ¼ cup)
6	cups water
	Salt
½	cup heavy cream
I	teaspoon dark brown sugar
	Pinch freshly grated nutmeg

1. Melt the butter in a large Dutch oven over medium-low heat until foaming. Add the shallot and cook, stirring frequently, until translucent, about 3 minutes. Add the squash scrapings and seeds, and cook, stirring occasionally, until the butter turns saffron color, about 4 minutes.

2. Add water and 1 teaspoon salt to the pot and

bring to a boil over high heat. Reduce the heat to medium-low, place the squash cut-side down in a steamer basket, and lower the basket into the pot. Cover and steam until the squash is completely tender, about 30 minutes. Take the pot off the heat, and use tongs to transfer the squash to a rimmed baking sheet. When cool enough to handle, use a large spoon to scrape the flesh from the skin. Reserve the squash flesh in a bowl and discard the skins.

3. Strain the steaming liquid through a mesh strainer into a second bowl; discard the solids in the strainer. (You should have 2½ to 3 cups of liquid.) Rinse and dry the pot.

4. Puree the squash in batches in the blender, pulsing on low and adding enough reserved steaming liquid to obtain a smooth consistency. Transfer the puree to the pot and stir in the remaining steaming liquid, cream, and brown sugar. Warm the soup over medium-low heat until hot, about 3 minutes. Stir in the nutmeg and adjust the seasonings, adding salt to taste. Serve immediately. (Soup can be refrigerated in an airtight container for several days. Warm over low heat until hot; do not boil.)

➤ VARIATIONS

Curried Squash Soup with Cilantro

Mix 4 tablespoons plain yogurt, 2 tablespoons minced fresh cilantro leaves, 1 teaspoon lime juice, and ⅛ teaspoon salt together in a small bowl. Refrigerate until needed. Follow recipe for Butternut Squash Soup, adding 2 teaspoons curry powder to the blender when pureeing the squash and liquid. Finish the soup as directed and ladle it into individual bowls. Spoon some of the cilantro-yogurt mixture into each bowl and serve immediately.

Squash Soup with Cinnamon-Sugar Croutons

A sprinkling of spicy but sweet croutons is a nice foil for the rich soup.

Adjust the oven rack to the middle position and heat the oven to 350 degrees. Remove crusts from 4 slices of white sandwich bread and cut bread into ½-inch cubes (you should have about 2 cups). Toss the bread cubes with 2 tablespoons melted butter in a medium bowl. In a small bowl, combine 4 teaspoons sugar and 1 teaspoon ground cinnamon; sprinkle over bread cubes and toss to combine. Spread the bread cubes in a single layer on parchment-lined baking sheet and bake until crisp, 8 to 10 minutes. (Croutons can be stored in an airtight container for several days.) Follow recipe for Butternut Squash Soup, sprinkling croutons over individual bowls of soup just before serving.

INGREDIENTS: Winter Squash Varieties

Butternut and acorn squash are the most commonly available winter squash varieties. In our tests, we found that while firm butternut squash makes excellent soup, acorn squash is too stringy and sour for this purpose. Of course, supermarkets and farmer's markets carry more varieties of squash than just your standard acorn and butternut. We were interested in learning how the different squash varieties would perform in our soup. Here are our top picks (ranked in order of preference) to use in our squash soup recipe. We do not recommend sugar pumpkin, spaghetti, or blue hubbard, which we found to be too fibrous and/or sour for use in soup.

CARNIVAL This squash is shaped like an acorn squash but has a yellow skin with green and orange stripes. The flesh is creamy, delicate, buttery, and sweet, and it produces a deep yellow soup.

DELICATA This squash is shaped like a zucchini and can be yellow or white with long green stripes. The flesh is sweet and has a ricelike flavor. It produces a beautiful pale orange soup.

BUTTERNUT This squash is shaped like a long-necked bell, and the skin is peach colored. The flesh is buttery and strong tasting and yields a lovely orange soup.

KABOCHA This squash is shaped like a small, squat pumpkin with dark green skin. The flesh is very thick and earthy, with a slightly sour or vegetal flavor. If using kabocha squash, use a 2½-pound squash and increase the brown sugar to 1 tablespoon.

SWEET DUMPLING This squash is shaped like an acorn squash but smaller, and the skin is yellow or white. The flesh is thin and has onion and corn overtones. If using sweet dumpling squash, increase the amount of squash to 5 pounds.

RED KURI This orange squash looks like an oblong and unridged pumpkin. The flesh is very mellow and delicate. If using red kuri squash, increase the brown sugar to 1 tablespoon.

CREAM OF TOMATO SOUP

RAINY SATURDAYS IN LATE WINTER BRING to mind the grilled cheese sandwiches and tomato soup of childhood. The sandwiches were made with squishy white bread and cheese from an oblong box. As for the soup, it came in a can, of course—and we all know which can. Long after our affection for other soups sealed in that small red and white icon has waned, our nostalgia for Campbell's cream of tomato soup persists. Few of us eat canned tomato soup these days, but some of us do have a vision of the perfect tomato soup. Our vision is a soup of Polartec softness, rich color, and a pleasing balance of sweetness and acidity.

To get a dose of reality, we opened a can of Campbell's. Though rich and tomatoey, it was also cloyingly sweet, not unlike a cream of ketchup soup. So we moved on to create a soup that would actually be as good as our childhood memories.

For our first tests, we used fresh out-of-season tomatoes. Arriving in the test kitchen, the tomatoes were cosmetically peerless, with gleaming red skins and crisp upright stems. But their taste was a different matter. Without exception, the soups they produced were anemic and completely lacking in tomato flavor. The soups containing flavor boosters such as carrots, celery, and onions failed even more strikingly to suggest a tomato soup. One made with a roux had the characteristics of a tomato gravy.

Not content to develop a recipe that would be worth making only during the one or two months of the year when tomatoes are in prime form, we turned to canned tomatoes. For our soup we selected fine canned organic diced tomatoes and added shallots, a bit of flour to give the finished product some body, a spoon of tomato paste and canned chicken broth to enrich the flavor, a splash of heavy cream and sherry for refinement, and a pinch of sugar for good measure. Though the resulting soup was dramatically better than those made with fresh winter tomatoes, it failed to make the cut; the flavor simply wasn't robust enough.

How do you get bigger flavor from canned tomatoes? If they were fresh and ripe, you might roast

them: The caramelization of sugar in the skins that occurs during roasting concentrates and intensifies the flavors. In the test kitchen, where almost any experiment is considered worth trying, we decided to roast canned tomatoes. We hoped that intense dry heat might evaporate the surface liquid and concentrate the flavor.

Leaving the above recipe otherwise unchanged, we switched from diced to whole tomatoes for ease of handling, drained and seeded them (reserving the juice for later), then laid them on a foil-covered rimmed baking sheet and sprinkled them with brown sugar, which we hoped would induce a surface caramelization. Only minutes after sliding our tray of tomatoes into a 450-degree oven, the test kitchen was filled with real tomato fragrance, and we knew we had done something right. The roasting made an extraordinary difference, intensifying the tomato flavor and mellowing the fruit's acidity. What's more, the rest of the soup

PREPARING TOMATOES FOR ROASTING

1. With your fingers, carefully open the whole tomatoes over a strainer set in a bowl and push out the seeds, allowing the juices to fall through the strainer and into the bowl.

2. Arrange the seeded tomatoes in a single layer on a foil-lined, rimmed baking sheet. The foil is essential; it keeps the tomatoes from scorching and sticking to the baking sheet. Let the roasted tomatoes cool slightly before trying to remove them from the foil.

could be prepared while the tomatoes roasted.

Only one minor visual detail marred our efforts. The intense flavor we'd achieved by roasting the tomatoes was not mirrored in the soup's color. The deep coronation red we admired while the soup simmered on the stovetop gave way to a faded circus orange during a round in the blender. The mechanical action of combining solids and liquids had aerated the soup and lightened the color. This wouldn't do. We decided to leave the rich tomato broth behind in the saucepan while pureeing the solids with just enough liquid to result in a soup of perfect smoothness. A finish of heavy cream and our vision of tomato soup had come to life.

Cream of Tomato Soup

SERVES 4

Use canned whole tomatoes that are not packed in puree; you will need some of the juice to make the soup. For information on specific brands, see right.

2	(28-ounce) cans whole tomatoes packed in juice, drained, 3 cups juice reserved
1½	tablespoons dark brown sugar
4	tablespoons unsalted butter
4	large shallots, minced
1	tablespoon tomato paste
	Pinch ground allspice
2	tablespoons all-purpose flour
1¾	cups homemade chicken stock or canned low-sodium chicken broth
½	cup heavy cream
2	tablespoons brandy or dry sherry
	Salt and cayenne pepper

1. Adjust the oven rack to the upper-middle position and heat the oven to 450 degrees. Line a rimmed baking sheet with foil. Seed and spread the tomatoes in a single layer on the foil (see illustrations on page 116). Sprinkle evenly with the brown sugar. Bake until all the liquid has evaporated and the tomatoes begin to color, about 30 minutes. Let the tomatoes cool slightly, then peel them off the foil; transfer to a small bowl and set aside.

2. Heat the butter over medium heat in a large saucepan until foaming. Add the shallots, tomato paste, and allspice. Reduce the heat to low, cover, and cook, stirring occasionally, until the shallots are softened, 8 to 10 minutes. Add the flour and cook, stirring constantly, until thoroughly combined, about 30 seconds. Whisking constantly, gradually add the chicken stock; stir in the reserved tomato juice and the roasted tomatoes. Cover, increase the heat to medium, and bring to a boil. Reduce the heat to low and simmer to blend flavors, stirring occasionally, about 10 minutes.

3. Pour the mixture through a strainer and into a medium bowl; rinse out the saucepan. Transfer the tomatoes and solids in the strainer to a blender; add 1 cup strained liquid and puree until smooth. Place the pureed mixture and remaining strained liquid in the saucepan. Add the cream and warm over low heat until hot, about 3 minutes. Off heat, stir in the brandy and season with salt and cayenne to taste. (Soup can be refrigerated in an airtight container for 2 days. Warm over low heat until hot; do not boil.) Serve immediately.

INGREDIENTS: Canned Whole Tomatoes

Canned whole tomatoes are the closest product to fresh. Whole tomatoes, either plum or round, are steamed to remove their skins and then packed in tomato juice or puree. We prefer tomatoes packed in juice; they generally have a fresher, more lively flavor. Puree has a cooked tomato flavor that can impart a slightly stale, tired flavor to the whole can.

To find the best canned whole tomatoes, we tasted 11 brands, both straight from the can and in a simple tomato sauce. Muir Glen (an organic brand available in most supermarkets and natural foods stores) and Progresso finished at the head of the pack. Either brand is an excellent choice in cream of tomato soup or any recipe that calls for canned whole tomatoes.

CREAMY MUSHROOM SOUP

MUSHROOMS ARE THE MEATIEST VEGETABLE: substantial, distinctive, and rich. That is why we are constantly surprised by the number of mushroom soups that, given such promising material, offer so little in return. Yet a superb mushroom soup is simple to achieve if you know what you're doing.

We believe a soup must be purposefully chunky or decidedly smooth. None of this lazy in-between stuff. In this case, we opted for a pureed soup finished with cream. We think a mushroom soup of this type should be like a fine warm sweater—not cashmere, but not nubby fisherman knit, either; richly textured and hued, not too thick, not too thin; not casual, but not dressy. Merino, perhaps, or alpaca.

The starting point was clear. Traditional French mushroom soups (and mushroom soups are traditionally French) use white button mushrooms sautéed in butter with onions or shallots. The sautéed mushrooms are simmered in a white veal or chicken stock, pureed, and then finished with cream and sherry. Nutmeg or thyme provides the narrow range of flavoring options.

Given this history, we did not feel constricted by the uniformity of recipes we found in our initial research. We had expected as much. A mushroom soup is obliged to have a faultlessly smooth texture and to taste of mushrooms. That's it. Additional "stuff" simply brings the soup off course. We also decided to rule out any combination of fresh wild mushrooms for the base of the soup; they are expensive and can be difficult to find. Instead, we wanted a recipe that would call on the real virtues of the white mushroom, a readily available ingredient that is often underestimated. On the other hand, a soupçon of dried mushrooms seemed a reasonable option if the flavor needed encouragement.

We began our testing with the mushrooms themselves. Coaxing forth their flavor would be the premier issue. In the past we had "sweated" sliced mushrooms in butter in a covered pan to soften them up and release their juices. But we were interested in seeing how roasting would affect their flavor in a soup. Roasted mushrooms appealed to us not only because they are a sublime eating experience but also because we saw them as a means of losing the chop-chop segment of the recipe altogether. Many people chafe at the idea of using a knife for what it was designed to do and are always on the lookout for a mechanical shortcut of some sort. We hoped that the roasting and subsequent shrinkage would reduce the mushrooms to manageably sized pieces that could be simmered in stock until spent and then pureed.

So against 2 pounds of roasted mushrooms we sliced and sautéed 2 pounds of raw mushrooms. Both batches were simmered in chicken stock and pureed, finished with cream, and tasted. To our surprise, the roasted mushroom soup was less flavorful than the soup made with sautéed mushrooms. Juices released during the roasting process had browned on the sheet pan and were, for all intents and purposes, irretrievable.

Our next attempt to minimize chopping was more mundane. A cook we knew also hated chopping mushrooms (though, to be fair, she was dealing with 10 to 15 pounds) and so one day made a soup by pulsing the mushrooms in a food processor before sautéing them. The unevenly sliced scraps

INGREDIENTS: Button Mushrooms

With more than 300 edible mushroom varieties, it's surprising that until recently most supermarkets carried only one type of fresh mushroom consistently: the white button *(Agaricus bisporus)*. The primary reason? Availability.

But the "everyday" nature of this mushroom should not blind us to its virtues. In fact, until the turn of the twentieth century, even this mushroom was considered rare and exotic. The French became the first to cultivate white mushrooms when seventeenth-century Parisian melon growers discovered that compost from their melon crops provided a favorable growing medium for mushrooms. Soon mushrooms (now grown in specially prepared caves) dotted the city, earning them the nickname *champignon de Paris*.

In the United States, florists in Pennsylvania first utilized the dark spaces under their greenhouse shelves for mushroom cultivation in the late nineteenth century. These efforts were followed in the twentieth century with the manufacture of mushroom "houses," which made cultivation easier by providing a stable, controlled environment similar to that of the French caves. Although other types of mushrooms are now cultivated (oyster, shiitake, and portobello, to name a few), the white button has become the world's most commonly cultivated fungus, with the United States leading global consumption. Whereas wild mushrooms enjoy only seasonal availability, mushroom cultivation ensures a consistent supply of that unique, meaty flavor.

became bruised and watery, and the resulting soup neither looked nor tasted good. Just to be sure, we repeated her effort; sure enough, the soup made with food-processed mushrooms had a blackish hue and an unfulfilled flavor. Though we cannot say precisely why this is the case, we can only assume that the food processor brings out the juices in a manner aggressive enough to do some damage to subsequent flavor and that the unevenly pulsed bits do not sauté at the same rate.

Butter was the obvious fat to go with here, earning high marks for flavor transport while requiring no application of high heat (which might have supported a call for olive oil, since it burns less easily). Six tablespoons of butter did the trick, an amount that shouldn't induce cardiac arrest in someone reading the ingredient list. Shallots were more delicate tasting and more supportive of the mushroom flavor than onions, although we did find that two small, minced garlic cloves brightened the flavor. Nutmeg was also in; thyme was out.

The sliced mushrooms required an initial toss in hot melted butter (which bore the translucent shimmer and perfume of the sautéed shallots and garlic and had been dusted with ground nutmeg), followed by prolonged cooking over low heat in a covered Dutch oven. This half-moist/half-dry heat in close quarters brings out flavors, and it is far superior to boiling a vegetable away in broth or water until softened. The technique is similar to cooking a chicken in a clay pot with only its juices to moisten it—what the French call *poêler*—and it brings forth intense flavor. In contrast, a soup made with sliced mushrooms that were sautéed in an uncovered skillet, and thus stripped of their liquid and browned, suffered in much the same way as the roasted mushrooms.

After the initial cooking of the button mushrooms, we added chicken stock and a pinch of dried porcini mushrooms, which torqued up the flavor. (Water alone, we discovered, would not produce the trophy flavor that even watery canned broth managed to impart.) Twenty minutes of measured simmering drained every last bit of fiber and flavor from the mushrooms and fused the small family of flavors together. Once run through the blender, the soup took on a beautiful deep taupe, provoking tasters to fantasize about paint colors and loveseat sofa fabric (a stark contrast with the institutional flecked beige that blights most mushroom soups). With no thickening to mar its innocence, the texture of the soup was light, but it had body from the puréed mushrooms and heavy cream. The cream and the splash of Madeira added at the close of business rounded out the flavors and added just the right touch of sweetness.

Creamy Mushroom Soup

SERVES 6 TO 8

To make sure that the soup has a fine, velvety texture, puree it hot off the stove, but do not fill the blender jar more than halfway, as the hot liquid may cause the lid to pop off the jar.

6	tablespoons unsalted butter
6	large shallots, minced (about ¾ cup)
2	small cloves garlic, minced
½	teaspoon freshly grated nutmeg
2	pounds white button mushrooms, wiped clean and sliced ¼ inch thick
3½	cups homemade chicken stock or canned low-sodium chicken broth
4	cups hot water
½	ounce dried porcini mushrooms, rinsed well
⅓	cup Madeira or dry sherry
I	cup heavy cream
2	teaspoons lemon juice
	Salt and ground black pepper
I	recipe Sautéed Wild Mushrooms (page 120) for garnish (optional)

1. Melt the butter in a large stockpot or Dutch oven over medium-low heat. When the foaming subsides, add the shallots and sauté, stirring frequently, until softened, about 4 minutes. Stir in the garlic and nutmeg and cook until fragrant, about 1 minute longer. Increase the heat to medium, add the sliced mushrooms, and stir to coat with butter. Cook, stirring occasionally, until the mushrooms release some liquid, about 7 minutes. Reduce the heat to medium-low, cover the pot, and cook, stirring occasionally, until the mushrooms have released all their liquid, about 20 minutes. Add the chicken stock, water, and porcini mushrooms. Cover, bring to a simmer, then

reduce the heat to low, and simmer until the mushrooms are fully tender, about 20 minutes.

2. Puree the soup in batches in a blender until smooth, filling the blender jar only halfway for each batch. Rinse and dry the pot. Return the soup to the pot. Stir in the Madeira and cream and bring to a simmer over low heat. Add the lemon juice and season to taste with salt and pepper. (Soup can be refrigerated in an airtight container for up to 4 days. Warm over low heat until hot; do not boil.) Serve, garnishing each bowl with some sautéed wild mushrooms if desired.

INGREDIENTS: "Wild" Mushrooms

To sprinkle our mushroom soup with a bit of textural interest, we chose four mushroom varieties to sauté: shiitake, oyster, cremini, and chanterelle. The first three are wild mushrooms that are now cultivated to be available year-round. The chanterelle is a wild mushroom available in the spring.

Though the stems of button mushrooms are perfectly usable, the stems of the wild mushrooms we used were tough, so we removed them. In each case, 8 ounces of untrimmed, uncooked mushrooms yielded 1 to 1½ cups of sautéed mushrooms, just the right amount to garnish a pot of soup. You can use any one variety of mushroom as a garnish, or you can mix the varieties. Because each has a distinct cooking time, each should be sautéed separately even if you plan to mix varieties for the garnish.

SHIITAKE is an esteemed mushroom of Japan and China, tan to dark brown in color. Our tasters described them as woody, with earthy lower notes, savory, and meaty.

OYSTER MUSHROOMS are beige, cream, or gray in color with ruffled edges. They are delicate and best cooked only briefly. Tasters described them as redolent of fried oysters, delicate and briny.

CREMINI MUSHROOMS have the same shape as white button mushrooms but are brown in color and more intensely flavored than their pale cousins. (They are actually small portobellos.) Tasters described them as rich and sweet, like a caramelized button mushroom.

CHANTERELLE MUSHROOMS are bright yellow to pale orange in color and grow under oak trees. Tasters found them nutty and fruity.

Sautéed Wild Mushrooms

MAKES ENOUGH TO GARNISH
6 TO 8 BOWLS OF SOUP

Float a few sautéed mushrooms in each bowl of soup for visual, textural, and flavor appeal.

2   tablespoons unsalted butter
8   ounces shiitake, chanterelle, oyster, or cremini mushrooms, stems trimmed and discarded, mushrooms wiped clean and sliced thin
     Salt and ground black pepper

1. Heat the butter in a medium skillet over low heat. When the foam subsides, add the mushrooms and sprinkle with salt and pepper to taste. Cover and cook, stirring occasionally, until the mushrooms release their liquid, about 10 minutes for shiitakes and chanterelles, about 5 minutes for oysters, and about 9 minutes for cremini.

2. Uncover and continue to cook, stirring occasionally, until the liquid released by the mushrooms has evaporated and the mushrooms are browned, about 2 minutes for shiitakes, about 3 minutes for chanterelles, and about 2 minutes for oysters and cremini. Use the mushrooms immediately as a garnish for bowls of soup.

MUSHROOM–BARLEY SOUP

CREAMY MUSHROOM SOUP IS REFINED AND sophisticated. But mushrooms can make a hearty, rugged soup, especially when barley is added to the pot. That said, mushroom-barley soup is often misrepresented as barley-mushroom soup, meaning that the mushroom flavor is weak and the barley takes over, creating more of a barley porridge than a barley-enhanced soup. We wanted to create a mushroom-barley soup that was all about the headiness of mushrooms, with the barley lending a bit of texture and thickening power. In addition, we wanted mushroom-barley soup to be able to stand on its own two feet without leaning on a time-consuming homemade beef stock—a common ingredient in most recipes.

We started by analyzing recipes and cooking a variety of mushroom-barley soups. One soup that showed promise started by sautéing diced beef in some oil, cooking the mushrooms and remaining vegetables in the rendered beef fat, and then adding the liquid component directly to the pan. While this soup tasted rich and full-bodied, the beef flavor overwhelmed the subtle earthiness of the mushrooms; from this point on, we ruled out using any beef in the soup.

The other quick conclusion we made concerned the ratio of barley to soup liquid. In recipes uncovered during our research, this ratio varied from 2 teaspoons to 2 tablespoons of barley per cup of liquid. Knowing that barley is a headstrong and somewhat tyrannical grain, we ventured a guess that the lower barley-to-liquid ratio would be more appropriate. As it turned out, about 1 tablespoon per cup of liquid proved best. This provided just the right interchange between the barley and the soup, allowing a couple of nuggets to find their way into each spoonful without overwhelming the other ingredients.

Now that we knew that we weren't going to include beef in our ingredient list and that just ½ cup of barley could be used in a pot of soup, we had to find a way to boost the soup's flavor and give it some complexity. We were working with a composite recipe that started by sautéing onions and shallots in vegetable oil. Sliced button mushrooms went into the pot next, followed by carrots and garlic once the mushrooms were tender. Chicken stock, barley, bay leaf, and thyme were added and the mixture was simmered until the barley was tender. We identified three different ingredients that might build flavor in this soup—tomato paste, wine, and dried porcini mushrooms.

While some tasters found the flavor of the tomato paste comforting, other tasters argued that its flavor and color (a burnished orange-red) was too much like canned soup. On the wine front, red wine muddied the flavors of the soup rather than bringing them together, whereas white wine made the soup base too harsh. It was the porcini broth (dried porcinis steeped in hot chicken stock) that won the crowd, providing a boost of mushroom essence and richness.

Up to this point, we had been using the supermarket staple, white button mushrooms, in all of our trials. With the soup basics in check, we decided to tinker with different mushroom varieties. Not wanting to get too esoteric, we stuck to mushroom varieties

SCIENCE: To Wash or Not to Wash Mushrooms

Common culinary wisdom dictates that mushrooms should never, ever be washed. Put these spongy fungi under the faucet or in a bowl, the dictum goes, and they will soak up water like a sponge. Like most cooks, we had always blindly followed this precept. But when we learned that mushrooms consist of more than 80 percent water, we began to question their ability to absorb yet more liquid. As we so often do in situations like this, we consulted the works of food scientist and author Harold McGee. Sure enough, in his book *The Curious Cook* (North Point Press, 1990), we found an experiment he had devised to test this very piece of accepted mushroom lore. We decided to duplicate McGee's work in our test kitchen.

We weighed out 6 ounces of white mushrooms and put them into a bowl, then added water to cover and let them sit. After five minutes we shook off the surface water and weighed them again. Our results replicated McGee's—the total weight gain for all the mushrooms together was ¼ ounce, which translated to about 1½ teaspoons of water.

We suspected that even this gain represented mostly surface moisture rather than absorption, so we repeated the experiment with 6 ounces of broccoli, which no one would claim to be an absorbent vegetable. The weight gain after a five-minute soak was almost identical—⅕ ounce—suggesting that most of the moisture was clinging to the surface of both vegetables rather than being absorbed by them.

As it turns out, then, mushrooms can be cleaned in the same way other vegetables are cleaned—rinsed under cold water. However, it's best to rinse them just before cooking and to avoid rinsing altogether if you are using them uncooked, since the surfaces of wet mushrooms turn dark and slimy when they're exposed to air for more than four to five minutes.

Of course, if the mushrooms are fairly clean (as is often the case with button mushrooms), you can simply wipe them with a damp paper towel. You don't have to wash them, but it's nice to know you can if need be.

that now make regular appearances in many grocery stores—portobellos, creminis, and shiitakes.

Prior to this undertaking, we thought our soup was pretty good. But when we tried the different mushroom varieties, we realized it had the potential to be even better. While the shiitakes added an unwelcome pungency (and in texture became similar to fat rubber bands), the creminis and the portobellos (which, as mentioned elsewhere, are actually just overgrown creminis) gave the soup bravado. The white button version paled in comparison with the versions made from these brown mushrooms. The creminis gave the soup an elegant look and somewhat "beefy" flavor, whereas the portobellos darkened the soup to an inky brown and gave it a more intense mushroom flavor.

Next, we examined how to cut the mushrooms. We tried slicing, dicing, and cutting the mushrooms into chunky quarters. For the smaller creminis, we preferred cutting the mushrooms into quarters. For the portobellos, however, it was important to dice them small, otherwise they sautéed on the outside but steamed on the inside and tasted rubbery.

Mushroom-Barley Soup

SERVES 6

This soup works well with either portobello or cremini mushrooms. The portobellos will provide a darker and more mushroomy liquid, whereas the creminis will yield a lighter broth and a rounder, more beefy flavor. See page 82 for more information about pearl barley.

½	ounce dried porcini mushrooms
9	cups homemade chicken stock or canned low-sodium chicken broth
¼	cup vegetable oil
1	large onion, chopped medium
2	medium shallots, chopped small
1	pound (about 7 medium) portobello caps, wiped clean and cut into ¼-inch dice, or 1 pound cremini mushrooms, stemmed and cut into quarters
1¼	teaspoons salt
2	medium carrots, peeled and chopped medium

3	medium cloves garlic, minced
½	cup pearl barley
1	bay leaf
1	teaspoon minced fresh thyme leaves or ¼ teaspoon dried thyme

1. Place the porcini mushrooms in a small bowl, cover with 1½ cups hot chicken stock, and soak until softened, about 20 minutes. Carefully lift the porcinis from the water, letting any grit stay on the bottom of the bowl (see illustration on page 85). Chop the porcinis. Strain the soaking liquid through a strainer lined with a paper towel and set over a measuring cup (see illustration on page 85). Set the porcinis and their soaking liquid aside.

2. Heat the oil in a large stockpot or Dutch oven over medium-high heat. Add the onion and shallots, reduce the heat to medium, and cook, stirring frequently, until translucent and just beginning to brown, about 5 minutes. Add the fresh mushrooms and ¼ teaspoon salt. Cook, stirring frequently, until the mushrooms are tender, 8 to 10 minutes. Add the carrots and garlic and cook until the garlic is fragrant but not browned, about 1 minute.

3. Add the remaining 7½ cups chicken stock along with the porcini soaking liquid, chopped porcinis, barley, bay leaf, thyme, and remaining 1 teaspoon salt. Bring to a boil, reduce the heat to low, cover, and simmer gently until the barley is tender, about 50 minutes. Remove and discard the bay leaf and adjust the seasonings. Serve immediately.

➤ VARIATION

Vegetarian Mushroom-Barley Soup

The only difference between the vegetarian adaptation of this recipe is that the porcinis are steeped directly in a quick mushroom stock, which is used as a substitute for the chicken stock. Buy whole portobello mushrooms—the stems are used in the stock recipe; likewise, if using cremini mushrooms, reserve the stems for the stock.

Prepare Quick Mushroom Stock (recipe follows). Follow recipe for Mushroom-Barley Soup, omitting step 1 and replacing the chicken stock and porcini soaking liquid in step 3 with the mushroom stock.

Quick Mushroom Stock

MAKES ABOUT 9 CUPS

This stock serves as the base for Vegetarian Mushroom-Barley Soup on page 122.

2	tablespoons vegetable oil
1	medium onion, chopped medium
	Several ounces reserved mushroom stems (see note on page 122), roughly chopped
3	medium cloves garlic, chopped
10	cups water
½	ounce dried porcini mushrooms

1. Heat the oil in a large stockpot or Dutch oven over medium-high heat. Add the onion, reduce the heat to medium, and cook, stirring frequently, until translucent and just beginning to brown, about 5 minutes. Add the mushroom stems and cook, stirring frequently until tender, about 8 to 10 minutes. Add the garlic and cook until fragrant, about 1 minute. Add the water and the porcini mushrooms. Bring to a boil, reduce the heat to low, cover, and simmer for 30 minutes.

2. Line a large strainer with cheesecloth or paper towels. Pour the stock through the strainer; discard the vegetables.

RUSTIC POTATO-LEEK SOUP

WE LOVE POTATOES IN ANY FORM, AND leeks, with their gentle taste of onion, are among our favorite soup aromatics. And we have always liked the classic creamy soup that French cooks make from potatoes and leeks. But sometimes this recipe seems a little too refined. At times we want these two ingredients at their most basic; we want to eat them while resting our elbows on a scarred, wooden table, a cantankerous piece of bread in one hand. So we decided to part company with the creamy French classic and take on the challenge of a more peasant-style, chunky French soup.

Ironically, the two ingredients that should make this soup great (potatoes and leeks) can also be its downfall. The potatoes should actually play only a supporting role; the leeks, though gritty and time-consuming to clean, are the real star of this soup. Cooking time is also crucial. Undercook the soup and the flavors will not meld; cook it too long and you will have a mixture of broken-down bits with little flavor or bite. These were the challenges we bore in mind when we set out.

We tested the potatoes first. (For more information on types of potatoes, see page 125.) Quickly eliminating high-starch, low-moisture baking potatoes, which broke down immediately, we duly rejected the flavorful, medium-starch Yukon Gold as well. These potatoes broke down, too—just not as quickly. We settled on waxy, low-starch Red Bliss potatoes, which held their texture and did not become waterlogged during cooking. Then we reduced the proportion of potatoes altogether, giving leeks the leading role.

Next we wanted to pump up the flavor of the soup. We decided to use not only the white part of the leek but also the light green part (the very dark green part is tough and should be discarded), and we left the chopped pieces large enough to create textural interest. A whopping 4 pounds of leeks used this way provided nonstop flavor. Water wasn't dynamic enough to stand up to it, so we used chicken stock instead.

But our real breakthrough came in the province of technique. We knew that potatoes and leeks would need different simmering times. Stewing the leeks over a low flame to coax out their flavor, we added the potatoes later, with the chicken stock, then simmered them until almost tender. At that point we removed the pot from the heat, allowing the potatoes to finish cooking in the stock's residual heat so they would not overcook and become mushy. The result: a soup with perfectly cooked potatoes, sweet and tender leeks, and an outspoken leek flavor. Because the potatoes were not cooked long enough to release their starch, we added a little flour with the leeks, giving the soup just the right amount of body to pull everything together.

Rustic Potato-Leek Soup

SERVES 6 TO 8

This soup is hearty enough to serve as a main course, perhaps accompanied by crusty bread and preceded or followed by salad. Leeks differ. If yours have large desirable white and light green sections, use 4 pounds of leeks; if they're short on these parts, go with 5 pounds.

4 to 5	pounds leeks (see note)
6	tablespoons unsalted butter
1	tablespoon all-purpose flour
5¼	cups homemade chicken stock or canned low-sodium chicken broth
1	bay leaf
1¾	pounds red potatoes (about 5 medium), peeled and cut into ¾-inch dice
	Salt and ground black pepper

1. Cut off the roots and tough dark green portion of the leeks, leaving the white portion and about 3 inches of the light green portion. Clean the leeks (see the illustrations at right). Slice the leeks in half lengthwise and chop into 1-inch pieces. (You should have about 11 cups.)

2. Heat the butter in a large stockpot or Dutch oven over medium-low heat until foaming. Stir in the leeks, increase the heat to medium, cover, and cook, stirring occasionally, until the leeks are tender but not mushy, 15 to 20 minutes; do not brown the leeks. Sprinkle the flour over the leeks and stir to coat evenly. Cook until the flour dissolves, about 2 minutes.

3. Increase the heat to high; whisking constantly, gradually add the stock. Add the bay leaf and potatoes, cover, and bring to a boil. Reduce the heat to medium-low and simmer, covered, until the potatoes are almost tender, 5 to 7 minutes. Remove the pot from the heat and let stand, covered, until the potatoes are tender and the flavors meld, 10 to 15 minutes. Discard the bay leaf and season with salt and pepper to taste. (Soup can be refrigerated in an airtight container for up to 2 days. Warm over low heat until hot; do not boil.) Serve immediately.

➤ VARIATIONS

Rustic Potato-Leek Soup with Kielbasa

Eight ounces of cooked ham, cut into ½-inch dice, can be substituted for the sausage, if desired. Whichever you choose, season the soup with care, since both ham and kielbasa are fully seasoned.

Follow recipe for Rustic Potato-Leek Soup, stirring in 8 ounces kielbasa sausage, cut into ½-inch slices, just before removing the pot from the heat in step 3. Proceed as directed.

Rustic Potato-Leek Soup with White Beans

Follow recipe for Rustic Potato-Leek Soup, reducing potatoes to 2 medium (about ¾ pound). Just before removing the pot from the heat in step 3, stir in 1 cup hot water and 1 cup canned cannellini beans that have been drained and rinsed well. Proceed as directed.

TWO WAYS TO CLEAN LEEKS

Leeks are often quite dirty and gritty, so they require thorough cleaning. There are two ways to do this. Both methods require that you first cut the green portion into quarters lengthwise, leaving the root end intact.

Hold the leek under running water and shuffle the cut layers like a deck of cards.

An alternative is to slosh the cut end of the leek up and down in a bowl of water.

INGREDIENTS: Potatoes

Although all vegetables vary by size and freshness, most markets carry only a single variety. Broccoli is broccoli, carrots are carrots. Even when there are several varieties (as with heirloom tomatoes), most varieties can be used interchangeably in recipes. Yes, one tomato might look a bit different or be a bit sweeter than another, but they all will taste fine in salads.

With potatoes, this is not the case. Make french fries with red potatoes and the fries will be greasy and heavy. Use russets in salad or corn chowder and they will fall apart into a soggy mess. The fact that dozens of potato varieties are grown in this country makes the question of which potato is best for a specific recipe even more confusing. At any time you may see as many as five or six kinds of potatoes in your supermarket. Go to a farmer's market and you may see a dozen varieties. Some potatoes are sold by varietal name (such as Red Bliss or Yukon Gold), but others are sold by generic name (all-purpose, baking, etc.).

To make sense of this confusion, it is helpful to group potatoes into three major categories based on their ratio of solids (mostly starch) to water. The categories are high-starch/low-moisture potatoes, medium-starch potatoes, and low-starch/high-moisture potatoes.

High-starch/low-moisture potatoes, such as russets or Idahos, will generally lose their shape when simmered in soups or stews. Because they have so little moisture, they tend to soak up liquid as they cook and will eventually disintegrate. This can be desirable (especially if you want the potatoes to thicken a soup).

Medium-starch potatoes, such as Yukon Golds and Yellow Finns, will do a better job of holding their shape but share many traits in common with high-starch potatoes.

Low-starch/high-moisture potatoes will hold their shape better than other potatoes when simmered. This category includes all red-skinned potatoes, such as Red Bliss and Red Creamer, as well as freshly dug potatoes, which are often labeled "new" potatoes. Low-starch potatoes should be selected when potatoes are to hold their shape in a soup or stew.

CORN CHOWDER

WHILE IT IS MOST EASILY APPRECIATED ON the cob, fresh corn also lends itself well to another American favorite: corn chowder. The ingredients in most corn chowder recipes are relatively standard and certainly simple enough. There are the corn and other vegetables, usually potatoes and onions at minimum; there are the liquids, water or corn or chicken stock enriched with some sort of dairy; and there's some sort of fat, be it butter, bacon, or the traditional favorite, salt pork. Most recipes also have in common a reliance on the time-honored technique of first cooking the onions in fat to develop flavor and then adding the liquids and vegetables. Comfortable with this basic approach, we decided to build our master recipe from the ground up. We would first test the fat, then the liquids, and finally the solids, determining how to season and thicken the chowder along the way.

We knew from the outset that we wanted our chowder to be loaded with fresh corn flavor. What became apparent after testing a few recipes is that the texture and flavor of the base (the dairy-enriched liquid) are also critical to a great chowder. The first contributor to the base is fat. Because lots of people haven't cooked with salt pork and some shy away from bacon, we were hoping that butter or oil would be adequate substitutes, but tests proved otherwise. Chowders prepared with corn oil were bland and insipid. Butter was better, but it failed to add complexity of flavor to the chowder. Surprisingly, rendered bacon fat also failed to add much interesting flavor.

Tradition, in the form of salt pork, served the chowder best, giving the base a deep, resonant flavor. Salt pork comes from the pig's belly and consists mostly of fat, striated with thin layers of meat. It can be confused with fatback, which is pure fat and comes from the pig's back. Make sure that what you buy at the market is salt pork; because it's both salted and cured and also contains meat, salt pork is more flavorful than fatback. (For more information on salt pork, see page 129.)

The next question concerning the fat was how to use it. What was the best way to render the fat? Was it necessary (or desirable) to cut up the salt pork into small pieces? Should the salt pork be removed from the pan after rendering, or is there an advantage to leaving it in the pot?

The chowder developed a truly delectable flavor when the salt pork stayed in the pot throughout cooking. Cutting it in bits, though, proved to be undesirable; we found those little pieces to be tough

REMOVING KERNELS FROM CORN COBS

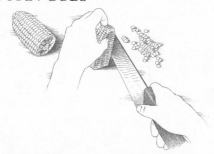

Tapered ears of corn can wobble on cutting boards, and kernels can fly around the kitchen. To work safely and more neatly, we cut the ear in half crosswise and then stand the half-ears on their cut surfaces, which are flat and stable.

and chewy. Our solution was to use two big chunks that could be removed easily at the end of cooking. One shortcoming of this technique was that the same amount of salt pork cut into a couple of big pieces produced less fat than all of those small pieces, and it wasn't quite enough to sweat the onions. We compensated by adding a little butter to the pot.

With this first important building block of flavor in place, we could go on to consider how best to infuse the chowder base with the flavor of corn. Corn stock, corn puree, corn juice, and corn pulp were all possibilities.

We made two quick stocks with corn cobs and husks, using water in one and chicken stock in the other. Although both brews had some corn flavor,

SCIENCE: Extending the Corn Chowder Season

Midsummer through early autumn is prime time for fresh corn, but corn chowder's appeal continues into the cold months. We wondered if we could extend the fresh corn chowder season and what would be the best way to do it. Could we simply freeze the chowder we made in September? Or would we need to freeze the corn and make the chowder on the spot? If so, what was the best way to freeze fresh corn?

For starters, we stocked the freezer with a quart of the chowder and three batches of just-harvested corn: one batch on the cob frozen raw; another batch of kernels, with the requisite amount of grated and scraped corn frozen separately, also raw; and another batch blanched on the cob before freezing.

Three months later, with winter now at hand, we removed what we hoped would be the sweet remains of summer from the freezer and got to work. The frozen chowder was easy to dismiss; its flavor was hollow and overly sweet, and the herbs tasted dried out and slightly moldy. In short, it was awful. Next, we made chowder from each of the batches of frozen corn. Chowder made from the corn frozen raw on the cob had a slightly stale freezer taste and looked curdled. Chowder made with pregrated and scraped corn and kernels was worse. Its flavor was stale and dull, it had a plastic breath, and this chowder, too, looked curdled. The chowder prepared with corn blanched on the cob and then frozen was a different story altogether. It conveyed the clean, fresh flavor of summer corn, and its texture was completely pleasing.

John Rushing, professor of food science at North Carolina State University, explained the chemistry behind what seemed

to us a small miracle. A good part of what gives fresh-picked corn its wonderful juiciness and flavor are its sugars. Once picked, however, these sugars start to break down, turning into starch. Primarily responsible for this unfortunate transformation, according to Rushing, are two groups of "marker" enzymes, peroxidase and catalase. Cold temperatures slow down the action of these enzymes considerably (which is why fresh-picked corn should go straight to the refrigerator and remain there until cooked), but the right amount of heat can stop them dead in their tracks. Blanching the corn completely disables the enzymes, thereby protecting the corn from decay. When we asked Rushing how long the blanched and frozen corn could be expected to maintain its quality, he said that deterioration from oxidation would become apparent after about six months.

Because freezing preserves quality but does not improve it, blanching the best just-picked corn you can find makes sense. Here's how to proceed when planning to use the corn for the chowder recipe: Husk 10 ears of corn and bring one gallon of water to boil in a large pot. Add half of the corn, return the pot to a boil, and cook for five minutes. Remove the cobs and place them immediately in a bowl of ice water for four minutes to stop the cooking action (a process known as shocking). Spread the cooled ears out on a clean kitchen towel to dry, and repeat blanching and shocking process with remaining corn. Place the dry corn in zipper-lock freezer bags, remove the air, seal the bags, then date and freeze. When preparing the chowder, cook the whole kernels in step 3 for just two to three minutes to obtain that wonderfully fresh corn crunch.

their overall effect on the chowder was minimal; making corn stock was clearly not worth the effort. We did learn, though, that water diluted the flavor of the chowder while chicken stock improved it. Chicken stock would be our liquid of choice for the base.

Looking for a quick and easy solution, we next tried pureeing the corn kernels and dumping them into the chowder. This wasn't going to work. The hulls made for an unpleasantly rough texture.

In our research, we identified grating and scraping as a good means of extracting flavor from corn to be used for chowder. This approach is time-consuming and messy, but the result convinced us that it was worth the effort. Here was one of the secrets to great corn chowder. The pulp was thick, lush, smooth-textured, and full of corn flavor. When added to the chowder, it improved both flavor and texture dramatically.

Our next concern was the dairy, and, as it turned out, the thickener to be used. A problem with the dairy component of chowder is its tendency to curdle when heated, with lower-fat products such as 2 percent milk more likely to curdle than high-fat products such as heavy cream. It's the protein component of dairy that causes curdling, and heavy cream is not susceptible because it has so much fat (about 40 percent); the protein molecules are thus completely surrounded by fat molecules, which keep the proteins from breaking down. But we could not rely entirely on heavy cream to prevent curdling, as our tasters rejected this version. In their collective

opinion, it tasted "like hot corn ice cream."

While some heavy cream was needed to give the base some depth of character, whole milk, which is wonderfully neutral and therefore capable of being infused with corn flavor, would make up the larger part of the dairy. This composition gave us some concern about curdling, which is where the thickening factor came in. We realized that the most practical thickener to use would be flour, which is known to help stabilize dairy proteins and thereby prevent curdling. Having a dual objective of both thickening the base and stabilizing the dairy made our work easier. To prevent curdling, the flour has to be in the pot before the dairy is added. The logical choice of technique, then, would be to make a roux, stirring the flour into the fat and onions at the beginning of the cooking process.

Determining the chowder solids was a relatively simple matter. Onions, potatoes, and corn kernels were a given; the questions were what variety of onion and potato and how much of each? All-purpose onions and leeks were serviceable, but Spanish onions proved best, adding flavor without dominating the other ingredients. The favorite potatoes were red potatoes, which remained firm and looked great with their skins left on. We celebrated the symmetry of batch 41 when we realized that 3 cups of kernels, 2 cups of potatoes, and 1 cup of cooked onion (the volume of two cups raw) was perfect. Whole corn kernels added authenticity to the chowder, and we learned that adding the kernels after the

MILKING CORN

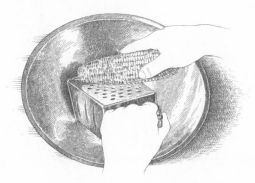

1. Start by grating the corn ears on a box grater.

2. Finish by firmly scraping any remaining kernels off the cob with the back of a butter knife.

potatoes have been cooked until tender, then cooking the kernels just briefly, resulted in a fresh-from-the-cob corn flavor. A bit of garlic added some depth and fullness, while thyme, parsley, and bay leaves helped to round out the flavors.

Corn Chowder

SERVES 6

Be sure to use salt pork, not fatback, for the chowder. Streaks of lean meat distinguish salt pork from fatback; fatback is pure fat. (See page 129 for more details.) We prefer Spanish onions for their sweet, mild flavor, but all-purpose yellow onions will work fine too.

10	medium ears fresh yellow corn, husks and silk removed
3	ounces salt pork, trimmed of rind (see illustration, right) and cut into two 1-inch cubes
1	tablespoon unsalted butter
1	large onion, preferably Spanish, chopped fine
2	medium cloves garlic, minced
3	tablespoons all-purpose flour
3	cups homemade chicken stock or canned low-sodium chicken broth
2	medium red potatoes (about 12 ounces), scrubbed (see illustration on page 81) and cut into 1/4-inch dice (about 2 cups)
1	medium bay leaf
1	teaspoon minced fresh thyme leaves or 1/4 teaspoon dried thyme
2	cups whole milk
1	cup heavy cream
2	tablespoons minced fresh parsley leaves
1 1/4	teaspoons salt
	Ground black pepper

1. Stand the corn on end. Using a chef's knife, cut the kernels from 4 ears of corn (see illustration on page 126). Transfer the kernels to a medium bowl and set aside. (You should have about 3 cups.) Following the illustrations on page 127, grate the kernels from the remaining 6 ears on the large holes of a box grater, then firmly scrape any pulp remaining on the cobs with the back of a butter knife. (You should have 2 generous cups of kernels and pulp.) Transfer the grated corn and pulp to a separate bowl and set aside.

2. Sauté the salt pork in a Dutch oven over medium-high heat, turning with tongs and pressing down on the pieces to render the fat, until the cubes are crisp and golden brown, about 10 minutes. Reduce the heat to low, stir in the butter and onion, cover the pot, and cook until the onion has softened, about 12 minutes. Remove the salt pork and reserve. Add the garlic and sauté until fragrant, about 1 minute. Stir in the flour and cook, stirring constantly, about 2 minutes. Whisking constantly, gradually add the stock. Add the potatoes, bay leaf, thyme, milk, grated corn and pulp, and reserved salt pork; bring to a boil. Reduce the heat to medium-low and simmer until the potatoes are almost tender, 8 to 10 minutes.

3. Add the reserved corn kernels and heavy cream and return to a simmer; simmer until the corn kernels are tender yet still slightly crunchy, about 5 minutes longer. Discard the bay leaf and salt pork. (Chowder can be refrigerated in an airtight container for up to 2 days. Warm over low heat until hot; do not boil.) Stir in the parsley, salt, and pepper to taste and serve immediately.

TRIMMING SALT PORK

Salt pork is usually sold with the rind attached, and you must remove the tough rind before slicing or chopping. Steady the salt pork with one hand, and with the other hand slide the blade of a sharp chef's knife between the rind and the fat, using a wide sawing motion to cut away the rind in one piece.

INGREDIENTS: Salt Pork

Some confusion exists about the difference between fatback and salt pork, a confusion we experienced at several markets where these products were not correctly labeled.

Salt pork comes from the belly of the pig (like bacon), and it has been cured or preserved in salt. It has streaks of meat running through it and is often rendered to make cracklings. Salt pork is fattier and chewier than bacon, but the two can often be used interchangeably. Note that bacon is usually smoked but that salt pork is not.

As its name implies, fatback comes from the back of the animal. Unlike salt pork, fatback is not smoked or cured; rather it is simply fresh fat. Fatback is generally used to lard meat—that is, to run strips of fat through lean meat to improve its flavor when roasted. Fatback doesn't contain meat and cannot be used as a substitute for salt pork or bacon.

SPRING VEGETABLE SOUP

ALONG WITH SPRING COMES A FRESH CROP of green vegetables, the likes of which haven't been seen in months. While chilly winds left over from winter are still knocking around, these new-sprung vegetables provide the makings for a classic soup.

Spring vegetable soup has several interpretations. Some consider it to be inherently vegetarian, while others use beef bones and meat for flavor. Many recipes go for something clear and brothy, while others aspire to a thickened puree. Some even take the time to note the importance of cutting the vegetables into tiny, perfect cubes for the ultimate presentation.

As we began to research and cook up some of these recipes, one obvious problem arose. None of them had a truly springlike character. The purees turned out too heavy, and the lighter soups had the tinny taste of the canned broth we used to make them. The vegetarian soups were sweet and bland, while the addition of beef bones muscled all spring flavors out of the way. As for the vegetables, most recipes simply packed in the standard, year-round varieties without paying much attention to the spring season. What ultimately emerged from these many disappointments was a clear idea of what spring vegetable soup should be. It should be simple and clean tasting, and it should make use of the tender, green vegetables of the new season. Moreover, it should be light and fresh yet substantial enough to serve as supper on a chilly night.

Our first tentative steps quickly taught us something about the inherent nature of a soup based on spring vegetables. While most other soups rely on their main ingredients for flavor, character, and overall heft, we soon found that spring vegetables are simply too delicate to carry this load. They are easily overcooked if simmered too long, and their flavors can be overpowered at the drop of a hat. To make a good spring soup, these tender vegetables would need the support of a broth that was rich and multidimensional, not characterized by any single, distinctive flavor. So we threw aside the idea of a heavy puree and focused on building a flavorful liquid base.

One solution to this problem would be to make a rich, savory vegetable stock, but we thought this would be too time consuming. We tried using canned vegetable broths, but they were incredibly thin and sweet, with an overwhelming taste of carrot. Beef stock gave the soup some heft but also imparted an unwanted meaty flavor that couldn't be quieted. Homemade chicken stock was delicious, but the soup was too chickeny, more like chicken vegetable soup. We wanted the broth to have more vegetable notes, and it seemed silly to start tinkering with good homemade stock.

We then tried using canned chicken broth, which, while not perfect, was promising, with a mellow and sturdy character. On its own it wasn't nearly balanced or flavorful enough, but we figured it would work well with a little doctoring. Looking for a quick way to give the chicken broth a rounder, fuller, vegetable flavor, we decided to borrow some techniques from our previous recipes for stock.

To start, we looked at our recipe for Quick Chicken Stock, which begins by cooking onions and chicken bones covered, over low heat, to encourage them to release their flavor. Not wanting any more chicken flavor, we tried using onions alone. The resulting broth was better, but still not there. Looking to our Vegetable Stock recipe, with its diverse selection of ingredients, we began to realize that it would take more than just onions to turn this canned broth around. Not wanting to cut or cook anything unnecessary, we worked our way stingily through a variety of other vegetables, from carrots and celery to dried mushrooms and cauliflower. In the end, we found a core group of vegetables was key. The hallowed trio of carrot, celery, and onion, with some extra help from shallots, leeks, and garlic, turned the boring canned chicken broth into something rich and satisfying. Parsley stems, a sprig of thyme, and a bay leaf also helped to reinforce the overall flavor change from canned to fresh. One by one we tried omitting each of the vegetables and herbs for the sake of simplicity, but we found that each made its own important contribution to the stock.

Now that we had decided on the vegetables for the stock, we wanted to streamline the process of making it. We tried using a food processor, but it produced an inferior result. The processed vegetables had a harsher edge and rougher flavor than those cut by hand. As it turns out, the blades of the food processor actually batter and tear the vegetables, eliciting an off, acidic flavor from the onions, leeks, and shallots. After going back to chopping by hand, we realized how important it is to cut these vegetables into small pieces so they can cook and release their flavors more quickly. It may take a couple of minutes more to cut the vegetables into petite pieces, but the resulting flavor and speedy cooking time are worth the extra effort.

Taking a cue from our other stock recipes, we tried sweating the vegetables lightly on their own first, before covering them with the canned broth. When the stock made from the sweated vegetables was compared with one in which the vegetables and stock were simply simmered together, the difference in flavor was dramatic. Once strained, the sweated stock had a full, round flavor, while the simmered stock tasted thin and one-dimensional. Sweating allows the vegetable cells to break down and release their flavor into the pot before the canned broth is added. This process is a good way to get flavor into the stock without taking the time for a long simmer. Finally, we had a quick stock that was chock-full of flavor without being overly sweet or meaty. Now we could focus on the main characters of this soup: spring vegetables.

Not wanting to clutter the soup with any vegetables that weren't essential, we steered toward a simple, clean soup filled only with vegetables of the season. Leeks, green peas, and baby spinach all made the cut quickly. Their tender flavors, different shapes, and varying shades of green made for a balanced and elegant spring lineup. Tomatoes, on the other hand, added unwelcome acidity, while fava beans involved too much work. Although chard, arugula, and asparagus were brightly colored and flavorful, their spicy, overpowering flavors and sulfuric aroma took over the otherwise delicate soup. Small, new red potatoes were a nice addition, giving the soup some body and a little variety in color. Scallions, celery, and carrots, on the other hand, managed only to crowd and distract.

Cooking the four finalists—leeks, peas, baby spinach, and red potatoes—was easy enough. The stock, still warm after being doctored and strained, was at the near-perfect temperature to poach this somewhat fragile foursome. The leeks and potatoes went in first; the spinach, peas, and herbs just before serving. The vegetables took well to this gentle cooking process, as the simmering stock brought out and reinforced the flavor of each. Garnished only with some chopped parsley and tarragon, the soup has an unmistakable spring flavor. It's a spring vegetable soup that lives up to its name.

Spring Vegetable Soup
SERVES 6

This soup uses canned chicken broth, but the broth is doctored with vegetables and herbs to brighten its flavor. Once completed, the soup is best served immediately.

STOCK

1	medium carrot, minced (about ⅓ cup)
1	stalk celery, minced (about ¼ cup)
2	medium onions, minced (about 1½ cups)
1	medium shallot, minced (about 2½ tablespoons)
1	medium leek, white and light green parts only, minced (see illustrations on page 124 to clean)
3	medium cloves garlic, unpeeled and crushed Vegetable cooking spray (see page 131)

7   cups (four 14½-ounce cans) canned low-sodium chicken broth
¼   teaspoon black peppercorns, crushed
1   sprig fresh thyme
5   parsley stems

SOUP

2   medium leeks, white and light green parts only, halved lengthwise, cut into 1-inch lengths (see illustrations on page 124 to clean)
6   small red potatoes, scrubbed (see illustration on page 81) and cut into ¾-inch chunks (about 1½ cups)
1   cup frozen peas, thawed
2   cups packed baby spinach
2   tablespoons chopped fresh parsley leaves
1   tablespoon chopped fresh tarragon leaves
    Salt and ground black pepper

1. FOR THE STOCK: Combine the carrot, celery, onions, shallot, leek, and garlic in a large heavy-bottomed stockpot or Dutch oven. Lightly spray the vegetables with cooking spray and toss to coat. Cover and cook the vegetables over medium heat, stirring frequently, until slightly softened and translucent, about 6 minutes. Add the broth, peppercorns, thyme sprig, and parsley stems. Increase the heat to medium-high and bring to a simmer. Simmer until the stock is flavorful, about 15 minutes. Strain the stock through a fine-mesh strainer; discard the solids. (Stock can be refrigerated in an airtight container for up to 3 days.)

2. FOR THE SOUP: Bring the stock to a simmer in a large saucepan over medium heat. Add the leeks and potatoes and simmer until the potatoes are tender, about 9 minutes. Stir in the peas, spinach,

parsley, and tarragon. Season to taste with salt and pepper. Serve immediately.

➤ VARIATION

Summer Vegetable Soup au Pistou

A pistou is a saucy French version of the Italian pesto that is often used as an accompaniment to vegetable soup. See page 135 for more information on how to bruise basil to release its flavor. See page 126 for tips on removing kernels from fresh ears of corn.

SOUP

1   recipe stock from Spring Vegetable Soup (preceding recipe)
1   medium zucchini (about 8 ounces), halved lengthwise and cut crosswise into half-moons ¼ inch thick
1½   cups fresh corn kernels (about 2 medium ears)
1   medium red bell pepper (about 8 ounces), stemmed, seeded, and cut into strips about 1 inch long and ⅛ inch wide
1½   cups packed arugula, stemmed and roughly chopped (about 2 ounces)
1   tablespoon chopped fresh parsley leaves
     Salt and ground black pepper

PISTOU

1½   cups packed fresh basil leaves, bruised
2   medium cloves garlic, peeled
7   tablespoons extra-virgin olive oil
     Salt and ground black pepper

1. FOR THE SOUP: Bring the stock to a simmer in a large saucepan over medium heat. Add the zucchini, corn, and red pepper and simmer until tender, about 5 minutes. Stir in the arugula and

---

INGREDIENTS: Vegetable Cooking Spray

Cooking sprays, most often used in low-fat cooking or to coat bakeware, have been around since the late 1950s. These convenient sprays consist of oil, soy lecithin, propellants, and sometimes silicone or grain alcohol. Under pressure, this combination of ingredients creates a stick-resistant spray that evenly distributes a minuscule amount of fat on a surface.

We found that a light mist of oil made all the difference when sweating vegetables for soup stock. Larger amounts of oil turned the stock cloudy, and smaller amounts were difficult to measure and work with. Although we were wary of food that comes packaged in an aerosol can, the convenient spray made quick work of coating vegetables with a negligible amount of fat.

There are several types of cooking spray on the market, as well as self-serve pumps that allow you to dispense your oil of choice. While all of the sprays we tried worked well with our Spring Vegetable Soup, we recommend avoiding any that are "flavored."

parsley. Season to taste with salt and pepper.

2. FOR THE PISTOU: While the soup is simmering, place the bruised basil, garlic, and oil in the workbowl of a food processor fitted with a steel blade and process until smooth, stopping as necessary to scrape down sides of bowl. Transfer the mixture to a small bowl and season to taste with salt and pepper.

3. To serve, ladle the soup into individual bowls and spoon a small dollop of pistou into each bowl. Serve immediately.

MINESTRONE

MINESTRONE IS NOT A LIGHT UNDERTAKING. Any way you cut it, there is a lot of dicing and chopping. Given the amount of preparation, we thought it was important to discover which steps and ingredients were essential and which we could do without. Could we simply add everything to the pot at once, or would precooking some of the vegetables be necessary? Was stock essential, or could we use water, as many traditional Italian recipes do? How many vegetables were enough? And which ones?

While we wanted to pack the soup with vegetables, we were also determined to create a harmonious balance of flavors. Minestrone should be a group effort, with each element pulling equal weight. From the start, we decided to jettison vegetables that were too bold (such as broccoli) as well as those that were too bland and would contribute no flavor to the soup (such as mushrooms).

But before tackling the issue of ingredients (we had come up with a list of more than 35 to test), we wanted to devise a basic technique. Our research turned up two possible paths. The majority of recipes dump the vegetables into a pot with liquid and simmer them until everything is tender. A smaller number of recipes call for sautéing some or most of the vegetables before adding the liquid along with those vegetables, such as spinach, that would not benefit from cooking in fat.

Although we expected the soup with sautéed vegetables to be more flavorful, it wasn't. We then prepared three more pots without sautéing any of the vegetables. We added homemade vegetable stock to one pot, homemade chicken stock to a second,

and water and the rind from a wedge of Parmesan cheese to the third.

The results were unexpected. The soup made with vegetable stock tasted one-dimensional and overwhelmingly sweet; because the vegetables were already sweet, using vegetable stock, which is also fairly sweet, did not help to balance the flavors. We realized we wanted the liquid portion of the soup to add a layer of complexity that would play off the vegetables. The soup made with chicken stock seemed to fit the bill. It was rich, complex, and delicious. However, the chicken flavor overwhelmed the vegetables. Diluting the stock with water wasn't the answer; this resulted in a rather bland soup. Ultimately, we preferred the soup made with water and the cheese rind. The cheese gave the broth a buttery, nutty flavor that contrasted nicely with the vegetables without overshadowing them.

We wanted the vegetables to soften completely but not lose their shape, and an hour of gentle simmering accomplished this. Much longer and the vegetables began to break down. Any less time over the flame and the vegetables were too crunchy. We liked the concentrating effect of simmering without the lid on the pot.

We also saw several recipes that added some fresh vegetables at the end of the cooking time. It sounded like a nice idea, but the fresh peas and green beans added 10 minutes before the soup was done tasted uncooked and bland compared with the vegetables that had simmered in the flavorful stock for an hour. For maximum flavor, all of the vegetables, even ones that usually require brief cooking times, needed to be added at the outset.

The addition of the cheese rind to the soup was an interesting find. During our research we also turned up two other flavor boosters that could be added up front: rehydrated porcini mushrooms with their soaking liquid and pancetta, unsmoked Italian bacon. We made a batch of soup with the porcinis but felt that, like the chicken stock, they overpowered the flavor of the vegetables.

Pancetta must be sautéed to render its fat and release its flavor. We cooked a little pancetta until crisp in some olive oil, then added the water and vegetables. Like the cheese rind, the pancetta contributed depth. While the soup made with the cheese rind was buttery and nutty, the soup with pancetta had a very subtle pork and spice flavor. We tried regular American bacon as well. It was stronger and lent the soup a smoky element. We preferred the subtler flavor of the pancetta, but either pancetta or smoked bacon is a significant improvement over water alone if you don't have a rind of Parmesan on hand.

Up until this point, we had focused on ingredients that went into the soup pot at the start. But many traditional Mediterranean recipes stir in fresh herbs or herb pastes just before the soup is served. Pesto is the most common choice. The first time we added pesto we were hooked. The heat of the soup releases the perfume of the basil and garlic and creates another delicious layer of flavor. A simple mixture of minced fresh rosemary, garlic, and extra-virgin olive oil was also delicious. As with the pesto, the oil here adds some fat to a soup that is otherwise very lean. The rosemary and garlic combo is very strong and must be used in smaller quantities than pesto.

Minestrone

SERVES 6 TO 8

The secret to this soup is adding the rind from a wedge of fresh Parmesan cheese, preferably Parmigiano-Reggiano, the Parmesan of Parmesans. It brings complexity and depth to a soup made with water instead of stock. (Rinds from which all the cheese has been grated can be stored in a zipper-lock bag in the freezer to use as needed.) To experiment with different vegetables or beans, see the chart on page 134.

2	small leeks (or 1 large), white and light green parts sliced thin crosswise (about ¾ cup) (see illustrations on page 124 to clean)
2	medium carrots, peeled and chopped small (about ¾ cup)
2	small onions, peeled and chopped small (about ¾ cup)
2	medium stalks celery, trimmed and chopped small (about ¾ cup)
1	medium baking potato, peeled and cut into ½-inch dice (about 1¼ cups)
1	medium zucchini, trimmed and chopped medium (about 1¼ cups)

3	cups stemmed spinach leaves, cut into thin strips
1	(28-ounce) can whole tomatoes packed in juice, drained and chopped
8	cups water
1	Parmesan cheese rind, about 5 by 2 inches
	Salt
1	(15-ounce) can cannellini beans, drained and rinsed
¼	cup Classic Pesto (page 134) or 1 tablespoon minced fresh rosemary mixed with 1 teaspoon minced garlic and 1 tablespoon extra-virgin olive oil
	Ground black pepper

1. Bring the vegetables, tomatoes, water, cheese rind, and 1 teaspoon salt to a boil in a large stockpot or Dutch oven. Reduce the heat to medium-low and simmer, uncovered, stirring occasionally, until the vegetables are tender but still hold their shape, about 1 hour. Remove and discard the cheese rind. (Soup can be refrigerated in an airtight container for 3 days. Reheat before proceeding with recipe.)

2. Add the beans and cook just until heated through, about 5 minutes. Remove the pot from the heat. Stir in the pesto. Adjust the seasonings, adding pepper and more salt, if necessary. Ladle the soup into bowls and serve immediately.

➤ VARIATIONS
Minestrone with Pancetta
Pancetta, unsmoked Italian bacon, can be used in place of a cheese rind to boost flavor in the soup. Because it has been smoked, American bacon can overwhelm the vegetables. To tone down some of the bacon's smokiness, cook bacon strips in simmering water for 1 minute.

Mince 2 ounces thinly sliced pancetta (or an equal amount of blanched bacon) and sauté in 1 tablespoon extra-virgin olive oil in a large stockpot or Dutch oven until crisp, 3 to 4 minutes. Proceed with recipe for Minestrone, adding the vegetables, tomatoes, and water but omitting the cheese rind.

Minestrone with Rice or Pasta

Adding pasta or rice makes this soup hearty enough to serve as dinner. If the soup seems too thick after adding the pasta or rice, stir in a little water.

Follow recipe for Minestrone or Minestrone with Pancetta until the vegetables are tender. Add ½ cup Arborio rice or small pasta shape, such as elbows, ditalini, or orzo. Continue cooking until the rice is tender but still a bit firm in the center of each grain, about 20 minutes, or until the pasta is al dente, 8 to 12 minutes, depending on the shape. Add the beans and proceed as directed.

Classic Pesto

MAKES ABOUT ³/₄ CUP

Basil often darkens in pesto, but you can boost the color by adding parsley. For sharper flavor, substitute 1 tablespoon finely grated Pecorino cheese for 1 tablespoon of the Parmesan.

¼	cup pine nuts, walnuts, or almonds
3	medium cloves garlic, unpeeled
2	cups packed fresh basil leaves
2	tablespoons fresh flat-leaf parsley leaves (optional)
7	tablespoons extra-virgin olive oil
	Salt
¼	cup finely grated Parmesan cheese

Varying the Vegetables and Beans in Minestrone

Our recipe for minestrone contains seven kinds of vegetables, plus tomatoes and cannellini beans. The aromatics—leeks, carrots, onions, and celery—are essential, as are the tomatoes. We like to add starchy potatoes, sweet zucchini, and leafy spinach, but this list is fairly subjective. What follows are some notes on other vegetables that were tested in this soup and well liked by tasters. Bell peppers and broccoli were judged too distinctive, while eggplant and white mushrooms added little flavor, so none of those four vegetables is recommended.

When making substitutions, keep in mind that our minestrone recipe has 2½ cups of solid vegetables (potatoes and zucchini) and three cups of leafy spinach. Follow similar proportions when using the vegetables below. As for the beans, white kidney beans, called cannellini beans in Italy, are the classic choice. But other white beans may be used, as well as red kidney, cranberry, or borlotti beans, all of which appear in various Italian recipes for minestrone.

VEGETABLE	TESTING NOTES	HOW TO USE
Cauliflower	While broccoli is too intensely flavored for minestrone, milder cauliflower can blend in.	Cut into tiny florets and use in place of potatoes or zucchini.
Escarole	This slightly bitter green works well with white beans and pasta.	Chop and use in place of spinach.
Green Beans	A standard ingredient in French versions of this soup.	Cut into ½-inch pieces and use in place of zucchini.
Kale	This assertive green can be overwhelming on its own, but when combined with spinach it gives the soup a pleasant edge.	Remove ribs and chop. Use up to 1½ cups in place of 1½ cups of the spinach.
Peas	The delicate flavor of fresh peas is wasted in this soup, so use frozen.	Add up to ½ cup in place of ½ cup of the zucchini or white beans.
Savoy Cabbage	Adds an earthy note.	Shred finely and use in place of spinach.
Swiss Chard	Similar to spinach, with a slightly more earthy flavor.	Remove ribs and chop. Use in place of spinach.
Turnips	Modest bitter edge helps balance the sweetness of some of the other vegetables.	Peel and cut into ½-inch dice. Use in place of potatoes.
Butternut Squash	Butternut squash is sweet, but in small quantities it is especially colorful and delicious.	Peel and cut into ½-inch dice. Use in place of potatoes or zucchini.

1. Toast the nuts in a small, heavy skillet over medium heat, stirring frequently, until just golden and fragrant, 4 to 5 minutes. Transfer the nuts to a plate.

2. Add the garlic to the empty pan. Toast, shaking the pan occasionally, until fragrant and the color of the cloves deepens slightly, about 7 minutes. Transfer the garlic to a plate, cool, peel, and chop.

3. Place the basil and parsley (if using) in a heavy-duty, gallon-sized, zipper-lock plastic bag. Pound the bag with the flat side of a meat pounder or rolling pin until all the leaves are bruised (see illustration, left).

4. Place the nuts, garlic, herbs, oil, and ½ teaspoon salt in the workbowl of a food processor. Process until smooth, stopping as necessary to scrape down the sides of the bowl. Transfer the mixture to a small bowl, stir in the cheese, and adjust the salt. (The surface of the pesto can be covered with a sheet of plastic wrap or a thin film of oil and refrigerated for up to 3 days.)

MAKING PESTO

Bruising herb leaves such as basil or parsley in a zipper-lock plastic bag with the flat side of a meat pounder (or rolling pin) is a quick but effective substitute for hand-pounding with a mortar and pestle and helps to release their flavor.

INGREDIENTS: Pesto

A swirl of pesto is delicious in minestrone, and it can be used to enliven countless other soups, especially those with vegetables, pasta, and/or beans. (Try a dollop in cream of tomato, white bean, or potato-leek soup.)

In our experience with pesto, the bright herbal fragrance of basil always hinted at more flavor than it really delivered. Also, although we love garlic, the raw article can have a sharp, acrid taste that overwhelms everything else in the sauce. So our goals were clear when developing a recipe for this simple sauce— heighten the flavor of the basil and subdue the garlic.

Traditionally, pesto is made in a mortar and pestle, which yields an especially silky texture and intense basil flavor. The slow pounding of the basil leaves (it takes 15 minutes to make pesto this way) releases their full flavor.

By comparison, blender and food-processor pestos can seem dull or bland, but if left with only a choice between the two, we prefer a food processor for several reasons. In a blender, ingredients tend to bunch up near the blade and do not become evenly chopped. Also, to keep solids moving in a blender, it is necessary to add more oil than is really needed to make pesto.

Since most Americans don't own a mortar and pestle (and those who do are unlikely to invest 15 minutes of pounding when the sauce can otherwise be made in seconds), we decided to focus on improving flavor in food-processor pesto. We tested chopping, tearing, and bruising basil leaves to release more of their flavor. In the end, we settled on packing basil leaves in a plastic bag and bruising them with a meat pounder or rolling pin.

We tried several approaches to tame the garlic—roasting, sautéing, and infusing oil with garlic flavor—but found them all lacking. What we did like was toasting whole cloves in a warm skillet. This tames the harsh garlic notes and loosens the skins from the cloves for easy peeling.

To bring out the full flavor of the nuts, we toasted them in a dry skillet before processing. (We then toasted the garlic in the empty pan.) Almonds are sweet but fairly hard, so they give pesto a coarse, granular texture. Walnuts are softer but still fairly meaty in texture and flavor. Pine nuts yield the smoothest, creamiest pesto. The choice is yours.

TUSCAN TOMATO AND BREAD SOUP

THOUGH NOT AS FAMILIAR TO AMERICANS as minestrone or pasta e fagioli, Tuscan tomato and bread soup (*pappa al pomodoro* in Italian) is a regional Italian favorite. On paper, pappa al pomodoro is a chicken stock and tomato soup finished with stale bread and basil, but in the pot, all of the ingredients meld together to form a thick and fragrant porridge-like stew. Though the texture sets this recipe apart from conventional American soups, its soft luxuriousness combined with simple, pleasing flavors make it worth exploring.

No doubt owing to the recipe's low profile in this country, we managed to dig up only two from our collection of Italian cookbooks. The rest were mostly personal recipes that we turned up during a search of the Web. Interestingly enough, each recipe had the same ingredient list: extra-virgin olive oil, red onion, garlic, chicken broth (canned), tomatoes (fresh or canned), Italian bread, and basil. Not one deviated. Some did differ in terms of preparation technique, though. In the case of the four recipes we chose to make, each had a base of onions and garlic sautéed in olive oil, was seasoned with salt and pepper, and garnished with basil; here the similarities ended.

Two of the recipes called for canned, imported Italian whole tomatoes passed through a food mill to puree them and remove their seeds. The result, a red sea of thick tomato juice, was added to the aromatics and chicken broth and simmered for 20 minutes. At this point the Italian bread, stale, crusty, and cubed, was mixed in and simmered for 20 minutes longer. Each soup (like the others to come) was then seasoned, garnished, and served with a healthy drizzle of good-quality extra-virgin olive oil. In terms of flavor, both soups were unanimously disliked for tasting tinny, acidic, and too tomatoey.

We next tested the recipes made with fresh tomatoes and learned a simple lesson: Don't make this soup with fresh tomatoes unless they are garden-fresh, summer tomatoes. Store-bought, off-season tomatoes were flavorless. If you do have access to garden-fresh tomatoes, by all means make the soup with them. Because we wanted to develop a recipe

that can be used year-round, we decided to press ahead with the canned tomatoes; the recipe that uses fresh tomatoes would be a variation.

Abandoning the food mill was the first step to success using canned tomatoes. Processing the tomatoes through the mill turned out a highly acidic, just-plain-too-tomatoey slurry. Pappa al pomodoro should not be tomato soup dressed in bread clothing; it should be a brothy soup containing tomatoes, finished with stale bread. There is quite a difference. With this in mind, we set out to explore our options. We made three batches with canned tomatoes—left whole, chopped, and crushed by hand—each drained of their packing liquid. In all three, we added the tomatoes to the broth and let them simmer for 20 minutes. All three of these soups were much better than their predecessors. The tomatoes now dotted the soup and accompanied, not consumed, the other flavors in each bite.

The soup made with tomatoes crushed by hand (by gently squeezing them through our fingers until small and uniform in size) got slightly higher marks for being more mellow tasting than the soups made with whole or chopped tomatoes. This was because when we crushed the tomatoes, some of the seeds, which are notoriously bitter, escaped, and never made it into the broth. The long, flat pieces of tomato (rather than three-dimensional chunks) were more smoothly incorporated into the soup and provided a nice contrast with the chunks of bread.

As stated earlier in this chapter, all canned tomatoes are not created equal (see page 117 for more information). We made two batches of soup: one with imported, whole Italian tomatoes packed in puree, the other with Muir Glen whole tomatoes packed in tomato juice. Drained, squeezed, and simmered in the broth, the two kinds of tomatoes made a notable difference. The Muir Glen tomatoes packed in juice were sweeter, lighter, and fresher tasting.

We now turned to the question of texture, which, we found, was related to the treatment of the bread. In the two initial recipes we had made with canned tomatoes, one used the whole loaf, crust and all, while the other called for removing the crust. The soup made with crust-free bread came out thin and runny, with the bread all but disintegrating as it simmered in the tomatoey broth. The soup made with the whole loaf got better marks. As the dry, hard crusts absorbed the stock, they softened without breaking down completely—turning into voluptuously soft, chewy dollops of bread. A few tasters were passionately drawn to this texture and commented that the soupy bread would never make it out of the pot because they intended to stand there and pluck out all of the "plump morsels." Crusty bread was the way to go, but a little refinement still seemed to be in order.

While tasters liked biting into chunks of bread, they wanted the overall texture to be slightly more homogenous. After testing different methods of breaking down the bread beyond merely simmering it in the broth, we found that a wire whisk did the best job. The whisk, patiently but vigorously passed through the soup, broke down the crust-free pieces, incorporating them into the base of the soup. The whisk was no match for the crusty pieces, though. While some got caught in the wires (they were then tapped out), they largely retained their dumpling-like shape and texture, giving the soup some tooth.

To streamline the process, we also tested slicing techniques and found it best to slice and cube the loaf of bread while it was fresh. Cubing an already-stale loaf was cumbersome and created excess crumbs that when added to the soup gave it a slimy texture. Slicing and cubing a fresh loaf and laying the cubes out to dehydrate for at least 24 hours eliminated the crumb issue. The cubes were solid and sturdy and held their own in the soup. If hard pressed for time, you can dry the cubes in a 250-degree oven for 30 minutes, or until hard, but not browned.

Adjusting the amounts of the few aromatics was easy; we knew they should complement one another, not do battle. Most of the recipes we looked at had similar ratios: 1 red onion to 3 cloves of garlic to 2 cups of chopped basil. The onion and garlic levels were just right—both flavors were subtle and soft. When we tested using red onion (which was part of every initial recipe) versus yellow onion, no one could detect a difference, so we decided to stick with tradition. Two cups basil, however, was too much; tasters found the flavor too potent. Working down in half-cup increments, we were all satisfied with a half cup. The clean, fresh taste of the basil

perfumed the soup without overwhelming it.

For a complete, authentic experience, it is important to serve pappa al pomodoro as the Italians do. Each bowl should always be drizzled with high-quality extra-virgin olive oil. The oil's fruitiness brings out and heightens the flavors in the soup. And, finally, remember that this is not minestrone—never sprinkle pappa al pomodoro with cheese. The strong flavor of cheese is quick to mute this soup's essential, unadulterated flavors.

Tuscan Tomato and Bread Soup
SERVES 4 TO 6

This humble Italian soup, known as pappa al pomodoro, requires good bread. We prefer to use Italian bread cubes staled for 1 to 2 days in this recipe, but you can stale fresh bread cubes quickly by putting them in a 250-degree oven until dry and hard, but not browned, about 30 minutes. This soup does not hold and should be served as soon as it is ready.

¼	cup extra-virgin olive oil, plus extra for drizzling over individual bowls
1	large red onion, chopped fine
3	large cloves garlic, minced
5½	cups homemade chicken stock or canned low-sodium chicken broth
2	(28-ounce) cans whole tomatoes packed in juice, juice drained and tomatoes crushed by hand (see illustrations on page 138)
1	loaf good-quality Italian bread, cut into 1-inch square cubes, spread in an even layer on rimmed baking sheet, and left to stale for 24 to 48 hours (about 9 heaping cups)
½	cup coarsely chopped fresh basil leaves Salt and ground black pepper

1. Heat the oil in a large stockpot or Dutch oven over medium-high until shimmering. Add the onion, reduce the heat to medium-low, and cook, stirring frequently, until the onions are slightly softened and translucent, about 6 minutes. Add the garlic and cook, stirring frequently, until soft and fragrant, about 1 minute longer. Add the chicken stock, scraping the bottom of the pot with a wooden spoon; increase the heat to high and bring the mixture to a simmer. Add

the tomatoes, cover, and simmer until the tomatoes soften and the stock turns red, about 20 minutes.

2. Stir in the bread cubes and press with a wooden spoon to submerge the bread in the liquid. Cover and simmer until the bread is softened, about 15 minutes. Stir the soup with a whisk to break bread down until a thick porridge-like texture is obtained.

3. Take the pot off the heat, stir in the basil, and season with salt and pepper to taste. Ladle the soup into individual bowls, drizzle with olive oil, and serve immediately.

➤ VARIATION

Fresh Tomato and Bread Soup

This soup is delicious when made with garden-fresh tomatoes. Italians serve it at room temperature when the weather is warm.

Core and roughly chop 2 pounds ripe fresh tomatoes. Follow recipe for Tuscan Tomato and Bread Soup, adding tomatoes with stock in step 2. Proceed as directed.

CRUSHING TOMATOES

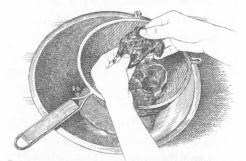

1. Empty the cans of whole tomatoes into a strainer and let the juice drain away in a bowl. With your fingertips, gently open each tomato and let the juice and seeds fall away.

2. Squeeze the opened tomato to break it into several rough pieces.

CALDO VERDE

CALDO VERDE IS A HEARTY PORTUGUESE soup made with greens, potatoes, and sausage. This soup gets its deep rich color from the greens, so that is where we began testing. Traditionally, the green of choice is the deep-colored *couve gallego*, a Galician cabbage native to the Iberian Peninsula that is similar to Tuscany's *cavolo nero*. But since neither of these is easily obtained in this country, we limited our tests to more available options: kale, collard greens, turnip greens, and Swiss chard.

For this series of tests, we weighed out equal amounts of greens and washed them thoroughly. Then we trimmed the tough stems from the leaves, stacked a few leaves on top of each other, rolled the stack tightly, and finely shredded the rolled stack into ⅛-inch slices, as directed in just about every recipe we found. We added the greens toward the end of the cooking process, hoping to avoid the bitter taste that can result from overcooking.

Turnip greens fared the worst. Their characteristically tender leaves nearly fell apart and became slimy during their short bath in the stock. In addition, the turnip greens imparted an unpleasant sour and "dirty" flavor that was impossible to ignore. We tried cutting the turnip greens into larger strips (¼ inch wide), hoping that this more substantial size would impede their disintegration and thereby inhibit development of the sour flavor. Unfortunately, the greens tasted just as bad as before.

Turning next to collard greens, we performed the same tests. Collard greens are somewhat less tender than turnip greens, and we predicted that they would perform better in the soup. The good news was that the taste was an improvement. The collards added a lovely peppery flavor to the soup. The bad news was that the texture was similar to the turnip greens, although not to the same degree. Once again we tried cutting the greens into slightly wider shreds, and this time there was a glimmer of hope. The collards kept their integrity for a few minutes longer, but by the time the soup was ladled into a bowl and we sat down to eat it, the greens had started to break down to an unpleasant texture. Finally, we tried a method from a published caldo verde recipe in which the collards are added to the soup off heat right before serving. The improvement was not substantial enough to warrant the use of this technique, so we moved on.

Next up for testing was Swiss chard. Tasters unanimously disliked the chard for its spinach-like flavor, which did not seem to belong in the caldo verde. Lessening the cooking time by any amount did not help—the earthy, mineral taste of the chard was out of place.

On to kale, which is by far the most commonly used green in caldo verde in this country—and for good reason. The kale, which has a more coarse, substantial texture than the other greens, resisted wilting and provided a more forgiving window of time in which it could cook. The kale also imparted a lovely sweet cabbage flavor to the soup that was both delicious and authentic. In the end, as we had done with the other greens, we shredded the kale into ¼-inch slices. This greatly increased the flavor of the kale.

Most caldo verde recipes call for either the very garlicky Portuguese linguiça or chorizo. Luckily, many supermarkets carry one or both of these sausages, but we also wanted to determine if there was a suitable substitute for cooks who cannot get their hands on either of these.

We made three soups and tested linguiça, chorizo, and smoked Polish kielbasa, which also has a bold garlic flavor. The linguiça contributed little flavor to the soup. In fact, most tasters were surprised to find that there was any sausage in the soup at all. Chorizo, on the other hand, made a big impact. The potent spices in the chorizo blended into the stock and made the soup spicy and very garlicky. The combination of the sweet cabbage-flavored kale and the hot, pungent chorizo made tasters swoon. The soup made with kielbasa was surprisingly good as well. Not as rich and full flavored as the soup made with chorizo, the soup made with kielbasa took on a sweet, spicy flavor.

A few recipes called for sautéing the sausage in oil before simmering it in the stock. We tried this and found that the sausage had lost its interesting flavor. Moreover, precooking the sausage turned the meat into tough little bites.

Traditionally, caldo verde is thickened by breaking down or mashing potato in the soup. Tasters liked soup in which the potato was not broken down completely. High-starch potatoes such as russets did not work well. They fell apart completely and gave the soup a granular mouthfeel. Medium-starch Yukon Gold potatoes fared better texturally but were a little too sweet for the soup. Low-starch boiling potatoes, such as Red Bliss, worked best—even after a vigorous boiling and coarse mashing, the potatoes held together. A number of recipes left the potatoes unpeeled, but we found that the soggy peels inevitably found their way onto a disappointed taster's spoon. Cutting the potatoes into 1-inch pieces cut down on the cooking time considerably.

Although not an essential part of caldo verde, we did find a few recipes that added fresh herbs such as bay, thyme, oregano, and savory. We tested these along with a caldo verde made without herbs. Tasters preferred the faint mint flavor of the savory but thought it became overpowering as they ate more of the soup. Instead of mincing the herb, we tried simmering a sprig of savory in the soup along with the sausage (which we were adding at the end so that the sausage would lose little flavor). After just 15 minutes, when the savory had given up just the right amount of flavor, we removed the sprig. Perfect soup.

Caldo Verde

SERVES 6

Using the right potatoes makes a tremendous difference in this recipe. For more information on potatoes see page 125. For tips on stemming and slicing kale, see page 140.

2	tablespoons extra-virgin olive oil, plus extra for drizzling over individual bowls
I	large onion, chopped medium
4	medium cloves garlic, minced
6	cups homemade chicken stock or canned low-sodium chicken broth
I	pound red potatoes (about 4 medium), peeled and cut into I-inch pieces Salt
8	ounces chorizo or smoked kielbasa sausage, halved lengthwise and cut crosswise into ¼-inch pieces
I	sprig fresh savory or oregano

6 ounces kale, stems removed and leaves
cut crosswise into ¼-inch strips (about
4½ packed cups)
Ground black pepper

1. Heat the oil in a large stockpot or Dutch oven over medium heat until shimmering. Add the onion and cook, stirring frequently, until softened, about 5 minutes. Add the garlic and sauté until fragrant, about 30 seconds.

2. Add 3 cups stock, the potatoes, and ½ teaspoon salt. Increase the heat to medium-high and bring to a boil. Reduce the heat and simmer until the potatoes are tender, about 15 minutes. Remove the pot from the heat and mash the potatoes in the liquid with a potato masher until no large chunks remain and the potatoes thicken the soup slightly.

3. Return the pot to medium-high heat. Add the remaining 3 cups stock, sausage, and savory and bring to a boil. Reduce the heat to medium-low, cover, and simmer to blend the flavors, about 15 minutes.

4. Remove and discard the savory. Stir in the kale and simmer until just tender, about 5 minutes. Adjust the seasonings with salt and pepper to taste. Serve immediately, drizzling each portion with olive oil, if desired.

MULLIGATAWNY SOUP

MULLIGATAWNY IS A PUREED VEGETABLE soup that originated in India during the British Raj. The soup is mildly spicy but not hot. There should be some faint sweetness as well, usually from coconut. The finished soup should be silky and elegant with potent yet balanced spices and aromatics.

We decided to start with the question of the liquid base. Research indicated that chicken stock, lamb stock, beef stock, vegetable stock, or water were possible choices. Tasters found vegetable stock too sweet and vegetal, and beef stock too strong, even a bit sour. Lamb stock was overpowering and ruled out because of the work involved in making it. In the end, we decided that chicken stock was the ideal base for the competing spices and vegetables. We found that canned broth was fine in this soup. Water made a tasty vegetarian soup that was not quite as rich as the versions made with chicken stock.

Curry powder, which is a blend of spices, is a central ingredient in mulligatawny soup. We wondered whether to use a prepackaged blend or whether to make our own. After experimenting with several homemade curry powders, we found that the end product was not worth the effort of toasting and grinding our own spices. If we had homemade curry powder on hand we would use it, but commercial curry powder is just fine with some modifications.

HANDLING KALE

1. Hold each leaf at the base of the stem over a bowl filled with water and use a sharp knife to slash the leafy portion from either side of the thick stem. Discard the stems, and then wash and dry the leaves.

2. Stack some leaves in a short pile, roll the leaves into a tight cylinder, and slice crosswise into strips ¼ inch wide.

We found it best to start with a good-quality curry powder (we like a Madras blend from south India) and then boost the flavor with a little additional ground cumin and some cayenne for a bit of heat.

We decided to focus next on the aromatics (garlic and ginger) and coconut. After testing various strategies for adding garlic and ginger flavor to this soup, we found that tasters preferred versions with most of the garlic and ginger sautéed in fat at the outset and a small amount of raw garlic and ginger added just before serving. To keep tasters from biting into a piece of raw garlic, we adopted a technique common in Indian cooking. We pureed the raw garlic and ginger with water so they could be fully incorporated into the soup for a fresh hit of flavor.

Coconut gives mulligatawny its distinctive sweet flavor and is authentically Indian along with the curry and ginger. Some recipes asked for coconut milk, others for fresh coconut meat, and still others added dried coconut, either sweetened or not. The coconut milk gave the soup a silky consistency but not much coconut flavor. Fresh coconut was not flavorful enough, either, and in any case was much too troublesome to prepare. Dried coconut was the best option, adding enough flavor to the soup without taking it over. Sweetened shredded coconut struck many tasters as odd, but unsweetened shredded coconut was delicious.

With our aromatics and spices under control it was time to test the vegetables, which would give the soup flavor, bulk, and color when pureed. We tested onions, carrots, celery, cauliflower, spinach, peas, potatoes, and bananas. Not surprisingly, we found that onions are a must in the soup. Carrots added color and sweetness, and the celery provided a cool flavor that contrasted nicely with the hot spices. Cauliflower was rejected for the cabbage-like flavor it gave to the soup. Spinach and peas did little to enhance the soup's flavor. In addition, they imparted an undesirable color when pureed.

Potato, which was originally added for flavor, also improved the soup's texture. When pureed, the potato added body to the soup, thickening it slightly. Upon recommendation from several sources, we tried using a banana instead of a potato. The banana produced soup with the same rich body as that made with the potato, but this soup had a richer, slightly sweet flavor that offset the heat from the ginger. Afraid that the banana flavor might be too strong, we held a blind taste test between the banana and the potato. Unanimously, the tasters preferred the soup made with the banana, although all were unable to identify the source of the flavor.

A single banana or potato gave the soup body but did not thicken it quite enough. Adding more banana or potato was the most obvious solution, but more bananas made the soup sweet and the potatoes became gritty in larger amounts. Several recipes suggest using pureed rice or lentils to thicken the soup, but we did not like the thick, porridge-like results. We finally settled on sprinkling flour over the sautéed aromatics to make a roux. One-quarter cup of flour gave the soup the perfect consistency—silky and substantial but not heavy.

Although a few sources said that pureeing was optional, we think that mulligatawny must be smooth. Chunks of meat can float in the finished soup (we developed one variation with chicken, another with lamb), but the soup itself is meant to be refined and smooth. A dollop of yogurt and shower of cilantro finishes the soup. Traditionally, mulligatawny is served over basmati rice or red lentils, although it can stand on its own.

Mulligatawny Soup

SERVES 6 TO 8

For freshness, puree some of the garlic and ginger with water in a blender, then leave this mixture in the blender while making the soup. The finished soup is pureed in the same blender, where it will pick up a hit of spicy raw garlic and ginger flavor.

4	medium cloves garlic, 2 peeled and 2 finely minced
I	piece fresh ginger (about 1½ inches), peeled and grated (about 1½ tablespoons)
¼	cup water
3	tablespoons unsalted butter
2	medium onions, chopped medium
I	teaspoon tomato paste

½ cup shredded unsweetened coconut

1½ tablespoons curry powder

1 teaspoon ground cumin

¼ teaspoon cayenne pepper

¼ cup all-purpose flour

7 cups homemade chicken stock or canned low-sodium chicken broth

2 medium carrots, peeled and chopped coarse

1 medium stalk celery, chopped coarse

1 medium very ripe banana (about 5 ounces), peeled, or 1 small boiling potato (about 5 ounces), peeled and cut into 1-inch pieces

Salt and ground black pepper

Plain yogurt for serving

2 tablespoons minced fresh cilantro leaves

1. Place 2 peeled whole garlic cloves, 2 teaspoons grated ginger, and water in a blender. Blend until smooth, about 25 seconds; leave mixture in the blender jar and set aside. (You will be pureeing the soup right in the blender with the garlic and ginger.)

2. Heat the butter in a large stockpot or Dutch oven over medium heat until foaming. Add the onions and tomato paste and cook, stirring frequently, until the onions are softened and beginning to brown, about 3 minutes. Stir in the coconut and cook until fragrant, about 1 minute. Add the minced garlic, remaining 2½ teaspoons ginger, curry powder, cumin, cayenne, and flour; stir until evenly combined, about 1 minute. Whisking constantly and vigorously, gradually add the chicken stock.

3. Add the carrots, celery, and whole banana to the pot. Increase the heat to medium–high and bring to a boil. Cover, reduce the heat to low, and simmer until the vegetables are tender, about 20 minutes.

4. Puree the soup in batches in the blender with the garlic and ginger until very smooth. Wash and dry the pot. Return the pureed soup to a clean pot and season to taste with salt and pepper. Warm the soup over medium heat until hot, about 1 minute. (Soup can be refrigerated in an airtight container for up to 3 days. Warm over low heat until hot; do not boil.) Ladle the soup into individual bowls, spoon a dollop of yogurt over each bowl, sprinkle with cilantro, and serve immediately.

➤ VARIATIONS

Mulligatawny Soup with Chicken

Basmati rice (page 312) makes a good accompaniment to this soup.

Follow the recipe for Mulligatawny Soup, adding 4 medium (about 1½ pounds) boneless, skinless chicken breasts to the simmering stock in step 3 just before covering the pot. Simmer until cooked through, about 20 minutes. With tongs, transfer the cooked chicken to cutting board, cool slightly, and cut crosswise into slices ¼ inch wide. Continue with the recipe, adding the reserved chicken to the pureed soup in the pot in step 4. Warm over medium heat until the chicken is hot, about 5 minutes. Garnish as directed and serve immediately.

Mulligatawny Soup with Lamb

This hearty, stewlike variation is especially good served with red lentils. It's also quite nice with basmati rice (page 312).

4 medium cloves garlic, 2 peeled and 2 finely minced

1 piece fresh ginger (about 1½ inches), peeled and grated (about 1½ tablespoons)

¼ cup water

5 pounds lamb shoulder chops, bone, fat, and gristle discarded; meat cut into 1½-inch pieces

2 tablespoons olive oil

7 cups homemade chicken stock or canned low-sodium chicken broth

3 tablespoons unsalted butter

2 medium onions, chopped medium

1 teaspoon tomato paste

½ cup shredded unsweetened coconut

1½ tablespoons curry powder

1 teaspoon ground cumin

¼ teaspoon cayenne pepper

¼ cup all-purpose flour

2 medium carrots, peeled and chopped coarse

1 medium stalk celery, chopped coarse

1 medium very ripe banana (about 5 ounces), peeled, or 1 boiling potato (about 5 ounces), peeled and cut into 1-inch pieces

Salt and ground black pepper

Plain yogurt for serving

2 tablespoons minced fresh cilantro leaves

1. Place 2 peeled whole garlic cloves, 2 teaspoons ginger, and water in a blender. Blend until smooth, about 25 seconds; leave mixture in the blender jar and set aside.

2. Heat a large stockpot or Dutch oven over medium-high heat until very hot, about 3 minutes. Add 1 tablespoon olive oil, swirl to coat the pan bottom, and add half of the lamb pieces. Cook until the lamb is well-browned, about 2 to 3 minutes. Transfer the browned lamb to a medium bowl with a slotted spoon. Add the remaining tablespoon oil to the pot, swirl to coat the pan bottom, add the remaining lamb, and cook until the lamb is well browned on all sides. Return all lamb to the pot and add the chicken stock, scraping up the browned bits from the pan bottom with a wooden spoon. Bring to a simmer, cover, reduce the heat to medium-low, and simmer until the lamb is tender, about 20 minutes. With a slotted spoon, transfer the lamb to a medium bowl, cover, and reserve. Pour the stock into another bowl and reserve.

3. Heat the butter in a large stockpot or Dutch oven over medium heat until foaming. Add the onions and tomato paste and cook, stirring frequently, until the onions are softened and beginning to brown, about 3 minutes. Stir in the coconut and cook until fragrant, about 1 minute. Add the minced garlic, remaining 2½ teaspoons ginger, curry powder, cumin, cayenne, and flour; stir well until evenly combined, about 1 minute. Whisking constantly and vigorously, gradually add the reserved stock used to cook the lamb.

4. Add the carrots, celery, and whole banana to the stock. Increase the heat to medium-high and bring to a boil. Cover, reduce the heat to low, and simmer until the vegetables are tender, about 20 minutes.

5. Puree the soup in batches in the blender with garlic and ginger until very smooth. Return the pureed soup to a clean pot and season to taste with salt and pepper. Add the lamb pieces and warm the soup over medium heat until the lamb is hot, about 5 minutes. Ladle the soup into individual bowls, spoon a dollop of yogurt over each bowl, sprinkle with cilantro, and serve immediately.

GARLIC SOUP

GARLIC SOUP IS POPULAR THROUGHOUT the Mediterranean. Originally a simple country dish, this soup can still be a humble affair, nothing more than garlic simmered in stock, or it can be rather complex, made with herbs, cream, eggs, and/or cheese. We knew we wanted a soup with rich (but not harsh) garlic flavor, but we had no preconceived notions about which style was best. To get a handle on the choices, we prepared four different types of garlic soup.

We prepared a classic *aigo bouido,* a French soup made by simmering garlic and herbs in chicken stock. The soup was thickened with beaten eggs just before serving. Tasters disliked the results, detecting a metallic taste in the garlic.

We then made two recipes with cream and sherry. In one recipe, whole heads of garlic were roasted in the oven and then peeled and added to the soup pot. In the other recipe, the whole heads of garlic were peeled, minced, and sautéed. Most tasters strongly disliked the soup flavored with roasted garlic, finding it overly sweet and scorched. The soup made with sautéed minced garlic was better, but no one liked the idea of all that peeling and mincing. Tasters found the sherry too strong tasting and did not like the cream (it conflicted with the garlic flavor).

The last test recipe was a Spanish soup that called for poaching minced garlic in olive oil until it was soft and mild tasting. The garlic and oil were added to the chicken stock, which was enriched with eggs just before serving. This recipe was certainly the most promising in terms of flavor, but, again, we didn't like the idea of prepping all of that garlic.

After this initial round of tests, we refined our goal. We wanted to develop a soup with a deep garlic flavor, more toasted than roasted, with a spicy, heady finish. As for the liquid, we wanted something clean and relatively thin, ruling out cream or bread as a thickener and the use of sherry at the finish. A little egg might be nice for body, but we did not want a final soup that was thick.

The Spanish-style soup came the closest to the flavor we were looking for. We wondered if we could get around the tiresome task of peeling and mincing four heads of garlic by smashing the heads and then poaching the garlic with the skin on, separating it out later by forcing the cloves through a fine-mesh strainer. We placed the four heads of garlic in one doubled-up, 1-gallon zipper-lock bag and used a rubber mallet to pulverize the heads into quarter-inch shards. We extracted the largest shreds of papery garlic skin and placed the garlic in a heavy-bottomed pot. Our only adjustment to the Spanish method was to add stock to the oil to compensate for the moisture-absorbing garlic skin.

After 35 minutes over low heat, the smashed garlic was quite soft and easily forced through a fine-mesh strainer. The method worked beautifully, resulting in a deeply flavorful garlic paste. We conducted a simple tasting of the paste simmered quickly in chicken stock, and tasters loved the flavor. Since the finished soup would be strained, we decided to add the garlic mixture, skins and all, to the stock.

The unanimously positive responses to the quick test of the paste simmered in stock showed that tasters favored a clean liquid base unencumbered by flavors that might interfere with or mute the garlic. Tasters ruled out aromatics like onion and celery as too sweet and strong. Herbaceousness, however, was appreciated, so we added a healthy dose of parsley, thyme, and bay leaves to the liquid (herbs were standard in many of the garlic soup recipes we found).

For body, we turned to Parmesan rinds. We knew from making other Mediterranean-style soups (such as minestrone; see page 132) that Parmesan rinds could add richness and depth without a discernible or possibly distracting flavor. We also added a bit of water so that the resulting soup would not taste overwhelmingly chickeny. Once the garlic mixture was added to the stock, we did not want to risk overcooking the garlic or developing a "boiled" flavor. To thoroughly incorporate the garlic and olive oil into the stock, we borrowed a technique from another olive oil–rich soup, bouillabaisse, and rapidly boiled the stock to encourage emulsion.

To finish the soup, we strained it, pushing on the solids to extract as much flavor as possible. We added hot red pepper flakes for a bit of color and spice. Some recipes recommended the addition of eggs as a garnish or a thickener, with some calling for whole poached eggs and some for beaten eggs. We decided to stir beaten eggs into the soup since tasters had liked this in our original testing. The soup cooled enough during the straining process to make tempering the egg mixture unnecessary, as long as the eggs were rapidly incorporated. (See the section on egg-lemon soup, page 48, for information on tempering.) Tasters suggested adding a little Parmesan to the eggs to elevate the faint nutty flavor the rinds had infused into the stock.

During the course of recipe development, tasters had liked a touch of raw garlic in the final soup. We first tried adding raw garlic paste to the soup pot, but this resulted in a boiled garlic taste if the leftover soup was later reheated. We thought of the spicy raw garlic bite of bruschetta and wondered if toasts made in a similar fashion could be added to the soup. Rubbing the toasts with whole raw cloves of garlic was much easier than making a garlic paste and, according to all the tasters, provided the proper garlicky kick. The toasts, cut into small croutons, also added a pleasing texture to this otherwise lean soup.

Garlic Soup
SERVES 6 TO 8

This recipe must be served once the eggs have been added. If you want to prepare the liquid base in advance, strain the liquid as directed in step 6 and then refrigerate in an airtight container for up to 2 days. When ready to serve, reheat the liquid, take the pan off the heat, cool slightly, and then stir in the egg mixture and hot red pepper flakes. If you like, the croutons can be made in advance and stored at room temperature in an airtight plastic bag.

GARLIC CROUTONS

4 slices hearty country-style bread cut ½ inch thick (about 6 ounces)

I medium clove garlic, peeled

SOUP

4 medium heads garlic (about 11 ounces total), smashed (see illustration on page 145)

½ cup extra-virgin olive oil

7 cups chicken stock, preferably homemade

2 cups water

2 Parmesan cheese rinds, each about 5 by 2 inches

4   sprigs fresh parsley

4   springs fresh thyme

2   bay leaves

2   large eggs, beaten lightly

2   tablespoons finely grated Parmesan cheese
    Salt and ground black pepper

¼   teaspoon hot red pepper flakes

1. FOR THE CROUTONS: Adjust the oven rack to the middle position and heat the oven to 400 degrees. Arrange the bread in a single layer on a rimmed baking sheet and bake until the bread is dry and crisp, about 10 minutes, turning over the bread slices halfway through the baking time. While still hot, rub the surface of the bread with the raw garlic clove. Cut the bread into ½-inch cubes and set aside.

2. FOR THE SOUP: Bring the smashed garlic, olive oil, and 1 cup chicken stock to a simmer in a small saucepan over low heat, stirring frequently. Cook until the garlic is soft enough to mash with the back of a spoon, about 35 minutes.

3. Meanwhile, bring the remaining 6 cups chicken stock, water, Parmesan rinds, parsley, thyme, and bay leaves to a boil in a large saucepan over high heat.

SMASHING GARLIC

The secret to garlic soup is releasing flavor from the individual cloves. Many recipes call for peeling and mincing several heads of garlic. We found we could get around this tedious step by smashing whole heads of garlic inside two 1-gallon zipper-lock plastic bags (doubled up to prevent leaks). Use a meat pounder, a rubber mallet, or the bottom of a small skillet to smash the cloves until they are reduced to ¼-inch-long shards or bits. Large pieces of skin should be picked out, but otherwise the entire mixture can be poached in oil. The remaining skins are removed when the broth is strained.

Reduce the heat to medium and simmer until the stock is flavorful, about 30 minutes.

4. Transfer the simmered garlic mixture to the pot with the chicken stock. Increase the heat to medium-high and boil until the garlic flavor is infused into the stock, about 10 minutes.

5. Meanwhile, beat the eggs and grated cheese in a small bowl with a fork until combined.

6. Strain the broth through a fine-mesh strainer, pushing on the solids with a spoon to extract all the liquid. Return the stock to a clean large saucepan (off heat) and season with salt and pepper to taste. Stir in the hot red pepper flakes and the egg mixture. Add several croutons to individual bowls, ladle the soup over the croutons, and serve immediately.

FRENCH ONION SOUP

MAKING TRADITIONAL FRENCH ONION SOUP is easily a two-day affair, with one day spent making the beef stock and the next toiling over the onions to finish the soup. And there's no guarantee that it will turn out right. We ended up with many crocks of flavorless onions floating in hypersalty beef bouillon and topped with globs of greasy melted cheese. We also had weak, watery soups. French onion soup should have a dark, rich liquid base, intensely flavored by a plethora of seriously cooked onions and covered by a crouton that is broth-soaked underneath and cheesy and crusty on top.

The first obstacle to success was the liquid. This soup is most commonly made with homemade beef stock. If the right stock is used (such as our Rich Beef Stock), the results can be delicious. But making beef stock takes at least three hours. We wondered if there was a way to get around this step.

We tested soups made with chicken stock, both homemade (which takes considerably less time to prepare than beef stock) and canned. Both were, well, too chickeny and just not right. Soups made with canned beef broth were terrible; it didn't have enough flavor to carry the day. After some experimentation, we devised a formula for a "cheater's" broth that combined canned beef and chicken broths with red wine (the secret ingredient). It had enough good, rich flavor to make an excellent soup base.

The next obvious step was to examine the onion factor. After a crying game of slicing many onions of several varieties and then sautéing away, we found Vidalias to be disappointingly bland and boring, white onions to be candy sweet and one-dimensional, and yellows to be only mildly flavorful, with a slight sweetness. Red onions ranked supreme. They were intensely oniony, sweet but not cloying, with subtle complexity and nuance.

It was exasperating that the onions took so long—nearly an hour—to caramelize. On top of that, they required frequent stirring to keep them from sticking to the bottom of the pot and burning. We found that adding salt to the onions as they began to cook helped to draw out some of the water and shaved about 10 minutes off the cooking time. But we began to wonder if it was necessary for the onions to be so caramelized. We tried, as one recipe suggested, sautéing them until just softened and col-ored, but they didn't brown enough to contribute much flavor to the soup. Maybe, we thought, a vig-orous sauté over high heat to achieve deep browning might do the trick. Not so. Onions cooked that way did not lose enough liquid and made the soup watery and bland. Besides, there is something wrong with onions in onion soup that have even an iota of crunch. We also tried roasting the onions, thinking that the even, constant heat of the oven might be the answer. Wrong again. Going in and out of the oven to stir the onions was an incredible hassle.

It was inattentiveness that caused us to let the drip-pings in a pot of onions go a little too far. The onions themselves weren't thoroughly caramelized, but all the goo stuck to the bottom of the pot was. We were sure that the finished soup would taste burnt but were surprised to find that it was, in fact, as sweet, rich, and flavorful as the soups we had been making with fully caramelized onions. To refine the technique we had stumbled on, we decided that medium-high heat was the way to go and that the drippings should be very, very deeply browned. There's no way around frequent stirring, but this method cut another 10 minutes off the onion-cooking time, bringing it down to just over 30 minutes.

With all those wonderful, tasty drippings stuck on the bottom of the pot, the deglazing process of adding the liquid and scraping up all the browned bits is crucial. Once the broth is added to the onions, we found that a simmering time of 20 minutes is needed to allow the onion flavor to permeate the broth and for the flavors to meld.

Many French onion soup recipes call for herbs. A couple of sprigs of fresh parsley, some thyme, and a bay leaf simmered in the soup rounded out the fla-vors and imparted freshness. We also tried a smidgen of garlic, but its flavor was far too distinct in a soup where onions should take center stage.

Finally, we tried a little flour as a thickener, stir-ring it into the onions after they were cooked. It added body to the soup, but it also bogged down the flavor and muddied its appearance. The soup was better without it. Having arrived at a soup that was rich, well-balanced, and full of fabulous onion flavor, it was time to move on to the crouton and the cheese, much to our tasters' delight.

Some recipes call for placing the crouton in the bottom of the bowl and ladling the soup over it. We disagree. We opt to set the crouton on top, so that only its bottom side is moistened with broth while its top side is crusted with cheese. The crouton can then physically support the cheese and keep it from sinking into the soup. To keep as much cheese as possible on the surface, we used two croutons, instead of only one, to completely fill the mouth of the bowl. A baguette can be cut on the bias as nec-essary to secure the closest fit in the bowl.

Traditionally, French onion soup is topped with Swiss, Gruyère, or Emmentaler cheese. We also ven-tured across the border to try Parmesan, Asiago, moz-zarella, and fontina. Plain Swiss cheese was neither outstanding nor offensive. It was gooey, bubbly, and mild, in characteristic Swiss flavor. Both Gruyère and Emmentaler melted to perfection and were sweet, nutty, and faintly tangy, but they also were very strong and pungent, overwhelming many tasters' palettes. We surprised ourselves by favoring the subdued Italian Asiago. Its flavor, like that of Gruyère and Emmentaler, was sweet and nutty, but without the pungent quality. Parmesan, too, was good, with a pleasant sweetness and saltiness, but without the nut-tiness of Asiago. The big losers were mozzarella and fontina. The former was extremely bland, too chewy, rubbery, and suggestive of pizza topping; the latter was very soft, almost wet and slippery, with no distinctive character.

Both Asiago and Parmesan are dry, not "melting," cheeses, so although we were leaning toward them in flavor, we were left wanting better texture. The obvious answer was to combine cheeses. We tried a layer of Swiss topped with a grating of Asiago. It was a winning combination of chewy goodness and nutty sweetness.

The final coup that weakens knees and makes French onion soup irresistible is a browned, bubbly, molten cheese crust. The quickest way to brown the cheese is to set the bowls on a rimmed baking sheet under the broiler, so heatsafe bowls are essential. Bowls or crocks with handles make maneuvering easier. This is no soup for fine china.

French Onion Soup

SERVES 6

For a soup that is resplendent with deep, rich flavors, use 8 cups of Rich Beef Stock (page 30) in place of the canned chicken and beef broths and red wine. Tie the parsley and thyme sprigs together with kitchen twine so they will be easy to retrieve from the soup pot. Slicing the baguette on the bias will yield slices shaped to fill the mouths of the bowls.

SOUP

2	tablespoons unsalted butter
5	medium red onions (about 3 pounds), sliced thin
	Salt
6	cups canned low-sodium chicken broth
1 ¾	cups canned low-sodium beef broth
¼	cup dry red wine
2	sprigs fresh parsley
1	sprig fresh thyme
1	bay leaf
1	tablespoon balsamic vinegar
	Ground black pepper

CHEESE-TOPPED CRUST

1	baguette, cut on the bias into ¾-inch slices (2 slices per serving)
4 ½	ounces Swiss cheese, sliced ¹⁄₁₆ inch thick
3	ounces Asiago cheese, grated

1. FOR THE SOUP: Melt the butter in a large stockpot or Dutch oven over medium-high heat. Add the sliced onions and ½ teaspoon salt and stir to coat the onions thoroughly with butter. Cook, stirring frequently, until the onions are reduced and syrupy and the inside of the pot is coated with a very deep brown crust, 30 to 35 minutes. Stir in the chicken and beef broths, red wine, parsley, thyme, and bay leaf, scraping the pot bottom with a wooden spoon to loosen the browned bits, and bring to a simmer. Simmer to blend flavors, about 20 minutes, and discard the herbs. Stir in the balsamic vinegar and adjust the seasonings with salt and pepper to taste. (The soup can be cooled to room temperature and refrigerated in an airtight container up to 2 days. Return to a simmer before finishing the soup with croutons and cheese.)

2. FOR THE CRUST: Adjust the oven rack to the upper-middle position and heat the broiler. Set serving bowls on a large rimmed baking sheet and fill each with about 1½ cups soup. Top each bowl with two baguette slices and divide the Swiss cheese slices, placing them in a single layer, if possible, on the bread. Sprinkle each bowl with about 2 tablespoons grated Asiago cheese. Place the baking sheet in the oven and broil until the cheese is well-browned and bubbly, about 10 minutes. Cool for 5 minutes and then serve immediately.

SCIENCE: Blue Onion Soup?

Red onions may be the best choice in terms of flavor, but they can turn onion soup an unappetizing bluish-gray color. This is because they contain anthocyanin, a water-soluble pigment that also causes red cabbage to discolor when cooked. This pigment is present in some other reddish fruits and vegetables as well, such as cherries and radishes.

When the fruit or vegetable is cooked in liquid, the anthocyanin leaches out. If the liquid is alkaline (as is the case with our soup), the anthocyanin turns blue. Adding some acid, either lemon juice or vinegar, to the soup at the end helps it to regain its reddish color. This may sound improbable, but when we stirred in 1 tablespoon of balsamic vinegar, the soup returned to a deep reddish brown. The vinegar also brightens the flavors in the soup.

SCIENCE: Cry Me a River

Every now and then, something will prompt you to think of a particular song. In our test kitchen, that something occurred every time we had to slice another batch of onions for another pot of soup, and the song that came to mind, of course, was Arthur Hamilton's "Cry Me a River." As we started humming it for the umpteenth time, we began to wonder if we could change our tune to Johnny Nash's "I Can See Clearly Now."

Over the past couple of years, we have compiled more than 20 ideas from reader correspondence, books, and conversations with colleagues all aimed at reducing tears while cutting onions. What better time than now, we thought, to put these ideas to the test?

The problem, it turns out, derives from the sulfuric compounds in onions. When an onion is cut, the cells that are damaged release sulfuric compounds as well as various enzymes, notably sulfoxide lyase. Those compounds, which are separated in the onion's cell structure, activate and mix to form the real culprit, a volatile new compound—thiopropanal sulfoxide. When thiopropanal sulfoxide evaporates into the air, it irritates the eyes and causes tearing. Some sources we consulted even claim that the irritants produce a very mild form of sulfuric acid in the eyes.

The two general methods that we found worked best were to protect our eyes by covering them with goggles or contact lenses or to introduce a flame near the cut onions. The goggles and contact lenses form a physical barrier that keeps the gases from irritating the eyes. The flame, which can be produced by either a lit candle or a gas burner, changes the activity of the thiopropanal sulfoxide by completely oxidizing it.

CHEDDAR CHEESE SOUP

WHEN MOST PEOPLE THINK OF CHEDDAR cheese soup, they think of a day-glo-colored, glue-like substance that comes out of a can and tastes something like nacho sauce. When made well, however, cheddar cheese soup is an elegant dish with layers of complementary flavors. It should burst with cheddar flavor, but the dairy element should not be overpowering. The color should be inviting and warm-yellow, not shocking orange. Using white cheddar instead of orange cheddar seemed a good start, but we knew the recipe would be more complicated to develop than simply choosing a cheese.

For our first tests we tried three recipes. The first was very simple, using a basic béchamel sauce that was finished with some cheese. Butter and flour were cooked to create a roux, milk was added to form the béchamel, and shredded cheese was stirred in at the end. The second recipe was essentially the same except that cream was used in place of the milk and some onions were sautéed in the butter. The third recipe was more complex. It began by sautéing mirepoix (diced onions, carrots, and celery) in butter. Flour was added to form a roux, but the liquid was a blend of milk and chicken stock. Aromatics (peppercorns, parsley stems, and a bay leaf) were simmered to add flavor to the soup, which was finished with cheese just before serving.

The results were as expected. The simpleton soup of béchamel with cheese had a boring, simple cheese flavor. It was also quite plain looking, almost blond. The second version with cream and onions had more heft and flavor and was better liked by tasters. However, it still wasn't all that good. The third soup was the best of the lot. The combination of the mirepoix, chicken stock, bay leaf, and parsley stems made this soup taste more interesting than the others, which were basically cheese melted in milk or cream. This third soup was not without problems, however. It lacked a good cheddar punch. This soup was also pureed, which some tasters liked and some did not. (Although the pureeing turns the soup smooth, it also makes it somewhat foamy.)

We came away from this initial round of testing with these observations. Cheddar cheese soup needs both sautéed vegetables (mirepoix) and chicken stock. Without both, the soup has a one-dimensional, lactose-heavy flavor that's hard to distinguish from good-quality nacho sauce.

We went back to our third test recipe (the one with the mirepoix) and started some experiments. We tried half-and-half in place of the milk and the soup improved greatly. The extra fat made the soup rich and luxurious. We saw no point in trying to use cream. The soup was already quite rich.

Although mirepoix had already shown itself to be necessary, there were two schools of thought on whether the soup should be smooth or slightly textured. Everyone liked the textured soup with bits of sautéed vegetables still visible, while some did not like the smooth soup. We decided to make pureeing an optional step.

Cheddar cheese is the focal point of this soup, and we fussed with the amount of cheese until we dared go no higher. We ended up with 12 ounces of cheese for 5 cups of liquid. Our recipe calls for more cheese than any recipe we uncovered in our research.

We tried a variety of white American cheddars in our recipe and, although there were differences, they all worked. We did not try any English cheddars because most are orange in color. As for the differences between mild, sharp, and extra-sharp, we found that an extra-sharp cheddar makes the soup piquant, while mild cheddar produces a bland soup. We decided to steer a middle course and use sharp cheddar cheese. Owing to the amount of cheese used, the soup does reflect the flavor of the cheese, whatever its quality or degree of sharpness. We found Cabot cheese, a nationally available supermarket brand from Vermont, to work particularly well.

Up until this point in our testing, we had based all of the soups on a roux. However, we had uncovered several recipes without any flour or a roux. Most of these recipes called for reducing half-and-half to thicken the soup. We were intrigued by these recipes and tried several. While this method does work, we found that it produces a soup that is much less stable. The roux provides a stable, starchy base into which we could easily load a lot of cheese without worrying about the soup separating, or curdling. So we experimented with the amount of flour and found that 2 tablespoons of flour and 3 tablespoons of butter make enough roux to thicken and stabilize 7 cups of soup without making it gummy.

After testing several seasonings, we decided to include a pinch of cayenne, a drizzle of dry sherry, and a sprinkle of fresh thyme. The cayenne adds a touch of heat and helps balance the richness in this soup. The dry sherry brought the various flavors together and gave the soup a more refined taste. The fresh thyme is a nice complement to the cheddar. No one really liked Worcestershire sauce or dry mustard, common additions in other recipes.

As for the cooking process, it is very easy to sauté the vegetables in some butter, add flour to make a roux, then whisk in the stock and half-and-half, add a bay leaf, and simmer until the vegetables are tender. The real trick to making this soup is in how you add the cheese. Even with a roux, this soup can easily separate because so much cheese is used. We found that if we removed the pot from the heat and allowed it to cool for a minute or two, the shredded cheese stirred right in without causing a problem.

The final soup is fantastic. It is elegant and has a great cheddar punch without being too thick or chalky. It's perfect on a winter's day. Best of all, it can be made—start to finish—in about 30 minutes.

Cheddar Cheese Soup

SERVES 4 TO 6

We like the little bits of cooked vegetables in this recipe. However, if you want a smooth soup, puree the base after the vegetables soften in step 2 and then pour it through a strainer; proceed as directed in step 3. This soup can be tricky to reheat and isn't the best candidate for making in advance. Leftovers can be refrigerated in an airtight container for 2 to 3 days. Reheat the soup in a saucepan over low heat, whisking frequently to prevent the soup from separating and curdling. Do not heat the soup above a bare simmer.

3	tablespoons unsalted butter
I	medium onion, minced
I	small shallot, minced
I	medium carrot, minced
I	small stalk celery, minced
I	medium clove garlic, minced
2	tablespoons all-purpose flour
2½	cups homemade chicken stock or canned low-sodium chicken broth
2½	cups half-and-half
I	bay leaf
	Pinch cayenne pepper
3	tablespoons dry sherry
12	ounces sharp white cheddar cheese, shredded (about 3 cups)
I	tablespoon minced fresh thyme leaves
	Salt and ground black pepper

1. Heat the butter in a large stockpot or Dutch oven over medium heat until foaming. Add the

onion and shallot and cook, stirring occasionally, until softened, about 4 minutes. Add the carrot, celery, and garlic and cook until the garlic is fragrant, about 1 minute. Add the flour and cook, stirring to coat the vegetables, until the mixture begins to brown on the bottom of the pot, about 2 minutes.

2. Gradually whisk in the chicken stock and half-and-half. Add the bay leaf and increase the heat to medium-high. Bring to a boil, reduce the heat to medium-low, and simmer until the vegetables soften, about 3 minutes.

3. Remove the pot from the heat. Stir in the cayenne and sherry and allow to cool slightly, about 2 minutes. Slowly whisk in the cheese and thyme until the cheese melts. Season with salt and pepper to taste and serve immediately.

➤ VARIATIONS

Smoked Cheddar Cheese Soup with Bacon

Smoked cheddar cheese is an excellent complement to the bacon, but regular cheddar cheese will work in this recipe.

Cut 4 bacon slices crosswise into ¼-inch strips and fry in a large stockpot or Dutch oven over medium-high heat until crisp, about 5 minutes. With a slotted spoon, transfer the bacon to a paper towel–lined plate and set aside. Follow recipe for Cheddar Cheese Soup, substituting the bacon fat in the pot for the butter; substituting 6 ounces smoked cheddar cheese, shredded (about 1½ cups), for an equal amount of sharp cheddar cheese; and reducing sherry to 2 tablespoons. Garnish each serving with bacon bits.

Cheddar and Ale Soup with Potato

The type of ale used can make a huge difference in this variation. We found that inexpensive, light-colored ales worked well and were universally pleasing, while heartier ales made a darker, more potent-tasting soup.

Follow recipe for Cheddar Cheese Soup, adding 1 medium Yukon Gold potato, peeled and cut into ¼-inch dice (about ⅔ cup), along with carrot, celery, and garlic; substituting 1½ cups ale for an equal amount of chicken stock; and reducing the sherry to 2 tablespoons.

7

PASTA AND BEAN SOUPS

PASTA AND BEANS MAKE ESPECIALLY HEARTY soups. Pasta and beans can be used singly or in combination, as in the case of the Italian soup pasta e fagioli (see page 155).

When it comes to soup, pasta is generally a team player. In Italian soups, small pasta shapes are cooked right in the soup pot, along with vegetables and plenty of stock. (The pasta soaks up liquid as it softens, so at the outset there must be plenty of liquid in the pot.) The starch from the pasta helps to thicken the soup and gives it body. In Asian soups, long noodles are cooked in a separate pot and then divided among individual bowls. Asian noodle soups are assembled in serving bowls, with vegetables, protein (beef, pork, shrimp, tofu, etc.), liquid, and garnishes scattered, ladled, or sprinkled over the noodles.

In contrast, legumes—including beans, lentils, and split peas—in a soup recipe are generally the focal point. Vegetables and pork products are added for depth, but they are generally cut quite small and used in limited amounts.

When beans are added in smaller amounts (such as in minestrone or pasta e fagioli), we have found that canned beans are a fine option. However, when making a bean soup, such as black bean soup or white bean soup, take the extra time to start with dried beans. Our tests revealed that soaking is not necessary, so most of these soups can be on the table in about two hours.

TUSCAN WHITE BEAN SOUP

WE HAVE OFTEN THOUGHT OF WHITE BEAN soup as a choice between soup with mushy, exploded beans in an unmemorable liquid or soup filled with beans reminiscent of pebbles. But when made right (as is usually the case in Italy), Tuscan white bean soup can be amazingly delicious. And it can be easy to make. This soup is a testament to restraint, comprising only two components: tender, creamy beans and a soup base perfumed with the fragrance of garlic and rosemary. We surmised that a soup so simple would be easy to duplicate. We had no idea.

We based our initial research on Italian recipes that used navy, great northern, or cannellini (white

kidney) beans. After cooking a few batches, we found that we preferred the larger size and appearance of the cannellini beans, so we centered our testing on them. Many of these recipes came with tips and warnings on how to achieve a cooked bean with perfect texture. "Always soak the beans overnight to ensure even cooking" and "Never salt the beans while they are cooking or they will become tough or split open" were common counsel. Surely these "rules" were established for a reason. They couldn't be merely rural myths, could they?

We decided to find out and started with rule number one: Always soak the beans. We cooked up three batches of beans. Prior to cooking, we soaked one batch overnight and another according to the "quick-soak" method (water and beans simmer for two minutes, then are taken off heat, covered, and allowed to sit in the water for one hour). We didn't presoak the third batch at all. The results were altogether disappointing. Both batches of soaked beans split or exploded. The unsoaked beans looked better, but their texture was uneven; by the time half of the beans were tender, the other half had overcooked and disintegrated.

We wondered what would happen if we cooked unsoaked beans until just barely done, then let them sit off the heat in their still-hot cooking liquid. Would the residual heat from the liquid finish cooking the beans without any splitting or bursting? The answer was yes. This batch produced perfectly cooked beans that were creamy but not soggy.

Now we took on rule number two: Never salt the beans during cooking. Recipes that warned against salting stated that it would cause the outer shell of the bean to toughen. We tested beans cooked in salted water and in unsalted water, and the salted beans were indeed slightly more toothsome on the outside. However, these beans were not any less cooked on the inside than the unsalted beans. In addition, the small amount of resistance that the salted beans had developed on the outside seemed to keep them from bursting. The beans were now softly structured on the outside and tooth-tender on the inside.

One other advantage of using salted water is flavor. The seasoned beans were simply much tastier than those cooked in unsalted water. We reasoned that by adding other ingredients to the cooking liquid, we could improve the flavor of the beans that much more. (See "Flavoring Beans" on page 160.) In our initial testing, tasters preferred the beans flavored with pork rather than chicken. But because meat is not called for in the finished soup (only the extracted flavor of the meat is used), we didn't want to use expensive cuts of pork, such as loin chops, only to throw out the meat later. We reasoned that a ham hock or bacon would do the job, but smoked meats, we found out, added an unwanted sugary-smoky flavor reminiscent of canned soup. We tried an unsmoked ham hock, but the flavor lacked the punch that we were looking for. Finally, we tried pancetta, a salt-cured, unsmoked Italian bacon. The pancetta gave the beans a welcome sweet and sour flavor, and the rendered fat boosted the pork flavor of the broth. Cutting the pancetta into large cubes made it easy to remove once the beans were cooked. Onion, garlic, and a bay leaf are the other traditional additions; their flavors permeated the beans.

So now we had perfectly cooked beans, full of flavor from the pork and aromatics. Surely the finished soup would take little more than some rosemary and a light drizzling of olive oil to finish. Wrong. Although the beans were delicious enough to be eaten on their own, the liquid base was lacking that bright, full garlic flavor we wanted. It was clear that we would have to add a second batch of vegetables toward the end of the cooking process.

We cooked another batch of beans with all of the accouterments, strained them from their cooking liquid, and allowed them to cool on the side while we proceeded. Sautéing was key to releasing the flavors from the aromatics quickly, and a short swim in the bean water helped to blend the flavors.

Now we needed to work in the flavor of rosemary, an herb traditional to white bean soup. We tried cooking the rosemary with the beans, but that produced a bitter, medicinal broth. Recalling a technique used in our shrimp bisque recipe, we allowed the herb to steep off heat in the hot liquid for just a few minutes at the finish of our recipe. It worked—just the right amount of bright, fresh rosemary flavor was infused into the soup.

Tuscan White Bean Soup
SERVES 6 TO 8

If possible, use fresh dried beans in this soup (see page 154 for details). For a more authentic soup, place a small slice of lightly toasted Italian bread in the bottom of each bowl and ladle the soup over. To make this a vegetarian soup, omit the pancetta and add a 4-ounce piece of Parmesan rind to the pot along with the halved onion and unpeeled garlic in step 1.

6	ounces pancetta, one 1-inch-thick slice, cut into 1-inch cubes
1	pound (2¼ cups) dried cannellini beans, rinsed and picked over
1	large onion, unpeeled and halved pole to pole, plus 1 small onion, chopped medium
4	medium cloves garlic, unpeeled, plus 3 medium cloves garlic, peeled and minced
1	bay leaf
	Salt and ground black pepper
¼	cup extra-virgin olive oil, plus extra for drizzling over individual bowls
1	sprig fresh rosemary

1. Cook the pancetta in a large stockpot or Dutch oven over medium heat until just golden, 8 to 10 minutes. Add 12 cups water, beans, halved onion, unpeeled garlic, bay leaf, and 1 teaspoon salt. Bring to a boil over medium-high heat. Cover the pot partially, reduce the heat to low, and simmer, stirring occasionally, until the beans are almost tender, 1 to 1¼ hours. Remove the pot from the heat, cover, and let stand until the beans are tender, about 30 minutes. Drain the beans, reserving the cooking liquid. (You should have about 5 cups; if not, add more water.) Discard the pancetta, onion, garlic, and bay leaf. Spread the beans in an even layer on a rimmed baking sheet and cool.

2. While the beans are cooling, heat the oil in the now-empty Dutch oven over medium heat until shimmering. Add chopped onion and cook, stirring occasionally, until softened, 5 to 6 minutes. Stir in the minced garlic and cook until fragrant, about 30 seconds. Add the cooled beans and cooking liquid, increase the heat to medium-high, and bring to a simmer. Submerge the rosemary sprig in the liquid, cover the pot, and let stand off heat for 15 to 20 minutes.

3. Discard the rosemary sprig and season to taste with salt and pepper. Ladle the soup into individual bowls and drizzle each bowl with olive oil. Serve immediately.

➤ VARIATION

White Bean Soup with Winter Vegetables

SERVES 10 TO 12

The addition of carrots, potatoes, leeks, celery, kale, and escarole makes this soup much more substantial.

6	ounces pancetta, one 1-inch-thick slice, cut into 1-inch cubes
1	pound (2¼ cups) dried cannellini beans, rinsed and picked over
1	large onion, unpeeled and halved pole to pole, plus 1 small onion, chopped medium
4	medium cloves garlic, unpeeled, plus 3 medium cloves garlic, minced
1	bay leaf
	Salt and ground black pepper
¼	cup extra-virgin olive oil, plus extra for drizzling over individual bowls
2	small carrots, chopped medium
2	stalks celery, chopped medium
2	small leeks, white and light green parts, cut crosswise into ½-inch pieces (see illustrations on page 124 to clean)
4	ounces kale, stems discarded and leaves cut into ½-inch strips (about 3 cups; see illustrations on page 140 to clean)
4	ounces escarole, stems discarded and leaves cut into ½-inch strips (about 3 cups)
2	small red potatoes, peeled and cut into ½-inch dice
1	(14½-ounce) can diced tomatoes, drained
1	sprig fresh rosemary

1. Cook the pancetta in a large stockpot or Dutch oven over medium heat until just golden, 8 to 10 minutes. Add 12 cups water, beans, halved onion, unpeeled garlic, bay leaf, and 1 teaspoon salt. Bring to a boil over medium-high heat. Cover the pot partially, reduce the heat to low, and simmer, stirring occasionally, until the beans are almost tender, 1 to 1¼ hours. Remove the pot from the heat, cover, and let stand until the beans are tender, about 30 minutes. Drain the beans, reserving the cooking liquid. (You should have about 5 cups. Add enough water to yield 9 cups.) Discard the pancetta, onion, garlic, and bay leaf. Spread the beans in an even layer on a rimmed baking sheet and cool.

2. While the beans are cooling, heat the oil in the now-empty Dutch oven over medium heat until shimmering. Add chopped onion, carrots, celery, and leeks and cook, stirring occasionally, until softened but not browned, about 7 minutes. Stir in the minced garlic and cook until fragrant, about 30 seconds. Add the bean cooking liquid, kale, and escarole, increase the heat to medium-high, and bring to a boil. Cover, reduce the heat to low, and simmer for 30 minutes. Add the potatoes and tomatoes, cover, and cook until the potatoes are tender, about 20

INGREDIENTS: "Fresh" Dried Beans

As one of our test cooks stood over pots of beans during the testing for Tuscan bean soup, she began to wonder if there was a way to tell if the beans were fresh. Noticing a pile of raw beans shriveling in a bowl of water, a colleague observed that beans shrivel when they are old. The test cook herself became aware that some of the beans she cooked were old when, instead of being creamy, their interiors were gritty or mealy. Because bean bags contain no "sell by" date, however, we were uncertain how to determine if the beans we pulled off the supermarket shelves were fresh.

For more information, we contacted legume expert Dr. Barry Swanson at Washington State University. Yes, shriveling during soaking is generally a sign of age, he told us. That is because beans should absorb moisture only through their hilum, the part of the bean that attaches to the pod. But beans are not handled with much care, Swanson said: "People think of them as piles of rocks or gravel." Beans that have been knocked around can develop holes in their seed coats. Even carefully handled beans develop these holes (called "checks") over time because of fluctuations in temperature, moisture, and fungi growth. These holes subsequently admit water, shriveling the bean. Dr. Swanson counsels that apart from soaking, there is no way to tell if the beans you buy are fresh. His advice: "If you find some fresh beans, buy some more."

RIBOLLITA

If you find yourself with a plethora of leftover bean soup, have no fear. In Tuscany, where nothing is wasted, leftover soup is not seen as a problem but rather as the last step in creating a delicious, homey dish called *ribollita*, Italian for "reboiled."

The leftover soup is warmed over medium-low heat. Slices of rustic day-old bread are submerged in the soup until completely softened, then the mixture is blended or mashed until very thick. True ribollita connoisseurs say that it must be thick enough to eat with a fork.

Don't be put off by the strange appearance of this dish—what ribollita lacks in beauty it more than makes up for in flavor. But do be sure to use a good-quality artisan or rustic bread when making ribollita; a fluffy, supermarket bread will result in a mushy, sloppy mess.

minutes. Add the cooled beans, increase the heat to medium-high, and bring to a simmer. Submerge the rosemary sprig in the liquid, cover the pot, and let stand off heat for 15 to 20 minutes.

3. Discard the rosemary sprig and season to taste with salt and pepper. Ladle the soup into individual bowls and drizzle each bowl with olive oil. Serve immediately.

➤ VARIATION

Quick Tuscan White Bean Soup

This quick variation uses canned beans and can be on the table in just 40 minutes. For information on buying canned beans, see page 157.

6	ounces pancetta, one 1-inch-thick slice, cut into 1-inch cubes
2	tablespoons extra-virgin olive oil, plus extra for drizzling over individual bowls
1	small onion, chopped medium
3	medium cloves garlic, minced
4	(15½-ounce) cans cannellini beans, drained and rinsed
	Salt and ground black pepper
1	sprig fresh rosemary

Cook the pancetta in a large stockpot or Dutch oven over medium heat until just golden, 8 to 10 minutes.

Discard the pancetta and add the oil to the pot with the pancetta fat. Add onion and cook, stirring occasionally, until softened, 5 to 6 minutes. Stir in the garlic and cook until fragrant, about 30 seconds. Add the beans, ½ teaspoon salt, and 3½ cups water. Increase the heat to medium-high and bring to a simmer. Submerge the rosemary in the liquid, cover the pot, and let stand off heat 15 to 20 minutes. Discard the rosemary and adjust the seasonings with salt and pepper. Ladle the soup into individual bowls and drizzle each bowl with olive oil. Serve immediately.

PASTA E FAGIOLI

PASTA E FAGIOLI (OR PASTA AND BEANS) IS a hearty, nutritious peasant soup made throughout Italy. The beans and pasta shapes used vary from region to region, but the broad outlines of this soup are the same. This soup is loaded with ingredients and is quite thick. The orange-red color comes from tomatoes, and each spoonful should be laden with pasta and beans. The soup is full of harmonious flavors, with no single taste standing out. The vegetables are used as accents and cut small. A drizzle of olive oil and dusting of grated Parmesan cheese are typical garnishes.

Most recipes follow a similar procedure. The aromatics (vegetables and often some pork product) are sautéed in olive oil. The tomatoes and broth go into the pot, followed by the beans and lastly the pasta. Our goal was to streamline the process and create a full-flavored soup that could be on the table in less than one hour.

Many authentic recipes call for pancetta, unsmoked Italian bacon. (Americanized recipes call for regular bacon.) For our first test, we sautéed 4 ounces of diced pancetta in ¼ cup of olive oil prior to adding the aromatic vegetables. We found this amount of fat to be excessive, and the resulting soup had an oily texture. We reduced the pancetta to 3 ounces and the olive oil to 1 tablespoon and then compared this soup with one made with 3 tablespoons of oil and no meat. All tasters felt that the pancetta added complexity to the soup. When diced small, the pancetta almost disappeared in the final soup. Its flavor lingered, though. Pancetta gave the soup a subtle pork flavor, but tasters did not mind the stronger, smokier flavor of regular bacon.

Most Italian recipes use the same quartet of aromatic vegetables—onions, celery, carrots, and garlic. Tasters liked the onions, celery, and garlic but were divided about the sweetness imparted by the carrots. We decided to use carrots with the kidney bean variation—the sweetness of the carrots balances the earthiness of the beans—but to omit this ingredient from the master recipe.

Once the aromatics have been sautéed, most recipes use tomatoes or stock to deglaze the pan. We also wanted to try white wine. The wine proved to be a bad idea; the tomatoes provide plenty of acidity, and adding wine just made the soup sour. Both the tomatoes and stock worked fine, but we liked the way the tomatoes and aromatics blended, so decided to add them to the pot first.

Pasta e fagioli usually starts with canned beans. The challenge is to get some flavor into them. We wondered if adding the beans to the tomato mixture (before the stock) would help infuse them with the flavors of the pancetta, oil, and vegetables. We prepared two batches of soup—one with beans and stock added simultaneously and one with beans added to the tomatoes and cooked for 10 minutes before the stock went into the pot. As we had hoped, simmering the beans in the thick tomato mixture infused them with flavor and was worth the extra step.

We next focused on the type of beans. Cranberry beans, a pink-and-white mottled variety, are especially popular in Italy. Since cranberry beans are hard to find in this country, we tested two common substitutes, pinto and red kidney beans. Neither bean has the sweet, delicate flavor of a cranberry bean, but tasters felt that the red kidneys were a closer approximation. Cannellini beans, also known as white kidney beans, are the other common choice in this soup. These oval-shaped beans are sweet and creamy. Since they are widely available, we decided to use them in the master recipe.

Our recipe was coming together, but we had a few more points to consider. Many versions of this soup rely on chicken stock. However, many of our tasters complained that the chicken flavor was too strong.

Was this chicken noodle soup with beans, they wondered? We decided some experiments were in order. First, we used water instead of chicken stock and added a Parmesan rind to pump up the flavor. This trick had worked well in our minestrone recipe. Tasters liked pasta e fagioli made this way. The cheese added flavor and body. As a final test, we decided to keep the Parmesan rind and use half water and half chicken stock. This combination produced the best soup—the flavors were rich but not chickeny, and the liquid had better body.

Our last area to investigate was pasta. Our tests showed that smaller shapes are best in this soup. Larger shapes crowded out the other ingredients and soaked up too much liquid. Ditalini (small tubes), tubetini (very small tubes), and orzo (rice-shaped pasta) were favorites among our tasters. We also liked conchigliette (very small shells with ridges), but this shape is hard to find. Elbows were acceptable but a bit on the large side.

Pasta e Fagioli
SERVES 6 TO 8

This hearty pasta and bean soup is so simple and delicious it is easy to understand why regional versions are found throughout Italy. We wanted ours to be quick cooking; by using canned beans the soup is prepared in less than one hour. Pancetta or bacon and the rind from a wedge of Parmesan infuse flavor into the broth. We preferred using half water and half chicken stock, but the bacon and cheese rind will flavor the soup nicely if stock is not available (use 2 quarts of water and increase the salt to 2 teaspoons). Combined with a green salad and some crusty bread, this soup makes an excellent dinner. Because of the pasta and beans, this soup does not hold well and should be served as soon as it is ready.

3	tablespoons extra-virgin olive oil
3	ounces bacon or pancetta, chopped fine
I	medium onion, chopped fine
I	medium stalk celery, chopped fine
4	medium cloves garlic, minced
I	teaspoon dried oregano
1/4	teaspoon hot red pepper flakes
2	(14 1/2-ounce) cans diced tomatoes
I	Parmesan cheese rind, about 5 inches by 2 inches

2 (15½-ounce) cans cannellini beans, drained and rinsed

4 cups homemade chicken stock or canned low-sodium chicken broth

1 teaspoon salt

8 ounces ditalini or other small pasta shape

¼ cup chopped fresh parsley leaves
Ground black pepper

1 cup freshly grated Parmesan cheese

1. Heat 1 tablespoon oil in a large stockpot or Dutch oven over medium–high heat. Add the bacon and sauté until browned, about 5 minutes. Add the onion and celery and cook, stirring occasionally, until the vegetables soften, 4 to 5 minutes. Add the garlic, oregano, and hot red pepper flakes, and sauté until fragrant, about 1 minute.

2. Add the tomatoes and scrape up any browned bits from the bottom of the pan. Add the cheese rind and the beans. Bring to a boil, reduce the heat to low, and simmer until the flavors meld, about 10 minutes. Add the chicken stock, 4 cups water, and salt. Raise the heat to high and bring to a boil. Add the pasta and cook until tender, about 8 minutes.

3. Off heat, remove and discard the cheese rind. Stir in most of the parsley and season with pepper and additional salt, if needed. Ladle the soup into individual bowls. Drizzle some of the remaining 2 tablespoons oil over each bowl and then sprinkle with parsley. Serve immediately, passing the grated cheese at the table.

➤ VARIATIONS
Tubetini and Chickpea Soup
Follow recipe for Pasta e Fagioli, substituting 1 tablespoon chopped fresh rosemary for the oregano, two 15½-ounce cans chickpeas for cannellini beans, and 8 ounces tubetini for ditalini.

Orzo and Kidney Bean Soup with Carrots
Follow recipe for Pasta e Fagioli, substituting 1 medium carrot, chopped small, for the celery, two 15½-ounce cans kidney beans for cannellini beans, and 8 ounces orzo for ditalini. Proceed as directed, increasing cooking time for pasta to 13 to 15 minutes.

INGREDIENTS: Canned Beans

So what about using canned beans in soups? In recipes that put beans center stage, we find that there is a real difference in flavor and texture between dried beans that you cook yourself and those out of a can. Beans from a can are much less flavorful. They taste of salt and not much else, compared with beans you cook yourself, which can take on the flavors of garlic, bay leaves, and other seasonings added to the water. Canned beans also tend to fall apart if simmered for any length of time, as required in our Black Bean Soup.

In recipes where beans are not the focal point and the cooking time is short, we find canned beans to be an acceptable shortcut. For instance, canned beans are fine in pasta e fagioli or minestrone. These soups have so many other ingredients that most people won't notice any flavor deficiencies in the canned beans.

We tested six leading brands of canned beans—both traditional and organic—to see if any brands would outperform the others in a soup recipe. We found that creamy, well-seasoned beans were preferred by the majority of tasters, in part because canned beans generally don't spend all that much time in the soup pot. If you want beans that are tender and flavorful in your soup, they should come out of the can with these qualities.

Our tasting panel found organic beans to be quite firm and chalky and to taste underseasoned. Green Giant and Goya beans were the top choices because they are creamy (but not mushy) and well seasoned.

BLACK BEAN SOUP

BLACK BEANS, ALSO CALLED TURTLE BEANS, are eaten widely in the Caribbean and Central and Latin America, and they often are served up in black bean soup. This peasant-style soup is robust, hearty, and earthy-tasting. Black beans have a wonderful creamy texture and a distinctive flavor. Their dark color provides a beautiful backdrop for a colorful array of garnishes.

We wanted to figure out how to build enough flavor to turn these beans into a satisfying bowl of soup. While we focused on flavor, we also paid close attention to texture. The perfect bean was tender without being mushy, with enough tooth to make a satisfying chew.

In pursuit of this perfect texture, we discovered that it was important to cook the beans in enough water; too little water and the beans on the top cooked more slowly than the beans underneath, and the whole pot took forever to cook. (Thirteen cups is sufficient water to cook 1 pound of beans.)

As we had done for our Tuscan White Bean soup, we did some further testing with black beans by comparing beans that had been soaked overnight with a batch of unsoaked, as well as with a batch softened by a "quick-soak" method in which the beans were brought to a boil, simmered two minutes, then covered to let stand for one hour off the heat. The quick-soak method caused a large percentage of the beans to burst during cooking. This reduced the chew we were after, so we nixed that method. Contrary to our expectations, overnight soaking decreased the cooking time by only about half an hour and didn't improve the texture. Because we are rarely organized enough to soak the night before, we no longer use this method.

The next theory to test was that salting toughens the skin of beans and lengthens the cooking time. We tested beans salted at the end of cooking, salted three-quarters of the way through cooking, and salted at the very beginning. In a blind tasting, we couldn't discern any difference in the skins, but only those beans salted from the beginning had enough salt for our taste, so for this soup we prefer to salt the beans from the outset. (See "Flavoring Beans" on page 160.)

Now that we had discovered how to cook beans with the texture we wanted, it was time to discover the best way to build more layers of flavor onto this base without drowning the earthy flavor of the beans. We determined that meat gave the beans a necessary depth of flavor. We tested cooking the beans with a ham hock, bacon, ham, and pork loin. We liked all four, and each gave the beans a slightly different flavor. The ham hock provided a smooth background taste, while bacon and ham produced a more assertive and salty flavor. Pork loin was the most subtle of the four choices. Since one ham hock is so inexpensive and flavors a whole pot of soup, we decided to use it in the master recipe. We include bacon in a variation.

In many Caribbean recipes, a sofrito is stirred in to flavor cooked beans. (A sofrito is a melange of vegetables—usually onion, garlic, and bell pepper—sautéed in olive oil until soft.) We found that this mixture adds another fresh layer without overpowering the flavor of the beans.

We ran several more experiments with flavorings. We tried adding sugar and found that we didn't like the additional sweetness. We also experimented with cumin, the traditional spice for black beans, simmered with the beans or mixed into the sofrito. The flavor of the spice got lost when simmered with the beans; we decided to save the cumin for the sofrito.

Black bean soup should be thick, not soupy. Some recipes use a blender or food processor to puree some of the beans and cooking liquid to create a thick texture. A few recipes blend all of the beans and create a soup that is essentially a thick puree, and others rely on some type of starch for thickening. At the outset, we decided we wanted our soup to have whole beans in it, so we dismissed the puree-only version. We did, however, try mashing beans into the sofrito; pureeing some of the beans (we tested various amounts) in the blender; breaking apart some of the beans in the food processor (we tested various amounts); and thickening with starch.

When either the blender or food processor was used, the resulting soup had a grayish brown color that was not as desirable as the more black color of the nonprocessed soups. These approaches also created more work, because the blender or food processor needed cleaning afterward. We found it simpler and easier to mash some of the beans with the sofrito using a potato masher. However, there was a limit to how many beans could go in the sauté pan at one time for mashing.

We considered combining the mashed beans with other classic approaches to thickening. A few recipes add flour to the sofrito, but we did not like this approach. The soup often cooked up too thick and was hard to manage. Cornstarch added at the end of the cooking seemed like a better option. The first time we tested cornstarch the results were fabulous. Not only did the soup thicken to a pleasing silky consistency, but also the color was outstanding. The blackish brown color of the beans appeared deeper and acquired an attractive sheen.

Finally, we found that acids play a key role in flavoring black beans. We tested red wine, balsamic and cider vinegars, as well as lime juice and lemon juice. We liked all of these additions except for the cider vinegar, which we found harsh.

Black Bean Soup

SERVES 6

This soup is best made a day ahead of serving so the flavors can meld. It will hold for three days in the refrigerator. Although the ham hock will probably hold just a tablespoon or two of meat, it's worth taking the time to remove this meat and adding it back to the soup. For a different effect, garnish the soup with shredded Monterey Jack cheese, diced seeded tomatoes, and minced jalapeño chile. Cornbread (page 328) is an excellent accompaniment to either version. For a meatier soup, make the variation with bacon that follows.

BEANS

1	pound (2¼ cups) dried black beans, rinsed and picked over
1	smoked ham hock (about ⅔ pound), rinsed
1	medium green bell pepper, stemmed, seeded, and quartered
1	medium onion, minced
6	medium cloves garlic, minced
2	bay leaves
1½	teaspoons salt

SOFRITO

2	tablespoons olive oil
1	medium onion, minced
1	small red bell pepper, stemmed, seeded, and minced
¾	teaspoon salt
8	medium cloves garlic, minced
2	teaspoons dried oregano
1	tablespoon ground cumin

FINISHING THE SOUP

2	tablespoons cornstarch
1	tablespoon lime juice
¼	cup sour cream
¼	cup roughly chopped fresh cilantro leaves
½	small red onion, minced
	Hot red pepper sauce (optional)

1. FOR THE BEANS: Place the beans, ham hock, green pepper, and 13 cups water in a large stockpot or Dutch oven. Bring to a boil over medium-high heat, reduce the heat to low, and skim the surface as scum rises. Stir in the onion, garlic, bay leaves, and salt and bring back to a simmer. Cook, partially covered, until the beans are tender but not splitting (taste several, as they cook unevenly), about 2 hours. Remove the ham hock from the pot. When cool enough to handle, remove and cut the meat into bite-sized pieces, discarding the bone, skin, and fat. Stir the meat back into the pot of beans.

2. FOR THE SOFRITO: Meanwhile, heat the oil in a large skillet over medium heat. Add the onion, red pepper, and salt, and sauté until the vegetables soften, 8 to 10 minutes. Add the garlic, oregano, and cumin and sauté until fragrant, 1 minute longer.

3. TO FINISH THE SOUP: Scoop 1½ cups beans and 2 cups cooking liquid into the pan with the sofrito. Mash the beans with a potato masher or fork until smooth. Simmer, uncovered, over medium heat, until the liquid is reduced and thickened, about 5 minutes. Return the sofrito mixture to the bean pot. Simmer, uncovered, until the flavors meld, about 15 minutes.

4. Blend the cornstarch and 2 tablespoons cold water together in a small bowl to form a smooth paste. Stir the paste into the soup and simmer until thickened, about 5 minutes. (Soup can be refrigerated in an airtight container for up to 3 days. Bring the soup to a simmer over low heat.) To serve, remove and discard the green pepper and bay leaves. Stir in the lime juice and adjust the seasonings. Ladle the soup into individual bowls, and garnish each bowl with a spoonful of sour cream, a generous sprinkling of cilantro, and some red onion. Serve immediately, passing hot red pepper sauce at the table if desired.

➤ VARIATION

Black Bean Soup with Balsamic and Bacon

For optimum flavor, cook the ham hock with the beans but don't bother trying to rescue the meat from the spent hock. The fried bits of bacon are more than sufficient. Although you can garnish this variation with sour cream, cilantro, and red onion, you might try finely chopped hard-boiled eggs and parsley instead.

Fry 4 ounces bacon, cut into ¼-inch strips, in a large skillet over medium heat until crisp and brown, about 5 minutes. Transfer bacon with a slotted spoon to a paper towel–lined plate; reserve bacon fat in skillet. Follow recipe for Black Bean Soup, discarding ham hock once the beans are tender in step 1 and cooking sofrito in bacon fat instead of olive oil in step 2. Add cooked bacon to the beans with the cornstarch slurry in step 4 and substitute 1 tablespoon balsamic vinegar for lime juice.

LENTIL SOUP

OUR IDEAL LENTIL SOUP IS THICK AND hearty, with lentils that are still intact. There are several different kinds of lentils, and many fall apart when simmered, so they are not appropriate in this kind of soup. With this mind, we started our investigations with the lentils.

We went to the local supermarket and to natural foods stores to see what was available. By far, brown and red lentils dominated the shelf space, although a few markets carried French green lentils, called *lentils du Puy*. We bought several bags of each kind and started testing.

Remarkably, all the lentils tasted more or less similar after cooking, but we found distinct differences in their texture. Red lentils come in varying shades of red, from light pink to a deep salmon, and look quite beautiful—in the bag, that is. When we cooked them, red lentils lost most of their color very quickly

---

SCIENCE: Flavoring Beans

Having found a technique for cooking beans that delivered the flavor we were looking for, we began to wonder what was actually going on in the pot. How does flavor get into the bean?

We found out that there are at least two processes going on as flavor develops in the bean. First, the bean itself develops flavor as it cooks. Beans are full of starch granules made up of layers of tightly packed starch molecules, arranged something like the layers of an onion. As the bean cooks, liquid seeps into the bean through the tiny white area on its side, the hilum, where the bean was originally connected to the pod. (The rest of the seed coat is impermeable unless it has been damaged in handling.) As the liquid leaks in, slowly at first and then more quickly, it gets in between the layers of starch, and the granules begin to swell. Eventually, the granules swell to the point of cracking, and the starch rushes into the bean in a process called gelatinization. This process not only alters the texture of the beans, it also improves their flavor. So, in cooking terms, a fully-cooked bean has more flavor than one that's not adequately cooked.

We went back into the kitchen to test this theory, tasting

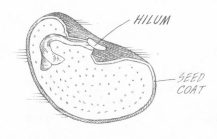

beans cooked in plain water every 10 minutes after the first hour of cooking until the beans burst. We found that the beans changed over time from a starchy, acrid taste with a chalky texture to a less acrid, rounder flavor with a velvety texture. Once the beans burst, they actually lost flavor, as if it were being washed away by the water.

So cooking itself changes the flavor and texture of the bean. But how do flavors outside the bean get infused into it? When you cook beans with vegetables and herbs, the water-soluble flavor compounds in those ingredients dissolve and flavor the water and then enter and swell the bean, thus flavoring it.

We wondered if it was necessary to introduce the flavorings at the outset of the cooking process. We cooked two batches of beans—one in plain water with bay leaves, garlic, and onions added to the pot once the beans were tender, the other in water flavored with bay leaves, garlic, and onions at the outset. The beans cooked with the flavorings from the outset tasted much better. Once the starch molecule has totally swollen, it ceases to take in water and therefore cannot absorb any flavorings.

and turned a pale yellow or khaki color. More important, these lentils also lost their texture quite rapidly. A matter of a few minutes was all it took to turn the red lentils to mush. They are suitable for a smooth soup, such as dal (see the recipe on page 162), but not for the chunky, rustic lentil soup we had in mind.

Brown lentils (sometimes tinged with green) can be found at most any supermarket. In our tests, these lentils held their shape and texture much better than their red relatives, although overcooking breaks them down as well. The advantage of using the brown lentils is that they maintain their integrity once the soup comes off the stove. They continued to soften but did not fall apart, as did the red lentils.

The French green lentils (lentils du Puy, not to be confused with plain green lentils, which are similar in texture to red lentils) were slightly smaller than the brown lentils we had found. We predicted that their smaller size would make them more prone to disintegration. We were wrong. These gray-green lentils are sold with their seed coat intact, and this keeps them from falling apart in the soup. Moreover, tasters thought these lentils gave the soup a "peppery" and "earthy" flavor that was well received.

Whether you decide to buy the brown or the French green lentils, we recommend that you buy them from a market with high turnover, since lentils will lose flavor with age. Most packaged lentils do not give any expiration date, so it makes sense to buy them from a store that you know specializes in natural foods and grains. We also found it imperative to wash and sort through the lentils carefully. Every package had at least a few stones mixed with the lentils.

Now that we knew which lentil was best for our soup, we were ready to test cooking methods. A few recipes recommended soaking the lentils for a few hours, but this was entirely unnecessary since the lentils cook up rather quickly. Sweating the lentils in a covered pan with the aromatic vegetables before adding the liquid was a technique found in quite a few Indian cookbooks. Sweating is said to strengthen the outer skin of the lentils. We tried this and were pleased with the results. Lentils that were sweated for about 10 minutes were firmer upon being simmered

in liquid than those that had been cooked only in liquid. It seems that sweating does indeed harden the lentil's outside layer of starch, producing soup with lentils that are tender on the inside yet do not fall apart.

We could now move on to the other ingredients in the soup. Our next test was pork, which the majority of recipes included in their ingredient lists. Ham bone, ham hock, prosciutto, pancetta, and bacon were all named. We found that the ham bone and hock added a nice smoky flavor to the soup, but the long simmering time required to extract the flavor didn't work with the rest of this reasonably quick recipe. Prosciutto and pancetta were expensive additions to the soup; their mild flavor didn't warrant their use. Finally, we tried bacon. We found the smoky flavor that we had liked in the ham, and the diced pieces of bacon provided a pleasant eating experience. Another advantage of using the bacon was the rendered bacon fat, which we used to sauté the aromatics.

Some recipes relied entirely on the pork (in this case bacon) to flavor the cooking water, but we found it necessary to use chicken stock to add flavor to the otherwise dull-tasting lentils. We also found we could brighten the flavor of the soup by adding a sizable amount of dry white wine (¾ cup). Tomatoes, garlic, onions, bay leaves, and fresh thyme were all substantive enough to round out the flavors.

Tasters were initially divided as to what they believed to be the proper texture for lentil soup. Many thought the soup should be completely pureed, while others thought the soup should remain rustic and untouched. In the end, we found that a happy medium worked best. We pureed a few cups of the soup and then added it back to the saucepan, thereby providing the whole lentils with a creamy contrast and the entire soup with a more interesting texture.

Many recipes call for the addition of vinegar or lemon juice just before the soup is served. We tested this and found that tasters preferred the flavor of balsamic vinegar against the smoky bacon and earthy lentils. The piquant character of the vinegar adds brightness and richness to the soup.

Lentil Soup

SERVES 4 TO 6

Common brown lentils work well in this recipe, although French green lentils (lentils du Puy, not to be confused with plain green lentils) are even better.

2	tablespoons vegetable oil
4	slices (about 4 ounces) bacon, diced
2	medium-large onions, chopped fine
2	medium carrots, peeled and chopped medium
3	medium cloves garlic, minced
1	bay leaf
1	teaspoon minced fresh thyme leaves
1	(14½-ounce) can diced tomatoes, drained and liquid reserved
1	cup lentils, rinsed and picked through
1	teaspoon salt
	Ground black pepper
¾	cup white wine
4	cups chicken stock, preferably homemade
1	tablespoon balsamic vinegar

1. Heat the oil in a large stockpot or Dutch oven over medium-high heat. When the oil is shimmering, add the bacon and cook, stirring occasionally, until the fat is fully rendered and the bacon is crisp, 3 to 4 minutes. Add the onions, carrots, garlic, bay leaf, thyme, and drained tomatoes, and cook until the vegetables begin to soften, about 2 minutes.

2. Stir in the lentils, salt, and a few grindings of pepper. Cover, reduce the heat to medium-low, and sweat the vegetables until softened and the lentils have become darker, 8 to 10 minutes.

3. Uncover, increase the heat to high, add the wine, and simmer for 1 minute. Add the stock, the juice from the canned tomatoes, and 1½ cups water. Bring to a boil, partially cover, and reduce the heat to low, simmering until the lentils are cooked but still hold their shape, 30 to 35 minutes. Remove and discard the bay leaf.

4. Place 3 cups soup in a blender and puree until smooth. Add the pureed soup back to a saucepan and stir in the vinegar. (Soup can be refrigerated in an airtight container for 2 days.) Warm over low heat until very hot. Serve immediately.

VARIATION
Indian Dal Soup

In India, dal is the generic name for all types of beans and dried peas as well as the dishes made with these legumes. This dal is made with split red lentils. These small lentils are bright orange-red when raw and a golden yellow color when cooked with turmeric. Red lentils do not hold their shape when cooked, so this soup is thick and creamy.

3	tablespoons unsalted butter
2	medium-large onions, chopped fine
3	medium cloves garlic, minced
1	tablespoon minced fresh ginger
1	teaspoon ground cumin
1	teaspoon ground coriander
1	teaspoon brown sugar
½	teaspoon turmeric
¼	teaspoon cayenne pepper
¼	teaspoon ground cinnamon
1	cup split red lentils, rinsed and picked through
1	teaspoon salt
4	cups chicken stock, preferably homemade
½	cup plain yogurt for serving
2	tablespoons chopped fresh cilantro leaves

1. Heat the butter in a large stockpot or Dutch oven over medium heat. When the butter melts, add the onions and cook until they soften, about 4 minutes. Add the garlic, ginger, cumin, coriander, brown sugar, turmeric, cayenne, and cinnamon and cook, stirring constantly, until fragrant, about 1 minute.

2. Stir in the lentils and salt. Add the stock and 1½ cups water and bring to a boil over high heat. Reduce the heat to low, partially cover, and simmer until the lentils are very soft and falling apart, about 35 minutes. (Soup can be refrigerated in an airtight container for 2 days.) Warm over low heat until very hot. Serve immediately, garnishing each bowl with a spoonful of yogurt and some cilantro.

Ham and Split Pea Soup

OLD-FASHIONED RECIPES FOR HAM AND split pea soup start with the bone from a large roast ham that has been nearly picked clean. The bone and some split peas are thrown in a pot with some water and cooked until the meat falls off the bone. By that time, the fat has discreetly melted into the liquid, and the peas have become creamy enough to thicken the soup.

We love split pea soup made this way, but times have changed. Except for the occasional holiday, most cooks rarely buy a bone-in ham, opting more often for the thin-sliced deli stuff. We wondered if we could duplicate this wonderful soup without buying a huge ham.

To confirm or disprove our belief that a ham stock is crucial to split pea soup, we made several pork stocks and pork-enhanced canned chicken broths. In addition to making stock the old-fashioned way from a meaty ham bone, we made stock from smoked pork necks, pork hocks (fresh and smoked), and smoked ham shanks. We also made cheater's stocks: kielbasa simmered in canned chicken broth, kielbasa simmered in water, bacon simmered in chicken broth, and bacon simmered in water.

The stocks based on hocks—fresh as well as smoked—were more greasy than flavorful. In addition, the hocks gave up very little meat, making it necessary to purchase an additional portion of ham to fortify the soup. Ham shanks, which include the hock, made a pleasant but lightweight stock that was a tad greasy and salty—both fixable problems had the stock been more stellar. Pork necks, which are not widely available, made a fairly flavorful but salty stock. All four cheater's stocks failed. Both the kielbasa- and bacon-enhanced chicken broths tasted strongly of overly processed meat, while the water-based versions tasted weak.

Not surprisingly, the stock made from the bone of a big ham was the winner. It was meaty and full-flavored, rich but not greasy, nicely seasoned without being overly salty, and smoky without tasting artificial. Unlike any of the other broths, this one sported bits of meat. And not just good meat—great meat.

The tender pieces of ham that fell away from the bone during cooking were not just a nice byproduct of the stock. They were the glory of our split pea soup. But was there a way around buying half a ham (with an average weight of about eight pounds) just to make a pot of soup?

After checking out the ham and smoked pork cases at several different stores, we discovered the picnic cut. Unlike what we generally refer to as ham, which comes from the back legs of the animal, the picnic comes from the shoulder and front legs. Smaller than a ham, the half-picnic weighs only 4½ pounds. After making a couple more pots of soup, we found that the picnic pork shoulder—with its bones, fat, rind, and meat—made outstanding stock, and after two hours of simmering, the meat was meltingly tender yet still potently flavorful.

Since we did not need the full picnic half for our pot of soup, we pulled off and roasted two of its meatier muscles for use in other dishes and used the remaining meat, bone, fat, and rind to make the soup. At around 99 cents a pound, a picnic shoulder is usually cheaper than a ham, and often cheaper than pork hocks, shanks, or neck bones as well. Here, we thought, was the modern solution. Rather than buy a ham for eating (and eating and eating) with a leftover bone for soup, instead purchase a picnic for soup, and roast the remaining couple of pounds for eating.

There are several ways to make ham and split pea soup. You can throw all the ingredients—ham bone, peas, and diced vegetables—into a pot and simmer until everything is tender. Or you can sauté the vegetables, then add the remaining ingredients and cook the soup until the ham and peas are tender. Alternatively, you can cook the ham bone and peas (or give the ham bone a head start) until ham and peas are tender and then add raw, sautéed, or caramelized vegetables to the pot, continuing to cook until the vegetables are tender and the flavors have blended.

Although we had hoped to keep the soup a straightforward one-pot operation, we found out pretty quickly that dumping everything in at the same time resulted in gloppy, overcooked peas and tired mushy vegetables by the time the ham was tender. For textural contrast in this smooth, creamy soup, we ultimately preferred fully—though not overly—cooked vegetables.

Our best soups were those in which the vegetables spent enough time in the pot for their flavors to blend but not so long that they had lost all of their individual taste. Of the soups with vegetables added toward the end of cooking, we preferred the one with the caramelized vegetables. The sweeter vegetables gave this otherwise straightforward meat-and-starch soup a richness and depth of flavor that made the extra step and pan worth the trouble.

Many pea soup recipes call for an acidic ingredient—vinegar, lemon juice, fortified wine such as sherry or Madeira, Worcestershire sauce, or sour cream—to bring balance to an otherwise rich, heavy soup. After tasting all of the above, we found ourselves drawn to balsamic vinegar. Unlike any of the other ingredients, balsamic vinegar's mildly sweet, mildly acidic flavor perfectly complemented the soup.

Ham and Split Pea Soup

SERVES 6

Use a small 2½-pound smoked picnic portion ham if you can find one. Otherwise, buy a half-picnic ham and remove some meat, which you can roast and use in sandwiches, salads, or omelets. (See illustrations, right.)

1	piece (about 2½ pounds) smoked, bone-in picnic ham
4	bay leaves
1	pound (2½ cups) split peas, rinsed and picked through
1	teaspoon dried thyme
2	tablespoons extra-virgin olive oil
2	medium onions, chopped medium
2	medium carrots, chopped medium
2	medium stalks celery, chopped medium
1	tablespoon unsalted butter
2	medium cloves garlic, minced
	Pinch sugar
3	small new potatoes, scrubbed (see illustration on page 81) and cut into ½-inch dice (about ¾ cup)
	Ground black pepper
	Minced red onion (optional)
	Balsamic vinegar

1. Place the ham, bay leaves, and 3 quarts water in a large stockpot or Dutch oven. Cover and bring to a boil over medium-high heat. Reduce the heat to low and simmer until the meat is tender and pulls away from the bone, 2 to 2½ hours. Remove the ham meat and bone from the pot. When the ham is cool enough to handle, shred the meat into bite-sized pieces and set aside. Discard the rind, fat, and bone.

2. Add the split peas and thyme to the ham stock. Bring back to a boil, reduce the heat, and simmer, uncovered, until the peas are tender but not dissolved, about 45 minutes.

3. While the ham is simmering, heat the oil in a large skillet over high heat until shimmering. Add the onions, carrots, and celery and sauté, stirring frequently, until most of the liquid evaporates and the vegetables begin to brown, 5 to 6 minutes. Reduce the heat to medium-low and add the butter, garlic, and sugar. Cook the vegetables, stirring frequently,

HANDLING A HALF-PICNIC HAM

A half-picnic ham is readily available in supermarkets but contains too much meat for a pot of soup. Our solution is to pull off several meaty sections of the ham and roast them for sandwiches, salads, and egg dishes.

1. With your fingers, loosen the large comma-shaped muscles on top of the picnic half.

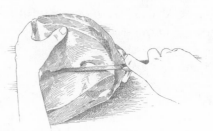

2. Use a knife to cut the membrane separating the comma-shaped muscles from the rest of the roast. The remaining meat and bone can be used to make soup.

until deeply browned, 30 to 35 minutes; set aside.

4. Add the sautéed vegetables, potatoes, and shredded ham to the pot with the split peas. Simmer until the potatoes are tender and peas dissolve and thicken soup to the consistency of light cream, about 20 minutes more. Season with ground black pepper to taste. (The soup can be refrigerated in an airtight container for 2 days. Warm the soup over low heat until hot.) Ladle the soup into bowls, sprinkle with red onion, if using, and serve, passing balsamic vinegar separately.

➤ VARIATION

Ham and Split Pea Soup with Caraway
Toast 1½ teaspoons caraway seeds in a small skillet over medium-high heat, stirring frequently, until fragrant and browned, about 4 minutes. Follow recipe for Ham and Split Pea Soup, substituting toasted caraway seeds for the dried thyme.

MISO SOUP

MISO SOUP, MADE WITH FERMENTED BEAN paste, is a Japanese restaurant standard. Order anything—except a soupy main dish—and some steaming, cloudy, swishing miso soup in a faux lacquered bowl is set down in front of you in a portion just large enough to whet your appetite. Miso soup is common in Japanese households, too, where it is considered a comfort food, akin to our chicken soup.

Served in a restaurant, miso soup is rarely judged, but it doesn't take a connoisseur to appreciate its subtleties and finer points. Bad miso soup is immediately identifiable as salty and hollow, with a one-dimensional flavor that is sometimes compensated for with MSG. This sort of institutional miso soup often begins life as an instant broth and ends in a salt explosion on the palate, with no redeeming qualities or interesting flavors. Good miso soup is alive with layers of sweet, smoky, briny, earthy flavors. The flavors linger and evolve in the mouth, and the soup is a pleasure to sip.

Just as chicken noodle soup has a base of chicken stock, miso soup has a base called *dashi,* which means "broth" in Japanese. A basic dashi is made from a simple combination of water, kombu (kelp), and dried bonito flakes (bonito is a type of fish). But unlike chicken stock, dashi can be made in fewer than 20 minutes. Miso is added to the strained dashi, and, with the addition of tofu or seaweed and a sprinkling of scallions, the soup is complete. Esoteric ingredients do not mean that miso soup is unapproachable for the home cook. All goods can likely be purchased in just a single trip to a Japanese or Asian grocer, well-stocked supermarket, or natural foods store.

With only two ingredients, excluding water, each component in dashi serves an important function. Kombu gives dashi saltiness, a bit of sweetness, and a briny ocean essence. It also gives the dashi a little body. Kombu is sold in dried sheets—several to a package—and the sheets are naturally dusted with a desirable whitish powder that by all accounts adds flavor. Bonito flakes give dashi smokiness and a savory fishy quality. They resemble wood shavings and are available in shavings of different sizes. Fine flakes are usually sold in small packets; they are sprinkled over foods and intended to be used as a garnish or condiment. Larger flakes are sold in bigger pillowy bags and are used primarily for making dashi.

Generally, dashi is a simple dish to prepare. Kombu and cold water are brought to a simmer, the kombu is removed, then the bonito flakes are added and cooked or steeped until the dashi is infused with their flavor. The details of the traditional process for making this broth found in several Japanese books seem overcomplicated. They often include wiping the kombu with a damp cloth before simmering and adding about ½ cup of cold water along with the bonito flakes, returning the liquid to a boil, and then straining immediately. Side-by-side tests could not give credence to these steps. The step of wiping the kombu did not overtly benefit the dashi, and there was no apparent advantage to adding cold water along with the bonito flakes. We opted instead to use the kombu straight out of the package and merely steep the bonito flakes in the liquid off heat for three to five minutes. Any longer and the smokiness and fishiness became overpowering.

After straining the dashi, miso is added to make miso soup. There are numerous kinds of miso, though for miso soup, shiromiso (white miso), is the type commonly used. We tried other types of miso and found that our tasters preferred white miso. (For more information on types of miso, see page 167.) We tested different amounts of white miso per cup of dashi and found that 2 tablespoons per cup produced the right amount of flavor.

Miso is a thick paste and is not easily dispersed in the dashi. We found it best to thin the miso with a small amount of dashi before adding it to the pot. Most recipes and books indicate that the dashi should be boiling or simmering before the thinned-out miso is added, to minimize the amount of time the miso is exposed to heat, which weakens its flavor. Our testing bore this out. We made three batches of miso soup. In the first batch, the soup was made according to the advised method of bringing the dashi to a simmer, then adding the miso; in the second, the miso was put into the dashi and brought to a simmer so as to give the miso prolonged heat exposure; and the third was made in the same manner as the first batch but was allowed to simmer for about two minutes. Indeed there were flavor differences. Soups two and

three suffered from the prolonged heat. The miso seemed to have lost some of its delicate flavor and subtle nuances. This time tradition won out.

Miso soup is not complete without some tofu or wakame (seaweed) or both in the bottom of the bowl. Adding these ingredients directly to the pot seemed the obvious thing to do, but we preferred to portion out the ingredients in individual bowls. This way, the delicate tofu does not get mangled during ladling, and the wakame that settles flat on the floor of the pot can be more evenly distributed. A sprinkling of sliced scallion and out goes the call "itadaki-masu," the Japanese equivalent of "bon appetit."

Miso Soup

SERVES 8 TO 10

This recipe can easily be halved. The dashi (broth) is best made just before making the soup, though it can be made ahead, cooled, and refrigerated in an airtight container for up to 2 days. Once the miso has been stirred into the simmering dashi, serve the soup immediately.

DASHI

2	pieces kombu, each about 4 inches long
2	cups loosely packed bonito flakes

SOUP

1	cup white miso
8	ounces silken tofu, cut into ½-inch cubes
1	tablespoon wakame flakes or four 6-inch strips wakame, soaked in cold water to cover for 15 minutes (if using strips, see illustrations, left)
3	scallions, sliced thin

1. Bring the kombu and 2 quarts water to a boil in a large saucepan over medium heat. When the water reaches a boil, discard the kombu and turn off the heat. Stir in the bonito flakes and let stand to infuse flavor, 3 to 5 minutes. Strain the broth through a fine-mesh strainer; reserve 1 cup of the dashi and return the remaining dashi to the pan.

2. Whisk the miso and the reserved 1 cup dashi in a small bowl until combined. Bring the dashi in the pan to a simmer over medium-high heat, then stir the miso mixture into the pan. Return to a simmer;

HANDLING WAKAME

Whether in flakes or strips, wakame (Japanese seaweed) should be soaked in cold water for about 15 minutes to soften. Wakame strips also need to be chopped after soaking.

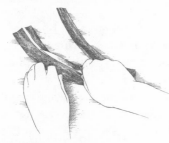

1. With a paring knife, cut out and discard the tough ribs that run the length of the wakame strips.

2. Once all of the ribs have been removed, roughly chop the wakame strips into ½-inch pieces.

immediately remove the pan from the heat.

3. Meanwhile, divide the tofu and wakame evenly among individual bowls. Ladle the soup into bowls, sprinkle with the scallions, and serve immediately.

INGREDIENTS: Miso

Most miso pastes are made from a combination of fermented soybeans and white rice. Some miso may contain just soybeans, while others may replace the white rice with brown rice or barley. Bear in mind that white miso (shiromiso) is the type commonly used to make miso soup. This and other types of miso and their flavor characteristics are described below. Miso is available in Japanese markets and natural foods stores as well as many supermarkets.

WHITE MISO (Shiromiso) White miso, which is used to make miso soup, is the type Westerners are most likely to be familiar with. It is brownish yellow in color—not pure white, as its name may lead you to believe—and its flavor is mellow, with a light sweetness, light saltiness, and delicacy that can range from fruity to nutty, depending on the brand. We tried making miso soup with the other types of miso in the test kitchen, and the soup made with white miso was the favorite of tasters.

BROWN OR RED MISO (Akamiso) Brown or red miso has a darker color and a saltier, more assertive flavor that lacks the delicate sweet quality of white miso. It has a meaty, roasted quality that makes a miso soup that tastes as if it had been splashed with a good dose of soy sauce.

BROWN RICE MISO (Genmaimiso) Like brown or red miso, brown rice miso is darker in color than white miso, and it lacks the subtleties of white miso. Brown rice miso has a strong saltiness, a soy sauce–like flavor, a hefty smokiness, and a few faint but detectable sour notes.

BARLEY MISO (Mugimiso) Barley miso resembles white miso in appearance, but its flavor is distinctly malty. Our tasters also identified sweet, nutty, and tea-like flavor characteristics. In spite of these flavors the soup made with barley miso seemed to lack some of the depth and backbone of the soup made with white miso.

JAPANESE NOODLE SOUP

JAPANESE NOODLE SOUPS ARE ONE-BOWL meals assembled just before being served. They include an assortment of ingredients that remain separate and distinct: soft, yielding noodles; flavorful protein; bright-colored, fresh-tasting greens; and a variety of garnishes—all served in a highly seasoned broth.

Although each component is by itself relatively easy to prepare, an entire recipe usually requires several pots and bowls, at least one for each component. Unlike Western soups, in which ingredients are typically simmered together in the same pot, these soups are assembled in individual servings. We found the best proportion of ingredients per serving to be 2 cups of broth combined with 1 cup of cooked noodles, 3 ounces of cooked protein, and 2 ounces of greens. We also found it best to use a large bowl for each person (1-quart capacity is ideal) and to pile the ingredients high, so they rise above the broth like a mountain island out of the sea.

There are many possibilities for the broth. After testing numerous options, we settled on three options—chicken stock with Japanese flavors, dashi, and mushroom dashi. For information on these choices, see the individual recipes that follow.

The Japanese eat noodles all the time. Noodles are a vital source of nutrients and calories. One of three types of Japanese noodle is usually found in these brothy soups: ramen, udon, or soba. Ramen and udon are made from wheat, while soba are made from buckwheat. (For more details on each type of noodle, see page 172.)

Traditionally, the Japanese cook all noodles by a process called *sashimizu,* or "add water." The idea is to add cold water to the pot occasionally to slow down the cooking process. Some sources indicate that this allows Japanese noodles, especially soba, to cook through to the core without the outside layers becoming soggy. We tested and dismissed this technique with wheat-based udon, finding that these noodles responded best to the traditional Western boiling method used for other kinds of wheat pasta. Because ramen are exceptionally thin, they are also quick-cooking, so the "add water" method is not required. We wondered, however, about soba.

We prepared several batches using the traditional Japanese method, adding a little cold water every time the water came to a boil. The noodles took about eight minutes to cook after the first boil. We then prepared several batches of noodles cooked as is the custom in the West. The noodles were done in about four minutes and tasted the same.

The next issue was rinsing. Most Japanese recipes instruct the cook to rinse the noodles under hot, warm, or cold water to wash away the excess starch. In our research, we ran across recipes in American cookbooks that did not rinse the noodles at all.

We started by preparing Japanese noodles without rinsing, which turned out to be a disaster. While Italian pasta should never be rinsed (the starch on the noodles helps the sauce adhere), Japanese noodles give off much more starch. We found that unrinsed noodles congealed into a starchy, gluey mass.

When we rinsed the noodles under hot water, we found that they softened further and became mushy. This makes sense—the noodles were continuing to cook. Rinsing the noodles under cold water was fine, but the noodles sometimes cooled down too much and were too chilled when covered with broth. Warm water washed away the starch without further cooking. It also kept the noodles at the right temperature for use in soups.

The protein component is fairly straightforward. Tender meat (often flank steak or pork tenderloin), seafood (especially shrimp), or tofu is added to these soups for flavor and nutritional heft. The protein should be cut into small pieces that will fit in a soup spoon or between two chopsticks.

The greens add a fresh taste and color to these soups. We found that the easiest way to incorporate them is to place them raw in the serving bowls and ladle very hot liquid, just below boiling, over them. The hot liquid wilts and softens the greens. Spinach and watercress are the most common choices, although tender Asian greens, such as tatsoi or mizuna, are also appropriate.

The garnishes are the final addition to the soup bowl. We have outlined several choices on page 171. Try several garnishes in combination; feel free to exercise some creativity here.

Japanese Noodle Soup

SERVES 4

Japanese noodle soups lend themselves well to mixing and matching component ingredients. The variations that follow are our favorite combinations, but you can easily assemble your own noodle soup by mixing and matching the liquid base, noodles, and protein from various recipes. This skeleton recipe demonstrates the basic technique.

I	recipe Japanese broth (recipes follow)
I	recipe Japanese noodles (recipes follow)
I	recipe meat, seafood, or tofu (recipes follow)
8	ounces spinach, watercress, tatsoi, or mizuna, stemmed and roughly chopped
	Garnishes of choice (see page 171)

1. Prepare the broth and hold in a covered pot over low heat.

2. Prepare the noodles and divide them among four 1-quart serving bowls.

3. Prepare the meat, seafood, or tofu and cook just prior to serving.

4. To serve, place the greens over the noodles and ladle 2 cups of broth into each bowl. Place some meat, seafood, or tofu on top of the greens, toward the center of each bowl. Sprinkle the garnishes on top and serve immediately.

➤ VARIATIONS

Udon with Chicken Stock, Roasted Five-Spice Pork, and Spinach

A small piece of pork tenderloin, brushed with a simple hoisin-based sauce and roasted, makes a good addition to Japanese noodle soup. To vary the flavors, substitute an equal amount of ground Sichuan peppercorns for the five-spice powder. If using canned broth, choose low-sodium or the soup will be too salty.

JAPANESE-STYLE CHICKEN BROTH

2	quarts homemade chicken stock or canned low-sodium chicken broth
6	medium cloves garlic, peeled
I	(3-inch) piece fresh ginger, peeled, cut into ⅛-inch rounds, and smashed (see illustration on page 26)

1/4   cup soy sauce

1   tablespoon sugar

NOODLES

12   ounces udon (see page 172)

ROASTED FIVE-SPICE PORK

1   tablespoon hoisin sauce

1   tablespoon sugar

1   tablespoon soy sauce

1 1/2   teaspoons five-spice powder

12   ounces pork tenderloin

8   ounces spinach, stemmed and roughly chopped
Garnishes of choice (page 171)

1. FOR THE BROTH: Place all ingredients in a medium saucepan over medium-high heat and bring to a boil. Reduce the heat to low and simmer, partially covered, to blend flavors, about 20 minutes. Remove the solids with a slotted spoon and discard. Cover and keep hot over very low heat.

2. FOR THE NOODLES: Bring 4 quarts of water to a boil in a large pot. Add the noodles and cook until al dente, 4 to 5 minutes. Drain and rinse under warm, running water to remove excess starch. Divide the noodles among four 1-quart serving bowls.

3. FOR THE PORK: Meanwhile preheat the oven to 350 degrees. Combine the hoisin sauce, sugar, soy sauce, and five-spice powder in a small bowl. Place the pork on a rimmed baking sheet and brush with the hoisin mixture. Roast until a thermometer inserted into the center reads 160 degrees, about 30 minutes. Let stand on a cutting board for 15 minutes. Slice thin and then halve the slices diagonally.

4. To serve, place the spinach over the noodles and ladle 2 cups of hot broth into each bowl. Place some pork on top of the spinach, toward the center of each bowl. Sprinkle the garnishes on top and serve immediately.

Soba with Dashi, Shrimp, and Watercress

Dashi is the classic broth used in Japanese noodle soups. On its own, however, the flavor is too plain. Enriched with soy sauce for saltiness as well as sugar and rice wine for sweetness, the flavors are quite satisfying and complex. This dashi is easy and quick to prepare. It requires three ingredients (kombu, bonito flakes, and mirin), not commonly found in Western homes but readily available at natural foods stores and Asian groceries. Dashi stores well in the refrigerator for up to two days. Note that because of the soy, rice wine, and sugar, this dashi recipe calls for fewer bonito flakes than the dashi used for miso soup. Shrimp add a beautiful coral color and delicate flavor to a bowl of noodles and broth. They are the easiest of the protein choices to add since they simply cook in the broth just prior to serving.

DASHI

2   pieces kombu, each about 4 inches long

1   cup loosely packed dried bonito flakes

1/2   cup soy sauce

2/3   cup rice wine

1   tablespoon sugar

NOODLES

1   tablespoon salt

12   ounces soba (see page 172)

SHRIMP

12   ounces shrimp, peeled, deveined if desired, and coarsely chopped

8   ounces watercress, stemmed and roughly chopped
Garnishes of choice (page 171)

1. FOR THE DASHI: Bring the kombu and 2 quarts water to a boil in a large saucepan over medium heat. When the water reaches a boil, discard the kombu and turn off the heat. Stir in the bonito flakes and let stand to infuse flavor, 3 to 5 minutes. Strain the broth through a fine-mesh strainer. Return the dashi to a clean saucepan. Add the soy sauce, rice wine, and sugar and bring almost to a boil over medium-high heat. Cover and keep hot over very low heat.

2. FOR THE NOODLES: Bring 4 quarts of water and salt to a boil in a large pot. Add the soba noodles and cook until al dente, 4 to 5 minutes. Drain and rinse under warm, running water to remove excess starch. Divide the noodles among four 1-quart serving bowls.

3. FOR THE SHRIMP: Stir the shrimp into the warm dashi, raise the heat to medium-low, and simmer until the shrimp are just pink, 1 to 2 minutes.

4. To serve, place the watercress over the noodles and ladle 2 cups of dashi and some shrimp into each bowl. Sprinkle the garnishes on top and serve immediately.

Ramen with Mushroom Dashi, Seared Beef, and Spinach

Aromatic slices of stir-fried flank steak lend a hearty flavor and substance to a bowl of noodles and broth. If you desire some heat and spice, add the optional chile.

MUSHROOM DASHI

8	Chinese black mushrooms or dried shiitake mushrooms
2	pieces kombu, each about 4 inches long
1	cup loosely packed dried bonito flakes
1/2	cup soy sauce
2/3	cup rice wine
1	tablespoon sugar

NOODLES

1	tablespoon salt
4	(3-ounce) packages instant ramen, flavor packets discarded (see page 172)

SEARED BEEF

12	ounces flank steak, sliced thin (see illustrations on page 174)
1	tablespoon soy sauce
1	tablespoon rice wine or sherry
1	tablespoon plus 1 teaspoon vegetable oil
1	tablespoon minced garlic
1	tablespoon minced fresh ginger
1 1/2	tablespoons minced jalapeño or other fresh chile (optional)

8	ounces spinach, stemmed and roughly chopped
	Garnishes of choice (page 171)

1. FOR THE DASHI: Soak the mushrooms in 2 cups hot water until softened, about 20 minutes. Lift the mushrooms from the water with a fork; trim and discard any tough stems, chop remaining pieces. Strain the soaking liquid through a strainer lined with a paper towel (see illustration on page 85). Reserve the mushrooms and strained liquid.

2. Meanwhile, bring the kombu and 2 quarts water to a boil in a large saucepan over medium heat. When the water reaches a boil, discard the kombu and turn off the heat. Stir in the bonito flakes and let stand to infuse flavor, 3 to 5 minutes. Strain the liquid through a fine-mesh strainer. Return the dashi to a clean saucepan. Add the mushrooms, strained mushroom soaking liquid, soy sauce, rice wine, and sugar and bring almost to a boil over medium-high heat. Cover and keep hot over very low heat.

3. FOR THE NOODLES: Bring 4 quarts of water and salt to a boil in a large pot. Add the ramen and stir once or twice in the first minute to separate noodles. Cook until just tender, 2 to 3 minutes. Drain and rinse under warm, running water to remove excess starch. Divide the noodles among four 1-quart serving bowls.

4. FOR THE MEAT: Meanwhile, toss the flank steak with soy sauce and rice wine in a medium bowl; set aside to marinate, stirring occasionally, for 15 minutes.

5. Heat a 12- or 14-inch nonstick skillet over high heat until very hot, 3 to 4 minutes. Add 1 tablespoon oil and swirl the oil so that it evenly coats the

---

INGREDIENTS: Soy Sauce

Few condiments are as misunderstood as soy sauce, the pungent, fragrant, fermented flavoring that's a mainstay in Asian cooking. Its simple, straightforward composition—equal parts soybeans and a roasted grain, usually wheat, plus water and salt—belies the subtle, sophisticated contribution it makes as an all-purpose seasoning, flavor enhancer, tabletop condiment, and dipping sauce.

The three products consumers are likely to encounter are regular soy sauce, light soy sauce (made with a higher percentage of water and hence lower in sodium), and tamari (made with fermented soybeans, water, and salt—no wheat). Tamari generally has a stronger flavor and thicker consistency than soy sauce. It is traditionally used in Japanese cooking.

In a tasting of leading soy sauces, we found that products aged according to ancient custom were superior to synthetic sauces, such as La Choy's, which are made in a day and almost always contain hydrolyzed vegetable protein. Our favorite soy sauce, Eden Selected Shoyu Soy Sauce (*shoyu* is the Japanese word for soy sauce), is aged for three years. Tasters also liked products made by San-J and Kikkoman.

bottom of the pan. Heat the oil until it just starts to shimmer and smoke. Drain the flank steak and add it to the pan. Stir-fry until seared and about three-quarters cooked, about 1 minute. Scrape the cooked flank steak and all the liquid into a clean bowl. Let the pan come back up to temperature, 1 to 2 minutes. Add the garlic, ginger, and jalapeño (if using). Drizzle with 1 teaspoon oil. Mash the aromatics into the pan with the back of a spatula. Cook until fragrant but not colored, about 10 seconds. Add the flank steak and the liquid back to the pan and stir-fry until the beef is sizzling hot and cooked medium-rare, about 1 minute.

6. To serve, place the spinach over the noodles and ladle 2 cups of dashi into each bowl. Place some beef on top of the spinach, toward the center of each bowl. Sprinkle the garnishes on top and serve immediately.

Udon with Mushroom Dashi, Ginger Tofu, and Watercress

For a change of pace, replace the ginger with an equal amount of garlic.

I	recipe Mushroom Dashi (see preceding recipe)	

NOODLES
12 ounces udon (page 172)

PAN-SEARED GINGER TOFU
12 ounces extra-firm tofu
I tablespoon soy sauce
I tablespoon rice wine
I tablespoon plus I teaspoon vegetable oil
I tablespoon minced fresh ginger

8 ounces watercress, stemmed and roughly chopped
  Garnishes of choice (see box at right)

1. Prepare the Mushroom Dashi and keep warm in a covered pan over very low heat.

2. FOR THE NOODLES: Bring 4 quarts of water to a boil in a large pot. Add the noodles and cook until al dente, 4 to 5 minutes. Drain and rinse under warm, running water to remove excess starch. Divide the noodles among four 1-quart serving bowls.

3. FOR THE TOFU: Meanwhile, wrap the tofu snugly in a clean kitchen towel, set it on a plate, and

let stand until cloth is soaking wet, about 10 minutes. Unwrap the tofu and cut it into ½-inch dice. Combine the soy sauce and rice wine in a medium bowl. Add the tofu and toss to combine. Let stand for 15 minutes, tossing once or twice.

4. Heat a 12- or 14-inch nonstick skillet over high heat until very hot, 3 to 4 minutes. Add 1 tablespoon oil and swirl the oil so that it evenly coats the bottom of the pan. Heat the oil until it just starts to shimmer and smoke. Drain the tofu and add it to the pan. Cook the tofu in a single layer until the sides touching the pan are golden brown, 1 to 2 minutes. Turn the tofu and repeat 2 more times. Clear the center of the pan and add the ginger. Drizzle with remaining 1 teaspoon oil and mash into pan with the back of a spatula. Cook until fragrant but not colored, about 10 seconds. Mix the ginger with the tofu.

5. To serve, place the watercress over the noodles and ladle 2 cups of dashi into each bowl. Place some tofu on top of the watercress, toward the center of each bowl. Sprinkle the garnishes on top and serve immediately.

GARNISHES FOR JAPANESE NOODLE SOUP

Garnishes add texture, flavor, color, and complexity to Japanese soups. They are very easy to incorporate, and it is pleasing to provide more than one in each soup bowl. We found we liked combinations of two or three garnishes best. The quantities listed below make enough for four servings of soup.

If you want to add heat to any of the soups, give each person some wasabi paste on a small plate so they can stir in as much as desired to individual bowls.

➤ 2 tablespoons sesame seeds, lightly toasted
➤ ½ cup mung bean sprouts
➤ 2 scallions, white and light green parts, sliced thin
➤ I sheet toasted nori (seaweed), cut in half crosswise and then into thin strips
➤ ¼ cup loosely packed fresh cilantro leaves
➤ I tablespoon Asian toasted sesame oil
➤ 2 tablespoons wasabi powder combined with 4 tablespoons water and set aside for 10 minutes

We used three kinds of dried Japanese noodles in soup, all of which are readily available in supermarkets and natural foods stores as well as in Asian markets.

UDON Udon noodles are white, slippery wheat noodles that are especially thick and starchy and should be well rinsed under warm, running water before serving. Udon noodles are typically made with quite a bit of salt. Some brands (especially those imported from Japan) contain as much as 4,000 milligrams of sodium per 12 ounces. Even domestic brands (a few natural foods companies sell udon) usually contain a lot of sodium. For this reason, there is no need to add salt to the cooking water for these noodles, and salt should be used sparingly in the soup.

SOBA Soba noodles are made from buckwheat, unlike ramen and udon noodles, which are made from wheat. Buckwheat is not related to wheat. In fact, it's not even a grain but rather a grass. The whole kernels, which are called kasha, are familiar to anyone with roots in Eastern Europe. Buckwheat flour has a robust, earthy flavor. Soba noodles are long and thin (like Italian linguine) but have a brownish-gray color. Their hearty flavor works well with strongly flavored ingredients.

In our testing, we found we preferred imported soba noodles over domestic brands. They are generally much darker in color and have a richer, stronger buckwheat flavor. In addition to point of origin, pay attention to the label. We preferred brands made with 100 percent buckwheat.

Like udon, soba are high in starch. Rinse with warm water after cooking to wash away the starch.

RAMEN Ramen are sold in cellophane packages in most American supermarkets. They have a distinctive wavy appearance and chewy texture. Ramen are called "instant" noodles because they cook so quickly, in just two to three minutes. They almost always come with a separate flavor packet, which we simply throw out. We prefer to make our stock and add meat, seafood, tofu, and vegetables.

In Japan, ramen noodles are available fresh and with egg in the dough. We are hard pressed to find fresh ramen in the United States and have to settle for the instant variety. Unlike fresh ramen, instant ramen never contain egg. Be wary of noodles with an unnaturally bright yellow color, which often comes from a list of chemicals and dyes. Read labels and avoid those with ingredients other than flour, water, and salt.

As with udon and soba noodles, rinse ramen with warm water after cooking to wash away the starch.

SOUTHEAST ASIAN NOODLE SOUP

A GOOD SOUTHEAST ASIAN NOODLE SOUP (the kind you get in a Vietnamese or Thai restaurant) starts with a homemade stock flavored with Asian spices and sauces. The stock is rich but not heavy and is filled with fettuccine-width rice noodles, maybe some paper-thin and barely cooked slices of beef, angled scallion slices, crisp bean sprouts, and lots of whole fresh mint, basil, and/or cilantro leaves.

This kind of soup is a terrific strategy for an everyday, home-cooked, one-pot meal that tastes anything but everyday. But we kept running into the inescapable fact that a stock of this caliber is impractical because it has to cook for several hours.

Faced with this dilemma in Western-style soups, it's often possible to substitute canned broth, even though it's no match for homemade. Western soups, like many of those in this book, are typically set up like a stew—sauté aromatics, add liquid and whatever major ingredient, season with herbs, and simmer for at least half an hour to cook the ingredients through and marry the flavors. By the time the soup is cooked, the flavor of the liquid has been substantially transformed by the ingredients cooked in it.

Unfortunately, this model doesn't work for Southeast Asian soups, which are generally collections of raw and cooked ingredients added to the bowl at the last minute, like a garnish, with little or no secondary cooking. So whereas the ingredients of a leek and potato soup are cooked until the edges of the flavors soften and merge, Southeast Asian soups are structured in a way that allows the flavorings to remain distinct and separate, just as they do in a stir-fry.

It seemed to us that the Southeast Asian model might be well suited to the use of canned broth, but for entirely different reasons. What if we cooked strong flavorings, such as garlic and ginger, in the broth before it was ladled into bowls? Could we punch up and disguise the pallid flavor of the canned broth? We had done this with our recipe for Improved Canned Chicken Broth with Asian Flavors (page 26); here we wanted to tailor the taste more closely to Southeast Asian flavors.

From past tastings, we knew that canned chicken broth is superior to canned beef broth. Starting with chicken broth, we added chopped garlic and fresh ginger and simmered for 20 minutes. The flavor of the broth was immeasurably improved, but we wanted to do less work. So instead of chopping, we merely crushed medallions of ginger and whole garlic cloves with the side of a chef's knife before simmering them in the canned broth; the result tasted just as good.

With this base to build on, we experimented with other ingredients to figure out how to get the taste we were looking for. We found that soy and fish sauces added much-needed body and depth of flavor; fish sauce, in particular, added just the right combination of salt and a musky sweetness. Cinnamon stick and star anise were also appropriate and tasty additions, especially when paired with beef.

We experimented with lemon grass to determine how best to use it. (For more information on lemon grass, see page 301.) First we chopped it and cooked it in the broth from the beginning. Then we did the same with larger pieces of lemon grass, bruised with the flat of the knife. As a last test, we minced the lemon grass and added it fresh at the end of the process. We settled on bruising, which released the flavor of the lemon grass while also being fast and efficient.

Satisfied with the broth, we turned our attention to the noodles. We found that boiled noodles, especially thin rice vermicelli, had a tendency to get mushy and, if left in the hot soup for any length of time, broke apart. Ultimately, we settled on soaking the noodles in very hot water—a simple process that did not overcook the noodles. We drained the noodles when they had softened to the point that they were tender but still had tooth.

Thin rice vermicelli require just 5 to 10 minutes of soaking. Thicker rice noodles (about the width of linguine or narrow fettuccine) take 10 to 15 minutes to soften up.

We were able to develop variations on the broth using chicken, shrimp, and beef. The cinnamon/star anise combination that worked so well with the beef seemed unlikely to work with chicken and shrimp, so we omitted the cinnamon. Lime juice and extra fish sauce compensated for its loss. So did the quantity of fresh herbs—we used cilantro and mint, but basil can be used as well—which are crucial for these soups and more effective in whole leaf form than chopped. Finally, we discovered that because the noodles are so bland and smooth, some crunchy vegetables, such as bean sprouts or napa cabbage, are needed for texture.

ASSEMBLING A SOUTHEAST ASIAN NOODLE SOUP

1. Once the noodles have been soaked in hot water and drained, divide them among individual bowls along with any sprouts or cabbage.

2. Add the meat, seafood, or chicken and then ladle in the hot broth.

3. Sprinkle the herbs and other flavorings of choice (scallions, chiles, peanuts, etc.) into each bowl and serve immediately.

Quick Southeast Asian Broth

MAKES ABOUT 5 CUPS

The secret to making superquick, Southeast Asian–style noodle soups is to enliven canned chicken broth with classic flavorings. Of course, you can use homemade chicken stock instead of canned broth, if you have it on hand. This basic broth is used as is in Southeast Asian Rice Noodle Soup with Beef (right). We altered the seasonings for its use in the recipes with shrimp and chicken that follow. Because in these recipes we cook the shrimp and chicken along with the other broth ingredients, the preparation of the broth has been incorporated into the recipes.

- 5 cups canned low-sodium chicken broth
- 4 medium cloves garlic, smashed and peeled
- 1 (2-inch) piece fresh ginger, peeled, cut into ¹/₈-inch rounds, and smashed (see illustration on page 26)
- 2 (3-inch) cinnamon sticks
- 2 star anise pods
- 2 tablespoons fish sauce
- 1 tablespoon soy sauce
- 1 tablespoon sugar

Bring all ingredients to a boil in a medium saucepan over medium-high heat. Reduce the heat to low and simmer, partially covered, to blend flavors, about 20 minutes. Remove the solids with a slotted spoon and discard. (Broth can be refrigerated in an airtight container for up to 1 day.)

Southeast Asian Rice Noodle Soup with Beef

SERVES 4

For this soup, be sure to have all the vegetables and herbs at hand ready for serving. Although the broth can be made in advance, the soup must be served as soon as the recipe is completed.

- 6 ounces thick rice noodles (see "Dried Rice Noodles" on page 176)
- 1 recipe Quick Southeast Asian Broth (left)
- 12 ounces flank steak, sliced crosswise into ¹/₄-inch strips (see illustrations, below)
  Salt and ground black pepper
- 1 tablespoon vegetable oil
- 2 cups mung bean sprouts
- 1 medium jalapeño chile, stemmed, seeded, and sliced thin
- 2 scallions, white and green parts, sliced thin on an angle
- ¹/₃ cup loosely packed basil leaves, torn in half if large
- ¹/₂ cup loosely packed fresh mint leaves, torn in half if large
- ¹/₂ cup loosely packed fresh cilantro leaves
- 2 tablespoons chopped roasted unsalted peanuts
  Lime wedges

1. Bring 4 quarts of water to a boil in a large pot. Off heat, add the rice noodles and let stand, stirring

---

SLICING FLANK STEAK

1. To make cutting flank steak easier, place the meat in the freezer for 15 minutes. Once the meat is firm, slice it into 2-inch-wide pieces.

2. Cut each 2-inch piece against the grain into very thin slices, not more than ¹/₄ inch thick.

occasionally, until tender, 10 to 15 minutes. Drain and distribute the noodles among four large soup bowls.

2. Bring the broth to a simmer in a medium saucepan. Cover and keep warm over low heat.

3. Season the steak slices with salt and pepper to taste. Heat the oil in a medium skillet over medium-high heat until shimmering. Add half of the steak slices in a single layer and sear until well browned, 1 to 2 minutes on each side; set aside. Repeat with the remaining slices.

4. Divide the bean sprouts and beef among the soup bowls. Ladle the hot broth into the bowls and garnish with the chile, scallions, herbs, and peanuts. Serve immediately, passing the lime wedges separately at the table.

Hot-and-Sour Rice Noodle Soup with Shrimp and Tomato

SERVES 4

Lemon grass is an essential ingredient in Southeast Asian cooking; it lends a subtle fragrant lemon essence without harsh citrus notes. Use fresh lemon grass if you can find it. Otherwise, substitute two pieces of water-packed lemon grass, bruised, or ½ teaspoon grated lemon zest (see page 301).

4	ounces thin rice noodles (see "Dried Rice Noodles" on page 176)
5	cups canned low-sodium chicken broth
4	medium cloves garlic, smashed and peeled
1	(2-inch) piece fresh ginger, peeled, cut into ⅛-inch rounds, and smashed (see illustration on page 26)
2	star anise pods
3	tablespoons fish sauce
1	tablespoon soy sauce
1	teaspoon sugar
1	stalk lemon grass, bruised (see illustration, right)
12	ounces shrimp, peeled, shells reserved
1 to 2	medium jalapeño chiles, stemmed, seeded if desired, and sliced thin
¼	cup lime juice
	Salt
2	cups mung bean sprouts
1	medium tomato, cored, halved across the equator, seeded, and cut into 12 wedges
2	scallions, green and white parts, sliced thin on an angle
½	cup loosely packed fresh mint leaves, torn in half if large
½	cup loosely packed fresh cilantro leaves

1. Bring 4 quarts of water to a boil in a large pot. Off heat, add the rice noodles, and let stand, stirring occasionally, until tender, 5 to 10 minutes. Drain and distribute the noodles among four large soup bowls.

2. Meanwhile, bring the broth, garlic, ginger, star anise, fish sauce, soy sauce, sugar, lemon grass, and shrimp shells to a boil in a medium saucepan over medium-high heat. Reduce the heat to low and simmer, partially covered, to blend flavors, about 15 minutes. Add the chile and simmer for 5 minutes longer. Remove the solids with a slotted spoon and discard.

3. Add the shrimp and simmer until opaque and cooked through, about 2 minutes. Remove the shrimp with a slotted spoon and set aside. Add the lime juice and season the broth with additional salt to taste if necessary. Cover and keep hot over low heat.

4. Divide the bean sprouts, tomato, and shrimp among the soup bowls. Ladle the hot broth into the bowls and garnish with the scallions and herbs. Serve immediately.

BRUISING LEMON GRASS

To bruise fresh lemon grass, smack the stalk with the back of a large chef's knife.

Southeast Asian Rice Noodle Soup with Chicken and Napa Cabbage

SERVES 4

We slightly altered the basic broth here, omitting the cinnamon, increasing the fish sauce, and decreasing the sugar. The chicken is cooked in the broth for added flavor.

6	ounces thick rice noodles (see "Dried Rice Noodles," below)
5	cups canned low-sodium chicken broth
4	medium cloves garlic, smashed and peeled
1	(2-inch) piece fresh ginger, peeled, cut into ⅛-inch rounds, and smashed (see illustration on page 26)
2	star anise pods
3	tablespoons fish sauce
1	tablespoon soy sauce
2	teaspoons sugar
12	ounces boneless, skinless chicken thighs, trimmed of excess fat
	Salt
½	medium napa cabbage, rinsed and sliced thin crosswise (about 4 cups)
2	scallions, white and green parts, sliced thin on an angle
½	cup loosely packed fresh mint leaves, torn in half if large
½	cup loosely packed fresh cilantro leaves
2	tablespoons chopped roasted unsalted peanuts
	Lime wedges

1. Bring 4 quarts of water to a boil in a large pot. Off heat, add the rice noodles, and let stand, stirring occasionally, until tender, 10 to 15 minutes. Drain and distribute the noodles among four large soup bowls.

2. Meanwhile, bring the broth, garlic, ginger, star anise, fish sauce, soy sauce, sugar, and chicken to a boil in a medium saucepan over medium-high heat. Reduce the heat to low and simmer until the chicken thighs are cooked through, about 10 minutes. Remove the chicken with a slotted spoon and set aside. When cool enough to handle, slice thinly. Continue to simmer the broth 10 minutes longer to blend flavors. Remove the solids with a slotted spoon and discard. Season the broth with additional salt to taste if necessary. Cover and keep hot over low heat.

3. Divide the cabbage and chicken among the soup bowls. Ladle the hot broth into the bowls and garnish with the scallions, herbs, and peanuts. Serve immediately, passing the lime wedges separately at the table.

INGREDIENTS: Dried Rice Noodles

Dried rice noodles are sold in two different styles: a thick, flat, fettuccine-width noodle and a very thin, thread-like noodle. It's confusing to try to buy these noodles by name. Because they're used in several Asian cuisines (including Chinese, Thai, and Vietnamese), they're marketed under several different Asian names. The English names are no more helpful because they're not standardized; you'll find the thicker noodles sold as "rice sticks" and the thread-like noodles sold as both "rice sticks" and "vermicelli." To further confuse matters, thin cellophane noodles made from mung beans are also marketed as "vermicelli." So don't bother with the names, just look for the shape of the noodle—all of the packages we've seen have been obligingly transparent.

The literature we read indicates that rice noodles are made from rice flour and water. But some of the packages we've seen list cornstarch in the ingredients as well as rice flour. In the fabrication of the noodles, rice flour may be stretched with or completely replaced by cornstarch, a cheaper ingredient. Noodles made with cornstarch break apart and stick together more readily than noodles made only with rice flour, so, if you have a choice, buy noodles made without cornstarch.

We found that boiled noodles have a tendency to get mushy and, if left in the soup for any length of time, to break apart. So we tried soaking for 15 minutes and then briefly submerging them in boiling water. This worked better but required two pots. Ultimately, we settled on soaking alone (in very hot water) because it was less complicated and worked just as well. We simply drained the noodles when they had softened to the point that they were tender but still had tooth. The only problem was that the noodles sometimes stuck together and then failed to soften properly. We were able to avoid this by stirring the noodles occasionally, especially at the beginning.

8

CHILLED SOUPS

WE GENERALLY THINK OF SOUPS AND STEWS in terms of cold-weather cooking. The exception, of course, is chilled soups, which are designed for summertime. These soups generally start with vegetables (although fruit is another option). They are meant to be served as a first course or a light lunch. (Fruit soups can also be served for dessert.)

There are a couple of points to keep in mind when preparing chilled soups. Cold temperatures dull flavors, so a chilled soup must be especially well seasoned. Although the refrigerator can be used to chill soups, this task can be accomplished more quickly over a bowl of ice water. Simply nestle the container with the hot soup (a wide container is best, since it will speed cooling) inside a larger bowl filled with ice cubes and cold water. Stir occasionally to help bring down the temperature of the soup in minutes rather than hours.

Temperature is a big part of the appeal of the soups in this chapter. On a hot summer day, nothing quite satisfies like an ice-cold bowl of soup. For maximum impact, chill individual bowls in the refrigerator for an hour or so before using them.

Finally, take the time to make the suggested garnishes. Many cold soups are pureed and benefit greatly from some texture, whether in the form of croutons, minced vegetables, or herbs. Even chilled soups that are not pureed, such as gazpacho, are improved by the addition of a simple garnish.

GAZPACHO

GAZPACHO IS HIGH SUMMER IN A BOWL. Popular on both sides of the Atlantic, this ice-cold, uncooked vegetable soup, made principally of tomatoes (whole and juice), cucumbers, bell peppers, and onions and seasoned with olive oil and vinegar, is sometimes referred to as "liquid salad" in its native Spain. That slang name may be more apt on these shores, though, as many American gazpacho recipes instruct the cook to simply puree all the vegetables together in the blender. Needless to say, the resulting mixture is more a thin vegetable porridge with an anonymous vegetal flavor, whereas we were looking for a soup with clearly flavored, distinct pieces of vegetable in a bracing tomato broth.

It's little wonder, then, that texture is one key to a great gazpacho. Philosophies about what is the right texture and how to achieve it vary considerably. Traditionally, gazpacho was thickened with water-soaked bread for extra body, but a number of the recipes we looked at skipped the bread altogether. Some recipes dictate straining the mixture to create a silky smooth texture, while others leave it chunky. With gorgeous summer produce and ingredients that remained constant from recipe to recipe, we knew that the basic flavor profile would not be a problem. That left thickening, method of manufacture as it related to both texture and flavor, and the best seasonings as the questions to explore.

In deference to tradition, we started by trying a number of bread-thickened gazpachos. No mater what kind of bread was used or how long it was soaked, tasters consistently favored breadless brews. The consensus among our palates was that the bread-thickened soups had a subtle but inescapable pastiness. It was the same with the gazpachos that were passed—rather laboriously, we might add—through a strainer. Their texture was too uniform for a soup that featured fresh vegetables.

With our preference for a chunky-style soup established, we had to figure out the best method for preparing the vegetables. Although it was a breeze to use, the blender broke the vegetables down beyond recognition, which was not at all what we wanted. The food processor method fared somewhat better, especially when we processed each vegetable separately, but still had distinct pros and cons. On the pro side were ease and the fact that the vegetables released some juice as they broke down, which helped flavor the soup. The cons were that no matter how we finessed the pulse feature, the vegetable pieces were neither neatly chopped nor consistently sized. This was especially true of the tomatoes, which broke down to a pulp. The texture of the resulting soup was more along the lines of a vegetable slushy, which might be acceptable given the ease of preparation, but was still not ideal. On balance, the food processor is a decent option, especially if you favor speed and convenience, so we've included a variation based on its use.

We pressed on to the old-fashioned, purist

method of hand chopping the vegetables. It does involve some extra work, but it went much more swiftly than we'd imagined, and the benefits to the gazpacho's texture were dazzling. Because the vegetable pieces were consistent in size and shape, they not only retained their individual flavors but also set off the tomato broth beautifully, adding immeasurably to the whole. This was just what we were after.

One last procedural issue we investigated was the resting time. Gazpacho is best served ice cold, and the chilling time also allows the flavors to develop and meld. We tasted every hour for eight hours and found that four hours was the minimum time required for the soup to chill and the flavors to blossom.

Several of the key ingredients and seasonings also bore some exploration. Tomatoes are a star player,

and we preferred beefsteak over plum because they were larger, juicier, and easier to chop. Gazpacho is truly a dish to make only when local tomatoes are plentiful. We made several batches using handsome supermarket tomatoes, but the flavor paled in comparison to those batches made with perfectly ripe, local farm-stand tomatoes. We considered skinning and seeding them, but not a single taster complained when we didn't, so we skipped the extra steps.

When it came to peppers, we preferred red over green for their sweeter flavor. But red was less popular in the onion department; tasters rejected red onions, as well as plain yellow, as too sharp. Instead, they favored sweet onions, such as Vidalia or Maui, and shallots equally. We did note, however, that any onion was overpowering (especially in the leftovers the next day) if used in the quantities recommended in most recipes, and the same was true of garlic, so we dramatically reduced the quantity of both. To ensure thorough seasoning of the whole mixture, we marinated the vegetables briefly in garlic, salt, pepper, and vinegar before adding the bulk of the liquid. These batches had more balanced flavors than the batches that were seasoned after all the ingredients were combined.

CUTTING TOMATOES INTO NEAT DICE

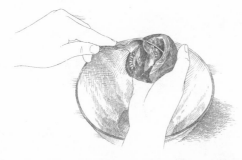

1. Core tomatoes and halve them pole to pole. Working over a bowl to catch all the juices, scoop out the inner pulp and seeds. Chop the tomato pulp into ¹/₄-inch cubes.

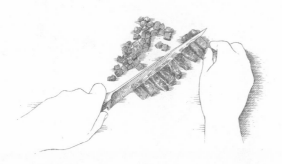

2. Cut tomato halves into ¹/₄-inch slices. Turn slices 90 degrees, so they are parallel with the edge of the work surface, and cut into ¹/₄-inch cubes.

The liquid component was also critical. Most recipes called for tomato juice, which we sampled both straight and mixed in various amounts with water and low-sodium canned chicken broth. The winning ratio was 5 cups of tomato juice thinned with 1 cup of water to make the 6-cup total we needed. The water cut the viscosity of the juice just enough to make it brothy and light, but not downright thin. Given our preference for ice-cold gazpacho, we decided to add ice cubes instead of straight water. The ice helped chill the soup while providing water as it melted. We also conducted a blind tasting of tomato juices in which Welch's showed very well. (See page 182 for additional details.)

Finally, a word about the two primary seasonings, vinegar and olive oil. Spain is a noted producer of sherry, so it follows that sherry vinegar is a popular choice for gazpacho. When we tasted it, along with champagne, red wine, and white wine vinegars, the sherry vinegar was our favorite by far, adding not only acidity but also richness and depth. If you find that your stock of sherry vinegar has run dry, white wine vinegar was the runner up and can be substituted. The oil contributes both flavor and a lush mouthfeel to this simple soup, and, in a word, only extra-virgin will do. Liquid or not, would you dress a beautiful summer salad with anything less?

Classic Gazpacho

SERVES 8 TO 10

This recipe makes a large quantity because the leftovers are so good, but it can be halved if you prefer. If Fresh Samantha juices are available in your grocery store, the company's Veggie Cha Cha vegetable juice makes an excellent gazpacho—use it in place of the tomato juice. Traditionally, diners garnish their own bowls with more of the same diced vegetables that are in the soup. If that appeals to you, cut some extra vegetables while you prepare those called for in the recipe. Additional garnish possibilities include croutons (see page 108), chopped pitted black olives, chopped hard-cooked eggs, and finely diced avocado.

3	ripe medium beefsteak tomatoes (about 1½ pounds), cored and cut into ¼-inch dice, following illustrations on page 179 (about 4 cups)
2	small red bell peppers (about 1 pound), cored, seeded, and cut into ¼-inch dice, following illustrations, right (about 2 cups)
2	small cucumbers (about 1 pound), one peeled and the other with skin on, both seeded and cut into ¼-inch dice, following illustrations on page 181 (about 2 cups)
½	small sweet onion (such as Vidalia, Maui, or Walla Walla) or 2 large shallots, peeled and minced (about ½ cup)
2	medium cloves garlic, minced
2	teaspoons salt
⅓	cup sherry vinegar
	Ground black pepper
5	cups tomato juice, preferably Welch's
1	teaspoon hot pepper sauce, such as Tabasco (optional)
8	ice cubes
	Extra-virgin olive oil for serving

1. Combine the tomatoes and their juices, bell peppers, cucumbers, onion, garlic, salt, vinegar, and pepper to taste in a large (at least 4-quart) nonreactive bowl. Let stand until the vegetables just begin to release their juices, about 5 minutes. Stir in the tomato juice, hot pepper sauce, if using, and ice cubes. Cover tightly. Refrigerate to blend flavors, at least 4 hours and up to 2 days.

2. Adjust the seasonings with salt and pepper and remove and discard any unmelted ice cubes. Serve cold, drizzling each portion with about 1 teaspoon extra-virgin olive oil and topping with the desired garnishes (see note).

➤ VARIATIONS
Quick Food Processor Gazpacho
Using the same ingredients and quantities as for Classic Gazpacho, core and quarter the tomatoes and process them in the workbowl of a food processor fitted with a steel blade until broken down into ¼- to ¾-inch pieces, about twelve 1-second pulses; transfer to a large bowl. Cut the cored and seeded peppers and seeded cucumbers into rough

CUTTING PEPPERS INTO NEAT DICE

1. Slice a ¾-inch section off both the tip and stem ends of the peppers. Make one slit in the trimmed shells, place skin-sides down, and open the flesh.

2. Scrape off seeds and membranes. Cut flesh into ¼-inch strips. Turn the strips 90 degrees, so they are parallel with the work surface edge, and cut into ¼-inch cubes.

1-inch pieces and process them separately until broken down into ¼- to ¾-inch pieces, about twelve 1-second pulses; add to the bowl with the tomatoes. Mince onion and garlic by hand, then add to bowl with vegetables along with salt, vinegar, and ground black pepper to taste; continue with recipe as directed.

Spicy Gazpacho with Chipotle Chiles and Lime

A garnish of finely diced avocado is a must here.

Follow recipe for Classic or Quick Food Processor Gazpacho, omitting optional hot pepper sauce and sherry vinegar and adding 2½ tablespoons minced chipotle chiles en adobo, ¼ cup minced fresh cilantro leaves, 6 tablespoons lime juice, and 2 teaspoons grated lime zest along with the tomato juice and ice cubes.

Gazpacho with Scallops and Shrimp

For maximum time efficiency, begin preparing the vegetables while the shrimp stock is simmering. Because of the seafood in this variation, this soup will keep for no more than a day. Garlic croutons (page 109) are an ideal garnish.

SEAFOOD

3	cups dry white wine
2	cups bottled clam juice
1½	teaspoons salt
¾	pound large shrimp, shelled and halved lengthwise, shells reserved
¾	pound small scallops, tendons removed (see illustration on page 253)
¼	cup extra-virgin olive oil
2	medium cloves garlic, minced
1	tablespoon lemon juice

GAZPACHO

3	ripe medium beefsteak tomatoes (about 1½ pounds), cored and cut into ¼-inch dice, following illustrations on page 179 (about 4 cups)
2	small red bell peppers (about 1 pound), cored, seeded, and cut into ¼-inch dice, following illustrations on page 180 (about 2 cups)
2	small cucumbers (about 1 pound), one peeled and the other with skin on, both seeded and cut into ¼-inch dice, following illustrations, right (about 2 cups)

½	small sweet onion (such as Vidalia, Maui, or Walla Walla) or 2 large shallots, peeled and minced (about ½ cup)
2	medium cloves garlic, minced
1½	teaspoons salt
⅓	cup sherry vinegar
	Ground black pepper
2½	cups tomato juice, preferably Welch's
1	teaspoon hot pepper sauce, such as Tabasco (optional)
8	ice cubes

1. FOR THE SEAFOOD: Bring the wine, clam juice, 1 teaspoon salt, and shrimp shells to a boil in a large sauté pan over medium-high heat. Cover the pan, reduce the heat to low, and simmer for 30 minutes. Strain the stock and discard the shells. Return the stock to a simmer over medium heat in the same saucepan. Add the reserved shrimp and scallops and poach until just barely cooked through, about 1½ minutes. With a slotted spoon, transfer the seafood to a small bowl, toss with oil, garlic, lemon juice, and remaining ½ teaspoon salt.

CUTTING CUCUMBERS INTO NEAT DICE

1. Cut a ¾-inch section off both ends of the cucumbers. Halve the cucumbers lengthwise and scoop out seeds with a spoon. Cut each seeded half lengthwise into ¼-inch strips.

2. Turn the strips 90 degrees and cut into even ¼-inch pieces.

Cool briefly, cover, and refrigerate the seafood. Bring the poaching liquid to a boil over high heat and boil until reduced to about 2½ cups; cool liquid and reserve.

2. FOR THE GAZPACHO: Combine the reserved seafood mixture, tomatoes, bell peppers, cucumbers, onion, garlic, salt, vinegar, and pepper to taste in a large (at least 4-quart) nonreactive bowl. Let stand until the vegetables just begin to release their juices, about 5 minutes. Stir in the reserved seafood stock, tomato juice, hot pepper sauce, if using, and ice cubes. Cover tightly and refrigerate to blend flavors, at least 4 hours and up to 1 day.

3. Adjust the seasonings with salt and pepper and remove and discard any unmelted ice cubes. Serve cold, garnishing with garlic croutons if desired.

INGREDIENTS: Tomato Juice

To drown ripe, hand-cut local vegetables in miserable tomato juice and call it gazpacho would be a travesty. So, after visits to several nearby supermarkets, we spread seven leading brands of tomato and tomato-based vegetable juices before us and blind-tasted our way to two winners. The lineup included tomato juices from R. W. Knudsen, Muir Glen, Campbell's, and Welch's and vegetable juices from V-8, Muir Glen, and Fresh Samantha, a small East Coast company still building toward national distribution. Tasters, among whom there was little accord, assessed the color, flavor, and viscosity of each juice, which they tried straight up and in gazpacho.

The dividing line was not drawn between the tomato and vegetable juices, as we might have suspected. Instead, juices perceived to be too thick, acidic, or salty were downgraded, and those thought to taste more tomatoey or fresh were favored. V-8, Knudsen, and two Muir Glen entries were judged too thick, with both Knudsen and Muir Glen Tomato Juice deemed too acidic and V-8 too salty. While Campbell's did not receive uniformly negative comments, neither did it rate within most tasters' top choices.

The juices rated tops, Fresh Samantha and Welch's, had distinctly different flavor profiles. Fresh Samantha was spicy and peppery but fresh tasting, while Welch's was judged straightforward, tomatoey, and mellow. Neither of these juices was "too thick" or "pasty," criticisms that felled every other juice in the pack.

WHITE GAZPACHO

WHEN AMERICANS HEAR THE WORD *GAZPACHO*, they invariably think tomatoes. But in Spain, gazpacho is often made without tomatoes or any vegetables at all. Traditional white gazpacho has seven ingredients: skinned almonds, olive oil, vinegar or lemon juice, garlic, bread, salt, and water. These ingredients are pureed, chilled, and garnished with halved, and sometimes skinned, green grapes. Some variations include pine nuts in addition to the almonds, egg yolks or whites for texture and frothiness, and melon or diced green apple for a garnish. But for the most part, white gazpacho recipes are fairly consistent, at least in terms of the ingredients.

To get a handle on this subject, we prepared three recipes from our research file that exhibited the greatest variation. The kitchen staff was horrified by the results. The soups were gummy and gritty and tasted closer to tahini or ranch-style salad dressing than chilled soup. Vinegar and garlic were the predominant flavors. Some tasters suggested that it wasn't worth continuing with recipe development. But other staffers insisted that white gazpacho, as they had tasted it in Spain, could be delicious.

Our goal here was clear: The soup needed to have a balanced acidity and sweetness, a smooth and creamy texture, and a refreshing spiciness. We started development from the ground up.

Several gazpacho recipes we had found during our research work used verjus, unfermented wine grape juice, for body and flavor. We have used verjus in the past and love it for its pleasant fruitiness, muted acidity, and dynamic flavor. We sensed that it was perfect for the job, and our hunch paid off, at least in part. White gazpacho made with verjus was outstanding: bright, strong, and fully flavored, without any cloying sweetness. The garlic flavor was piercing and clean.

Unfortunately, this test was only partly helpful. Verjus can be extraordinarily hard to find, so it was out of the question to call for it in our final recipe, but we could use it for inspiration. To approximate the flavor, we decided to puree and strain green grapes for their juice and to add a touch of lemon juice to balance out the sweetness. While far from the unique flavor of verjus, the grape juice was a good substitute.

It was important for us to keep in mind that grapes vary in ripeness, their tartness inconsistent. Our initial testing was with very unripe grapes, so we added only a little lemon juice. We bought ripe, sweet grapes for subsequent testing and increased the amount of lemon juice to approximate the desired tartness. The soup should be a bit tart but not puckery or sour.

For the almonds, we ended up choosing skinless, whole raw almonds. Many traditional recipes blanch or soak the skinned almonds prior to blending, but we found this step to be unnecessary. We lightly toasted one batch, but tasters were not thrilled. The toasted nut flavor clashed with the other flavors in the soup.

Our recipe was beginning to take shape. The bread was the last major issue to examine. While most recipes suggest a hearty country loaf as the best thickening agent, we wondered how other choices would perform. Sourdough bread was too strong and disrupted the delicate sweet/sour flavor of the gazpacho. Baguettes were wasteful; after the crust was removed and discarded there was very little crumb left over. We were happy with the results from a Pullman-style sandwich loaf, such as Pepperidge Farm. The bread is bland and has a tight crumb, which easily broke down into the gazpacho. Since this bread is so readily available, we decided to use it in our final recipe.

At this point, we realized that the gumminess tasters had so disliked in our early tests was caused by processing the bread too long. If the bread is fully incorporated into the soup, the texture becomes gummy. We found that adding soaked bread to the blender and pulsing it 10 times was just enough to combine and disperse some of the bread's starch. While not all of the bread was incorporated into the gazpacho, it added just enough starch to slightly thicken the soup.

After processing the bread, the soup was strained to attain a palatable consistency. We found that a fine-mesh strainer was crucial to achieving a silky smooth texture. We were surprised by the amount of solids (bread, almond, and grape) left after blending. If these solids were left in the gazpacho, the texture was grainy and unpleasant. The ideal white gazpacho should have the thickness and texture of heavy cream.

The traditional garnish for white gazpacho is halved white grapes. Because we included grapes in the soup itself, we looked for some alternatives. We found several traditional recipes with tart green apple or melon garnishes. Tasters liked the apple but were indifferent about the melon. The pale cream color of apple subtly accented the soup's slight green tinge. A few threads of mint further emphasized the green. A few crisp, garlicky croutons added a pleasing contrast to this silky soup.

White Gazpacho

SERVES 4 TO 6

Texture is a major consideration when preparing this refreshing soup. Don't overprocess the bread, and be sure to pass the soup through a fine-mesh strainer. Chop the apples for the garnish just before serving.

SOUP

4	ounces white sandwich bread (about 5 slices), crusts removed, and crumbled into ¼- to ½-inch pieces
4½	cups ice water
8	ounces whole, skinless almonds (about 1½ cups)
½	pound seedless green grapes, washed and stemmed (about 2 cups)
3	medium cloves garlic, peeled
1¼	teaspoons salt, plus more to taste
⅛	teaspoon cayenne pepper
1½	tablespoons lemon juice, plus additional to taste
2	tablespoons extra-virgin olive oil

GARNISH

1	small Granny Smith apple, peeled, cored, and chopped fine (about 1 cup)
1	tablespoon thinly sliced fresh mint leaves
2	cups Garlic Croutons (page 109)

1. Combine the bread crumbs and 1½ cups ice water in a medium bowl and set aside for several minutes to soften.

2. Place the almonds, grapes, garlic, salt, cayenne, lemon juice, and remaining 3 cups ice water in a blender. Blend until the mixture is completely liquefied, about 3 minutes. Add the breadcrumb mixture and olive oil and process until the mixture looks frothy

and a bit lumpy, about ten 1-second pulses. (Do not overprocess; the mixture should not become smooth.)

3. Strain the pureed mixture through a fine-mesh strainer set over a medium mixing bowl, pushing on the solids with a wooden spoon to extract all of the liquid. Discard the solids. Add salt and lemon juice to taste. Cover tightly and refrigerate until chilled, at least 3 hours and up to 1 day.

4. Ladle the gazpacho into bowls and garnish with apple, mint, and croutons. Serve immediately.

Vichyssoise

VICHYSSOISE SOUNDS SO REFINED, BUT its roots are really quite humble. Start with a rustic potato-leek soup, like our recipe in chapter 6, puree this chunky soup until it's supersmooth, add cream, and then chill. Given that we had already developed a great recipe for hot potato-leek soup, we figured vichyssoise would be a cinch.

Although easy to prepare, vichyssoise does have its problems. Sometimes vichyssoise can be gritty or too thick. At other times the dairy dominates the potato and leek flavors. We wanted to know which techniques we could use to avoid these problems and produce a flawlessly smooth, creamy soup bursting with potato and leek flavor.

Despite its French name, vichyssoise can claim American birthright—or at the very least dual citizenship. Louis Diat, a French chef working in New York in the early twentieth century, is credited with the invention of vichyssoise. After becoming popular in the United States, the soup made its way to France following World War II.

Perhaps because of its relatively recent invention, vichyssoise recipes are fairly similar. We did have some questions, though, starting with the potato. Although we liked red potatoes in our rustic potato-leek soup (they held their shape nicely in this chunky soup), we wondered if russet potatoes would be a better choice for a smooth soup. Sure enough, high-starch russets fell apart during the cooking process and helped promote the smooth texture we wanted. (For more information on potato varieties and their starch content, see page 125.)

Next, we considered the leeks. Many recipes add onions instead of leeks. We tested onions, leeks, and a mixture of the two. Tasters preferred a combination, with the leeks in the forefront to keep the onions from overpowering the other flavors in the soup. Sweating the onions and leeks in a covered pot over low heat brought out the full range of flavors in these vegetables. In contrast, recipes that just simmered the onions and leeks with the stock and potatoes made bland soups.

Once the leeks and onion had been sweated, it was time for the stock and potatoes to go into the pot. We found that we could omit the flour used in our hot potato-leek soup. Since cream would eventually be added to make vichyssoise, the soup would be plenty thick without any flour. Once the potatoes were tender, the soup was pureed in a blender. For ultimate smoothness, we found it necessary to run the pureed soup through a fine-mesh strainer.

Our final tests revolved around the cream. A few "light" recipes suggested using half-and-half, but we found the richness of cream to be a must. However, it was possible to use a lot less cream than many recipes suggest. (We found that large quantities obliterated the other flavors in the soup.) A single cup of cream gave the soup plenty of body and helped to create the luxurious mouthfeel it is known for.

Other than a thorough chilling, this soup required no more work once pureed and strained. We tried several garnishes and decided that tradition—in the form of minced chives—worked best.

Vichyssoise
SERVES 4 TO 6

Don't let the onion and leeks brown as they cook, or the color of the soup will be marred.

2   tablespoons unsalted butter
I   medium onion, chopped medium
    (about I cup)
4   medium leeks, white and light green parts only,
    sliced crosswise ¼-inch thick (about 4 cups,
    cleaned according to illustrations on page 124)
3   cups homemade chicken stock or canned
    low-sodium chicken broth
I   small russet potato (about 5 ounces), peeled
    and cut into ½-inch dice (about I cup)

1 cup heavy cream
   Salt and ground white pepper
2 tablespoons minced fresh chives

1. Melt the butter in a large stockpot or Dutch oven over medium-low heat. When the butter foams, stir in the onion and leeks. Reduce the heat to low, cover the pot, and cook, stirring frequently, until the vegetables are softened, about 10 minutes.

2. Add the stock and potato, increase the heat to medium-high, and bring the mixture to a boil. Reduce the heat to low, cover, and simmer until the potato pieces are completely tender, 10 to 15 minutes.

3. Working in batches, puree the mixture in a blender until it is liquefied and smooth, 1 to 2 minutes. Pour the puree through a fine-mesh strainer into a large bowl. Stir in the heavy cream and season with salt and pepper to taste. Cool to room temperature, then cover tightly and refrigerate until chilled, at least 4 hours and up to 2 days. Adjust the seasonings. Ladle the soup into individual bowls and sprinkle with chives. Serve immediately.

BORSCHT

LIKE HOT BORSCHT (SEE CHAPTER 4), chilled borscht begins with beets. But the soups are remarkably different, and not just because of the serving temperatures. Hot borscht is a grand affair, with several kinds of meat and vegetables floating in a ruby red beet broth. Chilled borscht is much simpler, with beets taking center stage. The beets are usually simmered in liquid until tender and then enriched with dairy to create a thick soup. Chilled borscht is basically cream of beet soup, served cold. Sometimes this smooth soup is served as is; more often it is enriched with grated beets, potatoes, herbs, and/or other garnishes.

Our goals here were to create a chilled soup bursting with beet flavor. Like hot borscht, chilled borscht relies on a complex balance of sweet and sour. Other ingredients would be added to enhance the beet flavor, but they would play supporting roles.

The first and most important issue to investigate was how to cook the beets. Our research uncovered two basic possibilities—roasting and boiling. We find that roasting concentrates the natural sugars in beets and makes them especially sweet. This is how we cook beets for salads and side dishes.

We roasted whole beets, slipped off their skins, grated the beets, and then cooked them in water with onion and garlic until extremely tender. The vegetables were pureed and enriched with cream and vinegar. The results were thoroughly disappointing. When we tasted the soup liquid before pureeing, it was extremely bland. The pureed soup was not much better. Although roasting is a great way to cook beets, it does not produce a flavorful liquid base on which to build a soup. For that, you must cook the beets in water, as done in the hot borscht recipe.

We now wondered how to prepare the beets before boiling. Should they be whole, diced, or grated? We started by cooking beets whole with their skins on until tender. When cool, we rubbed off the skins from the boiled beets with a paper towel. We then grated the beets and made soup with them. The results were quite good.

Since we wanted to cook grated beets in the soup, why not just peel and grate the beets before boiling them, as we did with hot borscht? We tried this approach twice, once cooking the beets in plain water and once in water flavored with salt, sugar, and vinegar. In both cases, we felt that the beets tasted washed out. (In hot borscht, the grated beets are cooked in homemade beef stock flavored with many other ingredients, so this does not happen.) For cold borscht, it was better to boil the beets whole until tender so they retained as much of their flavor as possible. We didn't even bother peeling the beets until after cooking them. Using a paper towel, we could rub the skins right off the cooked beets.

With our beet cooking method decided, we turned to the quantity of beets. We wanted our recipe to yield 2 quarts of soup and thus started out with 2 quarts of water. The recipes we had been working with called for one to two pounds of beets for this amount of liquid. We tested 1, 1½, and 2 pounds of beets. Two pounds of beets produced the best-tasting soup.

Although most chilled borscht recipes call for water as the liquid base, a few sources suggested chicken stock. We prepared two batches of soup—one with water, the other with homemade stock. The chicken flavor overwhelmed the beets, and tasters preferred the soup made with water. The water did need to be flavored, however.

We turned our attention to the ingredients responsible for creating the complex sweet-and-sour flavors that are the hallmark of good borscht. We tested lemon juice, red wine vinegar, and distilled white vinegar as well as when to add them to the soup. While the flavor of the lemon juice did not withstand prolonged cooking, we found that adding vinegar at the outset enhanced the flavor of the beets and the liquid. Both vinegars were good, although tasters preferred the clean, strong, sharp flavor of the distilled white vinegar. We found that a little lemon juice, added just before serving, provided a nice citrus kick.

As for the sugar, our tests revealed that it is best added directly to the beet cooking water, along with the vinegar. One-quarter cup brought out the sweetness in the beets and balanced the vinegar perfectly.

Although beets are the star, other vegetables do make an appearance in chilled borscht—typically onions, carrots, garlic, and/or potatoes. We found that onions added depth and complexity to the soup but could also overpower the beets. We tried using fewer onions but discovered that even one small onion was too strong. We finally hit upon the following solution: simmer a small onion whole with the beets for flavor but then discard it before pureeing the beets. This way the onion flavored the soup without taking over.

Carrots competed with the beets, both in terms of color and sweetness, and were dismissed. Garlic was much too pungent, even when we handled it like the onion and discarded a single clove after cooking the beets till tender. We liked potatoes as a garnish, but they muddied the texture if incorporated into the soup.

Our next step was to test thickening options. Several recipes we ran across used eggs to thicken the soup. The eggs were tempered by the addition of some of the beet cooking liquid and then stirred back into the soup pot to form a liaison. (See the Egg-Lemon Soup recipe in chapter 3 for more details on this technique.) Tasters roundly rejected this method. The egg flavor seemed out of place in this soup. In addition, the eggs curdled slightly and clung to the tiny bits of grated beet.

We identified a better option—dairy. Our choices were then to thicken the broth with dairy before stirring in the grated beets or to puree the beets and broth before adding the dairy. The former produced a better-looking soup. A brilliant pink broth offset strands of dark burgundy beets. The broth was now richly textured and creamy, and the beets were soft and tender, but the broth was not as flavorful as we might have liked. It tasted mostly of dairy, not beets. We realized that in terms of flavor, the latter option, pureeing beets and broth before adding dairy, was better because the beets were directly incorporated into the liquid base. What to do? We decided on a compromise: puree half the beets with the broth to make the soup base as flavorful as possible, then grate the remaining beets and stir them into the pureed soup for visual and textural appeal.

As for the particular dairy component to use, we tested heavy cream, sour cream, and yogurt. Yogurt was not rich enough to produce the soft, thick, and luxurious texture tasters wanted. Yogurt also had a strong tang that some tasters thought overpowered the sweetness of the beets. Sour cream and heavy

REMOVING BEET STAINS

When cut, beets stain everything they touch, including hands and cutting boards. To help remove these stains, sprinkle the stained area with salt, moisten with water, and then scrub with soap. The salt crystals help lift the beet juices away.

cream were tried separately and together. Both choices thickened and flavored the soup in desirable ways, but when equal amounts of sour cream and heavy cream were combined, the soup was superb. The texture was silky smooth, with lots of body, and the flavors were a perfect balance of tart and sweet. The sour cream is so thick that it must be added to the broth before the grated beets. If the grated beets are already in the broth the sour cream sticks to them, making it difficult to fully blend the sour cream into the soup.

Chopped fresh dill is the classic garnish for chilled borscht. We decided to stick with tradition in our master recipe but developed some nice options that require only a bit of extra work (see right). Consider serving chilled borscht alongside several garnishes in separate bowls. Each person can enhance the soup as desired, with boiled potatoes, onion, cucumber, hard-boiled egg, and/or an extra squeeze of lemon juice.

Chilled Borscht

SERVES 4 TO 6

This soup has a brilliant, deep pink broth that is thick with strips of burgundy beets. The classic garnish of a little dill adds a bright green contrast. Many other garnish options can add flavor and color to this soup; see right for suggestions. If possible, buy beets with the greens attached. Fresh tops mean fresh beets, and boiling the beets with some stem attached makes it easy to peel them. Medium-sized beets are best for this recipe. Small beets create more work, and large beets are sometimes tough.

2	pounds beets (6 medium), scrubbed and all but 1 inch of stems removed
1	small onion, peeled
1/4	cup distilled white vinegar
1/4	cup sugar
1 1/2	teaspoons salt
3/4	cup heavy cream
3/4	cup sour cream
1	tablespoon lemon juice
2	tablespoons chopped fresh dill

1. Place the beets, onion, 7 cups water, vinegar, sugar, and salt in a large saucepan. Bring to a boil

GARNISHING BORSCHT

Borscht lends itself to an assortment of garnishes that offer complementary flavor, texture, and color. Add one or two of the following garnishes (along with the dill) to each bowl of soup, or offer an assortment and let diners pick and choose as they like, garnishing their own bowls.

- 4 ounces small red potatoes, scrubbed, boiled until tender, and cut into 1/4-inch dice
- 1/2 large cucumber, seeded and cut into 1/4-inch dice
- 2 hard-cooked eggs, chopped fine
- 1/2 red onion, chopped fine
- 1 lemon, cut into wedges

over high heat. Reduce the heat to medium-low, cover partially, and simmer until the beets are tender and can be easily pierced with a skewer, about 45 minutes.

2. Remove and discard the onion. Transfer the beets to a cutting board and let cool slightly. Strain the liquid through a strainer lined with paper towel and reserve.

3. With a paper towel, rub the skin from beets. Grate half of the beets using the large holes on a box grater (see illustrations on page 80) or a food processor fitted with a shredding disk. Refrigerate the grated beets until cold. Cut the remaining beets into large chunks. Place half of the cut beets in a blender. Add just enough cooking liquid to cover them by 1 inch and blend until very smooth, about 2 minutes. Transfer this mixture to a large container. Repeat with the remaining beets. Stir the remaining cooking liquid into the pureed beets and refrigerate until cold, about 2 hours.

4. Remove the pureed beets and grated beets from the refrigerator. Whisk the heavy cream and sour cream into the pureed beets until smooth and fully blended. Stir in the grated beets. (Soup can be refrigerated in an airtight container for up to 3 days.) Stir in the lemon juice and adjust the seasonings. Ladle the soup into bowls and garnish with the dill and other garnishes as desired. Serve immediately.

CUCUMBER SOUP

CUCUMBER SOUP CAN BE BEAUTIFUL, ITS delicate green color and sweet, mild flavor making it a perfect first course or even light entrée on a hot summer day. Making good cucumber soup, however, can be tricky. The delicate cucumber flavor can easily be overpowered, yet if it is not rounded out by a few other ingredients, the soup can taste like a cucumber smoothie.

To start, we tried several recipes from various sources. Some instructed the cook to hand-chop the cucumbers, making a sort of watery raita. Others used the food processor, which we found turned the cucumbers to mush. Tasters preferred the smooth soup made using a blender then garnished with hand-chopped pieces for texture.

With our basic technique down, we started making soups from peeled and unpeeled cucumbers. As expected, the peel added some bitterness along with a speckled presentation tasters found unattractive. We then tested seeded versus unseeded cucumbers. Although the difference wasn't dramatic, the seeds added an acrid aftertaste, so we decided to omit them. We then tested European versus regular cucumbers. (European cucumbers are longer and thinner than the standard American cucumber and generally unwaxed.) The difference here was minor, but tasters preferred the sweeter, lighter flavor of the European cucumbers. Either cucumber, however, can be used.

We had been banking on garlic and shallots to round out the flavors of the soup, but both were simply too strong, especially after the soup had chilled. Still wanting some allium flavor, we moved on to scallions and found them to work well when the white ends weren't involved. Other recipes called for red onions, jalapeños, tomatoes, and spinach, but none of these was worth the effort; they all simply bullied the cucumber flavor.

Dairy is an important aspect of this soup, and most recipes use yogurt. We found that 1 cup of whole yogurt was perfect for 5 pounds of raw cucumber. When we used more than a cup of yogurt, it took over the soup, turning it into a dip. When we used less than that, the soup tasted more like a health food drink. We also found that it was better to whisk the yogurt into the soup; the blender made it incredibly foamy. Low-fat and nonfat yogurts were terrible, turning out flat, acidic soups. The extra fat in yogurt made from whole milk was a necessary ingredient.

The soup was now a bit thick, and we tried thinning it out with chicken stock and buttermilk, but both tasted out of place. In the end, water was best.

So far our soup was simple, containing only cucumbers, scallions, yogurt, and a little water. Some lemon juice added a good, citrus twang, while a little sugar helped bring out the cucumber flavor. Finished with a little salt and pepper, the soup was perfect.

The garnishes are an important part of this soup. They are the only way to dress it up without disturbing the fragile balance of flavors. While dill and diced cucumber are classic and easy, we found that small diced green apple with curry added perfumed, crunchy bites of sweet tartness. Mangoes added complementary color and fragrance; avocados and cilantro were also quite good.

Chilled Cucumber Soup
SERVES 6

We prefer long, thin European cucumbers in this recipe, but regular American cucumbers can be used. Don't prepare the garnish until you are ready to serve the soup. The variations make use of different garnishing ideas.

SOUP

5	pounds cucumbers, peeled, seeded (see illustration on page 189), and cut into 2-inch pieces (about 8 cups)
4	medium scallions, dark green parts only, chopped coarse (about ½ cup)
1	cup plain whole-milk yogurt
¼	teaspoon sugar
1	tablespoon lemon juice
1	teaspoon salt
	Pinch ground black pepper

CUCUMBER-DILL GARNISH

1	large cucumber (about 1 pound), peeled, seeded (see illustration on page 189), and cut into ½-inch cubes (about 2 cups)
1½	teaspoons chopped fresh dill
½	teaspoon lemon juice
¼	teaspoon salt

1. FOR THE SOUP: Toss the cucumbers with the scallions in a medium bowl. Puree half the cucumber-scallion mixture in a blender with 1¼ cups cold water until smooth, about 1 minute. Transfer the puree to a large nonreactive bowl. Puree the remaining cucumber-scallion mixture with 1¼ cups cold water and transfer it to the bowl with the first batch. Whisk in the yogurt, sugar, lemon juice, salt, and ground black pepper. Cover tightly and refrigerate until chilled, at least 1 hour or up to 12 hours.

2. FOR THE GARNISH: Dry the cucumber cubes between layers of paper towels. Toss cucumbers with dill, lemon juice, and salt in a small bowl.

3. To serve, divide the chilled soup among individual bowls. Sprinkle some of the cucumber and dill mixture over each bowl and serve immediately.

➤ VARIATIONS

Chilled Cucumber Soup with Mango and Mint

Toss 1 large mango, peeled and cut into ¼-inch cubes (about 1½ cups; see illustrations on page 238), with 2 teaspoons minced fresh mint leaves, ½ teaspoon lime juice, and ¼ teaspoon salt. Follow recipe for Chilled Cucumber Soup, replacing the cucumber garnish with the mango mixture.

Chilled Cucumber Soup with Curried Apples and Basil

Toss 2 Granny Smith apples, peeled, cored, and cut into ¼-inch dice (about 2 cups), with 1 tablespoon minced fresh basil leaves and ½ teaspoon curry powder. Follow recipe for Chilled Cucumber Soup, replacing the cucumber garnish with the apple mixture.

Chilled Cucumber Soup with Avocado and Cilantro

Halve and pit 2 avocados (about 12 ounces; see illustrations on page 190), scoop flesh from skins, and cut into ¼-inch dice (adapting technique shown on page 65). Toss with 1 tablespoon minced fresh cilantro leaves, ½ teaspoon lime juice, and ¼ teaspoon salt. Follow recipe for Chilled Cucumber Soup, substituting an equal amount of lime juice for lemon juice in the soup and replacing the cucumber garnish with the avocado mixture.

AVOCADO SOUP

A CHILLED AVOCADO SOUP SHOULD BE verdant green, buttery, delicate, and utterly delicious. Unfortunately, this soup often looks better than it tastes. Blindfolded, you would have a hard time telling what kind of soup you were eating.

Our goal was a soup that was pure, unfettered avocado. Unfortunately, every version we tried in restaurants or from cookbooks was everything but—from guacamole puree to Mexican ranch dressing. Even the most basic recipes were unappealing. Dairy

TESTING AVOCADOS FOR RIPENESS

A soft avocado is sometimes just soft rather than truly ripe. To be sure, try to flick the small stem off the avocado. If it comes off easily and you can see green underneath it, the avocado is ripe and ready to use. If the stem does not come off or if you see brown underneath after prying it off, the avocado is not ripe.

SEEDING CUCUMBERS

Peel and halve each cucumber lengthwise. Use a small spoon to remove the seeds and surrounding liquid from each cucumber half.

made an already-rich soup even richer as well as much too thick. Lime juice, sour cream, and buttermilk all introduced a sourness that magnified even the slightest suggestion of unripe avocado. Chili powder and tortilla chips evoked seven-layer dip. Cucumbers were refreshing, but even they detracted from the delicate flavor of the avocado. Chicken broth tasted, well, chickeny—not a desirable quality in a cold soup with a delicate vegetable base.

Each and every recipe was terrible, so we began our quest from square one, starting with nothing but the avocados. We would have no dairy, no broth, no spices, and no sour elements—just water, a few avocados, and some salt. After a quick puree in the blender, the resulting soup was smooth and rich and tasted like pure avocado.

In previous, unsatisfying versions, we noted that the coldest soups were the most refreshing, so we added some crushed ice to the working recipe. It created the perfect chill, which held up nicely over time, both in the fridge and out. Many recipes recommended citrus juice to prevent discoloration, but we found no such problem, even after six hours in the refrigerator.

While the soup was both rich and refreshing, we wanted to bring out some of the sweet, nutty elements of the avocado. With a suggestion from an avocado-milkshake fan, we decided to try a bit of sugar. Equal parts sugar and salt were perfect—

balancing the seasoning and enhancing the fruity nature of the avocado.

After trying to impart a bit of brightness to the soup, we decided that the avocado flavor was too delicate to stand up to any additional ingredients whatsoever. The only addition we deemed worthy was a simple infusion of lime. Steeping the zest from half of a lime for several hours resulted in muted floral tones and the merest suggestion of citrus, with none of the unappealing sour elements introduced by lime juice. We use the lime zest in a variation of the master recipe.

This simple soup, with its decadent neutral creamy base of green, seemed to cry out for creative garnishing. With the avocado milkshake still in mind, we found that a dollop of softly whipped cream enhanced the flavor and texture of the soup.

Since avocado is a fruit, many sources suggest using sweet garnishes and serving the soup as a first course or even dessert. We decided to try both sweet and savory garnishes. While unexpected, we all found the sweet versions to be brightly flavored and quite delicious. Savory additions worked well, too, making the soup more of a luncheon or first course than a dessert option. In all cases, the rich creaminess of the soup was texturally enhanced by the fresh garnishes.

Whether sweet or savory, chilled avocado soup is one of the most elegant dishes you can bring to the summer table. It's also one of the easiest to prepare.

PITTING AN AVOCADO

1. Start by slicing around the pit and through both ends with a chef's knife.

2. With your hands, twist to separate the avocado into two halves. Stick the blade of a chef's knife sharply into the pit. Lift the knife, twisting the blade if necessary to loosen, and remove the pit.

3. Don't pull the pit off the knife with your hands. Instead, use a large wooden spoon to pry the pit safely off the knife.

Chilled Avocado Soup

SERVES 8

We prefer Haas avocados (the dark-colored, bumpy-skinned variety), finding them superior in both flavor and texture. Be certain the avocados are ripe—they should give slightly when squeezed. (You might want to run the additional test on page 189.) See right for garnishing ideas, both sweet and savory. By adding or omitting the sugar to whipped cream, this soup can be taken in either a sweet or savory direction.

2	ripe avocados, halved and pitted (see illustrations on page 190)
1	cup ice cubes (about 10 cubes)
1	teaspoon salt
1	teaspoon sugar, plus 1½ teaspoons for whipping cream (optional)
½	cup heavy cream

1. Use a rubber spatula or soup spoon to scoop the avocado flesh into a blender; discard the avocado skins. Add ice cubes, 2 cups cold water, salt, and 1 teaspoon sugar to the blender and puree until smooth and liquefied, about 1 minute. (Soup can be refrigerated in an airtight container for up to 6 hours.)

2. Beat the cream in a large bowl with an electric mixer on low speed until small bubbles form, about 30 seconds. (If adding 1½ teaspoons sugar for sweet variation, do so at this stage.) Increase the speed to medium and continue beating until the beaters leave a trail in the cream, about 30 seconds more. Increase the speed to high and continue beating until the cream is smooth, thick, and nearly doubled in volume and forms very soft peaks, about 10 seconds.

3. Ladle the soup into bowls and garnish with a dollop of softly whipped cream. Serve immediately.

➤ VARIATION

Chilled Avocado-Lime Soup

Follow recipe for Chilled Avocado Soup, stirring 1 teaspoon grated lime zest into the pureed soup. Transfer it to a bowl, cover with plastic wrap, and refrigerate until the soup is infused with lime flavor, at least 2 and up to 6 hours. Pour the soup through a fine-mesh strainer just before serving.

GARNISHING AVOCADO SOUP

Whether serving avocado soup with sweet or savory garnishes, we think the soup tastes better with a dollop of softly whipped cream. In addition to the cream, we suggest serving the soup with a selection of garnishes on the side for individual diners to choose from; you can also sprinkle garnishes on top of the individual bowls just before they go to the table. Here are some suggestions, with preparation tips.

FOR SWEET AVOCADO SOUP

➤ **Brown sugar:** Finely crumbled.

➤ **Banana:** Peeled and cut crosswise into thin slices.

➤ **Watermelon:** Peeled, seeded, and cut into ¼-inch dice.

➤ **Mango:** Peeled, pitted, and cut into ¼-inch dice (see illustrations on page 238).

FOR SAVORY AVOCADO SOUP

➤ **Jícama:** Peeled and cut into ¼-inch dice.

➤ **Crabmeat:** Torn into small pieces.

➤ **Roasted fresh corn:** Heat a medium skillet over medium-high heat until hot, about 1 minute. Add kernels cut from 1 medium ear and stir constantly until browned, about 2 minutes. Remove corn from heat and cool slightly.

➤ **Sautéed scallops:** Remove tendons from 8 large sea scallops (see page 253) and season scallops with salt and pepper to taste. Heat a medium skillet over medium-high heat until hot, about 1 minute. Add ½ tablespoon butter and swirl to coat the pan bottom. Continue to heat pan until the butter begins to turn golden brown. Add the scallops, one at a time, flat-side down. Cook, adjusting the heat as necessary to prevent the butter from burning, until the scallops are well browned, 1½ to 2 minutes. Using tongs, turn the scallops, one at a time. Cook until medium-rare (sides firmed up and all but middle third of scallop opaque), 30 seconds to 1½ minutes longer, depending on size. Place one scallop in the center of each bowl of soup and serve immediately.

CHILLED FRUIT SOUP

FRUIT SOUP RECIPES ARE FAIRLY STRAIGHT-forward. The fruit is sweetened lightly, seasoned (with spices, lemon juice, or herbs), pureed, strained, and chilled. We identified four kinds of fruit soups—berry, cherry, stone fruit (plums, peaches, and apricots), and melon—and decided to develop a separate recipe for each.

The recipe for berry soup proved the most challenging to develop. We assembled five sample recipes, and tasters did not like a single one. These soups had problems with texture as well as flavor. Some were as thick as jam, others frothy, like smoothies, and still others were loaded with seeds. Some were too sweet and others barely tasted like fruit.

We made some initial decisions. Blackberries and raspberries were too expensive. We decided to stick with blueberries and strawberries. To eliminate the seeds from the strawberries, we poured the soup through a fine-mesh strainer or chinois (see chapter 1). Our task now was to unlock the flavor of the berries.

We tried several ways to release flavor from fresh berries, all with little success. Roasting dulled the flavors in the fruit, and poaching in sugar syrup caused the berries to release their pectin and created a soup with a gelatinous texture. Mashing fresh berries with some sugar (to help release their juices) was better but still not perfect. The texture was fine (not jammy or gelatinous), but the flavor was uneven. Unless the fruit was dead-on ripe, this technique resulted in soup with modest fruit flavor.

At this point, we started looking for other ideas. Someone in the kitchen suggested using individually quick-frozen fruit in place of fresh. We placed the unthawed fruit in a blender, added some sugar and lemon juice, and pureed the mixture until smooth. Once strained, the texture was too thick, but the flavors were intensely fruity. Hard to believe, but frozen fruit made better soup than fresh did.

This soup needed some liquid to achieve the right consistency. We tried dairy (cream and yogurt), but it just muddied the color and berry flavors. Sweet white wine was too harsh, grape juice was too sweet, and orange juice injected an unwelcome citrus flavor. Grape juice was the least offensive, and we wondered if pureed red grapes might work. Sure

enough, the grapes added enough liquid to thin the soup slightly without overpowering the berry flavor.

With our berry soup recipe developed, we moved onto cherry soup, which turned out to be much easier to perfect. We started with our favorite cobbler filling (jarred sour cherries cooked with a little red wine, sugar, and cornstarch) and simply pureed it. Once strained, this mixture proved to be extremely flavorful, smooth, and bright red. The cobbler filling has to be thickened with quite a lot of cornstarch, but we cut this amount back to just a tablespoon when making soup. (Without cornstarch, the soup was too loose, so we didn't eliminate this ingredient completely.) The soup was sweeter than it needed to be, so we trimmed the sugar back, too. A little cinnamon and almond extract highlighted the cherry flavor.

Stone fruits—plums, peaches, and nectarines—can make good fruit soups, but as with berry soups, we had to figure out how to release their flavor. We began work on this subject by testing several recipes. We concluded that simpler was better. Soups thickened with yogurt or cream had only a faint fruit flavor. Soups made by poaching fruit in wine were intriguing, but the emphasis was not on the fruit.

We started with the basics—fruit and sugar—to see how they could best be combined. Because stone fruits are quite firm, they must be cooked in some fashion before being pureed. (To make sure of this, we pureed raw plums with lemon juice and sugar and found the resulting mixture to be nearly tasteless.) Roasted plums produced a dull, lifeless soup. Poached fruit was better but not great. We increased the sugar, hoping this would intensify the fruit flavor. Unfortunately, more sugar just made the soup sweet. We next looked at the liquid element in the recipe (water) to see if we could do better. Orange juice was too acidic and wine too harsh, but white grape juice held some promise. White grape juice added floral notes and sweetness that complemented and enhanced the fruit flavor. We found that 1 part grape juice to 2 parts water was ideal.

Melon was our last category to investigate. Melons are so juicy that they are rarely cooked to make soup. Rather, the peeled and seeded fruit is usually pureed with sweetener and a little liquid until smooth and then strained. We tested sweet white wine, white grape juice, and plain water as the liquid element in this equation. The wine imparted bitterness and harshness, and the grape juice made the soup cloyingly sweet. The water was fine. But if we were going to use water, why not add ice and thereby make it unnecessary to chill the soup? Sure enough, 10 ice cubes did the trick—the soup had the perfect texture and was well chilled.

We had a few final tests. As expected, a hint of acidity (in the form of lemon juice) brought the melon flavor into focus. As for sweetener, several sources suggested honey instead of sugar. Our tasters preferred the floral notes added by the honey. As for more aggressive flavors, such as mint or ginger, we found they were best added with a light hand. Steeping bruised mint leaves or grated ginger in the finished soup for two hours (but not more than six) gave the herb and spice notes we wanted without overwhelming the delicate melon flavor.

Chilled Berry Soup

SERVES 4 TO 6

Individually quick-frozen berries deliver peak flavor. If you have fresh berries that are perfectly ripe, make the recipe variation that follows. Soup made with frozen berries can be served immediately but will be fairly thick. For a thinner consistency, refrigerate the soup until the fruit defrosts a bit more. If desired, add a dollop of whipped cream or scoop of vanilla ice cream.

4	cups frozen blueberries or strawberries
4	cups red grapes, stemmed and rinsed
¼	cup sugar
2	tablespoons lemon juice

Place the frozen berries, grapes, sugar, and lemon juice in a blender and blend until smooth and liquefied, about 1 minute. Pour the soup through a fine-mesh strainer set over a large bowl. Serve immediately. (Soup can be refrigerated in an airtight container for up to 1 day. Stir well just before serving.)

➤ VARIATIONS

Chilled Fresh Berry Soup

This soup needs to chill several hours before being served.

4	cups fresh blueberries or strawberries
¼	cup sugar
2	tablespoons lemon juice
4	cups red grapes, stemmed and rinsed

1. Rinse and pat dry the berries. If using strawberries, remove stems and slice. Mash the berries, sugar, and lemon juice in a large bowl with a potato masher, fork, or wooden spoon until the berries give up their juice and the sugar has mostly dissolved, about 4 minutes. Cover and refrigerate for 1 hour.

2. Transfer the berry mixture to a blender, add the grapes, and blend until liquefied and smooth, about 1 minute. Pour the soup through a fine-mesh strainer over a large bowl. Cover and refrigerate until chilled, at least 4 hours and up to 24 hours. Stir the soup well just before serving.

Chilled Berry Soup with Fresh Ginger

Follow recipe for Chilled Berry Soup or Chilled Fresh Berry Soup until all ingredients have been blended, but do not strain. Transfer the soup to a bowl and stir in 1 tablespoon minced fresh ginger. Cover and refrigerate at least 2 hours but no longer than 6 hours. Strain the soup through a fine-mesh strainer, stir the soup well, and serve immediately.

Chilled Berry Soup with Lemon Zest

Follow recipe for Chilled Berry Soup or Chilled Fresh Berry Soup until all ingredients have been blended, but do not strain. Transfer the soup to a bowl and stir in 2 teaspoons minced lemon zest. Cover and refrigerate at least 2 hours but no longer than 6 hours. Strain the soup through a fine-mesh strainer, stir the soup well, and serve immediately.

Chilled Cherry Soup

SERVES 4

We recommend Morello cherries for their superior flavor and color, but Montmorency will do if Morello are unavailable. Sweet Bing cherries cannot be used in this recipe.

2	(24-ounce) jars Morello or Montmorency sour cherries, drained (about 8 cups cherries), with 2 cups juice reserved
½	cup dry red wine

1   tablespoon cornstarch

¼   cup sugar

1   cinnamon stick

⅛   teaspoon almond extract (optional)

½   cup lightly sweetened whipped cream, sour cream, or crème fraîche (optional)

1. Whisk the reserved cherry juice, wine, cornstarch, sugar, and cinnamon together in a medium saucepan. Bring the mixture to a boil over medium-high heat. Reduce the heat to medium-low and simmer until slightly reduced and thickened, about 5 minutes. Remove the pan from the heat, stir in the almond extract, if using, and discard the cinnamon.

2. Working in batches, puree the drained cherries and juice mixture in a blender until smooth and liquefied, about 1 minute. Pour the soup through a fine-mesh strainer set over a large bowl, pressing on the solids with a rubber spatula to extract all the juices. Cool to room temperature, cover, and refrigerate the soup until chilled, at least 4 hours and up to 1 day. Stir well, ladle the soup into individual bowls, and garnish with whipped cream, sour cream, or crème fraîche, if desired. Serve immediately.

Chilled Stone Fruit Soup

SERVES 4 TO 6

This recipe can be made with ripe plums, peaches, or nectarines. If you like, garnish with a small scoop of vanilla ice cream or a dollop of lightly sweetened whipped cream.

4   pounds ripe plums, peaches, or nectarines (about 8 medium), pits discarded and fruit quartered lengthwise

¼   cup sugar

½   cup white grape juice

1. Bring the fruit, sugar, and 1 cup of water to a boil in a medium saucepan over medium-high heat. Reduce the heat to medium-low, cover, and simmer until the fruit has softened and the skins have begun to peel, 10 to 15 minutes.

2. Transfer the fruit and the cooking liquid to a blender, add the grape juice, and blend until liquefied and no chunks remain, about 1 minute. Pour the soup through a fine-mesh strainer into a medium bowl, pressing on the solids with a rubber spatula to extract all juices. Cool to room temperature, cover tightly, and refrigerate until chilled, at least 4 hours and up to 1 day. Stir well just before serving.

Chilled Melon Soup

SERVES 4 TO 6

With ice in the mix, this soup can be served straight from the blender as long as the fruit has been refrigerated. This soup makes a refreshing first course or dessert.

1   medium cold cantaloupe or ½ large honeydew (about 2½ pounds) seeded, peeled, and cut into 2-inch chunks (about 6 cups)

2   teaspoons honey

1   teaspoon lemon juice

1   cup ice cubes (about 10 cubes)

Place the melon, honey, lemon juice, and ice cubes in a blender and blend until the mixture is liquefied and smooth, 1 to 2 minutes. Pour the soup through a fine-mesh strainer. (The soup can be refrigerated for up to 1 day. Stir well before serving.) Ladle into individual bowls and serve immediately.

VARIATIONS

Chilled Melon Soup with Fresh Mint
Place 4 large sprigs of fresh mint in a plastic zipper-lock bag. With a rolling pin or rubber mallet, pound the mint until it is bruised and aromatic. Follow recipe for Chilled Melon Soup, pouring the pureed and strained soup in a large bowl or container. Submerge the bruised mint sprigs in the soup, cover, and refrigerate until the soup is infused with mint flavor, at least 2 hours but no longer than 6 hours. Discard the mint sprigs, stir the soup well, and serve.

Chilled Melon Soup with Fresh Ginger
Follow recipe for Chilled Melon Soup, but do not strain the soup. Transfer the soup to a bowl and stir in 1 teaspoon minced fresh ginger. Cover and refrigerate until the soup is infused with ginger flavor, at least 2 hours but no longer than 6 hours. Pour the soup through a fine-mesh strainer and serve.

PART 3

STEWS

9
MEAT STEWS

THIS CHAPTER COVERS STEWS MADE WITH beef, lamb, pork, and veal. Although each kind of meat and each stew has its own requirements, there are a few general points to keep in mind.

First and foremost, start with the right cut of meat. In our testing, we found that meat from the shoulder area of the animal usually has the best combination of flavor and texture. This meat is well marbled with fat, so it won't dry out during the stewing process. Other cuts are simply too lean to use in stews. They will become tough if cooked this way.

So why does shoulder meat generally make the best stews? Its intramuscular fat and connective tissue make it amenable to long, slow, moist cooking. When cooked in liquid, the connective tissue melts down into gelatin, making the meat tender. The fat in the meat helps as well, in two important ways. Fat carries the chemical compounds that our taste buds perceive as beef, lamb, pork, or veal flavor, and it also melts when cooked, lubricating the meat fibers as it slips between the cells, increasing tenderness.

In our tests, we found that buying roasts or chops and cutting them up for stew ourselves had distinct advantages over buying precut meat. Packages labeled "stew meat" in supermarkets often contain misshapen or small bits of meat. In addition, these packages may have scraps from various parts of the animal. To make sure that you have purchased the proper cut of meat and that it is divided into evenly sized chunks, take the five extra minutes to cut the meat yourself.

Browning the meat well is another key point to keep in mind. Meat stews generally begin by seasoning the chunks of meat with salt and pepper and then sautéing them in a film of oil. Don't rush this step. In our tests, meat that was only spottily browned didn't taste as good. Browning the meat and some of the vegetables, especially onions, adds flavor to the final dish.

How does browning work? In vegetables it is largely sugars and in meat sugars and proteins that caramelize, or brown, making the meat and vegetables taste better. In addition to flavoring the meat, proper browning covers the bottom of the pan with browned bits called *fond*. When liquid is added to the pot, the fond loosens and dissolves, adding flavor to the stew. This process is called *deglazing*. Wine and stock are the most common choices for deglazing the pan, but water works, too. Because the foundation of a stew's flavor comes from the fond and deglazing liquid, it is crucial that the meat be browned properly. In most recipes, to ensure proper browning, we sauté the meat in two batches. If all of the meat is put into the pot at once, the pieces crowd one another and steam, thus turning a pallid gray color rather than brown.

Contrary to popular belief, browning does not "seal in" the juices in meat. After browning, when the meat is slow-cooked, more and more juices are expelled as the internal temperature of the meat rises. By the time the meat is fork-tender, it has in fact shed most of its juices. As odd as it sounds, this is the beauty of a stew, since the surrounding liquid, which is served as a sauce, is enriched by these juices.

In our tests, we found the temperature of the stewing liquid to be crucial. We found it essential to keep the temperature of the liquid below 212 degrees. Boiled meat remains tough, and the outside becomes especially dry. Keeping the liquid at a simmer (rather than a boil) allows the internal temperature of the meat to rise slowly. By the time it is actually fork-tender, much of the connective tissue will have turned to gelatin. The gelatin, in turn, helps to thicken the stewing liquid.

To determine whether stews cook best on the stovetop or in the oven, we tried both, simmering a basic beef stew on the stovetop over low heat (with and without a flame-taming device to protect the pot from direct heat) and in a moderate oven. The flame-tamer device worked too well in distancing the pot from the heat; the stew juices tasted raw and boozy. Putting the pot right on the burner worked better, but we found ourselves constantly adjusting the burner to maintain a gentle simmer, and this method is prone to error. We had the most consistent results in the oven. We found that putting a covered Dutch oven in a 300-degree oven ensures that the temperature of the stewing liquid will remain below the boiling point, at about 200 degrees. (The oven must be kept at a temperature higher than 200 degrees because ovens are not completely efficient in transferring heat; a temperature of 300 degrees recognizes that some heat will be lost as it penetrates through the pot and into the stew.)

The beef, lamb, and one of the pork recipes in this chapter are conventional stews—large chunks of boneless meat accompanied by vegetables in a thickened sauce. The chapter concludes with three dishes that don't fit this definition.

For pozole (Mexico's most famous pork stew), a picnic roast is simmered, cooled, and then shredded. The veal stew in this chapter, osso buco, an Italian dish, uses shank meat rather than shoulder meat. Most cuts of veal, including the shoulder, are so mild-tasting that they become overwhelmed by the other flavors in a stew. Shanks are the exception to this rule. The meat is especially tasty, and the presence of the bone adds depth and complexity to the stewing liquid. The chapter concludes with cassoulet, a classic French dish that combines stewed meat, beans, sausage, and toasted bread crumbs. We've radically simplified this recipe, making it possible to prepare this grand dish at home.

A final note about our choice of liquids for use in meat stews. Few home cooks have meat stock on hand. They might make beef stock for beef soup because there's no other alternative, but they generally make only what they need for a particular recipe. In stews, with their many components, the liquid element is usually not as central as it is in soup. Beef stock is too much work for such recipes. We find that low-sodium canned chicken broth (which tastes better than canned beef broth; see page 27) is a fine option. If you have homemade chicken stock on hand, you can use some in these recipes. However, we have found that the differences between meat stews made with homemade chicken stock and those made with canned chicken broth are minimal.

HEARTY BEEF STEW

BEEF STEW SHOULD BE RICH AND SATISFYING. Our goal in developing a recipe for it was to keep the cooking process simple without compromising the stew's deep, complex flavor. We focused on these issues: What cuts of beef respond best to stewing? How much and what kind of liquid should you use? When and with what do you thicken the stew?

Experts tout different cuts as being ideal for stewing. We browned 12 different cuts of beef, marked them for identification, and stewed them in the same pot. (For more information on various beef cuts, see illustration on page 200.) Chuck proved to be the most flavorful, tender, and juicy. Most other cuts were too stringy, too chewy, too dry, or just plain bland. The exception was rib-eye steak, which made good stew meat but is too expensive a cut for this purpose.

Our advice is to buy a steak or roast from the chuck and cube it yourself. Precut stewing beef often includes irregularly shaped end pieces from different muscles that cannot be sold as steaks or roasts because of their uneven appearance. Because of the differences in origin, precut stewing cubes in the same package may not be consistent in the way they cook or taste. If you cut your own cubes from a piece of chuck, you are assured that all the cubes will cook in the same way and have the flavor and richness of chuck.

The names given to different cuts of chuck vary, but the most commonly used names for retail chuck cuts include boneless chuck-eye roasts, cross-rib roasts, blade steaks and roasts, shoulder steaks and roasts, and arm steaks and roasts. We particularly like chuck-eye roast, but all chuck cuts are delicious when cubed and stewed.

Having settled on our cut of beef, we started to explore how and when to thicken the stew. Dredging meat cubes in flour is a roundabout way of thickening stew. The floured beef is browned, then stewed. During the stewing process, some of the flour from the beef dissolves into the liquid, causing it to thicken. Although the stew we cooked this way thickened up nicely, the beef cubes had a "smothered steak" look.

We also tried two thickening methods at the end of cooking—a beurre manié (softened butter mixed with flour) and cornstarch mixed with water. Both methods are acceptable, but the beurre manié lightened the stew liquid's color, making it look more like pale gravy than rich stew juices. Also, the extra fat did not improve the stew's flavor enough to justify its addition. For those who prefer thickening at the end of cooking, we found that cornstarch dissolved in water did the job without compromising the stew's dark, rich color.

Pureeing the cooked vegetables is another thickening method. Once the stew is fully cooked, the meat is pulled from the pot and the juices and vegetables are pureed to create a thick sauce. Tasters felt this thickening method made the vegetable flavor too prominent.

Ultimately, though, we opted for thickening the stew with flour at the beginning—stirring it into the sautéing onions and garlic, right before adding the liquid. Stew thickened this way did not taste any better than that thickened at the end with cornstarch, but it was easier. There was no last-minute work; once the liquid started to simmer, the cook was free to do something else.

We next focused on stewing liquids. We tried water, wine, canned beef broth, canned chicken broth, combinations of these liquids, and beef stock. Stews made with water were bland and greasy. Stews made entirely with wine were too strong. The stew made from beef stock was delicious, but we decided that beef stew, which has many hearty ingredients contributing to its flavor profile, did not absolutely need beef stock, which is quite time-consuming to make. When we turned to canned broths, the chicken outscored the beef broth. (For more information about the problems with canned beef broth, see page 30.) The stew made entirely with chicken stock was good, but we missed the acidity and flavor provided by the wine. In the end, we preferred a combination of chicken stock and red wine.

We tested various amounts of liquid and found that we preferred stews with a minimum of liquid, which helps to preserve a strong meat flavor. With too little liquid, however, the stew may not cook evenly, and there may not be enough "sauce" to spoon over starchy accompaniments. A cup of liquid per pound of meat gave us sufficient sauce to moisten a mound of mashed potatoes or polenta without drowning them. We tested various kinds of wine and found that fairly inexpensive fruity, full-bodied young wines, such as Chianti or zinfandel were best. (See page 202 for more information on wine.)

To determine when to add the vegetables, we made three different stews, adding carrots, potatoes, and onions to one stew at the beginning of cooking and to another stew halfway through the cooking process. For our final stew, we cooked the onions with the meat but added steamed carrots and potatoes when the stew was fully cooked.

The stew with vegetables added at the beginning was thin and watery. The vegetables had fallen apart and given up their flavor and liquid to the stew. The beef stew with the cooked vegetables added at the last minute was delicious, and the vegetables were the freshest and most intensely flavored. However, it was more work to steam the vegetables separately. Also, vegetables cooked separately from the stew didn't really meld all that well with the other flavors and ingredients. We preferred to add the vegetables partway through the cooking process. They didn't fall apart this way, and they had enough time to meld with the other ingredients. There is one exception to this rule. Peas were added just before serving the stew to preserve their color and texture.

One final note: The meat passes from the tough to tender stage fairly quickly. Often at the 1¾-hour mark, we found that the meat would still be chewy. Fifteen minutes later it would be tender. Let the stew go another 15 minutes and the meat starts to dry out. Taste the meat often as the stew nears completion to judge when it's just right.

POSSIBLE CUTS FOR BEEF STEW

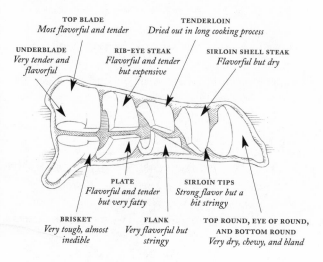

We stewed 12 different cuts of beef from every part of the cow. Chuck, which consists of the underblade and top blade, was the most flavorful and cooked up quite tender.

Hearty Beef Stew

SERVES 6 TO 8

Make this stew in an ovenproof Dutch oven, preferably with a capacity of 8 quarts but nothing less than 6 quarts. Choose one with a wide bottom; this will allow you to brown the meat in just two batches. See page 202 for information about choosing a red wine for use in this dish.

3	pounds beef chuck roast, trimmed and cut into 1½-inch cubes (see illustrations below)
	Salt and ground black pepper
3	tablespoons vegetable oil
2	medium onions, chopped coarse (about 2 cups)
3	medium cloves garlic, minced
3	tablespoons flour
1	cup full-bodied red wine
2	cups homemade chicken stock or canned low-sodium chicken broth
2	bay leaves
1	teaspoon dried thyme
4	medium red potatoes (about 1½ pounds), peeled and cut into 1-inch cubes
4	large carrots (about 1 pound), peeled and sliced ¼ inch thick
1	cup frozen peas (about 6 ounces), thawed
¼	cup minced fresh parsley leaves

1. Adjust the oven rack to lower-middle position and heat the oven to 300 degrees. Dry the beef thoroughly on paper towels, then season it generously with salt and pepper. Heat 1 tablespoon oil in a large ovenproof Dutch oven over medium-high heat until shimmering, about 2 minutes. Add half of the meat to the pot so that the individual pieces are close together but not touching. Cook, not moving the pieces until the sides touching the pot are well-browned, 2 to 3 minutes. Using tongs, turn each piece and continue cooking until most sides are well-browned, about 5 minutes longer. Transfer the beef to a medium bowl, add another 1 tablespoon oil to the pot, and swirl to coat the pan bottom. Brown the remaining beef; transfer the meat to the bowl and set aside.

2. Reduce the heat to medium, add the remaining tablespoon oil to the empty Dutch oven, and swirl to coat the pan bottom. Add the onions and ¼ teaspoon salt. Cook, stirring frequently and vigorously, scraping the bottom of the pot with a wooden spoon to loosen browned bits, until the onions have softened, 4 to 5 minutes. Add the garlic and continue to cook for 30 seconds. Stir in the flour and cook until lightly colored, 1 to 2 minutes. Add the wine, scraping up the remaining browned bits from the bottom and edges of the pot and stirring until the liquid is thick. Gradually add the stock, stirring constantly and scraping the pan edges to dissolve the flour. Add the bay leaves and thyme and bring to a simmer. Add the meat and return to a simmer. Cover

CUTTING STEW MEAT

To get stew meat pieces that are cut from the right part of the animal and regularly shaped, we suggest buying a boneless roast and cutting the meat yourself. A 3-pound roast, once trimmed, should yield 2¾ pounds of beef, the maximum amount that can be comfortably browned in a Dutch oven in two batches.

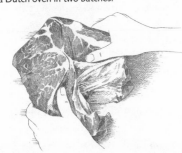  

1. Pull apart the roast at its major seams (delineated by lines of fat and silver skin). Use a knife as necessary.

2. With a paring knife, trim off excess fat and silver skin.

3. Cut the meat into cubes or chunks as directed in specific recipes.

and place the pot in the oven. Cook for 1 hour.

3. Remove the pot from the oven and add the potatoes and carrots. Cover and return the pot to the oven. Cook just until the meat is tender, about 1 hour. Remove the pot from the oven. (Stew can be covered and refrigerated up to 3 days. Bring to a simmer over medium-low heat.)

4. Add the peas, cover, and allow to stand for 5 minutes. Stir in the parsley, discard the bay leaves, adjust the seasonings, and serve immediately.

INGREDIENTS: Red Wine for Stew

When making a dish that uses red wine, our tendency is to grab whichever inexpensive, dry red is on hand, usually the leftover contents of a recently opened bottle. But we began to wonder what difference particular wines would make in the final dish and decided to investigate.

We called on the advice of several local wine experts, who gave us some parameters to work with when selecting red wines to use in a braise such as hearty beef stew or cacciatore. (The rules are slightly different when making some dishes, such as beef burgundy, that traditionally rely on a particular kind of wine. See page 210 for more details on choosing a red wine for this dish.)

When choosing a red wine for a basic stew, look for one that is dry (to avoid a sweet sauce) and with good acidity (to aid in breaking down the fibers of the meat). Keep in mind that any characteristic found in the uncooked wine will be concentrated when cooked.

From tests we ran, we found that softer, fruity wines such as Merlot yielded a "grape jelly" flavor, which most tasters thought was too sweet for beef stew or cacciatore. We also learned that it's best to avoid wines that have been "oaked," usually older wines; the oak flavor tends to become harsh and bitter as the wine is cooked.

BEEF GOULASH

THIS SIMPLE EASTERN EUROPEAN STEW HAS been around for centuries. The word *goulash* comes from the Hungarian *gulyas,* which means "herd of cattle." Originally, cattlemen seared and stewed beef until the liquid evaporated and then dried the meat in the sun. When needed, the meat was rehydrated with water and, depending on how much liquid was added, goulash, stew or soup was created. Goulash

stew—without the drying step—is the more popular version in the United States.

There are several versions of modern goulash stew. Beef, onions, garlic, and paprika are constants. Other possible ingredients include potatoes, tomatoes, and bell peppers. Our goal was to create a very simple stew with tender, flavorful beef and browned onions in an intensely flavored, rich sauce. The sauce would be thick and brownish red in color, both from the paprika and the good browning that the meat and onions would receive.

As with our Hearty Beef Stew, we found that chuck meat was the best choice because it cooks up tender and flavorful. Traditional recipes brown the beef in lard, and we found that the gentle pork flavor of good lard does add something to this dish. Given the fact that most cooks don't have lard on hand, we tried bacon fat as substitute. Tasters reacted negatively to goulash made with bacon fat. They said the smoky flavor imparted by the bacon was at odds with this stew. Vegetable oil turned out to be a better choice. Although not as flavorful as lard, oil will suffice.

On a related subject, we found that leaving a little fat attached to the pieces of meat boosts flavor and helps compensate for the missing pork flavor if lard is not used. You will need to defat the stew before serving, but this is easily done with a spoon.

In these early tests, we found that browning the meat well is essential to flavor development in goulash. The hearty, rich flavor and color of goulash is dependent on browning of the meat and onions and then deglazing the crusty, deep brown bits stuck to the bottom of the Dutch oven.

We found that adding a little salt with the onions caused them to release moisture and kept them from scorching. This moisture also helped to loosen the browned bits, a process that is completed once the liquid is added to the pan. Although onions are a must, the recipes we looked at were divided on the question of garlic. Tasters, however, were not. Everyone in the test kitchen liked garlic in this stew. Six cloves added depth and also balanced the sweetness of the paprika and onions.

Once the garlic was fragrant, it was time for the paprika to go into the pot. Sweet Hungarian paprika (see page 236 for more details) is essential in this recipe. We added the flour (to thicken the stew) at the same time.

Recipes uncovered in our research used an assortment of liquids, including water, beef stock, and chicken stock. We found that water created a bland stew. Homemade beef stock was delicious in this dish but required a large investment of time. We wondered if we could substitute canned broth without compromising the flavor too much. Canned beef broth tasted tinny and did not work in goulash. We had better results with canned chicken broth and, in fact, with homemade chicken stock. Both gave the stew good body, and the chicken flavor faded behind the beef and spices.

Some recipes also include wine in the mix, although authentic recipes do not. We tried varying amounts of red wine, and tasters felt that its flavor was too overpowering. Goulash should be soft and mellow; while red wine added complexity, it also made the stew acidic and a bit harsh. A few sources suggested white wine, but tasters were again unimpressed.

Our recipe was coming together—browned beef and onions, garlic and paprika for flavor, and chicken stock or canned broth as the liquid. We had two major issues to resolve—tomatoes and vegetables. We started with the tomatoes.

Many goulash recipes contain tomato, although the original dish (which dates back several centuries before the arrival of tomatoes from the New World) certainly did not. We decided to make four batches of goulash—one with canned diced tomatoes, one with plain tomato sauce, one with tomato paste, and one with no tomato product. The diced tomatoes and tomato sauce proved to be too dominant and made the stew reminiscent of beef cacciatore. Tomato paste, however, blended into the background and enhanced other flavors in the dish. Compared with the stew made without any tomatoes, the version with tomato paste was more complex and appealing. In fact, the tomatoes functioned a bit like wine in terms of adding depth, but they were also much more subtle than wine and thus more in tune with the spirit of goulash.

Vegetables were easy to incorporate into the dish. Tasters liked large chunks of red and green bell peppers, especially when added to the stew near the end of the cooking time. When added earlier (just after the onions are browned is a common choice), the peppers become mushy and fell apart. We found that if they are added to the stew while it is in the oven, the peppers soften without turning mushy.

We tested carrots, cabbage, celery, and green beans (ingredients used in some of the recipes we had collected) but did not like any of them in goulash. Potatoes were a different story. Several recipes added them to the stew pot with the liquid so they would fall apart and thicken the stew. Although we did not like this approach, we did like potatoes simmered in the stew until tender. Adding the potatoes partway through the oven cooking time yielded this result, so we decided to make the potatoes a variation.

Many Hungarian goulash recipes do not include sour cream, which seems more popular in German and Austrian versions. But our tasters all felt that the sour cream mellowed and enriched this stew. To prevent the sour cream from curdling, we combined the sour cream with a little hot stewing liquid to temper it and then stirred the mixture back into the stew pot.

Goulash is traditionally served over buttered egg noodles or spätzle. Egg noodles require almost no effort to cook and were our first choice. Mashed potatoes are not traditional, but they made an excellent accompaniment, too.

Beef Goulash

SERVES 6 TO 8

Goulash is like the Merlot of beef stews—mellow, with sweet overtones. If your tastes run more toward Zinfandel, add a pinch of hot paprika or cayenne pepper for a more complex, spicy version. The flavor from the beef fat adds something to this stew, so don't trim the meat too closely. We recommend removing external fat from the chuck roast but leaving internal fat alone unless it is excessively thick. Serve the stew over 1 pound of buttered egg noodles. Try tossing the noodles with 1 tablespoon of toasted caraway seeds for a distinctive and delicious flavor combination (caraway is an unusual and authentic touch).

I   (3 pound) beef chuck roast, trimmed and cut into 1½-inch cubes (see illustrations on page 201) Salt and ground black pepper

3 tablespoons vegetable oil or lard

3 medium-large onions, chopped coarse (about 5 cups)

6 medium cloves garlic, minced

5 tablespoons sweet paprika

¼ cup flour

3 cups homemade chicken stock or canned low-sodium chicken broth

2 tablespoons tomato paste

2 bay leaves

I teaspoon dried marjoram

I large red bell pepper, stemmed, seeded, and chopped coarse

I large green bell pepper, stemmed, seeded, and chopped coarse

½ cup sour cream

¼ cup minced fresh parsley leaves

1. Adjust the oven rack to the lower-middle position and heat the oven to 300 degrees. Dry the beef thoroughly on paper towels, then season it generously with salt and pepper. Heat 1 tablespoon oil in a large ovenproof Dutch oven over medium-high heat until shimmering, about 2 minutes. Add half of the meat to the pot so that the individual pieces are close together but not touching. Cook, not moving the pieces until the sides touching the pot are well-browned, 2 to 3 minutes. Using tongs, turn each piece and continue cooking until most sides are well-browned, about 5 minutes longer. Transfer the beef to a medium bowl, add another 1 tablespoon oil to the pot, and swirl to coat the pan bottom. Brown the remaining beef; transfer the meat to the bowl and set aside.

2. Reduce the heat to medium, add the remaining tablespoon oil to the empty Dutch oven, and swirl to coat the pan bottom. Add the onions and ¼ teaspoon salt. Cook, stirring frequently and vigorously, scraping the bottom of the pot with a wooden spoon to loosen browned bits, until the onions have softened and browned, about 8 minutes. Stir in the garlic and cook until fragrant, about 30 seconds. Add the paprika and flour and stir until the onions are evenly coated and fragrant, 1 to 2 minutes.

3. Stir in 1½ cups stock, scraping the pan bottom with a wooden spoon to loosen the remaining browned bits and stirring until the flour is incorporated and the liquid thickened. Gradually add the remaining stock, stirring constantly and scraping the pan edges to dissolve the flour. Stir in the tomato paste, bay leaves, marjoram, and ¾ teaspoon salt. Add the browned beef and accumulated juices, stir to blend and submerge the meat under the liquid. Increase the heat to medium, bring to a simmer, cover the pot, and place it in the oven. Cook for 1 hour and 20 minutes.

4. Remove pot from oven and stir in red and green peppers. Cover and return the pot to the oven. Cook until the meat is just tender, about 40 minutes. Remove the pot from the oven. If serving immediately, spoon off the fat that rises to the top. (Stew can be covered and refrigerated for up to 3 days. Spoon off the congealed fat and bring stew back to a simmer over medium-low heat.)

5. Place the sour cream in a medium bowl and stir in about ½ cup of the hot stewing liquid. Stir the sour cream mixture back into the stew. Stir in the parsley and season to taste with salt and pepper. Serve immediately.

➤ VARIATION

Beef Goulash with Potatoes and Caraway

With potatoes added, there's no need to serve this stew over noodles. Caraway is a traditional addition to Hungarian goulash.

Follow the recipe for Beef Goulash, reducing the amount of beef to 2½ pounds, adding 1 teaspoon caraway seeds with paprika and flour, and adding ¾ pound red potatoes, peeled and cut into 1-inch dice, after the stew has cooked in the oven for 1 hour. Proceed as directed.

CARBONNADE À LA FLAMMANDE

A BASIC BEEF STEW CAN BE ALTERED IN dozens of ways, usually by adding more ingredients to the pot. But you can also go the other way and strip beef stew down to its bare bones (to its beef). If you also trade in the carrots and potatoes for a plethora of onions and add a good dose of beer, you've created a Belgian beef stew called *carbonnade à la flammande*.

Beef, beer, and onions have an affinity—they're an ensemble with great appeal (think burger, onion rings, and a beer). In a carbonnade, the heartiness of beef melds with the soft sweetness of sliced onions in a broth that is deep and rich with the malty flavor of dark beer.

We made several versions of carbonnade and found that despite the simple and few ingredients, making a poor one is quite easy. We wound up with several batches of tough, tasteless beef and onions in a pale, insipid broth. Not quite what we had in mind.

We used the framework of our recipe for hearty beef stew to arrive at an improved carbonnade. The operations were as follows: The beef is browned in batches and set aside, the onions are sautéed in the empty pot, the flour is sprinkled over the onions, the liquid is added, the beef is returned to the pot, and the covered pot goes into the oven where it simmers until the beef is fork-tender.

In developing a recipe for carbonnade, the first departure from our beef stew recipe came with the selection of beef. For a basic beef stew, we prefer a chuck roast cut into 1½-inch chunks. A chuck roast is composed of a number of different muscles interwoven with intramuscular fat and connective tissue. This fat and tissue make for good texture and flavor, and the different muscles make for pieces of meat with uneven or differing textures, even when cooked.

The substance of carbonnade is purely beef and onion—there are no chunks of potatoes or carrots with which the beef competes. Consequently, we wanted smaller pieces of beef of a uniform texture that would be a better match for the soft, thinly sliced onions. Enter 1-inch-thick blade steaks (also called top blade or flatiron steaks)—small, long, narrow steaks cut from the shoulder (or chuck) area of the animal. Most blade steaks have a decent amount of fat marbling, which gives them good flavor as well as a tender texture. One taster described the blade steak in carbonnade as "buttery," a quality that is well-suited to this stew. The trade-off is that these smaller steaks are a bit more time-consuming to trim of silver skin and gristle, but they are well worth it.

Onions—and a good deal of them—go into a carbonnade. Two pounds was the right amount in relation to the amount of beef. We tried both white and red onions, but both were cloyingly sweet. Yellow onions tasted the best. After browning the beef, the floor of the pot was crusty with fond (browned bits). Do not underestimate the importance of the fond—it furnishes the stew with color and flavor. As we had done with goulash, we added ¼ teaspoon salt along with the thinly sliced onions to help release their moisture. This helps to keep the fond from burning and to loosen it from the pot when deglazing. Garlic is not an ingredient in all carbonnade recipes, but we liked its heady essence; a small amount is added to the onions only after the onions are cooked so that it does not burn.

The right beer is key to achieving a full, robust carbonnade. Beers of the light, lager persuasion, those commonly favored in America, lack guts—they result in light-colored, watery-tasting stews. We tried a number of different beers and found that reasonably dark ales, very dark ales, and stouts made the richest and best-tasting carbonnades. A few of our favorites were Chimay (a Trappist ale from Belgium), Newcastle Brown Ale, Anchor Steam (this beer cannot technically be classified as an ale), Samuel Smith Taddy Porter, and Guinness Extra Stout.

We tried making carbonnades with beer as the only liquid, but they lacked backbone and sometimes had an overwhelming bitterness, depending on the type of beer used. Equal parts chicken stock or canned broth and beer made a deeper, more solid-tasting stew. The addition of dried thyme and a bay leaf added herbal notes that complemented the other flavors. Just a bit of cider vinegar perked things up, and a bit of dark brown sugar rounded out the flavors.

Carbonnade à la Flammande

SERVES 6 TO 8

To make sure the beef browns well, dry the pieces thoroughly on paper towels. Don't bother making this stew with a light-colored beer—both the color and flavor will be insipid. We particularly liked Newcastle Ale, Anchor Steam Beer, and Chimay. For those who like a heavier beer, with a slightly bitter flavor, porter and stout are good.

3 to 3½	pounds top blade steaks, gristle removed and cut into 1-inch pieces (see illustrations below)
	Salt and ground black pepper
3	tablespoons vegetable oil
2	pounds medium onions, halved and sliced thin
2	medium cloves garlic, minced
3	tablespoons all-purpose flour
1½	cups homemade chicken stock or canned low-sodium chicken broth
1½	cups dark beer
¾	teaspoon dried thyme
1	bay leaf
1	tablespoon dark brown sugar
1	tablespoon cider vinegar

1. Adjust the oven rack to the lower-middle position and heat the oven to 300 degrees. Dry the beef thoroughly on paper towels, then season it generously with salt and pepper. Heat 1 tablespoon oil in a large ovenproof Dutch oven over medium-high heat until shimmering, about 2 minutes. Add half of the meat to the pot so that the individual pieces are close together but not touching. Cook, not moving the pieces until the sides touching the pot are well-browned, 2 to 3 minutes. Using tongs, turn each piece and continue cooking until most sides are well-browned, about 5 minutes longer. Transfer the beef to a medium bowl, add another 1 tablespoon oil to the pot, and swirl to coat the pan bottom. Brown the remaining beef; transfer the meat to the bowl and set aside.

2. Reduce the heat to medium-low, add the remaining tablespoon oil to the empty Dutch oven, and swirl to coat the pan bottom. Add the onions and ¼ teaspoon salt and cook, stirring occasionally and vigorously, scraping the bottom of the pot with a wooden spoon to loosen the browned bits, until the onions have released some moisture, about 5 minutes. Increase the heat to medium and cook, stirring occasionally and scraping the bottom of the pot, until the onions are limp, softened, and lightly browned, 12 to 14 minutes. Stir in the garlic and cook until fragrant, about 30 seconds. Add the flour and stir until the onions are evenly coated.

3. Stir in the stock, scraping the pan bottom and edges with a wooden spoon to loosen the browned bits. Gradually add the beer, stirring constantly and scraping the pan edges to dissolve the flour. Add the thyme, bay leaf, brown sugar, and cider vinegar as well as the browned beef and accumulated juices, pushing down on the beef to submerge the pieces;

TRIMMING BLADE STEAKS

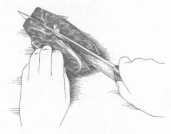

1. Each steak has a line of gristle running down the center that should be removed. To remove the gristle, halve each steak lengthwise, leaving the gristle on one half.

2. Cut away the gristle from the half to which it is still attached.

3. Cut the trimmed meat crosswise into 1-inch pieces.

sprinkle with salt and pepper, bring to a simmer, cover, and place in the oven. Cook until the beef is fork-tender, 1½ to 2 hours. Adjust the seasonings with salt and pepper to taste and serve. (Stew can be covered and refrigerated for several days. Bring back to a simmer over medium-low heat.)

BEEF BURGUNDY

IF THE LOUVRE WERE JUST A MUSEUM, then *boeuf à la bourguignonne* might be just beef stew. Both are French and utterly extraordinary, but only one can be enjoyed at home. We liken beef Burgundy more to a fabulous prime steak napped with a rich, silken red wine reduction sauce than to a mundane beef stew. The beef in beef Burgundy is cut into satisfyingly large chunks that become utterly tender. The braising liquid, brimming with voluptuous wine and infused with aromatic vegetables, garlic, and herbs, is finessed into a sauce of burgundy velvet studded with mushrooms and pearl onions. Beef Burgundy is earthy, big, robust, warm, and welcoming in a brooding sort of way.

At least that's what it is at its best. We have had versions that fell far short of this, with tough meat or a dull sauce with no flavor complexity. We wanted to find a way to bring this classic dish to its full potential in a home kitchen.

Recipes for beef Burgundy are very much alike. Aromatic vegetables (onions, garlic, and carrots), red wine, stock, herbs, mushrooms, and pearl onions are all requisite ingredients; their combinations and proportions and the variations in preparation and technique are where the recipes diverge.

We started by cooking up four recipes, and from these four we deduced a couple of things. First, marinating the beef in the red wine and herbs that will later go into the braise—a common recommendation in recipes—does not improve the flavor of the cooked meat. Second, the braising liquid requires straining to rid it of bits of aromatic vegetables and herbs so that it may become a silky sauce. We found that bundling in cheesecloth all the goods that must eventually come out of the pot made their extraction possible in one easy step. When wrapped in cheesecloth, however, the aromatic vegetables cannot first be sautéed—a customary step, the omission of which we feared would adversely affect the flavors of the braise. Remarkably, it did not. But perhaps this is why it took such generous amounts of chopped onions, carrots, and garlic as well as parsley, thyme, peppercorns, and bay leaves to create a balanced mélange of flavors.

The cut of beef best suited to the long braise of beef Burgundy is a chuck roast. It's the cut that almost every recipe calls for and the one we preferred in a regular beef stew because of its rich, meaty flavor. Because the beef in a beef Burgundy is cut into chunks larger than those in a beef stew—a good 1½ to 2 inches—we found it necessary to take extra care to trim off as much fat and silver skin as possible; larger pieces of beef also mean larger, more detectable bites of these undesirables.

Each and every beef Burgundy begins with either salt pork or bacon cut into lardons, or small strips, and fried to a crisp; the fat that results is used to brown the beef chunks. The crisped pork is added to the pot to simmer alongside the beef so that it can relinquish its flavors to the braise, providing a subtle, sweet underpinning and lending the sauce roundness and depth. We tried both bacon and salt pork and favored the cleaner, purer, more honest flavor of salt pork. Moreover, the thicker, more toothsome strips of salt pork had better texture than the lifeless, thin pieces of bacon. Although we prefer salt pork, it can be a challenge to find in grocery stores, so we decided to try thick-cut bacon. We reasoned that just as blanching salt pork removes excess salt that would otherwise crystallize on the surface during frying, blanching thick-cut bacon ought to calm its smoke and sugar. This worked well. The thick-cut bacon had more textural appeal than regular bacon and was a more acceptable substitute for salt pork.

As for the stock that goes into the braise, most recipes call for beef, preferably homemade. Because making beef stock is so time-consuming, we wanted to try canned broth. From past experience, we knew that canned beef broth does not make an acceptable substitute for homemade beef stock. Therefore, in all subsequent tests, we used what we have found to be the next best option—canned chicken broth—with excellent results. Still, beef Burgundy necessitates a good amount of liquid for braising, and too much chicken broth tasted too chickeny. Water was a fine filler, especially since the braising liquid is later reduced to create the sauce. We then tried something a bit unorthodox to boost flavor. Just a small amount of dried porcini mushrooms wrapped into the cheesecloth package delivered the meatiness and savory quality that homemade beef stock would conceivably have added. A modicum of tomato paste added color and sprightliness.

Wine was the next issue. Beef Burgundy does not exist without a healthy dose of it. We concluded after several batches that anything less than a whole bottle left the sauce lacking and unremarkable. After numerous experiments, we determined that a Burgundy, or at least a decent Pinot Noir, was indeed the wine of choice (see page 210 for more details). Though most recipes indicate that all of the wine should be added at the outset, one recipe, as well as one wine expert, recommended saving just a bit of the wine to add at the very end, just before serving. This late embellishment of raw wine vastly improved the sauce, brightening its flavor, giving it resonance. This sauce sang.

Midway through testing, we decided we needed an alternative to browning the meat in the Dutch oven, where it would eventually be braised. Browning in batches took too long, and the drippings, or fond, that are essential flavor providers frequently burned. Evidently, the small cooking surface of even a large Dutch oven was a liability. We took to browning the beef in two batches in a heavy, large 12-inch skillet. To keep the fond from going to waste, we deglazed the pan with a bit of water and poured it directly into the braising pot, where it would eventually marry with the broth and wine.

Next we went to work to find the best means of adding flour to thicken the braising liquid that must blossom into a velvety sauce. Tossing the beef in flour before browning interfered with the color the beef could attain and ultimately affected its flavor. We found it preferable to make a roux in the skillet and add broth and water to it, then have it join the beef, wine, and vegetable and herb bouquet in the braising pot. This afforded us the opportunity to cook the roux until it achieved a toasty brown color, which made a favorable impact on the flavor of the dish.

With everything assembled in the Dutch oven, into the oven it went, where the constant, all-encompassing heat produced an even simmer that required little attention. This was the time to prepare the mushrooms and pearl onions, both of which would later join the sauce. Peeling fresh pearl onions is a nuisance, but opening a bag isn't. We embraced already-peeled frozen pearl onions that, contrary to expectations, are not inferior in flavor or texture to fresh when browned, as they are when boiled. A brisk simmer in a skillet with some water, butter, and sugar, and then a quick sauté with the mushrooms created glazed beauties that were ready to grace the sauce. The final flourish was a swish of brandy that added richness and warmth to an already magnificent boeuf à la bourguignonne.

Beef Burgundy

SERVES 6

If you cannot find salt pork (see page 129 for more information), thick-cut bacon can be substituted. Cut it crosswise into ¼-inch pieces and treat it just as you would the salt pork, but note that you will have no rind to include in the vegetable and herb bouquet. To make this dish a day or two in advance, see Do-Ahead Beef Burgundy on page 210. Boiled potatoes are the traditional accompaniment, but mashed potatoes or buttered noodles are nice as well.

BEEF BRAISE

6	ounces salt pork, trimmed of rind (see illustration on page 128), rind reserved, and salt pork cut into ¼ inch by ¼ inch by 1-inch pieces
10	sprigs fresh parsley, torn into quarters
6	sprigs fresh thyme
2	medium onions, chopped coarse
2	medium carrots, chopped coarse
1	medium head garlic, cloves separated and crushed but unpeeled
2	bay leaves, crumbled
½	teaspoon black peppercorns
½	ounce dried porcini mushrooms, rinsed well (optional)
4 to 4¼	pounds beef chuck roast, trimmed and cut into 2-inch chunks (see illustrations on page 201)

Salt and ground black pepper

4 tablespoons unsalted butter, cut into 4 pieces

⅓ cup all-purpose flour

1¾ cups homemade chicken stock or canned low-sodium chicken broth

1 (750 ml) bottle wine, red Burgundy or Pinot Noir

1 teaspoon tomato paste

ONION AND MUSHROOM GARNISH

36 frozen pearl onions (about 7 ounces)

1 tablespoon unsalted butter

1 tablespoon sugar

½ teaspoon salt

10 ounces white mushrooms, whole if small, halved if medium, quartered if large

2 tablespoons brandy

3 tablespoons minced fresh parsley leaves

1. Bring the salt pork, reserved salt pork rind, and 3 cups water to a boil in a medium saucepan over high heat. Boil 2 minutes, then drain well.

2. Cut two 22-inch lengths of cheesecloth. Following illustrations below, wrap the parsley, thyme, onions, carrots, garlic, bay leaves, peppercorns, porcini mushrooms, and blanched salt pork rind in the cheesecloth and set in a large ovenproof Dutch oven. Adjust the oven rack to the lower-middle position and heat the oven to 300 degrees.

3. Set a 12-inch skillet with salt pork over medium heat; sauté until lightly brown and crisp, about 12 minutes. With a slotted spoon, transfer the salt pork to the Dutch oven. Pour off all but 2 teaspoons fat and reserve. Dry the beef thoroughly on paper towels, then season it generously with salt and pepper. Increase the heat to high and brown half of the beef in a single layer, turning once or twice, until deep brown, about 7 minutes; transfer the browned beef to the Dutch oven. Pour ½ cup water into the skillet and scrape the pan with a wooden spoon to loosen browned bits. When the pan bottom is clean, pour the liquid into the Dutch oven.

4. Dry the skillet and return it to high heat. Add 2 teaspoons reserved pork fat; swirl to coat the pan bottom. When the fat begins to smoke, brown the remaining beef in a single layer, turning once or twice, until deep brown, about 7 minutes; transfer the browned beef to the Dutch oven. Pour ½ cup water into the skillet and scrape the pan with a wooden spoon to loosen the browned bits. When the pan bottom is clean, pour the liquid into the Dutch oven.

5. Dry the now-empty skillet, set it over medium heat, and add the butter. When the foaming subsides, whisk in the flour until evenly moistened and pasty. Cook, whisking constantly, until mixture has a toasty aroma and resembles light-colored peanut butter, about 5 minutes. Gradually whisk in the chicken broth and 1½ cups water. Increase the heat to medium-high and bring to a simmer, stirring frequently, until thickened. Pour the mixture into the Dutch oven. Add 3 cups wine, tomato paste, and salt and pepper to taste to the Dutch oven and stir to combine. Set the Dutch oven over high heat and bring to a boil. Cover and place the pot in the oven.

MAKING A VEGETABLE AND HERB BOUQUET

1. Cut two 22-inch lengths of cheesecloth and unfold each piece once lengthwise so that each forms a two-ply, 22 by 8-inch piece.

2. Lay the cheesecloth in a medium bowl, stacking the sheets. Place the designated ingredients in the cheesecloth-lined bowl.

3. Gather the edges of the cheesecloth securely and fasten with kitchen twine. Trim excess cheesecloth with scissors if necessary.

Cook until the meat is tender, 2½ to 3 hours.

6. Remove the Dutch oven from the oven and, using tongs, transfer the vegetable and herb bouquet to a strainer set over the pot. Press the liquid back into the pot and discard the bouquet. With a slotted spoon, transfer the beef to a medium bowl; set aside. Allow the braising liquid to settle about 15 minutes, then, with a wide shallow spoon, skim fat off the surface and discard.

7. Bring the liquid in the Dutch oven to boil over medium-high heat. Simmer briskly, stirring occasionally to ensure that the bottom is not burning, until the sauce is reduced to about 3 cups and thickened to the consistency of heavy cream, 15 to 25 minutes.

8. While the sauce is reducing, bring the pearl onions, butter, sugar, ¼ teaspoon salt, and ½ cup water to a boil in a medium skillet over high heat. Cover, reduce the heat to medium-low, and simmer, shaking the pan occasionally, until the onions are tender, about 5 minutes. Uncover, increase the heat to high, and simmer until all liquid evaporates, about 3 minutes. Add the mushrooms and remaining ¼ teaspoon salt. Cook, stirring occasionally, until the liquid released by the mushrooms evaporates and the vegetables are browned and glazed, about 5

minutes. Transfer the vegetables to a large plate and set aside. Add ¼ cup water to the skillet and stir with a wooden spoon to loosen the browned bits. When the pan bottom and sides are clean, add the liquid to the reducing sauce.

9. When sauce has reduced to about 3 cups and thickened to the consistency of heavy cream, reduce the heat to medium-low. Stir the beef, mushrooms, and onions (and any accumulated juices), the remaining wine from the bottle, and the brandy into the Dutch oven. Cover the pot and cook until just heated through, 5 to 8 minutes. Adjust the seasonings with salt and pepper and serve, sprinkling individual servings with minced parsley.

➤ VARIATION
Do-Ahead Beef Burgundy
The braise can be made a day or two ahead, and the sauce, along with the onion and mushroom garnish, can be completed the day you intend to serve.

1. Follow recipe for Beef Burgundy through step 5. Using tongs, transfer the vegetable and herb bouquet to a mesh strainer set over the Dutch oven. Press the liquid back into pot and discard the bouquet. Let the beef cool to room temperature in the

---

INGREDIENTS: Does It Have to Be Burgundy?

Beef Burgundy is rightfully made with true Burgundy wine. This means a red wine made from the Pinot Noir grape grown in the French province of Burgundy. Characteristically, these wines are medium-bodied but also deep, rich, and complex, with earthy tones and a reticent fruitiness. They are also expensive. Throughout our testing, into each batch of beef Burgundy, we emptied a $12 bottle of Burgundy—the least expensive we could find. Quite frankly, it was making outstanding beef Burgundies. Nonetheless, we tried more costly, higher-quality Burgundies and found that they bettered the dish—a $30 bottle gave a stellar, rousing performance. We thought it worth exploring other wines, but, wanting to remain faithful to the spirit of the dish, we limited ourselves to Pinot Noirs made on the West Coast of the United States, which are slightly less expensive than Burgundies. We made beef Burgundies with domestic Pinot Noirs at three different price points, and even the least expensive wine—a $9 bottle—was perfectly acceptable, although its flavors were simpler and less intriguing than those of its Burgundian counterpart.

Both the Burgundies and the Pinot Noirs exhibited the same pattern: As the price of the wine increased, so did the depth, complexity, and roundness of the sauce. We can advise with some confidence to set your price, then seek out a wine—either Burgundy or Pinot Noir—that matches it. But if your allegiance is to a true Burgundy, be warned that they can be difficult to find because production is relatively limited. We also caution you to beware of several very inexpensive mass-produced wines from California of questionable constitutions that are sold as "Burgundy." They are usually made from a blend of grape varieties, and whether or not they actually contain so much as a drop of Pinot Noir is a mystery. We made a beef burgundy with one of these wines, and it resulted in a fleeting, one-dimensional, fruity, sweet sauce that, though palatable, lacked the deep, lavish flavors we have come to expect in a beef Burgundy.

braising liquid in the Dutch oven. The braise can be kept covered in the refrigerator for up to 2 days.

2. To complete the dish, use a slotted spoon to skim the congealed fat off the top and discard. Set the pot over medium-high heat and bring to a simmer. With a slotted spoon, transfer the beef to a medium bowl and set aside. Simmer the sauce briskly, stirring occasionally to ensure that the bottom is not burning, until reduced to about 3 cups and thickened to the consistency of heavy cream, 15 to 25 minutes.

3. Continue with recipe from step 8.

BEEF STROGANOFF

BEEF STROGANOFF LOOKS LIKE A STEW. IT tastes like a stew. It is served like a stew. But deconstructed, beef stroganoff is really a simple sauté and pan sauce combo in which meat and mushrooms are sautéed and then held on the side while a quick sauce is made. They are all reunited and joined with egg noodles in holy matrimony. The meat that goes into a stroganoff is tender stuff like filet mignon and sirloin rather than braising cuts such as chuck or brisket, which need time and patience to grow tender under a lid.

Stroganoff is nevertheless a tough dish to get right—for a couple of reasons. Because stroganoff is a pan sauce, it is a light proposition and hasn't time to gather the intensity of flavor a braise might; and, since it is served over noodles, the sauce must be thinner and cleaner than a microreduced buttery pan sauce. Whereas matters in the flavor department would be much simplified by the addition of homemade demi-glace (a highly concentrated sauce that takes hours to reduce), canned chicken broth and 10 minutes didn't get us very far.

Beef, mushrooms, onions, and sour cream are classic ingredients in a stroganoff. Beyond that there seem to be no standard seasonings, probably because the dish itself did not evolve naturally from Russian cuisine but was introduced to the Russian aristocracy by a French chef. The spoon of sour cream seems to have been thrown in as an afterthought to put a Russian spin on things.

There is an almost desperate "anything goes" feeling in some recipes for beef stroganoff. Different combinations of ingredients such as prepared mustard, paprika, Worcestershire sauce, cider vinegar, tomato paste, brown sugar, brandy, and sherry ultimately antagonized each other. Still, our impulse, like everyone else's, was to use as many flavor-building ingredients as possible in hopes of getting a little flirtation into the whole affair.

We first set up a basic recipe using 1 pound of beef, 6 ounces of mushrooms, ¼ quarter cup minced onions, 1 tablespoon of flour, 1 cup of chicken stock, and ½ cup sour cream, then went off to test cuts of beef (all steaks, really). Though we knew beef tenderloin was favored in stroganoff, we thought other steak cuts might bring more flavor to the pan. Toward that end, we made four stroganoffs, sautéing strips of sirloin, rib-eye, blade steak, and tenderloin. Our assumption proved faulty. While the improved flavor of fattier cuts is striking in a simple grilled format, it was altogether lost in a sauce rich with dairy. The other steaks were also unpleasantly chewy and at odds with the plush, velvety sauce and mushrooms, and the lush noodles.

Many recipes flour the meat to promote browning and thicken the sauce. But flouring left the sautéed meat lying in the sauce looking like swathed mummies. What worked far better was adding a single tablespoon of flour to the pan after the meat had been sautéed. We also found that broader strips of tenderloin (we were cutting them about a half inch thick to begin) often had a livery taste—even with the sour cream. By slicing them as thin as ⅛ inch, we were able to reduce the total weight of the meat to ¾ pound and surround each bite with flavorful browned edges. Since most beef stroganoff recipes feature strips of meat that appear to have been browned very little, if at all, we thought it would only be fair to try a batch of meat thrown in a skillet with no attention to browning. Sure enough, it looked just like the stroganoffs we had seen in hotel chafing dishes. Unfortunately, it tasted like them, too.

As for the mushrooms, we knew they would benefit from hot, dry heat, which would brown their edges and leave their insides silky and flavorful. There is no greater injustice wrought upon a mushroom than being sliced thin and boiled off in a sauce. We also wanted the mushrooms to have a presence equal to the beef, so we decided to use 12 ounces of button mushrooms and quarter or half them (depending on their size) rather than slice them.

We knew that the fond, or browned bits left in the pan after sautéing, would be critical to a flavorful sauce and that the sequence of the sauté would be key. We found it was better to start with the mushrooms (which, by the time they were finished, had barely colored the pan bottom), remove them from the pan, and then sauté the beef. By the time the beef had been browned and set aside with the mushrooms, a beautiful brown film covered the pan. It needed only to be lifted from the pan with a little liquid, or deglazed. Here red wine did the job nicely.

Aromatics were up next. At first we gave minced onions and shallots equal play. Though we favor sautéed shallots in sauces over onions 90 percent of the time for their mildness, in this case we found the shallots muted and ineffective. We liked the bright flavor of the onions and increased the amount to ½ cup.

Now came the gypsy caravan of flavorings and

SLICING TENDERLOIN FILET

For stroganoff, we usually buy two 6-ounce tenderloin filets and cut them into thin strips as shown.

1. Turn each filet on its side and cut it in half to yield two ¹/₂-inch-thick medallions.

2. Cut the medallions across the grain into ¹/₈-inch strips.

the finishing touch of liquid. In different combinations, singly, doubly, and in groups, we tried all the seasonings listed earlier. Despite our desire to pump flavor into the sauce, the only survivors were 1 teaspoon of tomato paste and 1½ teaspoons of dark brown sugar. We kept just a splash of chicken stock and added two jiggers of red wine and a big spoon of sour cream. This at last was stroganoff, recognizably retro, and, in the company of a bowl of hot, buttered noodles, pretty irresistible.

Beef Stroganoff
SERVES 4

Stroganoff is an elegant dish made with tender pieces of beef tenderloin and finished with a swirl of sour cream. Sour cream can curdle if added directly to hot liquid. To prevent this, temper the sour cream by stirring a little of the stewing liquid into it and then stirring the warmed sour cream mixture back in the pan with the stroganoff. Buttered egg noodles are the classic accompaniment to this recipe. About ½ pound of noodles will serve four.

2	teaspoons vegetable oil
12	ounces white mushrooms, whole if small, halved if medium, quartered if large
	Salt and ground black pepper
³/₄	pound beef tenderloin (about 2 filets), cut into ¹/₈-inch strips (see illustrations, left)
³/₄	cup dry red wine
1	tablespoon unsalted butter
1	small onion, minced (¹/₂ cup)
1	teaspoon tomato paste
1¹/₂	teaspoons dark brown sugar
1	tablespoon flour
¹/₂	cup homemade chicken stock or canned low-sodium chicken broth
¹/₃	cup sour cream

1. Heat a heavy 12-inch skillet over high heat for 2 minutes. Add 1 teaspoon oil and swirl the pan to coat the bottom. Add the mushrooms and cook over high heat without stirring for 30 seconds, thereafter shaking the pan occasionally until the mushrooms have browned lightly, about 3 minutes more. Season the mushrooms with salt and pepper

to taste and transfer them to a mixing bowl.

2. Return the pan to high heat, add the remaining teaspoon of oil, and swirl to coat the pan bottom. Place the tenderloin strips in the pan in a single layer, taking care that the strips are not touching, and sear them without turning until the meat is well-browned on one side, 2 to 2½ minutes. Turn the strips and sear the other sides until well-browned, about 1 minute more. Season the meat with salt and pepper to taste and transfer it to the mixing bowl with the mushrooms.

3. Return the pan to high heat and add ¼ cup wine to deglaze the pan, scraping up the browned bits on the pan bottom with a wooden spoon. Simmer and reduce the wine until it has become thick and glazed, about 30 seconds. Transfer the glaze to the mixing bowl with the mushrooms and beef, using a rubber spatula to scrape the pan clean.

4. Return the pan to medium heat and add the butter. When the butter foams, add the onion, tomato paste, and brown sugar, and cook, stirring frequently, until the onion is lightly browned, about 3 minutes. Stir in the flour and mix it well to incorporate with the other ingredients. Add the remaining ½ cup wine and the chicken stock and whisk vigorously until thickened, about 1½ minutes. Pour any reserved liquid from the mushrooms and the beef into the sauce and simmer just to incorporate. Spoon about ½ cup of the hot sauce into a small bowl with the sour cream, then add the mixture back into the sauce. Add the mushrooms and beef, and heat to warm through, about 1 minute. Season to taste with salt and pepper. Serve.

IRISH STEW

IRISH STEW IS A SIMPLE LAMB STEW THAT has sustained countless generations. At its most basic, Irish stew is made with just lamb, onions, potatoes, and water. There's no browning or precooking. The raw ingredients are layered in the pot and cooked until tender.

We prepared several variations of this basic dish and identified a couple of problems. First, by modern standards, it is bland. With no browning and so few ingredients, authentic Irish stew can't even compete with a good bowl of beef stew. Second, the potatoes break down and lose their shape after several hours of simmering. Although the potatoes do thicken the stew, modern palates generally prefer vegetables that are not so overcooked.

Our goals for this recipe were clear. While remaining true to the dish's humble roots—lamb and potatoes—we wanted to pump up the flavors (especially of the lamb) and find a way to thicken the stew without overcooking the potatoes.

We started with boneless lamb shoulder meat, figuring that the equivalent cut had worked well with beef stews. We browned the meat, replaced the water with chicken stock, added carrots and Worcestershire sauce for flavor (an ingredient suggested in a number of recipes), and thickened everything with flour. The results were better but not great. Browning helped intensify the lamb's flavor, but the chicken stock, carrots, and Worcestershire sauce tended to diminish this effect. The flour was a good idea, though, creating a nicely textured sauce.

For the next test, we browned the chunks of boneless shoulder meat, removed the meat from the pan, and cooked some onions until they were tender. We added some flour for thickening power and then some water. We let the stew cook for an hour before adding the potatoes, so they would not overcook. This stew was better—there were few distractions—but the lamb flavor was a bit weak. With so little else in the pot, the lamb has to carry the day, and this meat was not up to the task.

We started to think that shoulder meat was the wrong choice. We tested some boneless leg of lamb (the cut commonly sold as stew meat), and the results were extremely disappointing. The meat cooked up dry, tough, and not very flavorful. This cut has far less fat than the shoulder, making it a poor choice for stewing.

We were ready to throw in the towel when James Beard came to the rescue. In the course of our research, we found his recipe for Irish stew, which called for leaving the meat on the bone. We tested his recipe and were pleasantly surprised. The water and lamb bones had, in fact, created a rich-tasting stock. The meat itself was especially tasty, no doubt because it was cooked on the bone. Cooking whole chops (as Beard suggested) made this dish seem more like a braise than a stew. Also, Beard did not brown the meat, a step we had grown fond of in earlier tests.

We took a Chinese cleaver and cut shoulder chops into 2-inch pieces. Although this idea seemed promising, the hacked-up bones created some small splinters, which tasters felt were unappealing and even dangerous. Our next idea was to remove the meat from the bones and cut it into stew-sized chunks. The meat would be browned and then removed from the pot so that the onions could be cooked. When the meat was added back to the stew pot, we would throw in the uncooked lamb bones as well. As we had hoped, this strategy gave us excellent results.

Cutting the lamb meat into medium-sized chunks made this dish seem like a stew. Browning added flavor to the meat as well as the stew. The bones, which still had bits of meat attached to them, created a rich, heady sauce. Some tasters liked to gnaw on the meaty bones; others felt that bones have no place in a finished stew and should be discarded just before serving. The choice is yours.

We found it worthwhile to buy shoulder chops from the butcher. In most supermarkets, lamb shoulder chops are thin, often about ½ inch thick. At this thickness, the stew meat is too insubstantial. Ideally, we like chops cut 1½ inches thick, but 1-inch chops will suffice.

We had a few more tests to run. Although traditional recipes often layer raw onions into the pot with the meat, potatoes, and water, we knew that cooking the onions would be key. Tasters had liked stews made with softened onions, but further tests proved that browning the onions added even more depth to the final dish.

We generally prefer low-starch, red-skinned potatoes in stews because they hold their shape well. (For more information on potato varieties, see page 125.) However, in this dish the potatoes traditionally act as a thickener. Even though we had added some flour to the browned onions to thicken the sauce, we wondered if a higher-starch potato would be more appropriate in Irish stew. We decided to try this dish with russets and Yukon Golds as well as red potatoes.

Russets fell apart into a soupy mess and were universally panned. The red potatoes were fine, but the Yukon Golds stole the show. Tasters appreciated the buttery, rich flavor as well as the soft, creamy texture

they contributed to this simple stew.

Thyme and parsley are often added to Irish stew, and we saw no need to deviate from tradition. The parsley was best stirred in just before serving to maintain its bright, fresh flavor. At last, a hearty Irish stew worth eating.

Irish Stew

SERVES 6

The secret to this simple, hearty stew is to add the lamb bones to the pot. Bone-in shoulder chops weighing 4½ pounds will yield about 2½ pounds of boneless meat plus a pile of bones. Some meat will cling to the bones, and the choice is yours whether to remove the bones just before serving for a more refined dish or to include them for a casual eating experience. True Irish stew includes just meat and potatoes with some onions. We've added a recipe for a popular variation with carrots and turnips.

4½ pounds lamb shoulder chops, each 1 to 1½ inches thick (see page 216)
    Salt and ground black pepper
3   tablespoons vegetable oil
3   medium-large onions, chopped coarse (about 5 cups)
4   tablespoons flour
1   teaspoon dried thyme
6   medium Yukon Gold or red potatoes (about 2 pounds), peeled and cut into 1-inch cubes
¼   cup minced fresh parsley leaves

1. Adjust the oven rack to the lower-middle position and heat the oven to 300 degrees. Cut the meat from the bones and reserve the bones. Trim the meat of excess fat and cut it into 1½-inch cubes. Season the meat generously with salt and pepper.

2. Heat 1 tablespoon oil in a large ovenproof Dutch oven over medium-high heat until shimmering, about 2 minutes. Add half the meat to the pot so that the individual pieces are close together but not touching. Cook, not moving the pieces until the sides touching the pot are well-browned, 2 to 3 minutes. Using tongs, turn each piece and continue cooking until most sides are well-browned, about 5 minutes longer. Transfer the meat

to a medium bowl, add another 1 tablespoon oil to the pot, and swirl to coat the pan bottom. Brown the remaining lamb; transfer the meat to the bowl and set aside.

3. Reduce the heat to medium, add the remaining tablespoon oil, and swirl to coat the pan bottom. Add the onions and ¼ teaspoon salt and cook, stirring frequently and vigorously, scraping the bottom of the pot with a wooden spoon to loosen browned bits, until the onions have browned, about 8 minutes. Add the flour and stir until the onions are evenly coated, 1 to 2 minutes.

4. Stir in 1½ cups water, scraping the pan bottom and edges with a wooden spoon to loosen the remaining browned bits. Gradually add another 1½ cups water, stirring constantly and scraping the pan edges to dissolve the flour. Add the thyme and 1 teaspoon salt and bring to a simmer. Add the bones and then the meat and accumulated juices. Return to a simmer, cover, and place in the oven. Cook for 1 hour.

5. Remove the pot from the oven and place the potatoes on top of the meat and bones. Cover and return the pot to the oven and cook until the meat is tender, about 1 hour. If serving immediately, stir the potatoes into the liquid, wait 5 minutes, and spoon off any fat that rises to the top. (Stew can be covered and refrigerated for up to 3 days. Spoon off the congealed fat and bring back to a simmer over medium-low heat.)

BLADE CHOP AND ROUND BONE CHOP

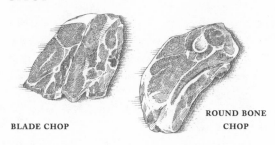

BLADE CHOP **ROUND BONE CHOP**

There are two kinds of shoulder chop. The blade chop is roughly rectangular in shape and contains a piece of the chine bone (backbone) and a thin piece of the blade bone. The arm, or round bone, contains a round cross-section of the arm bone so that the chop looks like a small ham steak. The round bone chop contains less fat and fewer muscles, making it easier to cut into meat for stews.

6. Stir in the parsley and adjust the seasonings. Remove the bones if desired. Serve immediately.

➤ VARIATIONS

Irish Stew with Carrots and Turnips
Follow recipe for Irish Stew, substituting ½ pound carrots, peeled and sliced ¼ inch thick, and ½ pound turnips, peeled and cut into 1-inch cubes, for 1 pound of the potatoes. Proceed as directed.

Italian-Style Lamb Stew with Green Beans, Tomatoes, and Basil
This peasant-style lamb stew has its roots in Sicily. Although it is more complex than traditional Irish stew, the approach to preparing it is identical. Tomatoes and green beans replace some of the potatoes to lighten up the dish.

4½	pounds lamb shoulder chops, each 1 to 1½ inches thick (see page 216)
	Salt and ground black pepper
3	tablespoons vegetable oil
3	medium-large onions, chopped coarse (about 5 cups)
3	medium cloves garlic, minced
4	tablespoons flour
½	cup dry white wine
1	tablespoon minced fresh rosemary
1	(14½-ounce) can diced tomatoes
4	medium Yukon Gold or red potatoes (about 1¼ pounds), peeled and cut into 1-inch cubes
¾	pound green beans, ends trimmed and halved
¼	cup minced fresh basil leaves

1. Adjust the oven rack to the lower-middle position and heat the oven to 300 degrees. Cut the meat from the bones and reserve the bones. Trim the meat of excess fat and cut it into 1½-inch cubes. Season the meat generously with salt and pepper.

2. Heat 1 tablespoon oil in a large ovenproof Dutch oven over medium-high heat until shimmering, about 2 minutes. Add half of the meat to the pot so that the individual pieces are close together but not touching. Cook, not moving the pieces until the sides touching the pot are well-browned, 2 to 3 minutes. Using tongs, turn each piece and continue cooking until most sides are well-browned, about 5 minutes longer. Transfer the meat to a medium bowl,

add another 1 tablespoon oil to the pot, and swirl to coat the pan bottom. Brown the remaining lamb; transfer the meat to the bowl and set aside.

3. Reduce the heat to medium, add the remaining tablespoon oil, and swirl to coat the pan bottom. Add the onions and ¼ teaspoon salt and cook, stirring frequently and vigorously, scraping the bottom of the pot with a wooden spoon to loosen browned bits, until the onions have softened, about 5 minutes. Add the garlic and cook until fragrant, about 30 seconds. Add the flour and stir until the onions are evenly coated, 1 to 2 minutes.

4. Stir in the wine and 1 cup water, scraping the pan bottom and edges with a wooden spoon to loosen the remaining browned bits. Gradually add another ¾ cup water, stirring constantly and scraping the pan edges to dissolve the flour. Add the rosemary, tomatoes, and 1 teaspoon salt and bring to a simmer. Add the bones and then the meat and accumulated juices. Return to a simmer, cover, and place in the oven. Cook for 1 hour.

5. Remove the pot from the oven and place the potatoes and green beans on top of the meat and bones. Cover, return the pot to the oven, and cook until the meat is tender, about 1 hour. If serving immediately, spoon off any fat that rises to the top. (Stew can be covered and refrigerated for up to 3 days. Spoon off the congealed fat and bring back to a simmer over medium-low heat.)

6. Stir in the basil and adjust the seasonings. Remove the bones if desired. Serve immediately.

LAMB TAGINE

TAGINES ARE FUNDAMENTAL TO THE CUISINES of Morocco, Algeria, and other North African countries. The term comes from the earthenware pot with a conical cover that has traditionally been used to prepare stews in this region. Most tagines are highly aromatic and feature a blend of sweet and savory ingredients. Most also contain some sort of fruit (often dried) as well as a heady mixture of ground spices, garlic, and cilantro. Lamb tagines are especially popular, although chicken or vegetables can take center stage.

Tagines differ widely from region to region. We decided to start with a classic, slow-simmering recipe typically prepared in Morocco. Our goal for this recipe was to develop a dish that kept the authentic flavors of Morocco but eliminated most of the fuss.

Many tagine recipes have incredibly long ingredient lists or call for pieces of equipment (such as the above-mentioned earthenware pot) that are unlikely to be found in American kitchens. We wanted to make this dish in a Dutch oven. As for the tagine itself, we wanted the lamb to be moist and succulent. The flavors and aromas would be heady, with a medley of spices blending together harmoniously. A few vegetables and fruits would provide depth and offer the characteristic sweet and savory components.

Given our results with Irish stew, we were weary of using boneless shoulder meat. However, our fears were unfounded. Given the abundance of flavors in this recipe, tasters did not miss the extra oomph

INGREDIENTS: Lamb Shoulder Chops

Lamb shoulder is sliced into two different cuts, blade and round bone chops (see illustrations on page 215). You'll find them sold in a range of thicknesses (from about one-half inch to more than one inch thick), depending on who's doing the butchering. (In our experience, supermarkets tend to cut them thinner, while independent butchers cut them thicker.) Blade chops are roughly rectangular in shape, and some are thickly striated with fat. Each blade chop includes a piece of the chine bone (the backbone of the animal) and a thin piece of the blade bone (the shoulder blade of the animal).

Round bone chops, also called arm chops, are more oval in shape and as a rule are substantially leaner than blade chops. Each contains a round cross-section of the arm bone so that the chop looks a bit like a little ham steak. In addition to the arm bone, there's also a tiny line of riblets on the side of each chop.

As to which chop is better, we found that it is easier to remove the meat in large chunks from round bone chops. The blade chops often contain a lot of intramuscular fat and, once trimmed, chops will yield irregularly shaped pieces of meat. That said, our lamb stews will still be delicious if made with blade chops.

provided by the bones we decided to include in our recipe for Irish stew. The shoulder meat was plenty tasty when seasoned so liberally with spices.

We were following our recipe for beef stew but noticed some changes at the outset. Although we found it helpful to pat beef dry with paper towels before browning, the same step caused problems with lamb. Unlike beef, which can be moist, lamb tends to be sticky, and the paper towels quickly became "glued" to the meat. Picking out the bits of paper was tedious, so we stopped drying the meat.

We focused on the spices next. Sweet, warm spices are typically used in North African cooking. Ground cinnamon and ginger were quickly voted in by tasters, as were paprika and cumin. Most everyone liked the addition of some fragrant coriander but tasters were divided about cayenne—some liked a little heat, but others did not. We decided to make this spice optional.

Although some sources suggested tossing the meat with the spices before browning it, we found that this caused the spices to burn. Other recipes add the spices with the liquid, but we found sautéing the spices in a little oil helps to bring out their flavor. It made sense to add the spices to the pot along with the flour—that is, once the onions and garlic were sautéed.

Adding the spices with the flour created a thick coating on the pan bottom. We found it essential to scrape the pan bottom when the liquid was added to incorporate the spices into the stew and develop their full flavor potential.

Although water is the traditional choice in Irish stew, we knew that we would have more options in a tagine. Some traditional recipes call for lamb stock, but we wondered how canned chicken broth would perform. Thankfully, canned chicken broth proved more than adequate in this dish. It adds body to the stew but doesn't compete with the lamb flavor, the way it had in Irish stew. We tested water in this recipe, but tasters felt that the stew suffered a bit, especially in terms of body.

Tomatoes are another constant in most tagines. We found that canned diced tomatoes provide an acidic contrast that heightened the other flavors. We tested several other vegetables, including summer squash, sweet potatoes, and potatoes. All were delicious, but none seemed essential in a basic tagine—the tomatoes

and onions could carry the day. We did like the addition of chickpeas, another common ingredient in many tagines. Canned chickpeas are fine in this dish as long as they are added near the end of the stewing time to keep them from becoming mushy.

As for fruits, we liked the soft texture and sweet flavor of most every dried fruit tested. Apricots were a unanimous favorite, but prunes, raisins, and currants were other good options.

Finally, we found that it was best to use a strong hand with the seasonings. Plenty of garlic and cilantro punched up the flavor and kept the sweet elements in check.

Lamb Tagine
SERVES 6 TO 8

If you can't find boneless lamb shoulder, you can purchase blade or arm chops and remove the meat yourself. Buy 4½ pounds of chops to yield the 2½ pounds of boneless meat needed for this recipe. Prunes, raisins, golden raisins, or currants can be substituted for the apricots. Serve over couscous or basmati rice (page 312).

2½	pounds boneless lamb shoulder, trimmed and cut into 1½-inch cubes
	Salt and ground black pepper
3	tablespoons olive oil
2	medium-large onions, chopped coarse (about 3 cups)
4	medium cloves garlic, minced
3	tablespoons flour
1½	teaspoons ground cumin
1	teaspoon ground cinnamon
1	teaspoon ground ginger
½	teaspoon ground coriander
⅛	teaspoon cayenne pepper (optional)
2¼	cups homemade chicken stock or canned low-sodium chicken broth
1	(14½-ounce) can diced tomatoes
1	cup dried apricots, roughly chopped
2	bay leaves
6	fresh cilantro sprigs (optional)
1	(15-ounce) can chickpeas, drained and rinsed
¼	cup minced fresh cilantro or parsley leaves
¼	cup toasted slivered almonds (optional)

1. Adjust the oven rack to the lower-middle position and heat the oven to 300 degrees. Season the lamb generously with salt and pepper.

2. Heat 1 tablespoon oil in a large ovenproof Dutch oven over medium-high heat until shimmering, about 2 minutes. Add half of the meat to the pot so that the individual pieces are close together but not touching. Cook, not moving the pieces until the sides touching the pot are well-browned, 2 to 3 minutes. Using tongs, turn each piece and continue cooking until most sides are well-browned, about 5 minutes longer. Transfer the meat to a medium bowl, add another 1 tablespoon oil to the pot, and swirl to coat the pan bottom. Brown the remaining lamb; transfer the meat to the bowl and set aside.

3. Reduce heat to medium, add the remaining tablespoon oil, and swirl to coat the pan bottom. Add the onions and ¼ teaspoon salt and cook, stirring frequently and vigorously, scraping the bottom of the pot with a wooden spoon to loosen browned bits, until the onions have softened, about 5 minutes. Stir in the garlic and cook until fragrant, about 30 seconds. Add the flour, cumin, cinnamon, ginger, coriander, and cayenne (if using), and stir until onions are evenly coated and fragrant, 1 to 2 minutes.

4. Gradually add the stock, scraping the pan bottom and edges with a wooden spoon to loosen the remaining browned bits and spices, and stirring until the flour is dissolved and the liquid thick. Stir in the tomatoes, apricots, bay leaves, and cilantro sprigs (if using) and bring to a simmer. Add the browned lamb and accumulated juices, pushing down the meat to submerge the pieces. Return to a simmer, cover, and place in the oven. Cook for 1 hour and 15 minutes.

5. Remove the pot from the oven and stir in the chickpeas. Cover and return the pot to the oven. Cook until the meat is tender and the chickpeas are heated through, about 15 minutes. If serving immediately, spoon off any fat that rises to the top. (Stew can be covered and refrigerated for up to 3 days. Spoon off the congealed fat and bring back to a simmer over medium-low heat.)

6. Discard the bay leaves and cilantro sprigs. Stir in the cilantro leaves and adjust the seasonings. Serve immediately, garnishing each bowl with almonds if desired.

PORK VINDALOO

VINDALOO HAS ROOTS IN GOA, A REGION on India's western coast that was once a Portuguese colony. Many local dishes, including vindaloo, are a blend of Indian and Portuguese ingredients and techniques. Vindaloo is most often made with pork but sometimes with chicken, beef, or vegetables. The word *vindaloo* is derived from a combination of Portuguese words—*vinho,* for wine vinegar, and *alhos,* for garlic. This stew is usually made with a mixture of warm spices (such as cumin and cardamom), chiles (usually in the form of cayenne and paprika), tomatoes, mustard seed, and vinegar.

When this stew is correctly prepared, the meat is tender, the liquid is thick and deep reddish-orange in color, and the flavors are complex. The heat of chiles is tamed by the sweetness of the aromatic spices and the acidity of the tomatoes and vinegar. Onions and garlic add pungency, while mustard seeds lend their unique flavor and crunch.

Most vindaloo recipes we tested were pretty good, but we noticed two recurring problems: meat that was dry and/or tough and flavors that were muddled. We decided to start with the meat component in this dish and then test the flavoring option.

Given our results with beef, we figured that pork shoulder would make the best stew. To test this proposition, we stewed various cuts of pork from the shoulder and loin, including several kinds of chops. The shoulder cuts were far superior to the loin. Like beef chuck, pork shoulder has enough fat to keep the meat tender and juicy during the long cooking process.

Pork shoulder is often called Boston butt or Boston shoulder in markets. The picnic also comes from the shoulder. For vindaloo, a boneless Boston butt was the best option because there was less waste. (A picnic roast can be used, but the bone, skin, and thick layer of fat will need to be discarded.) As with beef, we had the best results when buying a boneless roast and cutting it into cubes ourselves. When we purchased precut pork labeled "stew meat," the results were disappointing. The pieces were irregularly sized and seemed to have come from several parts of the animal. The resulting stew had pieces that were dry and others that were overcooked.

As expected, we found that browning enhanced

the flavor of the pork and the stewing liquid. We left a little room in the pot between pieces of meat and planned on a total of at least seven minutes to get each pork cube well-browned. We found that 3 pounds of pork cubes could be browned in two batches in a large Dutch oven and decided to limit the meat to this amount.

Spices are the cornerstone of this stew. Classic recipes included a combination of sweet and hot spices. We had the best results using small amounts of many spices, rather than larger amounts of fewer spices. For chile flavor, we used sweet paprika and cayenne. To give the stew its characteristic earthy qualities, we added cumin, cardamom, and cloves. The cardamom and cloves are highly sweet and aromatic, while the cumin hits lower, earthier notes. Mustard seeds, a spice used frequently in the cooking of South India, added pungency. Bay leaves brought a deep, herbaceous flavor to this stew and a hit of cilantro just before serving added freshness.

With our meat and spices chosen, we turned our attention to the liquid element. Most of the recipes we uncovered in our research called for water. The theory is that water is a neutral medium that allows the flavors of the meat and spices to come through as clearly as possible. We wondered, though, if chicken stock would add richness and body to the stewing liquid. We prepared two batches—one with water, the other with chicken stock. Tasters felt that the chicken stock added complexity and fullness without calling attention to itself.

Sweet and sour flavors are the final component of this stew. Diced canned tomatoes, with their juices, were far less work than fresh tomatoes (which needed to be peeled and seeded), and the canned tomatoes performed admirably. Two tablespoons of red wine vinegar and one teaspoon of sugar provided the right balance of sour and sweet. We tried adding the vinegar at the end of the cooking time (a step suggested in a few recipes), but tasters felt this stew was harsh. The vinegar needed time to soften and mix with the other flavors.

Although vindaloo is not fiery, it is spicy and is therefore best served over rice to help temper the intensity of flavors. Basmati rice was the ideal partner for this dish, but steamed long-grain rice was also a nice accompaniment.

Pork Vindaloo

SERVES 6 TO 8

This Indian dish of Portuguese ancestry is full of flavors— hot, sweet, spicy, and pungent—that all come together in a tantalizing dish. A piece of boneless Boston butt is easy to trim and cut into cubes. However, a bone-in picnic roast will also work nicely. In addition to the bone, a picnic roast typically is covered with skin and a thick layer of fat. When trimmed, a 5-pound picnic roast will yield the same amount of meat (about 2¾ pounds) as a 3-pound Boston butt. Premeasuring the flour with the spices makes it easy to add them to the pot. Serve with basmati rice (page 312).

1	(3-pound) boneless Boston butt roast (see page 220), trimmed and cut into 1½-inch cubes
	Salt and ground black pepper
3	tablespoons vegetable oil
3	medium-large onions, chopped coarse (about 5 cups)
8	medium cloves garlic, minced
3	tablespoons flour
1	tablespoon sweet paprika
¾	teaspoon ground cumin
½	teaspoon ground cardamom
¼	teaspoon cayenne pepper
¼	teaspoon ground cloves
1½	cups homemade chicken stock or canned low-sodium chicken broth
1	(14½-ounce) can diced tomatoes
2	bay leaves
1	teaspoon sugar
2	tablespoons red wine vinegar
1	tablespoon mustard seeds
¼	cup minced fresh cilantro leaves

1. Adjust the oven rack to lower-middle position and heat oven to 300 degrees. Season the meat generously with salt and pepper. Heat 1 tablespoon oil in a large ovenproof Dutch oven over medium-high heat until shimmering, about 2 minutes. Add half of the meat to the pot so that the individual pieces are close together but not touching. Cook, not moving the pieces until the sides touching the pot are well-browned, 2 to 3 minutes. Using tongs, turn each piece and continue cooking until most sides are well-browned, about 5 minutes longer. Transfer the

meat to a medium bowl, add another 1 tablespoon oil to the pot, and swirl to coat the pan bottom. Brown the remaining meat; transfer the meat to the bowl and set aside.

2. Reduce heat to medium, add the remaining tablespoon oil to the empty Dutch oven, and swirl to coat the pan bottom. Add the onions and ¼ teaspoon salt and cook, stirring frequently and vigorously, scraping the bottom of the pot with a wooden spoon to loosen browned bits, until the onions have softened, about 5 minutes. Stir in the garlic and cook until fragrant, about 30 seconds. Add the flour, paprika, cumin, cardamom, cayenne, and cloves. Stir until the onions are evenly coated and fragrant, 1 to 2 minutes.

3. Gradually add the stock, scraping the pan bottom and edges with a wooden spoon to loosen the remaining browned bits and dissolve the flour. Add the tomatoes, bay leaves, sugar, vinegar, and mustard seeds and bring to a simmer. Add the browned pork and accumulated juices, submerging the meat under the liquid. Return to a simmer, cover, and place in the oven. Cook for 2 hours.

4. Remove the pot from the oven. If serving immediately, spoon off any fat the rises to the top. (Stew can be covered and refrigerated for up to 3 days. Spoon off the congealed fat and bring back to a simmer over medium-low heat.) Remove the bay leaves, stir in the cilantro, and adjust the seasonings. Serve immediately.

BEST CUTS FOR PORK STEWS

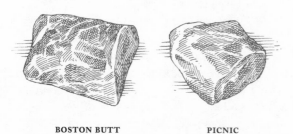

BOSTON BUTT   **PICNIC**

We found that cuts from the shoulder of the pig are the best for stewing. These cuts have enough fat to keep the meat moist as it cooks (the loin, for instance, is much too lean for stewing). We recommend buying a boneless Boston butt (also called a pork shoulder blade Boston roast) for vindaloo and buying a picnic roast (also called a pork shoulder arm picnic roast) for pozole.

POZOLE

POZOLE IS THE MEXICAN NAME FOR BOTH hominy (dried field corn kernels treated with lime and boiled until tender but still chewy) and the stew made with hominy and pork. The stew is made throughout Mexico and in several quite distinct incarnations. Pozole blanco (white pozole) is prepared without any chiles. Pozole rojo (red pozole) is made with dried red chiles and pozole verde (green pozole) with tomatillos, fresh green chiles, and cilantro. Pozole blanco seems fairly bland compared with the red and green versions, so we decided to focus on the latter two styles.

Whether red or green, pozole should have a complex, richly flavored broth with lots of body. The meat, which is shredded, must be exceedingly tender, while the hominy is toothsome and sweet. A garnish of chopped raw vegetables (lettuce, radishes, and herbs) is added at the table.

Although pozole has become popular in the United States, especially in the Southwest, most American cooks balk at preparing traditional recipes, many of which take 12 hours or more to execute. One of the culprits here is the hominy. If you begin with dried field corn, you must boil it with slaked lime to loosen the hulls. The corn is then washed to remove the hulls, and the germ is pinched off from each kernel by hand. Preparing hominy can take an entire afternoon. We wanted to figure out how to use canned, or precooked, hominy to save time.

Another concern we had when developing our pozole recipe was the meat. In Mexico, pozole is traditionally made with cuts rarely sold in American supermarkets (unsmoked pig's feet and pig's head, for example). We would have to find an acceptable substitute.

With these goals in mind, we started work on a red pozole recipe. (We figured that green pozole could be a variation of our red pozole.) The meat issue seemed like the first one to tackle.

Authentic pozole is made with bones from the head, neck, shank, and feet of the pig, supplemented with some boneless meat from the shoulder or loin. We wondered how important bones were to this dish. We prepared one batch with boneless shoulder meat only and another with a bone-in shoulder roast. (We chose the shoulder not only because of availability but because it has consistently proven to be the best cut for stewing.) The liquid of the pozole prepared without bones was weak in flavor and thin in texture. The version made with the bone-in shoulder roast had a distinctive, satisfying pork flavor. It was obvious to tasters that bones are key to developing rich, full-bodied pork flavor. In addition, the bones released a large amount of gelatin that gave the pozole a voluptuous body.

There are two cuts from the shoulder (see illustration on page 220). Since Boston butt is typically sold without the bone, we decided to use the picnic roast. We found that a 5-pound roast, once trimmed of its thick skin and fat, yielded just about three pounds of boneless meat—enough for the stew.

Pozole differs from other meat stews in that the meat is shredded rather than cubed. The meat is usually stewed in large chunks until it is tender enough to pull apart by hand. Just to make sure that tradition is best, we tried cubing the meat and then shredding it after cooking, but this process proved quite tedious. We then tried cooking the roast whole, but this increased the cooking time dramatically. Finally, we tried cutting the meat into large chunks, following the natural lines of the muscles as we removed the meat from the bone. This approach worked best. The stewing time was not excessive (two hours did the trick), and the meat was easy to shred. The sizes and shapes of these chunks varied from 3 by 1-inch strips to 4-inch cubes. From a 5-pound roast we obtained eight or nine randomly shaped chunks plus the bone, which had some pieces of meat tightly attached.

Pozole differs from most stews in another regard. Stew meat is typically browned to enhance the flavor of both the meat and the stewing liquid. In many pozole recipes, the meat is simply added raw to the simmering liquid. The reason is simple: Browning inhibits the shredding process and creates a firmer, crustier texture on the outside of each piece of meat. Another choice is to sweat the meat with some onions. We tried both simmering and sweating and found that the latter developed more flavor in the liquid without firming up the texture of the meat. To prevent the meat from burning or scorching on the outside, we cooked the onions first so they would release some liquid.

In addition to onion, garlic is the other aromatic ingredient typically added at the outset when making pozole. Once the onion is soft, the garlic goes into the pot and cooks just until fragrant. We found that gentle sweating, rather than browning, worked best for the alliums.

Once the meat was sweated, it was time to add the liquid and other seasonings. We tested water and canned chicken broth (figuring that homemade stock, while always good, wouldn't be necessary in such a highly flavored dish). Although the water was fine, the broth was superior, adding not only depth of flavor but also body to the stewing liquid. Tomatoes also added moisture to this dish. Although some versions of red pozole reserve the tomatoes as part of the garnish, our tasters liked the tomatoes cooked right into the stew. The acidity of the tomatoes created a more lively dish. (Note that for green pozole, the tomatoes are used as a garnish.)

Oregano is another main ingredient in pozole. Several varieties are grown in Mexico, all of which differ from the Mediterranean oregano popular in this country. Mexican oregano does not have the anise compounds found in Mediterranean varieties. Its flavor is more earthy and more potent. We tested pozole with dried Mexican, dried Mediterranean, and fresh Mediterranean oregano. (We were unable to purchase fresh Mexican oregano.) The dried Mediterranean oregano had a strong pizza-parlor flavor that was out of place in pozole. The fresh Mediterranean oregano was a better substitute for the dried Mexican oregano, which we prefer but which can be difficult to find.

The final component of the pozole to examine was the chiles. The red color comes from dried chiles, so we tested several possibilities—anchos, New Mexico reds, and pasillas. We removed stems and seeds from the dried chiles, soaked them in boiling water, and then pureed the chiles and soaking liquid to create a thick paste. (We tested toasting the chiles before soaking but found this step added little to this dish.) The paste was added to the pot once the meat was tender. We liked all three chiles but preferred the deep reddish brown color and rich, sweet, raisiny flavor of the anchos.

We also tested chile powder, sprinkling some into the pot once the onions, garlic, and meat had been sweated. Although the results weren't terrible, everyone in the test kitchen agreed that the pozole made with powder instead of a puree of whole chiles was less complex tasting and less appealing. It was worth spending the extra few minutes soaking and pureeing the anchos, as directed in our final recipe.

We found that it can be difficult to create a stew that pleases all tasters, especially when it comes to heat. For this reason, we mixed three-quarters of the ancho chile puree into the pozole and served the rest at the table with the other garnishes. Individuals who like spicy food could swirl extra chile puree into their bowls.

It was time to deal with the hominy. We started by preparing one batch of pozole with freshly rehydrated hominy (which took hours to prepare) and another batch with canned hominy (which took seconds to drain and rinse). The pozole with freshly cooked hominy was superb, but the pozole with canned hominy was pretty good. It was chewy (as hominy should be) and relatively sweet.

After a few more tests, we found that cooking the canned hominy in the stew for 40 to 45 minutes allowed the hominy to soak up some of the flavorful broth. Cooking canned hominy any longer made the texture suffer. The hominy became soggy when simmered for an hour or more.

Canned hominy comes in white and yellow varieties, depending on the type of field corn used. We tested white and yellow hominy and found that both types were fine. Flavor wasn't much of an issue; white and yellow hominy are both sweet and "corny" tasting. In terms of appearance, yellow hominy looked a bit better in green pozole, but the difference was slight. (The chile puree used to make red pozole makes it impossible to tell the difference between white and yellow hominy in this version.)

Our pozole recipe turned out to be remarkably simple—no more than an hour of hands-on work and a start-to-finish time of about three hours. The 10 minutes it took to prepare all the suggested garnishes was well worth it. The lettuce, radishes, cilantro, oregano, and lime juice all brightened the stew and turned it into a one-dish meal.

Pozole Rojo

SERVES 8 TO 10

This earthy tasting, full-flavored pork and hominy stew originated in Mexico, although it is now just as popular in the American Southwest. This stew is typically accompanied by an assortment of crunchy toppings (each in a small bowl) and warm tortillas. Ancho chiles (see page 279) are used to create a rich flavor and color in this dish. Mexicans use oregano liberally, but their varieties are different from Mediterranean oregano. If available, use dried Mexican oregano. If using Mediterranean oregano, fresh is a better substitute than dried.

STEW

1 (5-pound) bone-in picnic shoulder roast (see illustration on page 220)
  Salt and ground black pepper
2 tablespoons vegetable oil
2 medium-large onions, chopped coarse (about 3 cups)
5 medium cloves garlic, minced
1 (14½-ounce) can diced tomatoes
1 tablespoon chopped fresh oregano leaves or 1 teaspoon dried Mexican oregano
6 cups homemade chicken stock or canned low-sodium chicken broth
2 ounces dried ancho chiles (about 3 large)
3 (15-ounce) cans white or yellow hominy, drained and rinsed

GARNISHES

2 limes, cut into quarters
½ head romaine lettuce, sliced crosswise into thin strips
6 medium radishes, sliced thin
1 small onion, minced
  Roughly chopped fresh cilantro leaves
  Chopped fresh oregano leaves or dried Mexican oregano
¼ cup pureed ancho chiles (prepared with stew)
  Flour or corn tortillas, warmed

1. Adjust the oven rack to lower-middle position and heat oven to 300 degrees. Trim thick skin and excess fat from meat and cut along muscles to divide the roast into large pieces of various sizes; reserve the

bones. Season the meat generously with salt and pepper.

2. Heat the oil in a large ovenproof Dutch oven over medium heat. Add the onions and ¼ teaspoon salt. Cook, stirring frequently, until the onions have softened, about 4 minutes. Stir in the garlic and cook until fragrant, about 30 seconds.

3. Add the meat and bones and stir often until the meat is no longer pink on the outside, about 8 minutes. Add the tomatoes, oregano, stock, and ½ teaspoon salt. Increase the heat to medium-high and bring to a simmer. With a large spoon, skim off any scum. Cover, place in the oven, and cook until the meat is very tender, about 2 hours.

4. Meanwhile, remove the stems and seeds from the ancho chiles and soak in a medium bowl with 1½ cups boiling water until soft, about 20 minutes. Puree the chiles and soaking liquid in a blender until smooth. Pour the mixture through a strainer and reserve ¼ cup pureed anchos for garnish.

5. Remove the pot from the oven and remove the meat and bones from the stew. Stir in the hominy and the remaining pureed anchos. Cover and bring the stew to a simmer on top of the stove over medium-low heat. Cook until the hominy is hot and the flavors meld, about 30 minutes.

6. Meanwhile, when the meat is cool, shred it using your fingers or the tines of two forks; discard the bones. Stir the shredded meat into the stew. If serving immediately, spoon off any fat that rises to the top and then simmer until the meat is hot, about 10 minutes. (Stew can be covered and refrigerated for up to 3 days. Spoon off the congealed fat and bring back to a simmer over medium-low heat.) Taste to adjust seasonings. Ladle the stew into individual bowls and serve immediately with garnishes.

➤ VARIATION

Pozole Verde

Green pozole is lighter and more refreshing than its red cousin. It is prepared with cilantro, jalapeños, and tomatillos. These ingredients are cooked for a very short time; the flavors are bigger, brighter, and fresher tasting.

Follow the recipe for Pozole Rojo, eliminating the tomatoes and ancho chiles. While the pozole is simmering, puree 1 pound tomatillos, husked, washed, and quartered; 3 medium jalapeños, stemmed, seeded, and chopped coarse; ½ small onion, chopped coarse; and ½ cup water in a blender until smooth, 2 to 3 minutes. Add 2 bunches (about 5 cups) fresh cilantro leaves and stems and puree until smooth, about 2 minutes more. When the pozole comes out of the oven in step 5, remove the meat and stir in the hominy. Simmer as directed. Stir the tomatillo mixture into the stew along with shredded meat and simmer until hot, 10 to 15 minutes. Ladle the stew into individual bowls and serve immediately with garnishes, substituting diced tomato, diced avocado, and minced jalapeño for the cilantro, oregano, and ancho chile puree.

OSSO BUCO

OSSO BUCO, OR ITALIAN BRAISED VEAL shanks, is too venerable a recipe to be fiddled with. With some humility, we headed into the kitchen. We decided the best way to approach the dish was to perfect (and simplify, if possible) the cooking technique and to extract the most flavor from the simple ingredients: veal shanks (which are browned), aromatics (onions, carrots, and celery, all sautéed), and liquids (a blend of wine, stock, and tomatoes).

To start, we gathered three classic recipes and prepared each in the test kitchen. At the tasting, there was little consensus about these recipes, although white wine was clearly preferred to red wine. Tasters did, however, offer similar ideas as to what constituted the perfect osso buco: It would be rich in flavor and color and somewhat brothy but not stewy. This first goal is the reason why we prefer osso buco to veal stews made with boneless shoulder meat. While shoulder meat can be a bit wan, the shank is robust, and the bone adds tremendous flavor to the stewing liquid. With these traits in mind, we created a rough working recipe and set out to explore the two main components in this dish—the veal shanks and the braising liquid.

Most recipes we reviewed called for shanks from the upper portion of the hind leg cut into pieces between 1 and 1½ inches thick. We found that purchasing shanks is tricky, even when we special-ordered them. From one market, we received stunning shanks with a lovely pinkish blush, which were ideal except for the weight. Each shank weighed between 12 and 16 ounces—too large for individual servings. Part of the charm of osso buco is receiving an individual shank as a portion. We concluded that shanks should weigh 8 to 10 ounces (with the bone) and no more. At another market, the shanks were generally in the ideal weight range, but the butchering job was less than perfect. In the same package, shank widths varied from 1 to 2½ inches and were occasionally cut on an extreme bias, making tying difficult (explained shortly) and searing uneven.

The first step, then, was to shop carefully. We found a thickness of 1½ inches and a weight of 8 ounces to be ideal. We made sure all the shanks we bought were close to these specifications, with two nicely cut, flat sides to facilitate browning.

Preparing the meat for braising was the next step. Most recipes called for tying the shanks and dredging them in flour before searing. We found that tying a piece of butcher's twine around the equator of each shank did prevent the meat from falling apart and made for a more attractive presentation. When we skipped this step, the meat fell off the bone and floated about the pot.

Although we do not generally dredge meat in flour before browning, we felt we should at least try it, considering that the majority of osso buco recipes include this step. Tasters felt that the meat floured before searing was gummy and lacked depth. The flour on the meat browns instead of the meat itself, and the flour coating sometimes peeled off during the long braising time.

To develop the best flavor in the shanks, we seasoned them heavily with salt and pepper and seared them until a thick, golden brown crust formed. We seared the shanks in two batches (even if they could all fit in the pan at the same time) so that we could deglaze the pan twice with wine, thereby enriching the braising liquid doubly.

The most difficult part of developing this recipe was attaining an ideal braising liquid and sauce. Braising, by design, is a relatively inexact cooking method because the rates at which the liquid reduces can vary greatly. Some of the initial recipes we tried yielded far too much liquid, which was thin in both flavor and texture. In other cases, the liquid nearly evaporated by the time the meat was tender. We needed to create a foolproof, flavorful braising liquid

and cooking technique that would produce a rich sauce in a suitable volume and would not need a lot of last-minute finessing.

We experimented with numerous techniques to attain our ideal liquid, including reductions before braising and after braising (with the aromatics and without) and a reduction of the wine to a syrup during the deglazing process. In the end, we settled on the easiest method—natural reduction in the oven. The seal on most Dutch ovens is not perfectly tight, so the liquid reduces as the osso buco cooks. We found further simmering on the stovetop to be unnecessary as long as we started out with the right amount of liquid in the pot.

The braising liquid traditionally begins with meat stock and adds white wine and tomatoes. Since few cooks have homemade meat stock on hand and canned versions are horrid, we knew that canned chicken broth would be our likely starting point. Two cups (or one can) seemed like the right amount, and further tests confirmed this. To enrich the flavor of the broth, we used a hefty amount of diced onion, carrot, and celery. Tasters liked the large amount of garlic in one recipe, so we finely chopped about six cloves and added them to the pot prior to the stock. We rounded out the flavors with two bay leaves.

Early on in testing, we hoped to write the recipe in even amounts, using whole vegetables, one can of stock, one bottle of wine, etc. But an entire bottle of wine proved overwhelming. The resulting sauce was dominated by acidity. Some testers also felt that the meat was tougher than previous batches with less wine. We scaled the wine back to 2½ cups, about two-thirds of a bottle, and were happy with the results. More than half of the wine is used to deglaze the pot between searing batches of veal shanks and thus the final dish is not as alcoholic or liquidy as it might seem.

With the wine and stock amounts settled, we had to figure out how to best incorporate tomatoes. Most tasters did not like too much tomato because they felt it overwhelmed the other flavors. Fresh tomatoes are always a gamble outside of the summer months, so we chose canned, diced tomatoes, drained of their juice. This approach worked well, and the tomatoes did not overwhelm the sauce.

We still needed to figure out the ideal braising time. Several sources suggested cooking osso buco to an almost "pulled-pork" consistency. Tasters loved the meat cooked this way, but it was less than attractive—broken down and pot-roast-like. We wanted compact meat firmly attached to the bone, so we cooked the meat just until it was fork-tender but still clinging to the bone. Two hours in the oven produced veal that was meltingly soft but still affixed to the bone. With some of the larger shanks, the cooking time extended to about 2½ hours.

We experimented with oven temperature and found that 325 degrees reduced the braising liquid to the right consistency and did not harm the texture of the meat. While beef stews are best cooked at 300 degrees, veal shanks have so much collagen and connective tissue that they can be braised at a slightly higher temperature.

Just before serving, osso buco is sprinkled with gremolata—a mixture of minced garlic, parsley, and lemon zest. We were surprised to find variations on this classic trio. A number of recipes included orange zest mixed with lemon zest or on its own. Other recipes included anchovies. We tested three gremolatas: one traditional, one with orange zest mixed equally with lemon zest, and one with anchovies. Tasters liked all three but favored the traditional version.

In some recipes the gremolata is used as a garnish, and in others it is added to the pot just before serving. We compromised, stirring half the gremolata into the pot and letting it stand for five minutes so that the flavors of the garlic, lemon, and parsley would permeate the dish. We sprinkled the remaining gremolata on individual servings for a hit of freshness.

Osso Buco

SERVES 6

To keep the meat attached to the shank bone during the long simmering process, tie a piece of twine around the thickest portion of each shank before it is browned. Use a zester, vegetable peeler, or paring knife to remove the zest from a lemon and then mince it with a chef's knife. Osso buco is traditionally served with risotto alla Milanese (saffron-flavored risotto made with meat stock). Mashed potatoes or polenta (see chapter 14) are excellent options as well.

OSSO BUCO

6   veal shanks (8 to 10 ounces and 1½ inches thick each), dried thoroughly with paper towels and tied around equator with butcher's twine
     Salt and ground black pepper

6   tablespoons vegetable oil

2½   cups dry white wine

2   medium onions, cut into ½-inch dice (about 2 cups)

2   medium carrots, cut into ½-inch dice (about 1½ cups)

2   medium stalks celery, cut into ½-inch dice (about 1 cup)

6   medium cloves garlic, minced

2   cups homemade chicken stock or canned low-sodium chicken broth

2   small bay leaves

1   (14½-ounce) can diced tomatoes, drained

GREMOLATA

3   medium cloves garlic, minced

2   teaspoons minced lemon zest

¼   cup minced fresh parsley leaves

1. **FOR THE OSSO BUCO:** Adjust the oven rack to the lower-middle position and heat the oven to 325 degrees.

2. Heat a large ovenproof Dutch oven over medium-high heat until it is very hot, about 3 minutes. Meanwhile, sprinkle both sides of the shanks generously with salt and pepper. Add 2 tablespoons oil to the Dutch oven and swirl to coat the pan bottom. Place 3 shanks in a single layer in the Dutch oven and cook until they are golden brown on one side, about 5 minutes. Using tongs, flip the shanks and cook on the second side until golden brown, about 5 minutes longer. Transfer the shanks to a bowl and set aside. Off heat, add ½ cup wine to the Dutch oven, scraping the bottom with a wooden spoon to loosen any browned bits. Pour the liquid into the bowl with the shanks. Return pot to medium-high heat, add 2 tablespoons oil, and heat the oil until it is shimmering. Brown the remaining shanks, about 5 minutes per side, and transfer to the bowl with the other shanks. Off heat, add another 1 cup wine to the pot, scraping the bottom to loosen browned bits. Pour the liquid into the bowl with the shanks.

3. Set the pot over medium heat. Add the remaining 2 tablespoons oil and heat until the oil is shimmering. Add the onions, carrots, and celery and cook, stirring occasionally, until soft and lightly browned, about 9 minutes. Add the garlic and cook until lightly browned, about 1 minute longer. Increase the heat to high and stir in the chicken stock, juices from the veal shanks, and bay leaves. Add the tomato and veal shanks to pot (the liquid should just cover the shanks). Cover the pot and place it in the oven. Cook the shanks until the meat is easily pierced with a fork, but not falling off bone, about 2 hours. (Osso buco can be refrigerated for up to 2 days. Bring to a simmer over medium–low heat.)

4. FOR THE GREMOLATA: Combine the garlic, lemon zest, and parsley in a small bowl. Stir half of the gremolata into the pot, reserving the rest for garnish. Adjust the seasonings with salt and pepper to taste. Let the osso buco stand, uncovered, for 5 minutes.

5. Using tongs, remove the shanks from the Dutch oven, cut off and discard the butcher's twine, and place 1 veal shank in each bowl. Ladle some braising liquid over each shank and sprinkle with a portion of the remaining gremolata. Serve immediately.

CASSOULET

CASSOULET ORIGINATED IN LANGUEDOC, France, and each area of the region touts its version of the recipe as "the real thing." All versions contain beans, but that is where the agreement ends. Some prefer pork loin in their cassoulet, others use a shoulder of lamb, while still others use a combination of both. Mutton, duck, pheasant, garlic sausage, and even fish can be found in the different variations.

The best known and most often replicated type of cassoulet hails from Toulouse. This cassoulet must start with the preparation of confit. Meat or poultry, most often goose legs (the region of Toulouse also houses the foie gras industry, so goose is plentiful), is placed in a large container, sprinkled heavily with salt, and cured for 24 to 48 hours. This both preserves and tenderizes the meat. After this sojourn in salt, the meat is slowly simmered in its own fat, so that the flavor of the fat penetrates the spaces previously occupied by the juices. The finished confit may be used immediately or stored in an airtight container, covered in its own fat to prevent contamination.

But the intricacy of cassoulet doesn't end with the confit. Both pork loin and mutton must be slow-roasted for hours to become fully tender, and garlic sausages freshly made. The beans must be presoaked and then simmered with pork rinds to develop flavor. Finally, the entire mixture has to be combined in an earthenware pot and placed in a low-temperature oven to simmer slowly for several hours. A topping of fresh bread crumbs finishes the dish.

The result is nothing short of divine. But while this classic French dish can be replicated at restaurants, it is definitely not a dish for the casual home cook. The time investment alone is impractical, and it can be difficult to achieve a perfect balance of flavors. On more than one occasion we have eaten cassoulets that were overwhelmed by salt or swimming in fat, most often because of the confit and sausages. But we love this dish so much that we decided it would be worth the effort to try to streamline it without compromising its essential nature.

We accepted the hardest of the challenges first: conquer the confit. We eliminated the confit made from scratch as far too time-consuming. Assessing the other options, we created three cassoulets. One was prepared with braised duck leg confit (goose leg confit is less widely available) purchased through our butcher. The others we made with no confit at all, starting one version with sautéed and braised duck legs and the other with sautéed and braised chicken legs, which we most wanted to use in our recipe because they're so easy to find in the supermarket. The results were disheartening, although not surprising. The cassoulet made with the purchased confit was the clear favorite. Those made without it produced dishes more reminiscent of duck and chicken stews.

Unfortunately, ready-made confit is not widely available, so we wanted to develop a recipe that wouldn't rely on it. We arrived at the solution to the problem with some help from the confit itself.

Because confit is salt-cured and then cooked in its own fat, it retains an intense duck flavor when added to the cassoulet, contributing a rich, slightly smoky flavor that was noticeably absent from the dishes prepared with the sautéed and braised duck and chicken. The texture of the dish made with confit was superior as well, the flesh plump with flavor yet tender to the bite. The sautéed and braised duck and chicken became tough and gave up all of their flavor to the surrounding liquid. Taking an educated guess, we decided to adopt an approach often used in our test kitchen and brine the chicken. Because we had found when making other dishes that brining resulted in poultry that was both more moist and more flavorful, we reasoned that brining the chicken might bring it closer to the tender texture of confit. To approximate the confit's light smokiness, we decided to cook the legs briefly in bacon fat.

What resulted was just what we were hoping for: a suitable substitute for duck confit. The bacon added a smoky flavor, and it enhanced the flavors of the pork and sausage added later. The texture was spot-on for the confit; the chicken was plump and juicy, and the liquid was well-seasoned because of the brine. With this "mock" confit in hand, we proceeded.

Our next tests involved figuring out which meats to use and how to avoid the issue of slow-roasting. We wanted to be true to the original recipe and use either fresh pork or lamb. We decided to try stewing the meat in liquid entirely on top of the stove. This method yielded great results in terms of tenderness, but the meat had none of the depth of flavor that occurs with roasting. Searing the meat in some of the rendered bacon fat that we had used with the chicken legs took care of that problem.

Because we were now stewing the meat, we needed to use cuts that were appropriate for this method. We tried pork loin, the choice in so many cassoulet recipes, but the loin became waterlogged and tasteless during stewing. A suggestion from our butcher led us to try a blade-end roast, the part of the loin closest to the shoulder. This cut has more internal fat than the center loin and retained the moisture and flavor that was lost with the other cut. To facilitate quicker cooking, we cut the roast into 1-inch pieces. We put the lamb through similar tests. Lamb shoulder is the best cut for stewing, but it can be difficult to find in markets. We bought instead thick lamb shoulder chops, which we cut into 1-inch pieces. Finally, perfectly tender meat without the effort of roasting.

We tested four bean varieties, and the winner was the pale green flageolet bean. These small, French kidney-shaped beans have a creamy, tender texture and delicate flavor that perfectly enhance the cassoulet. We also parcooked the beans on top of the stove along with the rendered bacon fat and the aromatics to let them absorb as much flavor as possible in little time, an effort to duplicate the depth of flavor in the original.

After ruling out the use of hard-to-find French sausages, we found that both kielbasa and andouille sausages intensified the smokiness that we desired. We especially like the andouille sausage with the lamb and so decided to make this a variation to the master recipe, which we made with pork and kielbasa.

With the major problems out of the way, we were able to concentrate on streamlining the technique used to cook the dish. This proved to be quite simple. With the chicken, meat, and beans now modified for cooking on the stovetop, oven-braising became unnecessary. Cooking the dish entirely on the stove at a low simmer, with a quick finish in the oven to brown the bread crumbs, produced perfect results in a short amount of time. Stovetop cooking also necessitated the use of only one pot, down from the two to three used for the original. At last we had it: a quick cassoulet that was worthy of the name.

Simplified Cassoulet with Pork and Kielbasa

SERVES 8

For the most time-efficient preparation of the cassoulet, while the chicken is brining and the beans are simmering, prepare the remaining ingredients. If you can't find a boneless blade-end pork loin roast, use boneless Boston butt.

CHICKEN

- 1 cup kosher salt or ½ cup table salt
- 1 cup sugar
- 10 bone-in chicken thighs (about 3½ pounds), skin removed

TOPPING

- 6 slices good-quality white sandwich bread, cut into ½-inch dice (about 3 cups)
- 3 tablespoons unsalted butter, melted

CASSOULET

4	slices bacon (about 4 ounces)
I	pound dried flageolet or great Northern beans, picked over and rinsed
I	medium onion, peeled and left whole, plus I small onion, chopped
4	medium cloves garlic, 2 peeled and left whole, 2 peeled and minced
	Vegetable oil
I	pound boneless blade-end pork loin roast, trimmed of excess fat and silver skin and cut into 1-inch pieces
I	(14½-ounce) can diced tomatoes, drained
I	tablespoon tomato paste
I	tablespoon minced fresh thyme leaves
I	bay leaf
¼	teaspoon ground cloves
	Ground black pepper
1¾	cups homemade chicken stock or canned low-sodium chicken broth
I	cup dry white wine
½	pound kielbasa, halved lengthwise and cut into ¼-inch slices

1. FOR THE CHICKEN: In a gallon-sized zipper-lock plastic bag, dissolve the salt and sugar in 1 quart cold water. Add the chicken, pressing out as much air as possible, seal, and refrigerate until fully seasoned, about 1 hour. Remove the chicken from the brine, rinse thoroughly under cold water, and pat dry with paper towels. Refrigerate until ready to use.

2. FOR THE TOPPING: While the chicken is brining, adjust the oven rack to the upper-middle position and heat oven to 400 degrees. Mix the bread cubes and butter in a small baking dish. Bake, tossing occasionally, until light golden brown and crisp, 8 to 12 minutes. Cool to room temperature and set aside.

3. FOR THE CASSOULET: Cook the bacon slices over medium heat in a large ovenproof Dutch oven until just beginning to crisp and most of the fat has rendered, 5 to 6 minutes. Leaving the bacon slices in the pot, pour the bacon grease into a heatproof measuring cup and reserve. Return the pot to the heat and add the beans, 10 cups water, whole onion, and whole garlic cloves. Bring to a boil over medium-high heat, reduce the heat to low, cover partially, and simmer, stirring occasionally, until the beans are partially cooked and almost tender, 40 to 50 minutes. Reserving 1½ cups cooking liquid, drain the beans. Discard the onion, garlic, and bacon.

3. Add vegetable oil to reserved bacon grease to equal ¼ cup. In the now-empty pot, heat the oil mixture over medium-high heat until shimmering. Add half of chicken thighs, fleshy-side down; cook until first side is lightly browned, 3 to 4 minutes. Using tongs, turn the chicken and cook until lightly browned on second side, 2 to 3 minutes longer. Transfer the chicken to a large plate; repeat with the remaining thighs and set aside.

4. Drain off all but 2 tablespoons fat from the pot. Return the pot to medium heat, add the pork pieces, and cook, stirring occasionally, until lightly browned, about 5 minutes. Add the chopped onion and cook, stirring occasionally, until softened, 3 to 4 minutes. Add the minced garlic, tomatoes, tomato paste, thyme, bay leaf, cloves, and pepper to taste and cook until fragrant, about 1 minute. Stir in the chicken stock, wine, and 1 cup of reserved bean cooking liquid. Increase the heat to medium-high and bring to a boil, scraping up the browned bits from bottom of the pot with a wooden spoon. Add the chicken and beans. If the liquid does not fully cover the chicken and beans, add the remaining ½ cup reserved bean cooking liquid. Reduce the heat to low, cover, and simmer until the chicken is cooked through and the beans are tender, about 40 minutes. (Cassoulet can be covered and refrigerated for up to 2 days. Bring to a simmer over medium-low heat.)

5. Meanwhile, adjust the oven rack to the lower-middle position and heat the oven to 425 degrees. Off heat, gently stir in the kielbasa, and sprinkle the surface with bread crumbs. Bake, uncovered, until the topping is golden brown, about 10 minutes. Let the cassoulet rest 10 minutes, then serve.

➤ VARIATION

Simplified Cassoulet with Lamb and Andouille Sausage

Follow recipe for Simplified Cassoulet with Pork and Kielbasa, substituting 2 pounds lamb shoulder chops, trimmed, boned, and cut into 1-inch pieces, for pork, and ½ pound andouille for kielbasa.

10
CHICKEN STEWS

THREE STYLES OF CHICKEN STEW ARE COVERED in this chapter. The most traditional calls for bone-in parts (after extensive testing, our preference is for thighs), which are simmered (usually with vegetables) in a combination of wine, stock, and/or tomatoes. This technique yields a fair amount of thickened sauce, which can be used to moisten the chicken as well as an accompanying starch.

A second style starts with a whole bird that is poached to make stock. The meat is removed from the bird and then used with the stock as the basis for the stew. We find this method rather laborious and reserve it for dishes that must be made with boneless chicken meat, such as chicken and dumplings. It's simply too difficult to eat dumplings in a stew that contains bones.

A third style of chicken stew also starts with a whole bird. But in this case, the bird is cut up, browned, and then poached or simmered with a small amount of liquid to create a fricassee. The sauce for a fricassee is usually fairly thick and not terribly abundant. (See "What is a Fricassee?" on page 243 for more details.)

No matter which kind of chicken stew you make, try to start with the best-tasting chicken you can buy. (For the findings of our tasting of leading brands, see page 20.) Since the liquid component in a chicken stew is relatively small, you can generally use canned chicken broth in these recipes.

Hearty Chicken Stew

CHICKEN STEW IS A BIT HARD TO DEFINE. Say "beef stew" and most everyone can imagine large, boneless chunks of browned beef floating in a rich, dark sauce along with some vegetables. But what, exactly, is chicken stew? Is it a cut-up chicken that is browned and then braised? Is it a cut-up chicken that is stewed (to make homemade stock) and then cooled so the meat can be torn from the bones? Is it boneless breasts or thighs cut into chunks and browned and stewed like beef?

We started with a whole chicken that was cut up, browned, and then simmered in water to make stock. The liquid was strained and the meat removed from the breasts, legs, and thighs. This preparation produced a stew without bones, and the homemade stock was a nice bonus. But the dish required a lot of effort (pulling the meat off each bone is tedious), and the results were good but not great.

Our next thought was to follow our master recipe for meat stew, browning a cut-up chicken instead of cubes of boneless beef, lamb, or pork. We browned the chicken parts, removed them from the pot, sautéed some aromatic vegetables, deglazed (released the brown bits from) the pot with some wine, added stock, then simmered the vegetables and chicken until everything was tender. We encountered several problems with this method. The skin was crisp after browning, but it became flabby and not very appealing after stewing in liquid for the necessary half hour or so. In addition, the wings were unappetizing, containing mostly inedible skin and very little meat. Finally, the breast pieces were much too large to fit in a bowl (each piece would have to be cut in half crosswise), and they dried out during the stewing process.

We tried this recipe again using just breasts and legs. We cut the split breasts in half, browned all the parts, pulled off the skin, and then added the legs to the stew followed by the breasts. Although the breasts were less dry and stringy, we felt that the dark meat pieces, with their extra fat and connective tissue, were better suited to stewing. They had much more flavor, and their texture was more appealing. In addition, our tasters preferred the meatier thighs to the drumsticks, which tend to have more bone. The thighs are also easier to eat than the drumsticks, with the meat easily separating from the bones. We decided to abandon the breasts and drumsticks and concentrate on a stew made with thighs only.

This last test had revealed something interesting about the thighs. Removing the skin after the parts were browned was a must. The stew liquid was much less fatty, and since the skin was very soft and flabby and not really edible, there seemed little reason to serve it to people. We wondered if we should just start with boneless, skinless thighs—it certainly would be easier to eat a stew without bones. Unfortunately, when we browned boneless, skinless thighs, the outer layer of meat became tough and dry. Also, the skinless thighs tended to stick to the pan, even when we added quite a bit of oil. The skin acts as a cushion between the meat and pan.

With the skin on, we found we needed only 1 teaspoon of oil to brown the chicken. Putting the chicken in the pan with the skin-side down renders the fat quickly, and keeping the oil to a minimum allows for a stronger chicken flavor in the final dish. Since the skin will be discarded, the thighs must be seasoned liberally or the stew will be bland.

We had decided on the style of chicken stew and for the most part liked the master recipe for beef stew adapted to chicken. But we found that we could not simply take the beef stew recipe wholesale and just add chicken instead of beef.

First of all, beef stews usually taste best with red wine. Chicken generally matches up better with white wine. Also, because chicken requires less cooking time, we found that a stew made with 1 cup of wine and 2 cups of stock (as suggested in our meat stew recipes) was too alcoholic. Cutting the wine back to ½ cup and increasing the stock to 2½ cups keeps the stew from being too boozy. We also found that chicken's milder flavor calls for less aggressive seasoning. Therefore, we used half as much bay leaf and thyme as in our beef stew recipe.

Like beef stew, chicken stew responds best to subboiling temperatures, which are easier to maintain in a low oven. We had very inconsistent results on the stovetop. In some cases, the chicken was done in just 25 minutes, but at other times the chicken needed 40 minutes to cook through, despite the fact that the flame was set at the same temperature during all these tests. Oven heat is more consistent and surrounds the pot. As a result, the vegetables softened more evenly when we finished the stew in the oven.

Because chicken requires so much less time to cook than meat, vegetables are added before the chicken, not after. For instance, the carrots and potatoes get a 10-minute head start on the chicken so that they will be tender by the time the chicken is cooked through.

Hearty Chicken Stew
SERVES 4 TO 6

We recommend using bone-in chicken thighs in this recipe. As a second option, you may use boneless, skinless chicken thighs, although the outer layer of meat will toughen during browning. To substitute boneless, skinless thighs, add a few more tablespoons of vegetable oil during browning to keep them from sticking. You may need to use a metal spatula to loosen browned skinless thighs from the pan.

8	bone-in, skin-on chicken thighs (about 3 pounds), trimmed of excess skin and fat
	Salt and ground black pepper
I	teaspoon vegetable oil
I	large onion, chopped coarse
2	medium cloves garlic, minced
3	tablespoons flour
½	cup white wine
2½	cups homemade chicken stock or canned low-sodium chicken broth
I	bay leaf
½	teaspoon dried thyme
4	large carrots, peeled and sliced ¼ inch thick
4	medium red potatoes (about 1½ pounds), peeled and cut into ½-inch dice
I	cup frozen peas (about 6 ounces), thawed
¼	cup minced fresh parsley leaves

1. Adjust the oven rack to the lower-middle position and heat the oven to 300 degrees. Season the chicken liberally with salt and pepper to taste. Heat the oil in a large ovenproof Dutch oven over medium-high heat until shimmering but not smoking, about

SKINNING BROWNED CHICKEN

Once the chicken thighs have been browned and cooled, grasp the skin from one end and pull to separate the skin from the meat. Discard the skin.

2 minutes. Add four chicken thighs, skin-side down, and cook, not moving them until the skin is crisp and well-browned, about 5 minutes. Using tongs, flip the chicken and brown on the second side, about 5 minutes longer. Transfer the browned chicken to a large plate. Brown the remaining chicken thighs, transfer them to the plate, and set aside. When the chicken has cooled, remove and discard the skin (see illustration on page 231). With a spoon, remove and discard all but 1 tablespoon fat from the pan.

2. Add the onion to the empty Dutch oven and sauté over medium heat until softened, 4 to 5 minutes. Add the garlic and continue to cook for 30 seconds. Stir in the flour and cook until lightly colored, 1 to 2 minutes. Add the wine, scraping up any browned bits stuck to the pot. Add the stock, bay leaf, and thyme, and bring to a simmer. Add the carrots and potatoes, return to a simmer, and cook for 10 minutes. Add the chicken pieces and accumulated juices, submerging the chicken in the liquid. Return to a simmer, cover, and place the pot in the oven. Cook until the chicken is done, about 30 minutes. Remove the pot from the oven. (Stew can be covered and refrigerated for up to 3 days. Bring to a simmer over medium-low heat.)

3. Add the peas, cover, and let stand for 5 minutes. Stir in the parsley, discard the bay leaf, and adjust the seasonings. Serve immediately.

CRUMBLING SAFFRON THREADS

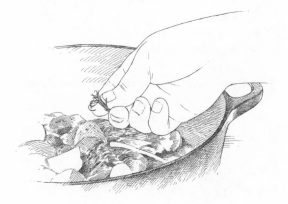

To release their flavor, crumble saffron threads between your fingers right over the stew pot.

➤ VARIATION

Chicken Stew with Leeks, Potatoes, and Saffron

Saffron gives this stew a yellow-orange hue and a rich, earthy flavor. Buy saffron threads (not powder), and crumble them yourself for the best flavor.

8	bone-in chicken thighs (about 3 pounds), trimmed of excess skin and fat
	Salt and ground black pepper
1	teaspoon vegetable oil
4	large leeks, light green and white parts, sliced thin (see illustrations on page 124 to clean)
2	medium cloves garlic, minced
3	tablespoons flour
½	cup white wine
2 ½	cups homemade chicken stock or canned low-sodium chicken broth
1	bay leaf
½	teaspoon dried thyme
¼	teaspoon saffron threads
4	large carrots, peeled and sliced ¼ inch thick
4	medium red potatoes (about 1 ½ pounds), peeled and cut into ½-inch dice
¼	cup minced fresh parsley leaves

1. Adjust the oven rack to the lower-middle position and heat the oven to 300 degrees. Season the chicken liberally with salt and pepper to taste. Heat the oil in a large ovenproof Dutch oven over medium-high heat until shimmering but not smoking, about 2 minutes. Add four chicken thighs, skin-side down, and cook, not moving them until the skin is crisp and well-browned, about 5 minutes. Using tongs, flip the chicken and brown on the second side, about 5 minutes longer. Transfer the browned chicken to a large plate. Brown the remaining chicken thighs, transfer them to the plate, and set aside. When the chicken has cooled, remove and discard the skin (see illustration on page 231). With a spoon, remove and discard all but 1 tablespoon fat from the pan.

2. Add the leeks to the empty Dutch oven and sauté over medium heat until softened, 4 to 5 minutes. Add the garlic and continue to cook for 30 seconds. Stir in the flour and cook until lightly colored, 1 to 2 minutes. Add the wine, scraping up any

browned bits stuck to the pot. Add the stock, bay leaf, and thyme, and bring to a simmer. Crumble the saffron threads between your fingers right over the pot to release flavor (see illustration on page 232). Add the carrots and potatoes, return to a simmer, and cook for 10 minutes. Add the chicken pieces and accumulated juices, submerging the chicken in the liquid. Return to a simmer, cover, and place the pot in the oven. Cook until the chicken is done, about 30 minutes. Remove the pot from the oven. (Stew can be covered and refrigerated for up to 3 days. Bring to a simmer over medium-low heat.)

3. Stir in the parsley, discard the bay leaf, and adjust the seasonings. Serve immediately.

CHICKEN CACCIATORE

CACCIATORE, WHICH MEANS "HUNTER-STYLE" in Italian, originally referred to a simple method of cooking fresh-killed game. Game hen or rabbit would be sautéed along with wild mushrooms, onions, and other foraged vegetables and then braised with wine or stock. Unfortunately, when translated by American cooks, cacciatore mutated into a generic pasty "red sauce" dish, often featuring sauces that are greasy and overly sweet along with dry, overcooked chicken. We knew there was a really good version of this dish to be found, and we were determined to discover it.

From the beginning we knew that we wanted a sauce that was just substantial enough to cling to the chicken; we didn't want the chicken to be swimming in broth, nor did we want a sauce reminiscent of Spackle. Another thing we wanted was a streamlined cooking method. This cacciatore would be easy enough to prepare on a weeknight and, we hoped, would necessitate the use of only one pot.

We began our work with a blind taste test. We gathered an abundance of recipes (every "Italian" cookbook seems to include some form of cacciatore), then selected what seemed to be the more "authentic" versions (no boneless, skinless chicken breasts, no jarred tomato sauces) written by prominent Italian cooks. All four of these recipes started with the same basic preparation, one that we would

also use for our working recipe. Chicken (a whole chicken cut up, in all but one of the recipes) was dredged in flour and sautéed in olive oil, then removed from the pan, which was then deglazed (lifting the browned bits from the pan bottom with a liquid) with either wine or stock. Vegetables—most often tomatoes, onions, and mushrooms—were added to the braise, and the dish was then left to cook until the meat was fall-apart tender.

As we reviewed the tasters' notes from this trial run, we noticed that two problems were common to all the recipes. For one, tasters found the dishes to be too greasy (nearly an inch of oil floated at the top of one dish), for another, they disliked the presence of chicken skin in the final product. The skin, which was crisp after the initial sauté, had become soggy and unappealing.

All of the recipes except one had other serious problems as well. One was too vegetal, another included black olives that proved too dominant a flavor, and a third had no tomatoes, an omission that tasters thought took the dish too far from what Americans consider to be a classic cacciatore. The fourth recipe was much more promising. It started off with chicken thighs rather than a whole, cut-up chicken and used a mixture made from equal parts flour and softened butter (beurre manié) to thicken the sauce. The dark thigh meat remained much more moist and plump than the fibrous, flavorless breast meat we had ended up with in the other recipes. (It was also much easier to simply buy a package of thighs than to cut up a whole chicken.) The thighs also gave the braising liquid a more intense flavor. Unfortunately, the beurre manié overthickened the sauce, giving it a gravylike consistency.

From the test results we were able to come to a few conclusions and devise a working recipe. Chicken thighs were in, but the flabby skin was out, and this, we hoped, would reduce the overabundance of grease in the dish. Wine (whether to use red or white was still to be determined) was the liquid of choice for braising, and the additional vegetables needed to be kept to a minimum—a combination of onions, mushrooms, and tomatoes was all that would be needed.

We assumed that the flabby skin issue could be solved by using skinless chicken thighs. But that assumption proved to be untrue. A batch made with skinless thighs, while good, lacked the intense flavor of the batches made with skin-on chicken. The rendered fat and juice from the chicken skin caramelized on the pan bottom, which, when deglazed, made a big contribution to the flavor of the sauce. In addition, the skin protected the flesh of the chicken from direct contact with the high heat, preventing the meat from forming a fibrous crust. As with our hearty chicken stew, we needed to lose the chicken skin only after its fat had been rendered.

We found that pulling the skin off the thighs after the initial sauté cost the dish none of its flavor while allowing us to serve the dish sans skin. Removing the skin before braising also eliminated the problem of excess grease. The fat from the skin is first rendered at a high heat, which helps to keep the skin from sticking to the pan bottom. The extra fat is then disposed of, but the caramelized bits are left behind for deglazing.

Next came the braising medium. Preliminary testing suggested that red wine would prevail. Most tasters liked its bold presence, although some thought the hearty flavor of the wine was a bit too harsh. We tried cutting the wine with small amounts of water, dry vermouth, and chicken stock and found that the latter buffered the strong presence of the wine and rounded out the flavors. (Since some tasters preferred the lighter, brothier taste of the version made with white wine, we decided to offer that as a variation on the master recipe.)

At this point the sauce was rich in flavor but lacking in substance. Truthfully, it was more like a broth; the vegetables and chicken were lost in the liquid. We remembered that the flour used to dredge the chicken thighs had been thrown away with the skin. We would have to introduce it somewhere else. A beurre manié was too complicated for this streamlined dish, so we ended up adding a little flour directly to the vegetables as they were finishing their sauté. The sauce was now silky and robust. On a whim we threw in a piece of a Parmesan cheese rind, an option we had noticed in one of the recipes tested earlier. The sauce, very good before, now surpassed all of our expectations. It was now substantial, lavish, and amply flavored.

We were finally down to the details of finishing.

Portobello mushrooms, bursting with the essence of red wine, added an earthy flavor and meaty chew. We also found that just about any herb would complement the recipe; we added sage just before serving for a mellow, woodsy flavor.

Chicken Cacciatore with Portobellos and Sage

SERVES 4

The Parmesan cheese rind is optional, but we highly recommend it for the robust, savory flavor it adds to the dish. An equal amount of minced fresh rosemary can be substituted for the sage. See page 202 for information about choosing a red wine for use in this dish.

8	bone-in chicken thighs (about 3 pounds), trimmed of excess skin and fat
	Salt and ground black pepper
1	teaspoon olive oil
1	medium onion, chopped small
6	ounces (3 medium) portobello mushroom caps, wiped clean and cut into ¾-inch dice
4	medium cloves garlic, minced
1½	tablespoons all-purpose flour
1½	cups dry red wine
½	cup homemade chicken stock or canned low-sodium chicken broth
1	(14½-ounce) can diced tomatoes, drained
2	teaspoons minced fresh thyme leaves
1	Parmesan cheese rind, about 4 by 2 inches (optional)
2	teaspoons minced fresh sage leaves

1. Adjust the oven rack to the lower-middle position and heat the oven to 300 degrees. Season the chicken liberally with salt and pepper to taste. Heat the oil in a large ovenproof Dutch oven over medium-high heat until shimmering but not smoking, about 2 minutes. Add four chicken thighs, skin-side down, and cook, not moving them until the skin is crisp and well-browned, about 5 minutes. Using tongs, flip the chicken and brown on the second side, about 5 minutes longer. Transfer the browned chicken to a large plate. Brown the remaining chicken thighs, transfer them to the plate, and set aside. When the chicken has cooled, remove and discard the skin (see illustration

on page 231). With a spoon, remove and discard all but 1 tablespoon fat from the pan.

2. Add the onion, mushrooms, and ½ teaspoon salt to the empty Dutch oven. Sauté over medium-high heat, stirring occasionally, until moisture evaporates and the vegetables begin to brown, 6 to 8 minutes. Add the garlic and sauté until fragrant, about 30 seconds. Stir in the flour and cook, stirring constantly, for about 1 minute. Add the wine, scraping the pot bottom with a wooden spoon to loosen the brown bits. Stir in the stock, tomatoes, thyme, cheese rind (if using), ½ teaspoon salt (omit salt if using cheese rind), and pepper to taste. Add the chicken pieces and accumulated juices, submerging the chicken in the liquid. Bring to a simmer, cover, and place the pot in the oven. Cook until the chicken is done, about 30 minutes. Remove the pot from the oven. (Stew can be covered and refrigerated for up to 3 days. Bring to a simmer over medium-low heat.)

3. Discard the cheese rind, stir in the sage, and adjust the seasonings. Serve immediately.

➤ VARIATION

Chicken Cacciatore with White Wine and Tarragon

This variation is based on chicken chasseur, the French version of Italian cacciatore.

Mince 3 large shallots; clean 10 ounces white mushrooms and quarter if large, halve if medium, or leave whole if small. Follow recipe for Chicken Cacciatore with Portobellos and Sage, substituting shallots for onions, white mushrooms for portobellos, dry white wine for red wine, and 2 teaspoons minced fresh tarragon for sage.

CHICKEN PAPRIKASH

THIS HUNGARIAN SPECIALTY HAS BEEN popular in this country for decades, and with good reason. The chicken is succulent, the flavors mellow and a bit sweet, and the color a vibrant red. Sour cream makes the sauce comforting but not overly rich, while paprika gives the stew its characteristic appearance and flavor.

Paprikash is a simple stew, but you wouldn't know it from all the recipes out there. Too many recipes have lengthy ingredient lists, and the resulting stews taste muddled. Our goal was to keep the focus on the main flavors—the chicken, the sour cream, and the paprika, with vegetables in the background. Another common problem with this dish is the sauce. In many versions, the sauce is thick and gluey. Ideally, the sauce will have the right consistency to coat egg noodles. A sauce that is too thick can't do this.

We began our tests by examining the chicken component. After several tests, we concluded that paprikash (like other chicken stews) is best made with bone-in thighs. White meat dried out in our tests, and drumsticks were not terribly meaty. We decided to replace the whole cut-up chicken called for in most recipes with eight thighs.

We focused on the paprika next (see page 236 for more details). Many recipes suggest seasoning the chicken with salt and paprika before browning. We tried this approach and were disappointed with the results. The wonderful paprika aroma that initially filled the kitchen soon turned to a smell of singed peppers. The flavor of the finished dish was bitter, and the color had morphed from bright red to burnt sienna. We decided to season the chicken with salt and black pepper and add the paprika later.

With our chicken browned and reserved, we started to test various vegetable options, including onions, peppers, carrots, tomatoes, and mushrooms. Onions were a must—their pungent flavor balanced the sweetness of the paprika. Tasters found both red and green peppers to be welcome additions to the pot. They enhanced the natural sweetness of the paprika and worked well with the onions and chicken. Long strips of peppers looked out of place in this dish, so we cut each cleaned pepper in half before slicing it thin. These shorter strips softened a bit more in the pot and proved easier to eat.

Tasters rejected carrots and mushrooms. Although tasty additions, neither seemed essential and so both were vetoed. Tomatoes, however, were deemed crucial to achieving a proper balance between the sweet and acidic components in this dish. Tomato paste muddied the colors and flavors, but tasters responded favorably to the addition of canned diced tomatoes. We found it best to drain the tomatoes so that their juice did not overwhelm the flavors of the other vegetables.

With the vegetables in place, we focused on the seasonings. We found it best to add the paprika to the pot once the onions and peppers had softened. A quick sauté in oil brought out the full flavor of this spice. We tried adding some garlic with the paprika but found its flavor oddly out of place with the mellow sweet flavors in paprikash. Tasters felt that a little dried marjoram was a worthy addition. We also added some flour to the pot at this point to help thicken the stew. A tablespoon of flour provided just enough thickening power.

Although the drained tomatoes provide a little moisture, most paprikash recipes call for some wine to deglaze the pan. We found red wine too harsh. White wine worked better with the other flavors.

Sour cream is the final component, added only when the chicken has completely stewed. It gives the sauce body and tang and has a thickening effect as well. Some sources suggest using heavy cream and sour cream. Although we liked the effect that the heavy cream had on the consistency of the sauce (it was velvety and smooth), we missed the tang of recipes made with just sour cream. In the end, we decided to finish the stew with ⅓ cup of sour cream.

If sour cream is added directly to the pot it can curdle. Tempering the sour cream (stirring some of the hot liquid from the stew pot together with the sour cream in a small bowl, then adding the warmed mixture to the pot) will prevent curdling. Once the sour cream goes into the pot, the stew should be served promptly.

INGREDIENTS: Paprika

Most cooks are familiar with paprika. They sprinkle this bright red spice made from dried red peppers on foods for visual appeal. They don't really think of paprika in terms of flavor, and that's a shame.

In Hungary, paprika is used as much for flavor as for color. Sweet Hungarian paprika has an earthy, mild flavor. (A hot version is not appropriate in most stews.) What makes sweet Hungarian paprika so good? Most experts cite the fact that a blend of mild peppers is used to make paprika in Hungary. In our kitchen, we found that stews made with Hungarian paprika had a fuller, more complex flavor than stews made with paprika from Spain or California.

Chicken Paprikash
SERVES 4

In this rendition of the Hungarian classic, the natural juices of chicken, bell peppers, onion, and tomatoes are released while stewing and then enriched with sour cream to create a dish especially comforting in cold weather. Use genuine sweet Hungarian paprika for the best flavor and most vibrant color. Buttered egg noodles are our favorite accompaniment, but rice or mashed potatoes are also good options.

8	bone-in chicken thighs (about 3 pounds), trimmed of excess skin and fat
	Salt and ground black pepper
I	teaspoon vegetable oil
I	large onion, halved and sliced thin
I	large red bell pepper, stemmed, seeded, halved widthwise, and cut into thin strips
I	large green bell pepper, stemmed, seeded, halved widthwise, and cut into thin strips
4	tablespoons paprika
¼	teaspoon dried marjoram
I	tablespoon flour
½	cup dry white wine
I	(14½-ounce) can diced tomatoes, drained
⅓	cup sour cream
2	tablespoons chopped fresh parsley leaves

1. Adjust the oven rack to the lower-middle position and heat the oven to 300 degrees. Season the chicken liberally with salt and pepper to taste. Heat the oil in a large ovenproof Dutch oven over medium-high heat until shimmering but not smoking, about 2 minutes. Add four chicken thighs, skin-side down, and cook, not moving them until the skin is crisp and well-browned, about 5 minutes. Using tongs, flip the chicken and brown on the second side, about 5 minutes longer. Transfer the browned chicken to a large plate. Brown the remaining chicken thighs, transfer them to the plate, and set aside. When the chicken has cooled, remove and discard the skin (see illustration on page 231). With a spoon, remove and discard all but 1 tablespoon fat from the pan.

2. Add the onion to the empty Dutch oven and sauté over medium heat until softened, about 5 minutes. Add the red and green peppers and sauté until the onions are browned and the peppers softened,

about 3 minutes. Stir in the paprika, marjoram, and flour and cook, stirring constantly, until fragrant, about 1 minute. Add the wine, scraping the pot bottom with a wooden spoon to loosen the brown bits. Stir in the tomatoes and 1 teaspoon salt. Add the chicken pieces and accumulated juices, nestling the chicken under the onion and peppers. Bring the liquid to a simmer, cover, and place the pot in the oven. Cook until the chicken is done, about 30 minutes. Remove the pot from the oven. (Stew can be covered and refrigerated for up to 3 days. Bring to a simmer over medium-low heat.)

3. Place the sour cream in a small bowl. Remove the chicken from the pot and place a portion on each plate. Stir a few tablespoons of the hot sauce into the sour cream and then stir the mixture back into the remaining peppers and sauce. Ladle the peppers and enriched sauce over the chicken, sprinkle with parsley, and serve immediately.

COUNTRY CAPTAIN CHICKEN

FOLKLORE ABOUT COUNTRY CAPTAIN CHICKEN abounds. Some claim that a sea captain toting spices brought the recipe from India in the early 1800s. The captain is said to have introduced the recipe (and the necessary spices) to residents of Savannah, Georgia which was then an important shipping port for the spice trade. Others say it is named for the captain of Indian troops (called country troops) who served the dish to British soldiers, also in the 1800s.

Whatever its origin, it is universally recognized as a favorite of President Franklin D. Roosevelt. In the 1940s, he enjoyed the stew at the Little White House at Warm Springs, Georgia, where he underwent treatment for paralysis. He liked it so much that he instructed his chef to serve it to Gen. George Patton when he visited the Little White House.

It is understandable that the comforting, curried flavor of country captain was such a favorite of F.D.R. The chicken stew is at once spicy, sweet, and fragrant, but not overpoweringly so. Almost all recipes call for tomatoes, garlic, onions, green peppers, curry powder, and raisins or currants, and cooks vary the dish with additional spices. With its playful

name, colorful look, and bright flavors, it has become a well-known dish, particularly in Georgia and other parts of the South.

Before beginning our tests, we narrowed the field a bit by choosing to make the stew with chicken thighs. While some recipes call for cut up whole chickens, we opted to use thighs only, since their dark, rich meat is flavorful and well suited to stewing. After making this decision, we prepared three different versions of this recipe. The differences between the three were significant.

The first recipe intrigued us with its unusual additions of bacon and orange juice, but tasters found it unbalanced in flavor. The bacon took over, and the orange juice was lost behind the curry powder. The stewing liquid reduced during cooking but was still quite thin—not very stewlike. In this recipe, raisins appeared as a garnish, but tasters agreed that the raisins were more pleasant when plumped while stewing rather than added at the table.

The second recipe was the simplest of the three, made with the most basic of ingredients, but it left tasters wanting more flavor, sweetness, and spice.

We liked the appearance, texture, and taste of the third recipe. The tender bites of stewed chicken, raisins, mango, and tomato with a final sprinkling of parsley won us over. The addition of flour made for a nicely thickened sauce. Another advantage of this recipe was that it removed the chicken skin after browning, while both of the other recipes left the skin on. Tasters unilaterally disliked chicken skin in the stew. The soft, flabby skin was always left behind, and stews made with the skin on were described as greasy. Our technique of quickly cooking the thighs with the skin on and later removing it proved best.

Many of the recipes that we looked at did not specify a certain type of curry powder, though varieties of curry are infinite. We tested standard yellow curry powder (the kind most frequently spotted on supermarket shelves) against hotter Madras-style curry powder as well as a homemade curry powder, ground just before cooking. Tasters preferred the Madras-style curry powder for the heat it offered up in contrast with the sweet, round flavors of the stew. The stew made with standard curry powder was bland in comparison. The one made with homemade curry powder was good, but it didn't seem worth the effort given how much we liked the version made with the premixed Madras-style curry.

During testing, tasters consistently enjoyed the traditional garnish of toasted almonds. Since the stew looks and tastes like party food, we also tested a host of traditional curry garnishes to serve along with it. Mango chutney is suggested in many recipes, but we found it too strong in flavor. Bananas, shredded coconut, green apple, and scallions complemented the sweet/hot flavors of the stew perfectly.

Country Captain Chicken

SERVES 6

For this recipe, we like to use Madras-style curry powder, which is hotter than standard curry powder. Toasted almonds are a traditional garnish, but it's fun to pass a variety of garnishes at the table (see page 239 for other ideas). Serve with regular long-grain rice or basmati rice (page 312).

8	bone-in chicken thighs (about 3 pounds), trimmed of excess skin and fat
	Salt and ground black pepper
I	teaspoon vegetable oil
2	large onions, chopped coarse
I	medium green bell pepper, stemmed, seeded, and chopped coarse
2	medium cloves garlic, minced
I ½	tablespoons sweet paprika
I	tablespoon Madras-style curry powder
¼	teaspoon cayenne pepper
3	tablespoons flour
I ½	cups homemade chicken stock or canned low-sodium chicken broth
I	(14½-ounce) can diced tomatoes
I	bay leaf
½	teaspoon dried thyme
½	cup raisins
I	ripe mango, peeled, pitted, and cut into ¼-inch dice (see illustrations below)
¼	cup minced fresh parsley leaves

1. Adjust the oven rack to the lower-middle position and heat the oven to 300 degrees. Season the chicken liberally with salt and pepper to taste. Heat the oil in a large ovenproof Dutch oven over medium-high heat until shimmering but not smoking, about 2 minutes. Add four chicken thighs, skin-side down, and cook, not moving them until the skin is crisp and well-browned, about 5 minutes. Using tongs, flip the chicken and brown on the second side, about 5 minutes longer. Transfer the browned chicken to a large plate. Brown the remaining chicken thighs, transfer them to the plate, and set aside. When the chicken has cooled, remove and discard the skin (see illustration on page 231). With a spoon, remove and discard all but 1 tablespoon fat from the pan.

2. Add the onions and bell pepper to the empty Dutch oven and sauté over medium heat until softened, 4 to 5 minutes. Stir in the garlic, paprika, curry powder, and cayenne and cook until the spices are fragrant, about 30 seconds. Stir in the flour and cook

HANDLING A MANGO

1. Mangoes are notoriously hard to peel, owing to their odd shape and slippery texture. Start by removing a thin slice from one end of the mango so it can sit flat on a work surface.

2. Hold the mango cut-side down and remove the skin in thin strips with a sharp paring knife or serrated knife, working from top to bottom.

3. Once the peel has been removed, cut down along one side of the flat pit to remove the flesh from one side of the mango. Do the same thing on the other side of the pit.

4. Trim around the pit to remove any remaining flesh. The flesh can now be sliced or diced as desired.

GARNISHES FOR
COUNTRY CAPTAIN

These garnishes are optional, but they are an easy way to dress up this stew. Use them singly or in combination.

➤ ½ cup sliced almonds, toasted

➤ 1 banana, peeled and cut into ¼-inch dice

➤ ½ cup sweetened shredded coconut

➤ 1 Granny Smith apple, cored and cut into ¼-inch dice

➤ 4 to 5 scallions, sliced thin

for 1 to 2 minutes. Add the stock, scraping up any browned bits stuck to the pot. Add the tomatoes, bay leaf, thyme, raisins, and mango, and bring to a boil. Reduce the heat and simmer for 10 minutes. Add the chicken pieces and accumulated juices, submerging the chicken in the liquid. Return to a simmer, cover, and place the pot in the oven. Cook until the chicken is done, about 30 minutes. Remove the pot from the oven. (The stew can be covered and refrigerated for up to 3 days. Bring to a simmer over medium-low heat.)

3. Stir in the parsley, discard the bay leaf, and adjust the seasonings. Serve immediately, with garnishes if desired.

Chicken and Dumplings

DESPITE AMERICA'S ONGOING LOVE AFFAIR with comfort food, chicken and dumplings, unlike its baked cousin, chicken pot pie, hasn't made a comeback. After making several dozen batches of dumplings, we think we know why.

As tricky as it can be to make pie pastry or biscuits for pot pie, dumplings are far more temperamental. With pot pie, dry oven heat and a rich sauce camouflage minor flaws in biscuits or pastry, whereas moist, steamy heat highlights gummy or leaden dumplings. What's more, pot pie, with its meat, vegetables, bread, and sauce, is a complete meal. Chicken and dumplings is, well, chicken and dumplings. A few hearty vegetables would make it a complete meal— just the selling point to attract today's busy cook.

Our mission in developing a recipe for chicken and dumplings was twofold. First, we wanted a recipe that was as foolproof and complete as that for a good chicken pot pie. Second, we wanted a dumpling that was light yet substantial, tender yet durable. But which style of dumpling to explore?

In different parts of the country, dumplings come in different shapes. They may be rolled thin and cut into strips, rolled thick and stamped out like biscuits, or shaped into round balls by hand. Could these three styles come from the same dough, or would we need to develop separate doughs to accommodate each style? Most flour-based dumplings are made of flour, salt, plus one or more of the following: butter, eggs, milk, and baking powder. Depending on the ingredient list, dumplings are usually mixed in one of three ways. The most common is a biscuit or pastry style in which cold butter is cut into the dry ingredients, then cold milk and/or eggs are stirred in until just mixed. Other dumplings are made by simply mixing wet into dry ingredients. Many of the eggier dumplings are made pâte-à-choux (puff-pastry) style, adding flour to hot water and butter, then whisking in eggs, one at a time.

We spent a full day making batch after batch of dumplings in some combination of the ingredients and three mixing methods outlined above. By the end of the day, we hadn't made a single dumpling that we really liked.

We finally made progress after looking at an entry in *Master Recipes* (Ballantine, 1987), in which author Stephen Schmidt cuts butter into flour, baking powder, and salt. Then, instead of adding cold liquid to the dry ingredients, he adds hot liquid to the flour-butter mixture. Dumplings made according to this method were light and fluffy, yet they held up beautifully during cooking. These were the firm yet tender dumplings we were looking for. This type of dumpling is a success because hot liquids, unlike cold ones, expand and set the starch in the flour, keeping it from absorbing too much of the cooking liquid. Now that we had the technique down, it was time to test the formula.

We thought that cake flour dumplings would be even lighter-textured than those made with all-purpose. In fact, just the opposite was true. They were tight, spongy little dumplings with a metallic, acidic aftertaste. The problem lies with the cake flour, not the baking powder. The process by which cake flour is chlorinated leaves it acidic. One of the benefits of acidic flour is that it sets eggs faster in baking, resulting in a smoother, finer-textured cake. This acidic flavor, less distracting in a batter rich with butter, sugar, and eggs, really comes through in a simple dumpling dough.

Although we were pretty sure that dumplings made with vegetable shortening wouldn't taste as good as those made with butter, we had high hopes for the ones made with chicken fat. After a side-by-side test of dumplings made with butter, shortening, and chicken fat, we selected those made with butter. The shortening dumpling tasted flat, like cooked flour and chicken stock, while the one made with chicken fat tasted like flour and stronger-flavored chicken stock. The butter gave the dumpling that extra flavor dimension it needed.

Liquids were simple. Dumplings made with chicken stock, much like those made with chicken fat, tasted too similar to the stewing liquid. Those made with water were dull. Because buttermilk tends to separate and even curdle when heated, buttermilk dumplings felt wrong. Whole milk dumplings were tender, with a pleasant biscuity flavor—our first choice.

Up to this point, we had made all of our dumplings by cutting the fat into the dry ingredients, then adding hot liquid. Because we were adding hot milk, we questioned why it was necessary to cut in the cold butter. Why couldn't we simply heat the milk and butter together and dump the mixture into the dry ingredients? A side-by-side tasting of dumplings made from the two different mixing techniques made us realize that cutting the butter into the flour was indeed an unnecessary step. The simpler route of adding the hot milk and melted butter to the dry ingredients actually yielded more substantial, better-textured dumplings.

Having decided on dumplings made with all-purpose flour, milk, butter, baking powder, and salt, we tested the formula by shaping it into balls, cutting it into biscuit shapes, and rolling it thin and cutting it into strips. Regardless of shape, we got the same consistent results: tender, sturdy dumplings.

We now turned our energies to updating the chicken part of the dish. Our first few attempts were disastrous. To make the dish clean and sleek, we left the chicken pieces on the bone, cut the vegetables into long, thin strips, and thickened the stewing liquid slightly. As we ate the finished product, we realized that we needed a knife (to cut the chicken off the bone), a fork (to eat the vegetables, dumplings, and meat), and a spoon (for the liquid). Although we wanted the dish to look beautiful, it had to be eater-friendly. This meant that the chicken had to come off the bone, the vegetables needed to be cut a little smaller, and the liquid would have to be reduced and thickened. As the dish evolved, we worked toward making it not only a one-dish, but also a one-utensil meal.

Boneless, skinless chicken breasts just didn't seem right for this dish. We wanted large chunks of both light and dark meat. Only a whole chicken would work. Because we wanted this dish to serve six to eight and because we preferred bigger chunks of meat, we chose the larger oven roasters over the small fryer hens. Because we had already developed a method for rich, flavorful chicken stock and perfectly poached chicken parts (see chapter 2), we simply adapted the technique to this recipe.

Our updated chicken and dumplings now needed vegetables, but where and how to cook them? In an attempt to streamline the process, we tried cooking the vegetables along with the poaching chicken parts. After fishing out hot, slightly overcooked vegetables from among the chicken parts and pieces, we decided this shortcut wasn't worth it. So we simply washed the pot, returned it to the stove, and let the vegetables steam for 10 minutes while removing the meat from the bone, straining the stock, and making the dumpling dough. Because the vegetables would cook again for a short time in the sauce, we wanted them slightly undercooked at this point. Steaming them separately gave us more control.

With our meat poached and off the bone, our stock degreased and strained, and our vegetables steamed, we were ready to complete the dish— almost like someone ready to stir-fry. We chose to thicken the sauce at the beginning of this final phase rather than at the end, because once our chicken, vegetables, and dumplings were added to the pot, thickening became virtually impossible.

To a roux (paste) of flour and chicken fat (once again, using every bit of the chicken to make the dish), we added our homemade stock and stirred until thickened. Although we needed 6 cups of stock to poach the chicken parts, we found this quantity of liquid made the dish much too saucy, more like chicken and dumpling soup. Pouring off 2 cups of stock to reserve for another use solved the problem.

We added the chicken and vegetables to the thickened sauce, then steamed the dumplings. The dumplings thus remained undisturbed, while the chicken and vegetables had an opportunity to marry with one another and the sauce. A few peas and a little parsley made the dish beautiful, and a little dry sherry or vermouth heightened the flavor. A touch of cream enriched and beautified, but the dish was equally good without it.

Chicken and Dumplings with Aromatic Vegetables

SERVES 6 TO 8

If you are in a hurry, you can poach boneless chicken breasts in low-sodium canned broth, pull the breast into large pieces, and skip step 1 below. This compromise saves time, but the results are not nearly as delicious.

POACHED CHICKEN AND
AROMATIC VEGETABLES

I	teaspoon vegetable oil
I	large roasting chicken (6 to 7 pounds) cut into 2 drumsticks, 2 thighs, and 2 breast pieces, each with skin removed; back, neck, and wings hacked with cleaver into I- to 2-inch pieces to make stock
I	large onion, cut into large chunks (not necessary to peel)
2	bay leaves
	Salt
3	stalks celery, trimmed and cut into I by ¹/₂-inch pieces
4	medium carrots, peeled and cut into I by ¹/₂-inch pieces
6	boiling onions, peeled and halved

4	tablespoons unsalted butter, softened, or chicken fat from the cooked chicken
6	tablespoons all-purpose flour
I	teaspoon dried thyme
2	tablespoons dry sherry or vermouth
¹/₄	cup heavy cream (optional)
³/₄	cup frozen peas, thawed
¹/₄	cup minced fresh parsley leaves
	Ground black or white pepper

BAKING POWDER DUMPLINGS

2	cups all-purpose flour
I	tablespoon baking powder
³/₄	teaspoon salt
3	tablespoons butter
I	cup milk

1. **FOR THE CHICKEN:** Heat oil in a large Dutch oven over medium-high heat until shimmering but not smoking, about 2 minutes. Add the hacked-up chicken pieces (back, neck, and wings) and onion chunks; sauté until the onion softens and the chicken loses its raw color, about 5 minutes. Reduce the heat to low, cover, and cook until the chicken pieces give up most of their liquid, about 20 minutes. Increase the heat to medium-high, add 6 cups hot water, skinned chicken parts (drumsticks, thighs, and breasts), bay leaves, and ³/₄ teaspoon salt, then bring to a simmer. Reduce the heat; continue to simmer, partially covered, until the stock is flavorful and the skinned chicken parts are just cooked through, about 20 minutes longer. Remove the skinned chicken parts and set aside. When cool enough to handle, remove the meat from the bones in 2- to 3-inch chunks. Strain the stock, discarding the hacked-up chicken pieces. Skim and reserve fat from stock and set aside 4 cups of stock, reserving extra for another use.

2. Bring ¹/₂ inch water to a simmer in the cleaned Dutch oven fitted with a steamer basket. Add the celery, carrots, and onions; cover and steam until just tender, about 10 minutes. Remove and set aside.

3. **FOR THE DUMPLINGS:** Mix the flour, baking powder, and salt in a medium bowl. Heat the butter and milk to a simmer and add to the dry ingredients. Mix with a fork or knead by hand two or three times until mixture just comes together. Following illustrations on page 242,

form the dough into desired shape; set aside.

4. **To finish the dish:** Heat the butter in cleaned Dutch oven over medium-high heat. Whisk in the flour and thyme; cook, whisking constantly, until flour turns golden, 1 to 2 minutes. Continuing to whisk constantly, gradually add the sherry, then the reserved 4 cups chicken stock; simmer until the gravy thickens slightly, 2 to 3 minutes. Stir in cream (if using) and chicken and vegetables; return to a simmer. Gently stir in the peas and parsley. Adjust the seasonings, including generous amounts of salt and pepper.

5. Lay the formed dumplings on the surface of the chicken mixture; cover and simmer until the dumplings are cooked through, about 10 minutes for strip dumplings and 15 minutes for balls and biscuit rounds. Ladle a portion of meat, sauce, vegetables, and dumplings into soup plates and serve immediately.

➤ VARIATION

Chicken and Herbed Dumplings with Aromatic Vegetables

Follow recipe for Chicken and Dumplings with Aromatic Vegetables, adding ¼ cup minced soft fresh herb leaves such as parsley, chives (or scallion greens), dill, or tarragon to dumpling mixture along with dry ingredients. If other herbs are unavailable, parsley alone can be used.

CHICKEN FRICASSEE

CHICKEN CAN BE ROASTED, SAUTÉED, GRILLED, fried, stir-fried, oven-fried, baked, poached, and smoked, but these days we rarely think about a simple fricassee. Why? Well, for one thing, most of us mistake it for some outdated Cordon Bleu preparation. In fact, a chicken fricassee is nothing more than a whole cut-up chicken poached in stock, after which a simple sauce is made from the liquid. It's simple, it's flavorful, and it's easy. So why has it been forgotten? In the case of many recipes for other traditional dishes, the answer is quite simple: They are either too time-consuming or no longer appeal to the modern palate. But this is not the case with chicken fricassee, which is neither time-consuming nor unappetizing. It seemed high time to resurrect chicken fricassee.

The process did involve solving some problems, however. The first was to define the parameters of the recipe. Fricassee has had a long history and many different interpretations. (For more information, see page 243.) In short, a French fricassee meant chicken (or sometimes vegetables) cooked in a white sauce. Over time, this dish evolved to become chicken poached in a clear liquid, usually chicken stock but sometimes water and/or wine. When the chicken was done, it was removed from the pan, and then a sauce was made from the poaching liquid. This simple definition was our starting point.

THREE SHAPES FOR DUMPLINGS

FLAT, NOODLELIKE DUMPLINGS
Roll dough ⅛ inch thick and cut into 2-inch by ½-inch strips.

BISCUITLIKE DUMPLINGS
Roll dough ½ inch thick. Use a 2-inch biscuit cutter or a round drinking glass top to cut dough rounds.

ROUND, PUFFY DUMPLINGS
Divide dough into 18 pieces. Roll each piece of dough into a rough round.

We had other considerations as well. We did not want an extremely rich sauce, preferring instead something lighter and more modern. We were also keen on developing a recipe that could be put together as quickly and simply as possible, making it a candidate for weeknight cooking. This would mean shortening cooking times and using the minimum number of pans and ingredients. We also wanted to make sure that the skin was appealing, which would require either sautéing or using skinless pieces of chicken. Producing moist chicken was also going to be important, as was producing a flavorful, well-balanced sauce that was neither too rich nor too acidic.

We started off with a blind taste test, choosing the lightest, most promising fricassee recipes we could find. The first was a classic French preparation in which the chicken pieces were lightly sautéed in butter and then simmered in equal amounts of chicken stock and white wine; the dish was then finished with a bit of heavy cream. The resulting sauce was judged too acidic, and the chicken's skin was unappealing. The second recipe was similar to the first except that the cooking liquid was a combination of water and chicken stock. This recipe also called for three large carrots and two large celery stalks. The sauce was thin and vegetal, with a carrot flavor so strong that it was unwelcome. The third recipe, the worst of the lot, called for 45 minutes of cooking in chicken stock, much too long to produce moist meat.

After these initial forays, we made three decisions: Chicken stock rather than water or wine was the preferred poaching liquid, we favored a light hand when finishing the sauce with cream, and the remaining ingredients had to be added with parsimony.

Now we were ready to create our own recipe. First, though, we had to decide whether we preferred a brown or white fricassee, the difference being a matter of whether the chicken is sautéed before being poached. A quick test confirmed that sautéing develops flavor and renders fat from the skin, some of which is used to flavor the sauce. We preferred a full-fledged sauté to the light sauté used in some of the recipes selected for the blind tasting; the higher heat made the skin crisper and the dish more flavorful.

At this point we had a working recipe. A whole chicken is cut up, seasoned liberally with salt and pepper, and sautéed in olive oil and butter. The chicken is then simmered in stock for about 20 minutes and removed from the liquid. Meanwhile, onions and mushrooms are sautéed in a second pan, and a sauce is then made with the poaching liquid, the vegetables, and a bit of heavy cream to finish. We decided to thicken the sauce using a basic roux, which is simply melted butter and flour cooked together over high heat.

The first test of this master recipe produced very good results. The sauce had a nice, rich flavor. By poaching the chicken in stock we had created a wonderful double stock. But there were still some problems. The sauce was too fatty, and it was also a bit flat, in need of some bite and contrast. We then substituted a half cup of white wine for the same amount of

---

WHAT IS A FRICASSEE?

The dictionary defines a fricassee as poultry stewed in sauce. This rather spare explanation is not incorrect, but it is less than complete. In the recipe contained in the 1915 edition of *The Fannie Farmer Cookbook*, the chicken is cooked in cream, removed, and a sauce is then made in the pot using chicken stock and additional cream. This method is quite close to the original interpretation of the French fricassee, which, according to *Larousse Gastronomique*, refers to chicken cooked in a white sauce, not merely poached in a liquid. So, at least until recently, fricassee was poultry stewed in a cream sauce.

As times have changed, so has the recipe. James Beard, for example, offers a white fricassee in which he starts by poaching the chicken in water and then makes a white sauce fortified with cream and egg yolks. This is still no recipe for a modern cook. But he also offers a brown fricassee recipe (in a brown fricassee, the chicken is sautéed before poaching) that is significantly lighter, the sauce finished with cream but no eggs. We think this kind of fricassee has the most appeal.

These days, modern cookbooks usually define a fricassee as chicken poached in stock from which a sauce is then made. The sauce can be merely a reduction, the stock simmered down to a more concentrated state, or it can be enriched with cream or other ingredients.

stock, using the wine to deglaze the pan after sautéing the onions and mushrooms. This helped, but we found that an additional squirt of lemon juice just before serving was also necessary for balance. We then tried substituting half-and-half for the cream, a change that made the sauce more balanced as well as lighter. We also tried making the sauce with no dairy. This version was acceptable, but the sauce lacked the silky feeling provided by the half-and-half and did not balance as nicely with the wine and lemon juice.

Since we like a choice of white or dark meat, we usually buy a whole chicken and cut it up in the test kitchen. However, chicken thighs work well, too. You can use skinless chicken parts if you like, but if you do so we suggest that you eliminate the sautéing step, simply starting the recipe by poaching in the chicken stock. This will result in a very good but somewhat less flavorful dish. We also learned that it was best to let the cooked chicken rest in a covered bowl rather than keeping it warm in an oven. A great deal of liquid escapes from the meat when left in a warm oven, resulting in dry chicken. For optimum flavor, we also took care to add back to the sauce any accumulated juices from the resting chicken.

Chicken Fricassee with Mushrooms and Onions

SERVES 4

We have divided the task of browning the chicken parts between a Dutch oven and a medium skillet that is later used to sauté the vegetables. This eliminates the need to brown in batches in one pot and shortens the cooking time by about 10 minutes. Fans of dark meat can substitute eight bone-in, skin-on thighs for the whole chicken.

1	whole chicken (3 to 4 pounds), cut into 2 wings, 2 drumsticks, and 2 thighs, with breast quartered (see illustrations on page 245) Salt and ground black pepper
2	tablespoons olive oil
4	tablespoons unsalted butter
2½	cups homemade chicken stock or canned low-sodium chicken broth
1	medium onion, chopped fine
10	ounces white mushrooms, left whole if small, halved if medium, quartered if large
½	cup dry white wine
3	tablespoons flour
1	cup half-and-half
1	teaspoon minced fresh thyme leaves
1½	tablespoons lemon juice
¼	teaspoon freshly grated nutmeg
¼	cup minced fresh parsley leaves

1. Season the chicken with salt and pepper to taste. Heat 1 tablespoon each olive oil and butter in both a large Dutch oven and medium skillet over medium-high heat. When foam subsides, add the chicken pieces, skin-side down, and cook until well-browned, 4 to 5 minutes on each side. Spoon off all but 2 tablespoons fat from the Dutch oven. Add the chicken from the skillet, arranging pieces in a single layer as much as possible. Add the stock, partially cover, and bring to a boil. Reduce the heat to low and simmer until chicken is fully cooked, 20 to 25 minutes. Remove the Dutch oven from the heat, transfer the chicken to a bowl, cover the bowl with foil, and set aside.

2. While the chicken is simmering, drain off all but 1 tablespoon fat from the now-empty skillet. Add the onion, mushrooms, and ¼ teaspoon salt and sauté over medium-high heat, stirring occasionally, until the mushroom liquid evaporates and the vegetables begin to brown, 6 to 8 minutes. Add the wine, scraping up any brown bits, and cook until almost all liquid evaporates, 2 to 3 minutes. Transfer the vegetables to a small bowl and set aside.

3. Set the Dutch oven with the chicken cooking liquid back over medium heat. Heat the remaining 2 tablespoons butter in now-empty skillet over medium heat until foaming. Add the flour and whisk until golden in color, about 1 minute. Add the half-and-half, whisking vigorously until smooth. Immediately whisk this mixture into the hot chicken cooking liquid in the Dutch oven and bring to a boil over medium-high heat. Reduce the heat to medium-low and simmer, stirring frequently, until thickened to the consistency of heavy cream, 6 to 8 minutes. Stir in mushroom mixture, thyme, lemon juice, and nutmeg and season with salt and pepper to taste.

4. Add the chicken and any accumulated juices to the Dutch oven and simmer until heated through, 2

to 3 minutes. Stir in 2 tablespoons parsley. Transfer the chicken pieces to serving platter or individual plates. Spoon sauce over chicken and sprinkle with remaining parsley. Serve immediately.

➤ VARIATION

Chicken Fricassee with Peas and Carrots
Follow recipe for Chicken Fricassee with Mushrooms and Onions, substituting 1 small carrot, diced small, for mushrooms. Sauté until vegetables begin to brown, 3 to 4 minutes. Reduce heat to low, add wine, cover, and cook until carrots are tender, 10 to 12 minutes. Stir in ½ cup thawed frozen peas, increase heat to medium-high, and cook until almost all liquid evaporates, 1 to 2 minutes. Transfer to small bowl; set aside. Continue with recipe, substituting peas and carrots for mushroom mixture in step 3.

COQ AU VIN

WE REMEMBER DISCOVERING COQ AU VIN in the late 1960s when French food was taking hold in American kitchens. This classic fricassee of cut-up chicken cooked in a red-wine sauce and finished with a garnish of bacon, tiny glazed pearl onions, and sautéed mushrooms was a giant step away from chicken cooked under a blanket of cream of mushroom soup. But if we've cooked coq au vin in the past 20 years, we don't remember; it simply isn't a dish that we make at home.

Why not, we wondered? As we thought back, we discovered that after falling in love with coq au vin at an early age, versions of the dish we had cooked and tasted since then had universally disappointed us. In high school it was enough that coq au vin seemed exotic. These days, if we're going to peel all those baby onions, we want to be thrilled with the results.

CUTTING UP A WHOLE CHICKEN

1. With a sharp chef's knife, cut through the skin around the leg where it attaches to the breast.

2. Using both hands, pop the leg out of its socket.

3. Use the chef's knife to cut through the flesh and skin to detach the leg from the body.

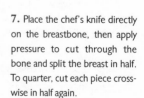

4. A line of fat separates the thigh and the drumstick. Cut through the joint at this point. Repeat steps I, 2, 3, and 4 with the other leg.

5. Bend the wing out from the breast and cut to remove it using a boning knife. Repeat with the other wing.

6. Using poultry shears, cut down along the ribs on both sides of the backbone to remove the backbone from the breast.

7. Place the chef's knife directly on the breastbone, then apply pressure to cut through the bone and split the breast in half. To quarter, cut each piece crosswise in half again.

And we didn't see why we couldn't be. At its best, coq au vin should be hugely tasty, the acidity of the wine rounded out by rich, salty bacon and sweet, caramelized onions and mushrooms. The chicken should soak up those same dark, rich flavors. We set about creating a recipe that would satisfy our appetite for a really great coq au vin.

We started out by cooking and tasting a number of recipes from French cookbooks. As we cooked, we noticed that the recipes fell into two categories: those that were simpler and more provincial in character, and those that were more complicated and promised a more refined taste. The recipes in the first category were versions of a straightforward brown fricassee (see "What Is a Fricassee?" on page 243). Tasting these simpler versions, we recognized them as the serviceable coq au vins of recent memory. The sauces were good but not extraordinary. The chicken tasted mostly like chicken. In short, the recipes weren't special enough to merit the time they demanded.

We moved on to testing a much more complicated recipe from Madeleine Kamman's *The New Making of a Cook* (William Morrow, 1998). This two-day affair was also a brown fricassee but with a much more elaborate sauce. The recipe began by combining red wine with veal stock and browned vegetables and reducing this mixture by about half. The chicken was then browned and the pan deglazed with the reduced wine mixture (in deglazing, liquid is added to a hot pan to remove the brown bits that remain from the previous round of cooking). Once the chicken was cooked, the sauce was strained, bound first with a beurre manié (a paste of mashed butter and flour), and then with a bit of chicken liver pureed with heavy cream; the bound sauce was finished with flambéed cognac.

Although it was built on the same basic model as the others, this dish was in a whole different league. It was what a good coq au vin ought to be—the sauce beautifully textured, clean flavored, and rich without being heavy or murky. The chicken was drenched in flavor. Though we were able to make it in just one day instead of the two that Kamman posited, the recipe unquestionably demanded more time, more last-minute fussing, and a lot more dishes (in addition to a blender) than the recipes we'd made before.

Still, this recipe got our attention. What was going on that made it so good? Were all of those steps actually necessary, or could we isolate one or two that really made the difference? Clearly there was something here to be learned about how to make a great red wine sauce, but in this recipe even the chicken tasted better. Why?

As we compared Kamman's recipe with the others, two techniques stood out. First, Kamman bound her sauce differently—with a beurre manié and chicken liver—rather than sprinkling the meat or vegetables with flour at the beginning. Kamman also used all chicken legs instead of both legs and breasts as the other recipes did. Finally, Kamman's recipe was the only one that reduced the wine with the stock and aromatics before adding the chicken; the others used raw wine.

We first tested a coq au vin bound with a beurre manié and compared it with one in which the vegetables were sprinkled with flour. We liked using the beurre manié far better because it gave us more control over the thickness of the sauce. With the latter technique, we were forced to choose a measurement of flour without knowing what the final measurement of liquid would be.

We found that we also agreed with Kamman's use of legs only. Not only do the legs add more flavor to the sauce because they cook longer than the breasts, but, as Kamman points out, the breasts don't cook long enough in the wine to take on much wine flavor; they taste insipid compared with the legs. Further testing demonstrated that thighs worked as well as whole legs.

Finally, we tested a recipe in which the wine was reduced by half before it was cooked with the chicken against a recipe in which the wine was added to the pan raw and reduced at the end, after the chicken was cooked. There was a readily discernible difference in taste between the two: The first sauce, in which the wine had been reduced early on, was much less astringent, tasting full and round; the other tasted raw and somewhat sweet in comparison. The better sauce tasted more of chicken as well, so the flavor was more interesting and complex. There was even a noticeable difference in the taste of the chicken itself. The chicken in the first test tasted better because it tasted of the cooked, reduced wine; the other had the harsh, sweet flavor of raw wine. In addition, it was a boon not to have to reduce the sauce at the end when we had other things to do.

Having determined that beurre manié, dark meat, and a preliminary reduction of the wine were key to the success of this dish, we ran some final tests to find out if the addition of cognac, chicken liver, or tomato paste improved the sauce enough to merit the extra trouble. While cognac was a refinement that we could taste, we liked the sauce well enough without it. The chicken liver mellowed the taste of the sauce by balancing the acidity of the wine, and it added body; but because its addition required two more steps and we liked the sauce without it, we nixed the liver. Tomato paste, however, was simple to whisk in, and, as it furnished some of the extra flavor and body that a true veal stock would add, we decided to use it.

Kamman's recipe also called for using pork brisket or pancetta in lieu of bacon, neither of which is smoked, as bacon is. We found it's not worth the extra trouble to find either.

Finally, we played with the proportions of chicken stock and wine to arrive at a sauce with a wine flavor that was rich and full but not overpowering. This, at last, was a relatively simple coq au vin that was truly worth making.

MAKING A BOUQUET GARNI

A bouquet garni is a classic French combination of herbs used to flavor many soups, stews, and sauces. Sprigs of fresh parsley and thyme along with a bay leaf are common ingredients. Tie the herbs together with a piece of kitchen twine so they can be easily removed from the pot when the soup or stew is done.

Coq au Vin
SERVES 4

If you have the time to blanch and skin them, fresh pearl onions are terrific. For more information, see illustrations on page 248. Serve over buttered egg noodles or mashed potatoes.

1	(750 ml) bottle medium-bodied, fruity red wine, such as Oregon Pinot Noir, Zinfandel, or a light Rhône valley wine
2½	cups homemade chicken stock or canned low-sodium chicken broth
6	ounces bacon (preferably thick-cut), cut crosswise into ¼-inch pieces
6 to 7	tablespoons unsalted butter, at room temperature
1	large carrot, chopped coarse
1	large onion, chopped coarse
2	medium shallots, peeled and quartered
2	medium cloves garlic, skin on and smashed
4	whole chicken legs, trimmed of excess skin and fat, thighs and drumsticks separated (see illustration 4 on page 245), or 8 bone-in chicken thighs (about 3 pounds), trimmed of excess skin and fat
	Salt and ground black pepper
2	sprigs fresh thyme, 10 parsley stems, and 1 bay leaf tied together to make bouquet garni (see illustration, left)
1½	teaspoons tomato paste
24	frozen pearl onions (evenly sized), thawed, or fresh pearl onions (see note)
½	pound white mushrooms, whole if small, halved if medium, quartered if large
2 to 3	tablespoons flour
2	tablespoons minced fresh parsley leaves

1. Bring red wine and chicken stock to a boil in a large, heavy saucepan, reduce heat to medium-high, and cook until reduced to about 4 cups, about 20 minutes.

2. Meanwhile, fry the bacon in a large Dutch oven over medium heat until the fat has rendered and bacon is golden brown, about 5 minutes. Transfer the bacon with slotted spoon to a paper towel–lined plate to drain; set aside. Heat 1 tablespoon butter

with rendered bacon fat; add the carrot, onion, shallots, and garlic and sauté until lightly browned, 10 to 15 minutes. Press the vegetables against the side of the pan with a slotted spoon to squeeze out as much fat as possible; transfer the vegetables to the pan with the reduced wine mixture (off heat) and discard all but 1 tablespoon fat from the Dutch oven.

3. Generously sprinkle the chicken pieces with salt and pepper to taste. Return the Dutch oven to a burner over medium-high heat and add another 1 tablespoon butter. When the butter has melted, add half the chicken pieces, skin-side down, and cook, not moving them until the skin is crisp and well-browned, about 5 minutes. Using tongs, flip the chicken and brown on the second side, about 5 minutes longer. Transfer the browned chicken to a large plate. Brown the remaining chicken pieces, transfer them to the plate, and set aside.

4. Pour off all the fat from the Dutch oven. Return the pan to the heat and add the wine-vegetable mixture. Bring to a boil, scraping up browned bits from the bottom of the pan with a wooden spoon. Add the browned chicken, bouquet garni, and tomato paste to the boiling wine mixture. Return to a boil, then reduce heat to low and simmer gently, partially covered. Turn the chicken once during cooking, until tender and infused with wine flavor, 45 to 60 minutes.

5. While the chicken and sauce are cooking, heat 2 tablespoons butter in a medium skillet over medium-low heat. Add the pearl onions and cook, stirring occasionally and reducing the heat if butter starts to brown too fast, until lightly browned and almost cooked through, 5 to 8 minutes. Add the mushrooms, season with salt to taste, cover, increase the heat to medium, and cook until the mushrooms release their liquid, about 5 minutes. Remove the cover, increase the heat to high, and boil until the liquid evaporates and the onions and mushrooms are golden brown, 2 to 3 minutes more. Transfer the onions and mushrooms to the plate with the bacon; set aside.

6. When the chicken is cooked, transfer to a large bowl or platter; cover with aluminum foil to keep warm. Strain the sauce through a fine-mesh strainer set over a large measuring cup, pressing on the solids with a wooden spoon to release as much liquid as possible; sauce should measure 2 to 3 cups. Return the sauce to the pan; skim as much fat as possible off surface. Counting 1 tablespoon each of butter and flour for each cup of sauce, mash 2 to 3 tablespoons each butter and flour in a small bowl or plate to make a smooth paste (beurre manié). Bring the sauce to a boil and whisk in beurre manié until smooth. Add the reserved chicken, bacon, onions and mushrooms. Adjust the seasonings, reduce the heat to medium-low, and simmer very gently to warm through and blend flavors, about 5 minutes. Check seasoning and adjust with additional salt and pepper if necessary; add the parsley. Transfer the chicken to a serving platter and pour the sauce over the chicken. Serve immediately.

PREPARING FRESH PEARL ONIONS

1. Start by cutting off a tiny bit of the root end with a small paring knife.

2. To keep the onions from falling apart, cut an X in the exposed root end of each onion. This will allow the layers to expand but still hold together when sautéed.

3. We find it easier to peel fresh pearl onions after they have been blanched in boiling water for 30 seconds. Use a slotted spoon to transfer the onions to a bowl of ice water to cool. Then drain the onions and slip off the skins.

11

SEAFOOD STEWS

FIND A COUNTRY THAT HAS A COASTLINE, and you will find a fish stew in its culinary repertoire. But whatever their geographic origin, fish stews are surprisingly easy for home cooks to prepare. Most recipes begin with stock. The next step is to make a flavor base, which usually entails cooking aromatic vegetables—onions, garlic, etc.—in some fat. The stock is added and then the vegetables and finally the fish.

Although the process is straightforward, we had one overarching question. Is fish stock essential? It turns out that the answer depends on the stew in question. For instance, bouillabaisse must be made with fish stock, both for flavor and body. Substitutions simply don't work in this recipe. Unlike meat or chicken stews, where the protein simmers for some time in the stew, fish can cook for only a few minutes, or it will dry out and fall apart. Since the fish does not have time to flavor the stew liquid, the liquid must start out tasting good. We found that New England fish stew also requires homemade stock.

In contrast, cioppino can be made without any stock. The bivalves in this stew release so much flavorful liquid (and there are a lot of tomatoes in the flavor base) that there's no need to add more liquid, in the form of fish stock or some substitute, to the mix. A Sicilian fish stew with tomatoes, olives, capers, and raisins has so much flavor that you can use our recipe for Cheater's Fish Stock in chapter 2.

The other general concern when preparing seafood stews is the seafood. You must buy from a trusted source, preferably one with a high turnover, which ensures freshness. While cooking can hide imperfections in meat and poultry, there is little the cook can do to salvage a tired piece of snapper or slimy, mushy shrimp. Of course, seafood that is past its prime can also be dangerous to your health, especially shellfish.

What should you look for at the seafood shop? Bivalves are sold alive. This means that clams and mussels should be tightly shut. Shrimp should be firm, not mushy, and have no black spots or yellowing. Scallops should be sticky and flabby, not floating in tons of milky white liquid. (For more information on buying shellfish, see specific boxes in this chapter and in chapter 5.) Buying fish fillets and steaks is a bit more complicated. Fish should smell like the sea, not fishy or sour. The flesh should look bright, shiny, and firm, not dull or mushy. When possible, try to get your fishmonger to slice steaks and fillets to order rather than buying precut pieces that may have been sitting for some time and lost fluids. Avoid fish that is shrink-wrapped, since the packaging makes it difficult to examine and smell the fish. Fish should be kept chilled until the minute you buy it, and you should get it home quickly and refrigerate immediately, preferably set over a bowl of ice.

BOUILLABAISSE

THE RISE OF BOUILLABAISSE FROM A STEW of sea scraps fishermen cooked on the beach to the well-clad restaurant celebrity we know today is a classic rags-to-riches tale. Bouillabaisse is heady, powerful stuff—a jeweled tapestry of fish and shellfish in a briny-sweet broth with tomato, wine, garlic, and saffron. The base of this soup should have enough melted collagen from its fish frames to leave a sticky varnish on the lips best removed by a big hit of white Côtes de Provence and a fine linen napkin. Its name alone suggests concentration and flavor: *bouillir* (to boil), *abaisser* (to reduce). And, indeed, bouillabaisse requires a good rollicking boil to emulsify the oils into its broth, making it thicker. Boldly colored and steaming in its plate, bouillabaisse is interrupted by a slab of toasted or stale baguette brushed with olive oil and garlic and anointed with a spicy, luxuriant red pepper aioli called *rouille*. It gives you more bang for your bite than anything else in the world.

On its way up the social ladder, bouillabaisse developed something of an attitude problem. For a while there was even talk that Americans couldn't make this dish. Why? The humble fish responsible for its origins (principally the firm, white-fleshed rascasse, among others) are native only to Mediterranean waters. The American home cook was also put off by the notion of creating a full-flavored fish stock from scratch, a crucial step in producing a first-class bouillabaisse. Finally, great bouillabaisse is predicated on the notion of finesse in cooking the fish to perfection, flavoring the broth delicately, and balancing a host of diverse ingredients, from orange zest to Pernod, saffron to fennel, mussels to sea bass. We expected the testing process to be more a matter of refinement and balance than one of making radical new discoveries.

At the outset of this investigation, we tested a substantial number of bouillabaisse recipes and found that although the extended family of famous fish soups, both Gallic and Italian, reflect minor regional and cultural differences, there were few rogue upstarts or egregious bastardizations. That being said, seemingly minor variations in the recipes made an enormous impact on the finished dish. What is the best method for creating a homemade stock quickly and easily? How does one infuse this liquid with a complex range of flavors without producing a dull, oily stew? Which combination of fish provides just the right texture and flavor, and how does one prevent overcooking? How does one make a superior rouille? Finally, are there any shortcuts—bottled clam juice and frozen fish came to mind—that have a place in a great bouillabaisse?

We quickly dispensed with the obvious shortcuts. A couple of quarts of bottled clam juice will not stand in the stead of real fish stock, just as a couple boxes of frozen fish fillets cannot replace a selection of good, fresh fish. Although there is nothing technically or procedurally difficult about making it, a superior bouillabaisse was going to require a reasonable investment of time and attention. The good news is that bouillabaisse constitutes a one-pot, three-course meal—soup, fish, and bread. You won't need to put another thing on the table. Our goal was to simplify whenever possible and enhance flavor at every turn to make bouillabaisse a frequent guest at the table.

A bouillabaisse has four preparatory phases. The first is marinating the cut-up fish in olive oil and other flavorings. The second is making the fish stock. The third is preparing the soup, where the fish stock bows to the supporting cast of flavors—tomatoes, leeks, fresh fennel, and so on—and welcomes the fish. The fourth is preparing the rouille and crouton.

Fish destined for the bouillabaisse pot are generally cut, then splashed with olive oil and other herbs or aromatics and left to repose before being poached. This flavor marinade brightens the underwater landscape of the stew in ways that plain fish chunks cannot. Fish, with its delicate raw flesh, is capable of absorbing flavors nicely. In terms of specifics, green, fruity extra-virgin olive oil got the better of the fish—milder stuff was better. We found that 4 tablespoons serviced the 3 pounds of fish very well (mussels are not marinated because they hide in their shells, refusing to absorb new flavors; scallops and shelled shrimp can be marinated with the rest of the crew). Taste tests determined that minced garlic, saffron threads, fresh chopped basil, and Pernod, along with sea salt and a tiny bit of red pepper flakes, made the ideal marinade and that four hours were necessary to reach full flavor penetration. The more interesting discovery, however, was made when the marinade was poured into the boiling stock with the fish. The oil and other liquids emulsified into the stock, lending it more of its customary richness. This method was superior to simply adding olive oil directly to the stew later, as was the common practice in the recipes we tested.

We had discarded the notion of bottled clam juice and also found that canned chicken broth just wasn't

CLEANING MUSSELS

Mussels often contain a weedy beard protruding from the crack between the two shells. It's fairly small and can be difficult to tug out of place. To remove it easily, trap the beard between the side of a small knife and your thumb and pull to remove it. The flat surface of a paring knife gives you some leverage to remove the beard.

going to do the trick. So we visited an obliging fishmonger up the street who put together packages of cleaned fish heads and frames for us to begin preliminary tests on fish stock. Though home cooks may be tempted to freeze whatever fish bones and scraps are left from dinner to make a stock, this is not a good idea. We found that not only are the bones from salmon and the like too oily to produce a clean-tasting stock (white fish is essential), but leftover scraps and bits from any fish are likely to lack the essential levels of collagen required to produce a rich, flavorful stock. Fish heads are particularly collagen-rich, so it is important to buy some of them as well. (Don't worry about catching the fish's eye and cringing—the fishmonger will have scraped it out.) Ask the fishmonger to remove the fish's gills and organs as well, and, while he's at it, have him cut the frames into manageable 5- or 6-inch slabs.

One of two techniques is often used in making fish stock. Some recipes simply simmer the ingredients, whereas others sweat the aromatics in butter or olive oil, then add the bones with wine, and, finally, water to simmer. To determine which method was best, we used 3 pounds of fish bones, carrots, celery, onions, leeks, garlic, mushrooms, parsley stems, white wine, and water and made side-by-side fish stocks, one sweated and simmered, the other merely simmered. The resulting 2-plus quarts were robust and flavorful in the sweated version, watery and wanting in the simmered. While not as flawlessly clear as the simmered stock, the sweated stock was translucent, finished, and ready to move on; the simmered stock would have needed a reduction by 50 percent to reach comparable flavor and texture. As for simmering time, an hour extracted every drop of flavor and liquid protein the soft, porous bones had to relinquish.

Our second interesting discovery came when customizing the stock for this recipe. Most bouillabaisse recipes add sautéed chunks of leeks, tomatoes, and fennel slices to the stew along with the fish. We found the physical presence of these vegetables an encumbrance when served up with the fish, so we decided to add them to the stock, not the stew (which also saved us the bother of having to sauté them). Their

flavor was rendered, and then they were summarily discarded so that the key players—the fish and shellfish—could shine undisturbed.

Now we had to choose just the right ingredients to make a fish stock perfectly suited for bouillabaisse. We dashed a quarter cup olive oil into a Dutch oven to sweat the vegetables: Onions and carrots remained in the lineup, but mushrooms brought nothing to the sultry flavors to come. We replaced celery with a Mediterranean native, fresh fennel—same clean flavor with a licorice twist. A signature player, the garlic was doubled to reach critical mass (three full heads). After 30 minutes under cover, these vegetables were exhausted. In went 3 pounds of fish frames and heads, sea salt, peppercorns, and a nice bottle of white Côtes de Provence. The bones were simmered and prodded (the prodding is useful in extracting collagen from the bones so that it can dissolve in the stock). Next came leeks, canned tomatoes and their juices, fresh thyme, bay leaves, and 4 cups of water. At the end of an hour we added a half teaspoon of saffron threads and large strips of zest from two oranges. Strained, this stuff was in-your-face-intense, its color a hot, tropical sunset.

SIMMERING VERSUS SWEATING

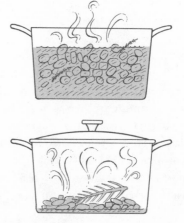

Some stocks are made by simmering fish bones and vegetables in water (top). Others begin by sweating (cooking fish bones and vegetables in butter or oil in a covered pot, bottom) and then add water. We found that sweating, then simmering, releases more flavor from the bones and vegetables than simmering alone.

With the stock in an advanced state of readiness, it was time to throw some fish in the pot. Nearly all bouillabaisse recipes emphasize that a variety of fish and shellfish are essential to bring character to the stew. They support the call for firm-fleshed fish and caution against using fish that are too delicate in constitution or too strong in flavor to complement any of the others.

We went back to the local fishmonger, hunting down everything from the top-billed red snapper (a warm water fish not native to New England) to lobster (certainly not an original, but would it work?). Boston is obviously not a bad place to be when looking for fish, and we were fortunate to be able to test upward of 20 different varieties. Certain fish simply have no place in a bouillabaisse, among them bluefish and mackerel—these guys lacked the politesse not to upstage everybody else. Others weren't worth the trouble required to get them suited up; besides being pricey and cumbersome, lobster failed to match any number of other entrants for flavor; squid was a nuisance to clean, and its chewy texture put it at odds with the group. Cod, Boston's great white hope, was too flaky and cooked too fast—it dissolved in the mouth.

Other fish fell out for the simple reason that their cooking times were too different. Sole was so thin that it overcooked right off. Clams required a separate pot to steam open. Once they had, their buff-colored shells and rubbery mollusk insides brought little to the party. Though many recipes suggest layering the fish in the pot, with longer cooking varieties going in first, the more delicate topping the stack, we wanted the liberty of adding fish to the boiling stock en masse and letting them poach to completion. (This "everyone-into-the-pool" simmer had one other advantage. It was easier to produce perfectly cooked fish since the timing was easier to control.)

In the end we found a lot to like and, by grouping favored fish in "flaky" and "firm" camps, were able to put together some winning combinations (see "Ingredients: Seafood for Bouillabaisse" on page 255). We concluded that at least six types of combined fish and shellfish were necessary to produce a first-class bouillabaisse and that 8 ounces per type of fish were required to satisfy 8 to 10 hungry diners.

As if bouillabaisse weren't already a glorious synthesis of flavors, two additions dive into the fray: a roasted red pepper and garlic mayonnaise, known as a rouille, and a large garlic crouton. The crouton is a raft on the stew, the rouille its passenger.

The croutons can be cut from a baguette or French country loaf, any bread that is rustic and honest—just not sourdough. The French typically use stale bread; we preferred ours broiled lightly on each side. In fact, we preferred the crouton brushed with olive oil and rubbed with raw garlic as well. The favored texture was crunchy on both exposed surfaces, with a light golden band along the edge of the crust and a yielding center.

For the rouille, we started with a large grill-roasted red pepper. Recipes use egg yolks and/or bread to bind the roasted pepper and create a thick sauce. We tested three preparations: 2 egg yolks and no bread, 1 egg yolk and 1 ounce bread, and 2 ounces bread and no egg yolk. The procedure is simple: The roasted pepper is seeded and divested of its burnt skin, then ground up in a food processor with 2 garlic cloves and the egg and/or bread. With the processor running, ½ cup olive oil is drizzled in.

REMOVING TENDONS FROM SCALLOPS

The small, rough-textured, crescent-shaped muscle that attaches the scallop to the shell will toughen when cooked. Remove the tendons before cooking the scallops, using your fingertips to peel each one away from the side of the scallop. (Some scallops may come with tendons removed.)

Tasters preferred the rouille made with bread alone. It had a note of sweetness that brushed up against the red pepper and melted potently into the broth when it slid off the crouton.

Now we had found what we were looking for: a richly scented homemade fish stock with complex flavors, just the right combination of readily available and perfectly cooked fish, a salmon-colored dollop of garlicky rouille, and a recipe that, although not simple, was well within the grasp of any cook eager to bring the clean, briny taste of the ocean to the table. It doesn't get much better than this.

Bouillabaisse

SERVES 8 TO 10

If you decide to make the fish stock ahead, it must be used within 2 days or frozen and defrosted. Use only the freshest fish. Monkfish, sea bass, and ocean perch or red snapper make up our favorite combination, but you can create your own according to the guidelines in the chart on page 255. The chopped vegetables for the stock must be fairly small (no larger than 1 inch in diameter) and evenly cut. The rouille must be made the day you are planning to serve the bouillabaisse.

FISH AND SHELLFISH MARINADE

8	ounces small shell-on shrimp, peeled and shells reserved for fish stock
8	ounces large sea scallops, tendons removed (see illustration on page 253) and each scallop halved
1½	pounds fish fillets, cut into 1- to 1½-inch cubes (see chart on page 255)
2	teaspoons sea salt or table salt
¼	teaspoon red pepper flakes
3	medium garlic cloves, minced or pressed through garlic press
½	teaspoon saffron threads
⅓	cup shredded basil leaves
4	tablespoons olive oil
3	tablespoons Pernod

FISH STOCK

1	small fennel bulb, chopped medium (about 2 cups)
1	large carrot, chopped medium (about 1 cup)
2	medium onions, chopped medium (about 2 cups)
4	tablespoons olive oil
3	heads garlic, outer papery skin removed, but heads intact
1	(750-ml) bottle dry white wine (preferably white Côtes de Provence)
2	(28-ounce) cans diced tomatoes with juice
2	large leeks (white and green parts included), split lengthwise, then chopped, washed thoroughly, and drained (about 4 cups)
3	pounds fish frames, gills removed and discarded (see illustrations on page 37), frames rinsed and cut into 6-inch pieces Reserved shrimp shells Stems from 1 bunch fresh parsley
5	sprigs fresh thyme
2	bay leaves
2	teaspoons whole black peppercorns
2	teaspoons sea salt or table salt Zest from 2 medium oranges removed in large strips with vegetable peeler
½	teaspoon saffron threads

STEW

2	pounds mussels, shells scrubbed and beards removed (see illustration on page 251) Salt and ground black pepper

1. Combine all fish and shellfish marinade ingredients in large nonreactive bowl; toss well, cover flush with plastic wrap, and refrigerate 4 hours.

2. Meanwhile, stir fennel, carrot, onions, and oil together in 8-quart heavy-bottomed stockpot or Dutch oven. Cover pot and set over medium-low heat; cook, stirring frequently, until vegetables are fragrant, about 15 minutes. Place garlic in large heavy-duty plastic bag and seal. Smash garlic with rolling pin or meat pounder until flattened. Add smashed garlic to vegetables and continue to cook, stirring frequently, until vegetables are dry and just beginning to stick, about 15 minutes more. (Take care not to let garlic burn.) Add wine and stir to scrape pot bottom, then add tomatoes and their juices, leeks, fish frames, shrimp shells, parsley stems, thyme, bay leaves, peppercorns, salt,

and 4 cups water. Bring to simmer over medium-high heat, reduce heat to medium-low, and simmer, pressing down on fish bones occasionally with wooden spoon to submerge, until stock is rich and flavorful, about 1 hour.

3. Strain stock through large fine-mesh strainer or chinois into large bowl or container (you should have about 9 cups); rinse and wipe out stockpot and return strained stock to pot. Bring stock to boil over high heat and simmer briskly until reduced to 8 cups, about 10 minutes. Off heat, add orange zest and saffron. Let stand 10 minutes to infuse flavors. Strain stock through mesh strainer and set aside.

4. Return fish broth to clean 8-quart stockpot and bring to rolling boil over high heat. Stir in marinated fish and shellfish along with mussels, cover pot, and return to simmer; simmer for 7 minutes, stirring a few times to ensure even cooking. Remove pot from heat, cover, and let stand until fish is cooked through and mussels have opened, about 2 minutes. Season to taste with salt and pepper; ladle into bowls, and float one garlic-rubbed crouton topped with dollop of rouille in each bowl. Serve immediately.

INGREDIENTS : Seafood for Bouillabaisse

While developing this recipe, we threw a ton of fish into our kettle. We wanted to see what worked, what didn't work, and what worked together. We also wanted to come up with textural combinations that pleased the palate and skated across the tongue. The fun of bouillabaisse is that one mouthful can contain buttery flakes of ocean perch, the bite of monkfish, the chew of a little mollusk, and the slippery firmness of shrimp. A tasting determined that a combination of three groups of seafood was best: firm-fleshed fish, flaky fish, and shellfish. Three fish and three shellfish make a great combination—or go with four fish and two shellfish if you prefer. Doubtless many freshwater fish would work well in this recipe, but we limited our testing to saltwater fish in the interest of time.

RECOMMENDED

For best results, choose at least one fish from each category:

FIRM	FLAKY	SHELLFISH
Chilean sea bass	hake	mussels
grouper	ocean perch	sea scallops
haddock	red snapper	shrimp
halibut	Thai snapper	
John Dory		
monkfish		
striped bass		
tilapia		

NOT RECOMMENDED

TOO OILY	INCOMPATIBLE COOKING RATES	TOO MEATY
bluefish	clams	mahi-mahi
mackerel	cod	swordfish
salmon	sole	tuna

Garlic-Rubbed Croutons
MAKES 10 CROUTONS
A single loaf of bread will be enough for both the croutons and rouille.

- 1 loaf (about 1 pound) country-style French bread, cut into ten ½-inch thick slices, remainder reserved for Rouille
- 6 medium garlic cloves, peeled and halved
- 3 tablespoons olive oil

Adjust oven rack (or broiler) to highest position and heat broiler. Arrange bread slices in single layer on baking sheet; broil until lightly toasted, about 1½ minutes. Flip slices and rub second side of each slice with raw garlic, then brush with olive oil. Broil until light golden brown, about 1½ minutes longer. Serve with bouillabaisse.

Rouille
MAKES ABOUT 1 CUP
This rouille is thickened with bread rather than eggs. Although it can be covered and set aside at room temperature for several hours, the sauce may separate. If this happens, simply throw the mixture back into the food processor to restore its creamy texture.

- 1 large red bell pepper (about 9 ounces), roasted, peeled, seeded, and cut into large pieces (about ⅔ cup)

2   ounces reserved bread, trimmed of crust and
     cut into large cubes (about 2 cups)

2   medium garlic cloves, minced finely or pressed
     through garlic press (about 2 teaspoons)

¹⁄₈ teaspoon cayenne pepper

¹⁄₂ cup olive oil

     Salt

In workbowl of food processor fitted with steel blade, process roasted pepper, bread cubes, garlic, and cayenne until smooth, about 20 seconds. With machine running, drizzle olive oil through feed tube; process until rouille has thick, mayonnaise-like consistency. Season to taste with salt. Serve with bouillabaisse.

Cioppino

CIOPPINO IS A SAN FRANCISCO SEAFOOD stew with roots that stretch to the shores of northern Italian fishing communities, where tomato and seafood stew was known as *ciuppin*. Bay Area lore is brimming with tales of Italian fishermen simmering the rich, red stew aboard small fishing boats as they headed back through the Golden Gate. On shore, cioppino was among the first signature dishes served in the city's earliest restaurants at Fisherman's Wharf.

Like many region-specific dishes, there is no one recipe for cioppino. Ingredients and technique vary radically from recipe to recipe. In fact, the stew is more a concept than a combination of specific ingredients. In our research, only one common thread surfaced—the stewing liquid is based on tomatoes. The rest of the ingredients seem to have depended entirely on the sea's daily bounty and the personal taste of the recipe's author. Thus armed with a collection of extremely different recipes, we set out to develop a streamlined cioppino recipe that seafood lovers could enjoy.

Initially, it became clear that many of the recipes for cioppino, especially those from popular cookbooks, were very similar to our bouillabaisse recipe. They called for fish stock; boasted long lists of fish, shellfish, and aromatics; and had intricate

and somewhat troublesome techniques for a stew that was said to have been "thrown together" on fishing boats and piers. Digging further, and into more obscure territory (the Internet and regional cookbooks), we turned up simpler, more straightforward recipes. These recipes were more appealing to us. We decided to make cioppino as simple as possible, in part to offer a recipe that would be less exacting than our version of bouillabaisse. Consequently, we decided to eliminate fish stock and fillets from our cioppino and concentrate on quick-cooking shellfish.

The simpler, more homespun recipes we uncovered had their own problems—a handful called for every dried herb imaginable, and some were nothing more than tomatoes and fish. We knew we wanted something fresher tasting and more complex than fish in tomato sauce. But we found four recipes that were promising. They were similar enough to compare but different enough for experimentation.

Three of the four contenders were universally panned. The procedures, while not difficult, proved to be time-consuming and yielded unevenly cooked seafood and thick, gloppy sauces. Tasters commented that these stews contained too many ingredients; they had to "fight their way" through them. And the extraneous ingredients—such as green peppers, leeks, carrots, and celery—competed entirely too much with the stew's tomato and seafood flavors. The taste of green pepper was especially forward.

These three recipes also called for native San Francisco Dungeness crabs. Fine if you are firing up the stove in Noe Valley, but not quite so easy for the rest of us. We did secure some of these crabs by mail order, but tasters actually found them extremely hard to eat in a stew (especially for those not accustomed or willing to pick meat from the crabs) and voted them out. For our shellfish, then, we settled on clams, mussels, shrimp, and scallops.

Of the four initial test recipes, one stood at the fore. It was a simple recipe that yielded a buttery, sweet tomato broth that was studded with a bounty of seafood—and no excessive or unwanted embellishments. Aromatics included only garlic (of which tasters wanted more), onions (which added a nice, sweet crunch), and parsley (which tasters thought too pedestrian).

The surprise ingredient in this test recipe was butter. The broth was finished with a pat, and it added a luxurious richness to the flavor and texture. Some tasters wanted less fat, but all still liked the addition of butter. With more testing, we found that butter is best incorporated at the outset so it has time to emulsify and blend with other ingredients. We decided to sauté the aromatic vegetables in a combination of butter and oil.

Another interesting finding from this round of tests concerned chicken broth. We had been using canned chicken broth, along with clam juice and canned diced tomatoes, to make the liquid for the stew. While the liquid was no doubt tasty, the chicken broth seemed like the odd man out. We wanted to see if its inclusion was really necessary.

The base, tomatoes, was a done deal. Tasters enjoyed the taste and presence of the bite-sized and sweet canned diced tomatoes, but we wondered if they would be able to detect any difference in stews made with all clam juice or all chicken broth in addition to the tomatoes. In the end, the differences were minimal, but most tasters favored the clam juice—the broth was sweeter, somewhat "fresher," and more fishlike. The chicken broth imparted a slightly salty, meaty flavor that, while not offensive, was not exactly winning, either. A simple combination of tomatoes, bottled clam juice, and juices reserved from the steamed clams and mussels did the trick.

Next we concentrated on the garlic, the heat, and the herbs. Tasters wanted more of everything. We played with the amounts of garlic, starting with a mere 3 tablespoons and taking it up to 6—and tasters still wanted more. Eight tablespoons thankfully appeased. We upped the heat by adding red pepper flakes to the sautéing onions and garlic in small increments until the tasters cried uncle. A touch of Tabasco added an extra kick and smokiness to the mix. As for

herbs, fresh oregano and thyme complemented the stew's basic flavors.

Seasoned with a healthy amount of salt and pepper, the broth had arrived. It was rich and tomatoey, super garlicky, with strong herbal accents and a good dose of the hot stuff.

At this point, we decided to backtrack and figure out the best way to cook the clams, mussels, shrimp, and scallops. It made sense to steam the clams and mussels before making the broth so that their juices would be available. On the other hand, it seemed best to cook the shrimp and scallops at the last minute, right in the cioppino broth.

We started with the clams and mussels. We had been cooking them in a combination of garlic, oil, vermouth, and wine to produce a highly charged broth. Could we lose any part of the regimen? The garlic and oil proved essential. Without it, the clams and mussels tasted flat. But were both vermouth and wine necessary? After a couple tests it became clear that they were not—tasters favored the vermouth-flavored broth. Though it was extremely hard to taste the difference, the vermouth added a bold, bracing flavor while the wine was a bit too fruity.

We wanted to make sure that the clams and mussels did not overcook. Pulling the clams and mussels off heat as soon as they opened kept them from overcooking. When added back to the stew pot, they would spend only enough time to warm through.

On the other hand, the shrimp and scallops needed to be cooked in the broth. We tried adding them to the simmering broth but found that we occasionally overcooked them. In the end, we discovered that the shrimp and scallops could be cooked perfectly and safely by residual heat. We pulled the simmering broth off the heat, added the shellfish (including the cooked clams and mussels), covered the pot, and let it stand for five minutes. The finished stew was magnificent—delicious, hearty, piquant and flavorful, and wholly satisfying. Best of all, this seafood stew can be on the table in less than one hour.

Cioppino

SERVES 6 TO 8

This all-seafood stew from California comes together rather quickly, so there's no place to break up the work and do something ahead. Since the cioppino can be on the table in less than hour, this isn't much of an obstacle to making this dish. Serve with crusty bread to soak up any extra tomato broth.

6 tablespoons extra-virgin olive oil

8 tablespoons coarsely chopped garlic (about 20 cloves)

1 cup dry vermouth

2 dozen littleneck clams, shells scrubbed (see illustration on page 89)

2 dozen mussels, shells scrubbed and beards removed (see illustration on page 251)

2 tablespoons unsalted butter

1 medium onion, chopped medium

1 teaspoon hot red pepper flakes

1 cup bottled clam juice

2 (14½-ounce) cans diced tomatoes

1 bay leaf

2 tablespoons minced fresh oregano leaves

2 tablespoons fresh thyme leaves

1 teaspoon Tabasco sauce

Salt and ground black pepper

1 pound sea scallops, tendons removed (see illustration on page 253)

1 pound medium shrimp, peeled

1. Heat a large stockpot or Dutch oven over medium-high heat until warmed. Add 2 tablespoons oil and 2 tablespoons garlic and cook until the garlic is fragrant but not browned, about 30 seconds. Add ½ cup vermouth and the clams. Cover and steam until the clams open completely, 6 to 7 minutes. Transfer the clams and the steaming liquid to a medium strainer set over a medium bowl. Return the empty stockpot to the burner and heat until warmed. Add 2 tablespoons oil and 2 tablespoons

---

INGREDIENTS: Scallops

Scallops offer several possible choices for the cook, both when shopping and when cooking. There are three main varieties: sea, bay, and calico. Sea scallops are available year-round throughout the country and are the best choice in most instances. Like all scallops, the product sold at the market is the dense, disk-shaped muscle that propels the live scallop in its shell through the water. The guts and roe are usually jettisoned at sea because they are so perishable. Ivory-colored sea scallops are usually at least an inch in diameter (and often much bigger) and look like squat marsh-mallows. Sometimes they are sold cut up, but we found that they can lose moisture when handled this way and are best purchased whole.

Smaller, cork-shaped bay scallops (about half an inch in diameter) are harvested in a small area from Cape Cod to Long Island. Bay scallops are seasonal—available from late fall through midwinter—and are very expensive, up to $20 a pound. They are delicious but nearly impossible to find outside of top restaurants and area fish markets.

Calico scallops are a small species (less than half an inch across) harvested in the southern United States and around the world. They are inexpensive (often priced at just a few dollars a pound) but generally not terribly good. Unlike sea and bay scallops, which are harvested by hand, calicos are shucked by machine steaming. This steaming partially cooks the scallops and gives them an opaque look. Calicos are often sold as "bays," but they are not the same thing. In our kitchen tests, we found that calicos are easy to overcook and often end up with a rubbery, eraser-like texture. Our recommendation is to stick with sea scallops, unless you have access to real bay scallops.

In addition to choosing the right species, you should inquire about processing when purchasing scallops. Most scallops (by some estimates up to 90 percent of the retail supply) are dipped in a phosphate-and-water mixture that may also contain citric and sorbic acids. Processing extends shelf life but harms the flavor and texture of the scallop. Its naturally delicate, sweet flavor can be masked by the bitter-tasting chemicals.

By law, processed scallops must be identified at the wholesale level, so ask your fishmonger. Also, look at the scallops. Scallops are naturally ivory or pinkish tan; processing turns them bright white. Processed scallops are slippery and swollen and usually sitting in milky white liquid at the store. Unprocessed scallops (also called dry scallops) are sticky and flabby. If they are surrounded by any liquid (and often they are not), the juices are clear, not white.

garlic and cook until the garlic is fragrant but not browned, about 10 seconds. Add the remaining ½ cup vermouth and the mussels. Cover and steam until the mussels open completely, 3 to 4 minutes. Transfer the mussels and their steaming liquid to the strainer with the clams. Set the strainer and reserved juices aside. Do not remove the shells.

2. Return the empty pot to the burner, raise the heat to medium-high, and heat until warmed. Add the remaining 2 tablespoons oil, butter, onion, remaining 4 tablespoons garlic, and hot red pepper flakes. Cook, stirring frequently, until the onion is soft and fragrant, about 4 minutes. Add the clam juice, diced tomatoes and their juices, bay leaf, and the reserved clam and mussel juices. Bring to a boil, reduce the heat, and simmer until the flavors blend, about 4 minutes. Add the oregano, thyme, Tabasco, and salt and pepper to taste.

3. Add the scallops and shrimp and press with a wooden spoon to submerge them in the liquid. Place the reserved clams and mussels in their shells on top of the shrimp and scallops. Cover and remove the pot from heat. Let stand until the shrimp are pink and the scallops are milky white, about 5 minutes. Ladle the shellfish and broth into shallow bowls and serve immediately.

INGREDIENTS: Mussels

Most mussels are now farmed either on ropes or along seabeds. You may also see "wild" mussels at the market. These mussels are caught the old-fashioned way—by dredging along the sea floor. In our tests, we found wild mussels to be extremely muddy and basically inedible. Rope-cultured mussels can cost up to twice as much as wild or bottom-cultured mussels, but we found them to be free of grit in our testing. Since mussels are generally inexpensive (no more than a few dollars a pound), we think clean mussels are worth the extra money. Look for tags, usually attached to bags of mussels, indicating how and where the mussels have been grown.

Even the cleanest mussels should be scrubbed under cold running water and debearded (see illustration on page 251). Don't debeard mussels until you are ready to cook them, as debearding can cause the mussel to die. Mussels kept in sealed plastic bags or under water also will die. Keep them in a bowl in the refrigerator and use them within a day or two for best results.

SICILIAN FISH STEW

IN SICILY, FISH IS OFTEN COMBINED WITH tomatoes and favorite local seasonings—olives, capers, raisins, and pine nuts—to create a heady, simple stew. Although easy to prepare, this recipe requires a careful balancing act. Add too much tomato and the dish feels like a pasta sauce. Finding the right mix of tomatoes and fish stock (the other liquid element) is key.

The other challenge is to create just the right blend of sweet, sour, and salty flavors. Many Sicilian dishes, including this one, demonstrate the strong influence of Arabic cooking in the region. The use of dried fruits and nuts in savory dishes is a telltale sign of Arab inspiration. Although these flavors are delicious, they must be used judiciously to keep them from upstaging each other as well as the fish.

We started our work on this recipe with the fish. Several sources suggested firm, white-fleshed fillets, such as snapper. Others pointed to either swordfish or tuna. We prepared a batch of stew with each kind of fish. Tasters felt that the mild flavor of snapper was lost amidst the bold flavors of the stew. Swordfish and tuna have more flavor, and are both well suited to this dish. In addition, the meaty texture of swordfish and tuna works better here—these fish stay firm and hold their shape, especially when cut into large chunks.

Most everyone in the test kitchen liked the beefy texture and meaty appearance of the tuna, although a few dissenters complained about the "fishy" flavor. Swordfish has a great texture and mild, sweet flavor that pleased everyone. We decided to use swordfish in the recipe and give tuna as an option. Either way, we found that 1½-inch cubes of fish offered the best combination of texture and appearance in the final dish. Smaller pieces of fish tended to fall apart, and larger chunks looked ungainly in serving bowls.

As for cooking the fish, we found it best to add the chunks once the stew is nearly done. To prevent overcooking, we simmer the fish until partially cooked and then turn off the heat and cover the pot. The fish finishes cooking by residual heat, thus greatly reducing the chance it will dry out. Needless to say, this stew must be served the second the fish is properly cooked. If the stew is held or reheated, the texture of the fish will decline dramatically.

With the fish chosen, we moved on to the liquid portion of the stew. Most every recipe we ran across when researching this dish called for canned tomatoes and fish stock. Ideally, we wanted the briny taste of the sea offset by the sweetness and acidity of tomatoes.

We started out with 2 cups of canned diced tomatoes and 4½ cups of stock. The resulting stew was too brothy and souplike. We cut back on the tomatoes, which helped reduce the volume but made the stew even more watery. For the next test, we increased the tomatoes to 3 cups and cut the stock way back, to just 2 cups. The finished stew looked better (it was red, not pale pink), and the texture was thicker. To our surprise, the briny flavor of the stock was still present. We had hit upon the right mix. The texture was thinner than tomato sauce but thicker than fish stock with a few bits of tomato, and the flavors of the tomato and stock were harmonized. Although this stew tastes best when made with homemade fish stock, we found that our cheater's stock (page 38), which starts with bottled clam juice, works fine, no doubt because of the presence of the tomatoes and other strong flavors.

It was time to examine the seasonings that give this stew its characteristic sweet, sour, and piquant flavors. Tasters preferred golden raisins to black raisins. We also found that the texture of the raisins was improved by simmering them in the stew rather than adding them at the end of the cooking process.

Pine nuts add a welcome crunch, and mint provides sweetness and fragrance. Some sources suggested stirring these ingredients right into the stew, while others preferred them as a garnish. We found that the texture of the nuts and fresh flavor of the mint was better preserved by using them as a garnish. For maximum flavor, we found it worthwhile to toast the nuts in a dry skillet until lightly colored.

We ran across several recipes that called for cayenne pepper or hot red pepper flakes. Most tasters felt that the heat was not necessary—the sweet and sour elements provide more than enough complexity. If you like, you can add some hot red pepper flakes, but we decided that this ingredient is optional.

Capers and green olives provide the sour, piquant elements in this recipe. We found that fair amounts of both ingredients are needed to achieve the desired effect. Recipes with a teaspoon of capers and a half dozen olives just didn't cut it. In the end, we added 2 tablespoons of capers and ½ cup of sliced green olives. Although some recipes called for adding these ingredients with the garnish, we felt they had more impact on the stew when simmered with the other ingredients.

Sicilian Fish Stew

SERVES 6 TO 8

Sweet and sour flavor combinations are at the heart of this stew and stand up well to stronger flavored fish like swordfish. Tuna is another favorite in Sicily and can be used with excellent results in this tomato-based stew. Add a pinch of red pepper flakes for heat, if desired. Serve with crusty bread or bruschetta—toasted slices of country bread rubbed with garlic and brushed with olive oil.

2	tablespoons extra-virgin olive oil
2	medium onions, chopped coarse
3	large cloves garlic, minced
½	cup dry white wine
2	(14½-ounce) cans diced tomatoes
2	large bay leaves
	Salt and ground black pepper
2	cups Fish Stock (page 37) or Cheater's Fish Stock (page 38)
¼	cup golden raisins
3	pounds swordfish steaks (1 to 1½ inches thick), trimmed of skin and cut into 1½-inch cubes
2	tablespoons drained capers
18	medium green olives, pitted and quartered lengthwise (about ½ cup)
¼	cup pine nuts, toasted
¼	cup coarsely chopped fresh mint leaves

1. Heat the oil in a large stockpot or Dutch oven. Add the onions and cook over medium heat until softened, about 5 minutes. Stir in the garlic and cook until aromatic, about 30 seconds. Add the wine and simmer until reduced by half, 2 to 3 minutes. Add the tomatoes, bay leaves, ½ teaspoon salt, and pepper to taste. Bring to a boil over high heat, reduce the heat, and simmer until the mixture has thickened to the consistency of tomato sauce, 15 to 20 minutes.

2. Add the fish stock and raisins and bring to a boil over high heat. Reduce the heat and simmer until the flavors meld, about 10 minutes.

3. Stir in the fish, capers, and olives and bring back to a simmer over medium heat. Simmer for 7 minutes, stirring a few times to ensure even cooking. Remove the pot from the heat, cover, and let stand until the fish is just cooked through, 2 to 3 minutes. Discard the bay leaves and adjust the seasonings. Serve immediately, garnishing each bowl with pine nuts and mint.

New England Fish Stew

IN NEW ENGLAND, FISH STEW IS SIMILAR to clam chowder. Chunks of white fish take the place of the clams, but otherwise the dishes are fairly similar—onions, potatoes, and bacon or salt pork floating in a briny, creamy broth. Still, there are some other, minor but important, differences. Clams shed so much juice that there's no need for fish stock. The firm, meaty white fish used in this hearty stew sheds no liquid, so fish stock is a must. The other important difference has to do with heft. The potatoes in a clam chowder are cut fairly small so they don't overwhelm the clams—you want everything to fit on the spoon at the same time. For a New England fish stew, the fish is cut into large chunks and the potatoes are often quite large, too. Also, the liquid is thicker and less plentiful. The resulting stew is a main course, not something you sip from a mug for lunch.

After preparing several versions of this stew, we noticed two problems that would need to be addressed. The first issue was the fish—in many recipes the fish fell apart into masses of small flakes. Some flaking was fine, but we wanted the fish to remain in large chunks when cooked. The second problem was the seasonings. Too many recipes added ingredients that had no place in this spartan stew. This was easy enough to fix. We jettisoned tomatoes, cayenne, and any other ingredients that just didn't feel right.

Given the importance of the fish, we decided to work on this question next. We had read several tips for keeping the fish from falling apart in the stew. One recipe suggested laying whole fillets on top of the liquid and letting the fish naturally fall apart into large chunks as it cooked. We found this method worked when there was a lot of liquid in the pot. However, we want a thicker stew, and when we tried cooking the fish this way in a pot with less liquid, the method failed. The potatoes pushed the fish up above the stew liquid and the fish consequently emerged from the pot a bit bland tasting—it had steamed above the liquid rather than poaching in it.

We found that cutting each fillet into 4-ounce pieces (roughly the size of your palm) yielded the best results. The pieces were small enough to sink down into the stew liquid but large enough to hold their shape, making for only a minimum of flaking.

With the fish issue resolved, we moved on to the seasonings. We found recipes with salt pork as well as those with bacon. We prepared pots with each pork product and tasters favored the smoky flavor of the bacon. Although salt pork is more traditional, we decided to listen to the crowd and use bacon in our stew. Once the bacon has been fried, we found it best to remove the crisp bits and then swirl them into the finished stew. If the stew is built on top of the bacon bits, they become flaccid and nearly tasteless. Adding them to the stew just before serving maximizes their flavor and crunch. Don't remove the bacon fat, though. We found that this fat was the best medium for cooking the onions, giving the stew a smoky flavor that vegetable oil could not match.

Once the onions have softened, the liquid and potatoes go into the pot. Homemade fish stock made a real difference in this dish. Cream is the other main liquid element in this stew. We tested half-and-half and whole milk but were disappointed with the results. The liquid was too thin, both in terms of consistency and flavor. In addition to cream and fish stock, we noticed that white wine was used in several recipes. Tasters agreed that the acidity of the white wine balanced the richness of the stock and the cream, so wine become part of our working recipe.

We found that a mix of 3 cups fish stock, ¾ cup cream, and ½ cup wine provided the ideal balance of flavors. There was a problem—the liquid was a bit thin. We tried using more cream, but then the dairy overwhelmed the other flavors. At this point, we decided to pick up a technique from our New England Clam Chowder recipe and stir some flour into the pot once the onions had softened. The flour did the trick, improving the texture of the stew liquid and stabilizing it.

Our recipe was nearly done, with only the potatoes and herbs to test. Red-skinned potatoes are the obvious choice for this dish, and they performed admirably when cut into 1-inch chunks. Although we had decided to keep our recipe simple, a couple of recipes recommended the addition of turnip, a good, old-fashioned New England vegetable, if not terribly usual in a fish stew. We tried turnip and liked it. Its gentle bitterness worked well with the other flavors in the stew.

As for the herbs, we limited ourselves to bay leaves, thyme, and a bit of parsley for freshness, stirred in just before serving. Our finished stew was restrained and dignified, just as you would expect, given its Yankee roots. But it was not austere. The combination of fish, onions, potatoes, bacon, and cream is hearty and satisfying, no matter where you live.

New England Fish Stew

SERVES 6 TO 8

Haddock is the best choice of fish for this recipe. It is traditional, and its firm flesh holds up well in the stew. Cod is next best, simply because it is so traditional and its mild sweet flavor is very similar to that of haddock; it's just a bit more flaky. Alternative fish choices are striped bass, hake, and halibut. We prefer thicker fillets, but you can use thinner fillets as long as you shave two or three minutes off the cooking time.

4 ounces sliced bacon, cut into ¼-inch pieces

2 medium onions, chopped coarse

3 tablespoons flour

½ cup dry white wine

3 cups Fish Stock (page 37)

¾ cup heavy cream

3 medium red potatoes (about 1 pound), scrubbed (see illustration on page 81) and cut into 1-inch cubes

3 medium white turnips (about 1 pound), peeled and cut into 1-inch cubes

½ teaspoon dried thyme

2 large bay leaves

Salt and ground black pepper

3 pounds haddock or cod fillets (¾ to 1 inch thick), rinsed, patted dry, and cut into 4-ounce pieces

¼ cup minced fresh parsley leaves

1. Fry the bacon in a large Dutch oven over medium-low heat until the fat renders and the bacon crisps, about 7 minutes. Remove bacon with slotted spoon and set on paper towel–lined plate. Add the onion to the bacon fat and sauté until softened, about 5 minutes. Stir in the flour and cook until the onions are well coated and flour is lightly colored, about 1 minute. Slowly add the wine and ½ cup fish stock, stirring constantly until the liquid is thick, about 1 minute. Continue adding the stock ¼ cup at a time, stirring all the time and scraping the pan bottom and edges to dissolve flour and loosen the browned bits.

2. Stir in the cream, potatoes, turnips, thyme, bay leaves, ½ teaspoon salt, and pepper to taste. Bring to a boil over high heat, reduce the heat to medium-low, and simmer until the potatoes and turnips are almost tender, about 15 minutes.

3. Add the fish pieces and bring back to a simmer over medium heat. Simmer for 7 minutes, stirring a few times to ensure even cooking. Remove the pot from the heat, cover, and let stand until the fish is just cooked through, 2 to 3 minutes. Remove and discard the bay leaves, stir in the bacon and parsley, and adjust the seasonings. Serve immediately.

12

VEGETABLE STEWS

MANY VEGETABLE STEWS CAN TASTE ONE-dimensional, much like a pan of sautéed vegetables with some broth. There is nothing wrong with these "stews," but they lack the intensity of a good meat, chicken, or fish stew. The biggest challenge when making vegetable stew is figuring out how to create rich, deep flavor. This task is even harder if you want to make a vegetarian vegetable stew (that is, one with no chicken stock). Nonetheless, we have had some good vegetarian stews in the past—dishes worth eating even if you like meat—and wanted to figure out what makes some vegetarian stews delicious and others bland and insipid.

Our plan for this chapter was to develop a classic recipe for hearty vegetable stew and then adapt it to use all root vegetables in one variation and spring vegetables in another variation. We would round out the chapter with recipes for mushroom ragoût and ratatouille. Together, these five stews offer a wide range of flavors. Each one demonstrates that a vegetable stew can be every bit as delicious as a stew made with meat, chicken, or fish.

HEARTY VEGETABLE STEW

OUR GOAL HERE WAS SIMPLE: CREATE A CLASSIC vegetable stew recipe that could then be adapted into a stew made with root vegetables or spring vegetables depending on the time of year and availability of ingredients. This hearty dish would have carrots, peas, and potatoes, but we wondered what other players would be needed to create a satisfying stew.

We started our testing by preparing a number of basic vegetable stews and devising a composite recipe. Early in the testing we learned that we preferred stews that started with onions, carrots, and celery sautéed in oil. (We tested butter but preferred the lighter flavor of olive oil with the vegetables.) For maximum flavor, we found it best to mince these vegetables and let them brown.

At this point, the larger vegetables, those that would hold their shape during cooking and form the backbone of the stew, could be added. High-moisture vegetables that are usually sautéed, such as mushrooms and red onions, should be added first.

We also found the addition of garlic and strong herbs, such as rosemary and thyme, added further depth to this base. The pot could then be deglazed with a little wine. We found that red wine overpowered the vegetables and vastly preferred white wine. We also found that too much wine made the stew boozy, no doubt because of the relatively short simmering time for vegetable stews. However, when we omitted white wine we felt the stew tasted flat. After some adjustment, we found that a half cup added just the right amount of flavor and acidity.

Once the wine had reduced, it was time to add the other liquids. We experimented with various liquids and liked the combination of vegetable stock and tomatoes. Homemade vegetable stock makes a delicious stew (see our recipe on page 34), but canned products are fine as long as you shop carefully. Vegetable stews tend to be sweet, so avoid stocks that are more sweet than savory. You can almost tell by looking at the broth how it will taste. If the color is bright orange, the broth was made with a lot of carrots and will be achingly sweet. (For more information on buying vegetable broth, see page 35.)

Tomatoes were another good addition to a vegetable stew, both for flavor and color. The acidity helped balance some of the sweetness of the vegetables, and the red color kept the stew from looking dull or brown.

Once the stock or broth, wine, and tomatoes had been added to the pot, carrots and potatoes were tossed in. We found it best to cut these vegetables quite large. Stews made with small diced vegetables did not feel hearty enough. One-inch pieces of potatoes and carrots gave the stew a heartier texture and appearance.

When the stew was almost done, delicate green vegetables such as peas were added. If using thawed frozen peas, turn off the heat and let residual heat in the covered pot warm the peas through. We found that frozen peas overcooked if they actually simmered in this stew.

Because different vegetables must go into the pot at different times, we prefer to cook vegetable stews on top of the stove. Vegetable stews can be simmered (not boiled—you don't want the veggies to fall apart) rather quickly, just until the vegetables are tender.

We found that vegetable stews taste watered down when the vegetables are cooked in too much liquid. It's best to cook the vegetables in just as much liquid as is necessary. While other stews are cooked covered, we preferred to cook vegetable stews partially covered to allow some of this liquid to reduce and concentrate in flavor. Cooking the stew with the cover ajar also allowed the liquid to thicken to a nice consistency.

Some sources suggest thickening vegetable stews with flour (like meat stews) or a cornstarch slurry. We tested both options and found that flour sometimes stuck inside tiny crevices in the vegetables (especially mushrooms) and imparted a raw floury taste to the stew. A little cornstarch (diluted in cold water) did a better job since it is smooth. Also, since cornstarch is added at the end of cooking, we could add a bit more or less if the vegetables had shed a bit more or less liquid than expected.

We found it best to add a little acid (we tested both lemon juice and balsamic vinegar and preferred the latter for its complexity and depth) just before serving the stew to balance the sweetness of the vegetables. Parsley finished things off nicely.

Unlike other stews, vegetable stews are best eaten immediately. The texture of the vegetables will suffer if the stews are held and reheated, and the flavors will become muddled. In terms of choosing an accompaniment, consider the stew itself. If the recipe has a lot of potatoes, it's best to avoid traditional stew accompaniments like mashed potatoes or polenta. Biscuits or a loaf of crusty bread—to soak up any stew liquid remaining in bowls—are a better option.

Hearty Vegetable Stew
SERVES 6

Portobello mushrooms give this all-purpose stew a rich, deep flavor that complements that of the other vegetables. The mushrooms also add a meaty texture and color to this hearty American-style stew.

2	tablespoons olive oil
1	medium onion, minced
1	medium carrot, minced
1	medium stalk celery, minced
1	medium red onion, chopped medium

9	medium portobello mushrooms (about 1¼ pounds), stems discarded, caps halved and then sliced ½ inch thick
10	ounces white mushrooms, stems trimmed and mushrooms halved
2	medium cloves garlic, minced
1	teaspoon minced fresh rosemary
½	teaspoon dried thyme
½	cup white wine
2½	cups vegetable stock, preferably homemade
1½	teaspoons salt
1	cup canned diced tomatoes
1	bay leaf
4	large carrots (about 1 pound), peeled, halved lengthwise, and cut into 1-inch pieces
4	medium red potatoes (about 1½ pounds), peeled, quartered lengthwise, and cut crosswise into 1-inch pieces (see illustrations on page 266)
1	tablespoon cornstarch
1	tablespoon cold water
1	cup frozen peas (about 6 ounces), thawed
¼	cup minced fresh parsley leaves
1	tablespoon balsamic vinegar

1. Heat the oil in a large Dutch oven over medium heat. Add the minced onion, carrot, and celery and sauté, stirring frequently, until the vegetables begin to brown, about 10 minutes.

2. Add the red onion and sauté until softened, about 5 minutes. Add the portobello and button mushrooms, raise the heat to medium-high, and sauté until the liquid they release has evaporated, about 10 minutes. Add the garlic, rosemary, and thyme and cook for 30 seconds. Add the wine, scraping up any browned bits stuck to the pot. Cook until the wine is reduced by half, about 2 minutes. Add the stock, salt, tomatoes, bay leaf, carrots, and potatoes, and bring to a boil. Reduce the heat and simmer, partially covered, until the carrots and potatoes are tender, about 35 minutes.

3. Mix the cornstarch with water to form a smooth paste. Stir the paste into the stew and cook until the liquid thickens, 1 to 2 minutes.

4. Turn off the heat, stir in the peas, cover, and let stand until the peas are hot, 3 to 4 minutes. Stir in the parsley and balsamic vinegar, discard the bay leaf, and adjust the seasonings. Serve immediately.

ROOT VEGETABLE STEW

WE WANTED TO TAKE OUR HEARTY VEGETABLE stew and change its character by removing the portobello mushrooms and increasing the amount and variety of root vegetables. We imagined that the stewing liquid would change, too. Tomatoes would seem out of place in such a wintery stew, while cream might be an appropriate addition. We decided to keep the remaining basic outlines of our hearty vegetable stew—sautéed mirepoix (onion, carrot, celery), garlic, herbs, and wine.

We began our testing with the vegetables. To the carrots and potatoes in the hearty vegetable stew, we added some turnips, parsnips, and sweet potatoes. These five root vegetables provided a good balance of colors, textures, and flavors. The turnips lent some pleasing bitterness, and parsnips brought a sweet but complex flavor to the pot. Sweet potatoes are a brightly colored addition, but we found that they cooked more quickly than the other vegetables and were best added to the pot after the others had partially softened.

At this point, we turned our attention to the liquid component of the stew. As with our hearty vegetable stew, white wine added complexity and brightness. We tried finishing the stew with cream, but much preferred a version made with cream added right after the wine. When used this way, the cream brought out the silky texture of the root vegetables. We tried reducing the cream by half once it was added to the pot (a trick often used in sauce making to increase richness) and liked the results. The thickened cream gave the stew a wonderful texture and flavor.

Although our stew was quite good, it was a bit too sweet. We were missing the meaty flavor of the portobello mushrooms. Since tasters felt that fresh mushrooms would be out of place in this stew, we decided to give dried mushrooms a shot. Sure enough, the earthy, pungent flavor of porcini proved to be the perfect foil to sweet root vegetables. We found it best to chop the soaked porcini quite small so that their flavor would diffuse in the stew. Reducing the cream with the mushrooms in the pot further brought out the mushroom flavor.

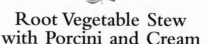

Root Vegetable Stew with Porcini and Cream
SERVES 6

Potatoes, parsnips, carrots, turnips, and sweet potatoes make this stew hearty and satisfying. Porcini mushrooms give the stew a smoky, earthy, meaty flavor that balances the sweetness of the vegetables. Heavy cream is reduced to thicken the liquid and enrich the flavors. See page 85 for tips on soaking dried mushrooms.

½	ounce dried porcini mushrooms
2	tablespoons olive oil
1	medium onion, minced
1	medium carrot, minced
1	medium stalk celery, minced
2	medium cloves garlic, minced
1	teaspoon minced fresh rosemary

PREPARING ROOT VEGETABLES

1. Cut potatoes, turnips, and sweet potatoes in half lengthwise, and then again in half lengthwise.

2. Cut each of the quarters crosswise at 1-inch intervals to yield large chunks.

½ teaspoon dried thyme

½ cup white wine

I cup heavy cream

I¼ cups vegetable stock, preferably homemade

I½ teaspoons salt

I bay leaf

3 medium turnips (about ¾ pound), peeled, quartered lengthwise, and cut crosswise into I-inch pieces (see illustrations on page 266)

3 large carrots (about ¾ pound), peeled, halved lengthwise, and cut into I-inch pieces

3 large parsnips (about ¾ pound), peeled, halved lengthwise, and cut into I-inch pieces

3 medium red potatoes (about I pound), peeled, quartered lengthwise, and cut crosswise into I-inch pieces (see illustrations on page 266)

I large sweet potato (about ¾ pound), peeled, quartered lengthwise, and cut crosswise into I-inch pieces (see illustrations on page 266)

¼ cup minced fresh parsley leaves

I tablespoon lemon juice

1. Place the porcini in a small bowl and cover with 1 cup hot tap water. Soak until softened, about 20 minutes. Carefully lift the mushrooms from the liquid with a fork. Wash the mushrooms under cold water if they feel gritty, then chop fine. Strain the soaking liquid through a strainer lined with a paper towel or coffee filter. Reserve the liquid separately.

2. Heat the oil in a large Dutch oven over medium heat. Add the minced onion, carrot, and celery and sauté, stirring frequently, until the vegetables begin to brown, about 10 minutes.

3. Add the chopped porcini, garlic, rosemary, and thyme and cook until fragrant, about 30 seconds. Add the wine, scraping up any browned bits stuck to the pot. Add the cream and cook until the liquid is reduced by half and almost syrupy, 3 to 4 minutes. Add the strained porcini liquid, stock, salt, bay leaf, turnips, carrots, parsnips, and red potatoes, and bring to a boil. Reduce the heat and simmer, partially covered, for 15 minutes. Add the sweet potato, bring back to a simmer, and cook until the vegetables are tender, about 20 minutes.

4. Stir in the parsley and lemon juice, discard the bay leaf, and adjust the seasonings. Serve immediately.

SPRING VEGETABLE STEW

A SPRING VEGETABLE STEW IS THE PERFECT choice for a cool April night. Palates have long tired of root vegetables and mushrooms, but the weather can still be quite cool. A warming stew with fennel, leeks, asparagus, and peas can provide a hint of spring without seeming too light and insubstantial.

Our goal for this recipe was to create a stew that looked and tasted like spring. We envisioned several shades of green contrasted with a few brightly colored root vegetables for heft. The stew would showcase the early vegetables of the growing season.

We started with the sautéed mirepoix (onion, carrot, and celery), garlic, and herbs that had worked so well in our hearty vegetable stew. Instead of the red onions and mushrooms, we decided to use leeks and fennel. We cut these vegetables into large chunks to create a stew-like texture. Although we had browned the onions and mushrooms, we felt that fennel and leeks would benefit from less heat. We wanted to preserve their bright color and decided to soften, rather than brown, these vegetables.

We decided to keep the carrots and potatoes in this stew but to use smaller amounts of each. Small red potatoes, with their skins on, felt more in tune with the other ingredients. The other greens, the peas and asparagus, would be added during the final phase of cooking.

We now turned our attention to the liquid element. Homemade stock or canned vegetable broth was a must, but we wondered about the wine and tomatoes. Although we worried that the wine might overwhelm the delicate spring vegetables, tasters preferred the version made with wine over the version made without wine. As long as the wine was reduced once it was added to the pot, its acidity stayed in check.

Tomatoes added flavor and color, but everyone agreed that they were out of place in a spring stew. We liked the version of this stew made without tomatoes, but we still missed their freshness and acidity. Lemon and herbs restored these traits to our final recipe.

Our recipe was almost done, but the stew seemed too thick. The cornstarch was overwhelming the delicate vegetables. We tried using cream (both reduced with the wine and stirred in just before serving), but the stew was still too thick and heavy. As a last resort, we tried thickening the finished stew with a little butter. The butter thickened the liquid ever so slightly and gave the stew a lustrous sheen. We decided to work the lemon into the butter and add them together for a final burst of flavor.

Spring Vegetable Stew with Fennel and Asparagus

SERVES 6

The delicate flavors and textures of spring vegetables blend beautifully in this aromatic stew enriched with lemon butter. Unless you can get just-picked fresh peas, frozen are a better option here. An equal amount of shelled and skinned fava beans makes a nice substitute for peas. Fresh chopped chives can be added as a garnish.

- 2   tablespoons olive oil
- 1   medium onion, minced
- 1   medium carrot, minced
- 1   medium stalk celery, minced
- 4   medium leeks, white and light green parts only, split lengthwise, and cut into 1-inch lengths (see illustrations on page 124 to clean)
- 1   large fennel bulb, fronds minced (about 2 tablespoons) and bulb cut into ¼-inch-thick strips (see illustrations below)
- 2   medium cloves garlic, minced
- 1   teaspoon minced fresh thyme leaves
- ½   cup white wine

- 2¼   cups vegetable stock, preferably homemade
- 1½   teaspoons salt
- 1   bay leaf
- 2   large carrots, peeled, halved lengthwise, and cut into 1-inch pieces
- 10   small red potatoes (about ¾ pound), scrubbed (see illustration on page 81) and quartered
- 4   tablespoons unsalted butter, softened
- 1   teaspoon minced lemon zest
- 1   tablespoon lemon juice
- 8   ounces medium spears asparagus, tough ends discarded and cut on the bias into 1-inch pieces
- 1   cup fresh or thawed frozen peas (about 6 ounces)
- 2   tablespoons minced fresh parsley leaves

1. Heat the oil in a large Dutch oven over medium heat. Add the minced onion, carrot, and celery and sauté, stirring frequently, until the vegetables begin to brown, about 10 minutes.

2. Reduce the heat to medium-low, add the leeks and fennel strips, and cook, stirring frequently, until softened, about 10 minutes. Add the garlic and thyme and cook until fragrant, about 30 seconds. Raise the heat to medium-high and add the wine, scraping up any browned bits stuck to the pot. Cook until the wine is reduced by half, about 2 minutes. Add the stock, salt, bay leaf, carrots, and potatoes, and bring to a boil. Reduce the heat and simmer, partially covered, until the vegetables are almost tender, about 25 minutes.

PREPARING FENNEL

1. Trim the feathery fronds and stems. Mince 2 tablespoons fronds and reserve. Discard the stems.

2. Trim slice from base and remove blemished outer layers. Cut in half through base and use knife to remove the pyramid-shaped core in each half.

3. Lay the cored fennel on a work surface and cut in half crosswise. Cut the fennel pieces into ¼-inch-thick strips.

3. Meanwhile, mix the butter with the lemon zest and juice in a small bowl; set aside.

4. Stir the asparagus into the pot, bring back to a simmer, and continue to cook until the vegetables are tender, about 3 minutes. Turn off the heat, stir in the peas, cover, and let stand for 3 to 4 minutes. Discard the bay leaf and stir in the butter mixture, fennel fronds, and parsley. Adjust the seasonings. Serve immediately.

MUSHROOM RAGOÛT

MUSHROOM RAGOÛT IS A DENSE, RICH, well-seasoned stew made with a variety of mushrooms. The focus of this stew is the mushrooms; unlike the other vegetable stews in this chapter, few other vegetables are included. Accordingly, this stew is called a *ragoût,* a meaty stew without large chunks of vegetables. (Minced vegetables can be used in the flavor base.) Typically, ragoûts are made with meat, poultry, or fish. Perhaps alone among vegetables, mushrooms have enough heft to be used in this way.

Mushroom ragoût is luxurious in texture with a hearty, deep brown color. Although we could imagine how wonderful this dish would be if prepared with an assortment of exotic wild mushrooms, we wanted our recipe to include only cultivated varieties found in the supermarket. We also wanted our version to be vegetarian and thought that some rehydrated dried mushrooms might provide an ideal liquid base. We knew an assortment of herbs would add complexity and a member or two of the allium family would add depth to the flavor. We wondered if we would be partial to a more hunter-style mushroom ragoût prepared with tomatoes or a refined variation prepared with cream. In the end, we made our master recipe with tomatoes and created a variation using cream.

We began our tests with the mushrooms. We wanted our ragoût to include mushrooms that offered variety in flavor, texture, and appearance. Portobello, cremini, white button, shiitake, and oyster mushrooms are typically found fresh in supermarkets. Creminis are baby portobellos, and test recipes revealed that including both was redundant for flavor. We preferred portobellos over creminis since they are meatier and can be cut into thick slices that offer an appealing visual contrast with the other mushroom choices. Portobellos have an abundance of dark brown gills on the underside of their caps. Some recipes called for removing the gills to keep them from marring the color of the finished dish. We tested removing the gills and decided this step was not worth the effort.

White button mushrooms taste bland compared with the intense, rich, sweet flavor of portobellos, but we found we liked them in the ragoût. Sautéing develops their flavor, but the true bonus of including this most common variety is in their value. They are the least expensive choice and, when cut in half, offer the most typically definitive mushroom look. We found the ragoût to be lacking visually without them.

Shiitakes have a thin cap, which is tan to dark brown in color. The stems are tough and so are always removed; the caps offered a savory, earthy flavor to the mix. We tried cutting the caps in quarters, but when cooked they were a bit spongy, so we sliced them instead.

Oyster mushrooms are much more delicate than the other mushroom types. Light beige and almost trumpet shaped with ruffled edges, oyster mushrooms may have acquired their name from their elusive briny flavor. Tasters loved the addition of oyster mushrooms in the ragoût. Their flavor contributed complementary and contrasting mushroom tones, but it was their appearance that won accolades. Their light color is deepened when cooked in a dark brown liquid, but their ruffled edges hold up, giving the ragoût a wild, exotic look. We found that packaged oyster mushrooms often contain a wide range of specimens. Some are very small, with the diameter of the trumpet heads being smaller than a quarter. Others are quite large, with diameters of about 3 inches. Since we wanted the shape and ruffled edges of these mushrooms to stand out from the crowd, we chose to not slice them thin but rather to include large pieces. The best approach was to cut them in half or in quarters, depending on their size.

Porcini mushrooms, also known as cepes, are rarely found fresh in this country, but they are available dried. They are treasured throughout Italy and France for good reason. Their flavor is smoky, pungent, rich, deep, earthy, and transcendent. Tasters loved the ragoûts in which dried porcinis were included. The ragoût benefited not just from the mushrooms but also from the water used to rehydrate them. When dried porcinis were not included in a test, we used either water or vegetable stock. The water diluted the mushroom flavors, while the vegetable stock added an odd, off taste that took away from the harmonious mingling of mushroom flavors.

We turned our attention to the aromatics. We next tried using the classic mirepoix combination of minced carrot, celery, and onions. The carrot and celery looked out of place in this stew, and their flavors and textures took away from the mushrooms rather than enhancing them. The carrot was too sweet and the celery too distinctive. We then did a number of tests focusing on alliums. This family of vegetables pairs beautifully with the mushrooms. They add depth and complexity in flavor. When cut small, members of the onion family disappear into the sauce and do not detract from the appearance of the ragoût. We tried regular yellow onions, shallots, garlic, and leeks. The leeks were the least favorite. They were a bit too delicate in flavor and texture. We thought tasters would prefer the more subtle, mild flavor of the shallots, but tests showed that the fuller flavor of regular yellow onions stood up nicely to the assortment of assertive mushroom flavors. Garlic is great with this mushroom mix. It adds a pungent note and depth to the flavor.

Most vegetable stews start with olive oil, but butter is commonly used in mushroom ragoûts. We tested both and found that tasters preferred the flavor of the butter. The butter also helped thicken the liquid in the stew.

Most mushroom stews also contain some alcohol. White wine is the common choice in other vegetable stews, but tasters did not like it in ragoût. It seemed too limp and just didn't have enough heft to brighten the flavors. We tried a dry red wine and found it made the ragoût too boozy and the flavors too strong and sharp. Next we tried dry Madeira and dry sherry. These fortified wines are often found in mushroom ragoût recipes, and testing them showed us why. They are stronger flavored than white wine but not as overpowering as red

wine. The Madeira was favored for its smooth, rich flavor, which blended more readily with the mushroom flavors.

Many mushroom ragoût recipes include tomatoes in one form or another. Their acidity adds a bright note that contrasts nicely with the hearty, earthy flavor of the mushrooms. Given that this dish is most often prepared in the fall and winter, when fresh garden tomatoes are not available, canned diced tomatoes or tomato paste are the most common options. We tested both and were surprised to discover that tasters liked both. The canned diced tomatoes added flecks of brilliant red color to the pot as well as a hint of freshness. The tomato paste added a desirable contrast in flavor, but its effects on texture and appearance were noticeably different from that of the diced tomatoes. The paste disappeared into the stew and thickened the liquid—a trait that we deemed positive. In the end, though, tasters missed the bright red bits of tomato; the stew made with tomato paste seemed too monochromatic. Diced tomatoes were added to our master recipe, just edging out the tomato paste.

With our main ingredients pretty much in hand, we began testing cooking methods. We found that browning brings out the flavors of the mushrooms, with one exception. The oyster mushrooms are so delicate that they will fall apart if sautéed for more than a minute or two. We decided to add them with the garlic.

As for herbs, we found this hearty ragoût to be an ideal vehicle for some of the more sturdy and strong-flavored choices. As the song says, we added parsley, sage, rosemary, and thyme. The parsley was used to add brightness to the stew just before serving. The other herbs went into the pot with the garlic.

Some sources indicate that mushroom ragoût is done once the liquid is added. Our tests showed that the mushrooms benefit from 10 minutes of simmering. Cooking the mushrooms in the stew liquid improves their texture and concentrates their flavor. Using butter and simmering the mushrooms uncovered helped to concentrate the flavors and thicken the texture of the liquid. But after 10 minutes of simmering, the liquid was still on the thin side. We tried stirring three additional tablespoons of butter into the ragout, and this worked perfectly. The extra butter, added at the end of cooking, enriched the flavor, thickened the texture, and gave the liquid a bit of a glossy shine.

We found that an acidic ingredient stirred into the pot of all of our vegetable stew recipes enlivens the flavors. We tried lemon juice, balsamic vinegar, and sherry vinegar with this mushroom ragoût. We first determined that 1 tablespoon—the amount used for the other stews—was too much. This made sense when we realized the yield of this ragoût is significantly less than that of the other stews. We cut the amount in half and tried again. Lemon juice was not potent enough, and the sherry vinegar was too sharp. Balsamic proved to be perfect—its rich, sweet but sharp flavor balances the deep tones of the mushrooms.

Mushroom Ragoût
SERVES 4 TO 6

Five types of mushrooms are combined to create this hearty, rich, rustic ragoût. They can be found in most supermarkets, and all are fresh except the porcinis. Dried porcinis add a smoky, earthy tone and when rehydrated provide a flavorful liquid for the stew. (See page 85 for tips on soaking dried mushrooms.) Since ragoûts are stews, it is common practice to serve them over an accompanying starch or, in the case of mushrooms, possibly alongside some protein. Mushroom ragoût is fabulous over polenta or mashed potatoes or tossed with pasta. It's also delicious in smaller portions served over a boneless chicken breast or even a steak.

½	ounce dried porcini mushrooms
5	tablespoons unsalted butter
I	medium onion, minced
7	medium portobello mushrooms (about I pound), stems discarded, caps halved and then sliced ½ inch thick
10	ounces white mushrooms, stems trimmed and mushrooms halved
4	ounces shiitake mushrooms, stems discarded, caps sliced thin
4	ounces oyster mushrooms, stems discarded, caps halved or quartered depending on size
3	medium cloves garlic, minced
I	teaspoon minced fresh rosemary
I	teaspoon minced fresh sage leaves
I	teaspoon minced fresh thyme leaves
¼	cup dry Madeira
I	cup canned diced tomatoes
I ½	teaspoons salt
2	tablespoons minced fresh parsley leaves
I	teaspoon balsamic vinegar

1. Place the porcini in a small bowl and cover with 1 cup hot tap water. Soak until softened, about 20 minutes. Carefully lift the mushrooms from the liquid with a fork. Wash the mushrooms under cold water if they feel gritty, then chop fine. Strain the soaking liquid through a strainer lined with a paper towel or coffee filter. Reserve the liquid separately.

2. Heat 2 tablespoons butter in a Dutch oven over medium heat. Add the onion and sauté, stirring frequently, until softened and lightly browned, about 10 minutes. Add the portobello, button, and shiitake mushrooms and sauté until the liquid they release has evaporated, about 10 minutes. Add the chopped porcini, oyster mushrooms, garlic, rosemary, sage, and thyme and cook until fragrant, about 30 seconds. Add the Madeira, scraping up any browned bits stuck to the pot. Add the reserved porcini soaking liquid, diced tomatoes, and salt and bring to a boil. Reduce the heat to low and simmer until the flavors concentrate, about 10 minutes. (Ragoût can be refrigerated in an airtight container for 3 or 4 days. Bring back to a simmer over medium-low heat.)

3. Stir in the remaining 3 tablespoons butter, parsley, and balsamic vinegar. Adjust the seasonings and serve immediately.

➤ VARIATION
Mushroom Ragoût with Cream
Cream replaces tomato to make a more refined variation of this dish. In our testing, we found it best to let the cream reduce and thicken rather than just adding it to the stew at the end of the cooking time. This variation is especially good over noodles.

Follow recipe for Mushroom Ragoût, replacing tomatoes with ½ cup heavy cream. Proceed as directed, omitting the 3 tablespoons butter stirred into the stew in step 3.

RATATOUILLE

SUMMER IN PROVENCE IS THE TIME FOR ratatouille, a medley of vegetables seasoned with garlic and fresh herbs. The lineup of vegetables can vary, but most recipes rely on summer's heavy hitters—eggplant, zucchini, tomatoes, and bell peppers—supplemented with onion. There are several styles of ratatouille (each Provençal cook seems to have a personal take on this dish) so we decided to start our testing by choosing a style to pursue.

A preliminary round of tests helped us to define this dish. Out were the gratin-style ratatouilles. Layered like lasagne and baked completely in the oven, they hardly resembled an exemplar ratatouille. While most tasters appreciated the simmered ratatouilles, they were not fond of their oily, slimy, watery texture. Cooking the vegetables in batches improved the dish, but there was much room for improvement. We wanted a ratatouille that maintained the integrity and flavor of each vegetable. Most of all, we wanted to keep the eggplant from becoming soggy or greasy (eggplant has a tendency to soak up oil like a sponge).

Although many traditional recipes call for bell peppers, tasters unanimously disliked the peppers' overwhelming flavor. In the interest of pleasing the masses, we omitted it. That left us with eggplant, zucchini, and tomatoes.

While most recipes we found called for globe eggplant, we found a few that called for either Japanese or Italian eggplant, stating that the flavor and texture of the latter two were superior to the standard globe. In a head-to-head comparison of the three, we found that neither the Japanese nor the Italian eggplant had anything on the globe eggplant—at least in this dish. In addition, Japanese and Italian eggplant can be somewhat harder to find as well as more expensive than the globe.

To address the potential soggy/greasy problem, we began by salting the eggplant to rid it of its extra moisture, a common practice. There are two schools of thought on the benefits of this procedure. One camp says that salting rids the eggplant of the inherent bitterness found in the liquid. The other camp suggests that ridding the very porous eggplant of much of its liquid makes it more compact, so it will not soak up oil quite so readily. We tested salted eggplant (cut into cubes and salted for 1½ hours) against unsalted eggplant, and tasters were not able to distinguish an appreciable difference in bitterness between the two. The salted eggplant did, however, fare much better when it came to soaking up less oil during sautéing. The unsalted eggplant, which needed a continuous feeding of oil to keep it from sticking to the pan, absorbed every bit of oil—almost one cup for two eggplants! In addition, the liquid left in the unsalted eggplant caused the cubes to steam rather than brown; the mixture became a soggy mess.

In addition to salting the eggplant, we found that pressing the cubes between several layers of paper towels helps to remove much of the remaining liquid from the eggplant, and further compacts its structure. When cooked and compared with eggplant that had been salted and merely patted dry, the salted and pressed eggplant soaked up nearly one-quarter cup less oil. The more compact cubes also better retained their shape.

As for the zucchini, we expected that we would need to use the same salting and pressing technique we used with the eggplant. After all, zucchini is mostly water—95 percent to be exact. Indeed, salting and pressing ridded the zucchini of its excess liquid, but this time tasters longed for a fresher flavor and a juicier, more plump texture.

We had read that dry heat (such as grilling or broiling) is the optimal method for cooking zucchini and often cancels the need for salting and pressing. We tested sautéed zucchini against broiled zucchini, and the differences were dramatic. Sautéed zucchini fell apart in the pan from steaming in its own juices. This zucchini was bland, limp, and slightly slimy. The broiled zucchini was much better, packed with flavor and still texturally interesting. On the downside, the zucchini started to burn a bit during the long time under the broiler (enough time to cause the evaporation of the liquid). We remedied this by roasting the zucchini in a 500-degree oven. The intense heat caused massive evaporation of liquid but eliminated the risk of burning.

At this point we did a bit of backtracking. We wondered whether the eggplant, if cooked using the same high-heat roasting method, would no longer need to be salted or pressed. Alas, this was not to be. Without the salting or pressing, the eggplant seemed very reluctant to give up any of its moisture, even under the persuasion of a 500-degree oven. Salting and pressing deepened the flavor of the eggplant, and the pieces were structurally firm and intact. We did nonetheless discover a big advantage to roasting rather than sautéing the eggplant. With the sauté method, the smallest amount of oil we could get away with was ½ cup. With the roasting method, we needed only 2 tablespoons oil to sufficiently coat both the zucchini and the eggplant before they were put in the oven.

With the eggplant and zucchini elements under control, it was time to move on to tomatoes. We preferred beefsteak tomatoes for their robust flavor, abundance of fleshy meat, and availability. Roma tomatoes did not work as well. Their gentler flavor became muted as they cooked down. We found that the tomatoes did not improve when roasted. While their flavor intensified as a result of the dehydration, they no longer carried the same fresh flavor that they had after sautéing. We found that it was necessary to sauté the tomatoes only until they just began to lose their structure, about 5 minutes.

Since we had decided to sauté the tomatoes, it seemed logical to sauté the onion and the garlic first, then add the tomatoes. The onion responded best to gentle heat—it softened and became golden. When we cooked the onion over higher heat, it browned and developed an overstrong flavor. As for the garlic,

tasters found that two cloves provided just enough punch; any more overpowered the other flavors.

Finally, we tested herbs. Quite a few recipes used solely basil. Some called for herbes de Provence, a dried mixture of several Mediterranean herbs. In the end, we went for a combination of fresh parsley, thyme, and basil in quite large amounts, for a total of 5 tablespoons. We first tried adding the herbs with the roasting vegetables, hoping to infuse the eggplant and zucchini with the flavor and aroma of the herbs. Ironically, the opposite occurred. Under a dry heat, the herbs lost all flavor and shriveled up to tiny specks. Adding the herbs at the very end of cooking preserved their bright color and flavor.

Ratatouille

SERVES 4 TO 6

You can serve ratatouille as a main course by adding couscous, pasta, or even focaccia along with a leafy salad. It's also an ideal summer side dish with lamb or chicken. See the illustrations below for tips on peeling the tomatoes.

2   medium globe eggplants (2 to 2½ pounds total), cut into 1-inch dice
     Salt
2   large zucchini (about 1½ pounds total), cut into 1-inch dice
¼   cup extra-virgin olive oil

PEELING TOMATOES

1. Place the cored tomatoes in a saucepan of boiling water, no more than five at a time. Boil until the skin splits and begins to curl around the cored area of the tomato, about 15 seconds for very ripe tomatoes or up to 30 seconds for firmer tomatoes. Remove the tomatoes from the water with a slotted spoon and place them in a bowl of ice water to stop the cooking process.

2. When the tomatoes are cool enough to handle, peel back the skins with a paring knife. Use the curled edges at the core as your point of departure.

1 large onion (about 8 ounces), cut into 1-inch
   pieces
2 medium cloves garlic, minced
3 medium ripe tomatoes, cored, peeled, and cut
   into 2-inch pieces
2 tablespoons chopped fresh parsley leaves
2 tablespoons chopped fresh basil leaves
1 tablespoon minced fresh thyme leaves
   Ground black pepper

1. Place the eggplant in a large colander set over a bowl. Sprinkle the eggplant with 2 teaspoons salt and toss to distribute the salt evenly. Let the eggplant stand for at least 1 hour and preferably 2 to 3 hours. Rinse the eggplant well to remove the salt and place on a triple thickness of paper towels. Cover with another triple layer of towels. Using your palms, press the eggplant firmly until it feels very firm when pressed between fingertips. Set aside.

2. Adjust the oven racks to the upper-middle and lower-middle positions and heat the oven to 500 degrees. Toss the eggplant and zucchini with 2 tablespoons oil in a large bowl. Divide the mixed vegetables between 2 parchment-lined rimmed baking sheets and season liberally with salt to taste. Place the baking sheets in the oven and roast the vegetables, stirring every 10 minutes, until the eggplant and zucchini are well-browned and very tender, 30 to 40 minutes. Remove from the oven and set aside.

3. Meanwhile, in a heavy-bottomed Dutch oven, heat the remaining 2 tablespoons oil over medium heat. Add the onion, reduce the heat to medium-low, and cook, stirring often, until the onion is golden and very soft, 15 to 20 minutes. Add the garlic and cook until just fragrant, about 30 seconds. Add the tomatoes and cook until their juices are released and tomatoes begin to break down, about 5 minutes.

4. Add the reserved eggplant and zucchini to the pot, stirring gently but thoroughly to coat until the vegetables are reheated. Add the parsley, basil, and thyme and season to taste with salt and pepper. (Ratatouille can be refrigerated in an airtight container for 3 or 4 days. Warm over medium-low heat.) Serve immediately.

13

CHILIS, GUMBOS, AND CURRIES

THIS CHAPTER INCLUDES THREE TYPES OF stews—chilis, gumbos, and curries—each of which is open to countless variation.

Defined in the broadest possible sense, a chili consists of meat, dried red chiles ground to a powder, and liquid and is more often than not seasoned with garlic, cumin, and oregano. But, of course, it's not that easy. Our research turned up numerous distinct styles of chili, the most prevalent of which were from Texas (chili con carne, with big chunks of beef and no beans) and Cincinnati (a sweeter, not terribly spicy version made with ground beef and served with spaghetti and beans). Vegetarian chilis are another common option. We cover all three styles in this chapter.

Gumbo is Louisiana's most famous stew. The broth is thick, and the flavors are heady and strong. Gumbo can include shrimp, crayfish, chicken, and/or sausage. No matter which main ingredients are chosen, the basic outlines of this dish remain the same.

The term *curry* encompasses a wide range of dishes made throughout Asia. Almost any Indian stew can be called a curry, and the term is used throughout Southeast Asia, where the dish takes on many different forms. In this chapter, we focus on two basic styles of curry—classic Indian curry with garlic, ginger, and spices and Thai curry with coconut milk.

CHILI CON CARNE

A STRICTLY TEXAN CHILI, KNOWN AS CHILI con carne, depends on either pureed or powdered ancho chiles, uses beef, excludes tomato, onion, and beans, and features a high proportion of meat to chiles. We wanted a chili that would be hearty, heavy on the meat, and spicy but not overwhelmingly hot. We wanted the sauce to have a creamy consistency somewhere between soup and stew. The flavors would be balanced so that no single spice or seasoning stood out or competed with the chile or beef.

Because chiles are the heart of chili con carne, we had to learn about the different types. After considerable testing and tasting, we settled on a combination of ancho and New Mexico Red for the dried chiles (see page 279 for more about dried chiles),

with a few jalapeños added for their fresh flavor and bite. Chilis made with toasted and ground whole dried chiles tasted noticeably fuller and warmer than those made with chili powder. The two main toasting methods are oven and skillet, and after trying both, we went to the oven simply because it required less attention and effort than skillet toasting. The chiles will puff in the oven, become fragrant, and dry out sufficiently after five to six minutes. One caveat, though: Overtoasted chiles can take on a distinctly bitter flavor, so don't let them go too long.

With the chiles chosen and toasted, the next big question was how best to prepare them. The two options were to rehydrate the toasted chiles in liquid and process them into a puree or to grind them into a powder. It didn't take long for us to select grinding as the preferred method. It was easier, faster, and much less messy than making the puree, which tasters felt produced a chili that was too rich, more like a Mexican enchilada sauce than a bowl of chili.

This felt like the right time to determine the best ratio of chile to meat. Many of the recipes we looked at suggested that a tablespoon of ground chile per pound of meat was sufficient, but we found these chilis to be bland and watery. Two tablespoons per pound of meat, on the other hand, produced chili with too much punch. We compromised: 1½ tablespoons per pound was the way to go.

There was little agreement in the recipes we had collected as to when the chili powder should be added. After running several tests, we found that sautéing the spices, including the chiles, was key to unlocking their flavor. We also discovered that blending the chili powder with water to make a paste kept it from scorching in the pot; this step is advised.

Since chuck is our favorite meat for stewing, we knew it would work best in chili. Still, there were some aspects of the meat question that had to be settled. Should the chuck be standard hamburger grind, coarser chili grind, hand-cut into tiny cubes, or a combination? The chili made from cubes of beef was far more appealing than those made from either type of ground beef (they both had a grainy, extruded texture). Most of the recipes we looked at specified that the meat should be cut into ¼-inch cubes. However, we found that larger 1-inch chunks gave the chili a satisfying chew. In addition, cutting a chuck roast into larger chunks was much, much faster and easier than breaking it down into a fussy, ¼-inch dice.

Next we set out to determine the best type, or types, of liquid for the chili. The main contenders were water, chicken stock, beef stock, beer, black coffee, and red wine. We tried each one on its own, as well as in any combination we felt made sense. The surprise result was that we liked plain water best, because it allowed the flavor of the chiles to come through in full force. Both stocks, whether on their own or combined in equal parts with each other or with water, muddied the chile flavors. All of the other liquids, used either alone or mixed with an equal part of chicken stock or water, competed with the chile flavor.

Another basic factor to determine was the garlic. Tasters agreed that three cloves were too few and eight were too many, so we settled on five. We found many recipes that called for powdered garlic rather than fresh. Out of obligation, we tested powdered versus fresh garlic and found fresh to be far superior.

Though common in modern recipes, Texas chili lore leaves tomatoes and onions out of the original formula. These two ingredients may break with tradition, but we found both to be essential. The acidity of the tomato and the sweetness of the onion, both used in small amounts, add interest and dimension to the chili. The batches we tested without them were decidedly dull. We tested various amounts and types of tomato products and determined that more than one cup pushed the flavor of the chili toward that of a spaghetti sauce. Products with a smooth consistency, such as canned crushed tomatoes or plain tomato sauce, helped create the smooth sauce we wanted.

We found that bacon lends the chili a subtly sweet, smoky essence that is most welcome. Other "secret" ingredients fell by the way side. Coke imparted a sourish, off taste. Brown sugar cut the heat of the chiles too much. An ounce of unsweetened chocolate gave the chili a rounder, deeper flavor, and 2 tablespoons of peanut butter made the sauce creamier and earthy tasting. Much as we liked both chocolate and peanut butter, we decided they were not essential.

Chili is generally thickened to tighten the sauce and make it smoother. Flour, roux (a paste of flour and melted butter), cornstarch, and masa harina (a flour ground from corn treated with lime, or calcium oxide) are the most common options. Dredging the meat in flour before browning and adding a roux along with the liquid were both effective, but these approaches made it more difficult to finesse the consistency of the finished product because both were introduced early in the cooking process. Roux added at the end of cooking left a faint taste of raw flour. We did prefer thickening at the end of cooking, though, because we could add thickener gradually until the chili reached the right consistency. We like chili thick enough to coat the back of a wooden spoon, like the custard base of homemade ice cream.

Our first choice for thickening was masa harina, added at the end of cooking. Masa both thickened the sauce and imparted a slightly sweet, earthy corn flavor to the chili. If masa harina is not available in your grocery store and you'd rather not mail-order it, use a cornstarch and water slurry. It brings no flavor to the chili, but it is predictable, easy to use, and gives the gravy a silky consistency and attractive sheen.

One last note: Time and time again, tasters observed that chili, like many stews, always improved after an overnight rest because the flavors blended and mellowed. If you are able to, cook your chili a day ahead. The result will be worth the wait.

Chili Con Carne
SERVES 6

To ensure the best chile flavor, we recommend toasting whole dried chiles and grinding them in a minichopper (see page 295) or spice-dedicated coffee grinder, all of which takes only 10 (very well-spent) minutes. Select dried chiles that are moist and pliant, like dried fruit.

To toast and grind dried chiles: Place chiles on a rimmed baking sheet in a 350-degree oven until fragrant and puffed, about 6 minutes. Cool, stem, and seed, tearing pods into pieces. Place pieces of the pods in a spice grinder and process until powdery, 30 to 45 seconds.

For hotter chili, boost the heat with a pinch of cayenne or a dash of hot pepper sauce near the end of cooking. Serve the chili with warm pinto or kidney beans, corn bread or chips, corn tortillas or tamales, rice, biscuits, or plain crackers. Top with chopped fresh cilantro, minced white onion, diced avocado, shredded cheddar or Jack cheese, or sour cream.

3 tablespoons ancho chili powder, or 3 medium pods (about ½ ounce), toasted and ground (see note)

3 tablespoons New Mexico Red chili powder, or 3 medium pods (about ¾ ounce), toasted and ground (see note)

2 tablespoons cumin seeds, toasted in a dry skillet over medium heat until fragrant, about 4 minutes, and ground

2 teaspoons dried oregano, preferably Mexican

4 pounds beef chuck roast, trimmed of excess fat and cut into 1-inch cubes

2 teaspoons salt, plus extra for seasoning

7 to 8 slices bacon (8 ounces), cut into ¼-inch dice

1 medium onion, minced

5 medium cloves garlic, minced

4 to 5 small jalapeño chile peppers, stemmed, seeded, and minced

1 cup canned crushed tomatoes or plain tomato sauce

2 tablespoons lime juice

5 tablespoons masa harina or 3 tablespoons cornstarch

Ground black pepper

1. Mix the chili powders, cumin, and oregano in a small bowl and stir in ½ cup water to form a thick paste; set aside. Toss the beef cubes with 2 teaspoons salt; set aside.

2. Fry the bacon in a large Dutch oven over medium-low heat until the fat renders and the bacon crisps, about 10 minutes. Remove the bacon with a slotted spoon to a paper towel–lined plate; pour all but 2 teaspoons fat from the pot into a small bowl; set aside. Increase the heat to medium-high; sauté the meat in four batches until well-browned on all sides, about 5 minutes per batch, adding additional 2 teaspoons bacon fat to pot as necessary. Set the browned meat aside.

3. Reduce the heat to medium and add 3 tablespoons bacon fat to the now-empty pot. Add the onion and sauté until softened, 5 to 6 minutes. Add the garlic and jalapeños and sauté until fragrant, about 1 minute. Add the chili powder mixture and

sauté until fragrant, 2 to 3 minutes. Add the reserved bacon and browned beef, crushed tomatoes, lime juice, and 7 cups water. Bring to a simmer. Continue to cook at a steady simmer until the meat is tender and the juices are dark, rich, and starting to thicken, about 2 hours.

4. Mix the masa harina with ⅔ cup water (or cornstarch with 3 tablespoons water) in a small bowl to form a smooth paste. Increase the heat to medium, stir in the paste, and simmer until thickened, 5 to 10 minutes. Adjust the seasoning generously with salt and ground black pepper to taste. (For best flavor, refrigerate in an airtight container overnight or for up to 5 days. Bring back to a simmer over medium-low heat.) Serve immediately.

➤ VARIATION

Smoky Chipotle Chili Con Carne

Grill-smoking the meat along with chipotle chiles gives this chili a distinct, but not overwhelming, smoky flavor. Be sure to start with a chuck roast that is at least 3 inches thick. The grilling is not meant to cook the meat but rather to flavor it by searing the surface and smoking it lightly.

1. To SMOKE THE MEAT: Puree 4 medium cloves garlic with 2 teaspoons salt. Rub the intact chuck roast with puree, and sprinkle evenly with 2 to 3 tablespoons New Mexico Red chili powder; cover and set aside. Meanwhile, build a hot fire in the grill. When you can hold your hand 5 inches above the grill surface for no more than 3 seconds, spread the hot coals to an area about the size of roast. Open the bottom grill vents, scatter 1 cup soaked mesquite or hickory wood chips over the hot coals, and set the grill rack in place. Place the meat over hot coals and grill-roast, opening the lid vents three-quarters of the way and covering so that the vents are opposite the bottom vents to draw smoke through and around the roast. Sear the meat until all sides are dark and richly colored, about 12 minutes per side. Remove the roast to bowl; when cool to the touch, trim and cut into 1-inch cubes, reserving juices.

2. To MAKE THE CHILI: Follow recipe for Chili Con Carne, omitting the browning of the beef cubes and substituting 5 minced canned chipotle peppers in adobo sauce for jalapeños. Add the grilled meat and juice with cooked bacon.

CINCINNATI CHILI

REDOLENT OF CINNAMON AND OTHER WARM spices, Cincinnati chili is unlike any chili served in Texas—or the rest of the country, for that matter. On sight alone, its sauciness makes it look more like a Sloppy Joe filling or some strange sauce for pasta. One taste reveals layers of spices you expect from Middle Eastern or North African cuisine, not food from the American heartland.

Legend has it that Cincinnati chili was created in the 1920s by a Macedonian immigrant named Athanas Kiradjieff. He ran a hot dog stand called the Empress, where he served his chili over hot dogs. This deluxe hot dog eventually morphed into the "five-way" concoction beloved by locals.

Cincinnati chili is as much about the garnishes, or "ways," as the chili itself. On its own, it is merely one-way Cincinnati chili. Served over buttered spaghetti, it is two-way. Add shredded cheddar cheese and it becomes three-way. With chopped onions, four-way, and the final garnish, for five-way chili, is warmed kidney beans.

To get a handle on this unusual chili, we tested a number of recipes, including one purporting to be from the original Empress Chili Parlor. We noticed two problems. First, most of the versions tested were much too greasy. Second, the myriad spices used in many recipes were overwhelming. Our goals were clear—cut the fat and figure out which spices were essential and which were not.

We focused on the meat element first. In most chili recipes, the meat is browned to build flavor and render some fat, which can be spooned off. Cincinnati chili is unique because it calls for boiling ground beef instead of browning it. The boiled meat had a texture described as "wormy" by most tasters, which, as odd as it sounds, pairs well with the pasta and other accompaniments. But boiling the meat can make it difficult to rid the meat of excess fat, particularly since traditional recipes use the blanching liquid as the base for the chili.

We decided to try replacing ground chuck (80 to 85 percent lean), which is the usual choice for chili, with ground round (90 percent lean). This idea sounded great, but tasters felt that the flavor of the chili made with ground round suffered. Ground chuck has a beefier flavor, so we would have to figure out some other way to eliminate the excess grease from the final dish.

For our next batch of chili, we added the beef to

INGREDIENTS: Dried Chiles

For the most part, chili con carne is based on fairly mild dried chiles. The most common of these are dark, mahogany red, wrinkly skinned ancho chiles, which have a deep, sweet, raisiny flavor; New Mexico Reds, which have a smooth, shiny, brick-red skin and a crisp, slightly acidic, earthy flavor; California chiles, which are very similar to New Mexico in appearance but have a slightly milder flavor; and long, shiny, smooth, dark brown pasilla chiles. Pasillas, which are a little hotter than the other three varieties, have grapey, herbal flavor notes, and, depending on the region of the country, are often packaged and sold as either ancho or mulato chiles.

We sampled each of these types, as well as a selection of preblended commercial powders, alone and in various combinations in batches of chili. Though the chilis made with individual chiles tasted much more pure and fresh than any of the premixed powders, they nonetheless seemed one-dimensional on their own. When all was said and done, the two-chile combination we favored was equal parts ancho (for its earthy, fruity sweetness and the stunning deep red color it imparted to the chili) and New Mexico (for its lighter flavor and crisp acidity).

Chile heat was another factor to consider. Hotter dried chiles that appear regularly in chili include guajillo, de árbol, pequin, japonés, and cayenne. Though we did not want to develop a fiery, overly hot chili, we did want a subtle bite to give the dish some oomph. We found that minced jalapeños, added with the garlic to the chili pot, supplied some heat and a fresh vegetable flavor.

ANCHO

CALIFORNIA

NEW MEXICO RED

PASILLA

salted, boiling water and blanched it for three minutes, or until an unappetizing raft of oily meat foam had risen to the surface. We then drained the beef and discarded the water—along with the fat. The resulting chili was grease-free but lacked the body and flavor that fat provides. We had gone too far. Next, we cut the blanching time back to only 30 seconds, and the results were much better. The chili was rich and fully flavored, without being slick or greasy. This method also retained the traditional "wormy" texture of the meat.

Like curries in India, the mixture of spices in Cincinnati chili varies from recipe to recipe (and house to house). Some mixes contain just two or three spices, while others embrace the entire spice cabinet and are more evocative of a Moroccan souk than an Ohio hot dog. We hoped to isolate the key flavors and create a streamlined spice mixture.

We had uncovered all kinds of incongruous combinations in our research, including one recipe that called for coriander, cardamom, turmeric, and nutmeg—a simply dreadful mixture. Tasters also objected to cloves and mace, both of which were deemed too overpowering. Chili powder, cinnamon, and cayenne pepper were essential, although the latter had to be used sparingly. Cincinnati chili should not be scorching hot.

Cumin, in addition to the small amount of cumin

SCIENCE: How Come You Don't Think It's Hot?

One enduring mystery among those partial to spicy food is why people have such varying tolerances for the heat of chile peppers. As it turns out, there are several reasons why your dinner companion may find a bowl of chili only mildly spicy while the same dish causes you to frantically summon a waiter for a glass of milk to cool the heat before you expire. (Milk, not water, is the thing to drink when you want to cool the fire in your mouth.)

Your dining partner may be experiencing "temporary desensitization." The phenomenon, discovered by Barry Green of the Monell Chemical Senses Institute in Philadelphia, occurs when you eat something spicy hot, then lay off for a few minutes. As long as you keep eating chiles, their effect keeps building. But if you take a break—even for as few as two to five minutes, depending on your individual susceptibility—you will be desensitized when you go back to eating the chiles. A dish with the same amount of chiles will not seem as hot the second time around.

The more likely explanation, however, is that people who find chiles intensely, punishingly hot simply have more taste buds. According to Linda Bartoshuk, a psychophysicist at the Yale School of Medicine, human beings can be neatly divided into three distinct categories when it comes to tasting ability: unfortunate "nontasters," pedestrian "medium tasters," and the aristocrats of the taste bud world, "supertasters."

This taste-detection pecking order appears to correspond directly to the number of taste buds a person possesses, a genetically predetermined trait that may vary by a factor of 100. Indeed, so radical is the difference between these three types that Bartoshuk speaks of them inhabiting different "taste worlds."

Bartoshuk and her colleagues discovered the extent of this phenomenon a few years ago when they carried out experiments using a dye that turns the entire mouth blue except for the taste papillae (structures housing taste buds and other sensory receptors). After painting part of subjects' tongues with the dye, they were rather stunned at the differences they saw. One poor taster had just 11 taste buds per square centimeter, while a supertaster had 1,100 in the same area.

Further experiments confirmed that the ability to taste intensely was in direct proportion to the number of taste buds. Researchers found that women were twice as likely as men to be supertasters, while men were nearly twice as likely as women to be nontasters.

What does this have to do with how hot you find chiles? It turns out that every taste bud in the mouth has a pain receptor literally wrapped around it. Along with the extra taste buds comes an extra ability to feel pain. As a result, supertasters have the capacity to experience 50 percent more pain from capsaicin, the chemical that gives chiles their heat.

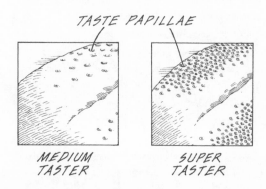

TASTE PAPILLAE

MEDIUM TASTER

SUPER TASTER

already blended into the chili powder, proved too much, so it was pulled. The cinnamon was not strong enough in early batches and was almost doubled in the final recipe. We were almost content with the basic spice mixture, but it needed a little more depth. After trying several ideas, a combination of black pepper and allspice proved winning. These spices added depth and, in conjunction with the rest of the spices, complexity.

Many recipes called for unsweetened chocolate, but we figured that cocoa powder would achieve much the same thing and would be easier to add along with the spices. (Further testing bore out the hypothesis.) Dried oregano rounded out our list of "spices." To further boost the flavors of our spice mixture, we toasted it in the pan with the onion and garlic before adding the liquid ingredients.

While the spices vary from recipe to recipe, the aromatics were consistently onion and garlic. Most recipes added them to the water with the meat. We decided to draw out a little more flavor and sweetness by sautéing them.

As far as the liquids go, most recipes call for tomato sauce and water. We tried to replace the generic canned tomato sauce suggested in most recipes with canned whole peeled tomatoes that we pureed in the blender. While the canned tomatoes made the chili taste a bit brighter, the chili made with canned tomato sauce was favored by most tasters.

Tasters felt that the water did little to improve the chili and wondered if it should be replaced. To add body, we tried using red wine as part of the liquid. We decided it was superfluous due to the strength of the rest of the flavors. In the end, we went with canned chicken broth for convenience' sake. To keep the chicken flavor from dominating, we used half chicken broth and half water. A small amount of cider vinegar (very traditional) brightened the broth. Some brown sugar added the necessary sweetness to balance the vinegar and spices.

With our chili perfected, we turned our attention to the garnishes. After several tests, we realized it was best to leave tradition alone. Sure, you could do without the beans or onions, but why compromise? Five-way Cincinnati chili is almost sacrosanct, so we did not consider any alterations.

Cincinnati Chili
SERVES 6 TO 8

Choose a can or jar of relatively plain tomato sauce—nothing too spicy or herbaceous. To warm the kidney beans, simmer them in water to cover for several minutes, then drain.

CHILI

- 2 teaspoons salt, plus more to taste
- 1½ pounds ground chuck
- 2 tablespoons vegetable oil
- 2 medium onions, chopped fine (about 2 cups)
- 2 medium cloves garlic, minced
- 2 tablespoons chili powder
- 2 teaspoons dried oregano
- 2 teaspoons cocoa powder
- 1½ teaspoons ground cinnamon
- ½ teaspoon cayenne pepper
- ½ teaspoon ground allspice
- ½ teaspoon ground black pepper
- 2 cups canned low-sodium chicken broth
- 2 tablespoons cider vinegar
- 2 teaspoons dark brown sugar
- 2 cups tomato sauce
- Tabasco sauce

ACCOMPANIMENTS

- 1 pound spaghetti, cooked, drained, and tossed with 2 tablespoons unsalted butter
- 12 ounces sharp cheddar cheese, shredded
- 1 (15-ounce) can red kidney beans, drained, rinsed, and warmed
- 1 medium onion, chopped fine (about 1 cup)

1. Bring 2 quarts of water and 1 teaspoon salt to a boil in a large saucepan. Add the ground beef, stirring vigorously to separate the meat into individual strands. As soon as the foam from the meat rises to the top (this takes about 30 seconds) and before the water returns to a boil, drain the meat into a strainer and set it aside.

2. Rinse and dry the empty saucepan. Heat the saucepan over medium heat and add the oil. When the oil is warm, about 1 minute, add the onions and cook, stirring frequently, until the onions are soft and browned around the edges, about 8 minutes. Add the garlic and cook until fragrant, about 1 minute. Stir in

the chili powder, oregano, cocoa, cinnamon, cayenne, allspice, black pepper, and remaining 1 teaspoon salt. Cook, stirring constantly, until the spices are fragrant, about 30 seconds. Stir in the chicken broth, vinegar, brown sugar, tomato sauce, and 2 cups water, scraping the bottom of the saucepan to loosen any browned bits. Add the blanched ground beef and increase the heat to high. As soon as the liquid boils, reduce the heat to medium-low and simmer, stirring occasionally, until the chili is deep red and has thickened slightly, about 1 hour. Adjust the seasonings, adding salt and Tabasco sauce to taste. (Chili can be refrigerated in an airtight container for up to 3 days. Bring back to a simmer over medium-low heat.)

3. Divide the buttered spaghetti among individual bowls. Spoon the chili over the spaghetti and top with the cheese, beans, and onion. Serve immediately.

VEGETARIAN CHILI

WHAT EXACTLY IS VEGETARIAN CHILI? BY definition, doesn't chili have to contain meat? After researching the subject thoroughly, we identified three basic styles of vegetarian chili—those that rely on a mixture of vegetables; those that rely on beans; and those that rely on a soy product to replicate the texture and feeling of meat.

We decided to make a couple of versions of each style to narrow the field. The vegetable-heavy chilis were the first to go. While we love vegetables, the recipes we had gathered were chock-full of zucchini, eggplant, tomatoes, and mushrooms, and all we could think was "ratatouille."

Next, we attacked the soy-based chilis. We went down the list of soy products and, based on their textures and flavors, started to rule some out. Even though tofu comes in a range of textures, none of them seemed right for chili. Silken and soft tofu disintegrated (as expected), but even extra-firm tofu crumbled into unappealing bits. Textured vegetable protein, or TVP, won no one over, but some tasters were intrigued by tempeh.

Tempeh is a tender but firm soybean cake made with fermented whole soybeans, sometimes mixed with other grains such as rice or millet. The texture certainly had potential, although the flavor was a bit bland. We decided to put the tempeh on hold and focus on the bean chilis, which were the real standouts in this first round of testing.

Most people, even nonvegetarians, expect to find at least one kind of bean in chili. When we prepared a vegetarian chili with several kinds of beans, tasters were impressed. We narrowed down a list of eight initial contenders to just three beans—red kidney, pinto, and black. All three have an earthy flavor and firm texture that work well in chili.

We also took a moment to consider whether or not to use canned beans. They are generally subject to scorn in the test kitchen, but we all agreed that in the case of chili, a dish packed with seasonings and aromatics, there was no need to worry about canned beans' lack of flavor. First and foremost, the beans needed to hold their shape and add body. This was easily accomplished by adding the beans at the end of the cooking process.

We moved on to consider the spice base. Most of our research recipes called for a host of dried herbs, including commercial chili powder, ground cumin, and dried oregano. But we wondered if a homemade chili powder, like the one used in our Chili con Carne recipe, would add more depth.

After conducting a dozen tests using toasted and pulverized dried ancho and New Mexico chiles, we concluded that this technique was not suited to vegetarian bean chili. Homemade chili powder has too much kick and simply overwhelms the flavor of the beans and vegetables. Without the strong meat presence, our homemade chili powder tasted hot and bitter. We also surmised that the fat in the Chili con Carne was tempering some of the chili powder heat. It seemed silly to add more oil to bean chili just to mellow the flavor of the chili powder.

We went back to the drawing board and decided to test commercial chili powder. Hoping to mellow the heat and bitterness of the chili powder, we decided to add a sweet red pepper to our base of onions and garlic. This worked nicely. We also wondered if some sweet frozen corn, added with the beans, would help tip the balance away from the bitter components. Tasters responded well to a chili made with three kinds of beans and corn. The flavor of the corn was great, and it had visual appeal, too.

Although the commercial chili powder was fine, the flavor of the final dish was a bit flat. We thought adding some whole cumin seeds would give the chili depth, and they did. A little cayenne pepper provided some heat, and brown sugar rounded out the other flavors.

We focused next on the liquid. Several recipes suggested using beer to build complexity in bean chili. Although beans and beer would seem to have a natural affinity, we found that beer added a sour note. We decided to stick with water and the customary tomatoes. Crushed tomatoes, rather than diced, were preferred for their smooth texture and body.

A sprinkle of cilantro and a squeeze of lime just before serving brightened the flavors. Everyone agreed that this bean chili was good. It was rich and highly flavorful, and it had a nice, sharp heat as well as some gentle sweetness.

It was time to return to the issue of the tempeh. We wondered if we could add some to the bean chili. It made sense to brown the tempeh (much as you might brown meat) before adding it to the pot. Tempeh soaks up flavors like a sponge, so it is usually marinated before cooking. We soaked the tempeh in a mixture of oil, garlic, smoky chipotle chiles, cumin, and salt. After broiling it for a few minutes on each side, the tempeh was crisp, spicy, and well seasoned. Tasters loved it—even plain, out of hand. But having to turn the broiler on bothered us. We wanted to keep the chili and its components in one place—on the stove. We browned the tempeh in a nonstick skillet and found it to be just as tasty as the broiled version. We sautéed the tempeh in large chunks (cakes cut in half) to get even browning and then cubed the browned tempeh before adding it to the chili.

But adding the tempeh to the chili as it was—with 3 cups of mix-and-match beans and 1 cup of corn—made it too thick and chunky. So we took out 2 cups of beans to alleviate the crowding. Everyone was happy, and the chili—with tempeh or without—was good enough, even for the die-hard meat eaters in the test kitchen. Recognizing that everyone might not want to include tempeh in their chili, we made this a variation on the master recipe.

Vegetarian Bean Chili
SERVES 4

Our favorite crushed tomatoes are made by Muir Glen, which calls its product ground tomatoes. As for the beans, we recommend a mix of pinto, black, and red kidney beans. Two 15-ounce cans will yield approximately three cups. Serve this chili over rice.

3	tablespoons vegetable oil
1	medium onion, chopped fine (about 1 cup)
1	large red bell pepper, stemmed, seeded, and chopped fine (about 1 1/4 cups)
8	medium cloves garlic, minced
1	tablespoon cumin seeds
3	tablespoons chili powder
1/4	teaspoon cayenne pepper
1	(28-ounce) can crushed tomatoes
1	teaspoon dried oregano
1	tablespoon brown sugar
3	cups canned beans (see note above), drained and rinsed
1	cup frozen corn kernels, thawed
1 1/2	teaspoons salt
1/4	cup coarsely chopped fresh cilantro leaves
1	tablespoon lime juice

1. Heat the oil in a large Dutch oven over medium-high heat until almost shimmering. Add the onion and cook until translucent and slightly softened, about 3 minutes. Add the red pepper and cook until it and the onion are soft and lightly browned around the edges, about 3 minutes. Add the garlic and cook until fragrant, about 1 minute. Push the vegetables to the perimeter of the pot so that the center of the pot is clear. Sprinkle the cumin seeds into the center of pot and cook for 30 seconds, stirring constantly. Stir the seeds and vegetables together and let cook until the cumin is fragrant, about 1 minute. Add the chili powder and cayenne pepper and stir to coat the vegetables. Cook until fragrant, about 1 minute.

2. Add 2 cups water and stir well to combine, scraping up any browned bits from the bottom of the pot. Bring to a boil, reduce the heat, and simmer until slightly thickened, about 5 minutes. Stir in the tomatoes, oregano, and brown sugar, and bring back

to a simmer. Simmer until slightly thickened, about 25 minutes.

3. Add the beans and corn and stir gently to incorporate. Remove the pot from the heat and stir in salt, cilantro, and lime juice. (Chili can be refrigerated in an airtight container for up to 3 days. Bring back to a simmer over medium-low heat.) Serve.

➤ VARIATION

Vegetarian Bean and Tempeh Chili
Canned chipotle chiles give this chili a nice smoky flavor.

1. Combine ½ cup vegetable oil, 4 large minced cloves garlic, 4 minced chipotle chiles in adobo sauce, 1 teaspoon ground cumin, and 1 teaspoon salt in a shallow bowl. Add two 8-ounce pieces tempeh, each cut in half crosswise, and toss to coat completely. Cover and marinate for at least 2 hours or up to 24 hours. (If marinating for more than a couple of hours, place bowl in the refrigerator.)

2. Follow recipe for Vegetarian Bean Chili through step 2. While the chili is simmering, heat a medium nonstick skillet over high heat for 2 minutes. Place the tempeh (coated with as much marinade as possible) in the pan and cook, turning once, until deeply browned and crisped, about 8 minutes. Transfer the tempeh to a cutting board. When cool enough to handle, cut the tempeh into ½-inch cubes.

3. Proceed with step 3 of the chili recipe, reducing the beans to 1 cup and adding the browned tempeh cubes with the beans and corn. Finish as directed.

GUMBO

WE HAD LONG KNOWN OF THE LEGENDARY soup/stew of Louisiana that is famous for both its complex flavor and its temperamental nature, but our experience with it was limited. That changed after we took a quick trip to southern Louisiana. In just over 48 hours, we covered a couple of hundred miles of bayou country, downed 15 bowls of gumbo, cooked alongside four native cooks, and interviewed two more. After returning, we dug up and studied about 80 recipes, and before long we learned that gumbo, like all great folk recipes, is

open to plenty of individual interpretation. Generally speaking, though, gumbo usually includes some combination of seafood, poultry, or small game along with sausage or some other highly seasoned, cured smoked pork. Also present is the Creole/Cajun "holy trinity" of onion, bell pepper, and celery. Quite often, gumbos are thickened with okra or ground dried sassafras leaves, known as filé (pronounced fee-LAY) powder. Last, but very important, most gumbos are flavored with a dark brown roux. For us, this roux is the heart of a good gumbo.

In classic French cooking, a roux is nothing more than flour cooked gently in some type of fat to form a paste that is used to thicken sauces. If the flour is just barely cooked, you have a white roux; if cooked to a light beige, you have a blond roux. When it reaches the color of light brown sugar, you have brown roux. Creole and Cajun cooks push that process to the outer limit. When they make roux, they keep cooking until the flour reaches a shade of very dark brown, sometimes just short of black. This breaks down the starches in the flour to the point where the roux offers relatively little thickening power. Instead, it imbues gumbo with a complex, toasty, smoky flavor and a deep, rich brown color that define the dish. The problem is that the flour can burn very easily, and the only safeguards against that are relatively low heat and constant stirring. This means that it often takes as long as an hour of constant stirring and careful attention to make a dark roux. Few of the home cooks we asked said they'd be willing to go to this trouble, so we had to shorten that time if we wanted a more practical recipe for gumbo.

Our goals for this project were falling into place, and there were three. First, the roux was key. We wanted to feature its flavor over the cacophony of other herbs and spices and to streamline its preparation. Once we had mastered the roux, we would have to determine the components and flavorings of the stew. As a starting point, we chose to feature shrimp over chicken or game (we would handle chicken in a variation) and to include sausage. Finally, we would have to decide whether to use okra or filé as a thickener, knowing that either would bring not only viscosity but also a distinct flavor to the dish.

The distinctive taste, color, and aroma of dark roux is a central characteristic of Creole and Cajun food. Most of the recipes we saw called for cooking the roux over low heat while stirring constantly for anywhere from 40 to 60 minutes. Since the roux truly does need to be stirred constantly as it cooks to avoid burning the flour, which will give the mixture a noticeable bitter taste, time was the first issue we had to tackle. We decided on 20 minutes as our limit for stirring. Any longer than that, we reasoned, and most cooks would probably skip over this dish. Just as important, tasters discerned little difference in flavor between gumbos made with the traditional low-heat, long-cooking roux and those with roux that were cooked faster and hotter.

To hit that 20-minute mark, we knew we'd have to increase the heat and probably preheat the oil before adding the flour. We also thought we'd try a microwave roux, instructions for which we'd seen along the way. For our testing, we began with the widely used 1-to-1 ratio of all-purpose flour to vegetable oil, using ½ cup of each.

Some cooks recommend heating the oil until it smokes and then cooking the roux over high heat. Though this method produced a very dark roux, about the color of bittersweet chocolate, in less than 10 minutes there was too much sizzle and smoke. The process felt out of control, and the specter of burned roux loomed large.

We slowed things down a bit, preheating the oil over medium-high heat for only about two minutes (to well below the smoke point) before adding the flour, then lowering the heat to medium to cook the roux. At the 20-minute stopping point, the roux had cooked to a deep reddish brown, about the color of a shelled pecan or a dirty penny. It had started to smoke once or twice, but it cooled fairly quickly when we removed it from the heat, stirred it for a minute, then returned it to the burner. In all, the process was much less nerve-wracking than the high-heat methods we had tried, and it yielded absolutely acceptable results. Unfortunately, though, another problem popped up. We began to have trouble incorporating the simmering stock into the roux. The roux and stock generally would mix smoothly, but sometimes they wouldn't, and the result was little globs of brown flour floating in a layer of oil at the surface of the liquid. Nonetheless, we pressed on with our testing of the roux.

We experimented with a number of fats—including bacon fat, sausage fat, butter, and different types of oil—and ended up preferring the flavor and ease of vegetable oil. We tried different ratios of fat to flour, varying them by as much as 6 tablespoons up and down from the ½-cup starting point, but none improved on the original 1-to-1 ratio in terms of either taste or performance. Switching the all-purpose flour from a high-protein, unbleached northern brand to a slightly lower-protein, bleached national brand improved the texture of the gumbo slightly, making it a little smoother and more satiny. The gumbo's consistency also benefitted from a thorough skimming of the foam from the surface of the liquid, both just after it had come to a boil and throughout the simmering time.

The microwave roux had seemed vaguely promising until the day we turned the test kitchen into a scene from a *Lethal Weapon* movie by putting a superheated, microwave-safe bowl with its smoking hot contents down on a damp counter. The bowl did not merely shatter; it exploded, literally raining glass shards and globs of fiery hot roux into every corner of the room. We were very lucky that no one was hurt, and, sure enough, a quick call to the test kitchens at Corning Consumer Products confirmed that they do not recommend heating oil in any Pyrex product for 10 minutes on high in the microwave.

Throughout the roux testing, the occasional separation of the flour and oil upon the addition of simmering liquid continued to perplex us. All along, we had followed the instructions in most of the recipes we'd studied to add simmering stock, which is about 200 degrees, to a hot roux-vegetable mixture, also about 200 degrees. But there is another, if less popular, school of thought. Food scientist and author of *On Food and Cooking* (Collier, 1984) Harold McGee and legendary New Orleans restaurateur Leah Chase had advised cooling either the roux or the stock before combining them. Sure enough, cooling the stock (which took less time than cooling the roux) did the trick. Room-temperature stock, at about 75 degrees, mixed into the hot roux beautifully; stock at about 150 degrees also mixed in very well and was only slightly less smooth than its cooler counterpart. In terms of the timing in the recipe, then, we decided to make a concentrated shrimp stock and cool it rapidly by adding ice water rather than making the full amount and allowing it to cool at its own slow pace. This quick-cooling technique brought the stock to about 110 degrees within minutes, and the gumbo made with this concentrated, then diluted stock easily passed muster with tasters.

McGee explained to us why this method succeeds. He said that the key to smooth incorporation is to thoroughly mix the roux into the liquid before the starch in the flour in the roux had a chance to swell up and gelatinize. Though much of the starch would have been broken down by the high heat of the oil before the stock was added, McGee estimated that the remaining starch would gelatinize somewhere around 160 degrees. Adding 200-degree stock to 200-degree roux would thus cause instant gelatinization. The result is disastrous: the globules of flour stick together in gluey clumps before they can be dispersed throughout the liquid. By adding cooler stock, the roux and the stock have time to blend thoroughly before the whole mixture comes up to temperature and the starch gelatinizes, resulting in the smooth consistency we were looking for.

The rest of the recipe development process focused on testing the wide range of ingredients and flavorings we encountered on our trip and in our research. First, we experimented with the liquid. Our testing thus far had been done with a simple shrimp stock made by simmering the shells in water. We tried boiling the shells in chicken stock instead of water, combining equal parts shrimp and chicken stock, adding bottled clam juice to the shrimp stock, and adding small amounts of white wine and beer to the gumbo. The clam juice did the trick, adding a depth of flavor that supplemented the 20-minute roux.

Two big flavoring questions concerned tomatoes—some say that gumbo just isn't gumbo without them—and garlic. Well, our tasters said that gumbo was just fine without tomatoes, but they gave the thumbs up to garlic, six cloves of it, in fact. Other seasonings in gumbo range from elaborate mixtures of herbs, spices, and sauces down to nothing more than salt. We tried what seemed like a hundred

seasoning variations and finally settled on a simple combination of dried thyme and bay leaves. Our experiments with different proportions of onion, bell pepper, and celery in the holy trinity notwithstanding, the classic ratio of 1 part celery to 2 parts pepper to 4 parts onion tasted best. We did, however, switch from the traditional green bell pepper to red peppers, preferring their sweeter, fuller flavor.

Next we considered the level of spicy heat, usually provided by either cayenne pepper alone or in combination with a hot pepper sauce such as Tabasco. The gumbos we tasted in Louisiana were only subtly spicy, with the pepper heat very much in the background. We wanted to feel a slight heat in the back of our throats after we had swallowed a couple of spoonfuls. A mere ½ teaspoon of cayenne did the trick for our tasters, all of whom favored the powder over the vinegary taste of bottled hot sauce.

Last, we considered whether to thicken the gumbo with okra or filé powder. We think both are probably acquired tastes. Thus far, everyone had been satisfied without either, and because both added distinct—and to some unwelcome—flavors, we decided to reserve them for the variations on the master recipe.

By the time we were finished cranking out pot after pot of gumbo, its once exotic southern flavor and aroma had become familiar, even comforting. With our early travails now just a memory, we're hooked on its deep, smoky flavor.

MAKING A ROUX

A long-handled, straight-edged wooden spatula is best for stirring the roux. Be sure to scrape the pan bottom and reach into the corners to prevent burning. The cooking roux will have a distinctive toasty, nutty aroma. If it smells scorched or acrid, or if there are black flecks in the roux, it has burned.

Creole-Style Shrimp and Sausage Gumbo

SERVES 6 TO 8

Making a dark roux can be dangerous. The mixture reaches temperatures in excess of 400 degrees. Therefore, use a deep pot for cooking the roux and long-handled utensils for stirring it, and be careful not to splash it on yourself. One secret to smooth gumbo is adding shrimp stock that is neither too hot nor too cold to the roux. For a stock that is at the right temperature when the roux is done, start preparing it before you tend to the vegetables and other ingredients, strain it, and then give it a head start on cooling by immediately adding ice water and clam juice. So that your constant stirring of the roux will not be interrupted, start the roux only after you've made the stock. Alternatively, you can make the stock well ahead of time and bring it back to room temperature before using it. Spicy andouille sausage is a Louisiana specialty that may not be available everywhere; kielbasa or any fully cooked smoked sausage makes a fine substitute. Gumbo is traditionally served over white rice.

1½	pounds small shrimp, shells removed and reserved
1	cup bottled clam juice
3½	cups ice water
½	cup vegetable oil
½	cup all-purpose flour, preferably bleached
2	medium onions, chopped fine
1	medium red bell pepper, stemmed, seeded, and chopped fine
1	medium stalk celery, chopped fine
6	medium cloves garlic, minced
1	teaspoon dried thyme
1	teaspoon salt
¼	teaspoon cayenne pepper
2	bay leaves
1	pound smoked sausage, such as andouille or kielbasa, sliced ¼ inch thick
½	cup minced fresh parsley leaves
4	medium scallions, white and green parts, sliced thin
	Ground black pepper

1. Bring the reserved shrimp shells and 4½ cups water to a boil in a stockpot or large saucepan over medium-high heat. Reduce the heat to medium-low and simmer for 20 minutes. Strain the stock and add the clam juice and ice water (you should have about 2 quarts of tepid stock, 100 to 110 degrees); discard the shells. Set the stock aside.

2. Heat the oil in a Dutch oven or large, heavy-bottomed saucepan over medium-high heat until it registers 200 degrees on an instant-read thermometer, 1½ to 2 minutes. Reduce the heat to medium and gradually stir in the flour with a wooden spatula or spoon, working out any lumps that form. Continue stirring constantly, reaching into corners of the pan, until the mixture has a toasty aroma and is deep reddish brown, about the color of an old copper penny or between the colors of milk chocolate and dark chocolate, about 20 minutes. (The roux will thin as it cooks; if it begins to smoke, remove the pan from the heat and stir the roux constantly to cool slightly.)

3. Add the onions, bell pepper, celery, garlic, thyme, salt, and cayenne to the roux and cook, stirring frequently, until the vegetables soften, 8 to 10 minutes. Add 1 quart reserved stock in slow, steady stream while stirring vigorously. Stir in the remaining stock. Increase the heat to high and bring to a boil. Reduce the heat to medium-low, skim off the foam on the surface, add the bay leaves, and simmer, uncovered, skimming any foam that rises to the surface, about 30 minutes. (Mixture can be covered and set aside for several hours. Reheat when ready to proceed.)

4. Stir in the sausage and continue simmering to blend flavors, about 30 minutes. Stir in the shrimp and simmer until cooked through, about 5 minutes. Off heat, stir in the parsley and scallions and adjust the seasonings with salt, ground black pepper, and cayenne to taste. Serve immediately.

VARIATIONS

Shrimp and Sausage Gumbo with Okra

Fresh okra can be used in place of frozen, though it tends to be more slippery, a quality that diminishes with increased cooking. Substitute an equal amount of fresh okra for frozen; trim the caps, slice the pods ¼ inch thick, and increase the sautéing time with the onion, bell pepper, and celery to 10 to 15 minutes.

Follow recipe for Creole-Style Shrimp and Sausage Gumbo, adding 10 ounces thawed frozen cut okra to the roux along with the onion, bell pepper, and celery. Proceed as directed.

Shrimp and Sausage Gumbo with Filé

Follow recipe for Creole-Style Shrimp and Sausage Gumbo, adding 1½ teaspoons filé powder along with the parsley and scallions after gumbo has been removed from heat. Let rest until slightly thickened, about 5 minutes. Adjust the seasonings and serve.

Chicken and Sausage Gumbo

If you like, add okra or filé to this recipe by following the directions in the variations above. Make sure the stock is tepid (100 to 110 degrees) before adding it to the roux.

10	bone-in chicken thighs (about 3½ pounds), trimmed of excess skin and fat
	Salt and ground black pepper
¼	cup plus 1 tablespoon vegetable oil, or more as needed
½	cup all-purpose flour
2	medium onions, chopped fine
1	medium red bell pepper, stemmed, seeded, and chopped fine
1	medium stalk celery, chopped fine
6	medium cloves garlic, minced
1	teaspoon dried thyme
¼	teaspoon cayenne pepper
6	cups homemade chicken stock or canned low-sodium broth, warmed slightly
2	bay leaves
1	pound smoked sausage, such as andouille or kielbasa, sliced ¼ inch thick
½	cup minced fresh parsley leaves
4	medium scallions, white and green parts, sliced thin

1. Season the chicken liberally with salt and pepper. Heat 1 tablespoon oil in a large Dutch oven over medium-high heat until shimmering but not smoking, about 2 minutes. Add five chicken thighs, skin-side down, and cook, not moving them until the skin is crisp and well-browned, about 5 minutes. Using tongs, flip the chicken and brown on the second side, about 5 minutes longer. Transfer the browned chicken to a large plate. Brown the remaining chicken thighs, transfer them to the plate, and set aside. Drain the fat from the pan and strain it through a fine-mesh strainer lined with cheesecloth and into a measuring cup. The remaining oil should be entirely free of any

---

INGREDIENTS: Okra and Filé

In a Creole or Cajun dark roux, most of the starch in the flour breaks down in the cooking, so it does more to flavor the stew than thicken it. That leaves the task to one of two other traditional Southern ingredients, okra and filé powder. (It's also possible, as we do in our master recipe, to go without either one for a slightly thinner stew. Both okra and filé powder are often an acquired taste.) One thing on which most Creole and Cajun cooks agree is that you should never use okra and filé together because the gumbo will get too thick or even gummy.

Okra pods, said to have been brought to the southern United States from Africa by the slave trade, are slender, green, usually about 3 inches in length, ridged in texture, tapered in shape, and often slightly fuzzy. The interior of the pods is sticky and mucilaginous, so once they are cut open, they thicken any liquid in which they are cooked. Okra's flavor is subtle, with hints of eggplant, green bean, and chestnut. In our gumbo testing, we could detect no taste difference between fresh and frozen.

The other possible thickener, filé powder, is made of ground dried sassafras leaves. It is said to have been introduced to the settlers of southern Louisiana by the native Choctaw Indians. Filé, also referred to in Louisiana as gumbo filé, adds both a gelatinous thickness and a subtle, singular flavor to gumbo. Though difficult to describe precisely, the flavor is distinctly earthy, with notes of straw, bay, marjoram, and oregano. Filé is as much a hallmark of authentic Louisiana cooking as dark roux and the holy trinity of onion, bell pepper, and celery. Filé is used in one of two ways. Diners can sprinkle a little bit onto their portion of gumbo right at the table, or the cook can stir some into the pot at the very last moment of cooking or even once the pot has come off the heat. In our recipe variation, we prefer to add it to the pot, which mellows the flavor somewhat. In stores that carry it, pale green filé powder is generally sold in tall, slender, 1-ounce jars.

---

particles. Add enough vegetable oil (about ¼ cup) to yield ½ cup total fat.

2. Heat the chicken fat/vegetable oil mixture in a clean Dutch oven over medium-high heat until it registers 200 degrees on an instant-read thermometer, about 1½ to 2 minutes. Reduce the heat to medium and gradually stir in the flour with a wooden spoon or spatula, working out any lumps that form. Continue stirring constantly, reaching into the corners of the pan, until the mixture has a toasty aroma and is a deep reddish brown, about the color of an old copper penny or between the colors of milk and dark chocolate, about 20 minutes. (The roux will thin as it cooks; if it begins to smoke, remove the pan from the heat and stir the roux constantly to cool slightly.)

3. Add the onions, bell pepper, celery, garlic, thyme, 1 teaspoon salt, and cayenne to the roux and cook, stirring frequently, until the vegetables soften, 8 to 10 minutes. Add the chicken stock in a slow, steady stream while vigorously stirring. Stir in 2 cups water and the bay leaves and place the browned chicken thighs in a single layer in the pot. Increase the heat to high and bring to a boil. Once boiling, reduce the heat to medium-low and skim any foam that rises to the surface. Simmer for 30 minutes.

4. Stir in the sausage and continue simmering to blend the flavors, about 30 minutes longer. Off heat, stir in the parsley and scallions and adjust the seasonings with salt, ground black pepper, and cayenne to taste. Serve immediately.

INDIAN CURRY

OUR GOAL IN CREATING A CURRY RECIPE was to translate the many dishes that earn this name (almost any Indian stew can be called a "curry") into a basic formula that could be easily adapted. In the process, we wanted to discover how to keep the flavors bright and clear. So many curries are dull and heavy-tasting.

Our usual resources were of little help. Cookbooks couldn't give us hands-on experience, explain why an ingredient was used this way in one recipe, that way in the next. Classic (that is, French) culinary training was worse than useless. Although we could

pick out distinctly Indian cooking techniques, the food didn't seem to be inspired by technique. While a French (or any Western) stew follows a series of commands—brown, deglaze, emulsify—an Indian curry seemed to waft on the whim of the cook from one ethereal fragrance to the next.

Ultimately, we found our way into the kitchens of two extraordinarily gifted cooks in New York City, one Indian and one Pakistani. Their food defined two key elements of curry making. One was a mysterious, complex, and highly personal dance of spice, flavor, and fragrance that is the soul of the cuisine. The other was a simple, accessible technique that provided a structure within which we could dance. The marriage of these two elements resulted in a quick, elegant formula for curry, the mood of which can be endlessly varied by substituting ingredients and adjusting the form and quantity of spice.

To begin this quest, we studied a recipe for meat curry from a favorite Indian cookbook. The dish was essentially a meat stew, flavored with onion, garlic, fresh ginger, ground coriander, cumin, turmeric, and cayenne and simmered in water with chopped tomato. It used techniques familiar enough, following the predictable route of browning the meat, browning the onions, adding the spices, then cooking for a couple of hours with the liquid.

But looking in other books, we found similar meat curries that used less familiar techniques: Spices were added and cooked at different points depending on whether they were dry or wet, whole or ground, and the meat was added to the mixture partway through the cooking process with no preliminary browning. At a loss, we went to locate an Indian cook we could talk to.

We found Usha Cunningham, a Bombay-born home cook with no restaurant training. We laid out for her the two styles of curry we had found and asked her to cook a curry, in her own style, based on the ingredients in the meat curry recipe we had originally studied. Usha agreed but was a little hesitant about the recipe—it was such a plain dish, she said, like a plain roast chicken for an American; didn't we want her to show us something a bit more interesting? No, we assured her, we needed to start simple, to get our feet on the ground. Later, when we tasted her own cooking, we understood her reaction. Her food was astonishingly complex—bold, intense, and bright, each bite exploding in layers of distinct, individual tastes of sweet and sour, bitter, salty, and fragrant. When we had recovered sufficiently to ask her how she got this result, Usha shrugged and suggested that it might be in the way she used her spices—that is, with a heavy hand, as an Italian cook might use fresh herbs.

And so we began. She started work like a French chef, doing all her chopping and grinding first off; once we started cooking there would be no time for prep. And, as we pressed clove after clove of garlic through her press, it was clear that she did indeed flavor heavily: about one tablespoon each of ground coriander and cumin and pureed garlic and ginger per pound of meat, substantially more than the amounts used in the recipes we had found in cookbooks. Then Usha hit the stove.

First she heated a duet of whole spices—cinnamon and cloves—in hot oil until the cinnamon unfurled and the cloves popped. She explained that this step infused the oil with the fragrance of the spices, thus flavoring everything else that came in contact with the oil.

Next she added sliced onion and cooked it until translucent, just to evaporate out the moisture and set the sweetness. It was sliced, rather than pureed or chopped, she said, because slicing was easier. She explained that as a general rule she cooked onions translucent for a lighter-tasting sauce, such as the one we were making that day with tomatoes, or to a rich brown color for heavier sauces, such as those based on yogurt or bound by ground nuts.

With the onions now cooked, she stirred in equal volumes of pureed garlic and ginger. Why pureed? Usha maintained that chopping was Western. While every Indian household would have a grinding stone to grind spices daily, she pureed the garlic and ginger with a little water in an electric minichopper until smooth (see page 295) or pressed the garlic through a press. This choice was in part based on speed and convenience. In addition, experience had shown her that puree, with no surfaces to burn, cooked more evenly than a mince and melted into the sauce for a smooth finish. And because a puree is wet where a mince is dry, this method gave her a cushion against burning.

Now Usha added bone-in lamb shoulder to the pan (what, no preliminary browning?) and cooked it for about 10 minutes, stirring almost constantly, to evaporate all the moisture from the pan. As she stirred, she explained that the idea behind this traditional Indian technique was to release the flavors of the aromatic ingredients into the oil and cook them into the meat. If the meat were browned first, as in a French stew, the caramelized crust might inhibit the meat from absorbing the flavors.

Now we were ready to add the ground spices. Usha explained that she ground the coriander and cumin herself from whole seed for better flavor but contented herself with preground turmeric (a rhizome like ginger) and cayenne.

She mixed the ground dried spices with enough water to form a paste, then added the paste to the pan. Now she cooked, stirring, until enough moisture had been cooked out of the ingredients to allow the oil to separate out and pool around the clumps of meat, onion, and spice paste. This, Usha explained, was the secret to a well-made curry. The spices must fry in this hot oil, uninhibited by liquid, to release and develop their flavors. Once the final stewing liquid was added, the flavor of the spices would develop no further. (Spices may also be pan-roasted separately, ground, and then folded in at the end, but we will leave that option to another day.) Once the oil had separated, Usha turned the heat down and cooked everything for several more minutes.

The spices cooked, Usha finished the curry with lots of chopped tomato (no water) and a handful of dried fenugreek leaves. She didn't consider the fenugreek seeds to be right for this particular curry. The leaves and seeds have different flavors, but their family resemblance is clear. Both are delicious with spinach, tomato, and sweet flavors.

We ate Usha's delicious curry with a pilaf of basmati rice, made with onion and whole spices. Usha showed us how to mash the curry and rice together with the tips of our fingers and then pop neat balls of the mixture into the mouth. (The less adventurous can mash with a fork as well.) The mashing opened up the flavors so effectively that the food had noticeably more flavor and fragrance than when eaten in the Western manner.

Smelling the spices cooking in Usha's kitchen, we

noticed that their fragrance had quite an effect on us. Whereas we like French food because it smells tasty in an earthy, comforting, body-satisfying way, we were entranced by Indian food because it was heady and dreamy. Sour, bitter, and sweet flavors that wouldn't appeal to us in French food (bitter fenugreek, for example) were exquisitely satisfying in Indian food.

We reasoned that it was this particular dreamy sensibility that Usha navigated while she cooked. (She herself described her experience in the kitchen as a sort of a trance.) As we understood her, she improvised by associating to ingredients rather than building the dish within a formula so that she hardly knew at the beginning where she'd end up. Even the dishes we tasted from her refrigerator defied categorization. While her ethereal tomato-meat concoction was certainly a stew, such a term didn't begin to describe the experience of eating it. So even as we talked and cooked, we knew there was little hope of walking out of her kitchen with a formula that could map out such an intuitive journey. We took good notes and went back to our test kitchen.

We spent the next week or so cooking curries with Usha's approach. We tested her method against the technique used in the meat curry we had started out with and determined that Usha's method did infuse more flavor into the meat. With no browning in batches, it was easy, too. We also worked to educate our nose and palate to the taste and smell of properly cooked spices, tasting and smelling raw spices and noting how their acrid fragrance and flavor transformed and mellowed with frying (see page 296 for more information on the science of frying spices). We were getting very close; often our curries were delicious, but almost as often they came out heavy and muddy-tasting. We had no idea why.

As luck would have it, schedules and deadlines were such that we couldn't cook with Usha again. So we sought out another cook, this time a Pakistani woman named Samia Ahad, who had cooked extensively in New York restaurant kitchens and was trained in French cooking.

Samia's food defined the other end of the spectrum. While Usha's genius lay in the ecstatic dance of her bright, bold, and complex flavors, Samia's lay in the elegant and understated simplicity of the food. She used spices sparingly, particularly the dry

ones, to produce in her curries a light, clean, aromatic, but everyday mood. Although the ingredients were the same, her curries were quite different from Usha's.

With Samia we found the cultural bridge we were looking for. Presumably, because her own restaurant work had required her to shuttle regularly between the cooking of two cultures, Samia had managed to translate the heady sensibility that inspired Usha's cuisine into a simple, accessible formula that invited endless variation. And she'd vastly condensed traditional technique as well.

Like Usha, Samia prepared all of her ingredients completely before cooking. Like Usha, she pureed garlic and ginger and sliced onion for convenience. She also ground her own cumin and coriander seed. However, she used only one-third of Usha's liberal quantity of aromatics: about a teaspoon (rather than a tablespoon) of pureed garlic and ginger and ground coriander and cumin per pound of meat. Also like Usha, Samia started by frying sliced onion in oil until translucent. (And like Usha, she reserved browned onion for heavier sauces.)

Then, to our surprise, Samia added most of the rest of her ingredients: all of the spices she had prepared as well as a pound of boneless cubed meat, salt, and ½ cup of chopped tomato. She cooked, stirring until the oil separated (about five minutes), and then cooked another 30 seconds to cook the spices completely. She explained, as had Usha, that this cooking of the spices was the heart of the dish. Then she added 2 cups of water and a halved chile pepper (she liked the flavor of the fresh chile better than that of cayenne) and simmered until tender, about 40 minutes.

We asked Samia how she got away with condensing all the steps at the end. She explained that contrary to traditional technique, her experience was that as long as the oil separated, allowing the spices to fry in the oil for about 30 seconds, there was no need for the long cooking. She further explained that her formula could be used as the base for many, many flavor combinations. We could fry whole spices before adding onion, as Usha had done. We could add any number of cubed vegetables. We could cook beef, lamb, chicken, fish, or shrimp this way. We could reduce the recipe to its bare roots—a very simple stew of protein, onion, garlic, ginger, turmeric (for some reason she always uses turmeric, she said), and water—or embellish it with more spices, vegetables, or legumes. That day, for example, she made a chicken variation using browned onion and ½ cup yogurt (instead of the tomato) and flavored the curry with double the amount of coriander, but no cumin. The technique was exactly the same, but the richness of the yogurt and the browned onion produced a different result altogether. We went back into the test kitchen and cooked a number of curries to test out what these two women had taught us.

First, we tested Usha's longer step-by-step cooking against Samia's condensed recipe and decided that, at least for this basic curry and for our taste buds, Samia's simplified method was as tasty, and far quicker. We also tried adding the tomato along with the water instead of reducing it with the spice; however, the reduced tomato in Samia's formula added structure to the sauce, and we liked the ease of adding everything at once.

We then tested a curry made with sliced onion against one made with chopped and found that slicing was vastly quicker. We also preferred the texture of the sauce with sliced onion. We ran the same comparison between chopped and pureed ginger and garlic. Not only was pureeing in a minichopper substantially easier than mincing, the wetness gave us a cushion against burning, just as Usha had explained.

Although up until now we had been cooking with bone-in lamb shoulder, we were sold on the ease of Samia's quicker-cooking boneless curries (40 minutes or fewer compared with 1½ to 2 hours), so we stuck to top sirloin, boneless leg of lamb, and chicken thigh. Shrimp also made a delicious curry and cooked in a flash.

We ran several experiments with spices. We compared a curry made with only ground spices with a curry using ground and whole spices. The comparison showed us that preground spices formed a kind of background wash; left whole, they came through as bright, individual flavors. (Thus, the cook can use the same spices to different effect.)

Then we cooked three curries to determine how long the combined ground spices needed to cook to develop their flavor: We tried 30 seconds, 5 minutes, and 10 minutes after the oil had separated. We found that 30 seconds was all it took. We also determined that the heavy, muddy taste of our early curries probably resulted from spices that had burned and turned bitter when they stuck to the bottom of the skillet. The spices were less likely to stick when cooked quickly, and the addition of yogurt or tomato obviated the need to make a paste.

Next we made a curry in which we added the stewing liquid before the oil had separated. Indeed, the curry tasted raw. Use your ear to help you recognize when the spices are frying in pure oil. The sound changes from the gentle sound of a simmer to the loud, staccato sound of frying.

Finally, we played around with the amount of spice. It seems that the quantity was more a matter of personal preference than of rule, more spice resulting in heavier flavor. For the master recipe that follows, we chose quantities that fell in between those given us by Usha and Samia simply because we liked that flavor. Precise quantities of wet spices are even less critical than of dry because their flavor is weaker, but we like equal quantities of garlic and ginger. In any event, the beauty of the formula is that it invites experimentation.

The method of the recipe that follows is largely the same as the one Samia demonstrated for us. As in standard French technique, it begins by heating the oil to provide a cooking medium. After that, however, it diverges completely from French style. Rather than browning the meat in the oil, we first sauté the whole spices, then the onions. The wet spices (ginger and garlic) are then added, along with the meat or fowl, and the moistening agent, either tomatoes or yogurt. All of these are cooked until the liquid evaporates, the oil separates, and the spices begin to fry and become fully aromatic. Greens in the form of either spinach or cilantro are then added, along with water and chile peppers, and the whole is cooked until the meat is tender, at which point the vegetables are added and cooked until tender.

The ingredients in the recipe are completely interchangeable, depending on what result you're looking for. The whole spice combination (cinnamon, cloves, cardamom, peppercorns, and bay leaf) can be abbreviated to cinnamon and cloves or to cinnamon, cloves, and cardamom, if you like. The cumin and the coriander can also be used crushed, as in the Beef Curry with Crushed Spices and Channa Dal variation. Let yourself be drawn into the trance of the spices and improvise combinations from there.

Indian Curry
SERVES 4 TO 6

This recipe is a basic formula that can be altered in hundreds of ways. See the variations that follow for flavor combinations that work especially well. With all curries, gather and prepare all of your ingredients before you begin. Garlic and ginger may be pureed by hand or in a minichop food processor. If pureeing by hand, use a garlic press, or mince the garlic and ginger with a knife on a cutting board, sprinkling with salt to break them down. If using a minichopper, process the garlic and ginger with 1 to 2 tablespoons of water until pureed. You can substitute a scant half teaspoon of cayenne pepper for the jalapeño, adding it to the skillet with the other ground dried spices. Feel free to increase the wet (garlic, ginger, onion, and jalapeño) or dry spice quantities. Serve the curry with basmati rice (page 312).

WHOLE SPICE BLEND

1 1/2	(3-inch) cinnamon sticks
4	cloves
4	green cardamom pods
8	peppercorns
1	bay leaf

1/4	cup vegetable or canola oil
1	recipe Whole Spice Blend (optional)
1	medium onion, sliced thin
4	large cloves garlic, pureed
1	(1 1/2-inch) piece fresh ginger, peeled and pureed
1 1/2	pounds top sirloin or boneless leg of lamb, trimmed and cut into 3/4-inch cubes, or 6 chicken thighs, skinned, or 1 1/2 pounds shrimp, peeled and deveined
2	teaspoons ground cumin
2	teaspoons ground coriander
1	teaspoon ground turmeric
1/2	teaspoon salt, plus more to taste
3	canned plum tomatoes, chopped, plus 1 tablespoon juice, or 2/3 cup canned crushed tomatoes, or 1/2 cup plain low-fat yogurt
2	bunches (1 1/2 pounds) spinach, stemmed, thoroughly washed, and chopped coarse (optional)
1	cup chopped fresh cilantro leaves (optional)
1	jalapeño chile, stemmed and cut in half through the stem end
1/2	cup Indian split peas (channa dal), or 4 medium boiling potatoes, peeled and cut into 3/4-inch dice, or 4 medium zucchini, cut into 1/2-inch dice, or 1 cup fresh or thawed frozen green peas
2 to 4	tablespoons chopped fresh cilantro leaves (use the lesser amount if you've already added the optional cilantro)

1. Heat the oil in a large deep skillet or sauté pan, preferably nonstick, over medium-high heat until hot but not smoking. If using the whole spice blend, add it to the oil and cook, stirring with wooden spoon until the cinnamon sticks unfurl and the cloves pop, about 5 seconds. Add the onion and sauté until softened, 3 to 4 minutes, or browned, 5 to 7 minutes, as desired. (If omitting whole spice blend, simply add onion to skillet and proceed with recipe.)

2. Stir in the garlic, ginger, selected meat (except shrimp), ground spices, 1/2 teaspoon salt, and tomatoes or yogurt. Cook, stirring almost constantly, until the liquid evaporates, the oil separates and turns orange, and the spices begin to fry, 5 to 7 minutes. Continue to cook, stirring constantly, until the spices smell cooked, about 30 seconds longer.

3. Stir in the optional spinach and/or cilantro. Add 2 cups water and the jalapeño and season with salt to taste. Bring to a simmer, reduce the heat, cover, and simmer until the meat is almost tender, 20 to 30 minutes for chicken, 30 to 40 minutes for beef or lamb.

4. Add the selected vegetable (except green peas), cover, and cook until vegetable and meat are tender, about 15 minutes. If using, add the shrimp and/or peas and simmer 3 minutes longer. Stir in the cilantro. Serve immediately.

Chicken Curry with Yogurt, Cilantro, and Zucchini

WHOLE SPICE BLEND

1½	(3-inch) cinnamon sticks
4	cloves
4	green cardamom pods
8	peppercorns
1	bay leaf

¼	cup vegetable or canola oil
1	recipe Whole Spice Blend
1	medium onion, sliced thin
4	large cloves garlic, pureed
1	(1½-inch) piece fresh ginger, peeled and pureed
6	chicken thighs, skinned
2	teaspoons ground cumin
2	teaspoons ground coriander
1	teaspoon ground turmeric
½	teaspoon salt, plus more to taste
½	cup plain low-fat yogurt
1	cup plus 2 tablespoons chopped fresh cilantro leaves
1	jalapeño chile, stemmed and cut in half through the stem end
4	medium zucchini, cut into ½-inch dice

1. Heat the oil in a large deep skillet or sauté pan, preferably nonstick, over medium-high heat until hot but not smoking. Add the whole spice blend and cook, stirring with wooden spoon until the cinnamon sticks unfurl and the cloves pop, about 5 seconds. Add the onion and sauté until browned, 5 to 7 minutes.

2. Stir in the garlic, ginger, chicken, ground spices, ½ teaspoon salt, and yogurt. Cook, stirring almost constantly, until the liquid evaporates, the oil separates and turns orange, and the spices begin to fry, 5 to 7 minutes. Continue to cook, stirring constantly, until spices smell cooked, about 30 seconds longer.

3. Stir in 1 cup chopped cilantro. Add 2 cups water and the jalapeño and season with salt to taste. Bring to a simmer, reduce the heat, cover, and simmer until the chicken is almost tender, 20 to 30 minutes.

4. Add the zucchini and cook until zucchini and chicken are tender, about 15 minutes. Stir in the remaining 2 tablespoons cilantro. Serve immediately.

Chicken Curry with Spinach and Fenugreek

¼	cup vegetable or canola oil
1	medium onion, sliced thin
4	large cloves garlic, pureed
1	(1½-inch) piece fresh ginger, peeled and pureed
6	chicken thighs, skinned
2	teaspoons ground cumin
2	teaspoons ground coriander
1	teaspoon ground turmeric
¼	teaspoon dried fenugreek
½	teaspoon salt, plus more to taste
3	canned plum tomatoes, chopped, plus 1 tablespoon juice, or ⅔ cup canned crushed tomatoes
2	bunches (1½ pounds) spinach, stemmed, thoroughly washed, and chopped coarse
1	jalapeño chile, stemmed and cut in half through the stem end
4	medium red potatoes (about 1½ pounds), peeled and cut into ¾-inch dice
4	tablespoons chopped fresh cilantro leaves

1. Heat the oil in a large deep skillet or sauté pan, preferably nonstick, over medium-high heat until hot but not smoking. Add the onion and sauté until softened, 3 to 4 minutes.

2. Stir in the garlic, ginger, chicken, ground spices, fenugreek, ½ teaspoon salt, and tomatoes. Cook, stirring almost constantly, until the liquid evaporates, the oil separates and turns orange, and the spices begin to fry, 5 to 7 minutes. Continue to cook, stirring constantly, until the spices smell cooked, about 30 seconds longer.

3. Stir in the spinach. Add 2 cups water and the jalapeño and season with salt to taste. Bring to a simmer, reduce the heat, cover, and simmer until the chicken is almost tender, 20 to 30 minutes.

4. Add the potatoes, cover, and cook until potatoes and chicken are tender, about 15 minutes. Stir in the cilantro. Serve immediately.

Shrimp Curry with Yogurt and Peas

¼	cup vegetable or canola oil
1	medium onion, sliced thin
4	large cloves garlic, pureed
1	(1½-inch) piece fresh ginger, peeled and pureed
2	teaspoons ground cumin
2	teaspoons ground coriander
1	teaspoon ground turmeric
½	teaspoon salt, plus more to taste
½	cup plain low-fat yogurt
1	cup plus 2 tablespoons chopped fresh cilantro leaves
1	jalapeño chile, stemmed and cut in half through the stem end
1	cup fresh or thawed frozen green peas
1½	pounds medium shrimp, peeled and deveined

1. Heat the oil in a large deep skillet or sauté pan, preferably nonstick, over medium-high heat until hot but not smoking. Add the onion and sauté until browned, 5 to 7 minutes.

2. Stir in the garlic, ginger, ground spices, ½ teaspoon salt, and yogurt. Cook, stirring almost constantly, until the liquid evaporates, the oil separates and turns orange, and the spices begin to fry, 5 to 7 minutes. Continue to cook, stirring constantly, until the spices smell cooked, about 30 seconds longer.

3. Stir in 1 cup cilantro. Add 2 cups water and the jalapeño and season with salt to taste. Bring to a simmer, reduce the heat, partially cover, and simmer until the sauce thickens, about 20 minutes.

4. Add the peas and shrimp and simmer until heated through and tender, about 3 minutes. Stir in remaining 2 tablespoons cilantro. Serve immediately.

EQUIPMENT: Minichopper

We spent a lot of time pressing garlic and grating ginger until we gave in and bought a Cuisinart Mini-Mate Plus Chopper/Grinder. Although this machine would seem to be a luxury, it makes curries so much easier to prepare that it may make the difference, over time, between cooking them or not. The motor and blade can handle garlic, ginger, chiles, and herbs, but don't expect much else. For instance, Parmesan cheese and nuts should be ground in a real food processor.

Lamb Curry with Whole Spices

	WHOLE SPICE BLEND
1½	(3-inch) cinnamon sticks
4	cloves
4	green cardamom pods
8	peppercorns
1	bay leaf
¼	cup vegetable or canola oil
1	recipe Whole Spice Blend
1	medium onion, sliced thin
4	large cloves garlic, pureed
1	(1½-inch) piece fresh ginger, peeled and pureed
1½	pounds boneless leg of lamb, trimmed and cut into ¾-inch dice
2	teaspoons ground cumin
2	teaspoons ground coriander
1	teaspoon ground turmeric
½	teaspoon salt, plus more to taste
½	cup plain low-fat yogurt
1	jalapeño chile, stemmed and cut in half through the stem end
4	medium red potatoes (about 1½ pounds), peeled and cut into ¾-inch dice
4	tablespoons chopped fresh cilantro leaves

1. Heat the oil in a large deep skillet or sauté pan, preferably nonstick, over medium-high heat until hot but not smoking. Add the whole spice blend and cook, stirring with wooden spoon until the cinnamon sticks unfurl and the cloves pop, about 5 seconds. Add the onion and sauté until softened, 3 to 4 minutes.

2. Stir in the garlic, ginger, lamb, ground spices, ½ teaspoon salt, and yogurt. Cook, stirring almost constantly, until the liquid evaporates, the oil separates and turns orange, and the spices begin to fry, 5 to 7 minutes. Continue to cook, stirring constantly, until the spices smell cooked, about 30 seconds longer.

3. Add 2 cups water and the jalapeño and season with salt to taste. Bring to a simmer, reduce the heat, cover, and simmer until the meat is almost tender, 30 to 40 minutes.

4. Add the potatoes, cover, and cook until the potatoes and lamb are tender, about 15 minutes. Stir in the cilantro. Serve immediately.

Lamb Curry with Figs and Fenugreek

¼	cup vegetable or canola oil
1	medium onion, sliced thin
4	large garlic cloves, pureed
1	(1½-inch) piece fresh ginger, peeled and pureed
1½	pounds boneless leg of lamb, trimmed and cut into ¾-inch cubes
2	teaspoons ground cumin
2	teaspoons ground coriander
1	teaspoon ground turmeric
½	teaspoon fenugreek leaves
½	teaspoon salt, plus more to taste
3	canned plum tomatoes, chopped, plus 1 tablespoon juice, or ⅔ cup canned crushed tomatoes
1	jalapeño chile, stemmed and cut in half through the stem end
¼	cup dried figs, chopped coarse
4	tablespoons chopped fresh cilantro leaves

1. Heat the oil in a large deep skillet or sauté pan, preferably nonstick, over medium-high heat until hot but not smoking. Add the onion and sauté until softened, 3 to 4 minutes.

2. Stir in the garlic, ginger, lamb, ground spices, fenugreek, ½ teaspoon salt, and tomatoes. Cook, stirring almost constantly, until the liquid evaporates, the oil separates and turns orange, and the spices begin to fry, 5 to 7 minutes. Continue to cook, stirring constantly, until the spices smell cooked, about 30 seconds longer.

3. Add 2 cups water, the jalapeño, and figs and season with salt to taste. Bring to a simmer, reduce the heat, cover, and simmer until the meat is tender, 40 to 50 minutes. Stir in the cilantro. Serve immediately.

Beef Curry with Crushed Spices and Channa Dal

Channa dal is the name for yellow Indian split peas, available at Indian specialty food shops. Diced potatoes or regular green split peas may be substituted for the channa dal.

2	teaspoons whole coriander seeds
1	teaspoon cumin seeds
¼	cup vegetable or canola oil
1	medium onion, sliced thin
4	large cloves garlic, pureed
1	(1½-inch) piece fresh ginger, peeled and pureed
1½	pounds top sirloin, trimmed and cut into ¾-inch cubes
1	teaspoon ground turmeric
½	teaspoon salt, plus more to taste
3	canned plum tomatoes, chopped, plus 1 tablespoon juice, or ⅔ cup canned crushed tomatoes
1	jalapeño chile, stemmed and cut in half through the stem end
½	cup Indian split peas (channa dal)
4	tablespoons chopped fresh cilantro leaves

1. Crush coriander and cumin in a mortar and pestle. Heat the oil in a large deep skillet or sauté pan, preferably nonstick, over medium-high heat until hot but not smoking. Add the coriander and cumin and cook, stirring with a wooden spoon, until fragrant, less than 5 seconds. Add the onion and sauté until softened, 3 to 4 minutes.

2. Stir in the garlic, ginger, beef, turmeric, ½ teaspoon salt, and tomatoes. Cook, stirring almost constantly, until the liquid evaporates, the oil separates and turns orange, and the spices begin to fry, 5 to 7 minutes. Continue to cook, stirring constantly, until the spices smell cooked, about 30 seconds longer.

3. Add 2 cups water and the jalapeño and season with salt to taste. Bring to a simmer, reduce the heat, cover, and simmer until the meat is almost tender, 30 to 40 minutes.

4. Add the channa dal, cover, and cook until channa dal and beef are tender, about 15 minutes. Stir in the cilantro. Serve immediately.

SCIENCE: Frying Spices

Why does proper curry require that the spices be fried in oil or pan-roasted while stewing leaves them tasting raw? The answer is heat, which causes a madhouse of chemical reactions in foods, including spices. With high heat, the chemicals in the spices break down and re-form into totally different compounds with new tastes and aromas. Simmering in a liquid, a spice can be heated to a maximum temperature of 212 degrees. Oil, however, can heat the spices to more than 400 degrees and, depending on the metal, a dry skillet can get even hotter than that.

THAI CURRY

LIKE MOST THAI FOOD, THAI CURRIES embrace a delicate balance of tastes, textures, temperatures, and color that come together to create a harmonious whole. Thai curries (basically any spicy stew is called a curry in Thailand) are considered signature dishes of this cuisine. Thai curries have their antecedents in India. As with their Indian counterparts, spices and liquid are simmered together to create a sauce, to which protein and vegetables are added (there's no browning of meat or deglazing of pans). However, there are several major differences between Indian and Thai curries.

Thai curries almost always contain coconut milk, which not only blends and carries flavors but also forms the backbone of the sauce. While Indian curries rely on a mixture of ground spices and fresh aromatics (like ginger and garlic), Thai curries tilt the balance toward the fresh aromatics. The aromatics are added in the form of a paste, which usually consists of garlic, ginger, shallots, lemon grass, kaffir lime leaves, shrimp paste, and chiles. These pastes can be quite involved and may require an hour of preparation. The curries themselves come together rather quickly and gently simmer for far less time than Indian curries.

With these differences in mind, we set out to explore the two most common types of Thai curries, made with green curry paste and with red curry paste. We wanted to understand the basic structure of the dish and figure out ways to simplify the process of making it. In doing so, we would need to find substitutes for some ingredients, such as kaffir lime leaves and shrimp paste, which are not readily available in most American supermarkets.

Our work was divided into three neat areas: developing recipes for the pastes; cooking the pastes to draw out their flavor (this would involve combining the pastes with the other seasonings, such as coconut milk and fish sauce); and incorporating the protein and vegetables into the curry. We started with the pastes.

Thai curry pastes are intensely flavored. They are used in stir-fries, soups, and sauces as well as curries. Traditionally, ingredients are pounded together in a mortar and pestle to form a smooth paste (see page 299 for more information on a mortar and pestle).

Since this process can take up to an hour and requires a tool most American cooks don't own, we wanted to develop paste recipes that could be assembled by other means. We tested a blender, food processor, and minichopper.

With its narrow base, a blender isn't the best tool for this job. The lack of liquid in the curry paste also presents a problem when using a blender. Large chunks just sat on top of each other as the blade went round and round. We tried adding a little oil or water to help mix the ingredients, but this didn't work either.

The food processor—though not perfect—did a much better job. You must make a lot of curry paste (2 cups, enough for four curry recipes) when using the food processor. (Curry paste holds for a long time, so there's some logic to buying and preparing ingredients once and then enjoying curry on four different occasions.) With smaller batches, the blade simply wouldn't engage the ingredients. Even with more ingredients in the workbowl, we found that a little oil or, better yet, coconut cream, was needed to help bring the ingredients together. We also had the best results when we minced or cut the aromatics fairly small before adding them to the food processor. Although this increased the prep time, it yielded a better sauce. Note, though, that curry paste prepared in a food processor will be a tad grainy, not silky smooth like one ground in a mortar and pestle.

In further testing, we found that a minichopper works just as well as a food processor. Owing to its smaller bowl size, the minichopper will produce about half as much curry paste as the food processor— enough for two of our curry recipes, not four.

It was time to test the ingredients themselves. We started with green curry paste. Hot Thai chiles, sometimes called bird chiles, are the basis for most green curry pastes. These tiny chiles are less than an inch long and offer an intriguing balance of heat and floral flavors. We tested several substitutions and found that serranos are the best candidates. Habaneros were too strong, and jalapeños, Anaheims, and poblanos too mild. Eventually, we decided to mix the Thai or serrano chiles with some jalapeños for extra moisture and bulk and an added flavor dimension.

Shallots, garlic, and ginger are constants in most curry pastes. We found that putting the garlic through a garlic press ensures the smoothest texture. After testing various ratios, we concluded that 2 parts shallots to 1 part each garlic and ginger lends pungency to the herbaceous green curry paste.

Toasted and ground coriander seeds, as well as fresh coriander roots, are other common additions to curry pastes. We found that cilantro leaves are too moist and floral to use as a substitute for the roots but that cilantro stems are fine. The stems are fairly dry and have a pungent, earthy flavor that's similar to the roots. We also liked the effect that ground cumin and pepper had on the pastes.

Lemon grass is an essential ingredient. We tried to prepare curry pastes without it, and tasters uniformly panned them. However, we did find a substitute for galangal, a rhizome related to ginger that's both peppery and sour: A combination of fresh ginger and lime juice added the necessary hot and sour notes. We found that the flavor of the lime juice is best preserved by adding it directly to the curry rather than to the curry paste.

Kaffir lime leaves have a clean, floral aroma. Many tasters compare it with lemon verbena. We found that lime zest approximates this flavor.

Shrimp paste—a puree of salted, fermented shrimp and other seasonings—adds a salty, fishy note to Thai curry pastes. Since this ingredient is very hard to find, we searched for substitutes. Anchovy paste was a reasonable solution, but adding fish sauce directly to the curry is traditional and adds the same kind of subtle fishy flavor. (See page 68 for more information on fish sauce.) We decided to make anchovy paste an optional ingredient in our curry pastes. It adds another layer of flavor but is not essential.

Red chile paste relies on a similar alignment of ingredients except for using equal parts of shallot, garlic and ginger and, of course, the chiles. Traditional recipes call for dried red chiles, soaked in hot water until softened. We found that pastes made with dried chiles alone seemed thin, lacking the body we were looking for. A combination of soaked dried chiles and fresh red jalapeños provided a more satisfying combination of flavor and body. We found that any hot, small dried red chile worked in our recipe. Dried red Thai chiles, also called bird chiles, are traditional, but japonés and de árbol chiles are equally hot and delicious.

Happy with our chile pastes, we shifted gears and started to test ways to cook them. Our goal was to figure out the best way to unlock the flavors of the pastes. Given our experience with Indian curry (see "Frying Spices" on page 296), we figured that frying the curry paste in fat would be key.

In our research, we ran across three different methods for cooking the curry paste—sautéing in oil, simmering in coconut milk, and cooking with the thick coconut cream that floats to the top of cans of coconut milk.

For our first test, we sautéed curry paste in peanut oil and then added the coconut milk. The aroma was good, but the sauce seemed thin and not as flavorful as we wanted. For our second test, we stirred curry paste into coconut milk and then brought the mixture to a simmer and let it cook until it thickened considerably. The flavors were subdued in this version, and the curry lacked the lustrous sheen we had come to expect. For our last test, we spooned off 1 cup of thick coconut cream from the top of a can of coconut milk. We mixed

INGREDIENTS: Store-Bought Curry Pastes

In Thailand, many cooks rely on curry pastes purchased at food markets or in small shops. In the United States, supermarket shoppers may see small jars of Thai curry paste. Red curry paste is more widely available, although we did find green curry paste in a few supermarkets. Of course, prepared curry pastes are a standard item in Southeast Asian markets.

How do store-bought pastes compare with homemade? We purchased red and green Thai Kitchen pastes at the supermarket and several other brands at a local Asian market. All of these store-bought curry pastes were more potent than our homemade versions, so we learned to use far less. We found that all of the brands tested, including Thai Kitchen, which is nationally available, made good curries. The flavors were not as full as the recipes made with our homemade pastes, but the time savings was significant. So if you see Thai Kitchen curry paste in the supermarket, don't hesitate to use this product.

this cream with curry paste in a pan and then turned on the heat. After about 10 minutes, the fat in the coconut cream separated out, and the paste began to fry in the oil. We let the curry paste fry in the oil until it was very aromatic, a process that took just one to two minutes. We added the remaining liquid ingredients, following with the protein and vegetables. The finished curry was thick and flavorful, with a glorious sheen.

Cooking the moisture out of the coconut cream is a somewhat magical process. At first the cream is bubbling away, but then it begins to separate into a solid mass that comes together like soft dough, and a liquid oil (the color of the curry paste) emerges. Listen for the change that takes place as the gentle sound of liquid simmering becomes the louder, more staccato sound of oil frying.

The fat separates from the solids in the coconut cream at different rates, depending on the thickness of the coconut cream, how much is being cooked, and the amount of moisture in the curry paste. The thicker the cream, or the more cream in the pan, the longer the process takes. Dry store-bought curry pastes speed up the process, while moist homemade pastes slow it down.

Once the coconut oil separates out from the cream, the curry paste need only fry in the oil for a minute or two. The remaining coconut milk, fish sauce, and brown sugar (tasters found that this ingredient tempered the heat of the chiles better than granulated white sugar) are then added to the pot. We found that simmering the sauce for five minutes allowed the flavors to blend.

At this point, the protein and vegetables are added to the abundant liquid and cooked directly in the sauce. Aside from gauging the timing so that slow-cooking items, such as potatoes, go into the pot before quick-cooking items, such as snow peas, the process is very simple. Once the protein and vegetables are cooked, a final garnish of fresh herbs (we found that a combination of basil and mint best approximates the flavor of Thai basil) finishes the dish.

Thai curries are saucy and hot and require a nice cushion of rice. Jasmine rice is the most traditional option, but regular long-grain rice works fine.

Rice noodles are another good idea (see "Dried Rice Noodles" on page 176 for more information). A pickled vegetable or cucumber relish rounds out the meal.

INGREDIENTS: Coconut Milk

Coconut milk is an essential ingredient in Thai curries. (See page 67 for definitions of coconut products, including coconut milk and coconut cream.) We wondered if it mattered which brand we chose.

We went to a local Asian market and purchased several brands recommended in Southeast Asian cookbooks, including Chao Koh and Mae Ploy. We also purchased Thai Kitchen, Kame, and A Taste of Thai brands, all of which are sold in supermarkets and natural foods stores. With one exception, we found that all of these brands had a nice thick layer of solid coconut cream on top. The only brand we don't recommend is A Taste of Thai. The coconut cream in this can was not solid (the texture was akin to crème fraîche) and less plentiful—²/₃ cup, not the ³/₄ to 1 full cup of thick, almost solid cream we found in other cans the same size.

EQUIPMENT: Mortar and Pestle

We found that a mortar and pestle create the smoothest, most flavorful and aromatic curry paste. Although making pastes this way is time-consuming, tasters found that pastes made with a mortar and pestle had a better texture than those made in a food processor. In addition, the pounding of the pestle in the mortar crushes cell walls and releases more aroma and flavor from individual ingredients.

But you must use a mortar and pestle made of stone, not clay. In addition, a wide mortar (8 inches is ideal) with a capacity of 2 cups is preferable. Plan on spending at least 45 minutes pounding ingredients to make the paste.

If you own a stone mortar and pestle, here's how to use it to prepare our Green Curry Paste and Red Curry Paste recipes: Cut all ingredient amounts in half and omit the coconut cream or oil. Begin by adding the garlic and salt to the mortar and pound until completely crushed. In the sequence listed, add each new ingredient only after the previous one is pounded to a puree and incorporated into the paste. If making red curry, add the soaked dried chiles right after adding the fresh chiles.

Green Curry Paste

MAKES ABOUT 2 CUPS, ENOUGH TO
PREPARE 4 CURRIES

*Thai green curry paste uses fresh green chiles and is prized
for its herbaceous, aromatic flavor. It is most often used in
poultry, seafood, and vegetable curries. Small green Thai
chiles, also called bird chiles, are less than an inch long and
provide the most authentic heat and herbal flavor. This recipe
is designed to be prepared in a food processor. Cut the quantities in half if using a minichopper. See illustrations on page
302 for tips on handling lemon grass. Although you can
store curry paste in a plastic container, the container will
absorb the flavor and color of the paste and cannot be reused
(even after washing) for other purposes. A glass container is
a better option.*

20	medium cloves garlic, put through a garlic press or minced very fine
1	teaspoon salt
1/4	cup minced cilantro stems
2	tablespoons ground coriander
2	teaspoons ground cumin
1/2	teaspoon ground white pepper
30	green Thai chiles or 15 green serranos, stemmed, seeded, and chopped coarse (about 3/4 cup)
4	large or 6 medium green jalapeño chiles, stemmed, seeded, and chopped coarse (about 3/4 cup)
3	tablespoons minced fresh ginger
3 to 4	stalks lemon grass, outer sheath removed, bottom 3 inches trimmed and minced (about 1/2 cup)
4	teaspoons minced lime zest (from 4 limes)
2	small shallots, chopped coarse (about 6 tablespoons)
1/2	teaspoon shrimp paste or anchovy paste (optional)
2	tablespoons coconut cream or peanut or canola oil

Place all ingredients in the workbowl of a food
processor and pulse 10 times, each pulse lasting 4 to
5 seconds; stop and use a spatula to push down the
ingredients every few pulses. Once the ingredients
begin to form a paste, process until smooth, stopping
occasionally to push down the ingredients, about 3
minutes. Store in a covered glass container or bowl
in the refrigerator for up to 1 month or in the
freezer for several months. (If freezing, divide the
curry paste into 1/2-cup amounts, so that one portion will make one recipe, and freeze individually.)

Red Curry Paste

MAKES ABOUT 2 CUPS, ENOUGH TO
PREPARE 4 CURRIES

*This paste is hotter and even more versatile than green curry
paste. Dried red chiles are traditionally used, but we found
a combination of dried and fresh red chiles created a better
texture. Red curry is delicious paired with beef, pork, duck,
chicken, and all types of seafood. This recipe is designed to
be prepared in a food processor. Cut the quantities in half if
using a minichopper. See the illustrations on page 302 for
tips on handling lemon grass.*

1/2	ounce dried small red chiles (Thai, japonés, or de árbol), stems snapped off, chiles broken in half, and seeds shaken out (about 1/2 cup)
20	medium cloves garlic, put through a garlic press or minced very fine
1	teaspoon salt
2	tablespoons minced cilantro stems
2	tablespoons ground coriander
2	teaspoons ground cumin
1/2	teaspoon ground black pepper
4	large or 6 medium fresh red jalapeño chiles, stemmed, seeded, and chopped coarse (about 3/4 cup)
3	tablespoons minced fresh ginger
3 to 4	stalks lemon grass, outer sheath removed, bottom 3 inches trimmed and minced (about 1/2 cup)
4	teaspoons minced lime zest (from 4 limes)
1	small shallot, chopped coarse (about 3 tablespoons)
1/2	teaspoon shrimp paste or anchovy paste (optional)
2	tablespoons coconut cream or peanut or canola oil

1. Place the dried red chiles in a small bowl and
pour hot water over to cover. Let stand until soft and
rehydrated, about 30 minutes. Remove the chiles, discarding the liquid. Dry the chiles with paper towels.

2. Place all ingredients in the workbowl of a food processor and pulse 10 times, each pulse lasting 4 to 5 seconds; stop and use a spatula to push down the ingredients every few pulses. Once the ingredients begin to form a paste, process until smooth, stopping occasionally to push down the ingredients, about 3 minutes. Store in a covered glass container or bowl in the refrigerator for up to 1 month or in the freezer for several months. (If freezing, divide the curry paste into ½-cup amounts, so that one portion will make one recipe, and freeze individually.)

INGREDIENTS: Lemon Grass

Lemon grass is an integral part of Southeast Asian cooking, imparting a rich, ethereal, lemony essence to many dishes. Most often it is trimmed to the lower third, the tough outer leaves stripped away, and the soft inner core chopped or minced, as in curries or the Thai Chicken and Coconut Soup on page 68. Or, if it is eventually to be removed, as in a stock, the stalk—leaves and all—can simply be bruised and used as is. This is the approach that we took, for example, in making the stock for Hot-and-Sour Rice Noodle Soup with Shrimp and Tomato on page 175.

Fresh lemon grass is a staple in many Asian grocery stores, but it is not always available elsewhere. We did find it in both dried and water-packed form at our local grocer and decided to test them. We cooked them in stocks and compared them with stocks made with fresh lemon grass and lemon zest. Here are our findings.

Fresh lemon grass was the most aromatic, infusing the stock with a delicate, lemony freshness that made it the clear favorite. The next best was the water-packed lemon grass. Although it lacked the crispness and clarity of fresh, this version still maintained lemon grass characteristics. Grated lemon zest finished a remote third. Better zest than dried lemon grass, though. While the stock made with lemon zest was flat and one-dimensional compared with those made with fresh or water-packed lemon grass, it was still, at the very least, lemony. Dried lemon grass was the dog, with a dull, "off" herbal quality; the stock made with it lacked not only freshness but also any lemon flavor.

Thai Curry
SERVES 4

This is more a formula than a specific recipe. See the variations for combinations of protein and vegetables that we especially like. Other proteins may be used, including sliced pork tenderloin, skinned and sliced boneless duck breast, clams, or mussels. If using shrimp, combine it with quick-cooking vegetables to prevent the shrimp from overcooking and becoming tough. For an all-vegetable curry, omit the beef, chicken, or shrimp and increase the vegetables to 8 cups. Adding the optional fresh chile will increase the heat. If you prefer milder food, reduce the amount of curry paste as desired. If you can find Thai basil, replace the basil and mint with equal amounts of it. Serve all curries with jasmine rice or rice noodles (see page 176 for information on the latter).

- 2 (14-ounce) cans coconut milk, not shaken
- ½ cup homemade or 2 tablespoons store-bought green or red curry paste
- 2 tablespoons fish sauce
- 2 tablespoons brown sugar
- 1½ pounds sliced beef, sliced chicken, or shelled shrimp
  Salt
- 5 cups sliced or chopped vegetables
- 1 fresh hot chile, stemmed, seeded, and quartered lengthwise (optional)
- 1 tablespoon lime juice
- ½ cup whole fresh basil leaves
- ½ cup whole fresh mint leaves

1. Carefully spoon off about 1 cup of the top layer of coconut cream from one can—this layer will be thick and possibly solid. Place the coconut cream and curry paste in a large Dutch oven and bring to a boil over high heat, whisking to blend, about 2 minutes. Maintain this brisk simmer and whisk frequently until almost all of the liquid evaporates, 3 to 5 minutes. Reduce the heat to medium-high and whisk constantly until the cream separates into a puddle of colored oil and coconut solids, 3 to 8 minutes. (You should hear the curry paste starting to fry in the oil.) Continue cooking until the curry paste is very aromatic, 1 to 2 minutes.

2. Whisk in the remaining coconut milk, fish

sauce, and brown sugar. Bring back to a brisk simmer and cook until the flavors meld and the sauce thickens, about 5 minutes. Season the beef, chicken, or shrimp with salt and stir it into the pot until the pieces are separated and evenly coated with the sauce, about 1 minute. Add the long-cooking vegetables, such as eggplant, potatoes, and cauliflower, and simmer for several minutes. Add the quick-cooking vegetables, such as bell peppers, snow peas, green beans, bamboo shoots, and mushrooms, and fresh chile (if using) and continue to simmer until the protein and vegetables are cooked. (The total cooking time once the protein is added will range from 7 to 15 minutes.) Off heat, stir in the lime juice, basil, and mint. Serve immediately.

➤ VARIATIONS

Red Curry with Beef and Eggplant

This classic Thai curry is rich in flavors, textures, and colors. If the curry paste is purchased or prepared ahead of time, total cooking time is less than 30 minutes. Freeze the beef for 15 minutes to make cutting easier.

2	(14-ounce) cans coconut milk, not shaken
½	cup homemade or 2 tablespoons store-bought red curry paste
2	tablespoons fish sauce
2	tablespoons brown sugar
1½	pounds flank or skirt steak, trimmed of excess fat and sliced thin against the grain (see illustrations on page 174)

	Salt
2	small Japanese eggplants (about 8 ounces total), halved lengthwise and sliced crosswise on the diagonal into ¼-inch-thick pieces (about 3 cups)
1	(8-ounce) can bamboo shoots, drained and rinsed
1	medium red bell pepper, stemmed, seeded, and cut into thin strips
1	fresh hot chile, stemmed, seeded, and quartered lengthwise (optional)
1	tablespoon lime juice
½	cup whole fresh basil leaves
½	cup whole fresh mint leaves

1. Carefully spoon off about 1 cup of the top layer of coconut cream from one can—this layer will be thick and possibly solid. Place the coconut cream and curry paste in a large Dutch oven and bring to a boil over high heat, whisking to blend, about 2 minutes. Maintain this brisk simmer and whisk frequently until almost all of the liquid evaporates, 3 to 5 minutes. Reduce the heat to medium-high and whisk constantly until the cream separates into a puddle of colored oil and coconut solids, 3 to 8 minutes. (You should hear the curry paste starting to fry in the oil.) Continue cooking until the curry paste is very aromatic, 1 to 2 minutes.

2. Whisk in the remaining coconut milk, fish sauce, and brown sugar. Bring back to a brisk simmer and cook until the flavors meld and the sauce thickens,

MINCING LEMON GRASS

1. Trim all but the bottom 3 to 4 inches of the lemon grass stalk.

2. Remove the tough outer sheath from the trimmed lemon grass. If the lemon grass is particularly thick or tough, you may need to remove several layers to reveal the tender inner portion of the stalk.

3. Cut the trimmed and peeled lemon grass in half lengthwise, then mince finely.

about 5 minutes. Season the beef with salt and add it to the pot, stirring until the pieces are separated and evenly coated with the sauce, about 1 minute. Stir in the eggplant and bring back to a brisk simmer over medium heat. Cook until the eggplant is almost tender, about 10 minutes. Stir in the bamboo shoots, bell pepper, and fresh chile (if using) and cook until these vegetables are crisp-tender, about 2 minutes. Off heat, stir in the lime juice, basil, and mint. Serve immediately.

Red Curry with Shrimp, Pineapple, and Peanuts

Fiery red curry paste is delectable with shrimp, sweet pineapple, and peanuts. Red peppers and snow peas add some crunch and bright color to this classic combination. If desired, try cashews instead of peanuts. For a more authentic appearance, leave the shells on the shrimp tails.

2	(14-ounce) cans coconut milk, not shaken
½	cup homemade or 2 tablespoons store-bought red curry paste
2	tablespoons fish sauce
2	tablespoons brown sugar
1½	pounds medium shrimp, shelled
	Salt
3	cups pineapple chunks (preferably 1-inch cubes)
4	ounces snow peas, trimmed
I	medium red bell pepper, stemmed, seeded, and cut into thin strips
I	fresh hot chile, stemmed, seeded, and quartered lengthwise (optional)
I	tablespoon lime juice
½	cup whole fresh basil leaves
½	cup whole fresh mint leaves
½	cup dry-roasted unsalted peanuts, chopped coarse

1. Carefully spoon off about 1 cup of the top layer of coconut cream from one can—this layer will be thick and possibly solid. Place the coconut cream and curry paste in a large Dutch oven and bring to a boil over high heat, whisking to blend, about 2 minutes. Maintain this brisk simmer and whisk frequently until almost all of the liquid evaporates, 3 to 5 minutes. Reduce the heat to medium-high and whisk constantly until the cream separates into a puddle of colored oil and coconut solids, 3 to 8 minutes. (You should hear the curry paste starting to fry in the oil.) Continue cooking until the curry paste is very aromatic, 1 to 2 minutes.

2. Whisk in the remaining coconut milk, fish sauce, and brown sugar. Bring back to a brisk simmer and cook until the flavors meld and the sauce thickens, about 5 minutes. Season the shrimp with salt and add the shrimp and pineapple to the pot, stirring until the pieces are separated and evenly coated with the sauce, about 1 minute. Bring back to a brisk simmer over medium heat. Cook until the shrimp is almost done, about 4 minutes. Stir in the snow peas, bell pepper, and fresh chile (if using) and cook until the vegetables are crisp-tender, about 2 minutes. Off heat, stir in the lime juice, basil, and mint. Garnish with the peanuts and serve immediately.

Green Curry with Chicken, Broccoli, and Mushrooms

Green curry paste is hard to find in supermarkets but can be made at home in about an hour. Freeze the chicken for 15 minutes to make it easier to cut.

2	(14-ounce) cans coconut milk, not shaken
½	cup homemade or 2 tablespoons store-bought green curry paste
2	tablespoons fish sauce
2	tablespoons brown sugar
1½	pounds boneless, skinless chicken breasts, trimmed of excess fat and sliced thin against the grain
	Salt
2½	cups broccoli florets (about 6 ounces)
4	ounces white or shiitake mushrooms, stems discarded and mushrooms quartered (about 2 cups)
I	medium red bell pepper, stemmed, seeded, and cut in half widthwise and then into thin strips
I	fresh hot chile, stemmed, seeded, and quartered lengthwise (optional)
I	tablespoon lime juice
½	cup whole basil leaves
½	cup whole mint leaves

1. Carefully spoon off about 1 cup of the top layer of coconut cream from one can—this layer will be thick and possibly solid. Place the coconut cream and curry paste in a large Dutch oven and bring to a boil over high heat, whisking to blend, about 2 minutes. Maintain this brisk simmer and whisk frequently until almost all of the liquid evaporates, 3 to 5 minutes. Reduce the heat to medium-high and whisk constantly until the cream separates into a puddle of colored oil and coconut solids, 3 to 8 minutes. (You should hear the curry paste starting to fry in the oil.) Continue cooking until the curry paste is very aromatic, 1 to 2 minutes.

2. Whisk in the remaining coconut milk, fish sauce, and brown sugar. Bring back to a brisk simmer and cook until the flavors meld and the sauce thickens, about 5 minutes. Season the chicken with salt and add it to the pot, stirring until the pieces are separated and evenly coated with the sauce, about 1 minute. Stir in the broccoli and mushrooms and bring back to a brisk simmer over medium heat. Cook until the vegetables are almost tender, about 5 minutes. Stir in the bell pepper and fresh chile (if using) and cook until these vegetables are crisp-tender, about 2 minutes. Off heat, stir in the lime juice, basil, and mint. Serve immediately.

Green Curry with Mixed Vegetables

Vegetarian curries are often prepared with green curry paste. In this version, red potatoes and cauliflower are cooked until tender and combined with crisp green beans, yellow squash, and red peppers.

2	(14-ounce) cans coconut milk, not shaken
½	cup homemade or 2 tablespoons store-bought green curry paste
2	tablespoons fish sauce
2	tablespoons brown sugar
2	cups cauliflower florets (about 6 ounces)
2	medium red potatoes (about 8 ounces), scrubbed (see illustration on page 81), quartered lengthwise and cut crosswise into ¼-inch-thick slices (about 3 cups)
4	ounces green beans, ends trimmed and cut into 2-inch lengths (about 1 cup)
1	small summer squash, halved lengthwise and cut crosswise into ¼-inch-thick slices (about 2 cups)
1	medium red bell pepper, stemmed, seeded, and cut in half widthwise and then into thin strips
1	fresh hot chile, stemmed, seeded, and quartered lengthwise (optional)
1	tablespoon lime juice
½	cup whole basil leaves
½	cup whole mint leaves

1. Carefully spoon off about 1 cup of the top layer of coconut cream from one can—this layer will be thick and possibly solid. Place the coconut cream and curry paste in a large Dutch oven and bring to a boil over high heat, whisking to blend, about 2 minutes. Maintain this brisk simmer and whisk frequently until almost all of the liquid evaporates, 3 to 5 minutes. Reduce the heat to medium-high and whisk constantly until the cream separates into a puddle of colored oil and coconut solids, 3 to 8 minutes. (You should hear the curry paste starting to fry in the oil.) Continue cooking until the curry paste is very aromatic, 1 to 2 minutes.

2. Whisk in the remaining coconut milk, fish sauce, and brown sugar. Bring back to a brisk simmer and cook until the flavors meld and the sauce thickens, about 5 minutes. Stir in the cauliflower and potatoes and bring back to a brisk simmer over medium heat. Cook the vegetables for 7 minutes. Stir in the green beans, squash, bell pepper, and fresh chile (if using) and cook until the cauliflower and potatoes are tender and the other vegetables are crisp-tender, about 3 minutes. Off heat, stir in the lime juice, basil, and mint. Serve immediately.

PART 4

ACCOMPANIMENTS

14

RICE, POTATOES, POLENTA,
BREADS, AND BISCUITS

THERE ARE MANY REASONS WHY WE LOVE soups and stews, including the fact that most of the recipes in this book make an excellent one-dish main course. But even the heartiest bowl of soup or stew needs something to round out the meal—a craggy hunk of homemade bread to sop up the last drops of chicken soup or perhaps a mound of mashed potatoes to accompany beef burgundy. This chapter includes the best recipes for our favorite accompaniments to soups and stews.

The chapter begins by looking at rice, mashed potatoes, and polenta. These dishes are generally served underneath or alongside stews. Rice is the perfect foil for something hot and spicy, like curry or chili. Mashed potatoes and polenta soak up the rich sauce from a stew and add a necessary carbohydrate element to what otherwise can be too rich on its own.

Soups generally call out for bread, and our favorite choices are a rustic white loaf or a more refined baguette. (Of course, breads also make a fine accompaniment to most stews.) Cornbread and biscuits can also be served with either soups or stews. Cornbread and chili are as traditional as cornbread and black bean soup. And who doesn't love a warm, buttery biscuit with a bowl of creamy tomato soup or a plate of hearty chicken fricassee? We've included two recipes for types of biscuits—a traditional recipe made with buttermilk and a quick, foolproof version with cream.

WHITE RICE

FEW FOODS ARE AS SATISFYING AS RICE that's been perfectly cooked. But this elemental food can be temperamental—it can resist the cook and be a pot of true grit or dissolve to an unpleasant, gummy mess. Advertisements stress perfect rice, but package instructions are unreliable when you want a tasty bowl of fluffy rice with nicely separate grains. We wanted to find an easy method for making really great long-grain white rice.

We started our tests by following the package directions on four brands of long-grain rice. The technique was a variation on the simmer-in-a-covered-pot method, with 1 cup rice cooked with 2 to 2½ cups water. Some of the instructions called for salt, some didn't, and there were recipes with and without butter. All the recipes were disappointing, the results mostly insipid, with mushy, frayed grains. There was gritty rice, there was fatty rice, but there was no rice we liked.

Next we tried a method popular with both French and Indian cooks—boiling the rice in a generous quantity of salted water, as if cooking pasta. Cooked this way, all brands of rice came to the table evenly done, with separate kernels, but they were also waterlogged and bland.

Then we experimented with baking the rice in casseroles, with 1¾ to 2½ parts water to 1 part rice, some with butter, salted and unsalted. Boiling water was poured over the rice, then the vessels were sealed with foil and baked for 25 to 30 minutes. The rice made with less water and salt was better. This result was somewhat beside the point, however, because baked rice, while slightly creamy, did not have the well-defined grains we wanted.

We next tried a routine advocated by Asian cooks, a combination of uncovered boiling and covered steaming. For this technique the quantity of water is gauged by the length of a finger joint—½ to ¾ inch—above the rice. First the water is boiled until it evaporates to the level of the grains, then the heat is turned down to low, the pot is covered, and cooking continues over low heat for 10 to 16 minutes. The four brands of long-grain rice took unevenly to this method, some better than others, but the rice was always sticky—easy to handle with chopsticks, but not the distinct grains we were looking for.

The perfect method still eluded us, but we had discerned a pattern. Less water and an even, gentle heat worked better. So we tried a pilaf method, because pilaf recipes generally use less water and produce distinct grains of rice. We first sautéed the rice in two teaspoons of butter or oil, then boiled it with water varying from one to two cups. After the water came to a boil, we covered the pan and let the rice simmer for 15 minutes, then removed it from the heat and let it rest a bit prior to serving. With this method, the rice cooked up light and tender but not mushy, with

INGREDIENTS: White Rice

Essentially, white rice is brown rice made convenient. Developed thousands of years ago, the technique of stripping the germ and bran from brown rice to get white rice saves 30 minutes in cooking time. In today's busy world, that can make a big difference. Yet rice manufacturers have made cooking long-grain white rice even more of a snap with five-minute instant varieties and boil-in-bag options. We could not help but wonder whether so much convenience could still taste good. We decided to find out with a blind taste test.

To avoid comparing apples and oranges, we limited the candidates in our tasting to nationally distributed brands or major regional brands of plain, nonaromatic, long-grain white rice products. This gave us a lineup of 13 products, including standard, instant, converted, and boil-in-bag.

To understand the differences between these products, it helps to first know what they have in common. To begin with, all the rices in our tasting were long-grain, which means that each kernel is about four times longer than its width when uncooked. (Other common types of rice include medium- and short-grain.) Long-grain white rice is characteristically "fluffy" and is the least sticky of the white rices. In part, this is because it contains a high percentage of amylose, a starch that keeps grains separate after cooking.

All the rices were also milled using the standard milling process in which the hull is removed and the grains are then rubbed together by machine to remove the bran and germ. (Rice with bran and germ left intact is brown rice.) These two processes create standard white rice. Converted and instant rice, however, are subjected to more processing.

The additional processing for converted rice is done before the milling. The unmilled rice is soaked in hot water, then steamed and dried in the husk. This technique is far from modern, dating back about 1,500 years in India, where rice was put in large pots of water, soaked, steamed, and laid out in the sun to dry. Still practiced today in rural parts of India, this method makes it easier to remove the hull. For modern cooks the primary advantage of this processing is that the rice remains firmer and more separate when it's cooked. Some of the starch in the outer portion of the kernel becomes gelatinized when it's steamed in the husk. The rice kernel then dries harder than it was in its original state, and nutrients are retained as they seep from the bran into the kernel. The harder starch makes it more difficult for water to penetrate, so it takes about five minutes more time for converted rice to cook. The result is firmer, more separate rice with a tan-yellow tint and a stronger flavor than standard rice.

On the opposite end of the spectrum is instant rice. To make it, milled rice is fully precooked and then dried very fast. This creates cracks or channels that facilitate the movement of water into the kernel as it cooks on the stove. You can actually see this if you look closely at kernels of instant rice, which tend to be light and porous, like miniature puffed rice. This process makes cooking rice as effortless as making instant soup—stir into boiling water, cover, and let rest off heat for five minutes.

The compromise between the firm, separate kernels of converted rice and the convenience of instant rice seems to be boil-in-bag products. These modern innovations are made by precooking converted rice. In other words, these rices are parboiled prior to hulling, then precooked and dried after hulling and the removal of the bran and germ. The idea is that the parboiling will create rice grains with a firmer texture resistant to breaking down and turning mushy, so that even though they are also precooked they will remain firm and separate during their final 10 minutes of cooking.

When it came to tasting, our panel decided that in the case of white rice, less is definitely more. Most of the top ratings went to standard rices that had not been subjected to any special processing to make them cook faster or end up with grains that were unusually separate. This result was not unexpected. What really surprised us, though, was the second-place finish of Uncle Ben's Boil-in-Bag rice, along with the sixth-place showing of Kraft's Boil-in-Bag. In both cases, the idea behind the dual processing of these rices really paid off. Tasters found the grains of Uncle Ben's, in particular, to be firm, perfectly unbroken, and nicely moist. The converted rices, on the other hand, did not fare as well, with testers downgrading them on both flavor and texture. As for instant rices, tasters found these products unpalatably mushy, and they noted that the individual kernels tended to fall apart and fray. We also detected off flavors.

So if you aren't opposed to preparing your rice in a plastic pouch, a boil-in-bag rice might be the best option when you're looking for convenience. The trade-off, however, is that you get less rice for your dollar and you cannot cook the rice along with other seasonings or ingredients. Standard long-grain white rice takes only 30 to 35 minutes to prepare (including resting time) and requires minimal attention, so the rest of your meal can be prepared as the rice cooks.

individual grains, and the sautéing added a rich dimension of flavor. No matter the brand of rice, we preferred the ratio of 1 cup rice to 1½ cups water. The kernels should be sautéed and stirred until some become milky white. For stronger, nutty flavors, the raw rice can be fried to a toasted golden brown.

Fine-tuning the method produced different nuances in the grain. In repeated tests we found the rice was less starchy when the pan was swirled to incorporate all the ingredients instead of stirred with a fork. When boiling water was added to the sautéed rice, the finished rice was sticky; add cold water and then heat to a boil for the best results.

We were curious to try the same formula (1 cup rice, 1½ cups water, ½ teaspoon salt) without sautéing. Fluffed with a fork, rice cooked in this manner was almost as fluffy as the pilaf-method rice, with a mild flavor that brings out the subtly floral, "ricey" aromatics. At a small sacrifice of texture, this is the ideal rice for many chicken stews and fish dishes.

There was some flexibility in cooking time, as long as the rice was allowed to rest, covered, after

---

EQUIPMENT: Two-Quart Saucepan

A medium saucepan (2 to 2½ quarts) is the best pot for preparing rice on top of the stove. Many of the jobs suited for a small saucepan (making rice or oatmeal, heating milk for cocoa) involve ingredients that stick and leave a mess in the pan, even when the recipe comes out right. Leave a pot of rice unattended or burn some pastry cream, and you may have to soak the pot for hours and then put in a lot of elbow grease to get it back in shape.

For these reasons, we recommend buying a nonstick two-quart saucepan. Choose a pan with some heft (in our testing of eight models, we found that 2 to 3 pounds is ideal for this size pan). Avoid really lightweight pans, which are prone to scorching, as well as heavy copper or enameled cast-iron saucepans, which are hard to maneuver because of their weight.

Last, look for pans with handles that won't become scorching hot. Our testers preferred pans with hollowed-out stainless steel handles (like those on All-Clad pans) or even cheap plastic handles (a saucepan never goes into the oven, so there's no need to buy something ovenproof anyway). Stay away from saucepans with solid metal handles, which became hot very quickly in our tests.

---

cooking. We got the most consistent results with a cooking time of 15 to 18 minutes from when the pot was sealed to the time the rice was done, with a 15-minute rest on the turned-off burner. (Don't pull the cover off the pot to peek.) Before serving, fluff the rice with a fork.

Fluffy White Rice
SERVES 4

This recipe is designed for 1 cup of raw rice in a tight-lidded pot. As you cook more rice, you should reduce the proportion of water. With 2 cups of rice, you can get these results with 2½ to 2¾ cups of water. But it is very hard to get a reliable result with less than a cup of rice, so do not halve this recipe. Serve white rice with chili, gumbo, or stew.

2	teaspoons unsalted butter or oil (vegetable or olive)
1	cup long-grain white rice (not converted)
1½	cups water
½	teaspoon salt

1. Heat the oil in a medium saucepan over medium heat. Add the rice and cook, stirring constantly, for 1 to 3 minutes, depending on desired amount of nutty flavor. Add the water and salt. Bring to a boil, swirling the pot to blend ingredients.

2. Reduce the heat to low, cover tightly, and cook until the liquid is absorbed, about 15 minutes.

3. Turn off the heat; let the rice stand on the burner, still covered, to finish cooking, about 15 minutes longer. Fluff with a fork and serve.

BASMATI RICE

ALTHOUGH CURRIES CAN BE SERVED WITH regular white rice, basmati rice is both traditional and preferable. Ideally, basmati rice has a nutty, highly aromatic flavor and cooks up with separate grains that are at once fluffy and firm to the bite. Two major questions surfaced as we researched traditional Indian recipes. Is it necessary to prepare the rice for cooking by soaking or rinsing it, and what is the best cooking method?

In the first series of tests, we examined the

tradition of presoaking the rice, which is believed to maximize grain elongation and prevent the rice grains from breaking during and after cooking. We tested basmati rice prepared with a 20-minute presoak in water as well as rice prepared with just a quick rinse and rice made with neither soaking nor rinsing. To make sure that our tests were not skewed because we had used more water overall with one method than another, we weighed the rice before and after rinsing and soaking, then subtracted 1 ounce of water for each ounce of increased rice weight to compensate for water that had been absorbed.

When we ran a taste test on these rice preparation methods, we were surprised. Presoaking resulted in overcooked rice and inconsistently sized grains, ranging from 10 to 15 millimeters, with a mushy texture because of water absorbed during soaking. Contrary to what we had expected from our research, many of the presoaked rice grains broke.

The texture and flavor of the rinsed rice was in the same league as that of the soaked: definitely less aromatic and flavorsome than the unsoaked rice. Grains ranged in length from 10 to 14 millimeters. Despite the claim of some cookbooks that rinsing produces a less sticky product, our tests found the opposite to be true.

Rice that was not soaked or rinsed was fluffy, and the grains were dry and separate with a firm, toothy texture and a consistent grain size of 11 to 12 millimeters. This rice also had the nuttiest flavor and the most intact grains. All in all, we preferred the unsoaked rice with its slightly shorter grain and firmer texture.

In the next series of tests we focused on the

SCIENCE: Starches in Rice

When buying rice, it is imperative to pay attention to the size of the grains. Rice can be classed as long-, medium-, or short-grain. Long-grain rice is about four times as long as it is wide. Medium-grain rice is twice as long as it is wide. Short-grain rice is round. In general, long-grain rice cooks up fluffy and separate, while medium- and short-grain rice tend to cling or become starchy. This is due to the ratio of the two main starches in the rice—amylose and amylopectin.

Long-grain rice contains between 23 and 26 percent amylose, a starch that does not gelatinize during cooking. With such a high amylose content, properly cooked long-grain rice remains dry and separate. Medium-grain has an average amylose content between 18 and 26 percent, and short-grain falls between 15 and 20 percent. As these numbers indicate, individual lots of rice behave differently, and our tests with different brands bore this out.

Medium-grain rice is a favorite for risotto, where some starchiness, but not too much, is wanted. But when making plain steamed rice to accompany gumbo, chili, or stew, we prefer long-grain rice because the individual grains cook up separately.

cooking method. The three methods we tested were steeped, pilaf, and boiled and drained. In the steeping method, which is the standard way of making rice, water is brought to a boil, rice and salt are added, the pot is stirred, returned to a simmer, and then covered until all the water has been absorbed. In the pilaf method, the rice is first cooked in oil that has been infused with spice and onions, then steeped in water. In the boiled and drained method, the rice is cooked in a large quantity of boiling water and then drained, just as pasta is cooked.

INGREDIENTS: Basmati Rice

Basmati rice has been grown in India and Pakistan for nearly 9,000 years. American versions of the aromatic rice can be found under the names of Texmati, Della, and Kasmati. After preparing a batch of each of these, we found that Texmati and Della do have a vague aromatic resemblance to Indian basmati rice, but the grains are wider and do not fully elongate. Instead, they tend to expand like standard long-grain rice, which grows in length by about 50 percent when cooked, compared with true basmati rice, which doubles in length. Kasmati rice, on the other hand, is a close cousin to Indian basmati. It is not as fluffy as the authentic Indian variety and the grains are somewhat sticky, but the flavor holds its own. Imported basmati is available in well-stocked supermarkets, natural foods stores, and Indian grocery stores. We found it to be superior to and more economical than the American varieties.

The pilaf and steeped versions each had their merits. With the pilaf, an infusion of flavors resulted in a dish that can truly stand alone. Our preference is for this method because of its dynamic flavors; it also produced more separate grains than the other methods. However, steeped basmati rice is a simpler method for everyday curries and produces a rice with an extremely fresh and nutty flavor. Our least favorite was the boiled and drained version; the nutty flavor was washed out, and the rice ended up bland and waterlogged.

We tried various ratios of water to rice and found 1 cup of rice to 1½ cups of water to be ideal. In terms of timing, we got the most consistent results with 15 to 18 minutes from the moment the pot is sealed to the point when the rice is done.

Basmati Rice, Pilaf Style

SERVES 4

This rice is the ideal accompaniment to curry, but it can be served at any meal at which regular white rice might be appropriate. If doubling the recipe, use just 2½ to 2¾ cups of water.

I	tablespoon canola, vegetable, or corn oil
I	(3-inch) stick cinnamon, halved
2	whole green cardamom pods
2	whole cloves
¼	cup thinly sliced onion
I	cup basmati rice
I½	cups water
I	teaspoon salt

1. Heat the oil in a medium saucepan over high heat until almost smoking. Add the cinnamon, cardamom, and cloves and cook, stirring until the cinnamon unfurls and the cardamom and cloves pop, 5 to 10 seconds. Add the onion and cook, stirring until translucent, about 2 minutes. Stir in the rice and cook, stirring until fragrant, about 1 minute.

2. Add the water and salt and bring to a boil. Reduce the heat, cover tightly, and simmer until all the water has been absorbed, about 17 minutes. Let stand, covered, for at least 10 minutes. Fluff with a fork and serve immediately.

MASHED POTATOES

MOST OF US WHO MAKE MASHED POTATOES would never consider consulting a recipe. We customarily make them by adding chunks of butter and spurts of cream until our conscience—or a backseat cook—tells us to stop. Not surprisingly, we produce batches of mashed potatoes that are consistent only in their mediocrity.

Great stew deserves great spuds. The right mashed potatoes can transform the humblest stew into a meal fit for king. For us, the consummate mashed potatoes are creamy, soft, and supple, yet with enough body to stand up to sauce from a stew. As for flavor, the sweet, earthy, humble potato comes first, then the buttery richness that keeps you coming back for more.

Potatoes are composed mostly of starch and water. The starch is in the form of granules, which in turn are contained in starch cells. The higher the starch content of the potato, the fuller the cells. In high-starch potatoes (russets are a good example), the cells are completely full—they look like plump little beach balls. In medium-starch (Yukon Golds) and low-starch potatoes (Red Bliss), the cells are more like underinflated beach balls. The space between these less-than-full cells is taken up mostly by water.

In our tests, we found that the full starch cells of high-starch potatoes are most likely to maintain their integrity and stay separate when mashed, giving the potatoes a delightfully fluffy texture. In addition, the low water content of these potatoes allows them to absorb milk, cream, and/or butter without becoming wet or gummy. Starch cells in lower-starch potatoes, on the other hand, tend to clump when cooked and break more easily, allowing the starch to dissolve into whatever liquid is present. The broken cells and dissolved starch tend to make sticky, gummy mashed potatoes.

We needed first to address the simple matter of the best way to cook the potatoes. We started by peeling and cutting some potatoes into chunks to expedite their cooking while cooking others unpeeled and whole. Even when mashed with identical amounts of butter, half-and-half (recommended by a number of trustworthy cookbooks), and salt, the two batches were wildly different. Those peeled and cut made mashed potatoes that were thin in taste and texture and devoid of potato flavor, while those cooked whole and peeled after cooking yielded mashed potatoes that were rich, earthy, and sweet.

We talked to several food scientists, who explained that peeling and cutting the potatoes before simmering increases the surface area through which they lose soluble substances, such as starch, proteins, and flavor compounds, to the cooking water. The greater surface area also enables lots of water molecules to bind with the potatoes' starch molecules. Combine these two effects and you've got bland, thin, watery mashed potatoes.

Next were the matters of butter and dairy. Working with 2 pounds of potatoes, which serves four to six, we stooped so low as to add only 2 tablespoons of butter. The potatoes ultimately deemed best in flavor by tasters contained 8 tablespoons. They were rich and full and splendid.

When considering dairy, we investigated both the kind and the quantity. Heavy cream made heavy mashed potatoes that were sodden and unpalatably rich, even when we scaled back the amount of butter. On the other hand, mashed potatoes made with whole milk were watery, wimpy, and washed out. When we tried adding more butter to compensate for the milk's lack of richness, the mixture turned into potato soup. Half-and-half, which we'd used in our original tests, was just what was needed, and 1 cup was just the right amount. The mashed potatoes now had a lovely light suppleness and a full flavor that edged toward decadent. Make sure to warm the half-and-half or it will cool down the potatoes.

The issues attending butter and dairy did not end there. We had heard that the order in which they are added to the potatoes can affect texture and that melted butter makes better mashed potatoes than softened butter. Determined to leave no spud unturned, we threw several more pounds into the pot. As it turns out, when the butter goes in before the dairy, the result is a silkier, creamier, smoother texture than when the dairy goes first; by comparison, the dairy-first potatoes were pasty and thick.

Using melted rather than softened butter made the potatoes even more creamy, smooth, and light.

With our curiosity piqued by the significant textural differences effected by minor differences in procedure, we again contacted several food scientists, who explained that when the half-and-half is stirred into the potatoes before the butter, the water in it works with the starch in the potatoes to make the mashed potatoes gluey and heavy. When the butter is added before the half-and-half, the fat coats the starch molecules, inhibiting their interaction with the water in the half-and-half added later and thereby yielding silkier, creamier mashed potatoes. The benefit of using melted butter results from its liquid form, which enables it to coat the starch molecules quickly and easily. This buttery coating not only affects the interaction of the starch molecules with the half-and-half, it also affects the starch molecules' interaction with each other. All in all, it makes for smoother, more velvety mashed potatoes.

There is more than one way to mash potatoes. In our testing, we had been using either a ricer or a food mill. We preferred the food mill because its large hopper accommodated half of the potatoes at a time. A ricer, which resembles an oversized garlic press, required processing in several batches. Both, however, produced smooth, light, fine-textured mashed potatoes.

A potato masher is the tool of choice for making chunky mashed potatoes, but it cannot produce smooth mashed potatoes on a par with those processed through a food mill or ricer. With a masher, potatoes mashed within an inch of their lives could not achieve anything better than a namby-pamby texture that was neither chunky nor perfectly smooth. The sentiment among our tasters was that mashed potatoes should be either smooth or coarse and craggy. Because of this, a masher is best left to make the coarser version.

There are two styles of potato mashers—one is a disk with large holes in it, the other a curvy wire loop. We found the disk to be more efficient for reducing both mashing time and the number of lumps in the finished product.

Mashed Potatoes

SERVES 4 TO 6

Russet potatoes make slightly fluffier mashed potatoes, but Yukon Golds have an appealing buttery flavor and can be used if you prefer. Mashed potatoes stiffen and become gluey as they cool, so they are best served piping hot. If you must hold mashed potatoes before serving, place them in a heat-proof bowl, cover the bowl tightly with plastic wrap, and set the bowl over a pot of simmering water. The potatoes will remain hot and soft-textured for about one hour. This recipe can be increased by half or doubled as needed. This recipe yields smooth mashed potatoes. If don't mind lumps, use a potato masher as directed in the variation.

- 2 pounds russet potatoes, scrubbed (see illustration on page 81)
- 8 tablespoons unsalted butter, melted
- I cup half-and-half, warmed
- I ½ teaspoons salt
  Ground black pepper

1. Place the potatoes in a large saucepan with cold water to cover by about 1 inch. Bring to a boil over high heat, reduce the heat to medium-low, and simmer until the potatoes are just tender when pricked with a thin-bladed knife, 20 to 30 minutes.

2. Set a food mill or ricer over now empty but still warm saucepan. Spear a potato with a dinner fork, then peel back the skin with a paring knife (see illustration 1, right). Repeat with remaining potatoes. Working in batches, cut peeled potatoes into rough chunks and drop into the hopper of the food mill or ricer (see illustration 2, right). Process or rice the potatoes into the saucepan.

3. Stir in the butter with a wooden spoon until incorporated. Gently whisk in the half-and-half, salt, and pepper to taste. Serve immediately.

➤ VARIATIONS

Lumpy Mashed Potatoes

We prefer silky, smooth mashed potatoes and therefore recommend using a food mill or ricer. If you like chunky mashed potatoes, a potato masher can be used.

Follow recipe for Mashed Potatoes, dropping the peeled potato chunks back in the warm saucepan and mashing with a potato masher until fairly

smooth. Proceed as directed, reducing the half-and-half to ¾ cup.

Garlic Mashed Potatoes

Toasted garlic contributes the truest, purest garlic flavor imaginable to mashed potatoes. Best of all, the garlic can be peeled after toasting, when the skins will slip right off. Just be sure to keep the heat low and to let the garlic stand off heat until fully softened.

Toast 22 small to medium-large garlic cloves (about ⅔ cup), skins left on, in a small, covered heavy-bottomed skillet over lowest possible heat, shaking pan frequently, until cloves are dark spotty brown and slightly softened, about 22 minutes. Remove pan from heat and let stand, covered, until cloves are fully softened, 15 to 20 minutes. Peel cloves and, with paring knife, cut off woody root end. Follow recipe

MAKING MASHED POTATOES

1. Hold the cooked potato with a dinner fork, then peel off the skin with a paring knife.

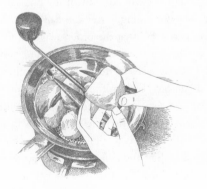

2. Cut the peeled potato into rough chunks and drop the chunks into the food mill.

for Mashed Potatoes, dropping peeled garlic cloves into food mill or ricer with peeled potatoes.

Mashed Potatoes with Parmesan and Lemon

Follow recipe for Mashed Potatoes, stirring in 1 cup grated Parmesan cheese and minced or grated zest from 1 lemon along with the half-and-half, salt, and pepper.

Mashed Potatoes with Root Vegetables

Most root vegetables are more watery than potatoes, so you will need less than the full cup of half-and-half.

Follow recipe for Mashed Potatoes, replacing 1 pound of potatoes with 1 pound of parsnips, rutabagas, celery root, carrots, or turnips that have been peeled and cut into 1½- to 2-inch chunks. Add the half-and-half, ¼ cup at a time, until the desired consistency is obtained.

Buttermilk Mashed Potatoes

Buttermilk gives mashed potatoes a pleasing tang and rich texture, even when less butter is used. If you prefer mashed potatoes with less fat, this is your best option.

Follow recipe for Mashed Potatoes, reducing the butter to 1 tablespoon and replacing the half-and-half with 1 cup warmed buttermilk.

POLENTA

IF YOUR MOTHER EVER COMPLAINED ABOUT slaving over a hot stove, she was probably talking about making polenta. Nothing more than cornmeal mush, polenta is made from dried, ground corn cooked in liquid until the starches in the corn have had enough time to hydrate and swell into soft, balloonlike structures. As an accompaniment to stew, this soft stage is the most delicious way to serve polenta.

The stiff polenta you often see in restaurants starts out as a soft mass but is spread into a thin layer on a baking sheet or marble surface, cooled until stiff, sliced, and then sautéed, fried, or grilled until it resembles a crouton. These crisp rectangles are rarely more than a garnish, but a smooth, piping hot mound of soft polenta can serve as a base for most stews—everything from ratatouille to chili.

Although making polenta sounds easy, the traditional Italian method for cooking it is a lot of work. The polenta must be slowly added to boiling salted water and then stirred constantly (to prevent scorching) during the entire 30- to 40-minute cooking time. Within minutes, you'll feel like you've been arm-wrestling Arnold Schwarzenegger. And 30 minutes of such constant stirring can seem like an eternity.

Of course, this assumes that you have avoided the biggest pitfall of all, the "seizing" problem at the beginning of the cooking process. Cornmeal is a starch, and starch thickens when it's mixed with water and heated. If this happens too quickly, the cornmeal seizes up in a solid, nearly immovable mass. We tested adding cornmeal to cold water, using more water, using less water, and using different grinds of cornmeal, all to no avail. Yes, we learned to prevent seizing (keep the water at a simmer and add the cornmeal very slowly), but we still needed to stir constantly for at least 30 minutes to prevent scorching.

This testing did, however, reveal some important information. We found that medium-grind cornmeal makes the best polenta. Finely ground cornmeal, such as the Quaker brand sold in many supermarkets, is too powdery and makes gummy polenta. Cornmeal with a texture akin to granulated sugar, not table salt, makes the best polenta. We also discovered that a ratio of 4 parts water to 1 part cornmeal delivers the right consistency. As for salt, 1 teaspoon is the right amount for 1 cup of cornmeal.

At this point in our testing, we started to explore alternative cooking methods. The microwave was a bust, yielding sticky, raw-tasting polenta. The pressure cooker was even worse—taking a long time and resulting in polenta stuck firmly to the pot.

We finally hit upon our solution when we prepared polenta in a double boiler. The polenta is cooked over simmering water so it cannot scorch or seize up the way it can when cooked over direct heat. There is only one drawback: The double-boiler method takes twice as long as the constant-stir method. However, since you need only stir the pot once every 10 to 15 minutes, we don't consider this much of a drawback, as long as you are around the kitchen anyway, cooking something else. Perhaps the best reason to use the double boiler to prepare polenta is the end result. To our palates, polenta prepared this way has a softer, lighter texture than polenta prepared according to the traditional recipe. It also tastes sweeter and more like corn.

Double-Boiler Polenta

SERVES 4

When stirring the polenta, there's no need to beat it vigorously; just move the cornmeal around, scraping the sides and bottom of the pan to ensure even cooking. Spoon any stew over a base of this polenta. This recipe can be increased by half or doubled as necessary, provided that your double boiler is large enough.

    4   cups boiling water
    I   teaspoon salt
    I   cup medium-grind cornmeal

1. Bring about 2 inches of water to a boil in the bottom of a double boiler. Reduce to a simmer and maintain throughout cooking process.

2. Set the top of the double boiler over the simmering water and add 4 cups boiling water. Add the salt, then gradually sprinkle the cornmeal into the water, whisking constantly to prevent the formation of lumps.

3. Cover and cook until the polenta is very soft and smooth, 1¼ to 1½ hours, stirring for several seconds every 10 to 15 minutes. (Once cooked, the polenta can be covered and set aside at room temperature for up to 4 hours. Reheat over simmering water, stirring in a little water if polenta has become too thick.)

➤ VARIATION

Polenta with Parmesan and Butter

This rich variation is especially good with vegetable stews.

Follow recipe for Double-Boiler Polenta, stirring in 4 tablespoons softened butter and ½ cup grated Parmesan cheese when the polenta is done.

INGREDIENTS: Instant Polenta

After testing dozens of ways to prepare polenta, we still had one question. What about "quick-cooking" or "instant" polenta? We tested several brands (all imported from Italy) and found that instant polenta is a great way to make polenta in a hurry. The flavor is good (although not nearly as good as double-boiler polenta), and it takes no more than 10 minutes.

Quick polenta, like quick grits or instant rice, has been cooked before, then dried out. All you need to do is reconstitute it with boiling water. Quick polenta costs at least three times as much as regular cornmeal and won't have the smooth texture and full corn flavor of double-boiler polenta. However, instant polenta is easy to prepare (just add to boiling water and simmer for several minutes), and the end result is good.

RUSTIC COUNTRY BREAD

FLOUR, WATER, YEAST, AND SALT. THAT'S ABOUT as simple as it gets in the kitchen, or so we thought when we set out to develop a reliable home recipe for a crusty, full-textured, European-style country bread. This is the kind of bread that is a main course all by itself; the first bite hits you with a heady burst of crackle and chew, an inspired whiff of yeast, and a hint of sourness.

Our first task was to determine which of the four types of country bread to test. These four types result from four different methods of leavening the bread: with a natural starter (a mixture of flour and water is left out for 24 hours, during which time the mixture attracts natural yeast spores from the air), a mixed starter (the starter in this case is a piece of dough reserved from a previously made kneaded batch), a standard yeast starter (where yeast is dissolved in warm water and then added to the dry ingredients), or a sponge starter (a "sponge" of flour, water, and yeast is left to ferment, then additional flour, water, and other ingredients are added in).

The first and second methods are inconvenient for home cooks. The third method does not provide enough time for the flavor to develop. The last method proved to be a good compromise.

In the *Chez Panisse Cookbook* (Random House, 1988), Paul Bertolli suggests making a sponge, covering it, and letting it sit out overnight before making the dough. We decided to follow this method. In his recipe, however, he uses only one-quarter of the sponge as a starter for his bread, reserving the rest for use in future loaves. Since most home cooks don't have the patience to keep a starter going in the refrigerator, we decided to deviate from his recipe by using the entire sponge.

This approach worked well. As we had expected, there was more flavor than with a quick rise using a greater amount of yeast. In fact, we only used ½ teaspoon of dry yeast (most recipes call for up to a tablespoon) for 6 cups of flour. We also varied the sponge recipe by increasing the percentage of whole wheat flour, using equal amounts of whole wheat and white flour for added flavor and texture.

The next element to consider was water. Professional bakers know that a high water content produces more texture and chew. To figure out the percentage of water in a bread recipe (as a percentage of the flour weight), you calculate the weight, in grams, of water in the recipe (each cup of water weighs 237.5 grams) and divide that by the weight of the flour (there are 130 grams in 1 cup of flour). After some research, we figured that a water content of 68 percent would be about right. The theory was that the higher percentage of water—most bread recipes run around 60 percent—would improve the chew. We tried this formula and got mediocre results. It was good bread, but without the big-league chew we wanted.

We then visited Iggy's Bakery just outside of Boston. The bread they make has a big chew, big crust, and big flavor. The chief baker told us we needed to push the water level even higher. He pointed to the plastic vats filled with rising dough. This dough was a sticky mass that would just about pour. This was a breakthrough. Our idea of bread dough had been a nonstick satin ball, easy to handle and more solid than liquid. But this stuff puddled and pulled, shimmered and shook. At Iggy's, they use a mixture of three flours—high protein, whole wheat, and rye—for optimum flavor and texture.

Back in the test kitchen, we increased the water percentage to near-dangerous levels. The revised recipe now had 2½ cups of water to 6 cups of flour, which brought the percentage of water to flour up to a whopping 76 percent, a percentage so high it borders on heresy. However, this high percentage was slightly counteracted by the fact that almost 30 percent of the total flour used was whole wheat and rye. We chose these flours for flavor, but both also absorb more water than white flour does.

Professional bakers use giant mixers and special shaping machines that easily handle very moist dough. Using consumer equipment in our test kitchen, the bread stuck to our hands, the wooden counter, the bowl, the damp dishtowel, and even the heavily floured peel (the shovel-like tool used to get breads in and out of the oven). We tried to knead the dough by hand, but this was almost impossible without adding lots of flour. Still, at the end of the day, the bread was vastly improved. Although a bit sticky, the inside had cavernous air holes and some real chew.

We now turned our attention more closely to the flour. Up until now, we had been using a professional baker's bread flour, which has a very high level of protein (about 14 percent). We decided to try both a regular bread flour and an all-purpose flour to see if protein content would have a noticeable effect on the finished product. The all-purpose flour yielded an extremely wet, unworkable dough; the dough made with regular bread flour was wetter than the high-protein loaf but still workable. Of most interest, however, was the fact that these lower-protein flours produced a chewier, crustier loaf, although we felt that the loaf made with all-purpose flour was a little too tough. After additional testing, it became clear that we had to adjust the recipe to accommodate the lower-protein flours, which can't absorb as much water as higher-protein flour. When we reduced the amount of water used in our "regular" bread flour dough to 2⅓ cups, the results were even better. Since this flour is sold in supermarkets, we decided to use it in our recipe.

Kneading by hand was not our first choice (it can be done, however). We tried using a food processor with a metal blade, which worked fine except that our $250 machine sounded like a lawnmower in a dense patch of weeds; all that was missing was a curl of blue smoke and the smell of burning rubber. The machine simply could not handle 6 cups of quicksand. We tried the recipe in two half-batches, which worked pretty well. We found that leaving the metal blade in the processor between batches is best (you won't get absolutely all of the first batch out of the processor bowl); otherwise your hands will get sticky and dough may ooze out around the center core of the bowl during the second batch. We also learned that the machine works great for the first 25 to 30 seconds and then starts to slow down. Our processor can just about handle it (although it seemed compelled to walk across the counter like a dog off its leash). We recommend that you process for no more than 30 seconds, which is enough time to knead the dough, and we recommend this method only for home cooks with a good heavy-duty processor.

The best solution was a heavy-duty standing mixer with a dough hook. We simply threw in the ingredients, mixed them briefly with a large, stiff rubber spatula, and then turned the machine on at the lowest setting for 15 minutes. We then transferred the dough to an oiled bowl to rise for about 2 hours, or until tripled in volume. Allowing the dough to triple in volume both improves flavor and helps the dough to develop more "muscle," which helps the bread to maintain its shape when baked.

Even after the dough was kneaded, it was a problem to handle. For the first rise, simply use a rubber spatula to transfer the wet dough to an oiled bowl or plastic tub. After rising for about 2 hours, use the same spatula to transfer the dough onto a lightly floured surface. Now flour both your hands and the dough (the latter lightly). Press the dough very gently into a round and then fold into a ball. Note that you should handle the dough as little as possible at this point both because it is still a little sticky (you'll be tempted to add extra flour) and because excessive handling is bad for rustic bread—you want an irregular texture with lots of air holes. This point goes for all bread making: Strong kneading after the first rise will harm the delicate structure of the dough.

The best way to move the dough from here on in is to use a large dough scraper, two metal spatulas, or a thin floured cookie sheet. The dough is now transferred, smooth-side down, into a colander or a basket that has been lined with a piece of muslin or linen that has been well-floured. The flour should be rubbed into the fabric so the dough will not stick. A banneton is a cloth-lined woven basket designed just for this purpose. You can purchase one or try making your own. Muslin (which is cheaper than linen) comes in different grades from fine (the most expensive) to coarse (the least expensive). Use the cheaper variety to line your basket, and make sure that it is 100 percent cotton and unbleached. A real banneton has the linen or muslin sewn right into the basket, an optional refinement. The basket we used was 4 inches high, 7 inches wide across the bottom, and 12 inches wide across the top. A colander is also a perfectly good option. It works well because it allows for air flow (the dough is more likely to stick to the muslin when sitting in a bowl).

For its second rise the dough needs to be covered. We tried a damp dish towel, but this simply stuck to the dough. It was like unwrapping a piece of saltwater taffy on a hot day. Aluminum foil was the test winner because the dough is less likely to stick, and it allows the dough to breathe and thus keeps it from rising too much. If the dough rises too much at this point you will end up with a fluffy texture (plastic wrap, for example, will cause too much rising). The foil gives the dough shape and allows you to transfer it easily to the peel when the second rise is completed.

We also wanted to try varying the amount of salt as well as the impact of other ingredients. Most recipes with 6 cups of flour use 2 teaspoons of salt, and this amount is just right. Next, we decided to try a little sweetness to both boost flavor and promote browning of the crust (sugar promotes browning). When we added 2 tablespoons of honey, the flavor was a bit better, and the crust turned a rich nut-brown.

The last major issue was the crust. The key, according to most experts, is steam. Just to test this theory, we baked one loaf with no steam at all, and the crust was thin and unappealing. This bread does need steam, but there are many ways in which to provide it. Some bakers use a spritzer and mist the outside of the dough every few minutes. Others throw ice cubes on the floor of the oven. Still others pour hot water into a pan at the beginning of baking. Our tests showed that hot water is the best option. We tested spritzing the bread every few minutes, and the results were poor—a thin, pliable crust. As for the ice cube method, why throw ice into an oven where you want lots of heat? Our tests confirmed that ice cubes lower oven temperature much more than hot water does, and a head-to-head test also proved that you get a better crust with hot water versus ice cubes. (A note to those who count themselves among the ice cube flingers: You could blow out the heating element in an electric oven if you don't throw the ice into a container. This also goes for throwing tap water onto the floor of the oven).

When adding a pan of hot water to the oven, be sure to use a small preheated pan and place it on a separate, lower rack. The theory among bread pros is that you want steam immediately, in the first few minutes of baking. A cold pan will not do the trick—the hot water will just sit there. By using enough water—2 cups—you get both instant steam and enough residual water to maintain a nice steamy

environment throughout the cooking process. A preheated pan will, however, vaporize some of the hot water in seconds, which leads to the issue of safety. Use thick oven mitts and wear a long-sleeved shirt when pouring the hot water into the pan. In sum: Use hot water, preheat the pan, and don't ever open the oven door for the first 20 minutes of baking—you'll let out steam.

Most recipes state that the bread should be baked to an internal temperature of 190 degrees. This produces undercooked bread, at least as far as our recipe goes. This bread needs to reach 210 degrees (use an instant-read thermometer pushed halfway into the bottom of the loaf). An undercooked loaf will be sticky inside and will not have developed the very dark brown crust we're after. If you do not have an

EQUIPMENT: Standing Mixer

Years ago, free-standing mixers were a kitchen staple. Your grand-mother probably had a "Mixmaster," which is used as a generic term for a free-standing mixer, though it is actually a brand name for the popular units manufactured by Sunbeam. As new food processors and more powerful hand mixers came onto the market, the large standing mixtures fell out of favor. And if all you want to do is whip egg whites or cream, or if you make cakes only from a mix, you really don't need a heavy-duty standing mixer.

However, if you like to bake, a standing mixer permits maximum flexibility. Models with the most options, such as a whisk, paddle, and dough hook, will open up the most possibilities for baking everything from cakes and cookies to breads.

Perhaps the best use for standing mixers is mixing and kneading bread dough. Standing mixers knead perfectly in about one-third the time of hand kneading, and with far more control and satisfaction than bread machines. (Hand-held mixers lack the stability and power to do a good job.) Some large food processors can knead bread dough, but they can handle only relatively small batches of dough.

Unfortunately, not all brands of standing mixers are helpful kitchen allies. In the process of testing seven of the top-selling standing mixers, we found that some models are simply too difficult and frustrating to work with to make them worthwhile purchases. Outdated engineering and poorly designed beaters and bowls made it a challenge, rather than a pleasure, to prepare baked goods in several of the models we used.

Three of the seven models were outstanding, and making

cakes, cookies, and bread with them was enjoyable and gratifying. The Rival Select KM210B was exceptional, performing every task flawlessly (albeit noisily). The two KitchenAid models tested (K5SS and K45SS) were outstanding as well, although the Rival's dough hook is better designed and kneaded bread dough more quickly. These three models are also the most expensive of the group at $300 to $400. Are they worth it? Yes. Each is designed for endurance, so it makes sense to spend the money up front; you will derive years of use and pleasure from these models.

Both the Rival Select and the two KitchenAid mixers operate by "planetary action," in which a wide, flat beater (called the paddle) moves around a stationary bowl. This proved the most effective way of blending ingredients, since the paddle reaches the sides as well as the center of the bowl and gathers particles quickly. As a result, there is little need to stop the machine and scrape the sides of the bowl.

Another critical point of comparison is stability. The Rival and KitchenAid models are heavy and barely vibrate even when put to the test of mixing stiff cookie and bread dough. A standing mixer you have to hold with one or two hands is not a labor-saving device.

The Rival and the KitchenAids were the best at kneading bread dough, performing the task quickly, smoothly, and efficiently, with the motors showing not the slightest sign of strain and without spilling any flour. All three models had the weight, stability, and power needed to make smooth, elastic, tender dough.

instant-read thermometer, just bake the bread until the crust starts to turn brownish-black in spots.

We also tested starting oven temperature. We first started the bread off in a 500-degree oven and then immediately turned the heat down to 400 degrees on the theory that the higher temperature offsets the drop in temperature caused by opening the oven door and adding the dough (the dough absorbs a great deal of heat quickly). The resulting crust was thin and disappointing. We also tested actually baking the bread at 500 degrees for the first 15 minutes and then reducing the temperature to 400. The crust was scorched. It cooked so fast that the interior had no time to cook properly. The best baking temperature turned out to be a constant 450 degrees.

Some final refinements: We found that cornmeal is vastly better than flour for coating a peel, especially when working with a wet dough. The dough will slide off easily. Also, use a very quick backward jerk when removing the peel.

Rustic Country Bread

MAKES 1 LARGE ROUND LOAF

Whole wheat and rye flours contribute to this bread's full flavor, and extra oven time gives the bread its thick crust. Because of its high water content, the bread will be gummy if pulled from the oven too soon. To ensure the bread's doneness, make sure its internal temperature reads 210 degrees by inserting an instant-read thermometer into the bottom of the loaf. Also look at the crust—it should be very dark brown, almost black. Because the dough is so sticky, a heavy-duty standing mixer is best for kneading, but food processor and hand-kneading instructions follow this recipe. Keep in mind that rising times vary depending on kitchen

temperature (the times listed below are minimums). You can vary the texture by increasing or decreasing the flour. For bread with a finer crumb and less chewy texture, increase the flour by ¼ cup increments. For coarser, chewier bread, decrease the flour by the same increments. You will need baking tiles or a stone for this recipe (see below for more information).

SPONGE

½	teaspoon active dry yeast (not rapid rise)
1	cup water (room temperature)
1	cup bread flour
1	cup whole wheat flour

DOUGH

3½	cups bread flour
½	cup rye flour
1⅓	cups water (room temperature)
2	tablespoons honey
2	teaspoons salt
	Coarse cornmeal for sprinkling on peel

1. FOR THE SPONGE: Stir the yeast into the water in a medium bowl until dissolved. Mix in the flours with a rubber spatula to create a stiff, wet dough. Cover with plastic wrap; let sit at room temperature for at least 5 hours, preferably overnight. (Can be refrigerated up to 24 hours; return to room temperature before continuing with recipe.)

2. FOR THE DOUGH: Mix the flours, water, honey, and sponge in the bowl of an electric mixer with a rubber spatula. Knead the dough, using the dough hook attachment, on lowest speed until the dough is smooth, about 15 minutes, adding the salt during the final 3 minutes. Transfer the dough to a large, lightly oiled container or bowl. Cover with plastic wrap; let

---

EQUIPMENT: **Baking Tiles or Stone**

If you like bread or pizza with a thin, crisp crust, we recommend that you invest $15 to $20 to line the bottom rack of your oven with unglazed quarry tiles made of terra cotta. These porous tiles absorb heat better than a metal baking sheet and thus transfer more heat to whatever food is cooked on them. Bread and pizza crusts become especially crisp and well-browned on the bottom when cooked on tiles. The tiles come in 6-inch squares and can be cut at a tile store to fit your oven rack perfectly. Look for tiles ½ inch thick.

A large rectangular pizza or baking stone (circular stones are generally smaller and not recommended) is also a good option. The chief drawback is size. In most home ovens, you can fit two medium pizzas or two loaves of bread on a tile-lined rack. However, most pizza stones can accommodate only one loaf or pizza at a time. If using a stone, be careful when sliding the bread or pizza into the oven. You don't want part of the loaf or pizza to hang off the stone.

rise until tripled in size, at least 2 hours.

3. Turn the dough onto a lightly floured surface. Dust the dough top and your hands with flour. Lightly press the dough into a round by folding the edges of the dough into the middle from the top, right, bottom, and left, sequentially, then gathering it loosely together. Transfer the dough, smooth-side down, to a colander or basket lined with heavily floured muslin or linen. Cover loosely with a large sheet of aluminum foil; let the dough rise until almost doubled in size, at least 45 minutes.

4. Meanwhile, adjust the oven rack to low-center position and arrange baking tiles to form a surface that is at least 18 by 12 inches, or place a large baking stone on rack. On lowest oven rack, place a small baking pan or cast-iron skillet to hold water. Heat the oven to 450 degrees.

5. Liberally sprinkle the coarse cornmeal over the entire surface of a baking peel. Invert the dough onto the peel and remove the muslin. Use scissors or a ser-rated knife to cut three slashes on the dough top.

6. Slide the dough from the peel onto the tiles or stone; remove the peel with a quick backward jerk. Carefully add 2 cups hot water to the preheated pan. Bake until an instant-read thermometer inserted in bread bottom registers 210 degrees and crust is very dark brown, 35 to 40 minutes, turning the bread around after 25 minutes if not browning evenly. Turn oven off, open the door, and let bread remain in the oven 10 minutes longer. Remove, then let cool to

---

EQUIPMENT: Peels

When trying to transfer dough to a preheated baking stone or tiles, a peel is almost a must. The long handle on the peel makes it easy to slide the dough onto tiles or a stone in a hot oven. Although a rimless metal baking sheet can be used in this fashion, the lack of a handle means your hands are that much closer to the oven heat.

When shopping for a peel, there are two choices. Aluminum peels with heat-resistant wooden handles are probably the bet-ter bet because they can be washed and cleaned easily. Peels made entirely of wood can mildew when washed, so it's best just to wipe them clean. Either way, make sure your peel measures at least 16 inches across so that it can accommodate a large dough round and still have room left around the edges.

---

room temperature before slicing, about 2 hours. To crisp crust, bake the cooled bread in a 450 degree oven for 10 minutes.

➤ VARIATIONS
Rustic Country Bread Kneaded in a Food Processor

Make the sponge as directed in recipe for Rustic Country Bread. Mix half the sponge and half the flours and honey in a food processor fitted with a metal blade. Pulse until roughly blended, three to four 1-second pulses. With the machine running, add half the water (⅔ cup) slowly through the feed tube; process until the dough forms a ball. Let sit for 3 minutes, then add half the salt and process to form a smooth dough, about 30 seconds longer. Transfer the dough to a large lightly oiled container or bowl, leaving the metal blade in the processor (some dough will remain under the blade). Repeat the process with remaining half of the ingredients. Proceed with the recipe as directed.

Rustic Country Bread Kneaded by Hand

Make the sponge as directed in recipe for Rustic Country Bread. Place the sponge and all dough ingredients, except 2 cups of the bread flour, in a large bowl. Stir the mixture with a wooden spoon to develop the gluten, about 5 minutes. Work in the reserved flour and then turn out onto a floured board. Knead by hand for 5 minutes, incorporating no more than an additional ¼ cup of flour as you work. The dough will be very wet and sticky. Proceed with the recipe as directed.

BAGUETTE

WHY MAKE BAGUETTES AT HOME? THERE ARE many reasons. First, it's still damned hard to find a really good one at your local bakery. Second, if you like to bake, it is a uniquely challenging and therefore uniquely satisfying experience when you get it right. Developing a recipe for the French baguette had long been contemplated by the test kitchen as a promising but risk-laden adventure. Everyone agreed that a great baguette was made from just four ingredients— flour, water, yeast, and salt—and that it must express excellence in its chief characteristics—crust, crumb, flavor, and color. It would have a thin, shattering crust of the deepest golden brown; an open, airy texture; a light, moist crumb; and fully developed flavor.

The first problem we had to figure out was, as bakers say, "rising" the dough. Real bread doughs (as opposed to quick breads, which are chemically leavened with baking soda or powder) depend on commercial yeast or a natural leavener to help them rise. Modern French bread uses a direct-rise method—one in which flour and water are mixed with commercial yeast, given a rise, punched down, shaped, allowed to rise again, and baked. But we found that an older method, one that prevailed before commercial yeast became affordable, appealed to us more.

This method, known as a pre-ferment, uses a small amount of yeast to rise a portion of dough for several hours or overnight. It is then refreshed with additional flour, yeast, and water, given some salt as well, mixed, and set to rise again.

We tried a number of apparently authentic French baguette recipes, using both the direct-rise and the pre-ferment methods. Although none of these baguettes swept us off our feet, the flavor and texture of the breads made from pre-fermented dough were definitely superior. Among the two or three types of pre-ferments, we chose the sponge method, which basically calls for a thinnish mixture of flour and water and a small amount of yeast. These ingredients are easily stirred together, and the resulting relatively liquid structure encounters little physical resistance to fermentation, so it rises fully (or ripens) in hours, not days.

Having determined our basic approach, we put together a rough recipe and began making bread. Because we wanted enough dough for two baguettes (more than enough to accompany a pot of soup), we started with a total of 3 cups of flour, using about a cup of it in the pre-ferment. Initially cavalier about the volume of water we stirred into the sponge (generally about one cup, with between ⅓ and ½ cup additional water in the final dough), our mishaps convinced us that correct early ratios of flour to water are critical to the behavior of the bread in later stages and that a scale was essential to ensure consistent results. As it turns out, what looks like a cup of flour

may be more or less on a given day, depending on factors such as humidity and the way the measuring cup is filled. On the other hand, 6 ounces of flour is always 6 ounces.

Any given bread type, moreover, has a correct proportion of ingredients. In a system known as the "baker's percentage," these proportions are predicated on the weight of the flour, which is judged to be 100 percent, with the other ingredients lining up behind. A correct baguette dough, for instance, is said to have a hydration of 62 to 65 percent. This means that for every 1 pound of flour there will be between 0.62 and 0.65 pounds of water. We found it necessary to weigh both flour and water to make sure the sponge had the correct consistency when we were ready to mix the dough. We settled on 6 ounces of both flour and water for the pre-ferment stage; this gave us a soft sponge that was still firm enough to require more water when we mixed the dough.

As for the yeast, we knew that we wanted to use as little as possible for greatest flavor development (using a lot of yeast results in bread that tastes more of yeast than of the flavorful byproducts of fermentation) but we weren't sure just how little. While we also knew that the sponge should double in volume and be pitted with small bubbles when ripe, we didn't know exactly how long this might take—it could reach this stage in as little as three hours or take as long as eight. Finally, we determined that a pinch of dry instant yeast was equal to the task of rising the sponge and that ½ teaspoon was enough to refresh the body of the dough. But we remained in a quandary about fermentation time until we came across Daniel Wing's exemplary book *The Bread Builders* (Chelsea Green, 1999) and his explanation of "the drop." This term refers to a sponge rising and then falling under its own weight. Far from representing deflation or exhaustion of the yeast, which seems logical and which we had previously supposed, the drop revitalizes the sponge and is a sign that the sponge is ready for action. The drop is a critical visual clue. By using warm water and a pinch of yeast, our sponge rose and dropped in about six hours in a 75-degree room.

The second phase of bread making is kneading,

or mixing. Mixing unites wet and dry ingredients and transforms them from a shaggy ball of dough to a satiny orb. Our preferred partner was the standing mixer outfitted with a dough hook. The thought of a food processor blade whizzing through dough seemed antithetic to the slow, measured pace of kneading. But we weren't keen on performing the entire operation by hand, either. Seasoned bakers will be familiar with the notion of gluten development, wherein flour and water join to form an interlocking protein structure that traps the gas that makes the dough rise. Kneading is the means to this end, and most recipes instruct the baker to knead the dough until it is smooth and elastic; others suggest a period of time by which mixing should be complete.

One thing we had not realized was how easily bread dough can overheat in a mixer. For the dough hook to engage just a small amount of dough, we had to mix at high speed. The sticky blob we ended up with once or twice was, we learned, a direct result of overheating—the dough was irreparably damaged and the character of the bread destroyed. By kneading with a dough hook instead of our hands, we had unwittingly distanced ourselves from some important tactile permutations that were taking place: the dough's temperature, its increasing elasticity and stretchiness, and its surface tackiness. At this point, we switched to hand kneading and began to experience the dough's transformation in a measured and controlled way. The process was pleasurable as well.

We never supposed we would be sprinkling a dough with water instead of flour. We had often made wet doughs—thinking the resulting crumb would be more open and moist—only to throw flour on them near the end. But this is a poor approach, as Daniel Wing cautions. Rather than working its way into the dough, the flour slides around on the surface. Real friction must be generated for proper gluten development. A relatively dry dough, vigorously hand-kneaded, on the other hand, welcomes incremental additions of water to bring it to the correct hydration. We discovered that a method of kneading used in Germany for strudel dough, known as crashing (in which the dough is picked up and flung repeatedly against the counter), worked beautifully to incorporate water. The doughs we produced using this technique had a texture far more satiny than did the wet doughs to which we added flour, and the bread had a far nicer crumb as well.

But perhaps the single most important contribution to our understanding of mixing came from Peter Reinhart's book *Crust and Crumb* (Ten Speed, 1998), in which he describes "windowpaning." In windowpaning, when you think the dough is fully kneaded, you stretch a small amount between your fingers. If it can be stretched until it is very thin, almost translucent, the dough has been adequately kneaded and can be set to rise. Should it tear while being stretched, more kneading is required. With the baker's percentage and the windowpane technique now firmly part of the plan, our results began to show significant improvement.

The next steps in bread making, which precede the final rise, are punching down and shaping. A fully risen dough should feel puffy and will not long bear the imprint of a finger. But punching down, experts agree, is a misleading term, inviting more force than is desirable. A gentle fist to the center of the dough does the trick. It is now ready to be scaled or divided and given a rough shape. We knew from experience that a covered rest of about 20 minutes is necessary to relax the dough again, giving it some workability. Attempts to shape long thin baguettes from freshly punched-down dough are frustrating because the dough feels tough and uncooperative and snaps back at you.

Having gotten this far, we had no idea that our most exciting discovery was right around the corner—in the refrigerator. Traditional wisdom holds that the second rise should take place in a warm, draft-free spot to encourage rapid rising and is accomplished in about half the time required for the first rise. So we were intrigued when we read about cool fermentation in Peter Reinhart's book. Cool fermentation retards, or slows down, the second rise—the formed loaves go into the refrigerator overnight and are baked the following day. With this method, the dough is thought to become better hydrated, to develop more flavor, and to achieve greater volume. Refrigeration also maintains humidity around the loaves, which keeps a skin from forming on the surface and inhibiting the rise. But surely the most dramatic contribution cold fermentation makes is to the crust.

The first baguettes we baked using overnight fermentation leapt beyond anything we had yet experienced. The surface of the crust was pitted with tiny bubbles and gave a sharp thrilling crackle when torn. Shards of crust sprayed the counter to reveal a creamy interior. But it was the flavor of the crust that rocketed this bread to stardom: It was incomparable. Though the French, as Reinhart wrote, believe a baguette's surface should be smooth and unblistered, we were untroubled by this breach of tradition. To us, this bread was the ultimate.

The final step in bread making is, of course, baking. Home baking is plagued by the problems that attend home ovens, which can neither deliver nor maintain heat in the same way that stone or brick does. We tried a number of baguette pans, both perforated and black (thought to improve browning), but by far the best means of conducting heat to the bread proved to be a large pizza stone (see page 320) that is preheated for a full 45 minutes in a hot oven. A stone is the closest home ovens can get to hearth ovens.

Transferring the baguettes to the stone was another matter. Precise placement is crucial. Once dough meets stone, there is no turning back—or over, as it were. We tried different approaches with calamitous results. Ultimately, the best approach proved to be using parchment paper and an inverted sheet pan to let the baguettes rise, then sliding the baguettes—paper and all—onto the stone.

Realizing that the goal of baking baguettes is to get a deep, golden brown crust in the short period of time it takes to finish the bread, we began experimenting with oven temperatures. Temperatures below 500 degrees produced inadequate browning of the crust or overbaked the interior. Even an initial temperature of 500 degrees accompanied by temperature reduction after a few minutes did not produce the color we wanted. Some recipes suggest leaving the bread in the oven for a few minutes after baking with the oven turned off to help set the crust, but our 12-ounce baguettes needed full, steady heat all along. In the end, 15 minutes at 500 degrees produced the crust and color we desired as well as a moist interior. The final temperature of the bread was around 208 degrees.

Ironically, all this research and testing (which produced well over 100 baguettes), distilled down to the four ingredients we began with—and our hands. It speaks to the deceptive simplicity of yeasted doughs: basic ingredients, the magic of yeast, a firm and gentle touch, and time can produce one of the greatest aromas and most satisfying foods in the world.

Bakery-Style French Baguettes

MAKES TWO 15 BY 3-INCH BAGUETTES

For this recipe you will need an instant-read thermometer, a scale, a lame (a tool for slashing bread dough) or single-edge razor blade, a rectangular pizza stone, and a spray bottle filled with water. We prefer SAF instant or Perfect Rise yeast, but other instant dry yeasts work as well. For the sponge, the ideal ambient temperature is 75 degrees; if it is cooler, fermentation will take longer. Do not add flour while kneading or shaping the dough.

This recipe should be started in the morning and will yield baguettes for breakfast the next day. The recipe variation uses altered rising times so that the baguettes are started in the afternoon and baked in time for dinner the next day. In either case, begin the recipe the day before you intend to serve the bread; the baguettes will emerge from the oven 20 to 24 hours after you start the sponge. The baguettes are best served within 2 hours after baking.

SPONGE

- 1/8 teaspoon instant dry yeast or 1/8 teaspoon regular active dry yeast
- 6 ounces (by weight) bottled or spring water, 110 to 115 degrees
- 6 ounces unbleached all-purpose flour, preferably King Arthur

DOUGH

- 1/2 teaspoon instant dry yeast or 3/4 teaspoon regular active dry yeast
- 4 ounces (by weight) bottled or spring water, 75 degrees, plus additional 2 teaspoons water if necessary
- 10 ounces unbleached all-purpose flour, preferably King Arthur
- 1 teaspoon salt

GLAZE

- 1 large egg white, beaten with 1 tablespoon water

1. **FOR THE SPONGE:** Combine the yeast, water, and flour in a medium bowl and stir together with a wooden spoon to form a thick batter. Scrape down the bowl with a rubber spatula. Cover with plastic wrap and punch a couple of holes in plastic wrap with a paring knife; let sponge stand at room temperature. After 4 to 5 hours, the sponge should be almost doubled in size and pitted with tiny bubbles. Let stand at room temperature until surface shows slight depression in center, indicating the drop, 2 to 3 hours longer. The sponge now is ready to use.

2. **FOR THE DOUGH:** To sponge, add the yeast and all but 2 tablespoons water. Stir briskly with a wooden spoon until the water is incorporated, about 30 seconds. Stir in the flour and continue mixing with a wooden spoon until a scrappy ball forms. Turn the dough onto a countertop and knead by hand, adding drops of water if necessary, until the dry bits are absorbed into dough, about 2 minutes. Dough will feel dry and tough. Stretch dough into rough 8 by 6-inch rectangle, make indentations in dough with fingertips, sprinkle with 1 tablespoon remaining water (see illustration 1, below), fold edges of dough up toward center to encase water, and pinch edges to seal. Knead dough lightly, about 30 seconds (dough will feel slippery as some water escapes but will become increasingly pliant as the water is absorbed). Begin crashing (vigorously flinging dough against countertop) and kneading dough alternately until soft and supple and surface is almost powdery smooth, about 7 minutes. Stretch dough again into rough 8 by 6-inch rectangle and make indentations with fingertips; sprinkle dough with salt and remaining tablespoon water. Repeat folding and sealing edges and crashing and kneading until dough is once again soft and supple and surface is almost powdery smooth, about 7 minutes. If dough still feels tough and nonpliant, knead in 2 additional teaspoons water.

3. Test the dough to determine if adequately kneaded by performing windowpane test. (Take a small piece of dough and stretch into a nearly translucent membrane.) If the dough tears before stretching thin, knead 5 minutes longer and test again. Gather the dough into a ball, place in a large bowl, and cover with plastic wrap. Let stand 30 minutes, then remove the dough from the bowl and knead gently to deflate, about 10 seconds; gather into a ball, return to the bowl, and replace plastic wrap. Let rise until doubled in bulk, about 1½ hours.

KEY STEPS TO MAKING A BAGUETTE

1. Add the remaining water.

2. Gently punch down the dough to release the gas.

3. Round the dough with half-circular motions.

4. Use the side of your hand to form an indentation.

5. Roll the sealed upper edge over your thumb.

6. Repeat this process several times to form a seam.

7. Stretch and roll the dough into a baguette shape.

8. Slash it diagonally.

4. Decompress the dough by gently pushing a fist in the center of the dough toward the bottom of the bowl (see illustration 2 on page 325); turn dough onto a work surface. With a dough scraper, divide dough into two 12-ounce pieces. Working one at a time, with second piece covered with plastic wrap on work surface, cup hands stiffly around dough and drag in short half-circular motions toward edge of counter (see illustration 3 on page 325) until dough forms rough torpedo shape with taut rounded surface, about 6½ inches long. (As you drag the dough, its tackiness will pull on the work surface, causing the top to scroll down and to the back to create a smooth, taut surface.) Repeat with second piece of dough. Drape plastic wrap over dough on work surface; let rest to relax dough, 15 to 20 minutes.

5. Meanwhile, line an inverted rimmed baking sheet with parchment paper. Working one at a time, with second piece covered with plastic wrap, roll torpedo seam-side up and press indentation along length of dough with side of outstretched hand (see illustration 4 on page 325). Working along length of dough, press thumb of one hand against dough while folding and rolling upper edge of dough down with other hand to enclose thumb (see illustration 5 on page 325). Repeat folding and rolling 4 or 5 times until upper edge meets lower edge and creates seam (see illustration 6 on page 325); press seam to seal. Dough will have formed cylinder about 12 inches long. Roll dough cylinder seam-side down; gently and evenly roll and stretch dough until it measures 15 inches long by 2½ inches wide (see illustration 7

on page 325). Place seam-side down on prepared baking sheet. Repeat with second dough piece. Space shaped dough pieces about 6 inches apart on baking sheet. Drape clean dry kitchen towel over dough and slide baking sheet into large clean garbage bag; seal to close. Refrigerate until dough has risen moderately, at least 12 but no longer than 16 hours.

6. TO BAKE: Remove one oven rack from oven; adjust second oven rack to lowest position. Place baking tiles or stone on rack in oven and heavy rimmed baking sheet on oven floor. Heat oven to 500 degrees. Remove baking sheet with baguettes from refrigerator and let baguettes stand covered at room temperature 45 minutes; remove plastic bag and towel to let surface of dough dry, then let stand 15 minutes longer. The dough should have risen to almost double in bulk and feel springy to the touch. Meanwhile, bring 1 cup water to simmer in small saucepan on stovetop.

7. With a lame or single-edge razor blade, make five ¼-inch deep diagonal slashes on each baguette (see illustration 8 on page 325). Brush baguette with egg glaze and mist with water. Working quickly, slide parchment sheet with baguettes off baking sheet and onto hot stone. Pour simmering water onto baking sheet on oven floor and quickly close oven door. Bake, rotating loaves front to back and side to side after 10 minutes, until deep golden brown and instant-read thermometer inserted into center of bread through bottom crust registers 205 to 210 degrees, about 5 minutes longer. Transfer to wire rack; cool 30 minutes.

SCIENCE: Steam Heat

Knowing steam to be essential to a great crust, we tried various approaches to produce a lot of steam when making our baguettes. We set a pan of water in the oven while it was preheating, we splashed hot water on a preheated sheet pan on the oven floor, and we tossed ice cubes onto a hot sheet pan on the oven floor. Against these tests we tried no steam at all. The baguettes baked at high temperatures with no steam had thin crusts, poor flavor, and an inferior crumb. The baguettes baked with steam throughout had thick, pale crusts and poor flavor. The baguettes baked using ice cubes to produce steam were subjected to inconstant and uneven steam, and the crust was second-rate. The best crust results by far were obtained by pouring about a cup of hot water into a sheet pan positioned on the oven floor—a tremendous amount of steam is produced for a very short period of time, and then vanishes. We also add water to the oven when making our Rustic Country Bread (see page 320). The principle being applied here—a moist environment improves the crustiness of bread crust—is the same; the technique and amount of water used are a bit different because the country-style bread spends much more time in the oven.

➤ VARIATION

Dinner Baguettes

The altered rising times in this variation will put the baguettes on the table at dinnertime.

Follow recipe for Bakery-Style French Baguettes, starting the sponge at about noon and using 75-degree water; let sponge rise 5 to 6 hours, then refrigerate overnight, 12 to 14 hours. In step 2, make dough using 110-degree water. Continue with recipe to knead, rise, and shape. Place shaped and covered dough in refrigerator until slightly risen, 7 to 10 hours. Continue with recipe from step 6.

CORNBREAD AND CORN MUFFINS

WHILE ALL CORNBREADS ARE QUICK TO make and bake, there are two very distinct types: Northern and Southern. The southern version uses 100 percent white cornmeal, making a cornbread that is crumbly, dry, and flat. This kind of cornbread is always baked in a cast-iron skillet. The northern version is sweeter, lighter, higher, and golden, which is achieved by adding sugar and combining white flour and yellow cornmeal. Both types of cornbread sport a brown crust, although southern cornbread crusts are also crisp and crunchy.

After an initial round of testing, we realized that we preferred something in between when serving cornbread with a bowl of chili or black bean soup. We decided to incorporate elements of both traditions into a single recipe. We liked the pure corn flavor of southern cornbread without the distraction of the sugar, but we wanted a crumb that was more moist and tender. Northern cornbread was more tender, but it was also fluffy, and the corn flavor was muted. Since it had more of the elements we liked, we decided to start out with a southern-style recipe that baked in a skillet.

The type of cornmeal was a natural place to begin our testing. We tested 11 different cornmeals—white and yellow—in a simple southern cornbread recipe. Before these tests, we would have bet that color was a regional idiosyncrasy that had little to do with flavor. But tasting proved otherwise. Cornbreads made with yellow cornmeal consistently had a more potent corn flavor than those made with white meal.

The grind of the cornmeal also affected flavor. Large commercial mills use huge steel rollers to grind dent corn (a hard, dry corn) into cornmeal. This is how Quaker, the leading supermarket brand, is produced. But some smaller mills scattered across the United States grind with millstones; this product is called stone-ground cornmeal. (If water is used as an energy source, the cornmeal may be labeled "water-ground.") Stone-ground cornmeal is usually a bit coarser than cornmeal processed through steel rollers.

These smaller millers may also choose not to degerm, or remove all of the germ, cleanly from the kernel, as commercial mills do. This makes their product closer to a whole-grain cornmeal. If the color is uniform, the germ has been removed. A stone-ground cornmeal with some germ will have flecks that are both lighter and darker than the predominant color, whether that's yellow or white. In our tests, we found the texture of cornbreads made with stone-ground meals to be more interesting, since the cornmeals were not of a uniform grind. More important, we found that cornbreads made with stone-ground cornmeal tasted much better than those made with the standard Quaker cornmeal.

Because of their higher moisture and oil content, stone-ground cornmeals spoil much faster than commercial, degerminated cornmeals; if not stored properly, they can turn rancid within weeks. If you buy some, wrap it tightly in plastic, or put it into a moisture-proof container, then refrigerate or freeze it. Degerminated cornmeals keep for a year if stored in a dry, cool place.

We were set on the cornmeal—yellow, preferably stone-ground. The next issue was flour. For cornbread with a rich corn flavor, we found that flour is best omitted. (For corn muffins, some flour is necessary; see page 329.)

Although we didn't want cornbread to taste like dessert, we wondered whether a little sugar might enhance the corn flavor. So we made three batches— one with no sugar, one with 2 teaspoons, and one with a heaping tablespoon. The higher-sugar bread was too sweet for our tastes, but 2 teaspoons of sugar seemed to enhance the natural sweetness of the corn without calling attention to itself.

So far all of our testing had been done with a composite recipe representative of most southern cornbread recipes. We had, however, run across a recipe that didn't quite fit the mold, and now seemed like the right time to give it a try.

In this simple version, boiling water is stirred into the cornmeal, modest amounts of milk, egg, butter, salt, and baking powder are stirred into the resulting cornmeal mush, and then the whole thing is baked. So simple, so lean, so humble, so backwater, this recipe would have been easy to pass over. Just one bite completely changed the direction of our pursuit. Unlike anything we had tasted so far, the crumb of this cornbread was incredibly moist and fine and bursting with corn flavor, all with no flour and very little fat.

We were pleased, but since the foundation of this bread was cornmeal mush, the crumb was actually more mushy than moist. In addition, the baking powder, the only dry ingredient left, got stirred into the wet batter at the end. This just didn't feel right.

After a few unsuccessful attempts to make this cornbread less mushy, we started thinking that this great idea was a bust. In a last attempt to salvage it, we decided to make mush out of only half the cornmeal and to mix the remaining cornmeal with the leavener. To our relief, the bread made this way was much improved. Decreasing the mush even further—from a half to a third of the cornmeal—gave us exactly what we were looking for. We made the new, improved cornbread with buttermilk and mixed a bit of baking soda with the baking powder, and it tasted even better. Finally, our recipe was starting to feel right.

With this new recipe in hand, we performed a few more tests. We tried vegetable oil, peanut oil, shortening, butter, and bacon drippings. Butter and bacon drippings were pleasant flavor additions and improved the texture of the cornbread by making it less crumbly.

Before conducting these cornbread tests, we didn't think it was possible to bake cornbread in too hot an oven, but after tasting breads baked on the bottom rack of a 475-degree oven, we found that a dark brown crust makes bitter bread. We moved the rack up a notch, reduced the oven temperature to 450 degrees, and were thus able to cook many loaves of cornbread to golden brown perfection.

One final question: Do you need to heat up the skillet before adding the batter? If you're not a southerner, the answer is no. Although the bread will not be as crisp in an unheated pan, it will ultimately brown up with a longer baking time. If you are a southerner, of course, the answer is yes. More than the color of the meal or the presence of sugar or flour, what makes cornbread southern is the batter hitting the hot fat in a cast-iron skillet.

Cornbread

SERVES 8

This cornbread is thin and crusty, making it the perfect accompaniment to soups, chili, or stews. Make sure that the water is at a rapid boil when it is added to the cornmeal. If you prefer a sweeter, more northern-style recipe, see the note to the corn muffin recipe on page 329. This crusty southern-style cornbread must be baked in a cast-iron skillet; cakier northern-style cornbread can be made in a cast-iron skillet or square baking pan.

4	teaspoons bacon drippings or 1 teaspoon vegetable oil plus 1 tablespoon unsalted butter, melted
1	cup yellow cornmeal, preferably stone-ground
2	teaspoons sugar
½	teaspoon salt
1	teaspoon baking powder
¼	teaspoon baking soda
½	cup rapidly boiling water
¾	cup buttermilk
1	large egg, beaten lightly

1. Adjust the oven rack to the lower-middle position and heat the oven to 450 degrees. Set an 8-inch cast-iron skillet with bacon drippings (or vegetable oil) in the heating oven.

2. Measure ⅓ cup cornmeal into a medium bowl. Whisk the remaining cornmeal, sugar, salt, baking powder, and baking soda together in small bowl; set aside.

3. Pour ¼ cup boiling water all at once into the ⅓ cup cornmeal; whisk quickly to combine.

Continue adding water, a tablespoon at a time, until the mixture forms a thick mush (see illustration below). Whisk in the buttermilk gradually, breaking up any lumps until smooth, then whisk in the egg. When the oven is preheated and the skillet very hot, stir the dry ingredients into the mush mixture until just moistened. Carefully remove the skillet from the oven. If using bacon drippings, pour it from the pan into the batter and stir to incorporate. If the pan has been greased with vegetable oil, stir the melted butter into the batter.

4. Quickly pour the batter into the heated skillet. Bake until golden brown, about 20 minutes. Remove from the oven and instantly turn the cornbread onto a wire rack; cool for 5 minutes. Serve warm or at room temperature.

➤ VARIATIONS

Cornbread with Chiles
Follow recipe for Cornbread, folding in 1 or 2 medium jalapeño chiles, seeded and minced, after the bacon drippings or melted butter has been incorporated.

Cornbread with Cheddar Cheese
Follow recipe for Cornbread, folding in 2 ounces (½ cup) shredded cheddar cheese after the bacon drippings or melted butter has been incorporated.

MAKING BATTER FOR CORNBREAD

We found that mixing part of the cornmeal with boiling water to make cornmeal mush is the key to great cornbread batter. However, the cornmeal mush must have just the right texture. The batter should neither clump nor be too thin. Ideally, the mush will be soft, like polenta. The consistency will be thick enough to give the batter body but pliable enough to accommodate wet ingredients easily.

Cornbread with Corn Kernels
Follow recipe for Cornbread, folding in ¾ cup fresh or thawed frozen corn kernels after the bacon drippings or melted butter has been incorporated.

Corn Muffins
MAKES 12

Sometimes you would rather serve a basket of corn muffins than hunks of cornbread with bowls of chili. Adding more sugar, another egg, and some cake flour turns cornbread into muffins. The flour and egg help create a cakier, less crumbly texture, while the sugar makes the muffins seem less savory. This batter is fairly thin; if you like, transfer the batter to a 1-quart measuring cup and pour it into the greased muffin tin. If you like a cakier, sweet cornbread, like those made in the North, bake this batter in a greased 8-inch cast-iron skillet or square pan for 25 minutes.

	Vegetable cooking spray or unsalted butter for greasing muffin tin
1¾	cups yellow cornmeal, preferably stone-ground
½	cup cake flour
½	cup sugar
¾	teaspoon salt
2	teaspoons baking powder
½	teaspoon baking soda
¾	cup rapidly boiling water
1¼	cups buttermilk
2	large eggs, beaten lightly
2	tablespoons unsalted butter, melted

1. Adjust the oven rack to the lower-middle position and heat the oven to 425 degrees. Spray a 12-hole muffin tin with vegetable cooking spray or coat lightly with butter.

2. Measure ½ cup cornmeal into a medium bowl. Whisk the remaining cornmeal, flour, sugar, salt, baking powder, and baking soda together in a small bowl; set aside.

3. Pour ⅓ cup boiling water all at once into the ½ cup cornmeal; whisk quickly to combine. Continue adding water, a tablespoon at a time, until the mixture forms a thick mush (see illustration, left). Whisk in the buttermilk gradually, breaking up any lumps until smooth, then whisk in the eggs. Stir the dry ingredients into the mush mixture until just

moistened. Stir in the melted butter just until incorporated. Ladle the batter into greased muffin tin, filling the holes almost to the rim.

4. Bake until the muffins are golden brown, 18 to 20 minutes. Set the tin on a wire rack to cool slightly, about 5 minutes. Remove the muffins from the tin and serve warm or at room temperature.

BUTTERMILK BISCUITS

BISCUITS ARE AMONG THE SIMPLEST OF ALL breads. They are made from a mixture of flour, leavener (baking powder or soda), salt, fat (usually butter or vegetable shortening), and liquid (milk, buttermilk, sour milk, yogurt, or cream). To make them, one cuts fat into the dry ingredients, as when making pie dough; the liquid is then stirred in until a dough forms. Biscuits are usually rolled out and cut, although they can also be shaped by hand or dropped onto a baking sheet by the spoonful.

We began our tests with the flour. We found that the kind of flour you choose has a great effect on the biscuit you end up with. The main factor here is the proportion of protein in the flour. Low-protein, or "soft," flour (such as cake flour or White Lily, a favored brand in the South) encourages a tender, cakelike texture as well as a more moist crumb. Higher-protein, or "strong," flour (such as all-purpose flour) promotes a crispier crust and a drier, denser crumb.

Tasters liked the crispier crust of the biscuits made with all-purpose flour and the tender, airy crumb of the biscuits made with cake flour. We

INGREDIENTS: Baking Soda and Baking Powder

Biscuits and cornbread, as well as muffins, cookies, cakes, pancakes, and waffles, get their rise from chemical leaveners—baking soda and baking powder—rather than yeast. Chemical leavenings react with acids to produce carbon dioxide, the gas that causes these baked goods to rise.

To do its work, baking soda relies on an acid in the recipe, such as buttermilk or molasses. It's important to use the right amount of baking soda. Use more baking soda than can be neutralized by the acidic ingredient, and you'll end up with a metallic-tasting, coarse-crumbed quick bread or cake. One cup of buttermilk will neutralize $1/2$ teaspoon of baking soda.

Baking powder is nothing more than baking soda (about one-quarter to one-third of the total makeup) mixed with a dry acid and double-dried cornstarch. The cornstarch absorbs moisture and keeps the two elements apart during storage, preventing premature production of the gas. When baking powder becomes wet, the acid comes into contact with the baking soda, producing carbon dioxide. Most commercial baking powders are "double-acting." In other words, they contain two kinds of acid—one that produces a carbon dioxide reaction at room temperature, the other responding only to heat.

In contrast, baking soda is only single-acting, as is homemade baking powder, which contains only one acid, cream of tartar. Baking soda reacts immediately on contact with an acid.

In a cake, for example, it is important to have an early release of carbon dioxide during the batter preparation so that small bubbles will be created to form the foundation of the cell structure. These cells expand during baking because of additional carbon dioxide production caused by the action of the second leavening acid, and the dough firms up into the final cake structure. Therefore, a double-acting agent is essential. In a cookie batter, however, especially one that has a good deal of structure from butter and eggs, the double-acting issue is less critical.

Since baking powder is nothing more than baking soda and acid, it's easy to convert a recipe from baking powder and milk to baking soda and buttermilk. Just divide the amount of baking powder by four to determine how much baking soda you should use and substitute buttermilk. For example, in a recipe calling for 2 teaspoons of baking powder and 1 cup of milk, you could substitute $1/2$ teaspoon of baking soda and 1 cup of buttermilk. There would be taste and textural differences, it is true, but the leavening action would be about the same.

One final note about baking soda: You may not want it to neutralize all the buttermilk's acidity. If you want to taste the buttermilk, you can substitute baking powder for some or all of the baking soda. Since baking powder has its own built-in acid to react with, the acidity of the buttermilk is allowed to come through. For example, in a recipe that calls for $1/2$ teaspoon of baking soda and 1 cup of buttermilk, the baking soda could be replaced with two teaspoons of baking powder. The leavening result would be the same, but the baked good would have a tangier flavor.

found that a combination of half cake flour and half all-purpose flour delivered the best results—a crisp crust and a tender crumb. If you don't have cake flour, all-purpose flour makes a fine biscuit as long as you add more liquid to the batter.

Fat makes biscuits tender, moist, smooth, and tasty. Butter, of course, delivers the best flavor, while vegetable shortening makes a slightly flakier biscuit with better holding powers. However, we don't think this gain in shelf life is worth the loss in flavor. Stick with unsalted butter when making biscuits.

We discovered that a proportion of ½ cup fat to 2 cups flour provides the best balance of tenderness and richness with structure. If you use less fat, your biscuits will rise well, but they will be tough and dry. If you use more, your biscuits will have a lovely texture, but they may end up a bit squat.

After mixing flour and leavening, you must "rub" the fat into the dry ingredients, making a dry, coarse mixture akin to large bread crumbs or rolled oats, with some slightly bigger lumps mixed in. This rubbing may seem unimportant, but in fact it is crucial to the proper rising of the biscuits. Gas released by the leavening during baking must have a space in which to collect; if the texture of the dough is homogeneous, the gas will simply dissipate. Melting fat particles create convenient spaces in which the gas can collect, form a bubble, and produce a rise. Proper rubbing breaks the fat into tiny bits and disperses it throughout the dough. As the fat melts during baking, its place

is taken up by gas and steam, which expand and push the dough up. The wider the dispersal of the fat, the more even the rising of the dough.

If, however, the fat softens and binds with the dry ingredients during rubbing, it forms a pasty goo, the spaces collapse, and the biscuits become leaden. Light, airy biscuits require cold, firm fat, which means rubbing must be deft and quick. Traditionally, biscuit makers pinch the cut-up fat into the dry ingredients, using only their fingertips—never the whole hand, which is too warm—and they pinch hard and fast, practically flinging the little bits of flour and fat into the bowl after each pinch. Less experienced cooks sometimes cut in the fat by scraping two knives in opposite directions or by using a bow-shaped pastry blender. We found, however, that there is no reason not to use the food processor for this task: pulsing the dry ingredients and the fat is fast and almost foolproof.

After the fat is cut in, liquid is added and the dough is stirred, just until the ingredients are bound, using a light hand so the gluten in the flour will not become activated. (Gluten development will cause the biscuits to be tough.) We found that buttermilk (or plain yogurt) gives biscuits the best flavor. It also creates a lighter, airier texture than does regular milk. That's because the acid in the buttermilk reacts with the leaveners to increase the rise.

Our biscuits are best formed by gently patting gobs of dough between your hands. If you prefer to roll and cut the biscuits (the traditional manner for shaping biscuit dough), the work surface, the dough, and the cutter must be generously floured. In tests, we found that the extra flour and handling make our biscuits heavier and somewhat dense.

Because they need quick heat, biscuits are best baked in the middle of the oven. Placed too close to the bottom, they burn on the underside and remain pale on top; set too near the oven roof, they do not rise well because the outside hardens into a shell before the inside has had a chance to rise properly. As soon as they are light brown, they are done. Be careful, as overcooking will dry them out. Biscuits are always at their best when served as soon as they come out of the oven. The dough, however, may be made some hours in advance and baked when needed; the biscuits will still rise well.

SHAPING BUTTERMILK BISCUIT DOUGH

Our buttermilk biscuit dough is too soft to roll and cut. Using a sharp knife or dough cutter, divide dough in quarters and then cut each quarter into thirds. With lightly cupped hands, gently shape each piece into a ball.

Buttermilk Biscuits

MAKES 12

Mixing the butter and dry ingredients quickly so the butter remains cold and firm is crucial to producing light, tender biscuits. The easiest and most reliable approach is to use a food processor fitted with a steel blade. Expect a soft and slightly sticky dough. The wet dough creates steam when the biscuits bake and promotes a light, airy texture. If the dough is too wet for you to shape the biscuits by hand, lightly flour your hands and then shape the biscuits.

I	cup all-purpose flour
I	cup plain cake flour
2	teaspoons baking powder
¹/₂	teaspoon baking soda
I	teaspoon sugar
¹/₂	teaspoon salt
8	tablespoons chilled unsalted butter, cut into ¹/₄-inch cubes (see illustrations below)
³/₄	cup cold buttermilk, or ³/₄ cup plus 2 tablespoons plain yogurt

1. Adjust the oven rack to the middle position and heat the oven to 450 degrees.

2. Place the flours, baking powder, baking soda, sugar, and salt in a large bowl or the workbowl of a food processor fitted with the steel blade. Whisk together or pulse six times.

3. If making by hand, use two knives, a pastry blender, or your fingertips to quickly cut in the butter until the mixture resembles coarse meal with a few slightly larger butter lumps. If using a food processor, remove the cover and distribute the butter evenly over the dry ingredients. Cover and pulse 12 times, each pulse lasting 1 second.

4. If making by hand, stir in the buttermilk with a rubber spatula or a fork until the mixture forms a soft, slightly sticky ball. If using a food processor, remove the cover and pour the buttermilk evenly over the dough. Pulse until the dough gathers into moist clumps, about eight 1-second pulses.

5. Transfer the dough to a lightly floured surface and quickly form into a rough ball. Be careful not to overmix. Using a sharp knife or dough cutter, divide the dough in quarters and then cut each quarter into thirds. Quickly and gently shape each piece into a rough ball (see illustration on page 331), and place on an ungreased baking sheet. (Baking sheet can be wrapped in plastic and refrigerated for up to 2 hours.)

6. Bake until the biscuit tops are light brown, 10 to 12 minutes. Serve immediately.

➤ VARIATION

Buttermilk Biscuits with All-Purpose Flour

We find that a blend of cake flour and all-purpose flour creates a light, airy, and tender biscuit. If you don't have cake flour on hand, you can use all-purpose flour alone, although the crumb will be coarser and the crust crispier because of the higher protein content in the flour.

Follow recipe for Buttermilk Biscuits, replacing the cake flour with an equal amount of all-purpose flour (for a total of 2 cups). Increase the buttermilk or yogurt by 2 tablespoons.

CUTTING BUTTER INTO SMALL CUBES

1. Cut the butter lengthwise into three even strips.

2. Separate the strips and then cut each lengthwise into thirds.

3. Stack the strips on top of each other, then cut them crosswise into ¹/₄-inch dice.

CREAM BISCUITS

OUR BUTTERMILK BISCUITS ARE EASY TO prepare; you can have biscuits on the table in 20 minutes. But many cooks are intimidated by this kind of biscuit because they are not comfortable with the traditional process of cutting butter into flour.

We wondered if we could come up with a recipe for homemade biscuits that could be made quickly and easily and that would not require cutting fat into flour. In short, was it possible to take the guesswork out of making biscuits to create a foolproof recipe?

We began with a basic recipe calling for 2 cups flour, 2 teaspoons baking powder, 1 tablespoon sugar, and ½ teaspoon salt. Now we had to figure out what to add to this mixture instead of butter or vegetable shortening to make a dough. We decided to try plain yogurt, sour cream, milk, milk combined with melted butter, and whipped heavy cream, an idea we borrowed from a scone recipe.

The biscuits made with yogurt and sour cream were a bit sodden in texture, those with the milk and milk/butter combination were tough and lifeless, and the whipped cream biscuit was too light, more confection than biscuit. This last approach also required another step—whipping the cream—which seemed like too much trouble for a simple recipe. So we tried using plain heavy cream, without whipping, and this biscuit was the best of the lot. (Cream biscuits are not our invention. James Beard included such a recipe in his seminal work *American Cookery* [Little, Brown, 1972].)

Next we decided to do a blind tasting, pitting the cream biscuits against our conventional buttermilk biscuit recipe, which requires cutting butter into the flour. The result? Both biscuits had their partisans. The cream biscuits were lighter and more tender. They were also richer tasting. The buttermilk biscuits were flakier and had the distinctive tang that many tasters associate with good biscuits. Although neither biscuit was sweet, the buttermilk version seemed more savory.

At this point, we decided that cream biscuits were a worthy (and easier) alternative to traditional buttermilk biscuits. Still, we were running into a problem with the shape of the biscuits, which spread far too much during baking. We have always followed the conventional advice about not overworking the dough. In our experience, the best biscuits are generally made from dough that is handled lightly. This is certainly true of buttermilk biscuits.

But cream biscuits, being less sturdy than those made with butter, become soft and "melt" during baking. In this case, we thought, a little handling might not be such a bad thing. So we baked up two batches: The first dough we patted out gingerly; the second dough we kneaded for 30 seconds until it was smooth and uniform in appearance. The results were remarkable. The more heavily worked dough produced much higher, fluffier biscuits than the lightly handled dough, which looked short and bedraggled.

We ran into a problem, though, when one batch of biscuits had to sit for a few minutes while we waited for the oven to heat up. During baking, the dough spread, resulting in biscuits with bottoms that were too wide and tops that were too narrow. Clearly, the biscuits had to be popped into the oven immediately after cutting. As for dough thickness, 1 inch provides a remarkably high rise, more appealing than biscuits that start out ½ inch thick. We also discovered that it was best to add just enough cream to hold the dough together. A wet dough does not hold its shape as well during baking.

Although we find it easy enough to quickly roll out this dough and then cut it into rounds with a biscuit cutter, you can simply shape the dough with your hands or push it into the bottom of an 8-inch cake pan. The dough can then be flipped onto the work surface and cut into wedges with a knife or dough scraper. We also tested making drop biscuits, a method in which the dough is simply scooped up and dropped onto a baking sheet. These biscuits did not rise very well and their shape was inferior. In addition to those drawbacks, we also found it more time-consuming to drop the batter in individual spoonfuls than to simply shape the dough in one piece.

Our final ingredient tests involved sugar (the tasters felt that 1 tablespoon was a bit much, so we dropped it to 2 teaspoons) and baking powder (which we found we could reduce to 1 teaspoon with no decrease in rise). For oven temperature, we tried 375, 400, and 425 degrees, and the latter was best for browning.

Now we had the simplest of biscuit recipes: Whisk together the flour, sugar, baking powder, and salt, add heavy cream, form the dough, knead it, cut it, and bake it. Serve them with a savory bowl of soup or stew. The rich reward will surprise you.

Cream Biscuits

MAKES 8

This recipe offers the quickest and easiest way to make biscuits. Bake the biscuits immediately after cutting them; letting them stand for any length of time can decrease the leavening power and thereby prevent the biscuits from rising properly in the oven.

2	cups all-purpose flour
2	teaspoons sugar
1	teaspoon baking powder
½	teaspoon salt
1½	cups heavy cream

1. Adjust the oven rack to the upper-middle position and heat the oven to 425 degrees. Line a rimmed baking sheet with parchment paper.

2. Whisk together the flour, sugar, baking powder, and salt in a medium bowl. Add 1¼ cups cream and stir with a wooden spoon until the dough forms, about 30 seconds. Transfer the dough from the bowl to the countertop, leaving all dry, floury bits behind in the bowl. In 1 tablespoon increments, add up to ¼ cup cream to the dry bits in the bowl, mixing with a wooden spoon after each addition, until moistened. Add these moistened bits to the rest of the dough and knead by hand just until smooth, about 30 seconds.

3. Following the illustrations below, cut the biscuits into rounds or wedges. Place the rounds or wedges on the parchment-lined baking sheet and bake until golden brown, about 15 minutes. Serve immediately.

> VARIATIONS

Cream Biscuits with Fresh Herbs

Use the herb of your choice in this variation.

Follow recipe for Cream Biscuits, whisking 2 tablespoons minced fresh herbs into the flour along with the sugar, baking powder, and salt.

Cream Biscuits with Cheddar Cheese

Follow recipe for Cream Biscuits, stirring ½ cup (2 ounces) sharp cheddar cheese cut into ¼-inch pieces into the flour along with the sugar, baking powder, and salt. Increase the baking time to 18 minutes.

TWO WAYS TO SHAPE CREAM BISCUIT DOUGH

  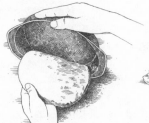 

ROUND BISCUITS
1. Pat the dough on a lightly floured work surface into a ¾-inch-thick circle.

2. Punch out dough rounds with a biscuit cutter. Push together the remaining pieces of dough, pat into a ¾-inch-thick round, and punch out several more biscuits. Discard the remaining scraps.

WEDGE BISCUITS
1. Press the dough into an 8-inch cake pan, then turn the dough out onto a lightly floured work surface.

2. With a knife or bench scraper, cut the dough into 8 wedges.

INDEX

A

Accompaniments, 305–34
  baguettes, 321–27
    Bakery-Style French, 324–26
    Dinner, 327
    key steps to making, 325
    steam heat for, 326
  buttermilk biscuits, 330–32
    with All-Purpose Flour, 332
    Master Recipe for, 332
    shaping dough for, 331
  cornbread, 327–29
    with Cheddar Cheese, 329
    with Chiles, 329
    with Corn Kernels, 329
    making batter for, 329
    Master Recipe for, 328–29
  Corn Muffins, 329–30
  cream biscuits, 333–34
    with Cheddar Cheese, 334
    with Fresh Herbs, 334
    Master Recipe for, 334
    two ways to shape, 334
  polenta, 315–16
    Double-Boiler, 316
    instant, 316
    with Parmesan and Butter, 316
  potatoes, mashed, 312–15
    Buttermilk, 315
    Garlic, 314–15
    Lumpy, 314
    making, 314
    Master Recipe for, 314
    with Parmesan and
      Lemon, 315
    with Root Vegetables, 315
  rice, basmati, 310–12
    Pilaf Style, 312
    tasting of, 311
  rice, white, 308–10
    Fluffy, 310
    tasting of, 309

Accompaniments *(cont.)*
    two-quart saucepan for, 310
  rustic country bread, 316–21
    Kneaded by Hand, 321
    Kneaded in Food
      Processor, 321
    Master Recipe for, 320–21
Ale and Cheddar Soup with
  Potato, 150
Almonds, in White Gazpacho, 183–84
Andouille Sausage, Simplified
  Cassoulet with Lamb and, 228
Apples, Curried, Chilled Cucumber
  Soup with Basil and, 189
Arugula, in Summer Vegetable Soup
  au Pistou, 131–32
Asian (cooking):
  chicken stock, 24–26
    Master Recipe for, 25
    with Sautéed Breast Meat, 25–26
  flavors
    Improved Canned Chicken
      Broth with, 26
    Oxtail Soup with, 77
  ingredients
    rice noodles, dried, 176
    soy sauce, 170
    wonton wrappers, 51
  see also Chinese cooking; Indian
    cooking; Japanese cooking;
    Southeast Asian cooking;
    Thai cooking
Asparagus:
  Chicken and Rice Soup with
    Spring Vegetables, 44
  snapping tough ends from, 110
  soup, cream of, 109–10
    recipe for, 109–10
  Spring Vegetable Stew with Fennel
    and, 268–69
Avgolemono (Greek egg-lemon
  soup), 48–50
  recipe for, 49–50

Avocado(s):
  Cucumber Soup with Cilantro
    and, 189
  dicing, 65
  pitting, 190
  soup, chilled, 189–91
    garnishes for, 191
    Lime, 191
    Master Recipe for, 191
    sweet vs. savory
      versions of, 190
  testing for ripeness, 189
  Tortilla Soup, 64–65

B

Bacon:
  Black Bean Soup with
    Balsamic and, 160
  Pancetta, Minestrone with, 133
  Smoked Cheddar Cheese
    Soup with, 150
Baguettes, 321–27
  Bakery-Style
    French, 324–26
  Dinner, 327
  key steps to making, 325
  steam heat for, 326
Baking powder, 330
  Dumplings, 241–42
Baking sheets, 4
Baking soda, 330
Baking tiles or stone, 320
Balsamic, Black Bean Soup with
  Bacon and, 160
Barley:
  Beef Soup with Mushrooms
    and, 73–74
  mushroom soup, 120–23
    Master Recipe for, 122
    Vegetarian, 122–23
  pearl, 82

Barley (cont.)
  Scotch broth, 81–83
    recipe for, 83
Basil:
  Chilled Cucumber Soup with
    Curried Apples and, 189
  Italian-Style Lamb Stew with
    Green Beans, Tomatoes
    and, 215–16
  pesto, 135
    Classic, 134–35
    making, 135
  releasing flavor of, 135
  Summer Vegetable Soup au
    Pistou, 131–32
Basmati rice, 310–12
  Pilaf Style, 312
  tasting of, 311
Bean(s):
  canned, 157
  cassoulet, 226–28
    Simplified, with Lamb and
      Andouille Sausage, 228
    Simplified, with Pork and
      Kielbasa, 227–28
  dried, freshness of, 154
  flavoring, 160
  vegetarian chili, 282–84
    Master Recipe for, 283–84
    with Tempeh, 284
  White, Rustic Potato-Leek Soup
    with, 124
Bean soups:
  black bean, 157–60
    with Balsamic and
      Bacon, 160
    Master Recipe for, 159
  ham and split pea, 163–65
    with Caraway, 165
    Master Recipe for, 164–65
  leftover, in ribollita, 155
  lentil, 160–62
    Dal, Indian, 162
    Master Recipe for, 162
  Minestrone, 133
  miso, 165–67
    recipe for, 166–67
  pasta e fagioli, 155–57
    Master Recipe for, 156–57
    Orzo and Kidney Bean Soup
      with Carrots, 157
    Tubetini and Chickpea
      Soup, 157
  white bean, Tuscan, 152–55
    Master Recipe for, 153–54
    Quick, 155
    with Winter Vegetables, 154–55
Beef:
  Barley Soup with
    Mushrooms, 73–74
  blade steaks, trimming, 206

Beef (cont.)
  borscht, hot, 77–81
    with Kielbasa, 81
    Master Recipe for, 80–81
  broth, canned, tasting of, 31
  Burgundy, 207–11
    Do-Ahead, 210–11
    making vegetable and herb
      bouquet for, 209
    Master Recipe for, 208–10
    wine for, 210
  carbonnade, 204–7
    à la Flammande, 206–7
  chili con carne, 276–78
    Master Recipe for, 277–78
    Smoky Chipotle, 278
  Cincinnati chili, 279–82
    recipe for, 281–82
  curry, Indian, 289–96
    with Crushed Spices and
      Channa Dal, 296
    Master Recipe for, 293
  curry, Thai, 297–304
    Master Recipe for, 301–2
    Red, with Eggplant, 302–3
  flank steak, slicing, 174
  flavor compounds in
    chicken vs., 30
  goulash, 202–4
    Master Recipe for, 203–4
    with Potatoes and
      Caraway, 204
  noodle soup, 72–74
    Master Recipe for, 72–73
    with Peas and Parsnips, 73
    with Spinach and
      Mushrooms, 73
  oxtails, buying, 75
  oxtail soup, 74–77
    with Asian Flavors, 77
    Master Recipe for, 76–77
    sherry for, 77
  Rice Noodle Soup with,
    Southeast Asian, 174–75
  and Ricotta Tortellini in Chicken
    Stock, 55
  Seared, Ramen with Mushroom
    Dashi, Spinach and, 170–71
  shank bones, handling, 30
  stew, hearty, 199–202
    recipe for, 199–202
  stews
    cuts for, 200
    cutting meat for, 201
    red wine for, 202
  stock, 28–30
    amount of meat required for, 30
    cut and type of meat in, 29
    Rich, 30
  stroganoff, 211–13
    recipe for, 212–13

Beef (cont.)
  tenderloin filet, slicing, 212
Beer:
  Ale and Cheddar Soup with
    Potato, 150
  carbonnade, 204–7
    à la Flammande, 206–7
Beet(s):
  borscht, chilled, 185–87
    garnishes for, 187
    recipe for, 187
  borscht, hot, 77–81
    with Beef and Kielbasa, 81
    Master Recipe for, 80–81
  handling, 80
  scrubbing, 81
  stains, removing, 186
Belgian carbonnade, 204–7
  à la Flammande, 206–7
Berry Soup, Chilled, 193
  with Fresh Berries, 193
  with Fresh Ginger, 193
  with Lemon Zest, 193
Biscuits:
  buttermilk, 330–32
    with All-Purpose Flour, 332
    Master Recipe for, 332
    shaping dough for, 331
  cream, 333–34
    with Cheddar Cheese, 334
    with Fresh Herbs, 334
    Master Recipe for, 334
    two ways to shape, 334
Bisques, 88
  lobster, 98–102
    with Coral, 102
    Master Recipe for, 101–2
  shrimp, 95–98
    recipe for, 96–98
Black bean soup, 157–60
  with Balsamic and Bacon, 160
  Master Recipe for, 159
Blade steaks, trimming, 206
Blenders, 4–5
  immersion, 5
  pureeing soup safely in, 108
Borscht:
  chilled, 185–87
    garnishes for, 187
    recipe for, 187
  hot, 77–81
    with Beef and Kielbasa, 81
    Master Recipe for, 80–81
Bouillabaisse, 250–56
  Garlic-Rubbed Croutons for, 255
  recipe for, 254–55
  Rouille for, 255–56
  seafood for, 255
Bouquet:
  garni, 247
  vegetable and herb, 209

Bread(s):
    baguettes, 321–27
        Bakery-Style French, 324–26
        Dinner, 327
        key steps to making, 325
        steam heat for, 326
    baking tiles or stone for, 320
    cornbread, 327–29
        with Cheddar Cheese, 329
        with Chiles, 329
        with Corn Kernels, 329
        making batter for, 329
        Master Recipe for, 328–29
    Corn Muffins, 329–30
    croutons, 108
        Buttered, 108
        Cinnamon-Sugar, Squash Soup
            with, 115
        Garlic, 109
        Garlic-Rubbed, 255
    crumbs, in Chicken Soup with
        Passatelli, 59–61
    kneading dough for
        in food processor,
            7–8, 317–18, 321
        in standing mixer, 318, 319
    peels for, 321
    rustic country, 316–21
        Kneaded by Hand, 321
        Kneaded in Food Processor,
            321
        Master Recipe for, 320–21
    and tomato soup, Tuscan, 136–38
        with Fresh Tomatoes, 138
        Master Recipe for, 137–38
    see also Biscuits
Broccoli:
    Green Curry with Mushrooms
        and, 303–4
    soup, cream of, 110–11
        preparing broccoli for, 111
        recipe for, 111
Broths, 16
    beef, canned, tasting of, 31
    chicken
        Japanese-Style, 168–69
        Southeast Asian, Quick, 174
        Udon with Roasted Five-Spice
            Pork, Spinach and, 168–69
    chicken, canned
        defatting, 28
        Improved, 26
        Improved, with Asian Flavors, 26
        tasting of, 27
    MSG (monosodium glutamate)
        in, 32
    Scotch. See Scotch broth
    stocks vs., 16
    vegetable, canned, tasting of, 35
Browning meat, 198
Buckwheat noodles. See Soba

Butter, cutting into small cubes, 332
Buttered Croutons, 108
Buttermilk:
    biscuits, 330–32
        with All-Purpose Flour, 332
        Master Recipe for, 332
        shaping dough for, 331
    Mashed Potatoes, 315
Butternut squash, 115
    cutting up, 114
    soup, 113–15
        with Cinnamon-Sugar
            Croutons, 115
        Curried, with Cilantro, 115
        Master Recipe for, 114–15

C

Cabbage:
    borscht
        with Beef and Kielbasa, 81
        Master Recipe for, 80–81
    Napa, Southeast Asian Rice
        Noodle Soup with Chicken
        and, 176
    savoy, in minestrone, 134
    shredding, 78
Cacciatore, chicken, 233–35
    with Portobellos and Sage, 234–35
    with White Wine and
        Tarragon, 235
Cajun cooking. See Creole and Cajun
    cooking
Caldo verde, 138–40
    recipe for, 139–40
Carbonnade, 204–7
    à la Flammande, 206–7
Carnival squash, 115
Carrot(s):
    Chicken Fricassee with
        Peas and, 245
    Hearty Vegetable Stew, 265
    Irish Stew with Turnips and, 215
    Mashed Potatoes with Root
        Vegetables, 315
    Minestrone, 133
    Orzo and Kidney Bean Soup
        with, 157
    Root Vegetable Stew with Porcini
        and Cream, 266–67
    scrubbing, 81
    soup, pureed, 111–13
        Curried, 113
        with Ginger, 113
        Master Recipe for, 112–13
        with Orange, 113
    Spring Vegetable Stew with Fennel
        and Asparagus, 268–69
    White Bean Soup with Winter
        Vegetables, 154–55

Casseroles, lidded, 6–7
Cassoulet, 226–28
    Simplified, with Lamb and
        Andouille Sausage, 228
    Simplified, with Pork and
        Kielbasa, 227–28
Cauliflower:
    Green Curry with Mixed
        Vegetables, 304
    in minestrone, 134
Celery:
    Minestrone, 133
    White Bean Soup with Winter
        Vegetables, 154–55
Celery root, in Mashed Potatoes with
    Root Vegetables, 315
Channa Dal, Beef Curry with
    Crushed Spices and, 296
Chanterelle mushrooms, 120
Cheater's Fish Stock, 38
Cheddar cheese:
    Cornbread with, 329
    Cream Biscuits with, 334
    soup, 148–50
        Ale and, with Potato, 150
        Master Recipe for, 149–50
        Smoked, with Bacon, 150
    Tortilla Soup, 64–65
Cheese:
    onion soup, French, 145–47
        recipe for, 147
    see also Cheddar cheese; Parmesan
        cheese
Cheesecloth, 17
Cheese graters, 5–6
Chef's knives, 8
Cherry Soup, Chilled, 193–94
Chicken:
    broth
        Japanese-Style, 168–69
        Southeast Asian, Quick, 174
        Udon with Roasted Five-
            Spice Pork, Spinach
            and, 168–69
    broth, canned
        defatting, 28
        Improved, 26
        Improved, with Asian
            Flavors, 26
        tasting of, 27
    browned, skinning, 231
    flavor compounds in beef vs., 30
    poultry shears for, 10
    safety concerns and, 23
    stock, 18–27
        amount of meat required for, 30
        Asian, 24–26
            Master Recipe for, 25
            with Sautéed Breast
                Meat, 25–26
        buying chicken for, 20–22

Chicken (cont.)
    chicken parts for, 19
    hacking up chicken for, 22
    Hot-and-Sour Soup, 85–86
    Quick, 22–23
    Quick, with Sautéed Breast
        Meat, 23
    for soup that needs chicken
        meat, 20, 42
    tips for, 18
    Traditional, 23–24
    tasting of, 20–22
    whole, cutting up, 245
Chicken soups, 41–70
    with coconut, Thai, 65–68
        recipe for, 68
    cream of (chicken velouté), 61–62
        recipe for, 62
    egg drop, 45–46
        recipe for, 46
    egg-lemon, 48–50
        with Chicken, 50
        with Cinnamon and
            Cayenne, 50
        Greek (Avgolemono), 49–50
        with Saffron, 50
    matzo ball, 56–59
        Herbed, 59
        Master Recipe for, 58–59
        shaping matzo balls for, 57
        Spiced, 59
    Mulligatawny, 142
    noodle, 42–45
        Master Recipe for, 44
        Rice Noodle, with Napa
            Cabbage, Southeast
            Asian, 176
        with Shells, Tomatoes, and
            Zucchini, 44
        three kinds of dried egg
            noodles for, 43
    with passatelli, 59–61
        recipe for, 59–61
    with Rice and Spring
        Vegetables, 44
    Straciatella, 47
    with tortellini, 53–56
        Fresh Egg Pasta for, 56
        making fresh pasta for, 54
        Master Recipe for, 55
        with Parsley-Cheese
            Tortellini, 55
        shaping tortellini for, 55
    tortilla, 62–65
        with Fried Corn Tortillas, 65
        Master Recipe for, 64–65
    with Wild Rice, Leeks, and
        Mushrooms, 44–45
    wonton, 50–53
        Master Recipe for, 52–53
        Shrimp, 53

Chicken stews, 229–48
    cacciatore, 233–35
        with Portobellos and
            Sage, 234–35
        with White Wine and
            Tarragon, 235
    cassoulet, 226–28
        Simplified, with Lamb and
            Andouille Sausage, 228
        Simplified, with Pork and
            Kielbasa, 227–28
    coq au vin, 245–48
        recipe for, 247–48
    country captain, 237–39
        garnishes for, 239
        recipe for, 238–39
    curry, Indian, 289–96
        Master Recipe for, 293
        with Spinach and
            Fenugreek, 294
        with Yogurt, Cilantro, and
            Zucchini, 294
    curry, Thai, 297–304
        Green, with Broccoli and
            Mushrooms, 303–4
        Master Recipe for, 301–2
    with dumplings, 239–42
        with Aromatic
            Vegetables, 241–42
        Herbed, with Aromatic
            Vegetables, 242
    fricassee, 242–45
        with Mushrooms and
            Onions, 244–45
        with Peas and Carrots, 245
    Gumbo, with Sausage, 288–89
    hearty, 230–33
        with Leeks, Potatoes, and
            Saffron, 232–33
        Master Recipe for, 231–32
    paprikash, 235–37
        recipe for, 236–37
Chickpea and Tubetini Soup, 157
Chile(s):
    Chipotle, Smoky, Chili con
        Carne, 278
    Chipotle, Spicy Gazpacho with
        Lime and, 181
    Cornbread with, 329
    dried, 279
    varying tolerance to
        heat of, 280
Chilis, 276–84
    Cincinnati, 279–82
        recipe for, 281–82
    con carne, 276–78
        Master Recipe for, 277–78
        Smoky Chipotle, 278
    vegetarian, 282–84
        Bean, 283–84
        Bean and Tempeh, 284

Chilled soups, 177–94
    avocado, 189–91
        garnishes for, 191
        Lime, 191
        Master Recipe for, 191
        sweet vs. savory versions of, 190
    borscht, 185–87
        garnishes for, 187
        recipe for, 187
    Carrot, Pureed, with Orange, 113
    cucumber, 188–89
        with Avocado and
            Cilantro, 189
        with Curried Apples and
            Basil, 189
        with Mango and Mint, 189
        Master Recipe for, 188–89
    fruit, 192–94
        Berry, 193
        Berry, with Fresh Berries, 193
        Berry, with Fresh Ginger, 193
        Berry, with Lemon Zest, 193
        Cherry, 193–94
        Melon, 194
        Melon, with Fresh Ginger, 194
        Melon, with Fresh Mint, 194
        Stone Fruit, 194
    gazpacho, 178–82
        Classic, 180
        Quick Food Processor, 180–81
        with Scallops and
            Shrimp, 181–82
        Spicy, with Chipotle Chiles
            and Lime, 181
    vichyssoise, 184–85
        recipe for, 184–85
    white gazpacho, 182–84
        recipe for, 183–84
Chilling:
    soups, 178
    stock quickly, 17, 18
China cap, 13–14
Chinese cooking:
    egg drop soup, 45–46
        recipe for, 46
    hot-and-sour soup, 84–86
        recipe for, 85–86
    wonton soup, 50–53
        Master Recipe for, 52–53
        Shrimp, 53
Chinois, 13–14
Chipotle chile(s):
    Smoky, Chili con Carne, 278
    Spicy Gazpacho with
        Lime and, 181
Chorizo, in Caldo Verde, 139–40
Chowders, 88
    clam, Manhattan, 91–94
        Italian Style, 94
        Master Recipe for, 93–94
        Quick Pantry, 94

Chowders (cont.)
  clam, New England, 88–91
    Master Recipe for, 90–91
    Quick Pantry, 91
    steaming clams for, 90
  corn, 125–28
    extending season for, 126
    milking corn for, 127
    recipe for, 128
    removing kernels from corn
      cobs for, 126
Cilantro:
  Cucumber Soup with Avocado
    and, 189
  Curried Squash Soup with, 115
Cincinnati chili, 279–82
  recipe for, 281–82
Cinnamon-Sugar Croutons, Squash
  Soup with, 115
Cioppino, 256–59
  recipe for, 258–59
Clam(s), 91
  buying by weight or number, 94
  chowder, Manhattan, 91–94
    Italian Style, 94
    Master Recipe for, 93–94
    Quick Pantry, 94
  chowder, New England, 88–91
    Master Recipe for, 90–91
    Quick Pantry, 91
    steaming clams for, 90
  Cioppino, 258–59
  grit issue and, 89, 91
  scrubbing, 89
Cleavers, 24
  using, 25
Coconut:
  chicken and, soup, Thai, 65–68
    recipe for, 65–68
  milk, 299
    cream of coconut and coconut
      cream compared to, 67
    and Shrimp Soup, Thai, 65–68
Cod, in New England Fish
  Stew, 262
Colanders, 13
Cookie sheets, 4
Cooking sprays, vegetable, 131
Coq au vin, 245–48
  recipe for, 247–48
Corn:
  chowder, 125–28
    extending season for, 126
    recipe for, 128
  cobs, removing kernels
    from, 126
  Kernels, Cornbread with, 329
  milking, 127
  Muffins, 329–30
  Summer Vegetable Soup au
    Pistou, 131–32

Corn (cont.)
  Tortillas, Fried, Tortilla Soup
    with, 65
Cornbread, 327–29
  with Cheddar Cheese, 329
  with Chiles, 329
  with Corn Kernels, 329
  making batter for, 329
  Master Recipe for, 328–29
Cornmeal. See Polenta
Country captain chicken, 237–39
  garnishes for, 239
  recipe for, 238–39
Cream:
  of asparagus soup, 109–10
    recipe for, 109–10
  biscuits, 333–34
    with Cheddar Cheese, 334
    with Fresh Herbs, 334
    Master Recipe for, 334
    two ways to shape, 334
  of broccoli soup, 110–11
    preparing broccoli for, 111
    recipe for, 111
  of chicken soup (chicken
    velouté), 61–62
    recipe for, 62
  Mushroom Ragoût with, 271
  Root Vegetable Stew with Porcini
    and, 266–67
  of tomato soup, 116–17
    recipe for, 117
Creamy:
  mushroom soup, 117–20
    recipe for, 119–20
  Pea Soup, 107–8
Cremini mushrooms, 120
Creole and Cajun cooking:
  gumbo, 284–89
    Chicken and
      Sausage, 288–89
    Shrimp and Sausage, Creole-
      Style, 287
    Shrimp and Sausage, with
      Filé, 288
    Shrimp and Sausage, with
      Okra, 287–88
  roux in, 284–86
Croutons, 108
  Buttered, 108
  Cinnamon-Sugar, Squash Soup
    with, 115
  Garlic, 109
  Garlic-Rubbed, 255
Cucumber(s):
  cutting into neat dice, 181
  gazpacho, 178–82
    Classic, 180
    Quick Food Processor, 180–81
    with Scallops and
      Shrimp, 181–82

Cucumber(s) (cont.)
  Spicy, with Chipotle Chiles
    and Lime, 181
  seeding, 189
  soup, chilled, 188–89
    with Avocado and Cilantro, 189
    with Curried Apples and
      Basil, 189
    with Mango and Mint, 189
    Master Recipe for, 188–89
Curried Apples, Chilled Cucumber
  Soup with Basil and, 189
Curried soups:
  Carrot, Pureed, 113
  mulligatawny, 140–43
    with Chicken, 142
    with Lamb, 142–43
    Master Recipe for, 141–42
  Squash, with Cilantro, 115
Curries (stews), 276
  country captain chicken, 237–39
    garnishes for, 239
    recipe for, 238–39
  Indian, 289–96
    Beef, with Crushed Spices and
      Channa Dal, 296
    Chicken, with Spinach and
      Fenugreek, 294
    Chicken, with Yogurt, Cilantro,
      and Zucchini, 294
    frying spices for, 296
    Lamb, with Figs and
      Fenugreek, 296
    Lamb, with Whole Spices, 295
    Master Recipe for, 293
    Shrimp, with Yogurt and
      Peas, 295
  Thai, 297–304
    coconut milk for, 299
    Green, with Chicken, Broccoli,
      and Mushrooms, 303–4
    Green, with Mixed
      Vegetables, 304
    Green Curry Paste for, 300
    lemon grass for, 301, 302
    Master Recipe for, 301–2
    Red, with Beef and
      Eggplant, 302–3
    Red, with Shrimp, Pineapple,
      and Peanuts, 303
    Red Curry Paste for, 300–301
    store-bought curry
      pastes for, 298
Curry pastes, store-bought, 68, 298

D

Dal Soup, Indian, 162
Dashi:
  in miso soup, 165–66

Dashi *(cont.)*
   Mushroom, Ramen with Seared
      Beef, Spinach and, 170–71
   Mushroom, Udon with Ginger
      Tofu, Watercress and, 171
   Soba with Shrimp, Watercress
      and, 169–70
Defatting:
   canned broth, 28
   stock, 17, 19
Delicata squash, 115
Dumplings:
   chicken and, 239–42
      with Aromatic Vegetables, 241–42
      Herbed, with Aromatic
         Vegetables, 242
   matzo ball(s)
      Chicken Soup with, 58–59
      Herbed, Chicken Soup
         with, 58–59
      shaping, 57
      soup, 56–59
      Spiced, Chicken Soup
         with, 58–59
   passatelli, chicken soup
      with, 59–61
      recipe for, 59–61
   three shapes for, 242
   wontons, shaping, 52
   wonton soup, 50–53
      Master Recipe for, 52–53
      Shrimp, 53
   wonton wrappers for, 51
Dutch ovens, 6–7

E

Eastern European cooking:
   beef goulash, 202–4
      Master Recipe for, 203–4
      with Potatoes and
         Caraway, 204
   borscht, chilled, 185–87
      garnishes for, 187
      recipe for, 187
   borscht, hot, 77–81
      with Beef and Kielbasa, 81
      Master Recipe for, 80–81
   chicken paprikash, 235–37
      recipe for, 236–37
Egg(s), 45
   drop soup, 45–46
      recipe for, 46
   lemon soup, 48–50
      with Chicken, 50
      with Cinnamon and
         Cayenne, 50
      Greek (Avgolemono), 49–50
      with Saffron, 50
   noodles, dried, three kinds of, 43

Egg(s) *(cont.)*
   Pasta, Fresh, 56
   Straciatella, 47
   tempering, 50
Eggplant:
   ratatouille, 272–74
      recipe for, 273–74
   Red Curry with Beef and, 302–3
Equipment, 3–14
   baking sheets, 4
   baking tiles or stone, 320
   blenders, 4–5
      immersion, 5
      pureeing soup safely in, 108
   cheese graters, 5–6
   cleavers, 24
      using, 25
   Dutch ovens/lidded
      casseroles, 6–7
   food processors, 7–8
      grating beets in, 80
      kneading bread dough
         in, 7–8, 317–18, 321
      pureeing with blender vs., 4–5
      shredding cabbage in, 78
   immersion blenders, 5
   knives, 8–9
   ladles, 9
   minichoppers, 295
   mixers, standing, kneading bread
      dough in, 318, 319
   mortars and pestles, 299
   oyster knives, 104
   peels, 321
   potato mashers, 313
   poultry shears, 10
   roasting pans, 10–11
   saucepans, two-quart, 310
   scales, 11–12
   skimmers, 12
   stockpots, 12–13
   strainers, 13–14
   vegetable peelers, 14
   zesters, 14
Escarole:
   in minestrone, 134
   White Bean Soup with Winter
      Vegetables, 154–55

F

Fatback, 129
Fennel:
   preparing, 268
   Spring Vegetable Stew with
      Asparagus and, 268–69
Fenugreek:
   Chicken Curry with Spinach
      and, 294
   Lamb Curry with Figs and, 296

Figs, Lamb Curry with Fenugreek
   and, 296
Filé, 288
   Shrimp and Sausage Gumbo
      with, 288
Fish:
   bouillabaisse, 250–56
      Garlic-Rubbed Croutons
         for, 255
      recipe for, 254–55
      Rouille for, 255–56
      seafood for, 255
   stew, New England, 261–62
      recipe for, 262
   stew, Sicilian, 259–61
      recipe for, 260–61
   stock (fish fumet), 35–38, 251–52
      Cheater's, 38
      cleaning fish frames for, 37
      fish for, 36
      recipes for, 37–38, 254–55
   see also Seafood soups;
      Seafood stews
Fish sauce, Southeast Asian, 68
Flambéing shrimp, 96
Flank steak, slicing, 174
Foam, causes of, 17
Food mills, 4
Food processors, 7–8
   grating beets in, 80
   kneading bread dough
      in, 7–8, 317–18, 321
   pureeing with blender vs., 4–5
   shredding cabbage in, 78
Freezing:
   corn for chowder, 126
   stock, 17
      in convenient
         portions, 20
French cooking:
   baguettes, 321–27
      Bakery-Style, 324–26
      Dinner, 327
      key steps to making, 325
      steam heat for, 326
   beef Burgundy, 207–11
      Do-Ahead, 210–11
      making vegetable and herb
         bouquet for, 209
      Master Recipe for, 208–10
      wine for, 210
   bouillabaisse, 250–56
      Garlic-Rubbed Croutons
         for, 255
      recipe for, 254–55
      Rouille for, 255–56
      seafood for, 255
   bouquet garni, 247
   cassoulet, 226–28
      Simplified, with Lamb and
         Andouille Sausage, 228

French cooking (cont.)
    Simplified, with Pork and
        Kielbasa, 227–28
    Chicken Cacciatore with White
        Wine and Tarragon, 235
    coq au vin, 245–48
        recipe for, 247–48
    onion soup, 145–47
        recipe for, 147
    ratatouille, 272–74
        recipe for, 273–74
    Rouille, 255–56
    Summer Vegetable Soup au
        Pistou, 131–32
    vichyssoise, 184–85
        recipe for, 184–85
Fricassees, 243
    chicken, 242–45
        with Mushrooms and
            Onions, 244–45
        with Peas and Carrots, 245
Fruit soup, chilled, 192–94
    Berry, 193
        with Fresh Berries, 193
        with Fresh Ginger, 193
        with Lemon Zest, 193
    Cherry, 193–94
    Melon, 194
        with Fresh Ginger, 194
        with Fresh Mint, 194
    Stone Fruit, 194

G

Galangal, 66
Garlic:
    Croutons, 109
    Gremolata, 225, 226
    Mashed Potatoes, 314–15
    -Rubbed Croutons, 255
    smashing, 145
    soup, 143–45
        recipe for, 144–45
Garnishes:
    Gremolata, 225, 226
    Pesto, Classic, 134–35
    Wild Mushrooms, Sautéed, 120
Gazpacho, 178–82
    Classic, 180
    Quick Food Processor, 180–81
    with Scallops and
        Shrimp, 181–82
    Spicy, with Chipotle Chiles and
        Lime, 181
    white, 182–84
        recipe for, 183–84
Ginger:
    mincing, 66
    Pureed Carrot Soup with, 113
    smashing, 26

Ginger (cont.)
    Tofu, Udon with Mushroom
        Dashi, Watercress and, 171
Gloves, "bathing" or "exfoliating," 81
Goulash, beef, 202–4
    Master Recipe for, 203–4
    with Potatoes and Caraway, 204
Grapes, in White Gazpacho, 183–84
Graters, cheese, 5–6
Gravy skimmers, 19
Greek egg-lemon soup
    (avgolemono), 48–50
    recipe for, 49–50
Green beans:
    Green Curry with Mixed
        Vegetables, 304
    Italian-Style Lamb Stew with
        Tomatoes, Basil and, 215–16
    in minestrone, 134
Green curry:
    with Chicken, Broccoli, and
        Mushrooms, 303–4
    with Mixed Vegetables, 304
    Paste, 300
Greens, in caldo verde, 138–40
    recipe for, 139–40
Gremolata, 225, 226
Gumbos, 276, 284–89
    Chicken and Sausage, 288–89
    okra and filé in, 288
    roux for, 284–86
    Shrimp and Sausage
        Creole-Style, 287
        with Filé, 288
        with Okra, 287–88

H

Haddock, in New England Fish
    Stew, 262
Ham:
    half-picnic, handling, 164
    and split pea soup, 163–65
        with Caraway, 165
        Master Recipe for, 164–65
Herb(ed)(s):
    bouquet garni, 247
    Dumplings, Chicken and, with
        Aromatic Vegetables, 242
    Fresh, Cream Biscuits
        with, 334
    and vegetable bouquet,
        making, 209
Hominy, in pozole, 220–23
    Rojo, 222–23
    Verde, 223
Hot-and-sour soup, 84–86
    recipe for, 85–86
    Rice Noodle, with Shrimp and
        Tomato, 175

Hungarian cooking:
    beef goulash, 202–4
        Master Recipe for, 203–4
        with Potatoes and
            Caraway, 204
    chicken paprikash, 235–37
        recipe for, 236–37

I

Immersion blenders, 5
Indian cooking:
    curry, 289–96
        Beef, with Crushed Spices and
            Channa Dal, 296
        Chicken, with Spinach and
            Fenugreek, 294
        Chicken, with Yogurt, Cilantro,
            and Zucchini, 294
        frying spices for, 296
        Lamb, with Figs and
            Fenugreek, 296
        Lamb, with Whole Spices, 295
        Master Recipe for, 293
        Shrimp, with Yogurt and
            Peas, 295
    Dal Soup, 162
    mulligatawny, 140–43
        with Chicken, 142
        with Lamb, 142–43
        Master Recipe for, 141–42
    pork vindaloo, 218–20
        recipe for, 219–20
Irish stew, 213–16
    with Carrots and
        Turnips, 215
    Master Recipe for, 214–15
Italian cooking:
    chicken cacciatore, 233–35
        with Portobellos and
            Sage, 234–35
        with White Wine and
            Tarragon, 235
    chicken soup with
        passatelli, 59–61
        recipe for, 59–61
    cioppino, 256–59
        recipe for, 258–59
    fish stew, Sicilian, 259–61
        recipe for, 260–61
    minestrone, 132–35
        Classic Pesto for, 134–35
        Master Recipe for, 133
        with Pancetta, 133
        with Rice or Pasta, 134
        varying vegetables and beans
            in, 134
    osso buco, 223–26
        recipe for, 225–26
Parmesan cheese, 60

Italian cooking (cont.)
  pasta e fagioli, 155–57
    Orzo and Kidney Bean Soup
      with Carrots, 157
    recipe for, 156–57
    Tubetini and Chickpea
      Soup, 157
  pesto, 135
    Classic, 134–35
    making, 135
  Ribollita, 155
  Straciatella, 47
  tomato and bread soup,
    Tuscan, 136–38
    with Fresh Tomatoes, 138
    Master Recipe for, 137–38
  tortellini soup, 53–56
    Master Recipe for, 55
    with Parsley-Cheese
      Tortellini, 55
  white bean soup, Tuscan, 152–55
    Master Recipe for, 153–54
    Quick, 155
    with Winter Vegetables, 154–55
Italian-style dishes:
  Lamb Stew with Green Beans,
    Tomatoes, and Basil, 215–16
  Manhattan Clam Chowder, 94

J

Japanese cooking:
  ingredients
    miso, 167
    noodles, 172
    soy sauce, 170
  miso soup, 165–67
    recipe for, 166–67
  noodle soup, 167–72
    garnishes for, 171
    Master Recipe for, 168
    noodles for, 172
    Ramen with Mushroom
      Dashi, Seared Beef, and
      Spinach, 170–71
    Soba with Dashi, Shrimp, and
      Watercress, 169–70
    Udon with Chicken Broth,
      Roasted Five-Spice Pork,
      and Spinach, 168–69
    Udon with Mushroom Dashi,
      Ginger Tofu, and
      Watercress, 171
Jasmine Rice and Turkey Soup,
  Spicy, 70
Jewish cooking:
  matzo ball(s)
    Chicken Soup with, 58–59
    Herbed, Chicken Soup
      with, 58–59

Jewish cooking (cont.)
    shaping, 57
    soup, 56–59
    Spiced, Chicken Soup
      with, 58–59
  matzo meal, 58
Julienning vegetables, 76

K

Kabocha squash, 115
Kaffir lime leaves, 66
Kale:
  Caldo Verde, 139–40
  handling, 140
  in minestrone, 134
  Turkey Soup with Potatoes,
    Linguiça and, 70
  White Bean Soup with Winter
    Vegetables, 154–55
Kidney Bean and Orzo Soup with
  Carrots, 157
Kielbasa:
  Borscht with Beef and, 81
  Caldo Verde, 139–40
  Rustic Potato-Leek Soup
    with, 124
  Simplified Cassoulet with Pork
    and, 227–28
Kneading bread dough:
  in food processor,
    7–8, 317–18, 321
  in standing mixer, 318, 319
Knife sharpeners, electric, 9
Knives, 8–9
  chef's, 8
  cleavers, 24
    using, 25
  oyster, 104
  paring, 8–9

L

Ladles, 9
Ladling, drip-free, 9
Lamb:
  cassoulet, 226–27
    Simplified, with Andouille
      Sausage, 228
  chops
    blade and round bone, 215
    shoulder, 216
  curry, Indian
    with Figs and Fenugreek, 296
    Master Recipe for, 293
    with Whole Spices, 295
  Irish Stew, 213–16
    with Carrots and Turnips, 215
    Master Recipe for, 214–15

Lamb (cont.)
  Mulligatawny Soup with, 142–43
  Scotch broth, 81–83
    recipe for, 83
  shanks, 83
  Stew, Italian-Style, with Green Beans,
    Tomatoes, and Basil, 215–16
  Stock, Rich, 83
  tagine, 216–18
    recipe for, 217–18
Leavening agents, 330
Leek(s):
  Chicken Soup with Wild Rice,
    Mushrooms and, 44–45
  Chicken Stew with Potatoes,
    Saffron and, 232–33
  cleaning, 124
  Minestrone, 133
  potato soup, rustic, 123–24
    with Kielbasa, 124
    Master Recipe for, 124
    with White Beans, 124
  Spring Vegetable Soup, 130–31
  Spring Vegetable Stew with Fennel
    and Asparagus, 268–69
  vichyssoise, 184–85
    recipe for, 184–85
  White Bean Soup with Winter
    Vegetables, 154–55
Leftover soup, in Ribollita, 155
Lemon:
  egg soup, 48–50
    with Chicken, 50
    with Cinnamon and
      Cayenne, 50
    Greek (Avgolemono), 49–50
    with Saffron, 50
  Mashed Potatoes with Parmesan
    and, 315
  zest
    Gremolata, 225, 226
    removing large strips of, 50
Lemon grass, 301
  bruising, 175
  mincing, 302
Lentil(s):
  soup, 160–62
    Dal, Indian, 162
    Master Recipe for, 162
  tasting of, 160–61
Lime:
  Avocado Soup, Chilled, 191
  Spicy Gazpacho with Chipotle
    Chiles and, 181–82
Linguiça, Turkey Soup with Potatoes,
  Kale and, 70
Lobster(s), 100
  bisque, 98–102
    with Coral, 102
    Master Recipe for, 101–2
  hard-shell vs. soft-shell, 98, 100

Lobster(s) *(cont.)*
   shells, cleaning, 102
   steamed, removing meat from, 99

M

Mango(es):
   Chilled Cucumber Soup with
      Mint and, 189
   handling, 238
Manhattan clam chowder, 91–94
   Italian Style, 94
   Master Recipe for, 93–94
   Quick Pantry, 94
Mashed potatoes. *See* Potatoes—
   mashed
Matzo ball(s):
   Chicken Soup with, 58–59
   Herbed, Chicken Soup
      with, 58–59
   shaping, 57
   soup, 56–59
   Spiced, Chicken Soup with, 58–59
Matzo meal, tasting of, 58
Meat and Ricotta Tortellini in
   Chicken Stock, 55
Meat cleavers, 24
   using, 25
Meat soups, 71–86
   Beef Barley, with
      Mushrooms, 73–74
   beef noodle, 72–74
      Master Recipe for, 72–73
      with Peas and Parsnips, 73
      with Spinach and
         Mushrooms, 73
   borscht, hot, 77–81
      with Beef and Kielbasa, 81
      Master Recipe for, 80–81
   hot-and-sour, 84–86
      recipe for, 85–86
   oxtail, 74–77
      with Asian Flavors, 77
      Master Recipe for, 76–77
      sherry for, 77
   Ramen with Mushroom Dashi,
      Seared Beef, and Spinach, 170
   Scotch broth, 81–83
      recipe for, 83
Meat stews, 197–228
   beef
      cutting meat for, 201
      possible cuts for, 200
      trimming blade steaks for, 206
   beef, hearty, 199–202
      recipe for, 201–2
   beef Burgundy, 207–11
      Do-Ahead, 210–11
      making vegetable and herb
         bouquet for, 209

Meat stews *(cont.)*
      Master Recipe for, 208–10
      wine for, 210
   beef goulash, 202–4
      Master Recipe for, 203–4
      with Potatoes and
         Caraway, 203–4
   beef stroganoff, 211–13
      Master Recipe for, 212–13
      slicing tenderloin filet for, 212
   best cuts for, 198
   browning meat for, 198
   carbonnade, 204–7
      à la Flammande, 206–7
   cassoulet, 226–28
      Simplified, with Lamb and
         Andouille Sausage, 228
      Simplified, with Pork and
         Kielbasa, 227–28
   chili, Cincinnati, 279–82
      recipe for, 281–82
   chili con carne, 276–78
      Master Recipe for, 277–78
      Smoky Chipotle, 278
   cooking on stovetop vs. in oven, 198
   cooking temperature for, 198
   curry, Indian, 289–96
      Beef, with Crushed Spices and
         Channa Dal, 296
      frying spices for, 296
      Lamb, with Figs and
         Fenugreek, 296
      Lamb, with Whole Spices, 295
      Master Recipe for, 293
   curry, Thai, 297–304
      coconut milk for, 299
      Green Curry Paste for, 300
      lemon grass for, 301, 302
      Master Recipe for, 301–2
      Red, with Beef and
         Eggplant, 302–3
      Red Curry Paste for, 300–301
      store-bought curry pastes
         for, 298
   gumbos, 276, 284–89
      Chicken and Sausage, 288–89
      okra and filé in, 288
      roux for, 284–86
      Shrimp and Sausage, Creole-
         Style, 287
      Shrimp and Sausage, with
         Filé, 288
      Shrimp and Sausage, with
         Okra, 287–88
   Irish stew, 213–16
      with Carrots and Turnips, 215
      Master Recipe for, 214–15
   Lamb, Italian-Style, with Green
      Beans, Tomatoes, and
      Basil, 215–16
   lamb tagine, 216–18

Meat stews *(cont.)*
      recipe for, 217–18
   liquids for, 199
   osso buco, 223–26
      recipe for, 225–26
   pork, best cuts for, 220
   pork vindaloo, 218–20
      recipe for, 219–20
   pozole, 220–23
      Rojo, 222–23
      Verde, 223
   red wine for, 202
Melon Soup, Chilled, 194
   with Fresh Ginger, 194
   with Fresh Mint, 194
Mexican cooking:
   pozole, 220–23
      Rojo, 222–23
      Verde, 223
   tortilla soup, 62–65
      with Fried Corn Tortillas, 65
      Master Recipe for, 64–65
Minestrone, 132–35
   Classic Pesto for, 134–35
   Master Recipe for, 133
   with Pancetta, 133
   with Rice or Pasta, 134
   varying vegetables and
      beans in, 134
Minichoppers, 295
Mint, Chilled Cucumber Soup with
   Mango and, 189
Miso, 167
   soup, 165–67
      recipe for, 166–67
Mixers, standing, kneading bread
   dough in, 318, 319
Monkfish, in Bouillabaisse, 254–55
Moroccan lamb tagine, 216–18
   recipe for, 217–18
Mortars and pestles, 299
MSG (monosodium glutamate), 32
Muffins, Corn, 329–30
Mulligatawny soup, 140–43
   with Chicken, 142
   with Lamb, 142–43
   Master Recipe for, 141–42
Mushroom(s):
   barley soup, 120–23
      Master Recipe for, 122
      Vegetarian, 122–23
   Beef Barley Soup with, 73–74
   Beef Noodle Soup with Spinach
      and, 73
   button, 118
   Chicken Fricassee with Onions
      and, 244–45
   Chicken Soup with Wild Rice,
      Leeks and, 44–45
   Dashi, Ramen with Seared Beef,
      Spinach and, 170–71

Mushroom(s) *(cont.)*
 Dashi, Udon with Ginger Tofu,
  Watercress and, 171
 dried, rehydrating, 85
 Green Curry with Broccoli
  and, 303–4
 Hearty Vegetable
  Stew, 265
 Porcini, Root Vegetable Stew with
  Cream and, 266–67
 Portobello, Chicken Cacciatore
  with Sage and, 234–35
 ragoût, 269–71
  with Cream, 271
  Master Recipe for, 271
 soup, creamy, 117–20
  garnish for, 120
  recipe for, 119–20
 Stock, Quick, 123
 washing, 121
 "wild," 120
 Wild, Sautéed, 120
Mussels, 259
 Bouillabaisse, 254–55
 Cioppino, 258–59
 cleaning, 252

N

Napa Cabbage, Southeast Asian Rice
 Noodle Soup with Chicken
 and, 176
Nectarine Soup, Chilled, 194
New England:
 clam chowder, 88–91
  Master Recipe for, 90–91
  Quick Pantry, 91
  steaming clams for, 90
 fish stew, 261–62
  recipe for, 262
Noodle(s):
 beef soup, 72–74
  Master Recipe for, 72–73
  with Peas and Parsnips, 73
  with Spinach and
   Mushrooms, 73
 chicken soup, 42–45
  Master Recipe for, 44
  with Shells, Tomatoes, and
   Zucchini, 44
  three kinds of dried egg
   noodles for, 43
 egg, dried, three
  kinds of, 43
 Japanese, 172
 rice, dried, 176
 soup, Japanese, 167–72
  garnishes for, 171
  Master Recipe for, 168
  noodles for, 172

Noodle(s) *(cont.)*
 Ramen with Mushroom
  Dashi, Seared Beef, and
  Spinach, 170–71
 Soba with Dashi, Shrimp, and
  Watercress, 169–70
 Udon with Chicken Broth,
  Roasted Five-Spice Pork,
  and Spinach, 168–69
 Udon with Mushroom Dashi,
  Ginger Tofu, and
  Watercress, 171
 soup, Southeast Asian, 172–76
  assembling, 173
  dried rice noodles for, 176
  Hot-and-Sour Rice Noodle, with
   Shrimp and Tomato, 175
  Rice Noodle, with
   Beef, 174–75
  Rice Noodle, with Chicken
   and Napa Cabbage, 176
 Turkey Soup, 69–70

O

Okra, 288
 Shrimp and Sausage Gumbo
  with, 287–88
Onion(s):
 carbonnade, 204–7
  à la Flammande, 206–7
 gazpacho, 178–82
  Classic, 180
  Quick Food Processor, 180–81
  with Scallops and
   Shrimp, 181–82
  Spicy, with Chipotle Chiles
   and Lime, 181
 Minestrone, 133
 pearl, fresh, preparing, 248
 reducing tears while cutting, 148
 Root Vegetable Stew with Porcini
  and Cream, 266–67
 soup, blue color of, 147
 soup, French, 145–47
  recipe for, 147
Orange, Pureed Carrot Soup
 with, 113
Orzo and Kidney Bean Soup with
 Carrots, 157
Osso buco, 223–26
 recipe for, 225–26
Oxtail(s):
 buying, 75
 soup, 74–77
  with Asian Flavors, 77
  Master Recipe for, 76–77
  sherry for, 77
Oyster(s):
 shucked, buying, 103

Oyster(s) *(cont.)*
 stew, 103–4
  recipe for, 104
Oyster knives, 104
Oyster mushrooms, 120
 Mushroom Ragoût, 271

P

Pancetta, Minestrone with, 133
Pans:
 roasting, 10–11
 saucepans, two-quart, 310
Pappa al pomodoro (Tuscan tomato and
 bread soup), 136–38
 with Fresh Tomatoes, 138
 Master Recipe for, 137–38
Paprika, 236
 chicken paprikash, 235–37
  recipe for, 236–37
Paring knives, 8–9
Parmesan cheese:
 cheese graters for, 5–6
 Chicken Soup with
  Passatelli, 59–61
 Mashed Potatoes with Lemon
  and, 315
 Polenta with Butter and, 316
 rinds, flavoring soup with, 132, 133
 Straciatella, 47
 tasting of, 60
Parsley:
 Gremolata, 225, 226
 Ricotta Tortellini in Chicken
  Stock, 55
Parsnips:
 Beef Noodle Soup with Peas
  and, 73
 Mashed Potatoes with Root
  Vegetables, 315
 Root Vegetable Stew with Porcini
  and Cream, 266–67
Passatelli, chicken soup with, 59–61
 recipe for, 59–61
Pasta:
 Egg, Fresh, 56
 fresh, 54
 Minestrone with, 134
 Shells, Chicken Soup with
  Tomatoes, Zucchini and, 44
Pasta e fagioli, 155–57
 Master Recipe for, 156–57
 Orzo and Kidney Bean Soup with
  Carrots, 157
 Tubetini and Chickpea
  Soup, 157
Pasta and bean soups, 151–76
 noodle, Japanese, 167–72
  garnishes for, 171
  Master Recipe for, 168

Pasta and bean soups (cont.)
    noodles for, 172
    Ramen with Mushroom
        Dashi, Seared Beef, and
        Spinach, 170–71
    Soba with Dashi, Shrimp, and
        Watercress, 169–70
    Udon with Chicken Broth,
        Roasted Five-Spice Pork,
        and Spinach, 168–69
    Udon with Mushroom Dashi,
        Ginger Tofu, and
        Watercress, 171
noodle, Southeast
    Asian, 172–76
    assembling, 173
    dried rice noodles for, 176
    Hot-and-Sour Rice Noodle,
        with Shrimp and
        Tomato, 175
    Rice Noodle, with
        Beef, 174–75
    Rice Noodle, with Chicken
        and Napa Cabbage, 176
pasta e fagioli, 155–57
    Master Recipe for, 156–57
    Orzo and Kidney Bean Soup
        with Carrots, 157
    Tubetini and Chickpea
        Soup, 157
tortellini, 53–56
    Master Recipe for, 55
    with Parsley-Cheese
        Tortellini, 55
Pea(s):
    Beef Noodle Soup with Parsnips
        and, 73
    Chicken and Rice Soup with
        Spring Vegetables, 44
    Chicken Fricassee with Carrots
        and, 245
    fresh and frozen, tasting of, 107
    Hearty Vegetable Stew, 265
    in minestrone, 134
    Shrimp Curry with Yogurt
        and, 295
    soup (sweet), 106–9
        Buttered Croutons for, 108
        Creamy, 107–8
        Garlic Croutons for, 109
    split, and ham soup, 163–65
        with Caraway, 165
        Master Recipe for, 164–65
    Spring Vegetable Soup, 130–31
    Spring Vegetable Stew with Fennel
        and Asparagus, 268–69
Peach Soup, Chilled, 194
Peanuts, Red Curry with Shrimp,
    Pineapple and, 303
Peelers, vegetable, 14
Peels, 321

Peppers (bell):
    cutting into neat dice, 180
    gazpacho, 178–82
        Classic, 180
        Quick Food Processor, 180–81
        with Scallops and
            Shrimp, 181–82
        Spicy, with Chipotle Chiles
            and Lime, 181
    ratatouille, 272–74
        recipe for, 273–74
    red
        Green Curry with Mixed
            Vegetables, 304
        Rouille, 255–56
        Summer Vegetable Soup au
            Pistou, 131–32
Peppers (chile). See Chile(s)
Perch, ocean, in
    Bouillabaisse, 254–55
Pesto, 135
    Classic, 134–35
    making, 135
Pineapple, Red Curry with Shrimp,
    Peanuts and, 303
Pistou, Summer Vegetable
    Soup au, 131–32
Plum Soup, Chilled, 194
Polenta, 315–16
    Double-Boiler, 316
    instant, 316
    with Parmesan and Butter, 316
Porcini mushrooms:
    dried, rehydrating, 85
    Mushroom Ragoût, 271
    Root Vegetable Stew with Cream
        and, 266–67
Pork:
    bacon
        Black Bean Soup with
            Balsamic and, 160
        Pancetta, Minestrone with, 133
        Smoked Cheddar Cheese Soup
            with, 150
    cassoulet, 226–28
        Simplified, with Kielbasa
            and, 227–28
    ham, half-picnic, handling, 164
    ham and split pea soup, 163–65
        with Caraway, 165
        Master Recipe for, 164–65
    hot-and-sour soup, 84–86
        recipe for, 85–86
    pozole, 220–23
        Rojo, 222–23
        Verde, 223
    and Ricotta Tortellini in Chicken
        Stock, 55
    Roasted Five-Spice, Udon with
        Chicken Broth, Spinach
        and, 168–69

Pork (cont.)
    salt, 129
        trimming, 128
    stews, best cuts for, 220
    vindaloo, 218–20
        recipe for, 219–20
    wonton soup, 50–53
        Master Recipe for, 52–53
    see also Sausage
Portobello mushrooms:
    Chicken Cacciatore with Sage
        and, 234–35
    Hearty Vegetable Stew, 265
    Mushroom Ragoût, 271
Portuguese caldo verde, 138–40
    recipe for, 139–40
Potato(es), 125
    Beef Goulash with Caraway
        and, 204
    caldo verde, 138–40
        recipe for, 139–40
    Cheddar and Ale Soup with, 150
    Chicken Stew with Leeks, Saffron
        and, 232–33
    Green Curry with Mixed
        Vegetables, 304
    Hearty Vegetable Stew, 265
    leek soup, rustic, 123–24
        with Kielbasa, 124
        Master Recipe for, 124
        with White Beans, 124
    mashed, 312–15
        Buttermilk, 315
        Garlic, 314–15
        Lumpy, 314
        making, 314
        Master Recipe for, 314
        with Parmesan and Lemon, 315
        with Root Vegetables, 315
    Minestrone, 133
    releasing starch from, 94
    Root Vegetable Stew with Porcini
        and Cream, 266–67
    scrubbing, 81
    Spring Vegetable Soup, 130–31
    Spring Vegetable Stew with Fennel
        and Asparagus, 268–69
    Turkey Soup with Linguiça, Kale
        and, 70
    vichyssoise, 184–85
        recipe for, 184–85
    White Bean Soup with Winter
        Vegetables, 154–55
Potato mashers, 313
Pots:
    Dutch ovens/lidded casseroles, 6–7
    stockpots, 12–13
Poultry shears, 10
Pozole, 220–23
    Rojo, 222–23
    Verde, 223

Pureeing soups:
  with blender vs. food mill or food
    processor, 4–5
  safely, 108

R

Ragoût, mushroom, 269–71
  with Cream, 271
  Master Recipe for, 271
Ramen, 172
  with Mushroom Dashi, Seared
    Beef, and Spinach, 170–71
Ratatouille, 272–74
  recipe for, 273–74
Red curry:
  with Beef and Eggplant, 302–3
  Paste, 300–301
  with Shrimp, Pineapple, and
    Peanuts, 303
Red kuri squash, 115
Red snapper, in Bouillabaisse, 254–55
Ribollita, 155
Rice:
  basmati, 310–12
    Pilaf Style, 312
    tasting of, 311
  Chicken Soup with Spring
    Vegetables and, 44
  Jasmine, and Turkey Soup,
    Spicy, 70
  Minestrone with, 134
  starches in, 311
  white, 308–10
    Fluffy, 310
    tasting of, 309
    two-quart saucepan for, 310
Rice noodle(s):
  dried, 176
  soup, Southeast Asian, 172–76
    assembling, 173
    with Beef, 174–75
    with Chicken and Napa
      Cabbage, 176
    Hot-and-Sour, with Shrimp
      and Tomato, 175
Ricotta:
  and Meat Tortellini in Chicken
    Stock, 55
  Parsley Tortellini in Chicken
    Stock, 55
Roasting pans, 10–11
Root vegetable(s):
  Mashed Potatoes with, 315
  preparing, 266
  Scotch Broth, 83
  scrubbing, 81
  stew, 266–67
    with Porcini and Cream, 266–67
  see also specific root vegetables

Rouille, 255–56
Roux:
  for gumbo, 284–86
  for velouté, 61
Rutabagas, in Mashed Potatoes with
  Root Vegetables, 315

S

Safety concerns:
  chicken, 23
  chilling stock quickly, 17
Saffron:
  Chicken Stew with Leeks,
    Potatoes and, 232–33
  Egg-Lemon Soup with, 50
  threads, crumbling, 232
Sage, Chicken Cacciatore with
  Portobellos and, 234–35
Salt, adding to stocks, 17
Salt pork, 129
  trimming, 128
Saucepans, two-quart, 310
Sauces:
  Pesto, Classic, 134–35
  Rouille, 255–56
Sausage:
  Andouille, Simplified Cassoulet
    with Lamb and, 228
  caldo verde, 138–40
    recipe for, 139–40
  gumbo, 284–89
    Chicken and, 288–89
    Shrimp and, Creole-
      Style, 287
    Shrimp and, with Filé, 288
    Shrimp and, with
      Okra, 287–88
  kielbasa
    Borscht with Beef and, 81
    Caldo Verde, 139–40
    Rustic Potato-Leek Soup
      with, 124
    Simplified Cassoulet with Pork
      and, 227–28
  Linguiça, Turkey Soup with
    Potatoes, Kale and, 70
Savoy cabbage, in minestrone, 134
Scales, 11–12
Scallops, 258
  Bouillabaisse, 254–55
  Cioppino, 258–59
  Gazpacho with Shrimp
    and, 181–82
  removing tendons from, 253
Science of cooking:
  beans
    dried, freshness of, 154
    flavoring, 160
  chicken safety, 23

Science of cooking (cont.)
  chiles, varying tolerance to heat
    of, 280
  corn chowder season,
    extending, 126
  flavor compounds in beef vs.
    chicken, 30
  foam, causes of, 17
  frying spices, 296
  MSG (monosodium
    glutamate), 32
  mushrooms, washing, 121
  onion(s)
    reducing tears while
      cutting, 148
    soup, blue color of, 147
  starches, 46
  steam heat, 326
Scotch broth, 81–83
  recipe for, 83
Sea bass, in Bouillabaisse, 254–55
Seafood soups, 87–104
  clam chowder, Manhattan, 91–94
    Italian Style, 94
    Master Recipe for, 93–94
    Quick Pantry, 94
  clam chowder, New
    England, 88–91
    Master Recipe for, 90–91
    Quick Pantry, 91
    steaming clams for, 90
  Gazpacho with Scallops and
    Shrimp, 181–82
  lobster bisque, 98–102
    with Coral, 102
    Master Recipe for, 101–2
  oyster stew, 103–4
    recipe for, 104
  Shrimp and Coconut Milk,
    Thai, 68
  shrimp bisque, 95–98
    recipe for, 96–98
  Shrimp Wonton, 53
  Soba with Dashi, Shrimp, and
    Watercress, 169–70
Seafood stews, 88, 249–62
  bouillabaisse, 250–56
    Garlic-Rubbed Croutons
      for, 255
    recipe for, 254–55
    Rouille for, 255–56
    seafood for, 255
  cioppino, 256–59
    recipe for, 258–59
  curry, Indian, 289–96
    frying spices for, 296
    Master Recipe for, 293
    Shrimp, with Yogurt and
      Peas, 295
  curry, Thai, 297–304
    coconut milk for, 299

Seafood stews *(cont.)*
 Green Curry Paste for, 300
 lemon grass for, 301, 302
 Master Recipe for, 301–2
 Red, with Shrimp, Pineapple,
  and Peanuts, 303
 Red Curry Paste for, 300–301
 store-bought curry pastes
  for, 298
gumbos, 276, 284–89
 okra and filé in, 288
 roux for, 284–86
 Shrimp and Sausage, Creole-
  Style, 287
 Shrimp and Sausage, with
  Filé, 288
 Shrimp and Sausage, with
  Okra, 287–88
New England fish stew, 261–62
 recipe for, 262
oyster. *See* Seafood soups
Sicilian fish stew, 259–61
 recipe for, 260–61
Seaweed (wakame), handling, 166
Sharpening steels, 9
Shells, Chicken Soup with Tomatoes,
 Zucchini and, 44
Sherry, 77
Shiitake mushrooms, 120
 dried, rehydrating, 85
 Mushroom Ragoût, 271
Shrimp, 97
 bisque, 95–98
  recipe for, 96–98
 Bouillabaisse, 254–55
 Cioppino, 258–59
 and Coconut Milk Soup,
  Thai, 68
 curry, Indian:
  Master Recipe for, 293
  with Yogurt and Peas, 295
 curry, Thai:
  Master Recipe for, 301–2
  Red, with Pineapple and
   Peanuts, 303
 flambéing, 96
 Gazpacho with Scallops
  and, 181–82
 gumbo, 284–89
  Sausage and, Creole-Style, 287
  Sausage and, with Filé, 288
  Sausage and, with
   Okra, 287–88
 Hot-and-Sour Rice Noodle Soup
  with Tomatoes and, 175
 Soba with Dashi, Watercress
  and, 169–70
 Wonton Soup, 53
Sicilian fish stew, 259–61
 recipe for, 260–61
Side dishes. *See* Accompaniments

Simmering, gentle or slow, 17
Skimmers, 12
Smoked Cheddar Cheese Soup with
 Bacon, 150
Soba, 172
 with Dashi, Shrimp, and
  Watercress, 169–70
Soups, 39–194
 pureeing safely, 108
 stews vs., xiii
 see also Chicken soups; Chilled
  soups; Meat soups; Pasta and
  bean soups; Seafood soups;
  Vegetable soups
Southeast Asian cooking:
 Broth, Quick, 174
 noodle soup, 172–76
  assembling, 173
  dried rice noodles for, 176
  Hot-and-Sour Rice Noodle,
   with Shrimp and
   Tomato, 175
  Rice Noodle, with Beef, 174–75
  Rice Noodle, with Chicken
   and Napa Cabbage, 176
 see also Thai cooking
Soy sauce, 170
Spanish cooking:
 gazpacho, 178–82
  Classic, 180
  Quick Food Processor, 180–81
  with Scallops and
   Shrimp, 181–82
  Spicy, with Chipotle Chiles
   and Lime, 181
 white gazpacho, 182–84
  recipe for, 183–84
Spices, frying, 296
Spinach:
 Beef Noodle Soup with
  Mushrooms and, 73
 Chicken Curry with Fenugreek
  and, 294
 Minestrone, 133
 Ramen with Mushroom Dashi,
  Seared Beef and, 170–71
 Spring Vegetable Soup, 130–31
 Udon with Chicken Broth,
  Roasted Five-Spice Pork
  and, 168–69
Spring vegetable(s):
 Chicken and Rice Soup with, 44
 soup, 129–32
  recipe for, 130–31
 stew, 267–69
  with Fennel and
   Asparagus, 268–69
Squash (summer):
 Green Curry with Mixed
  Vegetables, 304
 see also Zucchini

Squash (winter):
 butternut, 115
  cutting up, 114
 butternut, soup, 113–15
  with Cinnamon-Sugar
   Croutons, 115
  Curried, with Cilantro, 115
  Master Recipe for, 114–15
 in minestrone, 134
 varieties of, 115
Standing mixers, kneading bread
 dough in, 318, 319
Starches:
 releasing from potatoes, 94
 in rice, 311
 science of, 46
Steam heat, 326
Stews, 195–304
 soups vs., xiii
 see also Chicken stews; Chilis;
  Curries; Gumbos; Meat stews;
  Seafood stews; Vegetable stews
Stockpots, 12–13
Stocks, 15–38
 beef, 28–30
  amount of meat required
   for, 30
  cut and type of meat in, 29
  Rich, 30
 broths vs., 16
 canned. *See* Broths
 chicken, 18–27
  amount of meat required
   for, 30
  Asian, 24–26
  Asian, Master Recipe for, 25
  Asian, with Sautéed Breast
   Meat, 25–26
  buying chicken for, 20–22
  chicken parts for, 19
  hacking up chicken for, 22
  Quick, 22–23
  Quick, with Sautéed Breast
   Meat, 23
  for soup that needs chicken
   meat, 20, 42
  tips for, 18
  Traditional, 23–24
 chilling quickly, 17, 18
 cooking temperature for, 17
 defatting, 17, 19
 fish (fish fumet), 35–38, 251–52
  Cheater's, 38
  cleaning fish frames for, 37
  fish for, 36
  recipes for, 37–38, 254–55
 foam on
  cause of, 17
  skimming off, 12, 16–17
 freezing, 17
  in convenient portions, 20

Stocks (cont.)
homemade vs. canned, 16
ingredient quality and, 16
Lamb, Rich, 83
MSG (monosodium glutamate)
in, 32
Mushroom, Quick, 123
salting, 17
skimmed vs. unskimmed, 16–17
straining, 17
equipment for, 13–14
Turkey, Basic, 69
vegetable, 31–34
canned (broth), 35
recipe for, 34
Stone Fruit Soup, Chilled, 194
Stones, baking, 320
Straciatella, 47
Strainers, 13–14
Straining stocks, 17
Stroganoff, beef, 211–13
Master Recipe for, 212–13
slicing tenderloin
filet for, 212
Summer Vegetable Soup au
Pistou, 131–32
Sweet dumpling squash, 115
Sweet potatoes, in Root Vegetable
Stew with Porcini and
Cream, 266–67
Swiss chard, in minestrone, 134
Swordfish, in Sicilian Fish
Stew, 260–61

T

Tagine, lamb, 216–18
recipe for, 217–18
Tamari, 170
Tarragon, Chicken Cacciatore with
White Wine and, 234–35
Tastings:
beans, canned, 157
beef broth, canned, 31
chicken, 20–22
chicken broth, canned, 27
matzo meal, 58
Parmesan cheese, 60
peas, fresh and frozen, 107
polenta, instant, 316
rice
basmati, 311
white, 309
shrimp, 97
tomato juice, 182
vegetable broth, canned, 35
wonton wrappers, 51
Techniques:
asparagus, snapping tough ends
from, 110

Techniques (cont.)
avocados
dicing, 65
pitting, 190
testing for ripeness, 189
basil, releasing flavor of, 135
beef
blade steaks, trimming, 206
flank steak, slicing, 174
shank bones, handling, 30
tenderloin filet, slicing, 212
beet(s)
handling, 80
stains, removing, 186
bouquet garni, making, 247
butter, cutting into small cubes, 332
butternut squash, cutting up, 114
cabbage, shredding, 78
chicken
browned, skinning, 231
whole, cutting up, 245
chilling
soups, 178
stock quickly, 17, 18
clams, scrubbing, 89
cleavers, using, 25
corn
cobs, removing kernels from, 126
freezing for chowder, 126
milking, 127
cucumbers
cutting into neat dice, 181
seeding, 189
defatting
canned broth, 28
stock, 19
eggs, tempering, 50
fennel, preparing, 268
fish frames, cleaning for stock, 37
freezing
corn for chowder, 126
stock in convenient
portions, 20
garlic, smashing, 145
ginger
mincing, 66
smashing, 26
ham, half-picnic, handling, 164
julienning vegetables, 76
kale, handling, 140
ladling, drip-free, 9
leeks, cleaning, 124
lemon grass
bruising, 175
mincing, 302
lemon zest, removing large
strips of, 50
lobster(s)
shells, cleaning, 102
steamed, removing meat
from, 99

Techniques (cont.)
mangoes, handling, 238
meat, cutting for stew, 201
mushrooms, dried, rehydrating, 85
mussels, cleaning, 252
onions, fresh pearl, preparing, 248
peppers, cutting into neat
dice, 180
potatoes
releasing starches from, 94
scrubbing, 81
pureeing soups safely, 108
root vegetables, scrubbing, 81
saffron threads, crumbling, 232
salt pork, trimming, 128
scallops, removing tendons
from, 253
shrimp, flambéing, 96
stocks
canned, defatting, 28
chilling quickly, 17, 18
freezing in convenient
portions, 20
straining, 17
tomatoes
crushing, 138
cutting into neat dice, 179
peeling, 273
preparing for roasting, 116
vegetable and herb bouquet,
making, 209
wakame, handling, 166
Tempeh and Bean Vegetarian
Chili, 284
Tenderloin filet, slicing, 212
Thai cooking:
chicken and coconut soup, 65–68
recipe for, 68
curry, 297–304
coconut milk for, 299
Green, with Chicken, Broccoli,
and Mushrooms, 303–4
Green, with Mixed
Vegetables, 304
Green Curry Paste for, 300
lemon grass for, 301, 302
Master Recipe for, 301–2
Red, with Beef and
Eggplant, 302–3
Red, with Shrimp, Pineapple,
and Peanuts, 303
Red Curry Paste for, 300–301
store-bought curry pastes
for, 298
ingredients
coconut milk, cream of
coconut, and coconut
cream, 67, 299
curry paste, 68, 298
fish sauce, 68
lemon grass, 301

Thai cooking *(cont.)*
　Shrimp and Coconut Milk Soup, 68
Tiles, baking, 320
Tofu:
　Ginger, Udon with Mushroom
　　Dashi, Watercress and, 171
　Miso Soup, 166–67
Tomato(es):
　and bread soup, Tuscan, 136–38
　　with Fresh Tomatoes, 138
　　Master Recipe for, 137–38
　canned whole, 117
　Chicken Soup with Shells,
　　Zucchini and, 44
　crushing, 138
　cutting into neat dice, 179
　gazpacho, 178–82
　　Classic, 180
　　Quick Food Processor, 180–81
　　with Scallops and
　　　Shrimp, 181–82
　　Spicy, with Chipotle Chiles
　　　and Lime, 181
　Hot-and-Sour Rice Noodle Soup
　　with Shrimp and, 175
　Italian-Style Lamb Stew with
　　Green Beans, Basil and, 215–16
　juice, tasting of, 182
　Minestrone, 133
　peeling, 273
　preparing for roasting, 116
　ratatouille, 272–74
　　recipe for, 273–74
　soup, cream of, 116–17
　　recipe for, 117
Tortellini:
　Fresh Egg Pasta for, 56
　making fresh pasta for, 54
　shaping, 55
　soup, 53–56
　　Master Recipe for, 55
　　with Parsley-Cheese
　　　Tortellini, 55
Tortilla soup, 62–65
　with Fried Corn Tortillas, 65
　Master Recipe for, 64–65
Tubetini and Chickpea Soup, 157
Tunisian Egg-Lemon Soup with
　Cinnamon and Cayenne, 50
Turkey:
　soup, 69–70
　　with Jasmine Rice, Spicy, 70
　　Noodle, 69–70
　　with Potatoes, Linguiça, and
　　　Kale, 70
　Stock, Basic, 69
Turnips:
　Irish Stew with Carrots and, 215
　Mashed Potatoes with Root
　　Vegetables, 315
　in minestrone, 134

Turnips *(cont.)*
　Root Vegetable Stew with Porcini
　　and Cream, 266–67
　scrubbing, 81
Tuscan cooking:
　Ribollita, 155
　tomato and bread soup, 136–38
　　with Fresh Tomatoes, 138
　　Master Recipe for, 137–38
　white bean soup, 152–55
　　Master Recipe for, 153–54
　　Quick, 155
　　with Winter Vegetables, 154–55

U

Udon, 172
　with Chicken Broth, Roasted Five-
　　Spice Pork, and Spinach, 168–69
　with Mushroom Dashi, Ginger
　　Tofu, and Watercress, 171

V

Veal:
　osso buco, 223–26
　　recipe for, 225–26
　Tortellini Soup, 55
Vegetable(s):
　broth, canned, tasting of, 35
　and herb bouquet, making, 209
　julienning, 76
　Mixed, Green Curry with, 304
　root
　　Mashed Potatoes with, 315
　　preparing, 266
　　Scotch Broth, 83
　　scrubbing, 81
　stock, 31–34
　　canned (broth), 35
　　recipe for, 34
　Winter, White Bean Soup
　　with, 154–55
　see also specific vegetables
Vegetable cooking sprays, 131
Vegetable peelers, 14
Vegetable soups, 105–50
　asparagus, cream of, 109–10
　　recipe for, 109–10
　broccoli, cream of, 110–11
　　preparing broccoli for, 111
　　recipe for, 111
　butternut squash, 113–15
　　with Cinnamon-Sugar
　　　Croutons, 115
　　Curried, with Cilantro, 115
　　Master Recipe for, 114–15
　caldo verde, 138–40
　　recipe for, 139–40

Vegetable soups *(cont.)*
　carrot, pureed, 111–13
　　Curried, 113
　　with Ginger, 113
　　Master Recipe for, 112–13
　　with Orange, 113
　cheddar cheese, 148–50
　　Ale and, with Potato, 150
　　Master Recipe for, 149–50
　　Smoked, with Bacon, 150
　corn chowder, 125–28
　　extending season for, 126
　　milking corn for, 127
　　recipe for, 128
　　removing kernels from corn
　　　cobs for, 126
　garlic, 143–45
　　recipe for, 144–45
　minestrone, 132–35
　　Classic Pesto for, 134–35
　　Master Recipe for, 133
　　with Pancetta, 133
　　with Rice or Pasta, 134
　　varying vegetables and beans
　　　in, 134
　mulligatawny, 140–43
　　with Chicken, 142
　　with Lamb, 142–43
　　Master Recipe for, 141–42
　mushroom, creamy, 117–20
　　recipe for, 119–20
　mushroom-barley, 120–23
　　Master Recipe for, 122
　　Vegetarian, 122–23
　onion, French, 145–47
　　recipe for, 147
　pea (sweet), 106–9
　　Buttered Croutons for, 108
　　Creamy, 107–8
　　Garlic Croutons for, 109
　potato-leek, rustic, 123–24
　　with Kielbasa, 124
　　Master Recipe for, 124
　　with White Beans, 124
　pureeing safely, 108
　spring, 129–32
　　recipe for, 130–31
　　Summer, au Pistou, 130–31
　tomato, cream of, 116–17
　　recipe for, 117
　tomato and bread, Tuscan, 136–38
　　with Fresh Tomatoes, 138
　　Master Recipe for, 137–38
Vegetable stews, 263–74
　Green Curry with Mixed
　　Vegetables, 304
　hearty, 264–65
　　recipe for, 265
　mushroom ragoût, 269–71
　　with Cream, 271
　　Master Recipe for, 271

Vegetable stews *(cont.)*
  ratatouille, 272–74
    recipe for, 273–74
  root, 266–67
    with Porcini and Cream, 266–67
  spring, 267–69
    with Fennel and
      Asparagus, 268–69
Vegetarian dishes:
  chili, 282–84
    Bean, 283–84
    Bean and Tempeh, 283–84
  Green Curry with Mixed
    Vegetables, 304
  Mushroom-Barley Soup, 122–23
Velouté, chicken, 61–62
  recipe for, 62
Vichyssoise, 184–85
  recipe for, 184–85
Vindaloo, pork, 218–20
  recipe for, 219–20

W

Wakame, handling, 166
Watercress:
  Soba with Dashi, Shrimp
    and, 169–70

Watercress *(cont.)*
  Udon with Mushroom Dashi,
    Ginger Tofu and, 171
White bean(s):
  Minestrone, 133
  Rustic Potato-Leek Soup
    with, 124
  soup, Tuscan, 152–55
    Master Recipe for, 153–54
    Quick, 155
    with Winter
      Vegetables, 154–55
White gazpacho, 182–84
  recipe for, 183–84
Wild Rice, Chicken Soup with Leeks,
  Mushrooms and, 44–45
Wine:
  beef Burgundy, 207–11
    red wine for, 210
  coq au vin, 245–48
  red, for stew, 202
  sherry, 77
  White, Chicken Cacciatore with
    Tarragon and, 234–35
Winter Vegetables, White Bean Soup
  with, 154–55
Wonton(s):
  shaping, 52
  soup, 50–53

Wonton(s) *(cont.)*
  Master Recipe for, 52–53
  Shrimp, 53
  wrappers, 51

Y

Yogurt:
  Chicken Curry with Cilantro,
    Zucchini and, 294
  Shrimp Curry with Peas
    and, 294

Z

Zesters, 14
Zucchini:
  Chicken Curry with Yogurt,
    Cilantro and, 294
  Chicken Soup with Shells,
    Tomatoes and, 44
  Minestrone, 133
  ratatouille, 272–74
    recipe for, 273–74
  Summer Vegetable Soup au
    Pistou, 131–32

A Note on Conversions

SOME SAY COOKING IS A SCIENCE AND AN art. We would say that geography has a hand in it, too. Flour milled in the United Kingdom and elsewhere will feel and taste different from flour milled in the United States. So we cannot promise that the loaf of bread you bake in Canada or England will taste the same as a loaf baked in the States, but we can offer guidelines for converting weights and measures. We also recommend that you rely on your instincts when making our recipes. Refer to the visual cues provided. If the bread dough hasn't "come together in a ball," as described, you may need to add more flour— even if the recipe doesn't tell you so. You be the judge. For more information on conversions and ingredient equivalents, visit our Web site at www.cooksillustrated.com and type "conversion chart" in the search box.

The recipes in this book were developed using standard U.S. measures following U.S. government guidelines. The charts below offer equivalents for U.S., metric, and Imperial (U.K.) measures. All conversions are approximate and have been rounded up or down to the nearest whole number. For example:

1 teaspoon = 4.9292 milliliters, rounded up to 5 milliliters

1 ounce = 28.3495 grams, rounded down to 28 grams

Volume Conversions

U.S.	METRIC
1 teaspoon	5 milliliters
2 teaspoons	10 milliliters
1 tablespoon	15 milliliters
2 tablespoons	30 milliliters
¼ cup	59 milliliters
⅓ cup	79 milliliters
½ cup	118 milliliters
¾ cup	177 milliliters
1 cup	237 milliliters
1¼ cups	296 milliliters
1½ cups	355 milliliters
2 cups	473 milliliters
2½ cups	592 milliliters
3 cups	710 milliliters
4 cups (1 quart)	0.946 liter
1.06 quarts	1 liter
4 quarts (1 gallon)	3.8 liters

Weight Conversions

OUNCES	GRAMS
½	14
¾	21
1	28
1½	43
2	57
2½	71
3	85
3½	99
4	113
4½	128
5	142
6	170
7	198
8	227
9	255
10	283
12	340
16 (1 pound)	454

Conversions for Ingredients Commonly Used in Baking

Baking is an exacting science. Because measuring by weight is far more accurate than measuring by volume, and thus more likely to achieve reliable results, in our recipes we provide ounce measures in addition to cup measures for many ingredients. Refer to the chart below to convert these measures into grams.

INGREDIENT	OUNCES	GRAMS
I cup all-purpose flour*	5	I42
I cup whole-wheat flour	5½	I56
I cup granulated (white) sugar	7	I98
I cup packed brown sugar (light or dark)	7	I98
I cup confectioners' sugar	4	II3
I cup cocoa powder	3	85
Butter†		
4 tablespoons (½ stick, or ¼ cup)	2	57
8 tablespoons (I stick, or ½ cup)	4	II3
I6 tablespoons (2 sticks, or I cup)	8	227

*U.S. all-purpose flour, the most frequently used flour in this book, does not contain leaveners, as some European flours do. These leavened flours are called self-rising or self-raising. If you are using self-rising flour, take this into consideration before adding leavening to a recipe.

† In the United States, butter is sold both salted and unsalted. We generally recommend unsalted butter. If you are using salted butter, take this into consideration before adding salt to a recipe.

Oven Temperatures

FAHRENHEIT	CELSIUS	GAS MARK (IMPERIAL)
225	I05	¼
250	I20	½
275	I30	I
300	I50	2
325	I65	3
350	I80	4
375	I90	5
400	200	6
425	220	7
450	230	8
475	245	9

Converting Temperatures from an Instant-Read Thermometer

We include doneness temperatures in many of our recipes, such as those for poultry, meat, and bread. We recommend an instant-read thermometer for the job. Refer to the table at left to convert Fahrenheit degrees to Celsius. Or, for temperatures not represented in the chart, use this simple formula:

Subtract 32 degrees from the Fahrenheit reading, then divide the result by 1.8 to find the Celsius reading.

EXAMPLE:
"Roast until the juices run clear when the chicken is cut with a paring knife or the thickest part of the breast registers 160 degrees on an instant-read thermometer." To convert:

160° F − 32 = 128°
128° ÷ 1.8 = 71° C (rounded down from 71.11)